THE COLLECTED WORKS OF
G.K. CHESTERTON

VII

THE COLLECTED WORKS OF
G. K. CHESTERTON

VII

THE BALL AND THE CROSS

MANALIVE

THE FLYING INN

With Introduction and Notes by
Iain T. Benson

IGNATIUS PRESS   SAN FRANCISCO

Frontispiece: Bust of GKC by Maria Petre,
National Portrait Gallery, London

© 2004 Ignatius Press, San Francisco
ISBN 0–89870–997–0 (HB)
ISBN 0–89870–998–9 (PB)
Library of Congress control number 85–81511
Printed in the United States of America

CONTENTS

MANALIVE
PART I
THE ENIGMAS OF INNOCENT SMITH

PART II
THE EXPLANATIONS OF INNOCENT SMITH

THE FLYING INN

GENERAL EDITORS' INTRODUCTION

When asked to comment on Chesterton's works of fiction, novelist and critic Anthony Burgess stated "they are as entertaining as when they were first written and the substructure of farce and fantasy—a concern with free will, Western civilization, and the ultimate mysteries of Religion—is not less valid in the age of superstates and nuclear deterrents and brainwashing than it was in Chesterton's more innocent heyday."

In this volume Iain Benson introduces three of Chesterton's novels to which Mr. Burgess referred. These works were penned on the eve of the First World War.

In Volume VI of the Collected Works, we included an early version of *The Ball and The Cross* that had been serialized in *The Commonwealth*, the magazine of the Christian Social Union. The 1905 serial is basically the first eight chapters of the novel, but concludes abruptly with a very different ninth chapter. Chesterton slightly revised the early chapters and then added eleven new chapters to form the complete novel, which was published in 1909.

Manalive, first published in 1912, describes the trials and tribulations of Innocent Smith, an allegorical being like Christian in *The Pilgrim's Progress*. Reviewing the work in the March 1, 1912, edition of London's *The Daily News*, R. A. Scott James concluded that in *Manalive* "Mr. Chesterton has given us some good fun, some good old fashioned moral philosophy and a very wholesome sermon."

Published on January 22, 1914, *The Flying Inn* contains songs that originally appeared in *The New Witness* and were later published separately in the 1915 edition of *Wine, Water and Song*. "In respect of its high sprits and invention, its lavish paradox and frank absurdity", *The Observer* concluded in 1914, "*The Flying Inn* is as good as anything Mr. Chesterton has done."

Iain Benson, a noted Vancouver lawyer, served as chairman of the civil liberties section of the Canadian Bar Association in British

Columbia. His articles have appeared in numerous periodicals and he served as a contributing editor to *A Time to Choose Life: Women, Abortion and Human Rights.*

GEORGE J. MARLIN
RICHARD P. RABATIN
General Editors

DALE AHLQUIST
PATRICIA AZAR
JOE MYSAK
Associate Editors

A NOTE ON THE TEXTS

The first part of *The Ball and the Cross* was originally published in a serialized version in *The Commonwealth*, the magazine of the Christian Social Union. The episodes appeared from volume 10, number 3, of March 1905, to volume 11, number 11, of November 1906. They appeared regularly every month until February 1906, then in April, June and finally November 1906, when the episode concluded with the words "to be continued". However, no further episodes appeared. The serialized version differs only in minor ways from the version published by John Lane Company of New York in 1909. The first English edition, published in London by Wells, Gardner and Darton, appeared in February 1910 and was republished in 1984 by Boydell Press, again, with only slight alterations from the first American and English editions.

The first English edition contained two cancelled pages and an erratum slip. The erratum change has been incorporated in the text that is used here (with an explanatory note). The cancellations involved the title page (the reason for the change is not clear) and a later page that contains a variation between the first American and English editions. Again, this change is the subject of a short note in the text in this volume.

The text used here is that of the first English edition published by Wells, Gardner and Darton. The serialized version was published in volume VI of the Collected Works, compiled and introduced by Denis J. Conlon and published by Ignatius Press in 1991. I have benefitted from Professor Conlon's annotations to that edition and have, for the most part, used them here with minor adjustments and additions.

Man Alive was first published by Thomas Nelson and Sons in London in 1912 in "Nelson's New Two-shilling Novels", and it is the text for the first English edition that is used in this volume.

The Flying Inn was first published by Methuen and Company in London in 1914, and it is the text for the first English edition that is used in this volume.

A NOTE ON THE NOTES

Chesterton never used footnotes, and he would be surprised and amused that we are propping up some of his pages with these little annotations. We have decided, however, both in deference to G. K. C. and for the training of the reader, to let the vast majority of the pages stand on their own and leave a host of generally familiar names and references unannotated. As a rule, therefore, notes are furnished only for references clearly crucial to the context and of sufficient obscurity to send even the well-educated reader to the encyclopedia, lest the thread of narrative or argument be lost.

INTRODUCTION

By Iain T. Benson

As a Christian apologist, G. K. Chesterton was a romantic. And as a writer of romances, he was a Christian apologist. His apologetics are filled with elves and dragons and angels, and "the Romance of Orthodoxy", while his novels are for the most part philosophical and religious debates in which Christianity is defended from all angles. He really does both things at once in both kinds of books. *Orthodoxy* (1908), his first great work of apologetics, is inextricably connected to three novels that were to follow: *The Ball and the Cross* (1909), *Manalive* (1912) and *The Flying Inn* (1914). To read *Orthodoxy* and then these three novels is to see each of his theological arguments set out in a series of stories and parables.

In *Orthodoxy*, Chesterton discusses the despair of modern philosophy: "It does not really believe that there is any meaning in the universe; therefore it cannot hope to find any romance; its romances have no plots." [1] The three novels here are certainly romantic, certainly have interesting plots and certainly are antidotes to despair. But primarily they have the air of being philosophical debates that have found a good story into which to set themselves. Naturally, they are the same debates with which Chesterton was concerned his whole life. There is a certain lack of realism about the novels. The character development is of secondary importance to what is said and argued. There is little interest in the psychological aspects of the characters—a point that probably wins Chesterton as many fans as he loses on this score.

The three novels in this volume are philosophical adventures designed to make us see life—not simply to see life, but see it in a new and brighter light, to see it more abundantly. As one of the novels suggests,

[1] G. K. Chesterton, *Orthodoxy*, in *The Collected Works of G. K. Chesterton*, vol. 1 (San Francisco: Ignatius Press, 1986), 362.

to be alive is not the same as being merely alive, in the same way that to have eyes is not the same thing as to see, and to have a mind is not the same thing as to understand.

Chesterton is convinced that what we think about little things will influence how we think about bigger things. How we consider the lilies will have a great deal to do with how we consider our fellow man and our homes and our communities. Everything is connected. And everything in Chesterton's books is connected. As Maisie Ward, his most important biographer, put it, "Chesterton's was a philosophy universal and unified and [found] exceedingly varied techniques of expression. But the whole of it was in a sense in each of them—in each book, almost in each poem." [2]

There is a common element of strangeness in the three novels. *The Ball and the Cross* actually has more in common with *The Man Who Was Thursday* than with the other *Manalive* or *The Flying Inn* in terms of the metaphysical weirdness in which figures appear and disappear suddenly or turn out to be someone else. Yet the themes of the latter two books are also strange. In *Manalive*, an innocent man is put on trial for supposed crimes. In the second, there is a plot to Islamize England by banning alcohol. There is a parallel of an Odyssey-like adventure in both novels. In *Manalive*, Innocent Smith travels around the world so that he can see his own home and wife with a vividness that only his absence could have reawakened. In *The Flying Inn*, a pub owner and his friend have a harum-scarum jaunt around England with a barrel of rum and a wheel of cheddar, trying to keep the traditions of the common man alive in the midst of legislation to outlaw their pleasures.

All three novels in this volume urge us to see the so-called common things as distinctly uncommon. As in a famous Father Brown story in which the murdering postman is unnoticed except by the observant priest-detective, these books make us see common things with a startling, if not shocking, new perspective. They are designed to give us a good shake. The wind in the opening scene of *Manalive* blows in with an untamed, elemental force that has the newness of baptism. The uncontrollable aspect of nature can provide the means

---

[2] Maisie Ward, *Gilbert Keith Chesterton* (London: Sheed and Ward, 1943), 190.

for us to see our lives afresh. It is the same kind of wind that once blew Chesterton's hat off, leading to his famous observation: "An adventure is only an inconvenience rightly considered. An inconvenience is only an adventure wrongly considered." [3]

All three novels are about inconveniences of one sort or another. Sometimes the inconvenience is on a grand scale, as in the opening scene of *The Ball and the Cross*, in which Michael the monk has been thrown out of Professor Lucifer's flying ship and hangs precariously from the cross atop St. Paul's Cathedral. Sometimes the inconvenience is almost farcical, as in *The Flying Inn*, in which the two heroes keep setting up a portable pub, one step ahead of the authorities who are trying to arrest them. But every inconvenience is of the same primary nature: it is evil's attempt to derail goodness. Sometimes the most disarming weapon is to laugh in evil's face.

In each novel, the paradoxes pile up. Reality has to be sacrificed because reality is not real. While tradition brings an order that offers liberty, modern philosophies offer a liberty in chains. The human attempts to build new societies end up, as Chesterton shows in all three novels, as a threat to human freedom in all respects. He shows the folly of false ideas, simply by letting them play themselves out. As he says elsewhere, "The best way to destroy a Utopia is to establish it." [4]

Chesterton sees that there can never be a progress without standards against which to measure progress. Without a standard, changes are simply change. Each of the novels deals with false claims to progress where the standards that are the real standards—human nature, religion, faith, basic human longings—are being swept away by false creeds and even falser prophets, many of whom Chesterton names explicitly (Shaw, Nietzsche, Tolstoy, Schopenhauer, and so forth).

As Chesterton argues in *Orthodoxy*, every modern idea when taken to its logical conclusion ends in madness. In *The Ball and the Cross*, we learn that the insane asylum is run by a group of doctors headed by Professor Lucifer, who, as the name would indicate, is the devil himself.

---

[3] See Chesterton's essay "On Running after One's Hat", in *All Things Considered* (New York: Sheed and Ward, 1955), 28.

[4] Cited in Ward, *Gilbert Keith Chesterton*, 589.

The whole world that their science has created is, in fact, mad. The reader knows that while the entire society has gone mad, there is more in common between the novel's two main characters, an atheist and a Catholic, who know what they do and do not believe, than there is between a group of scientists who have cut science free of its philosophical and theological moorings.

These novels are Chesterton's attempt to share his clarity of vision with us, to help us recover the ability to see the things that have been obscured by modern philosophy. It is sometimes done in a dramatic fashion, as in *Manalive* when Innocent Smith risks everything to prove that Professor Eames' philosophy is a lie that he not only does not live by but that he *cannot* live by. The fact that Professor Eames' realization is achieved dramatically should not be surprising. When the blind regain their sight it is always dramatic.

Let us consider the novels, one at a time.

The Ball and the Cross (1909)

In the opening scene of *The Ball and the Cross*, a holy and scholarly monk named Michael is held captive in the flying machine of one Professor Lucifer. The discussion between the two occupies relatively few pages, yet their exchange sets the theme for the entire novel.

The monk argues that the truths from tradition and religion are still true, while the Professor argues that science has rendered religion obsolete. The debate centers around the nature of the ball and the cross on the top of St. Paul's Cathedral. The ball represents one kind of philosophy that is round and pleasant from all sides, and the cross represents another that is about contradiction and sharp edges and definition. Lucifer argues that the ball should be on top of the cross because it is the superior philosophy. Michael explains what would happen if the ball were to be put on top of the cross: "It would fall down." It is the same argument that Chesterton puts forth in *Orthodoxy*: that if we attempt to wreck Christianity we do not wreck Christianity; we wreck everything else.

Lucifer is not pleased with the points that Michael makes, and so he throws him out of the flying ship. Michael is left dangling danger-ously from the cross on top of the cathedral. The monk has an epiphany and realizes (in a way that foreshadows Innocent Smith, the hero of *Manalive*) the exquisite beauty and rightness of each thing as it is. He sees the loveliness of creation and makes an observation, in his sanctity, that frames the story of the novel that is about to begin:

> The new and childlike world which he had seen so suddenly, men had not seen at all. Here they were still at their old bewildering, pardonable, useless quarrels, with so much to be said on both sides, and so little that need be said at all. A fierce inspiration fell on him suddenly; he would strike them where they stood with the love of God. They should not move till they saw their own sweet and startling existence. They should not go from that place till they went home embracing like brothers and shouting like men delivered.[5]

Almost unnoticed is the fact, mentioned as a sort of aside at the end of the episode, that Michael the monk, "the happiest man in the world", is taken away and put in an asylum. For, as T. S. Eliot wrote, "humankind cannot bear very much reality."[6] Chesterton might have responded: "What else is there to bear?" It is well to keep this brief image in mind, because the asylum figures again at the end of the novel.

From this strange, theoretical and theatrical introduction, the scene shifts, with a shattering of glass, to the earthly plane and two new protagonists who are a bit more mundane: a Scottish Roman Catholic named Evan MacIan, and an atheist newspaper editor named James Turnbull. The latter has, in an article displayed in his office window, "insulted the Mother of God". So MacIan challenges Turnbull to a duel.

England, not surprisingly, frowns upon dueling, and so the two are constantly being prevented from carrying out the duel. Ironically, England also frowns on any passionate conviction for or against a belief in God. Atheism is considered bad taste, but so is Roman Catholicism. Although the two duelists do not know it yet, they are united in their firm convictions. In the meantime, they are trying to kill each other like gentlemen without being interrupted.

[5] See below, 50.
[6] T. S. Eliot, "Burnt Norton", in *Four Quartets* (1936), part 1.

But the duel before the duel, or rather the interruptions to the duel, is where the real meat is. MacIan and Turnbull have an ongoing philosophical fight while trying to find a place to wage the physical fight. The novel shares a quality with the other two in that it proceeds in a strange, almost dreamlike way in which day blends into day and distances blur and scenes change without a very plausible continuity. Time passes, though how much time is not clear, but there is suddenly another sunset or sunrise to set a mood, if not to mark another day.

Maisie Ward and others have commented upon the frequency of sunsets in Chesterton's writing. It is Chesterton the artist who sees the sunset and sunrises, the picturesque backgrounds against which to describe the action of the scenes. Sunrise and sunset are the edges of the day, the place where the light meets the dark, the place of conflict and continuance. Some commentators have tired of Chesterton's sunsets and sunrises. However, that is because they are not strong enough to exult in monotony. As Chesterton says in *Orthodoxy*, like the child who always says "Do it again!" to the adult, God is strong enough to exult in monotony. God says every day "Do it again!" to the sun, and every night "Do it again!" to the moon.

The novels are short because Chesterton does not spend a lot of time dressing and undressing his characters or explaining the menus (though we do get the occasional mention of various French wines) and all the other intricate details that fascinate most novelists. We have almost the sense of watching "toy theatre" proceedings, as the two duelists dash from staged encounter to staged encounter while discussing theology. Instead of using the points of the sword, they skewer each other with philosophical points, which is why, as one commentator has noted, "the interruptions are more important than the duel they interrupt." [7] The action, or lack of action, or potential action, is simply a device in which to deliver the different points of view. In the same way the supporting characters in the novel appear like puppets in a toy theatre, who "deliver their speeches then disappear stage left or right as the case may be": [8] a Tol-

---

[7] Ian Boyd, *The Novels of G. K. Chesterton: A Study in Art and Propaganda* (London: Elek, 1975), 29.

[8] Ibid.

stoyan pacifist, a Nietzschean decadent academic, a yokel advocate for common sense, an attractive female get-away-car driver, and so on. They each serve as a foil for the philosophical discussion that is taking place at that moment. We learn little of the characters themselves, except what their philosophy says of them, which was actually what Chesterton thought was the most important thing you can learn about anyone.

If the characters are one-dimensional, they make up for the fact by being able to talk a good talk. The historical, theological and literary references come thick and fast, and sometimes we have the sense of a well-stocked brain throwing off references as a Catherine Wheel firework throws off sparks. The conversation between the Catholic Scotsman and the atheist Englishman runs the gamut from ancient civilization to a rather detailed debate about English and Scottish Jacobites. Contemporary (Tolstoy and Shaw) and not so recent (Lucretius and Atlantis), French, German, South African and Russian sources jostle as examples for points being made. All is grist for this running debate.

And what is the theme of the debate? We will let Turnbull tell it:

> This man and I are alone in the modern world in that we think that God is essentially important. I think He does not exist; that is where the importance comes in for me. But this man thinks that He does exist, and thinking that very properly thinks Him more important than anything else. Now we wish to make a great demonstration and assertion—something that will set the world on fire like the first Christian persecutions. If you like, we are attempting a mutual martyrdom.[9]

Like Innocent Smith in *Manalive*, MacIan says that in smashing the atheist's window he has "woken up the world".[10] The story shows a change occurring in both men however little we get a real sense of their personalities. In the course of their improbable adventures they begin to like one another, and the complexity of the relationship between the man Turnbull and the man MacIan makes a deeper point missed by the doctors of the asylum and Professor Lucifer, and all the doubters who hold the dogmas of those who think they have no dogmas.

[9] See below, 99.
[10] See below, 81.

The novel is apocalyptic. Preceding R. H. Benson's *Lord of the World*
(1907) and many later works along this line (the most recent of which
are Michael O'Brien's novels in our own day), Chesterton sees the
intermeddling by the state with its wrong version of right, tending
toward a dehumanizing of mankind. In many places in his writings,
Chesterton foresaw the coming of "eugenics and other evils", the
evils all connected to an erroneous idea about the human person. He
saw that when respect for the sanctity of life is overthrown, respect
for human dignity will soon decline and will eventually disappear like
a Cheshire cat's smile, a floating image without substance.

When Professor Lucifer returns at the conclusion of the novel and
plucks Turnbull from inside the asylum walls, we are treated to a clear
view of Chesterton's didactic purpose. He offers Turnbull a chance to
assist in destroying "the Pope and all the kings",[11] in Lucifer's planned
revolution. What is about to occur, we are told, is "the last war of the
world", and it is the last war "because if it does not cure the world
forever, it will destroy it".[12]

When Turnbull realizes that, in the revolution being shown to him
below the flying machine, poor people are being burned out of their
homes because they are unemployable, he says this is wrong because
it interferes with "rights".

Lucifer agrees with Turnbull that life is sacred, but adds "lives are not
sacred. We are improving Life by removing lives."[13] As we approach
the centenary of the writing of this novel, we see the same views expressed
today in the modern mantra of "Every child a wanted child." What Chesterton criticized in the seeds of eugenics has grown root and branch into
a hundred malformed and disgusting shapes. Like R. H. Benson, whose
novel also refers to both euthanasia and a master figure in a flying ship,
Chesterton knew that what was euphemistically called "birth control"
could lead to what is euphemistically called "choice".

Turnbull, the atheist, rejects as a nightmare this vision of Lucifer's.
On meeting MacIan again, the two shake hands. Both are soon incar-

---

[11] See below, 209.
[12] See below, 211.
[13] See below, 214.

cerated deeper in the asylum's cells. But, after time there, MacIan
announces to a silent and thoughtful Turnbull,

> "Let the rationalists run their own race, and let us see where *they* end.
> If the world has some healthy balance other than God, let the world
> find it. Does the world find it? Cut the world loose," he cried with a
> savage gesture. "Does the world stand on its own end?" Does it stand,
> or does it stagger?" ... "There must be some round earth to plant the
> cross upon. But here is the awful difference—that the round world will
> not consent even to continue round. The astronomers are always tell-
> ing us that it is shaped like an orange, or like an egg, or like a German
> sausage. They beat the old world about like a bladder and thump it
> into a thousand shapeless shapes. Turnbull, we cannot trust the ball to
> be always a ball; we cannot trust reason to be reasonable. In the end the
> great terrestrial globe will go quite lop-sided, and only the cross will
> stand upright."[14]

Recalling the inverted image of the ball teetering on the cross, first
mentioned by the holy monk to Lucifer in the first few pages of the
book, the answer to MacIan's rhetorical question is clear: both the
ball *and* the cross are necessary, and it is the genius of this novel that,
as we follow MacIan and Turnbull, we see why Chesterton was able
to show that what unites the two men and shatters the scientistic
stratagems against humanity is love.

When the day of wrath comes, as it must in all apocalyptic works,
Lucifer, or "the Master", as he is now openly known, explains that
the story of the attempted duel for the honor of the Virgin has been,
in Orwellian fashion, erased. All those who knew anything about it
have been diagnosed as insane and, in Stalinist manner, removed for
their own good. But his boast is premature. The Revolution comes,
but not the one he imagined. Rather, the one that ultimately brings
them all, Turnbull included, to their knees.

At the beginning of this novel, the holy Michael was hanging from
the cross upon the ball at the top of St. Paul's, during which time he
had an epiphany of seeing all of creation in all its glory. Near the end
of the novel, when Michael is in the asylum, he awakes one morning

---

[14] See below, 247–48.

feeling "like a baby", as Scrooge awakes on Christmas morning in
A Christmas Carol. Chesterton's image of rebirth is a vivid one:

> Only once or twice in life is it permitted to a man thus to see the very
> universe from outside, and feel existence itself as an adorable adventure
> not yet begun. As they found this shining escape out of that hellish
> labyrinth they both had simultaneously the sensation of being babes
> unborn, of being asked by God if they would like to live upon the
> earth. They were looking in at one of the seven gates of Eden.[15]

Manalive (1912)

One of Chesterton's friends said that *Manalive* is "above all things a
hymn to life. It is the acid test of a Chestertonian." [16] Like *The Ball
and the Cross*, Chesterton erects a series of improbable events on which
to hang his philosophical arguments. He uses these events to identify
the false roads of thought that lead, like Lear's reflections on the heath,
to madness and death. Chesterton proposes the alternative route, a set
of affirmations that lead to sanity and life. The tale is essentially a
religious one, yet told in a parable with no overt religious references.
The controversies in *Manalive* are not the explicitly religious controversies in *The Ball and the Cross*. But it is a sacramental tale nonetheless.

Innocent Smith should be one of the most famous fictional characters in twentieth-century literature. From the moment he blows in
with the wind at the beginning of the novel, he offers a refreshing
perspective on everything. And he has the courage to challenge people to see if they really believe what they profess.

Chesterton uses Innocent Smith to take on the academic community, which is rife with hypocrisy, not at all living up to its own creed.
He pokes great fun at the academic mind that "reflects infinity and is
full of light by the simple process of being shallow and standing still".[17]

Chesterton, who never attended college, often uses Oxford and
Cambridge as symbols of intellectual confusion or waywardness. Thus,
in *The Ball and the Cross*, it is the Oxford philosophy don Morrice

---

[15] See below, 228–29.
[16] Ward, *Gilbert Keith Chesterton*, 370.
[17] See below, 346.

Wimpey who has the decadent and dangerous views. In *The Flying Inn*, both Hibbs However (who advocates vivisection on pauper children as long as it is done by "fully qualified practitioners") and Jon Leveson (the Secretary of The Committee of the Imperial Commission of Liquor Control) had both decided to be moderate politicians "when at Cambridge". And here in *Manalive*, the "Cambridge philosopher" Professor Emerson Eames is a pessimist of weary brilliance and "a student of Schopenhauer". Clearly, for Chesterton, the marvels of higher education have to be carefully balanced with the steady weight of common sense. If a little learning is a dangerous thing, then a lot of learning can be a positive menace!

Manalive contains some of the finest comic turns in twentieth-century literature, and each one turns on Innocent Smith's frank statement: "I am going to hold a pistol to the head of Modern Man. But I shall not use it to kill him—only to bring him to life." [18]

In this mission, bullets are for pessimists, or, as Smith says, "pills for pale people",[19] and laughter is something positive and bracing, a kind of wake-up call.

Innocent Smith is both innocent and, in a way, everyman (hence "Smith"). His very initials, which Chesterton makes a point of mentioning being printed on the side of his bag, are "I. S.", as if to heighten the fact the he simply "is". It will be recalled that in his masterful work on St. Thomas Aquinas, Chesterton notes that all of Thomas' philosophy might be said to proceed from the fact of being itself (*esse*). For the essence of Smith is that he *is*, and he knows and celebrates that fact and wants everyone else to experience their own "is" and "is-ing" as well. He has a mission that is similar to but different from that of a priest:

> "I don't deny," he said, "that there should be priests to remind men that they will one day die. I only say that at certain strange epochs it is necessary to have another kind of priests, called poets, actually to remind men that they are not dead yet." [20]

[18] See below, 355.
[19] See below, 354.
[20] See below, 378.

Innocent Smith, of course, is much like Chesterton himself. Indeed, it is impossible not to see the autobiographical aspects to these two large men. They are both larger than life, outside any academic role, and sweep exuberantly onto the scene with a mission to wake up an altogether sleeping world around themselves. Perhaps more than any character in the novels, one gets a sense that Chesterton has put his own philosophy of life into the failed undergraduate from Brakespeare College. It is not too much to say that, in Smith, Chesterton might well be describing his own sense of vocation, of meaning, of fun, of divine purpose. No doubt Chesterton's descriptions of Innocent's love of his wife come from Chesterton's descriptions of his own love for his own wife, Frances.

In Innocent Smith we also see the fear of disillusionment, the knowledge of where pessimism can lead, that were episodes in Chesterton's own life. He himself wrestled with the pessimism, pantheism, doubt and relativism that plagued the intellectuals of the late nineteenth century. His essay "The Diabolist" describes this dark period of his youth, when "right" and "wrong" were in the balance, and he held on to sanity, as he said, "by a thin thread of thanks".

For when Innocent Smith confronts Emerson Eames, his pessimistic philosophy professor at Cambridge, it is not just the loss of his own soul he fears; he is concerned also about the soul of his teacher. And the pistol shows them both that life is preferable to dissolution, life is preferable to suicide, and all doubt is, at bottom, just a pose.

Chesterton is speaking, and still speaks, to our modern/postmodern world in which few could actually continue to live with what they think they believe. They live in spite of what they believe, or perhaps more accurately, despite what they profess to believe. As a result, they are only half alive. That is the tragedy that *Manalive* seeks to overcome.

Like Innocent Smith, we also have a choice between genuine laughter and the cynical counterfeit that leads to despair. Innocent Smith makes the right choice. "He lashed his soul with laughter to prevent it falling asleep." [21] This affirmation of joy and hope and the rejection of suffocating pessimism reflect a passage from *Orthodoxy*:

[21] See below, 379.

Seriousness is not a virtue. It would be a heresy, but a much more sensible heresy, to say that seriousness is a vice. It is really a natural trend or lapse into taking one's self gravely, because it is the easiest thing to do. It is much easier to write a good *Times* leading article than a good joke in *Punch*. For solemnity flows out of men naturally; but laughter is a leap. It is easy to be heavy: hard to be light. Satan fell by the force of gravity.[22]

What place is there in a world of mere convention for a person like Innocent Smith, who, like Chesterton, "has broken the conventions but has kept the commandments"? We live in a world where most people do the exact opposite. As Chesterton says in his wonderful essay "On Lying in Bed", a man will change his philosophy all the time, "but his lunch does not change".[23]

We need the refreshing wind of *Manalive* to wake us up, to remind us of the purpose of life and the tremendous riot of life. There is a glory to be attained. Innocent Smith attains it. He finds Paradise, and finds it in the most surprising place: home. Chesterton explains why marriage is a sacrament better than any theologian has ever done.

The central theme of the novel, perhaps the central theme in all of Chesterton's writing, is best explained in Innocent Smith's description of himself:

> I have become a pilgrim to cure myself of being an exile.... I think God has given us the love of special places, of a hearth and of a native land, for a good reason.... God bade me love one spot and serve it, and do all things however wild in praise of it, so that this one spot might be a witness against all the infinities and the sophistries, that Paradise is somewhere and not anywhere, is something and not anything.[24]

The Flying Inn (1914)

The years spanned by the writing of these three novels were years of major change in Chesterton's life. He and his wife moved out of London to settle in the quiet town of Beaconsfield. He stepped out of

[22] Chesterton, *Orthodoxy*, 326.
[23] "On Lying in Bed", in *Tremendous Trifles* (New York: Sheed and Ward, 1955), 51.
[24] See below, 397–98.

the rush and commotion of Fleet Street and into a setting where he was able to produce a flood of writing that included weekly columns in several newspapers, poetry, biography, and literary criticism as well. The quiet setting may have allowed for more writing, but it did not slow Chesterton down in any other respect. In the midst of the writing was an increasingly busy life of lecturing and public debates. He debated both politics and religion, as he took on socialists and capitalists and atheists and Theosophists.

There was another important event during this time that played a key role in Chesterton's life: the event known as the Marconi Scandal. Maisie Ward says the affair made up an important element in Chesterton's "mental history".[25] And Chesterton himself, in his Autobiography, went so far as to say that the Scandal would be regarded as a landmark in English history, dividing the epoch up into the pre- and post-Marconi periods.

What was the Marconi Scandal? It was a case of "insider trading" on behalf of some highly placed British government officials, including the Attorney General, Sir Rufus Isaacs. The deal was engineered by Sir Rufus' brother, Godfrey, who was managing director of the Marconi Wireless Company of London. The Isaacs brothers were Jewish.

The government was about to award a major contract to Marconi Wireless, and before the public knew about the contract, Sir Rufus agreed with his brother to purchase 10,000 shares at two pounds per share. Rufus thought it would have been improper to have bought from Godfrey, who was in direct negotiation with the government for a lucrative contract on behalf of his company, so he bought from another brother, Harry, who had bought from Godfrey. Of his ten thousand shares, Rufus immediately sold one thousand to the Chancellor of the Exchequer, David Lloyd George, and another thousand to the Chief Whip of the Liberal Party then in office. When the government contract was publicly awarded to Marconi Wireless, the stock of course dramatically increased in value.

Cecil Chesterton, G. K.'s brother and editor of a paper called the *New Witness*, went on the warpath and exposed the scandal for every-

---

[25] Ward, *Gilbert Keith Chesterton*, 331.

thing it was. He attacked the credibility of the government officials involved and the financial chicanery of Godfrey Isaacs who sued Cecil for libel. The subsequent trial involved, among other things, G. K. Chesterton giving testimony.

Oddly enough, the point of the libel action was not the truth or falsity of Cecil's printed accusations but whether or not such accusations caused harm to Godfrey Isaacs' reputation. Cecil lost. He might have faced a prison term, but was let off with a minimal fine. In the meantime, a parliamentary committee investigated the conduct of the members involved in the deal, and it made findings of "grave improprieties" against Rufus Isaacs and the others. Despite this, the Report was not adopted, the vote splitting along party lines. When the matter went to the House of Commons for a vote by the entire body, the action failed again, splitting along party lines. The careers of the main individuals were not damaged, with Lloyd George going on to become Prime Minister, and Rufus Isaacs obtaining a peerage as Lord Reading and becoming Lord Chief Justice and later Viceroy of India.

G. K. Chesterton was troubled for the rest of his life by the fact that men who had willfully abused the public trust for their own personal gain, or as Maisie Ward puts it, men who were "dominant in the councils of England"[26] who had "no very nice sense of cleanliness"[27] not only went unpunished, but were actually rewarded. And to add true insult to injury, his brother was the only person prosecuted in connection with the Marconi Scandal. The specter of financial corruption (and certainly Jewish financial corruption) was one that Chesterton had often fretted about prior to the Marconi Scandal. When a clear-cut case of it was then exposed, Chesterton was enormously frustrated that not only was there no justice, but there was no public cry for justice: all the major newspapers simply looked the other way. In *The Flying Inn*, Chesterton exacts a little revenge.

The target in the novel is the pervasiveness of political corruption, which, left unchecked, can affect every aspect of the common

[26] Ibid., 362.
[27] Ibid.

man's life, as those in power take away the privileges of the poor as a way of controlling them and take away their traditions as a way of demoralizing them, turning them into soulless slaves. Chesterton rightly points out that the political machinations of the powerful are tied to spiritual ambitions. The character of Lord Ivywood in *The Flying Inn* is no less a Lucifer-like character than Professor Lucifer himself in *The Ball and the Cross*. Ivywood's tools for attacking the Christian culture of England are a combination of restrictive laws and fashionable new styles of religiosity. He brings in an Islamic holy man, Misysra Ammon, who, in the opening scene of the novel, preaches on a beach, expounding on a transparently bogus theory that every word in the English language is derived from Islam. But Lord Ivywood soon elevates M. Ammon to a position of influence, with his exotic Islamism, bolstered by a hypocritical vegetarianism and supposed teetotalism. Through clever parliamentary manipulation, Ivywood, "the most handsome man in England", bans the sale of alcohol, which is to destroy what is for Chesterton a quintessential part of England—the pint and the pub. Suddenly, the people who still think they live in a culture framed by democracy find themselves dominated by the Imperial Commission of Liquor Control, a tool of the powerfully connected elite. Underlying the attack on alcohol, however, is a deeper purpose: the complete eradication of England's Christian culture. You cannot serve God and M. Ammon. Lord Ivywood is willing to do anything to bring about his new world. The combination of Eastern exoticism, financial corruption, and obsession with control eventually drives him insane. Chesterton, as he does in *Orthodoxy*, once again demonstrates that a bad philosophy taken to its logical ends leads to madness.

The heroes of the novel, opposing the evil Lord Ivywood, are Captain Dalroy, representing honor and chivalry, and Humphrey Pump, representing the virtues of the common man. Dalroy is a swashbuckling Irish adventurer and former sailor, Pump is a rural pub owner. They set off to save English inns against a serpentine law that has banned not inns, but inn signs, which effectively outlaws the inns themselves. The two heroes wander through England, literally with a movable feast. The novel has a riot of incidents, punctuated by rousing drinking songs.[28] Chesterton likes nothing if not a good fight against evil: "The finding and fighting of positive evil is the beginning of all fun—and even of all farce."[29]

And that is the point lost by so many commentators on this novel: it is a farce. Some readers think some of the laughter is sardonic, and Chesterton is clearly letting off an enormous amount of steam in the wake of the Marconi Scandal. There are minor characters in the book who are Jewish and who represent corrupt financial dealings, but they are minor. If Chesterton were the anti-Semite his critics claim he was, he would have made the evil Lord Ivywood a Jew. But the object of Chesterton's wrath is not the Jews. It is the rich and powerful and godless, who extend their power through corruption, who prey on the powerless, and who are the enemies of Christian culture. It is understandable, perhaps, that some readers do not find it a laughing matter. But, incredibly, Chesterton does.

Chesterton demonstrates his gift for satire in the second chapter of the book with an excellent parody of a certain kind of political speech, where Ivywood promises "peace with honour" when his intentions are anything but honorable. The eerie thing about the speech, however, is how it foreshadows Neville Chamberlain's famous Munich Agreement with Hitler, where he promised "peace in our time". Chesterton's satire was on the mark and still is, as the oleaginous words of politicians continue to confuse and cover up the truth to this day. C. S. Lewis affirms the idea:

> Is Lord Ivywood obsolete? The doctrinaire politician, aristocratic yet revolutionary, inhuman, courageous, eloquent, turning the vilest treacheries and the most abominable oppressions into periods that echo with lofty magnanimity—is this out of date?[30]

Lewis wrote a short newspaper article entitled "Willing Slaves of the Welfare State" that is reminiscent of Chesterton and Belloc's criticism

---

[28] These drinking songs were later published as *Wine, Water, and Song* (1915).
[29] See below, 566.
[30] C. S. Lewis, "Notes on the Way", *Time and Tide*, Nov. 9, 1946, p. 1071, cited in Boyd, *Novels*, 71.

of socialist and capitalist governmental public policy. Evidently he did not think Chesterton's portrayal of Ivywood extreme.

There is a revolution at the end of the novel, but it has rightly been described as "inconclusive". All that seems to happen at the novel's end is the defeat of the Turkish army. There is not a grand description of what society will look like or on what principles it will proceed after the mob overtakes Ivywood's mansion. The final battle proceeds with more of a whimper than a bang.

It is debatable whether or not the actual writing is tired-sounding, but if it is, it might be revealing Chesterton's own fatigue. Shortly after completing the novel, Chesterton suffered a complete physical collapse, which left him semi-comatose for months. The *Flying Inn* was very nearly Chesterton's last book. However, he recovered completely and picked up the pen again and continued his astonishing literary output. When he "rose again" (at Easter 1915) he seemed to have recovered more of the spirit of Innocent Smith that is absent from the biting and bitter satire of *The Flying Inn*.

Yet *The Flying Inn* deserves to be remembered for its positive message, not its negative ones. It is an affirmation of the common man and common pleasures and common virtues. The image of the inn itself is important: the place where men gather as men, to share their joys and sorrows, to laugh and sing and toast. The inn sign is truly a vital sign. And it recalls Chesterton's great work on Dickens, that concludes with the wonderful promise that someday we will meet Dickens and all his characters—just as we shall someday meet Chesterton and all his characters—in the Inn at the end of the world.

ACKNOWLEDGMENTS

I would like to thank George Marlin for inviting me to undertake this work several years ago. Professor David Lyle Jeffrey was one of the first people with whom I discussed Chesterton, and his early encouragement meant a great deal. Aidan Mackey, bookseller and scholar, provided books and sage advice over the last twenty-three years. Professor David Schneiderman, of the University of Toronto Law School, located many scarce titles for me in early years. Aidan Benson and Hilary and Robin Butler provided their assistance in tracking down and capturing certain fugitive references in the current volume. Malcolm Muggeridge, Joseph Pearce, Michael and Bernadette Coren, Philip Marchand, Barbara Davies and Jack Swan all assisted with ideas and encouragement over the years and contributed in various ways (that might surprise them!) to this volume.

To our children—Aidan, Rowen, Callum, Alasdair, Cairstie, Piers and Sisley—go thanks for all the time they let their father exist, more or less undisturbed, in his "office" out back beside the slope of the ancient Fort. To the Board of the Centre for Cultural Renewal I am particularly grateful for allowing me the time in France during which this, amongst other things, has been completed.

Beyond all, however, it is to my wife, Eleanor Morag Maxwell Benson, who continues to give what no one can. To her, who first read these novels with a view to annotation, this current work is dedicated with love, thanks and not a little joy.

Iain T. Benson
Rue du Bourg,
Lourdes, France
January 2003

THE BALL AND THE CROSS

1909

I

A DISCUSSION SOMEWHAT IN THE AIR

The flying ship of Professor Lucifer sang through the skies like a silver arrow; the bleak white steel of it, gleaming in the bleak blue emptiness of the evening. That it was far above the earth was no expression for it; to the two men in it, it seemed to be far above the stars. The professor had himself invented the flying machine, and had also invented nearly everything in it. Every sort of tool or apparatus had, in consequence, to the full, that fantastic and distorted look which belongs to the miracles of science. For the world of science and evolution is far more nameless and elusive and like a dream than the world of poetry or religion; since in the latter images and ideas remain themselves eternally, while it is the whole idea of evolution that identities melt into each other as they do in a nightmare.

All the tools of Professor Lucifer were the ancient human tools gone mad, grown into unrecognisable shapes, forgetful of their origin, forgetful of their names. That thing which looked like an enormous key with three wheels was really a patent and very deadly revolver. That object which seemed to be created by the entanglement of two corkscrews was really the key. The thing which might have been mistaken for a tricycle turned upside down was the inexpressibly important instrument to which the corkscrew was the key. All these things, as I say, the professor had invented; he had invented everything in the flying ship, with the exception, perhaps, of himself. This he had been born too late actually to inaugurate, but he believed, at least, that he had considerably improved it.

There was, however, another man on board, so to speak, at the time. Him, also, by a curious coincidence, the professor had not invented, and him he had not even very greatly improved, though he had fished him up with a lasso out of his own back garden, in Western Bulgaria, with the pure object of improving him. He was an exceedingly holy man, almost entirely covered with white hair. You could see nothing but his eyes, and he seemed to talk with them. A monk of immense learning and acute intellect he had made himself happy in a little stone hut and a little stony garden in the Balkans, chiefly by writing the most crushing refutations and exposures of certain heresies, the last professors of which had been burnt (generally by each other) precisely 1,119 years previously. They were really very plausible and thoughtful heresies, and it was really a creditable or even glorious circumstance, that the old monk had been intellectual enough to detect their fallacy; the only misfortune was that nobody in the modern world was intellectual enough even to understand their argument. The old monk, one of whose names was Michael, and the other a name quite impossible to remember or repeat in our Western civilisation, had, however, as I have said, made himself quite happy while he was in a mountain hermitage in the society of wild animals. And now that his luck had lifted him above all the mountains in the society of a wild physicist, he made himself happy still.

"I have no intention, my good Michael," said Professor Lucifer, "of endeavouring to convert you by argument. The imbecility of your traditions can be quite finally exhibited to anybody with mere ordinary knowledge of the world, the same kind of knowledge which teaches us not to sit in draughts or not to encourage friendliness in impecunious people. It is folly to talk of this or that demonstrating the rationalist philosophy. Everything demonstrates it. Rubbing shoulders with men of all kinds——"

"You will forgive me," said the monk, meekly from under loads of white beard, "but I fear I do not understand; was it in order that I might rub my shoulder against men of all kinds that you put me inside this thing?"

"An entertaining retort, in the narrow and deductive manner of the Middle Ages," replied the Professor, calmly, "but even upon your own basis I will illustrate my point. We are up in the sky. In your religion and all the religions, as far as I know (and I know everything), the sky is made the symbol of everything that is sacred and merciful. Well, now you are in the sky, you know better. Phrase it how you like, twist it how you like, you know that you know better. You know what are a man's real feelings about the heavens, when he finds himself alone in the heavens, surrounded by the heavens. You know the truth, and the truth is this. The heavens are evil, the sky is evil, the stars are evil. This mere space, this mere quantity, terrifies a man more than tigers or the terrible plague. You know that since our science has spoken, the bottom has fallen out of the Universe. Now, heaven is the hopeless thing, more hopeless than any hell. Now, if there be any comfort for all your miserable progeny of morbid apes, it must be in the earth, underneath you, under the roots of the grass, in the place where hell was of old. The fiery crypts, the lurid cellars of the under-world, to which you once condemned the wicked, are hideous enough, but at least they are more homely than the heaven in which we ride. And the time will come when you will all hide in them, to escape the horror of the stars."

"I hope you will excuse my interrupting you," said Michael, with a slight cough, "but I have always noticed——"

"Go on, pray go on," said Professor Lucifer, radiantly, "I really like to draw out your simple ideas."

"Well, the fact is," said the other, "that much as I admire your rhetoric and the rhetoric of your school, from a purely verbal point of view, such little study of you and your school in human history as I have been enabled to make has led me to—er—rather singular conclusion, which I find great difficulty in expressing, especially in a foreign language."

"Come, come," said the Professor, encouragingly, "I'll help you out. How did my view strike you?"

"Well, the truth is, I know I don't express it properly, but somehow it seemed to me that you always convey ideas of that kind with most eloquence, when—er—when——"

"Oh! get on," cried Lucifer, boisterously.

"Well, in point of fact when your flying ship is just going to run into something. I thought you wouldn't mind my mentioning it, but it's running into something now."

Lucifer exploded with an oath and leapt erect, leaning hard upon the handle that acted as a helm to the vessel. For the last ten minutes they had been shooting downwards into great cracks and caverns of cloud. Now, through a sort of purple haze, could be seen comparatively near to them what seemed to be the upper part of a huge, dark orb or sphere, islanded in a sea of cloud. The Professor's eyes were blazing like a maniac's.

"It is a new world," he cried, with a dreadful mirth. "It is a new planet and it shall bear my name. This star and not that other vulgar one [1] shall be 'Lucifer, sun of the morning.' Here we will have no chartered lunacies, here we will have no gods. Here man shall be as innocent as the daisies, as innocent and as cruel—here the intellect——"

"There seems," said Michael, timidly, "to be something sticking up in the middle of it."

"So there is," said the Professor, leaning over the side of the ship, his spectacles shining with intellectual excitement. "What can it be? It might of course be merely a——"

Then a shriek indescribable broke out of him of a sudden, and he flung up his arms like a lost spirit. The monk took the helm in a tired way; he did not seem much astonished for he came from an ignorant part of the world in which it is not uncommon for lost spirits to shriek when they see the curious shape which the Professor had just seen on the top of the mysterious ball, but he took the helm only just in time, and by driving it hard to the left he prevented the flying ship from smashing into St. Paul's Cathedral.

A plain of sad-coloured cloud lay along the level of the top of the Cathedral dome, so that the ball and cross looked like a buoy riding on a leaden sea. As the flying ship swept towards it, this plain of cloud looked as dry and definite and rocky as any grey desert. Hence it gave to the mind and body a sharp and unearthly sensation when the ship cut and sank into the cloud as into any common mist, a thing without resistance. There was, as it were, a deadly shock in the fact that there was no shock. It was as if they had cloven into ancient cliffs like so much butter. But sensations awaited them which were much stranger than those of sinking through the solid earth. For a moment their eyes and nostrils were stopped with darkness and opaque cloud; then the darkness warmed into a kind of brown fog. And far, far below them the brown fog fell until it warmed into fire. Through the dense London atmosphere they could see below

[1] He is referring to the planet Venus when it appears as the morning star.

them the flaming London lights; lights which lay beneath them in squares and oblongs of fire. The fog and fire were mixed in a passionate vapour; you might say that the fog was drowning the flames; or you might say that the flames had set the fog on fire. Beside the ship and beneath it (for it swung just under the ball), the immeasurable dome itself shot out and down into the dark like a combination of voiceless cataracts. Or it was like some cyclopean sea-beast sitting above London and letting down its tentacles bewilderingly on every side, a monstrosity in that starless heaven. For the clouds that belonged to London had closed over the heads of the voyagers sealing up the entrance of the upper air. They had broken through a roof and come into a temple of twilight.

They were so near to the ball that Lucifer leaned his hand against it, holding the vessel away, as men push a boat off from a bank. Above it the cross already draped in the dark mists of the borderland was shadowy and more awful in shape and size.

Professor Lucifer slapped his hand twice upon the surface of the great orb as if he were caressing some enormous animal. "This is the fellow," he said, "this is the one for my money."

"May I with all respect inquire," asked the old monk, "what on earth you are talking about?"

"Why this," cried Lucifer, smiting the ball again, "here is the only symbol, my boy. So fat. So satisfied. Not like that scraggy individual, stretching his arms in stark weariness." And he pointed up to the cross, his face dark with a grin. "I was telling you just now, Michael, that I can prove the best part of the rationalist case and the Christian humbug from any symbol you liked to give me, from any instance I came across. Here is an instance with a vengeance. What could possibly express your philosophy and my philosophy better than the shape of that cross and the shape of this ball? This globe is reasonable; that cross is unreasonable. It is a four-legged animal, with one leg longer than the others. The globe is inevitable. The cross is arbitrary. Above all the globe is at unity with itself; the cross is primarily and above all things at enmity with itself. The cross is the conflict of two hostile lines, of irreconcilable direction. That silent thing up there is essentially a collision, a crash, a struggle in stone. Pah! that sacred symbol of yours has actually given its name to a description of desperation and muddle. When we speak of men at once ignorant of each other and frustrated by each other, we say they are at cross-purposes. Away with the thing! The very shape of it is a contradiction in terms."

"What you say is perfectly true," said Michael, with serenity. "But we like contradictions in terms. Man is a contradiction in terms; he is a beast whose superiority to other beasts consists in having fallen. That cross is, as you say, an eternal collision; so am I. That is a struggle in stone. Every form of life is a struggle in flesh. The shape of the cross is irrational, just as the shape of the human animal is irrational. You say the cross is a quadruped with one limb longer than the rest. I say man is a quadruped who only uses two of his legs."

The Professor frowned thoughtfully for an instant, and said: "Of course everything is relative, and I would not deny that the element of struggle and self-contradiction, represented by that cross, has a necessary place at a certain evolutionary stage. But surely the cross is the lower development and the sphere the higher. After all it is easy enough to see what is really wrong with Wren's architectural arrangement." [2]

"And what is that, pray?" inquired Michael, meekly.

"The cross is on top of the ball," said Professor Lucifer, simply. "That is surely wrong. The ball should be on top of the cross. The cross is a mere barbaric prop; the ball is perfection. The cross at its best is but the bitter tree of man's history; the ball is the rounded, the ripe and final fruit. And the fruit should be at the top of the tree, not at the bottom of it."

"Oh!" said the monk, a wrinkle coming into his forehead, "so you think that in a rationalistic scheme of symbolism the ball should be on top of the cross?"

"It sums up my whole allegory," said the professor.

"Well, that is really very interesting," resumed Michael, slowly, "because I think in that case you would see a most singular effect, an effect that has generally been achieved by all those able and powerful

---

[2] Sir Christopher Wren (1632–1723) was the English architect who designed the new St. Paul's Cathedral (1675–1710) and fifty other London churches after the great fire of London (1666).

systems which rationalism, or the religion of the ball, has produced to lead or teach mankind. You would see, I think, that thing happen which is always the ultimate embodiment and logical outcome of your logical scheme."

"What are you talking about?" asked Lucifer. "What would happen?"

"I mean it would fall down," said the monk, looking wistfully into the void.

Lucifer made an angry movement and opened his mouth to speak, but Michael, with all his air of deliberation, was proceeding before he could bring out a word.

"I once knew a man like you, Lucifer," he said, with a maddening monotony and slowness of articulation. "He took this——"

"There is no man like me," cried Lucifer, with a violence that shook the ship.

"As I was observing," continued Michael, "this man also took the view that the symbol of Christianity was a symbol of savagery and all unreason. His history is rather amusing. It is also a perfect allegory of what happens to rationalists like yourself. He began, of course, by refusing to allow a crucifix in his house, or round his wife's neck, or even in a picture. He said, as you say, that it was an arbitrary and fantastic shape, that it was a monstrosity, loved because it was paradoxical. Then he began to grow fiercer and more eccentric; he would batter the crosses by the roadside; for he lived in a Roman Catholic country. Finally in a height of frenzy he climbed the steeple of the Parish Church and tore down the cross, waving it in the air, and uttering wild soliloquies up there under the stars. Then one still summer evening as he was wending his way homewards, along a lane, the devil of his madness came upon him with a violence and transfiguration which changes the world. He was standing smoking, for a moment, in the front of an interminable line of palings, when his eyes were opened. Not a light shifted, not a leaf stirred, but he saw as if by a sudden change in the eyesight that this paling was an army of innumerable crosses linked together over hill and dale. And he whirled up his heavy stick and went at it as if at an army. Mile after mile along his homeward path he broke it down and tore it up. For he hated the cross and every paling is a wall of crosses. When he returned to his house he was a literal madman. He sat upon a chair and then started up from it for the cross-bars of the carpentry repeated the intolerable image. He flung himself upon a bed only to remember that this, too, like all workmanlike things, was constructed on the accursed plan. He broke his furniture because it was made of crosses. He burnt his house because it was made of crosses. He was found in the river."

Lucifer was looking at him with a bitten lip.

"Is that story really true?" he asked.

"Oh, no," said Michael airily. "It is a parable. It is a parable of you and all your rationalists. You begin by breaking up the Cross; but you end by breaking up the habitable world. We leave you saying that nobody ought to join the Church against his will. When we meet you again you are saying that no one has any will to join it with. We leave you saying that there is no such place as Eden. We find you saying that there is no such place as Ireland. You start by hating the irrational and you come to hate everything, for everything is irrational and so——"

Lucifer leapt upon him with a cry like a wild beast's. "Ah," he screamed, "to every man his madness. You are mad on the cross. Let it save you."

And with a herculean energy he forced the monk backwards out of the reeling car on to the upper part of the stone ball. Michael, with as abrupt an agility, caught one of the beams of the cross and saved himself from falling. At the same instant Lucifer drove down a lever and the ship shot up with him in it alone.

"Ha! ha!" he yelled, "what sort of a support do you find it, old fellow?"

"For practical purposes of support," replied Michael, grimly, "it is at any rate a great deal better than the ball. May I ask if you are going to leave me here?"

"Yes, yes. I mount! I mount!" cried the Professor in ungovernable excitement. "Altiora peto.[3] My path is upward."

"How often have you told me, Professor, that there is really no up or down in space?" said the monk. "I shall mount up as much as you will."

---

[3] *Altiora peto* is Latin for "I seek the higher things."

"Indeed," said Lucifer, leering over the side of the flying ship. "May I ask what you are going to do?"

The monk pointed downward at Ludgate Hill. "I am going," he said, "to climb up into a star."

Those who look at the matter most superficially regard paradox as something which belongs to jesting and light journalism. Paradox of this kind is to be found in the saying of the dandy, in the decadent comedy, "Life is much too important to be taken seriously." [4] Those who look at the matter a little more deeply or delicately see that paradox is a thing which especially belongs to all religions. Paradox of this kind is to be found in such a saying as "The meek shall inherit the earth." But those who see and feel the fundamental fact of the matter know that paradox is a thing that belongs not to religion only, but to all vivid and violent practical crises of human living. This kind of paradox may be clearly perceived by anybody who happens to be hanging in mid-space, clinging to one arm of the Cross of St. Paul's.

Father Michael in spite of his years, and in spite of his asceticism (or because of it, for all I know), was a very healthy and happy old gentleman. And as he swung on a bar above the sickening emptiness of air, he realised; with that sort of dead detachment which belongs to the brains of those in peril, the deathless and hopeless contradiction which is involved in the mere idea of courage. He was a happy and healthy old gentleman and therefore he was quite careless about it. And he felt as every man feels in the taut moment of such terror that his chief danger was terror itself; his only possible strength would be a coolness amounting to carelessness, a carelessness amounting almost to a suicidal swagger. His one wild chance of coming out safely would be in not too desperately desiring to be safe. There might be footholds down that awful façade, if only he could not care whether they were footholds or no. If he were foolhardy he might escape; if he were wise he would stop where he was till he dropped from the cross like a stone. And this antinomy kept on repeating itself in his mind, a

---

[4] The decadent comedy is possibly a reference to the play *The Importance of Being Ernest* (1895) by Oscar Wilde (1854–1900), to whom this quotation (not in that play) is attributed.

contradiction as large and staring as the immense contradiction of the Cross; he remembered having often heard the words, "Whosoever shall lose his life the same shall save it." He remembered with a sort of strange pity that this had always been made to mean that whoever lost his physical life should save his spiritual life. Now he knew the truth that is known to all fighters, and hunters, and climbers of cliffs. He knew that even his animal life could only be saved by a considerable readiness to lose it.

Some will think it improbable that a human soul swinging desperately in mid-air should think about philosophical inconsistencies. But such extreme states are dangerous things to dogmatise about. Frequently they produce a certain useless and joyless activity of the mere intellect, thought not only divorced from hope but even from desire. And if it is impossible to dogmatise about such states, it is still more impossible to describe them. To this spasm of sanity and clarity in Michael's mind succeeded a spasm of the elemental terror; the terror of the animal in us which regards the whole universe as its enemy; which, when it is victorious, has no pity, and so, when it is defeated has no imaginable hope. Of that ten minutes of terror it is not possible to speak in human words. But then again in that damnable darkness there began to grow a strange dawn as of grey and pale silver. And of this ultimate resignation or certainty it is even less possible to write; it is something stranger than hell itself; it is perhaps the last of the secrets of God. At the highest crisis of some incurable anguish there will suddenly fall upon the man the stillness of an insane contentment. It is not hope, for hope is broken and romantic and concerned with the future; this is complete and of the present. It is not faith, for faith by its very nature is fierce, and as it were at once doubtful and defiant; but this is simply a satisfaction. It is not knowledge, for the intellect seems to have no particular part in it. Nor is it (as the modern idiots would certainly say it is) a mere numbness or negative paralysis of the powers of grief. It is not negative in the least; it is as positive as good news. In some sense, indeed, it is good news. It seems almost as if there were some equality among things, some balance in all possible contingencies which we are not permitted to know lest we should learn indifference to good and evil, but which is sometimes shown to us for an instant as a last aid in our last agony.

Michael certainly could not have given any sort of rational account of this vast unmeaning satisfaction which soaked through him and filled him to the brim. He felt with a sort of half-witted lucidity that the cross was there, and the ball was there, and the dome was there, that he was going to climb down from them, and that he did not mind in the least whether he was killed or not. This mysterious mood lasted long enough to start him on his dreadful descent and to force him to continue it. But six times before he reached the highest of the outer galleries terror had returned on him like a flying storm of darkness and thunder. By the time he had reached that place of safety he almost felt (as in some impossible fit of drunkenness) that he had two heads; one was calm, careless, and efficient; the other saw the danger like a deadly map, was wise, careful, and useless. He had fancied that he would have to let himself vertically down the face of the whole building. When he dropped into the upper gallery he still felt as far from the terrestrial globe as if he had only dropped from the sun to the moon. He paused a little, panting in the gallery under the ball, and idly kicked his heels, moving a few yards along it. And as he did so a thunderbolt struck his soul. A man, a heavy, ordinary man, with a composed indifferent face, and a prosaic sort of uniform, with a row of buttons, blocked his way. Michael had no mind to wonder whether this solid astonished man, with the brown mustache and the nickel buttons, had also come on a flying ship. He merely let his mind float in an endless felicity about the man. He thought how nice it would be if he had to live up in that gallery with that one man for ever. He thought how he would luxuriate in the nameless shades of this man's soul and then hear with an endless excitement about the nameless shades of the souls of all his aunts and uncles. A moment before he had been dying alone. Now he was living in the same world with a man; an inexhaustible ecstasy. In the gallery below the ball Father Michael had found that man who is the noblest and most divine and most lovable of all men, better than all the saints, greater than all the heroes—man Friday.[5]

In the confused colour and music of his new paradise, Michael heard only in a faint and distant fashion some remarks that this beautiful solid man seemed to be making to him; remarks about something or other being after hours and against orders. He also seemed to be asking how Michael "got up" there. This beautiful man evidently felt as Michael did that the earth was a star and was set in heaven.

At length Michael sated himself with the mere sensual music of the voice of the man in buttons. He began to listen to what he said, and even to make some attempt at answering a question which appeared to have been put several times and was now put with some excess of emphasis. Michael realised that the image of God in nickel buttons was asking him how he had come there. He said that he had come in Lucifer's ship. On his giving this answer the demeanour of the image of God underwent a remarkable change. From addressing Michael gruffly, as if he were a malefactor, he began suddenly to speak to him with a sort of eager and feverish amiability as if he were a child. He seemed particularly anxious to coax him away from the balustrade. He led him by the arm towards a door leading into the building itself, soothing him all the time. He gave what even Michael (slight as was his knowledge of the world) felt to be an improbable account of the sumptuous pleasures and varied advantages awaiting him downstairs. Michael followed him, however, if only out of politeness, down an apparently interminable spiral of staircase. At one point a door opened. Michael stepped through it, and the unaccountable man in buttons leapt after him and pinioned him where he stood. But he only wished to stand; to stand and stare. He had stepped as it were into another infinity, out under the dome of another heaven. But this was a dome of heaven made by man. The gold and green and crimson of its sunset were not in the shapeless clouds but in shapes of cherubim and seraphim, awful human

[5] Man Friday was the first human encountered by Crusoe after many years of isolation on his island in *Robinson Crusoe* (1719), a novel by Daniel Defoe (1660–1731).

shapes with a passionate plumage. Its stars were not above but far below, like fallen stars still in unbroken constellations; the dome itself was full of darkness. And far below, lower even than the lights, could be seen creeping or motionless, great black masses of men. The tongue of a terrible organ seemed to shake the very air in the whole void; and through it there came up to Michael the sound of a tongue more terrible; the dreadful everlasting voice of man, calling to his gods from the beginning to the end of the world. Michael felt almost as if he were a god, and all the voices were hurled at him.

"No, the pretty things aren't here," said the demi-god in buttons, caressingly. "The pretty things are downstairs. You come along with me. There's something that will surprise you downstairs; something you want very much to see."

Evidently the man in buttons did not feel like a god, so Michael made no attempt to explain his feelings to him, but followed him meekly enough down the trail of the serpentine staircase. He had no notion where or at what level he was. He was still full of the cold splendour of space, and of what a French writer has brilliantly named the "vertigo of the infinite," [6] when another door opened, and with a shock indescribable he found himself on the familiar level, in a street full of faces, with the houses and even the lamp-posts above his head. He felt suddenly happy and suddenly indescribably small. He fancied he had been changed into a child again; his eyes sought the pavement seriously as children's do, as if it were a thing with which something satisfactory could be done. He felt the full warmth of that pleasure from which the proud shut themselves out; the pleasure which not only goes with humiliation, but which almost is humiliation. Men who have escaped death by a hair have it, and men whose love is returned by a woman unexpectedly, and men whose sins are forgiven them. Everything his eye fell on it feasted on, not æsthetically, but with a plain, jolly appetite as of a boy eating buns. He relished the squareness of the houses; he liked their clean angles as if he had just

[6] No French source has been located for this quotation, but it has been attributed to the Dutch painter Vincent van Gogh (1853–1890).

cut them with a knife. The lit squares of the shop windows excited him as the young are excited by the lit stage of some promising pantomime. He happened to see in one shop which projected with a bulging bravery on to the pavement some square tins of potted meat, and it seemed like a hint of a hundred hilarious high teas in a hundred streets of the world. He was, perhaps, the happiest of all the children of men. For in that unendurable instant when he hung, half slipping, to the ball of St. Paul's, the whole universe had been destroyed and recreated.

Suddenly through all the din of the dark streets came a crash of glass. With that mysterious suddenness of the Cockney mob, a rush was made in the right direction, a dingy office, next to the shop of the potted meat. The pane of glass was lying in splinters about the pavement. And the police already had their hands on a very tall young man, with dark, lank hair and dark, dazed eyes, with a grey plaid over his shoulder, who had just smashed the shop window with a single blow of his stick.

"I'd do it again," said the young man, with a furious white face. "Anybody would have done it. Did you see what it said? I swear I'd do it again." Then his eyes encountered the monkish habit of Michael, and he pulled off his grey tam o'shanter with the gesture of a Catholic.

"Father, did you see what they said?" he cried, trembling. "Did you see what they dared to say? I didn't understand it at first. I read it half through before I broke the window."

Michael felt he knew not how. The whole peace of the world was pent up painfully in his heart. The new and childlike world which he had seen so suddenly, men had not seen at all. Here they were still at their old bewildering, pardonable, useless quarrels, with so much to be said on both sides, and so little that need be said at all. A fierce inspiration fell on him suddenly; he would strike them where they stood with the love of God. They should not move till they saw their own sweet and startling existence. They should not go from that place till they went home embracing like brothers and shouting like men delivered. From the Cross from which he had fallen fell the shadow of its fantastic mercy; and the first three words he spoke in a voice like a silver trumpet, held men as still as stones. Perhaps if he had spoken there for an hour in his illumination he might have founded a religion on Ludgate Hill.[7] But the heavy hand of his guide fell suddenly on his shoulder.

"This poor fellow is dotty," he said good-humouredly to the crowd. "I found him wandering in the Cathedral. Says he came in a flying ship. Is there a constable to spare to take care of him?"

There was a constable to spare. Two other constables attended to the tall young man in grey; a fourth concerned himself with the owner of the shop, who showed some tendency to be turbulent. They took the tall young man away to a magistrate, whither we shall follow him in an ensuing chapter. And they took the happiest man in the world away to an asylum.

[7] Ludgate Hill is the major road running alongside St. Paul's Cathedral in London.

II

THE RELIGION OF THE
STIPENDIARY MAGISTRATE

The editorial office of "The Atheist" [8] had for some years past become less and less prominently interesting as a feature of Ludgate Hill. The paper was unsuited to the atmosphere. It showed an interest in the Bible unknown in the district, and a knowledge of that volume to which nobody else on Ludgate Hill could make any conspicuous claim. It was in vain that the editor of "The Atheist" filled his front window with fierce and final demands as to what Noah in the Ark did with the neck of the giraffe. It was in vain that he asked violently, as for the last time, how the statement "God is Spirit" could be reconciled with the statement "The earth is His footstool." It was in vain that he cried with an accusing energy that the Bishop of London was paid £12,000 a year for pretending to believe that the whale swallowed Jonah. It was in vain that he hung in conspicuous places the most thrilling scientific calculations about the width of the throat of a whale. Was it nothing to them all they that passed by? Did his sudden and splendid and truly sincere indignation never stir any of the people pouring down Ludgate Hill? Never. The little man who edited "The Atheist" would rush from his shop on starlit evenings and shake his fist at St. Paul's in the passion of his holy war upon the holy place. He might have spared his emotion. The cross at the top of St. Paul's and "The Atheist" shop at the foot of it were alike remote from the world. The shop and the Cross were equally uplifted and alone in the empty heavens.

To the little man who edited "The Atheist," a fiery little Scotchman, with fiery, red hair and beard, going by the name of Turnbull,[9] all this decline in public importance seemed not so much sad or even

---

[8] *The Atheist* is fictitious but seems to reflect the tone of *The Freethinker*, edited by George William Foote (1850–1915).

[9] The figure of Turnbull is probably based on Archie MacGregor, a denizen of Bedford Park and a friend of Yeats. Chesterton described him as "a fighting atheist ... defending against the new ethic of Nietzsche the old ethic of Naboth".

mad, but merely bewildering and unaccountable. He had said the worst thing that could be said; and it seemed accepted and ignored like the ordinary second best of the politicians. Every day his blasphemies looked more glaring, and every day the dust lay thicker upon them. It made him feel as if he were moving in a world of idiots. He seemed among a race of men who smiled when told of their own death, or looked vacantly at the Day of Judgment. Year after year went by, and year after year the death of God in a shop in Ludgate became a less and less important occurrence. All the forward men of his age discouraged Turnbull. The socialists said he was cursing priests when he should be cursing capitalists. The artists said that the soul was most spiritual, not when freed from religion, but when freed from morality. Year after year went by, and at last a man came by who treated Mr. Turnbull's secularist shop with a real respect and seriousness. He was a young man in a grey plaid, and he smashed the window.

He was a young man, born in the Bay of Arisaig, opposite Rum and the Isle of Skye. His high, hawklike features and snaky black hair bore the mark of that unknown historic thing which is crudely called Celtic, but which is probably far older than the Celts, whoever they were. He was in name and stock a Highlander of the Macdonalds; but his family took, as was common in such cases, the name of a subordinate sept as a surname, and for all the purposes which could be answered in London, he called himself Evan MacIan. He had been brought up in some loneliness and seclusion as a strict Roman Catholic, in the midst of that little wedge of Roman Catholics which is driven into the Western Highlands. And he had found his way as far as Fleet Street,[10] seeking some half-promised employment, without having properly realised that there were in the world any people who were not Roman Catholics. He had uncovered himself for a few moments before the statue of Queen Anne, in front of St. Paul's Cathedral, under the firm impression that it was a figure of the Virgin Mary. He was somewhat surprised at the lack of deference shown to the figure by the people bustling by. He did not understand that their one essential historical principle, the one law truly graven

[10] Fleet Street is the street in London known as being where the leading British papers were located until the mid 1980s.

on their hearts, was the great and comforting statement that Queen Anne is dead.[11] This faith was as fundamental as his faith, that Our Lady was alive. Any persons he had talked to since he had touched the fringe of our fashion or civilisation had been by a coincidence, sympathetic or hypocritical. Or if they had spoken some established blasphemies, he had been unable to understand them merely owing to the preoccupied satisfaction of his mind.

On that fantastic fringe of the Gaelic land where he walked as a boy, the cliffs were as fantastic as the clouds. Heaven seemed to humble itself and come closer to the earth. The common paths of his little village began to climb quite suddenly and seemed resolved to go to heaven. The sky seemed to fall down towards the hills; the hills took hold upon the sky. In the sumptuous sunset of gold and purple and peacock green cloudlets and islets were the same. Evan lived like a man walking on a borderland, the borderland between this world and another. Like so many men and nations who grow up with nature and the common things, he understood the supernatural before he understood the natural. He had looked at dim angels standing knee-deep in the grass before he had looked at the grass. He knew that Our Lady's robes were blue before he knew the wild roses round her feet were red. The deeper his memory plunged into the dark house of childhood the nearer and nearer he came to the things that cannot be named. All through his life he thought of the daylight world as a sort of divine débris, the broken remainder of his first vision. The skies and mountains were the splendid off-scourings of another place. The stars were lost jewels of the Queen. Our Lady had gone and left the stars by accident.

His private tradition was equally wild and unworldly. His great-grandfather had been cut down at Culloden,[12] certain in his last instant

---

[11] "Queen Anne is dead" is a semi-proverbial riposte to stale news with the meaning "Tell me something new". Queen Anne (1702–1714) was the last of the Stuart line and died without having children, and the succession passed to the House of Hanover or of Brunswick.

[12] Culloden Moor, northeast of Inverness Scotland, was the site of the final decisive battle of the Jacobite rebellion, when on April 16, 1746, the Highlanders of Bonnie Prince Charlie (Prince Charles Edward Stuart, grandson of James II and known as the Young Pretender) were defeated by the forces of the Duke of Cumberland.

that God would restore the King.[13] His grandfather, then a boy of ten, had taken the terrible claymore from the hand of the dead and hung it up in his house, burnishing it and sharpening it for sixty years, to be ready for the next rebellion. His father, the youngest son and the last left alive, had refused to attend on Queen Victoria in Scotland.[14] And Evan himself had been of one piece with his progenitors; and was not dead with them, but alive in the twentieth century. He was not in the least the pathetic Jacobite of whom we read, left behind by a final advance of all things. He was, in his own fancy, a conspirator, fierce and up to date. In the long, dark afternoons of the Highland winter, he plotted and fumed in the dark. He drew plans of the capture of London on the desolate sand of Arisaig.

When he came up to capture London, it was not with an army of white cockades,[15] but with a stick and a satchel. London overawed him a little, not because he thought it grand or even terrible, but because it bewildered him; it was not the Golden City or even hell; it was Limbo. He had one shock of sentiment, when he turned that wonderful corner of Fleet Street and saw St. Paul's sitting in the sky.

"Ah," he said, after a long pause, "that sort of thing was built under the Stuarts!" Then with a sour grin he asked himself what was the corresponding monument of the Brunswicks[16] and the Protestant Constitution.[17] After some warning, he selected a sky-sign of some pill.

[13] The king referred to is James III, the Old Pretender (1688–1766), father of Bonnie Prince Charlie (1720–1788).

[14] Things Scottish were rediscovered (by English society) when George IV visited Edinburgh to be greeted by chieftains organized for the occasion by Sir Walter Scott. Even George IV wore a kilt. However, some Scottish nationalists refused to take part because they did not recognize the Hanoverian monarchs, and so, when Queen Victoria and Prince Albert became the hub of a Scottish cult at Balmoral Castle, many Scots refused to join in.

[15] "White Cockades" referred to the badge that the Highlanders and later the Jacobites wore in their hats.

[16] The Brunswicks were the Royal House of Hanover, which in the person of George I acceded to the English throne in 1714, and by the Act of Union in 1707, to the Scottish throne.

[17] The Protestant Constitution was basically the Bill of Rights of 1689, assented to by William III and Mary II when they accepted the throne, taken together with the Act of Settlement of 1701. Both documents laid down the succession and debarred Roman Catholics from the throne.

Half an hour afterwards his emotions left him with an emptied
mind on the same spot. And it was in a mood of mere idle investigation that he happened to come to a standstill opposite the office of
"The Atheist." He did not see the word "atheist," or if he did, it is
quite possible that he did not know the meaning of the word. Even as
it was, the document would not have shocked even the innocent Highlander, but for the troublesome and quite unforeseen fact that the
innocent Highlander read it stolidly to the end; a thing unknown
among the most enthusiastic subscribers to the paper, and calculated
in any case to create a new situation.

With a smart journalistic instinct characteristic of all his school, the
editor of "The Atheist" had put first in his paper and most prominently in his window an article called "The Mesopotamian Mythology and its Effects on the Syriac Folk Lore." Mr. Evan MacIan began
to read this quite idly, as he would have read a public statement beginning with a young girl dying in Brighton and ending with Bile Beans.[18]
He received the very considerable amount of information accumu-
lated by the author with that tired clearness of the mind which children have on heavy summer afternoons—that tired clearness which
leads them to go on asking questions long after they have lost interest
in the subject and are as bored as their nurse. The streets were full of
people and empty of adventures. He might as well know about the
Gods of Mesopotamia as not; so he flattened his long, lean face against
the dim bleak pane of the window and read all there was to read
about the Mesopotamian Gods. He read how the Mesopotamians had
a God named Sho (sometimes pronounced Ji), and that he was
described as being very powerful, a striking similarity to some expressions about Jahveh, who is also described as having power. Evan had
never heard of Jahveh in his life, and imagining him to be some other
Mesopotamian idol, read on with a dull curiosity. He learnt that the
name Sho, under its third form of Psa, occurs in an early legend which
describes how the deity, after the manner of Jupiter on so many occasions, seduced a Virgin and begat a hero. This hero, whose name is
not essential to our existence, was, it was said, the chief hero and

---

[18] Bile beans were a proprietary pick-me-up and general panacea.

Saviour of the Mesopotamian ethical scheme. Then followed a paragraph giving other examples of such heroes and Saviours being born of some profligate intercourse between God and mortal. Then followed a paragraph—but Evan did not understand it. He read it again and then again. Then he did understand it. The glass fell in ringing fragments on to the pavement, and Evan sprang over the barrier into the shop, brandishing his stick.

"What is this?" cried little Mr. Turnbull, starting up with hair aflame. "How dare you break my window?"

"Because it was the quickest cut to you," cried Evan, stamping. "Stand up and fight, you crapulous coward. You dirty lunatic, stand up, will you? Have you any weapons here?"

"Are you mad?" asked Turnbull, glaring.

"Are you?" cried Evan. "Can you be anything else when you plaster your own house with that God-defying filth? Stand up and fight, I say."

A great light like dawn came into Mr. Turnbull's face. Behind his red hair and beard he turned deadly pale with pleasure. Here, after twenty lone years of useless toil, he had his reward. Some one was angry with the paper. He bounded to his feet like a boy; he saw a new youth opening before him. And as not unfrequently happens to middle-aged gentlemen when they see a new youth opening before them, he found himself in the presence of the police.

The policemen, after some ponderous questionings, collared both the two enthusiasts. They were more respectful, however, to the young man who had smashed the window, than to the miscreant who had had his window smashed. There was an air of refined mystery about Evan MacIan, which did not exist in the irate little shopkeeper, an air of refined mystery which appealed to the policemen, for policemen, like most other English types, are at once snobs and poets. MacIan might possibly be a gentleman, they felt; the editor manifestly was not. And the editor's fine rational republican appeals to his respect for law, and his ardour to be tried by his fellow citizens, seemed to the police quite as much gibberish as Evan's mysticism could have done. The police were not used to hearing principles, even the principles of their own existence.

The police magistrate, before whom they were hurried and tried, was a Mr. Cumberland Vane, a cheerful, middle-aged gentleman, honourably celebrated for the lightness of his sentences and the lightness of his conversation. He occasionally worked himself up into a sort of theoretic rage about certain particular offenders, such as the men who took pokers to their wives, talked in a loose, sentimental way about the desirability of flogging them, and was hopelessly bewildered by the fact that the wives seemed even more angry with him than with their husbands. He was a tall, spruce man, with a twist of black moustache and incomparable morning dress. He looked like a gentleman, and yet, somehow, like a stage gentleman.

He had often treated serious crimes against mere order or property with a humane flippancy. Hence, about the mere breaking of an editor's window, he was almost uproarious.

"Come, Mr. MacIan, come," he said, leaning back in his chair, "do you generally enter your friends' houses by walking through the glass?" (Laughter.)

"He is not my friend," said Evan, with the stolidity of a dull child.

"Not your friend, eh?" said the magistrate, sparkling. "Is he your brother-in-law?" (Loud and prolonged laughter.)

"He is my enemy," said Evan, simply; "he is the enemy of God."

Mr. Vane shifted sharply in his seat, dropping the eye-glass out of his eye in a momentary and not unmanly embarrassment.

"You mustn't talk like that here," he said, roughly, and in a kind of hurry, "that has nothing to do with us."

Evan opened his great, blue eyes; "God," he began.

"Be quiet," said the magistrate, angrily, "it is most undesirable that things of that sort should be spoken about—a—in public, and in an ordinary Court of Justice. Religion is—a—too personal a matter to be mentioned in such a place."

"Is it?" answered the Highlander, "then what did those policemen swear by just now?"

"That is no parallel," answered Vane, rather irritably; "of course there is a form of oath—to be taken reverently—reverently, and there's an end of it. But to talk in a public place about one's most sacred and private sentiments—well, I call it bad taste. (Slight applause.) I call it irreverent. I call it irreverent, and I'm not specially orthodox either."

"I see you are not," said Evan, "but I am."

"We are wandering from the point," said the police magistrate, pulling himself together.

"May I ask why you smashed this worthy citizen's window?"

Evan turned a little pale at the mere memory, but he answered with the same cold and deadly literalism that he showed throughout.

"Because he blasphemed Our Lady."

"I tell you once and for all," cried Mr. Cumberland Vane, rapping his knuckles angrily on the table, "I tell you, once for all, my man, that I will not have you turning on any religious rant or cant here. Don't imagine that it will impress me. The most religious people are not those who talk about it. (Applause.) You answer the questions and do nothing else."

"I did nothing else," said Evan, with a slight smile.

"Eh," cried Vane, glaring through his eye-glass.

"You asked me why I broke his window," said MacIan, with a face of wood. "I answered, 'Because he blasphemed Our Lady.' I had no other reason. So I have no other answer." Vane continued to gaze at him with a sternness not habitual to him.

"You are not going the right way to work, Sir," he said, with severity. "You are not going the right way to work to—a—have your case treated with special consideration. If you had simply expressed regret for what you had done, I should have been strongly inclined to dismiss the matter as an outbreak of temper. Even now, if you say that you are sorry I shall only——"

"But I am not in the least sorry," said Evan, "I am very pleased."

"I really believe you are insane," said the stipendiary, indignantly, for he had really been doing his best as a good-natured man, to compose the dispute. "What conceivable right have you to break other people's windows because their opinions do not agree with yours? This man only gave expression to his sincere belief."

"So did I," said the Highlander.

"And who are you?" exploded Vane. "Are your views necessarily the right ones? Are you necessarily in possession of the truth?"

"Yes," said MacIan.

The magistrate broke into a contemptuous laugh.

"Oh, you want a nurse to look after you," he said. "You must pay £10."

Evan MacIan plunged his hands into his loose grey garments and drew out a queer looking leather purse. It contained exactly twelve sovereigns. He paid down the ten, coin by coin, in silence, and equally silently returned the remaining two to the receptacle. Then he said, "May I say a word, your worship?"

Cumberland Vane seemed half hypnotised with the silence and automatic movements of the stranger; he made a movement with his head, which might have been either "yes" or "no." "I only wished to say, your worship," said MacIan, putting back the purse in his trouser pocket, "that smashing that shop window was, I confess, a useless and rather irregular business. It may be excused, however, as a mere preliminary to further proceedings, a sort of preface. Wherever and whenever I meet that man," and he pointed to the editor of "The Atheist," "whether it be outside this door in ten minutes from now, or twenty years hence in some distant country, wherever and whenever I meet that man, I will fight him. Do not be afraid, I will not rush at him like a bully, or bear him down with any brute superiority. I will fight him like a gentleman; I will fight him as our fathers fought. He shall choose how, sword or pistol, horse or foot. But if he refuses, I will write his cowardice on every wall in the world. If he had said of my mother what he said of the Mother of God, there is not a club of clean men in Europe that would deny my right to call him out. If he had said it of my wife, you English would yourselves have pardoned me for beating him like a dog in the market place. Your worship, I have no mother; I have no wife. I have only that which the poor have equally with the rich; which the lonely have equally with the man of many friends. To me this whole strange world is homely, because in the heart of it there is a home; to me this cruel world is kindly, because higher than the heavens there is something more human than humanity. If a man must not fight for this, may he fight for anything? I would fight for my friend, but if I lost my friend, I should still be there. I would fight for my country, but if I lost my country, I should still exist. But if what that devil dreams were true, I should not be—I should burst like a bubble and be gone. I could not live in that imbecile universe. Shall I not fight for my own existence?"

The magistrate recovered his voice and his presence of mind. The first part of the speech, the bombastic and brutally practical challenge, stunned him with surprise; but the rest of Evan's remarks, branching off as they did into theoretic phrases, gave his vague and very English mind (full of memories of the hedging and compromise in English public speaking) an indistinct sensation of relief, as if the man, though mad, were not so dangerous as he had thought. He went into a sort of weary laughter.

"For Heaven's sake, man," he said, "don't talk so much. Let other people have a chance (laughter). I trust all that you said about asking Mr. Turnbull to fight, may be regarded as rubbish. In case of accidents, however, I must bind you over to keep the peace."

"To keep the peace," repeated Evan, "with whom?"

"With Mr. Turnbull," said Vane.

"Certainly not," answered MacIan. "What has he to do with peace?"

"Do you mean to say," began the magistrate, "that you refuse to . . ."

The voice of Turnbull himself clove in for the first time.

"Might I suggest," he said, "that I, your worship, can settle to some extent this absurd matter myself. This rather wild gentleman promises that he will not attack me with any ordinary assault—and if he does, you may be sure the police shall hear of it. But he says he will not. He says he will challenge me to a duel; and I cannot say anything stronger about his mental state than to say that I think that it is highly probable that he will. (Laughter.) But it takes two to make a duel, your worship (renewed laughter). I do not in the least mind being described on every wall in the world as the coward who would not fight a man in Fleet Street, about whether the Virgin Mary had a parallel in Mesopotamian mythology. No, your worship. You need not trouble to bind him over to keep the peace. I bind myself over to keep the peace, and you may rest quite satisfied that there will be no duel with me in it."

Mr. Cumberland Vane rolled about, laughing in a sort of relief.

"You're like a breath of April air, sir," he cried. "You're ozone after that fellow. You're perfectly right. Perhaps I have taken the thing too seriously. I should love to see him sending you challenges and to see you smiling. Well, well."

Evan went out of the Court of Justice free, but strangely shaken, like a sick man. Any punishment or suppression he would have felt as natural; but the sudden juncture between the laughter of his judge and the laughter of the man he had wronged, made him feel suddenly small, or at least, defeated. It was really true that the whole modern world regarded his world as a bubble. No cruelty could have shown it, but their kindness showed it with a ghastly clearness. As he was brooding, he suddenly became conscious of a small, stern figure, fronting him in silence. Its eyes were grey and awful, and its beard red. It was Turnbull.

"Well, sir," said the editor of "The Atheist," "where is the fight to be? Name the field, sir."

Evan stood thunderstruck. He stammered out something, he knew not what; he only guessed it by the answer of the other.

"Do I want to fight? Do I want to fight?" cried the furious Freethinker. "Why, you moonstruck scarecrow of superstition, do you think your dirty saints are the only people who can die? Haven't you hung atheists, and burned them, and boiled them, and did they ever deny their faith? Do you think we don't want to fight? Night and day I have prayed—I have longed—for an atheist revolution—I have longed to see your blood and ours in the streets. Let it be yours or mine?"

"But you said ..." began MacIan.

"I know," said Turnbull, scornfully. "And what did you say? You damned fool, you said things that might have got us locked up for a year, and shadowed by the coppers for half a decade. If you wanted to fight, why did you tell that ass you wanted to? I got you out, to fight if you want to. Now, fight if you dare."

"I swear to you, then," said MacIan, after a pause. "I swear to you that nothing shall come between us. I swear to you that nothing shall be in my heart or in my head till our swords clash together. I swear it by the God you have denied, by the Blessed Lady you have blasphemed; I swear it by the seven swords in her heart. I swear it by the Holy Island where my fathers are, by the honour of my mother, by the secret of my people, and by the chalice of the Blood of God."

The atheist drew up his head. "And I," he said, "give my word."

III

SOME OLD CURIOSITIES

The evening sky, a dome of solid gold, unflaked even by a single
sunset cloud, steeped the meanest sights of London in a strange and
mellow light. It made a little greasy street off St. Martin's Lane look as
if it were paved with gold. It made the pawnbroker's half-way down
it shine as if it were really that Mountain of Piety[19] that the French
poetic instinct has named it; it made the mean pseudo-French book-
shop, next but one to it, a shop packed with dreary indecency, show
for a moment a kind of Parisian colour. And the shop that stood
between the pawnshop and the shop of dreary indecency, showed
with quite a blaze of old world beauty, for it was, by accident, a shop
not unbeautiful in itself. The front window had a glimmer of bronze
and blue steel, lit, as by a few stars, by the sparks of what were alleged
to be jewels; for it was in brief, a shop of bric-a-brac and old curiosities. A row of half burnished seventeenth century swords ran like
an ornate railing along the front of the window; behind was a darker
glimmer of old oak and old armour; and higher up hung the most
extraordinary looking South Sea tools or utensils, whether designed
for killing enemies or merely for cooking them, no mere white man
could possibly conjecture. But the romance of the eye, which really
on this rich evening, clung about the shop, had its main source in the
accident of two doors standing open, the front door that opened on
the street and a back door that opened on an odd green square of
garden, that the sun turned to a square of gold. There is nothing
more beautiful than thus to look as it were through the archway of a
house; as if the open sky were an interior chamber, and the sun a
secret lamp of the place.

I have suggested that the sunset light made everything lovely. To
say that it made the keeper of the curiosity shop lovely would be a

---

[19]"Mountain of Piety" is from the French *Mont de piété*, which in turn is derived
from the Italian *Monte di pietà*.

tribute to it perhaps too extreme. It would easily have made him beautiful if he had been merely squalid; if he had been a Jew of the Fagin type. But he was a Jew of another and much less admirable type; a Jew with a very well sounding name. For though there are no hard tests for separating the tares and wheat of any people; one rude but efficient guide is that the nice Jew is called Moses Solomon, and the nasty Jew is called Thornton Percy. The keeper of the curiosity shop was of the Thornton Percy branch of the chosen people; he belonged to those Lost Ten Tribes[20] whose industrious object is to lose themselves. He was a man still young, but already corpulent, with sleek dark hair, heavy handsome clothes, and a full, fat, permanent smile, which looked at the first glance kindly, and at the second cowardly. The name over his shop was Henry Gordon, but two Scotchmen who were in his shop that evening could come upon no trace of a Scotch accent.

These two Scotchmen in this shop were careful purchasers, but free-handed payers. One of them who seemed to be the principal and the authority (whom, indeed, Mr. Henry Gordon fancied he had seen somewhere before), was a small, sturdy fellow, with fine grey eyes, a square red tie and a square red beard, that he carried aggressively forward as if he defied any one to pull it. The other kept so much in the background in comparison that he looked almost ghostly in his grey cloak or plaid, a tall, sallow, silent young man.

The two Scotchmen were interested in seventeenth century swords. They were fastidious about them. They had a whole armoury of these weapons brought out and rolled clattering about the counter, until they found two of precisely the same length. Presumably they desired the exact symmetry for some decorative trophy. Even then they felt the points, poised the swords for balance and bent them in a circle to see that they sprang straight again; which, for decorative purposes, seems carrying realism rather far.

---

[20] The Lost Ten Tribes of Israel were the ten tribes forming the Kingdom of Israel, as opposed to the kingdom of Judah, which was made up of the other two tribes after the death of Solomon (ca. 930 B.C.). After defeat by the Chaldeans, they were transported to captivity in Babylon, but when Cyrus granted freedom to the Jews only the two tribes of Judah returned. The fate of the ten tribes is unknown, but they were no doubt assimilated.

"These will do," said the strange person with the red beard. "And perhaps I had better pay for them at once. And as you are the challenger, Mr. MacIan, perhaps you had better explain the situation."

The tall Scotchman in grey took a step forward and spoke in a voice quite clear and bold, and yet somehow lifeless, like a man going through an ancient formality.

"The fact is, Mr. Gordon, we have to place our honour in your hands. Words have passed between Mr. Turnbull and myself on a grave and invaluable matter, which can only be atoned for by fighting. Unfortunately, as the police are in some sense pursuing us, we are hurried, and must fight now and without seconds. But if you will be so kind as to take us into your little garden and see fair play, we shall feel how——"

The shopman recovered himself from a stunning surprise and burst out:

"Gentlemen, are you drunk? A duel! A duel in my garden. Go home, gentlemen, go home. Why, what did you quarrel about?"

"We quarrelled," said Evan, in the same dead voice, "about religion." The fat shopkeeper rolled about in his chair with enjoyment.

"Well, this is a funny game," he said. "So you want to commit murder on behalf of religion. Well, well my religion is a little respect for humanity, and——"

"Excuse me," cut in Turnbull, suddenly and fiercely, pointing towards the pawnbroker's next door. "Don't you own that shop?"

"Why—er—yes," said Gordon.

"And don't you own that shop?" repeated the secularist, pointing backward to the pornographic bookseller.

"What if I do?"

"Why, then," cried Turnbull, with grating contempt. "I will leave the religion of humanity confidently in your hands; but I am sorry I troubled you about such a thing as honour. Look here my man. I do believe in humanity. I do believe in liberty. My father died for it under the swords of the Yeomanry.[21] I am going to die for it, if need be, under that sword on your counter. But if there is one sight that makes

---

[21] Yeomanry: a yeoman is a person who holds and cultivates a small landed estate; historically it meant a person who owned land of annual value of forty shillings. On occasion, members of this group could become members of the volunteer cavalry forces raised from this class to support the civil authorities (1794–1908).

me doubt it it is your foul fat face. It is hard to believe you were not meant to be ruled like a dog or killed like a cockroach. Don't try your slave's philosophy on me. We are going to fight, and we are going to fight in your garden, with your swords. Be still! Raise your voice above a whisper, and I run you through the body."

Turnbull put the bright point of the sword against the gay waist-coat of the dealer, who stood choking with rage and fear, and an astonishment so crushing as to be greater than either.

"MacIan," said Turnbull, falling almost into the familiar tone of a business partner, "MacIan, tie up this fellow and put a gag in his mouth. Be still, I say, or I kill you where you stand."

The man was too frightened to scream, but he struggled wildly, while Evan MacIan, whose long, lean hands were unusually power-ful, tightened some old curtain cords round him, strapped a rope gag in his mouth and rolled him on his back on the floor.

"There's nothing very strong here," said Evan, looking about him. "I'm afraid he'll work through that gag in half an hour or so."

"Yes," said Turnbull, "but one of us will be killed by that time."

"Well, let's hope so," said the Highlander, glancing doubtfully at the squirming thing on the floor.

"And now," said Turnbull, twirling his fiery moustache and fin-gering his sword, "let us go into the garden. What an exquisite sum-mer evening!"

MacIan said nothing, but lifting his sword from the counter went out into the sun.

The brilliant light ran along the blades, filling the channels of them with white fire; the combatants stuck their swords in the turf and took off their hats, coats, waistcoats, and boots. Evan said a short Latin prayer to himself, during which Turnbull made something of a parade of lighting a cigarette which he flung away the instant after, when he saw MacIan apparently standing ready. Yet MacIan was not exactly ready. He stood staring like a man stricken with a trance.

"What are you staring at?" asked Turnbull. "Do you see the bobbies?"

"I see Jerusalem," said Evan, "all covered with the shields and stan-dards of the Saracens."

"Jerusalem!" said Turnbull, laughing. "Well, we've taken the only inhabitant into captivity."

And he picked up his sword and made it whistle like a boy's wand.

"I beg your pardon," said MacIan, drily. "Let us begin."

MacIan made a military salute with his weapon, which Turnbull copied or parodied with an impatient contempt; and in the stillness of the garden the swords came together with a clear sound like a bell. The instant the blades touched, each felt them tingle to their very points with a personal vitality, as if they were two naked nerves of steel. Evan had worn throughout an air of apathy, which might have been the stale apathy of one who wants nothing. But it was indeed the more dreadful apathy of one who wants something and will care for nothing else. And this was seen suddenly; for the instant Evan engaged he disengaged and lunged with an infernal violence. His opponent with a desperate promptitude parried and riposted; the parry only just succeeded, the riposte failed. Something big and unbearable seemed to have broken finally out of Evan in that first murderous lunge, leaving him lighter and cooler and quicker upon his feet. He fell to again, fiercely still, but now with a fierce caution. The next moment Turnbull lunged; MacIan seemed to catch the point and throw it away from him, and was thrusting back like a thunderbolt, when a sound paralysed him; another sound beside their ringing weapons. Turnbull, perhaps from an equal astonishment, perhaps from chivalry, stopped also and forbore to send his sword through his exposed enemy.

"What's that?" asked Evan, hoarsely.

A heavy scraping sound, as of a trunk being dragged along a littered floor, came from the dark shop behind them.

"The old Jew has broken one of his strings, and he's crawling about," said Turnbull. "Be quick! We must finish before he gets his gag out."

"Yes, yes, quick! On guard!" cried the Highlander. The blades crossed again with the same sound like song, and the men went to work again with the same white and watchful faces. Evan, in his impatience, went back a little to his wildness. He made windmills, as the French duellists say, and though he was probably a shade the better fencer of the two, he found the other's point pass his face twice so close as almost to graze his cheek. The second time he realised the actual possibility of defeat and pulled himself together under a shock of the sanity of anger. He narrowed, and, so to speak, tightened his operations: he fenced (as the swordman's boast goes), in a wedding ring; he turned Turnbull's thrusts with a maddening and almost mechanical click, like that of a machine. Whenever Turnbull's sword sought to go over that other mere white streak it seemed to be caught in a complex network of steel. He turned one thrust, turned another, turned another. Then suddenly he went forward at the lunge with his whole living weight. Turnbull leaped back, but Evan lunged and lunged and lunged again like a devilish piston rod or battering ram. And high above all the sound of the struggle there broke into the silent evening a bellowing human voice, nasal, raucous, at the highest pitch of pain. "Help! Help! Police! Murder! Murder!" The gag was broken; and the tongue of terror was loose.

"Keep on!" gasped Turnbull. "One may be killed before they come."

The voice of the screaming shopkeeper was loud enough to drown not only the noise of the swords but all other noises around it, but even through its rending din there seemed to be some other stir or scurry. And Evan, in the very act of thrusting at Turnbull, saw something in his eyes that made him drop his sword. The atheist, with his grey eyes at their widest and wildest, was staring straight over his shoulder at the little archway of shop that opened on the street beyond. And he saw the archway blocked and blackened with strange figures.

"We must bolt, MacIan," he said abruptly. "And there isn't a damned second to lose either. Do as I do."

With a bound he was beside the little cluster of his clothes and boots that lay on the lawn; he snatched them up, without waiting to put any of them on; and tucking his sword under his other arm, went wildly at the wall at the bottom of the garden and swung himself over it. Three seconds after he had alighted in his socks on the other side, MacIan alighted beside him, also in his socks and also carrying clothes and sword in a desperate bundle.

They were in a by-street, very lean and lonely itself, but so close to a crowded thoroughfare that they could see the vague masses of vehicles going by, and could even see an individual hansom cab passing the corner at the instant. Turnbull put his fingers to his mouth like a gutter-snipe[22] and whistled twice. Even as he did so he could hear the loud voices of the neighbours and the police coming down the garden.

The hansom swung sharply and came tearing down the little lane at his call. When the cabman saw his fares, however, two wild-haired men in their shirts and socks with naked swords under their arms, he not unnaturally brought his readiness to a rigid stop and stared suspiciously.

"You talk to him a minute," whispered Turnbull, and stepped back into the shadow of the wall.

"We want you," said MacIan to the cabman, with a superb Scotch drawl of indifference and assurance, "to drive us to St. Pancras Station—verra quick."

"Very sorry, sir," said the cabman, "but I'd like to know it was all right. Might I arst where you come from, Sir?"

A second after he spoke MacIan heard a heavy voice on the other side of the wall, saying: "I suppose I'd better get over and look for them. Give me a back."

"Cabby," said MacIan, again assuming the most deliberate and lingering lowland Scotch intonation, "if ye're really verra anxious to ken whar a' come fra', I'll tell ye as a verra great secret. A' come from Scotland. And a'm gaein' to St. Pancras Station. Open the doors, cabby."

The cabman stared, but laughed. The heavy voice behind the wall said: "Now then, a better back this time, Mr. Price." And from the shadow of the wall Turnbull crept out. He had struggled wildly into his coat (leaving his waistcoat on the pavement) and he was with a fierce pale face climbing up the cab behind the cabman. MacIan had no glimmering notion of what he was up to, but an instinct of discipline, inherited from a hundred men of war, made him stick to his own part and trust the other man's.

"Open the doors, cabby," he repeated, with something of the obstinate solemnity of a drunkard, "open the doors. Did ye no hear me say St. Pancras Station?"

---

[22] A gutter-snipe is a street urchin.

The top of a policeman's helmet appeared above the garden wall. The cabman did not see it, but he was still suspicious and began:

"Very sorry, sir, but ..." and with that the catlike Turnbull tore him out of his seat and hurled him into the street below, where he lay suddenly stunned.

"Give me his hat," said Turnbull in a silver voice, that the other obeyed like a bugle. "And get inside with the swords."

And just as the red and raging face of a policeman appeared above the wall, Turnbull struck the horse with a terrible cut of the whip and the two went whirling away like a boomerang.

They had spun through seven streets and three or four squares before anything further happened. Then, in the neighbourhood of Maida Vale, the driver opened the trap and talked through it in a manner not wholly common in conversations through that aperture.

"Mr. MacIan," he said shortly and civilly.

"Mr. Turnbull," replied his motionless fare.

"Under circumstances such as those in which we were both recently placed there was no time for anything but very abrupt action. I trust therefore that you have no cause to complain of me if I have deferred until this moment a consultation with you on our present position or future action. Our present position, Mr. MacIan, I imagine that I am under no special necessity of describing. We have broken the law and we are fleeing from its officers. Our future action is a thing about which I myself entertain sufficiently strong views; but I have no right to assume or to anticipate yours, though I may have formed a decided conception of your character and a decided notion of what they will probably be. Still, by every principle of intellectual justice, I am bound to ask you now and seriously whether you wish to continue our interrupted relations."

MacIan leant his white and rather weary face back upon the cushions in order to speak up through the open door.

"Mr. Turnbull," he said, "I have nothing to add to what I have said before. It is strongly borne in upon me that you and I, the sole occupants of this runaway cab, are at this moment the two most important people in London, possibly in Europe. I have been looking at all the streets as we went past, I have been looking at all the shops as we went past, I have been looking at all the churches as we went past. At first, I felt a little dazed with the vastness of it all. I could not understand what it all meant. But now I know exactly what it all means. It means us. This whole civilisation is only a dream. You and I are the realities."

"Religious symbolism," said Mr. Turnbull, through the trap, "does not, as you are probably aware, appeal ordinarily to thinkers of the school to which I belong. But in symbolism as you use it in this instance, I must, I think, concede a certain truth. We *must* fight this thing out somewhere; because, as you truly say, we have found each other's reality. We *must* kill each other—or convert each other. I used to think all Christians were hypocrites, and I felt quite mildly towards them really. But I know you are sincere—and my soul is mad against you. In the same way you used, I suppose, to think that all atheists thought atheism would leave them free for immorality—and yet in your heart you tolerated them entirely. Now you *know* that I am an honest man, and you are mad against me, as I am against you. Yes, that's it. You can't be angry with bad men. But a good man in the wrong—why one thirsts for his blood. Yes, you open for me a vista of thought."

"Don't run into anything," said Evan, immovably.

"There's something in that view of yours, too," said Turnbull, and shut down the trap.

They sped on through shining streets that shot by them like arrows. Mr. Turnbull had evidently a great deal of unused practical talent which was unrolling itself in this ridiculous adventure. They had got away with such stunning promptitude that the police chase had in all probability not even properly begun. But in case it had, the amateur cabman chose his dizzy course through London with a strange dexterity. He did not do what would have first occurred to any ordinary outsider desiring to destroy his tracks. He did not cut into by-ways or twist his way through mean streets. His amateur common sense told him that it was precisely the poor street, the side street, that would be likely to remember and report the passing of a hansom cab, like the passing of a royal procession. He kept chiefly to the great roads, so full of hansoms that a wilder pair than they might easily have passed in the press. In one of the quieter streets Evan put on his boots.

Towards the top of Albany Street the singular cabman again opened the trap.

"Mr. MacIan," he said, "I understand that we have now definitely settled that in the conventional language honour is not satisfied. Our action must at least go further than it has gone under recent interrupted conditions. That, I believe, is understood."

"Perfectly," replied the other with his bootlace in his teeth.

"Under those conditions," continued Turnbull, his voice coming through the hole with a slight note of trepidation very unusual with him, "I have a suggestion to make, if that can be called a suggestion, which has probably occurred to you as readily as to me. Until the actual event comes off we are practically in the position if not of comrades, at least of business partners. Until the event comes off, therefore, I should suggest that quarrelling would be inconvenient and rather inartistic; while the ordinary exchange of politeness between man and man would be not only elegant but uncommonly practical."

"You are perfectly right," answered MacIan, with his melancholy voice, "in saying that all this has occurred to me. All duellists should behave like gentlemen to each other. But we, by the queerness of our position, are something much more than either duellists or gentlemen. We are, in the oddest and most exact sense of the term, brothers—in arms."

"Mr. MacIan," replied Turnbull, calmly, "no more need be said." And he closed the trap once more.

They had reached Finchley Road before he opened it again.

Then he said, "Mr. MacIan, may I offer you a cigar. It will be a touch of realism."

"Thank you," answered Evan—"You are very kind." And he began to smoke in the cab.

IV

A DISCUSSION AT DAWN

The duellists had from their own point of view escaped or conquered the chief powers of the modern world. They had satisfied the magistrate, they had tied the tradesman neck and heels, and they had left the police behind. As far as their own feelings went they had melted into a monstrous sea; they were but the fare and driver of one of the million hansoms that fill London streets. But they had forgotten something; they had forgotten journalism. They had forgotten that there exists in the modern world, perhaps for the first time in history, a class of people whose interest is not that things should happen well or happen badly, should happen successfully or happen unsuccessfully, should happen to the advantage of this party or the advantage of that party, but whose interest simply is that things should happen.

It is the one great weakness of journalism as a picture of our modern existence, that it must be a picture made up entirely of exceptions. We announce on flaring posters that a man has fallen off a scaffolding. We do not announce on flaring posters that a man has not fallen off a scaffolding. Yet this latter fact is fundamentally more exciting, as indicating that that moving tower of terror and mystery, a man, is still abroad upon the earth. That the man has not fallen off a scaffolding is really more sensational; and it is also some thousand times more common. But journalism cannot reasonably be expected thus to insist upon the permanent miracles. Busy editors cannot be expected to put on their posters, "Mr. Wilkinson Still Safe," or "Mr. Jones, of Worthing, Not Dead Yet." They cannot announce the happiness of mankind at all. They cannot describe all the forks that are not stolen, or all the marriages that are not judiciously dissolved.[23] Hence the

---

[23] "Judiciously dissolved" is a typographical error for "judicially dissolved", which is how it originally appeared in the serially published version. The error appeared in the first American edition of the work and was not changed in any later publication.

complete picture they give of life is of necessity fallacious; they can only represent what is unusual. However democratic they may be, they are only concerned with the minority.

The incident of the religious fanatic who broke a window on Ludgate Hill was alone enough to set them up in good copy for the night. But when the same man was brought before a magistrate and defied his enemy to mortal combat in the open court, then the columns would hardly hold the excruciating information, and the headlines were so large that there was hardly room for any of the text. The "Daily Telegraph" headed a column, "A Duel on Divinity," and there was a correspondence afterwards which lasted for months, about whether police magistrates ought to mention religion. The "Daily Mail," in its dull, sensible way, headed the events, "Wanted to fight for the Virgin." Mr. James Douglas,[24] in "The Star," presuming on his knowledge of philosophical and theological terms, described the Christian's outbreak under the title of "Dualist and Duellist." The "Daily News" inserted a colourless account of the matter, but was pursued and eaten up for some weeks, with letters from outlying ministers, headed "Murder and Mariolatry." But the journalistic temperature was steadily and consistently heated by all these influences; the journalists had tasted blood, prospectively, and were in the mood for more; everything in the matter prepared them for further outbursts of moral indignation. And when a gasping reporter rushed in in the last hours of the evening with the announcement that the two heroes of the Police Court had literally been found fighting in a London back garden, with a shop-keeper bound and gagged in the front of the house, the editors and sub-editors were stricken still as men are by great beatitudes.

The next morning, five or six of the great London dailies burst out simultaneously into great blossoms of eloquent leader-writing. Towards the end all the leaders tended to be the same, but they all began differently. The "Daily Telegraph," for instance began, "There will be

[24] James Douglas (1867–1940) was the literary critic and later editor of *The Star* and afterward editor of *The Sunday Express*. He was well known to Chesterton, whose poetic volume *The Wild Knight* he had reviewed in 1900.

little difference among our readers or among all truly English and law-abiding men touching the etc., etc." The "Daily Mail" said, "People must learn, in the modern world, to keep their theological differences to themselves. The fracas, etc., etc." The "Daily News" started, "Nothing could be more inimical to the cause of true religion than etc., etc." The "Times" began with something about Celtic disturbances of the equilibrium of Empire, and the "Daily Express" distinguished itself splendidly by omitting altogether so controversial a matter and substituting a leader about goloshes.

And the morning after that, the editors and the newspapers were in such a state, that, as the phrase is, there was no holding them. Whatever secret and elvish thing it is that broods over editors and suddenly turns their brains, that thing had seized on the story of the broken glass and the duel in the garden. It became monstrous and omnipresent, as do in our time the unimportant doings of the sect of the Agapemonites,[25] or as did at an earlier time the dreary dishonesties of the Rhodesian financiers.[26] Questions were asked about it, and even answered, in the House of Commons. The Government was solemnly denounced in the papers for not having done something, nobody knew what, to prevent the window being broken. An enormous subscription was started to reimburse Mr. Gordon, the man who had been gagged in the shop. Mr. MacIan, one of the combatants, became for some mysterious reason, singly and hugely popular as a comic figure in the comic papers and on the stage of the music halls. He was always represented (in defiance of fact), with red whiskers, and a very

[25] The sect of Agapemone had no connection with early Christians but was an institution called the Abode of Love, founded at Charlwich near Bridgewater in Somerset in 1848 by English clergyman and eccentric Henry James Prince (1811–1899). Here he and his followers lived on a communal basis, professing spiritual doctrines and sharing everything, including their wives. In 1859 the group moved to Spaxton, Somerset, which had fifteen-foot-high walls and an increased number (two hundred) of "spiritual wives".

[26] Rhodesian financiers and their "dreary dishonesties" is not so much a reference to Rhodesia as to the Transvaal and in particular to Johannesburg, where the maltreatment of certain financiers claiming British nationality was a contributory factor, along with friction between the British Colonies of Cape Colony and Natal and the Dutch (Boer) republics of Orange Free State and Transvaal, to the Boer War of 1899–1902.

red nose, and in full Highland costume. And a song, consisting of an unimaginable number of verses, in which his name was rhymed with flat iron, the British Lion, sly 'un, dandelion, Spion (with Kop in the next line),[27] was sung to crowded houses every night. The papers developed a devouring thirst for the capture of the fugitives; and when they had not been caught for forty-eight hours, they suddenly turned the whole matter into a detective mystery. Letters under the heading, "Where are They," poured in to every paper, with every conceivable kind of explanation, running them to earth in the Monument,[28] the Twopenny Tube,[29] Epping Forest,[30] Westminster Abbey, rolled up in carpets at Shoolbreds,[31] locked up in safes in Chancery Lane.[32] Yes, the papers were very interesting, and Mr. Turnbull unrolled a whole bundle of them for the amusement of Mr. MacIan as they sat on a high common to the north of London,[33] in the coming of the white dawn.

The darkness in the east had been broken with a bar of grey; the bar of grey was split with a sword of silver and morning lifted itself laboriously over London. From the spot where Turnbull and MacIan were sitting on one of the barren steeps behind Hampstead, they could see the whole of London shaping itself vaguely and largely in the grey and growing light, until the white sun stood over it and it lay at their feet, the splendid monstrosity that it is. Its bewildering squares and parallelograms were compact and perfect as a Chinese puzzle; an enor-

[27] Spion Kop is a hill in South Africa, scene of a battle in the Boer War.

[28] The Monument is a memorial to the Great Fire of London (1666) and is situated on the site of the outbreak of the fire in Pudding Lane near London Bridge. The Monument was constructed by Christopher Wren in 1671–1677.

[29] The Twopenny Tube is the London Underground Railway, more particularly the Circle Line, where there was a flat-rate fare of twopence.

[30] Epping Forest is an area of woodland and heath to the northeast of London, much of which is open to the public.

[31] The "carpets at Shoolbreds" refers to James Shoolbred and Company, a grocer's and general emporium situated at 156 Tottenham Court Road.

[32] Chancery Lane is where the Public Records Office used to be situated and is in the center of London's legal district.

[33] "High common to the north of London" is likely the slope above Parliament Hill Fields, which is between Highgate and Hampstead on Hampstead Heath.

mous hieroglyphic which man must decipher or die. There fell upon
both of them, but upon Turnbull more than the other, because he
knew more what the scene signified, that quite indescribable sense as
of a sublime and passionate and heart-moving futility, which is never
evoked by deserts or dead men or men neglected and barbarous, which
can only be invoked by the sight of the enormous genius of man
applied to anything other than the best. Turnbull, the old idealistic
democrat, had so often reviled the democracy and reviled them justly
for their supineness, their snobbishness, their evil reverence for idle
things. He was right enough; for our democracy has only one great
fault; it is not democratic. And after denouncing so justly average
modern men for so many years as sophists and as slaves, he looked
down from an empty slope in Hampstead and saw what gods they are.
Their achievement seemed all the more heroic and divine, because it
seemed doubtful whether it was worth doing at all. There seemed to
be something greater than mere accuracy in making such a mistake as
London. And what was to be the end of it all? what was to be the
ultimate transformation of this common and incredible London man,
this workman on a tram in Battersea, this clerk on an omnibus in
Cheapside? Turnbull, as he stared drearily, murmured to himself the
words of the old atheistic and revolutionary Swinburne who had intoxicated his youth:

> "And still we ask if God or man
> Can loosen thee Lazarus;
> Bid thee rise up republican,
> And save thyself and all of us.
> But no disciple's tongue can say
> If thou can'st take our sins away."[34]

Turnbull shivered slightly as if behind the earthly morning he felt
the evening of the world, the sunset of so many hopes. Those words
were from "Songs before Sunrise." But Turnbull's songs at their best
were songs after sunrise, and sunrise had been no such great thing

[34] Algernon Charles Swinburne (1837–1909) was an English poet and critic. The
slightly misquoted lines come from the section "Before a Crucifix", from the longer
work "Songs before Sunrise" (1871).

after all. Turnbull shivered again in the sharp morning air. MacIan was also gazing with his face towards the city, but there was that about his blind and mystical stare that told one, so to speak, that his eyes were turned inwards. When Turnbull said something to him about London, they seemed to move as at a summons and come out like two householders coming out into their doorways.

"Yes," he said, with a sort of stupidity. "It's a very big place."

There was a somewhat unmeaning silence, and then MacIan said again:

"It's a very big place. When I first came into it I was frightened of it. Frightened exactly as one would be frightened at the sight of a man forty feet high. I am used to big things where I come from, big mountains that seem to fill God's infinity, and the big sea that goes to the end of the world. But then these things are all shapeless and confused things, not made in any familiar form. But to see the plain, square, human things as large as that, houses so large and streets so large, and the town itself so large, was like having screwed some devil's magnifying glass into one's eye. It was like seeing a porridge bowl as big as a house, or a mouse-trap made to catch elephants."

"Like the land of the Brobdingnagians," [35] said Turnbull, smiling.

"Oh! Where is that?" said MacIan.

Turnbull said bitterly, "In a book," and the silence fell suddenly between them again.

They were sitting in a sort of litter on the hillside; all the things they had hurriedly collected, in various places, for their flight, were strewn indiscriminately round them. The two swords with which they had lately sought each other's lives were flung down on the grass at random, like two idle walking-sticks. Some provisions they had bought last night, at a low public house, in case of undefined contingencies, were tossed about like the materials of an ordinary picnic, here a packet of chocolate, and there a bottle of wine. And to add to the disorder

[35] The land of the Brobdingnagians is one of the places visited by Lemuel Gulliver on one of his voyages in the fantastic novel *Gulliver's Travels* (1726), written by Anglo-Irish poet and satirist Jonathan Swift (1667–1745). In that land, everything was of gigantic size.

finally, there were strewn on top of everything, the most disorderly of modern things, newspapers, and more newspapers, and yet again newspapers, the ministers of the modern anarchy. Turnbull picked up one of them drearily, and took out a pipe.

"There's a lot about us," he said. "Do you mind if I light up?"

"Why should I mind?" asked MacIan.

Turnbull eyed with a certain studious interest, the man who did not understand any of the verbal courtesies; he lit his pipe and blew great clouds out of it.

"Yes," he resumed. "The matter on which you and I are engaged is at this moment really the best copy in England. I am a journalist, and I know. For the first time, perhaps, for many generations, the English are really more angry about a wrong thing done in England than they are about a wrong thing done in France."

"It is not a wrong thing," said MacIan.

Turnbull laughed. "You seem unable to understand the ordinary use of the human language. If I did not suspect that you were a genius, I should certainly know you were a blockhead. I fancy we had better be getting along and collecting our baggage."

And he jumped up and began shoving the luggage into his pockets, or strapping it on to his back. As he thrust a tin of canned meat, anyhow, into his bursting side pocket, he said, casually:

"I only meant that you and I are the most prominent people in the English papers."

"Well, what did you expect?" asked MacIan, opening his great grave blue eyes.

"The papers are full of us," said Turnbull, stooping to pick up one of the swords.

MacIan stooped and picked up the other.

"Yes," he said, in his simple way. "I have read what they have to say. But they don't seem to understand the point."

"The point of what?" asked Turnbull.

"The point of the sword," said MacIan, violently, and planted the steel point in the soil like a man planting a tree.

"That is a point," said Turnbull, grimly, "that we will discuss later. Come along."

Turnbull tied the last tin of biscuits desperately to himself with string; and then spoke, like a diver girt for plunging, short and sharp.

"Now, Mr. MacIan, you must listen to me. You must listen to me, not merely because I know the country, which you might learn by looking at a map, but because I know the people of the country, whom you could not know by living here thirty years. That infernal city down there is awake; and it is awake against us. All those endless rows of windows and windows are all eyes staring at us. All those forests of chimneys are fingers pointing at us, as we stand here on the hillside. This thing has caught on. For the next six mortal months they will think of nothing but us, as for six mortal months they thought of nothing but the Dreyfus case.[36] Oh, I know it's funny. They let starving children, who don't want to die, drop by the score without looking round. But because two gentlemen, from private feelings of delicacy, do want to die, they will mobilise the army and navy to prevent them. For half a year or more, you and I, Mr. MacIan, will be an obstacle to every reform in the British Empire. We shall prevent the Chinese being sent out of the Transvaal and the blocks being stopped in the Strand. We shall be the conversational substitute when any one recommends Home Rule, or complains of sky signs. Therefore, do not imagine, in your innocence, that we have only to melt away among those English hills as a Highland cateran[37] might into your god-forsaken Highland mountains. We must be eternally on our guard; we must live the hunted life of two distinguished criminals. We must expect to be recognised as much as if we were Napoleon escaping from

---

[36] The [Alfred] Dreyfus (1859–1935) case involved a French officer of Jewish background condemned to Devil's Island, French Guiana, in 1894 for allegedly selling secrets to the Germans. The flimsiness of the evidence against him encouraged Emile Zola to write *J'Accuse!* The Court of Appeal quashed the sentence in 1906, but in 1905 when Chesterton was writing, the affair was still a matter for debate and dispute and public opinion in both England and France was sharply divided over Dreyfus' guilt or innocence. German military documents unearthed in 1930 proved Dreyfus innocent.

[37] A Highland cateran was a Highland irregular-fighting man, brigand or marauder.

Elba. We must be prepared for our descriptions being sent to every tiny village, and for our faces being recognised by every ambitious policeman. We must often sleep under the stars as if we were in Africa. Last and most important we must not dream of effecting our—our final settlement, which will be a thing as famous as the Phoenix Park murders,[38] unless we have made real and precise arrangements for our isolation—I will not say our safety. We must not, in short, fight; until we have thrown them off our scent, if only for a moment. For, take my word for it, Mr. MacIan, if the British Public once catches us up, the British Public will prevent the duel, if it is only by locking us both up in asylums for the rest of our days."

MacIan was looking at the horizon with a rather misty look.

"I am not at all surprised," he said, "at the world being against us. It makes me feel I was right to——"

"Yes?" said Turnbull.

"To smash your window," said MacIan. "I have woken up the world."

"Very well, then," said Turnbull, stolidly. "Let us look at a few final facts. Beyond that hill there is comparatively clear country. Fortunately, I know the part well, and if you will follow me exactly, and, when necessary, on your stomach, we may be able to get ten miles out of London, literally without meeting any one at all, which will be the best possible beginning, at any rate. We have provisions for at least two days and two nights, three days if we do it carefully. We may be able to get fifty or sixty miles away without even walking into an inn door. I have the biscuits and the tinned meat, and the milk. You have the chocolate, I think? And the brandy?"

"Yes," said MacIan, like a soldier taking orders.

"Very well, then, come on. March. We turn under that third bush and so down into the valley." And he set off ahead at a swinging walk.

---

[38] The Phoenix Park murders involved the murders in 1882 of the Irish chief secretary and his undersecretary by "the Invincibles", a terrorist gang of Irish Nationalists, the members of which were later arrested and five of them hanged.

Then he stopped suddenly; for he realised that the other was not following. Evan MacIan was leaning on his sword with a lowering face, like a man suddenly smitten still with doubt.

"What on earth is the matter?" asked Turnbull, staring in some anger.

Evan made no reply.

"What the deuce is the matter with you?" demanded the leader, again, his face slowly growing as red as his beard; then he said, suddenly, and in a more human voice, "Are you in pain, MacIan?"

"Yes," replied the Highlander, without lifting his face.

"Take some brandy," cried Turnbull, walking forward hurriedly towards him. "You've got it."

"It's not in the body," said MacIan, in his dull, strange way. "The pain has come into my mind. A very dreadful thing has just come into my thoughts."

"What the devil are you talking about?" asked Turnbull.

MacIan broke out with a queer and living voice.

"We must fight now, Turnbull. We must fight now. A frightful thing has come upon me, and I know it must be now and here. I must kill you here," he cried, with a sort of tearful rage impossible to describe. "Here, here, upon this blessed grass."

"Why, you idiot," began Turnbull.

"The hour has come—the black hour God meant for it. Quick, it will soon be gone. Quick!"

And he flung the scabbard from him furiously, and stood with the sunlight sparkling along his sword.

"You confounded fool," repeated Turnbull. "Put that thing up again, you ass; people will come out of that house at the first clash of the steel."

"One of us will be dead before they come," said the other, hoarsely, "for this is the hour God meant."

"Well, I never thought much of God," said the editor of "The Atheist," losing all patience. "And I think less now. Never mind what God meant. Kindly enlighten my pagan darkness as to what the devil *you* mean."

"The hour will soon be gone. In a moment it will be gone," said the madman. "It is now, now, now that I must nail your blaspheming body to the earth—now, now that I must avenge Our Lady on her vile slanderer. Now or never. For the dreadful thought is in my mind."

"And what thought," asked Turnbull, with frantic composure, "occupies what you call your mind?"

"I must kill you now," said the fanatic, "because——"

"Well, because," said Turnbull, patiently.

"Because I have begun to like you."

Turnbull's face had a sudden spasm in the sunlight, a change so instantaneous that it left no trace behind it; and his features seemed still carved into a cold stare. But when he spoke again he seemed like a man who was placidly pretending to misunderstand something that he understood perfectly well.

"Your affection expresses itself in an abrupt form," he began, but MacIan broke the brittle and frivolous speech to pieces with a violent voice. "Do not trouble to talk like that," he said. "You know what I mean as well as I know it. Come on and fight, I say. Perhaps you are feeling just as I do."

Turnbull's face flinched again in the fierce sunlight, but his attitude kept its contemptuous ease.

"Your Celtic mind really goes too fast for me," he said; "let me be permitted in my heavy Lowland way to understand this new development. My dear Mr. MacIan, what do you really mean?"

MacIan still kept the shining sword-point towards the other's breast.

"You know what I mean. You mean the same yourself. We must fight now or else——"

"Or else?" repeated Turnbull, staring at him with an almost blinding gravity.

"Or else we may not want to fight at all," answered Evan, and the end of his speech was like a despairing cry.

Turnbull took out his own sword suddenly as if to engage; then planting it point downwards for a moment, he said, "Before we begin, may I ask you a question?"

MacIan bowed patiently, but with burning eyes.

"You said, just now," continued Turnbull, presently, "that if we did not fight now, we might not want to fight at all. How would you feel about the matter if we came not to want to fight at all?"

"I should feel," answered the other, "just as I should feel if you had drawn your sword, and I had run away from it. I should feel that because I had been weak, justice had not been done."

"Justice," answered Turnbull, with a thoughtful smile, "but we are talking about your feelings. And what do you mean by justice, apart from your feelings?"

MacIan made a gesture of weary recognition! "Oh, Nominalism,"[39] he said, with a sort of sigh, "we had all that out in the twelfth century."

"I wish we could have it out now," replied the other, firmly. "Do you really mean that if you came to think me right, you would be certainly wrong?"

"If I had a blow on the back of my head, I might come to think you a green elephant," answered MacIan, "but have I not the right to say now, that if I thought that I should think wrong?"

"Then you are quite certain that it would be wrong to like me?" asked Turnbull, with a slight smile.

"No," said Evan, thoughtfully, "I do not say that. It may not be the devil, it may be some part of God I am not meant to know. But I had a work to do, and it is making the work difficult."

"And I suppose," said the atheist, quite gently, "that you and I know all about which part of God we ought to know."

MacIan burst out like a man driven back and explaining everything.

"The Church is not a thing like the Athenæum Club,"[40] he cried. "If the Athenæum Club lost all its members, the Athenæum Club would dissolve and cease to exist. But when we belong to the Church we belong to something which is outside all of us; which is outside

[39] Nominalism holds that universals have no existence independently of being thought and are mere names, representing nothing that really exists. It was associated with the work of William of Ockham (ca. 1285–1349), who was excommunicated in 1328 and whose work was subsequently a significant influence on Luther.

[40] The Athenæum Club is a gentleman's club in Pall Mall, London, founded (1824) originally for men of distinction in literature, art and learning.

everything you talk about, outside the Cardinals and the Pope. They belong to it, but it does not belong to them. If we all fell dead suddenly, the Church would still somehow exist in God. Confound it all, don't you see that I am more sure of its existence than I am of my own existence? And yet you ask me to trust my temperament, my own temperament, which can be turned upside down by two bottles of claret or an attack of the jaundice. You ask me to trust that when it softens towards you and not to trust the thing which I believe to be outside myself and more real than the blood in my body."

"Stop a moment," said Turnbull, in the same easy tone, "even in the very act of saying that you believe this or that, you imply that there is a part of yourself that you trust even if there are many parts which you mistrust. If it is only you that like me, surely, also, it is only you that believe in the Catholic Church."

Evan remained in an unmoved and grave attitude.

"There is a part of me which is divine," he answered, "a part that can be trusted, but there are also affections which are entirely animal and idle."

"And you are quite certain, I suppose," continued Turnbull, "that if even you esteem me the esteem would be wholly animal and idle?" For the first time MacIan started as if he had not expected the thing that was said to him. At last he said:

"Whatever in earth or heaven it is that has joined us two together, it seems to be something which makes it impossible to lie. No, I do not think that the movement in me towards you was ... was that surface sort of thing. It may have been something deeper ... something strange. I cannot understand the thing at all. But understand this and understand it thoroughly, if I loved you my love might be divine. But in that I hate you, my hatred most certainly is divine. No, it is not some trifle that we are fighting about. It is not some superstition or some symbol. When you wrote those words about Our Lady, you were in that act a wicked man doing a wicked thing. If I hate you it is because you have hated goodness. And if I like you ... it is because you are good."

Turnbull's face wore an indecipherable expression.

"Well, shall we fight now?" he said.

"Yes," said MacIan, with a sudden contraction of his black brows, "yes, it must be now."

The bright swords crossed, and the first touch of them, travelling down blade and arm, told each combatant that the heart of the other was awakened. It was not in that way that the swords rang together when they had rushed on each other in the little garden behind the dealer's shop.

There was a pause, and then MacIan made a movement as if to thrust, and almost at the same moment Turnbull suddenly and calmly dropped his sword. Evan stared round in an unusual bewilderment, and then realised that a large man in pale clothes and a Panama hat was strolling serenely towards them.

V

THE PEACEMAKER

When the combatants, with crossed swords, became suddenly conscious of a third party, they each made the same movement. It was as quick as the snap of a pistol, and they altered it instantaneously and recovered their original pose, but they had both made it, they had both seen it, and they both knew what it was. It was not a movement of anger at being interrupted. Say or think what they would, it was a movement of relief. A force within them, and yet quite beyond them, seemed slowly and pitilessly washing away the adamant of their oath. As mistaken lovers might watch the inevitable sunset of first love, these men watched the sunset of their first hatred.

Their hearts were growing weaker and weaker against each other. When their weapons rang and reposted in the little London garden, they could have been very certain that if a third party had interrupted them something at least would have happened. They would have killed each other or they would have killed him. But now nothing could undo or deny that flash of fact, that for a second they had been glad to be interrupted. Some new and strange thing was rising higher and higher in their hearts like a high sea at night. It was something that seemed all the more merciless, because it might turn out an enormous mercy. Was there, perhaps, some such fatalism in friendship as all lovers talk about in love? Did God make men love each other against their will?

"I'm sure you'll excuse my speaking to you," said the stranger, in a voice at once eager and deprecating.

The voice was too polite for good manners. It was incongruous with the eccentric spectacle of the duellists which ought to have startled a sane and free man. It was also incongruous with the full and healthy, though rather loose physique of the man who spoke. At the first glance he looked a fine animal, with curling gold beard and hair, and blue eyes, unusually bright. It was only at the second glance that the mind felt a sudden and perhaps unmeaning irritation at the way in

87

which the gold beard retreated backwards into the waist-coat, and the way in which the finely shaped nose went forward as if smelling its way. And it was only, perhaps, at the hundredth glance that the bright blue eyes, which normally before and after the instant seemed brilliant with intelligence, seemed as it were to be brilliant with idiocy. He was a heavy, healthy looking man,[41] who looked all the larger because of the loose, light coloured clothes that he wore, and that had in their extreme lightness and looseness, almost a touch of the tropics. But a closer examination of his attire would have shown that even in the tropics it would have been unique; but it was all woven according to some hygienic texture[42] which no human being had ever heard of before, and which was absolutely necessary even for a day's health. He wore a huge broad-brimmed hat, equally hygienic, very much at the back of his head, and his voice coming out of so heavy and hearty a type of man was, as I have said, startlingly shrill and deferential.

"I'm sure you'll excuse my speaking to you," he said. "Now, I wonder if you are in some little difficulty which, after all, we could settle very comfortably together? Now, you don't mind my saying this, do you?"

The faces of both combatants remained somewhat solid under this appeal. But the stranger, probably taking their silence for a gathering shame, continued with a kind of gaiety:

"So you are the young men I have read about in the papers. Well, of course, when one is young, one is rather romantic. Do you know what I always say to young people?"

A blank silence followed this gay inquiry. Then Turnbull said in a colourless voice:

"As I was forty-seven last birthday, I probably came into the world too soon for the experience."

---

[41] This line, in an erratum slip in the first English edition, changed what had been printed in it and the first U.S. edition (but not the serialized publication) as: "He was a heavy, healthy working man."

[42] There was a tendency among certain groups to wear only fabrics such as mohair or camel hair fashioned in designs such as those of Dr. Jaeger, a German physician who believed that wearing wool next to the skin had a purifying effect on the body. Bernard Shaw bought his knickerbocker suits from Jaeger.

"Very good, very good," said the friendly person. "Dry Scotch humour. Dry Scotch humour. Well now. I understand that you two people want to fight a duel. I suppose you aren't much up in the modern world. We've quite outgrown duelling, you know. In fact, Tolstoy[43] tells us that we shall soon outgrow war, which he says is simply a duel between nations. A duel between nations. But there is no doubt about our having outgrown duelling."

Waiting for some effect upon his wooden auditors, the stranger stood beaming for a moment and then resumed:

"Now, they tell me in the newspapers that you are really wanting to fight about something connected with Roman Catholicism. Now, do you know what I always say to Roman Catholics?"

"No," said Turnbull, heavily. "Do *they?*" It seemed to be a characteristic of the hearty, hygienic gentleman that he always forgot the speech he had made the moment before. Without enlarging further on the fixed form of his appeal to the Church of Rome, he laughed cordially at Turnbull's answer; then his wandering blue eyes caught the sunlight on the swords, and he assumed a good-humoured gravity.

"But you know this is a serious matter," he said, eyeing Turnbull and MacIan, as if they had just been keeping the table in a roar with their frivolities. "I am sure that if I appealed to your higher natures ... your higher natures. Every man has a higher nature and a lower nature. Now, let us put the matter very plainly, and without any romantic nonsense about honour or anything of that sort. Is not bloodshed a great sin?"

"No," said MacIan, speaking for the first time.

"Well, really, really!" said the peacemaker.

"Murder is a sin," said the immovable Highlander. "There is no sin of bloodshed."

"Well, we won't quarrel about a word," said the other, pleasantly.

"Why on earth not?" said MacIan, with a sudden asperity. "Why shouldn't we quarrel about a word? What is the good of words if they

---

[43] Count Leo Nikolayevich Tolstoy (1828–1910) was a Russian writer, aesthetic philosopher, moralist and mystic. Chesterton here gently mocks what he had, about the same period, devastatingly critiqued as "Tolstoy and the Cult of Simplicity".

aren't important enough to quarrel over? Why do we choose one word more than another if there isn't any difference between them? If you called a woman a chimpanzee instead of an angel, wouldn't there be a quarrel about a word? If you're not going to argue about words, what are you going to argue about? Are you going to convey your meaning to me by moving your ears? The Church and the heresies always used to fight about words, because they are the only things worth fighting about. I say that murder is a sin, and bloodshed is not, and that there is as much difference between those words as there is between the word 'yes' and the word 'no'; or rather more difference, for 'yes' and 'no,' at least, belong to the same category. Murder is a spiritual incident. Bloodshed is a physical incident. A surgeon commits bloodshed."

"Ah, you're a casuist!" said the large man, wagging his head. "Now, do you know what I always say to casuists ... ?"

MacIan made a violent gesture; and Turnbull broke into open laughter. The peacemaker did not seem to be in the least annoyed, but continued in unabated enjoyment.

"Well, well," he said, "let us get back to the point. Now Tolstoy has shown that force is no remedy; so you see the position in which I am placed. I am doing my best to stop what I'm sure you won't mind my calling this really useless violence, this really quite wrong violence of yours. But it's against my principles to call in the police against you, because the police are still on a lower moral plane, so to speak, because, in short, the police undoubtedly sometimes employ force. Tolstoy has shown that violence merely breeds violence in the person towards whom it is used, whereas Love, on the other hand, breeds Love. So you see how I am placed. I am reduced to use Love in order to stop you. I am obliged to use Love."

He gave to the word an indescribable sound of something hard and heavy, as if he were saying "boots." Turnbull suddenly gripped his sword and said, shortly, "I see how you are placed quite well, sir. You will not call the police. Mr. MacIan, shall we engage?" MacIan plucked his sword out of the grass.

"I must and will stop this shocking crime," cried the Tolstoian, crimson in the face. "It is against all modern ideas. It is against the principle of love. How you, sir, who pretend to be a Christian ..."

MacIan turned upon him with a white face and bitter lip. "Sir," he said, "talk about the principle of love as much as you like. You seem to me colder than a lump of stone; but I am willing to believe that you may at some time have loved a cat, or a dog, or a child. When you were a baby, I suppose you loved your mother. Talk about love, then, till the world is sick of the word. But don't you talk about Christianity. Don't you dare to say one word, white or black, about it. Christianity is, as far as you are concerned, a horrible mystery. Keep clear of it, keep silent upon it, as you would upon an abomination. It is a thing that has made men slay and torture each other; and you will never know why. It is a thing that has made men do evil that good might come; and you will never understand the evil, let alone the good. Christianity is a thing that could only make you vomit, till you are other than you are. I would not justify it to you even if I could. Hate it, in God's name, as Turnbull does, who is a man. It is a monstrous thing, for which men die. And if you will stand here and talk about love for another ten minutes it is very probable that you will see a man die for it."

And he fell on guard. Turnbull was busy settling something loose in his elaborate hilt, and the pause was broken by the stranger.

"Suppose I call the police?" he said, with a heated face.

"And deny your most sacred dogma," said MacIan.

"Dogma!" cried the man, in a sort of dismay. "Oh, we have no *dogmas*, you know!"

There was another silence, and he said again, airily:

"You know, I think, there's something in what Shaw[44] teaches about no moral principles being quite fixed. Have you ever read 'The Quintessence of Ibsenism?' Of course he went very wrong over the war."

Turnbull, with a bent, flushed face, was tying up the loose piece of the pommel with string. With the string in his teeth, he said, "Oh, make up your damned mind and clear out!"

---

[44] George Bernard Shaw (1856–1950), Anglo-Irish playwright and author and friend of Chesterton (though the two disagreed in many fundamental respects), was very much in favor of the British side of the Boer War; Chesterton was not. The *Quintessence of Ibsenism* was published in 1891.

"It's a serious thing," said the philosopher, shaking his head. "I must be alone and consider which is the higher point of view. I rather feel that in a case so extreme as this ..." and he went slowly away. As he disappeared among the trees, they heard him murmuring in a sing-song voice, "New occasions teach new duties," out of a poem by James Russell Lowell.[45]

"Ah," said MacIan, drawing a deep breath. "Don't you believe in prayer now? I prayed for an angel."

"I am afraid I don't understand," answered Turnbull.

"An hour ago," said the Highlander, in his heavy meditative voice, "I felt the devil weakening my heart and my oath against you, and I prayed that God would send an angel to my aid."

"Well?" inquired the other, finishing his mending and wrapping the rest of the string round his hand to get a firmer grip.

"Well?"

"Well, that man was an angel," said MacIan.

"I didn't know they were as bad as that," answered Turnbull.

"We know that devils sometimes quote Scripture and counterfeit good," replied the mystic. "Why should not angels sometimes come to show us the black abyss of evil on whose brink we stand. If that man had not tried to stop us ... I might ... I might have stopped."

"I know what you mean," said Turnbull, grimly.

"But then he came," broke out MacIan, "and my soul said to me: 'Give up fighting, and you will become like That. Give up vows and dogmas, and fixed things, and you may grow like That. You may learn, also, that fog of false philosophy. You may grow fond of that mire of crawling, cowardly morals, and you may come to think a blow bad, because it hurts, and not because it humiliates. You may come to think murder wrong, because it is violent, and not because it is unjust. Oh, you blasphemer of the good, an hour ago I almost loved you! But do not fear for me now. I have heard the word Love pronounced in *his* intonation; and I know exactly what it means. On guard!'"

---

[45] James Russell Lowell (1819–1891) was an American poet, essayist and diplomat. The quoted portion comes from the poem "The Present Crisis" (1844) at line 86.

The swords caught on each other with a dreadful clang and jar, full of the old energy and hate; and at once plunged and replunged. Once more each man's heart had become the magnet of a mad sword. Suddenly, furious as they were, they were frozen for a moment motionless.

"What noise is that?" asked the Highlander, hoarsely.

"I think I know," replied Turnbull

"What? ... What?" cried the other.

"The student of Shaw and Tolstoy has made up his remarkable mind," said Turnbull, quietly. "The police are coming up the hill."

VI

THE OTHER PHILOSOPHER

Between high hedges in Hertfordshire, hedges so high as to create a kind of grove, two men were running. They did not run in a scampering or feverish manner, but in the steady swing of the pendulum. Across the great plains and uplands to the right and left of the lane, a long tide of sunset light rolled like a sea of ruby, lighting up the long terraces of the hills and picking out the few windows of the scattered hamlets in startling blood-red sparks. But the lane was cut deep in the hill and remained in an abrupt shadow. The two men running in it had an impression not uncommonly experienced between those wild green English walls; a sense of being led between the walls of a maze.

Though their pace was steady it was vigorous; their faces were heated and their eyes fixed and bright. There was, indeed, something a little mad in the contrast between the evening's stillness over the empty country-side, and those two figures fleeing wildly from nothing. They had the look of two lunatics, possibly they were.

"Are you all right?" said Turnbull, with civility. "Can you keep this up?"

"Quite easily, thank you," replied MacIan. "I run very well."

"Is that a qualification in a family of warriors?" asked Turnbull.

"Undoubtedly. Rapid movement is essential," answered MacIan, who never saw a joke in his life.

Turnbull broke out into a short laugh, and silence fell between them, the panting silence of runners.

Then MacIan said: "We run better than any of those policemen. They are too fat. Why do you make your policemen so fat?"

"I didn't do much towards making them fat myself," replied Turnbull, genially, "but I flatter myself that I am now doing something towards making them thin. You'll see they will be as lean as rakes by the time they catch us. They will look like your friend, Cardinal Manning." [46]

"But they won't catch us," said MacIan, in his literal way.

"No, we beat them in the great military art of running away," returned the other, "They won't catch us unless——"

MacIan turned his long equine face inquiringly. "Unless what?" he said, for Turnbull had gone silent suddenly, and seemed to be listening intently as he ran as a horse does with his ears turned back.

"Unless what?" repeated the Highlander.

"Unless they do—what they have done. Listen." MacIan slackened his trot, and turned his head to the trail they had left behind them. Across two or three billows of the up and down lane came along the ground the unmistakable throbbing of horses' hoofs.

"They have put the mounted police on us," said Turnbull, shortly. "Good Lord, one would think we were a Revolution."

"So we are," said MacIan, calmly. "What shall we do? Shall we turn on them with our points?"

"It may come to that," answered Turnbull, "though if it does, I reckon that will be the last act. We must put it off if we can." And he stared and peered about him between the bushes. "If we could hide somewhere the beasts might go by us," he said. "The police have their faults, but thank God they're inefficient. Why, here's the very thing. Be quick and quiet. Follow me."

He suddenly swung himself up the high bank on one side of the lane. It was almost as high and smooth as a wall, and on the top of it the black hedge stood out over them as an angle, almost like a thatched roof of the lane. And the burning evening sky looked down at them through the tangle with red eyes as of an army of goblins.

Turnbull hoisted himself up and broke the hedge with his body. As his head and shoulders rose above it they turned to flame in the full glow as if lit up by an immense firelight. His red hair and beard looked almost scarlet, and his pale face as bright as a boy's. Something

[46]Cardinal Henry Edward Manning (1808–1892) was the Archdeacon of Chichester (1840) who converted to Roman Catholicism in 1851 and became Archbishop of Westminster in 1865. He was made a cardinal in 1875 and, as contemporary portraits show, was notable for his cadaverousness.

violent, something that was at once love and hatred, surged in the strange heart of the Gael below him. He had an unutterable sense of epic importance, as if he were somehow lifting all humanity into a prouder and more passionate region of the air. As he swung himself up also into the evening light he felt as if he were rising on enormous wings.

Legends of the morning of the world which he had heard in childhood or read in youth came back upon him in a cloudy splendour, purple tales of wrath and friendship, like Roland and Oliver,[47] or Balin and Balan,[48] reminding him of emotional entanglements. Men who had loved each other and then fought each other; men who had fought each other and then loved each other, together made a mixed but monstrous sense of momentousness. The crimson seas of the sunset seemed to him like a bursting out of some sacred blood, as if the heart of the world had broken.

Turnbull was wholly unaffected by any written or spoken poetry; his was a powerful and prosaic mind. But even upon him there came for the moment something out of the earth and the passionate ends of the sky. The only evidence was in his voice, which was still practical but a shade more quiet.

"Do you see that summer-house-looking thing over there?" he asked shortly. "That will do for us very well."

Keeping himself free from the tangle of the hedge he strolled across a triangle of obscure kitchen garden, and approached a dismal shed or lodge a yard or two beyond it. It was a weather-stained hut of grey wood, which with all its desolation retained a tag or two of trivial ornament, which suggested that the thing had once been a sort of summer-house, and the place probably a sort of garden.

"That is quite invisible from the road," said Turnbull, as he entered it, "and it will cover us up for the night."

---

[47] Roland and Oliver were the two heroes in *The Song of Roland* and several other medieval epics.

[48] Balin and Balan were two brothers, both knights, whose deeds and death at each other's hands are recounted in a medieval French *chanson de geste*, and in works by Sir Thomas Malory, *Morte d'Arthur* (1485); Tennyson, *Balin and Balan* (1885); and Swinburne, *Tale of Balen* (1896).

MacIan looked at him gravely for a few moments. "Sir," he said, "I ought to say something to you. I ought to say——"

"Hush," said Turnbull, suddenly lifting his hand; "be still, man."

In the sudden silence, the drumming of the distant horses grew louder and louder with inconceivable rapidity, and the cavalcade of police rushed by below them in the lane, almost with the roar and rattle of an express train.

"I ought to tell you," continued MacIan, still staring stolidly at the other, "that you are a great chief, and it is good to go to war behind you."

Turnbull said nothing, but turned and looked out of the foolish lattice of the little windows, then he said, "We must have food and sleep first."

When the last echo of their eluded pursuers had died in the distant uplands, Turnbull began to unpack the provisions with the easy air of a man at a picnic. He had just laid out the last items, put a bottle of wine on the floor, and a tin of salmon on the window-ledge, when the bottomless silence of that forgotten place was broken. And it was broken by three heavy blows of a stick delivered upon the door.

Turnbull looked up in the act of opening a tin and stared silently at his companion. MacIan's long, lean mouth had shut hard.

"Who the devil can that be?" said Turnbull.

"God knows," said the other. "It might be God."

Again the sound of the wooden stick reverberated on the wooden door. It was a curious sound, and on consideration did not resemble the ordinary effects of knocking on a door for admittance. It was rather as if the point of a stick were plunged again and again at the panels in an absurd attempt to make a hole in them.

A wild look sprang into MacIan's eyes and he got up half stupidly, with a kind of stagger, put his hand out and caught one of the swords. "Let us fight at once," he cried, "it is the end of the world."

"You're overdone, MacIan," said Turnbull, putting him on one side. "It's only some one playing the goat. Let me open the door."

But he also picked up a sword as he stepped to open it.

He paused one moment with his hand on the handle and then flung the door open. Almost as he did so the ferrule of an ordinary bamboo cane came at his eyes, so that he had actually to parry it with the naked weapon in his hands. As the two touched, the point of the stick was dropped very abruptly, and the man with the stick stepped hurriedly back.

Against the heraldic background of sprawling crimson and gold offered him by the expiring sunset, the figure of the man with the stick showed at first merely black and fantastic. He was a small man with two wisps of long hair that curled up on each side, and seen in silhouette, looked like horns. He had a bow tie so big that the two ends showed on each side of his neck like unnatural stunted wings. He had his long black cane still tilted in his hand like a fencing foil and half presented at the open door. His large straw hat had fallen behind him as he leapt backwards.

"With reference to your suggestion, MacIan," said Turnbull, placidly, "I think it looks more like the Devil."

"Who on earth are you?" cried the stranger in a high shrill voice, brandishing his cane defensively.

"Let me see," said Turnbull, looking round to MacIan with the same blandness. "Who are we?"

"Come out," screamed the little man with the stick.

"Certainly," said Turnbull, and went outside with the sword, MacIan following.

Seen more fully, with the evening light on his face, the strange man looked a little less like a goblin. He wore a square pale-grey jacket suit, on which the grey butterfly tie was the only indisputable touch of affectation. Against the great sunset his figure had looked merely small: seen in a more equal light it looked tolerably compact and shapely. His reddish-brown hair, combed into two great curls, looked like the long, slow curling hair of the women in some pre-Raphaelite pictures. But within this feminine frame of hair his face was unexpectedly impudent, like a monkey's.

"What are you doing here?" he said, in a sharp small voice.

"Well," said MacIan, in his grave childish way, "what are *you* doing here?"

"I," said the man, indignantly, "I'm in my own garden."

"Oh," said MacIan, simply, "I apologise."

Turnbull was coolly curling his red moustache, and the stranger stared from one to the other, temporarily stunned by their innocent assurance.

"But, may I ask," he said at last, "what the devil you are doing in my summer-house?"

"Certainly," said MacIan. "We were just going to fight."

"To fight!" repeated the man.

"We had better tell this gentleman the whole business," broke in Turnbull. Then turning to the stranger he said firmly, "I am sorry, sir, but we have something to do that must be done. And I may as well tell you at the beginning and to avoid waste of time or language, that we cannot admit any interference."

"We were just going to take some slight refreshment when you interrupted us ..."

The little man had a dawning expression of understanding and stooped and picked up the unused bottle of wine, eyeing it curiously.

Turnbull continued:—

"But that refreshment was preparatory to something which I fear you will find less comprehensible, but on which our minds are entirely fixed, sir. We are forced to fight a duel. We are forced by honour and an internal intellectual need. Do not, for your own sake, attempt to stop us. I know all the excellent and ethical things that you will want to say to us. I know all about the essential requirements of civil order: I have written leading articles about them all my life. I know all about the sacredness of human life; I have bored all my friends with it. Try and understand our position. This man and I are alone in the modern world in that we think that God is essentially important. I think He does not exist; that is where the importance comes in for me. But this man thinks that He does exist, and thinking that very properly thinks Him more important than anything else. Now we wish to make a great demonstration and assertion—something that will set the world on fire like the first Christian persecutions. If you like, we are attempting a mutual martyrdom. The papers have posted up every town against us. Scotland Yard[49] has fortified every police station with our enemies;

---

[49] Scotland Yard is the headquarters of the London Metropolitan Police, named after the street in London on which it was first situated.

we are driven therefore to the edge of a lonely lane, and indirectly to taking liberties with your summer-house in order to arrange our ..."

"Stop!" roared the little man in the butterfly necktie. "Put me out of my intellectual misery. Are you really the two tomfools I have read of in all the papers? Are you the two people who wanted to spit each other in the Police Court? Are you? Are you?"

"Yes," said MacIan, "it began in a Police Court."

The little man slung the bottle of wine twenty yards away like a stone.

"Come up to my place," he said. "I've got better stuff than that. I've got the best Beaune within fifty miles of here. Come up. You're the very men I wanted to see."

Even Turnbull, with his typical invulnerability, was a little taken aback by this boisterous and almost brutal hospitality.

"Why ... sir ..." he began.

"Come up! Come in!" howled the little man, dancing with delight. "I'll give you a dinner. I'll give you a bed! I'll give you a green smooth lawn and your choice of swords and pistols. Why, you fools, I adore fighting! It's the only good thing in God's world! I've walked about these damned fields and longed to see somebody cut up and killed and the blood running. Ha! Ha!"

And he made sudden lunges with his stick at the trunk of a neighbouring tree so that the ferrule made fierce prints and punctures in the bark.

"Excuse me," said MacIan suddenly with the wide-eyed curiosity of a child, "excuse me, but ..."

"Well?" said the small fighter, brandishing his wooden weapon.

"Excuse me," repeated MacIan, "but was that what you were doing at the door?"

The little man stared an instant and then said: "Yes," and Turnbull broke into a guffaw.

"Come on!" cried the little man, tucking his stick under his arm and taking quite suddenly to his heels. "Come on! Confound me, I'll see both of you eat and then I'll see one of you die. Lord bless me, the gods must exist after all—they have sent me one of my day-dreams! Lord! A duel!"

He had gone flying along a winding path between the borders of the kitchen garden, and in the increasing twilight he was as hard to follow as a flying hare. But at length the path after many twists betrayed its purpose and led abruptly up two or three steps to the door of a tiny but very clean cottage. There was nothing about the outside to distinguish it from other cottages, except indeed its ominous cleanliness and one thing that was out of all the custom and tradition of all cottages under the sun. In the middle of the little garden among the stocks and marigolds there surged up in shapeless stone a South Sea Island idol. There was something gross and even evil in that eyeless and alien god among the most innocent of the English flowers.

"Come in!" cried the creature again. "Come in! it's better inside!"

Whether or no it was better inside it was at least a surprise. The moment the two duellists had pushed open the door of that inoffensive, whitewashed cottage they found that its interior was lined with fiery gold. It was like stepping into a chamber in the Arabian Nights. The door that closed behind them shut out England and all the energies of the West. The ornaments that shone and shimmered on every side of them were subtly mixed from many periods and lands, but were all oriental. Cruel Assyrian bas-reliefs ran along the sides of the passage; cruel Turkish swords and daggers glinted above and below them; the two were separated by ages and fallen civilisations. Yet they seemed to sympathise since they were both harmonious and both merciless. The house seemed to consist of chamber within chamber and created that impression as of a dream which belongs also to the Arabian Nights themselves. The innermost room of all was like the inside of a jewel. The little man who owned it all threw himself on a heap of scarlet and golden cushions and struck his hands together. A negro in a white robe and turban appeared suddenly and silently behind them.[50]

"Selim," said the host, "these two gentlemen are staying with me to-night. Send up the very best wine and dinner at once. And Selim,

[50] The comparison here with Lord Ivywood's House in *The Flying Inn* is notable. *Arabian Nights*: see below, *Flying Inn*, 524 and *Manalive*, 288, n. 11. Chesterton referred frequently to the *Arabian Nights* as capturing an exotic otherness that was at once both attractive and dangerous. This was known as "orientalism".

one of these gentlemen will probably die to-morrow. Make arrangements, please."

The negro bowed and withdrew.

Evan MacIan came out the next morning into the little garden to a fresh silver day, his long face looking more austere than ever in that cold light, his eyelids a little heavy. He carried one of the swords. Turnbull was in the little house behind him, demolishing the end of an early breakfast and humming a tune to himself, which could be heard through the open window. A moment or two later he leapt to his feet and came out into the sunlight, still munching toast, his own sword stuck under his arm like a walking-stick.

Their eccentric host had vanished from sight, with a polite gesture, some twenty minutes before. They imagined him to be occupied on some concerns in the interior of the house, and they waited for his emergence, stamping the garden in silence—the garden of tall, fresh country flowers, in the midst of which the monstrous South Sea idol lifted itself as abruptly as the prow of a ship riding on a sea of red and white and gold.

It was with a start, therefore, that they came upon the man himself already in the garden. They were all the more startled because of the still posture in which they found him. He was on his knees in front of the stone idol, rigid and motionless, like a saint in a trance or ecstasy. Yet when Turnbull's tread broke a twig, he was on his feet in a flash.

"Excuse me," he said with an irradiation of smiles, but yet with a kind of bewilderment. "So sorry ... family prayers ... old fashioned ... mother's knee. Let us go on to the lawn behind."

And he ducked rapidly round the statue to an open space of grass on the other side of it.

"This will do us best, Mr. MacIan," said he. Then he made a gesture toward the heavy stone figure on the pedestal which had now its blank and shapeless back turned toward them. "Don't you be afraid," he added, "he can still see us."

MacIan turned his blue, blinking eyes, which seemed still misty with sleep (or sleeplessness), towards the idol, but his brows drew together.

The little man with the long hair also had his eyes on the back view of the god. His eyes were at once liquid and burning, and he rubbed his hands slowly against each other.

"Do you know," he said, "I think he can see us better this way. I often think that this blank thing is his real face, watching, though it cannot be watched. He! he! Yes, I think he looks nice from behind. He looks more cruel from behind, don't you think?"

"What the devil is the thing?" asked Turnbull gruffly.

"It is the only Thing there is," answered the other. "It is Force."

"Oh!" said Turnbull shortly.

"Yes, my friends," said the little man, with an animated countenance, fluttering his fingers in the air, "it was no chance that led you to this garden; surely it was the caprice of some old god, some happy, pitiless god. Perhaps it was his will, for he loves blood; and on that stone in front of him men have been butchered by hundreds in the fierce, feasting islands of the South. In this cursed, craven place I have not been permitted to kill men on his altar. Only rabbits and cats, sometimes."

In the stillness MacIan made a sudden movement, unmeaning apparently, and then remained rigid.

"But to-day, to-day," continued the small man in a shrill voice. "Today his hour is come. To-day his will is done on earth as it is in heaven. Men, men, men will bleed before him to-day." And he bit his forefinger in a kind of fever.

Still, the two duellists stood with their swords as heavily as statues, and the silence seemed to cool the eccentric and call him back to more rational speech.

"Perhaps I express myself a little too lyrically," he said with an amicable abruptness. "My philosophy has its higher ecstasies, but perhaps you are hardly worked up to them yet. Let us confine ourselves to the unquestioned. You have found your way, gentlemen, by a beautiful accident, to the house of the only man in England (probably) who will favour and encourage your most reasonable project. From Cornwall to Cape Wrath this country is one horrible, solid block of humanitarianism. You will find men who will defend this or that war in a distant continent. They will defend it on the contemptible ground of commerce or the more contemptible ground of social good. But do not fancy that you will find one other person who will comprehend a strong man taking the sword in his hand and wiping out his enemy. My name is Wimpey, Morrice Wimpey. I had a Fellowship at Magdalen.[51] But I assure you I had to drop it, owing to my having said something in a public lecture infringing the popular prejudice against those great gentlemen, the assassins of the Italian Renascence. They let me say it at dinner and so on, and seemed to like it. But in a public lecture ... so inconsistent. Well, as I say, here is your only refuge and temple of honour. Here you can fall back on that naked and awful arbitration which is the only thing that balances the stars—a still, continuous violence. *Væ Victis!*[52] Down, down, down with the defeated! Victory is the only ultimate fact. Carthage *was* destroyed, the Red Indians are being exterminated: that is the single certainty. In an hour from now that sun will still be shining and that grass growing, and one of you will be conquered; one of you will be the conqueror. When it has been done, nothing will alter it. Heroes, I give you the hospitality fit for heroes. And I salute the survivor. Fall on!"

The two men took their swords. Then MacIan said steadily: "Mr. Turnbull, lend me your sword a moment."

Turnbull, with a questioning glance, handed him the weapon. MacIan took the second sword in his left hand and, with a violent gesture, hurled it at the feet of little Mr. Wimpey.

"Fight!" he said in a loud, harsh voice, "Fight me now!"

---

[51] Magdalen College, Oxford (1458). Here Chesterton pokes fun at the distinction between what is said among academics and what might be acceptable by "the common man" outside the ivory towers. It is useful to compare the philosophy of Oxford don Morrice Wimpey here with that of the "Cambridge philosopher" Professor Emerson Eames in the novel *Man Alive*. In the *Flying Inn*, both Hibbs However (who advocated vivisection on pauper children as long as by "fully qualified practitioners") and Jon Leveson (the Secretary of the Committee of the Imperial Commission of Liquor Control) had both decided to be moderate politicians "when at Cambridge".

[52] This is Latin for "Cursed be the defeated!", or "Suffering to the conquered!", Brennus' words as he threw his sword into the scales weighing gold intended to buy off the Gauls and secure their departure (see *Titus Livius, History of Rome* vol. 5, bk. 48). Morrice Wimpey's embrace of power recalls Nietzsche's "will to power" (see *The Flying Inn*, page 652, n. 43).

Wimpey took a step backward, and bewildered words bubbled on his lips.

"Pick up that sword and fight me," repeated MacIan, with brows as black as thunder.

The little man turned to Turnbull with a gesture, demanding judgment or protection.

"Really, sir," he began, "this gentleman confuses ..."

"You stinking little coward," roared Turnbull, suddenly releasing his wrath. "Fight, if you're so fond of fighting! Fight, if you're so fond of all that filthy philosophy! If winning is everything, go in and win! If the weak must go to the wall, go to the wall! Fight, you rat! Fight, or if you won't fight—run!"

And he ran at Wimpey, with blazing eyes.

Wimpey staggered back a few paces like a man struggling with his own limbs. Then he felt the furious Scotchman coming at him like an express-train, doubling his size every second, with eyes as big as windows and a sword as bright as the sun. Something broke inside him, and he found himself running away, tumbling over his own feet in terror, and crying out as he ran.

"Chase him!" shouted Turnbull as MacIan snatched up the sword and joined in the scamper. "Chase him over a county! Chase him into the sea! Shoo! Shoo! Shoo!"

The little man plunged like a rabbit among the tall flowers, the two duellists after him. Turnbull kept at his tail with savage ecstasy, still shooing him like a cat. But MacIan, as he ran past the South Sea idol, paused an instant to spring upon its pedestal. For five seconds he strained against the inert mass. Then it stirred; and he sent it over with a great crash among the flowers, that engulfed it altogether. Then he went bounding after the runaway.

In the energy of his alarm the ex-Fellow of Magdalen managed to leap the paling of his garden. The two pursuers went over it after him like flying birds. He fled frantically down a long lane with his two terrors in his trail till he came to a gap in the hedge and went across a steep meadow like the wind. The two Scotchmen, as they ran, kept up a cheery bellowing and waved their swords. Up three slanting meadows, down four slanting meadows on the other side, across another road, across a heath of snapping bracken, through a wood, across another road, and to the brink of a big pool, they pursued the flying philosopher. But when he came to the pool his pace was so precipitate that he could not stop it, and with a kind of lurching stagger, he fell splash into the greasy water. Getting dripping to his feet, with the water up to his knees, the worshipper of force and victory waded disconsolately to the other side and drew himself on to the bank. And Turnbull sat down on the grass and went off into reverberations of laughter. A second afterward the most extraordinary grimaces were seen to distort the stiff face of MacIan, and unholy sounds came from within. He had never practised laughing, and it hurt him very much.

VII

THE VILLAGE OF GRASSLEY-IN-THE-HOLE

At about half-past one, under a strong blue sky, Turnbull got up out of the grass and fern in which he had been lying, and his still intermittent laughter ended in a kind of yawn.

"I'm hungry," he said shortly. "Are you?"

"I have not noticed," answered MacIan. "What are you going to do?"

"There's a village down the road, past the pool," answered Turnbull. "I can see it from here. I can see the whitewashed walls of some cottages and a kind of corner of the church. How jolly it all looks. It looks so—I don't know what the word is—so sensible. Don't fancy I'm under any illusions about Arcadian virtue[53] and the innocent villagers. Men make beasts of themselves there with drink, but they don't deliberately make devils of themselves with mere talking. They kill wild animals in the wild woods, but they don't kill cats to the God of Victory. They don't——" He broke off and suddenly spat on the ground.

"Excuse me," he said; "it was ceremonial. One has to get the taste out of one's mouth."

"The taste of what?" asked MacIan.

"I don't know the exact name for it," replied Turnbull. "Perhaps it is the South Sea Islands, or it may be Magdalen College."

There was a long pause, and MacIan also lifted his large limbs off the ground—his eyes particularly dreamy.

"I know what you mean, Turnbull," he said, "but ... I always thought you people agreed with all that."

"Agreed with all what?" asked the other.

"With all that about doing as one likes, and the individual, and Nature loving the strongest, and all the things which that cockroach talked about."

[53] Arcadia is the mountainous district in the Peloponnese of southern Greece. In poetic fantasy it represents a pastoral paradise, the home of song loving and virtuous shepherds.

Turnbull's big blue-gray eyes stood open with a grave astonishment.

"Do you really mean to say, MacIan," he said, "that you fancied that we, the Free-thinkers, that Bradlaugh,[54] or Holyoake,[55] or Ingersoll,[56] believe all that dirty, immoral mysticism about Nature? Damn Nature!"

"I supposed you did," said MacIan calmly. "It seems to me your most conclusive position."

"And you mean to tell me," rejoined the other, "that you broke my window, and challenged me to mortal combat, and tied a tradesman up with ropes, and chased an Oxford Fellow across five meadows—all under the impression that I am such an illiterate idiot as to believe in Nature!"

"I supposed you did," repeated MacIan with his usual mildness; "but I admit that I know little of the details of your belief—or disbelief."

Turnbull swung round quite suddenly, and set off toward the village.

"Come along," he cried. "Come down to the village. Come down to the nearest decent inhabitable pub. This is a case for beer."

"I do not quite follow you," said the Highlander.

"Yes, you do," answered Turnbull. "You follow me slap into the inn-parlour. I repeat, this is a case for beer. We must have the whole of this matter out thoroughly before we go a step farther. Do you know that an idea has just struck me of great simplicity and of some cogency. Do not by any means let us drop our intentions of settling our differences with two steel swords. But do you not think that with

[54] Charles Bradlaugh (1833–1891) was an English politician, radical secularist and religious sceptic. He was an advocate of birth control and published a pamphlet on this subject for which he was prosecuted, unsuccessfully, for obscenity. He was M.P. for Northampton (1880–1891).

[55] George Jacob Holyoake (1817–1906) was an English secularist and editor of *The Reasoner*. He wrote about the lives of secularist Tom Paine (1851) and utilitarian John Stuart Mill (1873) and a book on *English Secularism* (1896). He was the last person imprisoned in England on a charge of atheism (1842).

[56] Robert Green Ingersoll (1833–1899) was an American lawyer and agnostic who became attorney general for Illinois (1867–1869). He was a noted agnostic lecturer and writer of many books that attacked Christian beliefs, including *Why I Am an Agnostic* (1896).

two pewter pots we might do what we really have never thought of doing yet—discover what our difference is?"

"It never occurred to me before," answered MacIan with tranquillity. "It is a good suggestion."

And they set out at an easy swing down the steep road to the village of Grassley-in-the-Hole.

Grassley-in-the-Hole was a rude parallelogram of buildings, with two thoroughfares which might have been called two high streets if it had been possible to call them streets. One of these ways was higher on the slope than the other, the whole parallelogram lying aslant, so to speak, on the side of the hill. The upper of these two roads was decorated with a big public-house, a butcher's shop, a small public-house, a sweetstuff shop, a very small public-house, and an illegible sign-post. The lower of the two roads boasted a horse-pond, a post-office, a gentleman's garden with very high hedges, a microscopically small public-house, and two cottages. Where all the people lived who supported all the public-houses was in this, as in many other English villages, a silent and smiling mystery. The church lay a little above and beyond the village, with a square gray tower dominating it decisively.

But even the church was scarcely so central and solemn an institution as the large public-house, the Valencourt Arms. It was named after some splendid family that had long gone bankrupt, and whose seat was occupied by a man who had invented an hygienic bootjack; but the unfathomable sentimentalism of the English people insisted on regarding the Inn, the seat and the sitter in it, as alike parts of a pure and marmoreal antiquity. And in the Valencourt Arms festivity itself had some solemnity and decorum; and beer was drunk with reverence, as it ought to be. Into the principal parlour of this place entered two strangers, who found themselves, as is always the case in such hostels, the object, not of fluttered curiosity or pert inquiry, but of steady, ceaseless, devouring ocular study. They had long coats down to their heels, and carried under each coat something that looked like a stick. One was tall and dark, the other short and red-haired. They ordered a pot of ale each.

"MacIan," said Turnbull, lifting his tankard, "the fool who wanted us to be friends made us want to go on fighting. It is only natural that the fool who wanted us to fight should make us friendly. MacIan, your health!"

Dusk was already dropping, the rustics in the tavern were already lurching and lumbering out of it by twos and threes, crying clamorous good-nights to a solitary old toper that remained, before MacIan and Turnbull had reached the really important part of their discussion.

MacIan wore an expression of sad bewilderment not uncommon with him. "I am to understand, then," he said, "that you don't believe in nature."

"You may say so in a very special and emphatic sense," said Turnbull. "I do not believe in nature, just as I do not believe in Odin.[57] She is a myth. It is not merely that I do not believe that nature can guide us. It is that I do not believe that nature exists."

"Exists?" said MacIan in his monotonous way, settling his pewterpot on the table.

"Yes, in a real sense nature does not exist. I mean that nobody can discover what the original nature of things would have been if things had not interfered with it. The first blade of grass began to tear up the earth and eat it; it was interfering with nature, if there is any nature. The first wild ox began to tear up the grass and eat it; he was interfering with nature, if there is any nature. In the same way," continued Turnbull, "the human when it asserts its dominance over nature is just as natural as the thing which it destroys."

"And in the same way," said MacIan almost dreamily, "the superhuman, the supernatural is just as natural as the nature which it destroys."

Turnbull took his head out of his pewter-pot in some anger.

"The supernatural, of course," he said, "is quite another thing; the case of the supernatural is simple. The supernatural does not exist."

"Quite so," said MacIan in a rather dull voice; "you said the same about the natural. If the natural does not exist the supernatural obviously can't." And he yawned a little over his ale.

Turnbull turned for some reason a little red and remarked quickly, "That may be jolly clever, for all I know. But every one does know

---

[57] Odin was, in Scandinavian mythology, the supreme god and creator.

that there is a division between the things that as a matter of fact do commonly happen and the things that don't. Things that break the evident laws of nature——"

"Which does not exist," put in MacIan sleepily. Turnbull struck the table with a sudden hand.

"Good Lord in heaven!" he cried——

"Who does not exist," murmured MacIan.

"Good Lord in heaven!" thundered Turnbull, without regarding the interruption. "Do you really mean to sit there and say that you, like anybody else, would not recognise the difference between a natural occurrence and a supernatural one—if there could be such a thing? If I flew up to the ceiling——"

"You would bump your head badly," cried MacIan, suddenly starting up. "One can't talk of this kind of thing under a ceiling at all. Come outside! Come outside and ascend into heaven!"

He burst the door open on a blue abyss of evening and they stepped out into it: it was suddenly and strangely cool.

"Turnbull," said MacIan, "you have said some things so true and some so false that I want to talk; and I will try to talk so that you understand. For at present you do not understand at all. We don't seem to mean the same things by the same words."

He stood silent for a second or two and then resumed.

"A minute or two ago I caught you out in a real contradiction. At that moment logically I was right. And at that moment I knew I was wrong. Yes, there is a real difference between the natural and the supernatural: if you flew up into that blue sky this instant, I should think that you were moved by God—or the devil. But if you want to know what I really think ... I must explain."

He stopped again, abstractedly boring the point of his sword into the earth, and went on:

"I was born and bred and taught in a complete universe. The supernatural was not natural, but it was perfectly reasonable. Nay, the supernatural to me is more reasonable than the natural; for the supernatural is a direct message from God, who is reason. I was taught that some things are natural and some things divine. I mean that some things are mechanical and some things divine. But there is the great difficulty,

Turnbull. The great difficulty is that, according to my teaching, you are divine."

"Me! Divine?" said Turnbull truculently. "What do you mean?"

"That is just the difficulty," continued MacIan thoughtfully. "I was told that there was a difference between the grass and a man's will; and the difference was that a man's will was special and divine. A man's free will, I heard, was supernatural."

"Rubbish!" said Turnbull.

"Oh," said MacIan patiently, "then if a man's free will isn't supernatural, why do your materialists deny that it exists?"

Turnbull was silent for a moment. Then he began to speak, but MacIan continued with the same steady voice and sad eyes:

"So what I feel is this: Here is the great divine creation I was taught to believe in. I can understand your disbelieving in it, but why disbelieve in a part of it? It was all one thing to me. God had authority because he was God. Man had authority because he was man. You cannot prove that God is better than a man; nor can you prove that a man is better than a horse. Why permit any ordinary thing? Why do you let a horse be saddled?"

"Some modern thinkers disapprove of it," said Turnbull a little doubtfully.

"I know," said MacIan grimly; "that man who talked about love, for instance."

Turnbull made a humorous grimace; then he said: "We seem to be talking in a kind of short-hand; but I won't pretend not to understand you. What you mean is this: that you learnt about all your saints and angels at the same time as you learnt about common morality, from the same people, in the same way. And you mean to say that if one may be disputed, so may the other. Well, let that pass for the moment. But let me ask you a question in turn. Did not this system of yours, which you swallowed whole, contain all sorts of things that were merely local, the respect for the chief of your clan, or such things; the village ghost, the family feud, or what not? Did you not take in those things, too, along with your theology?"

MacIan stared along the dim village road, down which the last straggler from the inn was trailing his way.

"What you say is not unreasonable," he said. "But it is not quite true. The distinction between the chief and us did exist; but it was never anything like the distinction between the human and the divine, or the human and the animal. It was more like the distinction between one animal and another. But——"

"Well?" said Turnbull.

MacIan was silent.

"Go on," repeated Turnbull; "what's the matter with you? What are you staring at?"

"I am staring," said MacIan at last, "at that which shall judge us both."

"Oh, yes," said Turnbull in a tired way, "I suppose you mean God."

"No, I don't," said MacIan, shaking his head. "I mean him."

And he pointed to the half-tipsy yokel who was ploughing down the road.

"What do you mean?" asked the atheist.

"I mean him," repeated MacIan with emphasis. "He goes out in the early dawn; he digs or he ploughs a field. Then he comes back and drinks ale, and then he sings a song. All your philosophies and political systems are young compared to him. All your hoary cathedrals, yes, even the Eternal Church on earth is new compared to him. The most mouldering gods in the British Museum are new facts beside him. It is he who in the end shall judge us all."

And MacIan rose to his feet with a vague excitement.

"What are you going to do?"

"I am going to ask him," cried MacIan, "which of us is right."

Turnbull broke into a kind of laugh. "Ask that intoxicated turnip-eater——" he began.

"Yes—which of us is right," cried MacIan violently. "Oh, you have long words and I have long words; and I talk of every man being the image of God; and you talk of every man being a citizen and enlightened enough to govern. But if every man typifies God, there is God. If every man is an enlightened citizen, there is your enlightened citizen. The first man one meets is always man. Let us catch him up."

And in gigantic strides the long, lean Highlander whirled away into the gray twilight, Turnbull following with a good-humoured oath.

The track of the rustic was easy to follow, even in the faltering dark; for he was enlivening his wavering walk with song. It was an interminable poem, beginning with some unspecified King William, who (it appeared) lived in London town and who after the second rise vanished rather abruptly from the train of thought. The rest was almost entirely about beer and was thick with local topography of a quite unrecognisable kind. The singer's step was neither very rapid nor, indeed, exceptionally secure; so the song grew louder and louder and the two soon overtook him.

He was a man elderly or rather of any age, with lean gray hair and a lean red face, but with that remarkable rustic physiognomy in which it seems that all the features stand out independently from the face; the rugged red nose going out like a limb; the bleared blue eyes standing out like signals.

He gave them greeting with the elaborate urbanity of the slightly intoxicated. MacIan, who was vibrating with one of his silent, violent decisions, opened the question without delay. He explained the philosophic position in words as short and simple as possible. But the singular old man with the lank red face seemed to think uncommonly little of the short words. He fixed with a fierce affection upon one or two of the long ones.

"Atheists!" he repeated with luxurious scorn. "Atheists! I know their sort, master. Atheists! Don't talk to me about 'un. Atheists!"

The grounds of his disdain seemed a little dark and confused; but they were evidently sufficient. MacIan resumed in some encouragement:

"You think as I do, I hope; you think that a man should be connected with the Church; with the common Christian——"

The old man extended a quivering stick in the direction of a distant hill.

"There's the church," he said thickly. "Grassley old church that is. Pulled down it was, in the old squire's time, and——"

"I mean," explained MacIan elaborately, "that you think that there should be some one typifying religion, a priest——"

"Priests!" said the old man with sudden passion. "Priests! I know 'un. What they want in England? That's what I say. What they want in England?"

"They want you," said MacIan.

"Quite so," said Turnbull, "and me; but they won't get us. MacIan, your attempt on the primitive innocence does not seem very successful. Let me try. What you want, my friend, is your rights. You don't want any priests or churches. A vote, a right to speak is what you———"

"Who says I a'n't got a right to speak?" said the old man, facing round in an irrational frenzy. "I got a right to speak. I'm a man, I am. I don't want no votin' nor priests. I say a man's a man; that's what I say. If a man a'n't a man, what is he? That's what I say, if a man a'n't a man, what is he? When I sees a man, I sez 'e's a man."

"Quite so," said Turnbull, "a citizen."

"I say he's a man," said the rustic furiously, stopping and striking his stick on the ground. "Not a city or owt else. He's a man."

"You're perfectly right," said the sudden voice of MacIan, falling like a sword. "And you have kept close to something the whole world of to-day tries to forget."

"Good-night."

And the old man went on wildly singing into the night.

"A jolly old creature," said Turnbull; "he didn't seem able to get much beyond that fact that a man is a man."

"Has anybody got beyond it?" asked MacIan.

Turnbull looked at him curiously. "Are you turning an agnostic?" he asked.

"Oh, you do not understand!" cried out MacIan. "We Catholics are all agnostics. We Catholics have only in that sense got as far as realising that a man is a man. But your Ibsens[58] and your Zolas[59] and your Shawls[60] and your Tolstoys[61] have not even got so far."

---

[58] Henrik Ibsen (1828–1906) was a Norwegian dramatist.
[59] Emile Zola (1840–1902) was a French novelist.
[60] Shaw: see n. 44, above.
[61] Tolstoy: see n. 43, above.

VIII

AN INTERLUDE OF ARGUMENT

Morning broke in bitter silver along the gray and level plain; and
almost as it did so Turnbull and MacIan came out of a low, scrubby
wood on to the empty and desolate flats. They had walked all night.

They had walked all night and talked all night also, and if the subject had been capable of being exhausted they would have exhausted
it. Their long and changing argument had taken them through districts and landscapes equally changing. They had discussed Haeckel[62]
upon hills so high and steep that in spite of the coldness of the night
it seemed as if the stars might burn them. They had explained and
re-explained the Massacre of St. Bartholomew[63] in little white lanes
walled in with standing corn as with walls of gold. They had talked
about Mr. Kensit[64] in dim and twinkling pine woods, amid the bewildering monotony of the pines. And it was with the end of a long
speech from MacIan, passionately defending the practical achieve-
ments and the solid prosperity of the Catholic tradition, that they
came out upon the open land.

MacIan had learnt much and thought more since he came out of
the cloudy hills of Arisaig. He had met many typical modern figures
under circumstances which were sharply symbolic; and, moreover, he
had absorbed the main modern atmosphere from the mere presence
and chance phrases of Turnbull, as such atmospheres can always be

[62]Ernest Haeckel (1834–1919) was a German naturalist known as "the German
Darwin" for his enthusiastic support of Darwinism.

[63] The massacre of St. Bartholomew's Eve was a plan hatched by Catherine de
Medici, the Cardinal Duke of Guise, Charles IX and the Duke of Anjou (later Henry
III) to destroy the power of the Protestant Huguenots by slaughtering thousands
of them when they gathered in Paris on August 24, 1572, to celebrate the marriage
of the Huguenot Henri de Navarre (later Henry IV) to Marguerite de Valois, sister of Charles IX.

[64]John Kensit (1853–1902) was a political agitator and founder of the Protestant
Truth Society, one of whose purposes is "to take a stand against the growing influence
of Romanism within the church". He was fatally wounded in a religious riot in Liverpool.

absorbed from the presence and the phrases of any man of great mental vitality. He had at last begun thoroughly to understand what are the grounds upon which the mass of the modern world solidly disapprove of her creed; and he threw himself into replying to them with a hot intellectual enjoyment.

"I begin to understand one or two of your dogmas, Mr. Turnbull," he had said emphatically as they ploughed heavily up a wooded hill. "And every one that I understand I deny. Take any one of them you like. You hold that your heretics and sceptics have helped the world forward and handed on a lamp of progress. I deny it. Nothing is plainer from real history than that each of your heretics invented a complete cosmos of his own which the next heretic smashed entirely to pieces. Who knows now exactly what Nestorius[65] taught? Who cares? There are only two things that we know for certain about it. The first is that Nestorius, as a heretic, taught something quite opposite to the teaching of Arius,[66] the heretic who came before him, and something quite useless to James Turnbull, the heretic who comes after. I defy you to go back to the Freethinkers of the past and find any habitation for yourself at all. I defy you to read Godwin[67] or Shelley[68] or the deists of the eighteenth century[69] or the

[65] Nestorius (died ca. A.D. 451) became Patriarch of Constantinople in A.D. 428. He taught that in Jesus Christ there were two separate persons, a divine one and a human one, a heresy condemned by the general Councils of Ephesus (431) and Chalcedon (451).

[66] Arius (ca. A.D. 250–336) was a priest at Alexandria who taught that Jesus was not coeternal with God the Father but created by him and, therefore, inferior, a heresy condemned by the Council of Nicea (325), which gave rise to the Niceaen and Athenasian Creeds.

[67] William Godwin (1756–1836) was an English political writer, novelist and romantic traditionalist who influenced Shelley.

[68] Percy Bysshe Shelley (1792–1822) was an English poet and writer and leader in the Romantic movement. Godwin's daughter by Mary Wollstonecraft became the second sixteen-year-old with whom Shelley eloped following the first wife's drowning suicide.

[69] The deists of the eighteenth century believed that God created the universe and man, but has since had nothing to do with them (a *Deus absconditus* point of view). The term originally meant belief in a god known through natural religion and reason rather than revelation or teaching.

nature-worshipping humanists of the Renaissance, without discovering that you differ from them twice as much as you differ from the Pope. You are a nineteenth-century sceptic, and you are always telling me that I ignore the cruelty of nature. If you had been an eighteenth-century sceptic you would have told me that I ignore the kindness and benevolence of nature. You are an atheist, and you praise the deists of the eighteenth century. Read them instead of praising them, and you will find that their whole universe stands or falls with the deity. You are a materialist, and you think Bruno[70] a scientific hero. See what he said and you will think him an insane mystic. No, the great Freethinker, with his genuine ability and honesty, does not in practice destroy Christianity. What he does destroy is the Freethinker who went before. Freethought may be suggestive, it may be inspiriting, it may have as much as you please of the merits that come from vivacity and variety. But there is one thing Freethought can never be by any possibility—Freethought can never be progressive. It can never be progressive because it will accept nothing from the past; it begins every time again from the beginning; and it goes every time in a different direction. All the rational philosophers have gone along different roads, so it is impossible to say which has gone furthest. Who can discuss whether Emerson[71] was a better optimist than Schopenhauer[72] was pessimist? It is like asking if this corn is as yellow as that hill is steep. No; there are only two things that really progress; and they both accept accumulations of authority. They may be progressing uphill or down; they may be growing steadily better or steadily worse; but they have steadily increased in certain definable matters; they have steadily advanced in a certain definable

[70] Giordano Bruno (1550–1600), an Italian philosopher who taught in Paris, attempted to reconcile scholasticism with Aristotelianism. He was buried in Rome after becoming a Calvinist.

[71] Ralph Waldo Emerson (1803–1882), American poet and essayist, was an idealist in philosophy, a rationalist in religion and an advocate of individualism and spiritual independence.

[72] Arthur Schopenhauer (1788–1860) was a German philosopher known for his theories and publications on the will and on pessimism, which were a significant influence on both Nietzsche and Freud.

direction; they are the only two things, it seems, that ever *can* progress. The first is strictly physical science. The second is the Catholic Church."

"Physical science and the Catholic Church!" said Turnbull sarcastically; "and no doubt the first owes a great deal to the second."

"If you pressed that point I might reply that it was very probable," answered MacIan calmly. "I often fancy that your historical generalisations rest frequently on random instances; I should not be surprised if your vague notions of the Church as the persecutor of science were a generalisation from Galileo.[73] I should not be at all surprised if, when you counted the scientific investigations and discoveries since the fall of Rome, you found that a great mass of them had been made by monks. But the matter is irrelevant to my meaning. I say that if you want an example of anything which has progressed in the moral world by the same method as science in the material world, by continually adding to without unsettling what was there before, then I say that there *is* only one example of it. And that is Us."

"With this enormous difference," said Turnbull, "that however elaborate be the calculations of physical science, their net result can be tested. Granted that it took millions of books I never read and millions of men I never heard of to discover the electric light. Still I can see the electric light. But I cannot see the supreme virtue which is the result of all your theologies and sacraments."

"Catholic virtue is often invisible because it is the normal," answered MacIan. "Christianity is always out of fashion because it is always sane; and all fashions are mild insanities. When Italy is mad on art the Church seems too Puritanical; when England is mad on Puritanism the Church seems too artistic. When you quarrel with us now you class us with kingship and despotism; but when you quarrelled with us first it was because we would not accept the divine despotism of Henry VIII.[74] The Church always seems to be behind the times, when it is really beyond the times; it is waiting till the last fad shall have seen its last summer. It keeps the key of a permanent virtue."

[73] Galileo Galilei (1564–1642) was the Italian astronomer, mathematician and natural philosopher who affirmed the Copernican system with the sun at its center; as a result, he was brought before the Inquisition, but under threat of torture he recanted.

[74] Henry VIII (1491–1547) was king of England from 1509 to 1547.

"Oh, I have heard all that!" said Turnbull with genial contempt. "I have heard that Christianity keeps the key of virtue, and that if you read Tom Paine[75] you will cut your throat at Monte Carlo. It is such rubbish that I am not even angry at it. You say that Christianity is the prop of morals; but what more do you do? When a doctor attends you and could poison you with a pinch of salt, do you ask whether he is a Christian? You ask whether he is a gentleman, whether he is an M.D.—anything but that. When a soldier enlists to die for his country or disgrace it, do you ask whether he is a Christian? You are more likely to ask whether he is Oxford or Cambridge at the Boat Race. If you think your creed essential to morals why do you not make it a test for these things?"

"We once did make it a test for these things," said MacIan smiling, "and then you told us that we were imposing by force a faith unsupported by argument. It seems rather hard that having first been told that our creed must be false because we did use tests, we should now be told that it must be false because we don't. But I notice that most anti-Christian arguments are in the same inconsistent style."

"That is all very well as a debating-club answer," replied Turnbull good-humouredly, "but the question still remains: Why don't you confine yourself more to Christians if Christians are the only really good men?"

"Who talked of such folly?" asked MacIan disdainfully. "Do you suppose that the Catholic Church ever held that Christians were the only good men? Why, the Catholics of the Catholic Middle Ages talked about the virtues of all the virtuous Pagans until humanity was sick of the subject. No, if you really want to know what we mean when we say that Christianity has a special power of virtue, I will tell you. The Church is the only thing on earth that can perpetuate a type of virtue and make it something more than a fashion. The thing is so

---

[75] Tom Paine (1737–1809) was an English radical political writer, who, while in America, wrote the pamphlet *Common Sense*, a strong defense of American independence. Later he returned to Europe, took French nationality and became a member of the National Convention. While imprisoned in France, he wrote *The Rights of Man*. He died in New York, and his remains were subsequently returned to England by William Cobbett.

plain and historical that I hardly think you will ever deny it. You cannot deny that it is perfectly possible that to-morrow morning, in Ireland or in Italy, there might appear a man not only as good but good in exactly the same way as St. Francis of Assisi. Very well, now take the other types of human virtue; many of them splendid. The English gentleman of Elizabeth was chivalrous and idealistic. But can you stand still here in this meadow and *be* an English gentleman of Elizabeth? The austere republican of the eighteenth century, with his stern patriotism and his simple life, was a fine fellow. But have you ever seen him? have you ever seen an austere republican? Only a hundred years have passed and that volcano of revolutionary truth and valour is as cold as the mountains of the moon. And so it is and so it will be with the ethics which are buzzing down Fleet Street at this instant as I speak. What phrase would inspire the London clerk or workman just now? Perhaps that he is a son of the British Empire on which the sun never sets; perhaps that he is a prop of his Trades Union, or a class, conscious[76] proletarian something or other; perhaps merely that he is a gentleman when he obviously is not. Those names and notions are all honourable; but how long will they last? Empires break; industrial conditions change; the suburbs will not last for ever. What will remain? I will tell you. The Catholic Saint will remain."

"And suppose I don't like him," said Turnbull.

"On my theory the question is rather whether he will like you: or more probably whether he will ever have heard of you. But I grant the reasonableness of your query. You have a right, if you speak as the ordinary man, to ask if you will like the saint. But as the ordinary man you do like him. You revel in him. If you dislike him it is not because you are a nice ordinary man, but because you are (if you will excuse me) a sophisticated prig of a Fleet Street editor. That is just the funny part of it. The human race has always admired the Catholic virtues, however little it can practise them; and oddly enough it has admired most those of them that the modern world most sharply disputes.

---

[76] Note typographical error that was not picked up in earlier editions but was corrected in volume 6 of the *Collected Works*. The text should contain the word "class-conscious" without the comma.

You complain of Catholicism for setting up an ideal of virginity; it did nothing of the kind. The whole human race set up an ideal of virginity; the Greeks in Athene, the Romans in the Vestal fire, set up an ideal of virginity. What then is your real quarrel with Catholicism? Your quarrel can only be, your quarrel really only is, that Catholicism has *achieved* an ideal of virginity; that it is no longer a mere piece of floating poetry. But if you, and a few feverish men, in top hats, running about in a street in London, choose to differ as to the ideal itself, not only from the Church, but from the Parthenon whose name means virginity, from the Roman Empire which went outwards from the virgin flame, from the whole legend and tradition of Europe, from the lion who will not touch virgins, from the unicorn who respects them, and who make up together the bearers of your own national shield, from the most living and lawless of your own poets, from Massinger,[77] who wrote the 'Virgin Martyr,' from Shakespeare, who wrote 'Measure for Measure'—if you in Fleet Street differ from all this human experience, does it never strike you that it may be Fleet Street that is wrong?"

"No," answered Turnbull; "I trust that I am sufficiently fair-minded to canvass and consider the idea; but having considered it, I think Fleet Street is right, yes—even if the Parthenon is wrong. I think that as the world goes on new psychological atmospheres are generated, and in these atmospheres it is possible to find delicacies and combinations which in other times would have to be represented by some ruder symbol. Every man feels the need of some element of purity in sex; perhaps they can only typify purity as the absence of sex. You will laugh if I suggest that we may have made in Fleet Street an atmosphere in which a man can be so passionate as Sir Lancelot and as pure as Sir Galahad. But, after all, we have in the modern world erected many such atmospheres. We have, for instance, a new and imaginative appreciation of children."

[77] Philip Massinger (1583–1640) was an English dramatist best known as the author of *A New Way to Pay Old Debts*. He wrote *The Virgin Martyr* (1622) in collaboration with Thomas Dekker (1570–1632). It is the story of Dorothea, who dies a martyr rather than give up her love, Antonius, or her religion.

"Quite so," replied MacIan with a singular smile. "It has been very well put by one of the brightest of your young authors, who said: 'Unless you become as little children ye shall in no wise enter the kingdom of heaven.' [78] But you are quite right; there is a modern worship of children. And what, I ask you, is this modern worship of children? What, in the name of all the angels and devils, is it except the worship of virginity? Why should any one worship a thing merely because it is small or immature? No; you have tried to escape from this thing, and the very thing you point to as the goal of your escape is only the thing again. Am I wrong in saying that these things seem to be eternal?"

And it was with these words that they came in sight of the great plains. They went a little way in silence, and then James Turnbull said suddenly, "But I *cannot* believe in the thing." MacIan answered nothing to the speech; perhaps it is unanswerable. And indeed they scarcely spoke another word to each other all that day.

[78] Lk 18:17.

IX

THE STRANGE LADY

Moonrise with a great and growing moon opened over all those flats, making them seem flatter and larger than they were, turning them to a lake of blue light. The two companions trudged across the moonlit plain for half an hour in full silence. Then MacIan stopped suddenly and planted his sword-point in the ground like one who plants his tent-pole for the night. Leaving it standing there, he clutched his black-haired skull with his great claws of hands, as was his custom when forcing the pace of his brain. Then his hands dropped again and he spoke.

"I'm sure you're thinking the same as I am," he said; "how long are we to be on this damned seesaw?"

The other did not answer, but his silence seemed somehow solid as assent; and MacIan went on conversationally. Neither noticed that both had instinctively stood still before the sign of the fixed and standing sword.

"It is hard to guess what God means in this business. But He means something—or the other thing, or both. Whenever we have tried to fight each other something has stopped us. Whenever we have tried to be reconciled to each other, something has stopped us again. By the run of our luck we have never had time to be either friends or enemies. Something always jumped out of the bushes."

Turnbull nodded gravely and glanced round at the huge and hedge-less meadow which fell away toward the horizon into a glimmering high road.

"Nothing will jump out of bushes here anyhow," he said.

"That is what I meant," said MacIan, and stared steadily at the heavy hilt of his standing sword, which in the slight wind swayed on its tempered steel like some huge thistle on its stalk.

"That is what I meant; we are quite alone here. I have not heard a horse-hoof or a footstep or the hoot of a train for miles. So I think we might stop here and ask for a miracle."

"Oh! Might we?" said the atheistic editor with a sort of gusto of disgust.

"I beg your pardon," said MacIan, meekly. "I forgot your prejudices." He eyed the wind-swung sword-hilt in sad meditation and resumed: "What I mean is, we might find out in this quiet place whether there really is any fate or any commandment against our enterprise. I will engage on my side, like Elijah, to accept a test from heaven. Turnbull, let us draw swords here in this moonlight and this monstrous solitude. And if here in this moonlight and solitude there happens anything to interrupt us—if it be lightning striking our sword-blades or a rabbit running under our legs—I will take it as a sign from God and we will shake hands for ever."

Turnbull's mouth twitched in angry humour under his red moustache. He said: "I will wait for signs from God until I have any signs of His existence; but God—or Fate—forbid that a man of scientific culture should refuse any kind of experiment."

"Very well, then," said MacIan, shortly. "We are more quiet here than anywhere else; let us engage." And he plucked his sword-point out of the turf.

Turnbull regarded him for a second and a half with a baffling visage almost black against the moonrise; then his hand made a sharp movement to his hip and his sword shone in the moon.

As old chess-players open every game with established gambits, they opened with a thrust and parry, orthodox and even frankly ineffectual. But in MacIan's soul more formless storms were gathering, and he made a lunge or two so savage as first to surprise and then to enrage his opponent. Turnbull ground his teeth, kept his temper, and waiting for the third lunge, and the worst, had almost spitted the lunger when a shrill, small cry came from behind him, a cry such as is not made by any of the beasts that perish.

Turnbull must have been more superstitious than he knew, for he stopped in the act of going forward. MacIan was brazenly superstitious, and he dropped his sword. After all, he had challenged the universe to send an interruption; and this was an interruption, whatever else it was. An instant afterward the sharp, weak cry was repeated. This time it was certain that it was human and that it was female.

MacIan stood rolling those great blue Gaelic eyes that contrasted with his dark hair. "It is the voice of God," he said again and again.

"God hasn't got much of a voice," said Turnbull, who snatched at every chance of cheap profanity. "As a matter of fact, MacIan, it isn't the voice of God, but it's something a jolly sight more important—it is the voice of man—or rather of woman. So I think we'd better scoot in its direction."

MacIan snatched up his fallen weapon without a word, and the two raced away toward that part of the distant road from which the cry was now constantly renewed.

They had to run over a curve of country that looked smooth but was very rough; a neglected field which they soon found to be full of the tallest grasses and the deepest rabbit holes. Moreover, that great curve of the countryside which looked so slow and gentle when you glanced over it, proved to be highly precipitous when you scampered over it; and Turnbull was twice nearly flung on his face. MacIan, though much heavier, avoided such an overthrow only by having the quick and incalculable feet of the mountaineer; but both of them may be said to have leapt off a low cliff when they leapt into the road.

The moonlight lay on the white road with a more naked and electric glare than on the grey-green upland, and though the scene which it revealed was complicated, it was not difficult to get its first features at a glance.

A small but very neat black-and-yellow motor-car was standing stolidly, slightly to the left of the road. A somewhat larger light-green motor-car was tipped half way into a ditch on the same side, and four flushed and staggering men in evening dress were tipped out of it. Three of them were standing about the road, giving their opinions to the moon with vague but echoing violence. The fourth, however, had already advanced on the chauffeur of the black-and-yellow car, and was threatening him with a stick. The chauffeur had risen to defend himself. By his side sat a young lady.

She was sitting bolt upright, a slender and rigid figure gripping the sides of her seat, and her first few cries had ceased. She was clad in close-fitting dark costume, a mass of warm brown hair went out in two wings or waves on each side of her forehead; and even at that distance it could be seen that her profile was of the aquiline and eager sort, like a young falcon hardly free of the nest.

Turnbull had concealed in him somewhere a fund of common-sense and knowledge of the world of which he himself and his best friends were hardly aware. He was one of those who take in much of the shows of things absent-mindedly, and in an irrelevant reverie. As he stood at the door of his editorial shop on Ludgate Hill and meditated on the non-existence of God, he silently absorbed a good deal of varied knowledge about the existence of men. He had come to know types by instinct and dilemmas with a glance; he saw the crux of the situation in the road, and what he saw made him redouble his pace.

He knew that the men were rich; he knew that they were drunk; and he knew, what was worst of all, that they were fundamentally frightened. And he knew this also, that no common ruffian (such as attacks ladies in novels) is ever so savage and ruthless as a coarse kind of gentleman when he is really alarmed. The reason is not reconidite; it is simply because the police-court is not such a menacing novelty to the poor ruffian as it is to the rich. When they came within hail and heard the voices, they confirmed all Turnbull's anticipations. The man in the middle of the road was shouting in a hoarse and groggy voice that the chauffeur had smashed their car on purpose; that they must get to the Cri that evening, and that he would jolly well have to take them there. The chauffeur had mildly objected that he was driving a lady. "Oh! we'll take care of the lady," said the red-faced young man, and went off into gurgling and almost senile laughter.

By the time the two champions came up, things had grown more serious. The intoxication of the man talking to the chauffeur had taken one of its perverse and catlike jumps into mere screaming spite and rage. He lifted his stick and struck at the chauffeur, who caught hold of it, and the drunkard fell backward, dragging him out of his seat on the car. Another of the rowdies rushed forward booing in idiot excitement, fell over the chauffeur, and, either by accident or design, kicked him as he lay. The drunkard got to his feet again; but the chauffeur did not.

The man who had kicked kept a kind of half-witted conscience or cowardice, for he stood staring at the senseless body and murmuring words of inconsequent self-justification, making gestures with his hands as if he were arguing with somebody. But the other three, with a mere whoop and howl of victory, were boarding the car on three sides at once. It was exactly at this moment that Turnbull fell among them like one fallen from the sky. He tore one of the climbers backward by the collar, and with a hearty push sent him staggering over into the ditch upon his nose. One of the remaining two, who was too far gone to notice anything, continued to clamber ineffectually over the high back of the car, kicking and pouring forth a rivulet of soliloquy. But the other dropped at the interruption, turned upon Turnbull and began a battering bout of fisticuffs. At the same moment the man crawled out of the ditch in a masquerade of mud and rushed at his old enemy from behind. The whole had not taken a second; and an instant after MacIan was in the midst of them.

Turnbull had tossed away his sheathed sword, greatly preferring his hands, except in the avowed etiquette of the duel; for he had learnt to use his hands in the old street-battles of Bradlaugh.[79] But to MacIan the sword even sheathed was a more natural weapon, and he laid about him on all sides with it as with a stick. The man who had the walking-stick found his blows parried with promptitude; and a second after, to his great astonishment, found his own stick fly up in the air as by a conjuring trick, with a turn of the swords-man's wrist. Another of the revellers picked the stick out of the ditch and ran in upon MacIan, calling to his companion to assist him.

"I haven't got a stick," grumbled the disarmed man, and looked vaguely about the ditch.

"Perhaps," said MacIan, politely, "you would like this one." With the word the drunkard found his hand that had grasped the stick suddenly twisted and empty; and the stick lay at the feet of his companion on the other side of the road. MacIan felt a faint stir behind him; the girl had risen to her feet and was leaning forward to stare at the fighters. Turnbull was still engaged in countering and pommelling with the third young man. The fourth young man was still engaged

---

[79]Bradlaugh: see n. 54, above.

with himself, kicking his legs in helpless rotation on the back of the car and talking with melodious rationality.

At length Turnbull's opponent began to back before the battery of his heavy hands, still fighting, for he was the soberest and boldest of the four. If these are annals of military glory, it is due to him to say that he need not have abandoned the conflict; only that as he backed to the edge of the ditch his foot caught in a loop of grass and he went over in a flat and comfortable position from which it took him a considerable time to rise. By the time he had risen, Turnbull had come to the rescue of MacIan, who was at bay but belabouring his two enemies handsomely. The sight of the liberated reserve was to them like that of Blucher at Waterloo;[80] the two set off at a sullen trot down the road, leaving even the walking-stick lying behind them in the moonlight. MacIan plucked the struggling and aspiring idiot off the back of the car like a stray cat, and left him swaying unsteadily in the moon. Then he approached the front part of the car in a somewhat embarrassed manner and pulled off his cap.

For some solid seconds the lady and he merely looked at each other, and MacIan had an irrational feeling of being in a picture hung on a wall. That is, he was motionless, even lifeless, and yet staringly significant, like a picture. The white moonlight on the road, when he was not looking at it, gave him a vision of the road being white with snow. The motor-car, when he was not looking at it, gave him a rude impression of a captured coach in the old days of highwaymen. And he whose whole soul was with the swords and stately manners of the eighteenth century, he who was a Jacobite[81] risen from the dead, had an overwhelming sense of being once more in the picture, when he had so long been out of the picture.

In that short and strong silence he absorbed the lady from head to foot. He had never really looked at a human being before in his life.

[80] Gebhart Leberecht von Blücher (1742–1819), Prussian field marshal, completed Wellington's victory at the Battle of Waterloo (1815) by his timely appearance on the field when his Prussians pursued the fleeing enemy all through the night.

[81] Jacobites were the supporters of the deposed James II and his descendants in their claim to the British throne after the Revolution of 1688. The Jacobites drew most of their support from Catholic clans of the Scottish Highlands.

He saw her face and hair first, then that she had long suede gloves; then that there was a fur cap at the back of her brown hair. He might, perhaps, be excused for this hungry attention. He had prayed that some sign might come from heaven; and after an almost savage scrutiny he came to the conclusion that this one did. The lady's instantaneous arrest of speech might need more explaining; but she may well have been stunned with the squalid attack and the abrupt rescue. Yet it was she who remembered herself first and suddenly called out with self-accusing horror:

"Oh, that poor, poor man!"

They both swung round abruptly and saw that Turnbull, with his recovered sword under his arm-pit, was already lifting the fallen chauffeur into the car. He was only stunned and was slowly awakening, feebly waving his left arm.

The lady in the long gloves and the fur cap leapt out and ran rapidly toward them, only to be reassured by Turnbull, who (unlike many of his school) really knew a little science when he invoked it to redeem the world. "He's all right," said he; "he's quite safe. But I'm afraid he won't be able to drive the car for half an hour or so."

"I can drive the car," said the young woman in the fur cap with stony practicability.

"Oh, in that case," began MacIan, uneasily; and that paralysing shyness which is a part of romance induced him to make a backward movement as if leaving her to herself. But Turnbull was more rational than he, being more indifferent.

"I don't think you ought to drive home alone, ma'am," he said, gruffly. "There seem to be a lot of rowdy parties along this road, and the man will be no use for an hour. If you will tell us where you are going, we will see you safely there and say good-night."

The young lady exhibited all the abrupt disturbance of a person who is not commonly disturbed. She said almost sharply and yet with evident sincerity: "Of course I am awfully grateful to you for all you've done—and there's plenty of room if you'll come in."

Turnbull, with the complete innocence of an absolutely sound motive, immediately jumped into the car; but the girl cast an eye at MacIan, who stood in the road for an instant as if rooted like a tree.

Then he also tumbled his long legs into the tonneau, having that sense of degradedly diving into heaven which so many have known in so many human houses when they consented to stop to tea or were allowed to stop to supper. The slowly reviving chauffeur was set in the back seat; Turnbull and MacIan had fallen into the middle one; the lady with a steely coolness had taken the driver's seat and all the handles of that headlong machine. A moment afterward the engine started, with a throb and leap unfamiliar to Turnbull, who had only once been in a motor during a general election, and utterly unknown to MacIan, who in his present mood thought it was the end of the world. Almost at the same instant that the car plucked itself out of the mud and whipped away up the road, the man who had been flung into the ditch rose waveringly to his feet. When he saw the car escaping he ran after it and shouted something which, owing to the increasing distance, could not be heard. It is awful to reflect that, if his remark was valuable, it is quite lost to the world.

The car shot on up and down the shining moonlit lanes, and there was no sound in it except the occasional click or catch of its machinery; for through some cause or other no soul inside it could think of a word to say. The lady symbolised her feelings, whatever they were, by urging the machine faster and faster until scattered woodlands went by them in one black blotch and heavy hills and valleys seemed to ripple under the wheels like mere waves. A little while afterward this mood seemed to slacken and she fell into a more ordinary pace; but still she did not speak. Turnbull, who kept a more common and sensible view of the case than any one else, made some remark about the moonlight; but something indescribable made him also relapse into silence.

All this time MacIan had been in a sort of monstrous delirium, like some fabulous hero snatched up into the moon. The difference between this experience and common experiences was analogous to that between waking life and a dream. Yet he did not feel in the least as if he were dreaming; rather the other way; as waking was more actual than dreaming, so this seemed by another degree more actual than waking itself. But it was another life altogether, like a cosmos with a new dimension.

He felt he had been hurled into some new incarnation: into the midst of new relations, wrongs and rights, with towering responsibilities and almost tragic joys which he had as yet had no time to examine. Heaven had not merely sent him a message; Heaven itself had opened around him and given him an hour of its own ancient and star-shattering energy. He had never felt so much alive before; and yet he was like a man in a trance. And if you had asked him on what his throbbing happiness hung, he could only have told you that it hung on four or five visible facts, as a curtain hangs on four or five fixed nails. The fact that the lady had a little fur at her throat; the fact that the curve of her cheek was a low and lean curve and that the moonlight caught the height of her cheek-bone; the fact that her hands were small but heavily gloved as they gripped the steering-wheel; the fact that a white witch light was on the road; the fact that the brisk breeze of their passage stirred and fluttered a little not only the brown hair of her head but the black fur on her cap. All these facts were to him certain and incredible, like sacraments.

When they had driven half a mile farther, a big shadow was flung across the path, followed by its bulky owner, who eyed the car critically but let it pass. The silver moonlight picked out a piece or two of pewter ornament on his blue uniform; and as they went by they knew it was a serjeant of police. Three hundred yards farther on another policeman stepped out into the road as if to stop them, then seemed to doubt his own authority and stepped back again. The girl was a daughter of the rich; and this police suspicion (under which all the poor live day and night) stung her for the first time into speech.

"What can they mean?" she cried out in a kind of temper; "this car's going like a snail."

There was a short silence, and then Turnbull said: "It is certainly very odd; you are driving quietly enough."

"You are driving nobly," said MacIan, and his words (which had no meaning whatever) sounded hoarse and ungainly even in his own ears.

They passed the next mile and a half swiftly and smoothly; yet among the many things which they passed in the course of it was a clump of eager policemen standing at a cross-road. As they passed, one of the policemen shouted something to the others; but nothing else happened. Eight hundred yards farther on, Turnbull stood up suddenly in the swaying car.

"My God, MacIan!" he called out, showing his first emotion of that night. "I don't believe it's the pace; it couldn't be the pace. I believe it's us."

MacIan sat motionless for a few moments and then turned up at his companion a face that was as white as the moon above it.

"You may be right," he said at last; "if you are I must tell her."

"I will tell the lady if you like," said Turnbull, with his unconquered good temper.

"You!" said MacIan, with a sort of sincere and instinctive astonishment. "Why should you—no, I must tell her, of course——"

And he leant forward and spoke to the lady in the fur cap.

"I am afraid, madam, that we may have got you into some trouble," he said, and even as he said it it sounded wrong, like everything he said to this particular person in the long gloves. "The fact is," he resumed, desperately, "the fact is, we are being chased by the police." Then the last flattening hammer fell upon poor Evan's embarrassment; for the fluffy brown head with the furry black cap did not turn by a section of the compass.

"We are chased by the police," repeated MacIan, vigorously; then he added, as if beginning an explanation, "You see, I am a Catholic."

The wind whipped back a curl of the brown hair so as to necessitate a new theory of aesthetics touching the line of the cheek-bone; but the head did not turn.

"You see," began MacIan, again blunderingly, "this gentleman wrote in his newspaper that Our Lady was a common woman, a bad woman, and so we agreed to fight; and we were fighting quite a little time ago—but that was before we saw you."

The young lady driving the car had half turned her face to listen; and it was not a reverent or a patient face that she showed him. Her Norman nose was tilted a trifle too high upon the slim stalk of her neck and body.

When MacIan saw that arrogant and uplifted profile pencilled plainly against the moonshine, he accepted an ultimate defeat. He had expected the angels to despise him if he were wrong, but not to despise him so much as this.

"You see," said the stumbling spokesman, "I was angry with him when he insulted the Mother of God, and I asked him to fight a duel with me; but the police are all trying to stop it."

Nothing seemed to waver or flicker in the fair young falcon profile; and it only opened its lips to say, after a silence: "I thought people in our time were supposed to respect each other's religion."

Under the shadow of that arrogant face MacIan could only fall back on the obvious answer: "But what about a man's irreligion?" The face only answered: "Well, you ought to be more broadminded."

If any one else in the world had said the words, MacIan would have snorted with his equine neigh of scorn. But in this case he seemed knocked down by a superior simplicity, as if his eccentric attitude were rebuked by the innocence of a child. He could not dissociate anything that this woman said or did or wore from an idea of spiritual rarity and virtue. Like most others under the same elemental passion, his soul was at present soaked in ethics. He could have applied moral terms to the material objects of her environment. If some one had spoken of "her generous ribbon" or "her chivalrous gloves" or "her merciful shoe-buckle," it would not have seemed to him nonsense.

He was silent, and the girl went on in a lower key as if she were momentarily softened and a little saddened also. "It won't do, you know," she said; "you can't find out the truth in that way. There are such heaps of churches and people thinking different things nowadays, and they all think they are right. My uncle was a Swedenborgian." [82]

MacIan sat with bowed head, listening hungrily to her voice but hardly to her words, and seeing his great world drama grow smaller and smaller before his eyes till it was no bigger than a child's toy theatre.

"The time's gone by for all that," she went on; "you can't find out the real thing like that—if there is really anything to find——" and she sighed rather drearily; for, like many of the women of our wealthy

---

[82] Emanuel Swedenborg (1688–1772) was a Swedish mystic, theologian and scientist. He had religious revelations and wrote some thirty volumes of these in Latin. His followers organized a society in London called the Church of the New Jerusalem, and his writings were influential to William Blake, English poet and artist.

class, she was old and broken in thought, though young and clean enough in her emotions.

"Our object," said Turnbull, shortly, "is to make an effective demonstration"; and after that word, MacIan looked at his vision again and found it smaller than ever.

"It would be in the newspapers, of course." said the girl. "People read the newspapers, but they don't believe them, or anything else, I think." And she sighed again.

She drove in silence a third of a mile before she added, as if completing the sentence: "Anyhow, the whole thing's quite absurd."

"I don't think," began Turnbull, "that you quite realise—Hullo! hullo—hullo—what's this?"

The amateur chauffeur had been forced to bring the car to a staggering stoppage, for a file of fat, blue policemen made a wall across the way. A serjeant came to the side and touched his peaked cap to the lady.

"Beg your pardon, miss," he said with some embarrassment, for he knew her for a daughter of a dominant house, "but we have reason to believe that the gentlemen in your car are———" and he hesitated for a polite phrase.

"I am Evan MacIan," said that gentleman, and stood up in a sort of gloomy pomp, not wholly without a touch of the sulks of a schoolboy.

"Yes, we will get out, serjeant," said Turnbull, more easily; "my name is James Turnbull. We must not incommode the lady."

"What are you taking them up for?" asked the young woman, looking straight in front of her along the road.

"It's under the new act," said the serjeant, almost apologetically. "Incurable disturbers of the peace."

"What will happen to them?" she asked, with the same frigid clearness.

"Westgate Adult Reformatory," he replied, briefly.

"Until when?"

"Until they are cured," said the official.

"Very well, serjeant," said the young lady, with a sort of tired common-sense. "I am sure I don't want to protect criminals or go against the law; but I must tell you that these gentlemen have done me a considerable service; you won't mind drawing your men a little farther off while I say good-night to them. Men like that always misunderstand."

The serjeant was profoundly disquieted from the beginning at the mere idea of arresting any one in the company of a great lady; to refuse one of her minor requests was quite beyond his courage. The police fell back to a few yards behind the car. Turnbull took up the two swords that were their only luggage; the swords that, after so many half duels, they were now to surrender at last. MacIan, the blood thundering in his brain at the thought of that instant of farewell, bent over, fumbled at the handle and flung open the door to get out.

But he did not get out. He did not get out, because it is dangerous to jump out of a car when it is going at full speed. And the car was going at full speed, because the young lady, without turning her head or so much as saying a syllable, had driven down a handle that made the machine plunge forward like a buffalo and then fly over the landscape like a greyhound. The police made one rush to follow, and then dropped so grotesque and hopeless a chase. Away in the vanishing distance they could see the serjeant furiously making notes.

The open door, still left loose on its hinges, swung and banged quite crazily as they went whizzing up one road and down another. Nor did MacIan sit down; he stood up stunned and yet staring, as he would have stood up at the trumpet of the Last Day. A black dot in the distance sprang up a tall black forest, swallowed them and spat them out again at the other end. A railway bridge grew larger and larger till it leapt upon their backs bellowing, and was in its turn left behind. Avenues of poplars on both sides of the road chased each other like the figures in a zoetrope.[83] Now and then with a shock and rattle they went through sleeping moonlit villages, which must have stirred an instant in their sleep as at the passing of a fugitive earthquake. Sometimes in an outlying house a light in one erratic, unexpected window would give them a nameless hint of the hundred

[83] A zoetrope is an optical toy in the form of a cylinder with a series of pictures on the inner surface that give an impression of continuous motion when viewed through slits with the cylinder rotating.

human secrets which they left behind them with their dust. Sometimes even a slouching rustic would be afoot on the road and would
look after them, as after a flying phantom. But still MacIan stood up
staring at earth and heaven; and still the door he had flung open flapped
loose like a flag. Turnbull, after a few minutes of dumb amazement,
had yielded to the healthiest element in his nature and gone off into
uncontrollable fits of laughter. The girl had not stirred an inch.

After another half mile that seemed a mere flash, Turnbull leant
over and locked the door. Evan staggered at last into his seat and hid
his throbbing head in his hands; and still the car flew on and its driver
sat inflexible and silent. The moon had already gone down, and the
whole darkness was faintly troubled with twilight and the first movement of beasts and fowls. It was that mysterious moment when light
is coming, as if it were something unknown whose nature one could
not guess—a mere alteration in everything. They looked at the sky
and it seemed as dark as ever; then they saw the black shape of a tower
or tree against it and knew that it was already grey. Save that they
were driving southward and had certainly passed the longitude of London, they knew nothing of their direction; but Turnbull, who had
spent a year on the Hampshire coast in his youth, began to recognize
the unmistakable but quite indescribable villages of the English south.
Then a white witch fire began to burn between the black stems of the
fir-trees; and, like so many things in nature, though not in books on
evolution, the daybreak, when it did come, came much quicker than
one would think. The gloomy heavens were ripped up and rolled
away like a scroll, revealing splendors, as the car went roaring up the
curve of a great hill; and above them and black against the broadening
light, there stood one of those crouching and fantastic trees that are
first signals of the sea.

X

THE SWORDS REJOINED

As they came over the hill and down on the other side of it, it is not too much to say that the whole universe of God opened over them and under them, like a thing unfolding to five times its size. Almost under their feet opened the enormous sea, at the bottom of a steep valley which fell down into a bay; and the sea under their feet blazed at them almost as lustrous and almost as empty as the sky. The sunrise opened above them like some cosmic explosion, shining and shattering and yet silent; as if the world were blown to pieces without a sound. Round the rays of the victorious sun swept a sort of rainbow of confused and conquered colours—brown and blue and green and flaming rose-colour; as though gold were driving before it all the colours of the world. The lines of the landscape down which they sped, were the simple, strict, yet swerving, lines of a rushing river; so that it was almost as if they were being sucked down in a huge still whirlpool. Turnbull had some such feeling, for he spoke for the first time for many hours.

"If we go down at this rate we shall be over the sea cliff," he said.

"How glorious!" said MacIan.

When, however, they had come into the wide hollow at the bottom of that landslide, the car took a calm and graceful curve along the side of the sea, melted into the fringe of a few trees, and quietly, yet astonishingly, stopped. A belated light was burning in the broad morning in the window of a sort of lodge- or gate-keepers' cottage; and the girl stood up in the car and turned her splendid face to the sun.

Evan seemed startled by the stillness, like one who had been born amid sound and speed. He wavered on his long legs as he stood up; he pulled himself together, and the only consequence was that he trembled from head to foot. Turnbull had already opened the door on his side and jumped out.

The moment he had done so the strange young woman had one more mad movement, and deliberately drove the car a few yards farther. Then she got out with an almost cruel coolness and began pulling off her long gloves and almost whistling.

"You can leave me here," she said, quite casually, as if they had met five minutes before. "That is the lodge of my father's place. Please come in, if you like—but I understood that you had some business."

Evan looked at that lifted face and found it merely lovely; he was far too much of a fool to see that it was working with a final fatigue and that its austerity was agony. He was even fool enough to ask it a question. "Why did you save us?" he said, quite humbly.

The girl tore off one of her gloves, as if she were tearing off her hand. "Oh, I don't know," she said, bitterly. "Now I come to think of it, I can't imagine."

Evan's thoughts, that had been piled up to the morning star, abruptly let him down with a crash into the very cellars of the emotional universe. He remained in a stunned silence for a long time; and that, if he had only known, was the wisest thing that he could possibly do at the moment.

Indeed, the silence and the sunrise had their healing effect, for when the extraordinary lady spoke again, her tone was more friendly and apologetic. "I'm not really ungrateful," she said; "it was very good of you to save me from those men."

"But why?" repeated the obstinate and dazed MacIan, "why did you save us from the other men? I mean the policemen?"

The girl's great brown eyes were lit up with a flash that was at once final desperation and the loosening of some private and passionate reserve.

"Oh, God knows!" she cried. "God knows that if there is a God He has turned His big back on everything. God knows I have had no pleasure in my life, though I am pretty and young and father has plenty of money. And then people come and tell me that I ought to do things and I do them and it's all drivel. They want you to do work among the poor; which means reading Ruskin[84] and feeling self-righteous in the best room in a poor tenement. Or to help some

---

[84]John Ruskin (1819–1900) was an English author and art critic known for his art and social criticism.

cause or other, which always means bundling people out of crooked houses, in which they've always lived, into straight houses, in which they quite as often die. And all the time you have inside only the horrid irony of your own empty head and empty heart. I am to give to the unfortunate, when my whole misfortune is that I have nothing to give. I am to teach, when I believe nothing of all that I was taught. I am to save the children from death, and I am not even certain that I should not be better dead. I suppose if I actually saw a child drowning I should save it. But that would be from the same motive from which I have saved you, or destroyed you, whichever it is that I have done."

"What was the motive?" asked Evan, in a low voice.

"My motive is too big for my mind," answered the girl.

Then, after a pause, as she stared with a rising colour at the glittering sea, she said: "It can't be described, and yet I am trying to describe it. It seems to me not only that I am unhappy, but that there is no way of being happy. Father is not happy, though he is a Member of Parliament——" She paused a moment and added with the ghost of a smile: "Nor Aunt Mabel, though a man from India has told her the secret of all creeds. But I may be wrong; there may be a way out. And for one stark, insane second, I felt that, after all, you had got the way out and that was why the world hated you. You see, if there were a way out, it would be sure to be something that looked very queer."

Evan put his hand to his forehead and began stumblingly: "Yes, I suppose we do seem——"

"Oh, yes, you look queer enough," she said, with ringing sincerity. "You'll be all the better for a wash and brush up."

"You forget our business, madam," said Evan, in a shaking voice; "we have no concern but to kill each other."

"Well, I wouldn't be killed looking like that if I were you," she replied, with inhuman honesty.

Evan stood and rolled his eyes in masculine bewilderment. Then came the final change in this Proteus,[85] and she put out both her

---

[85] Proteus was a minor sea god who had the power of prophecy but who would assume different shapes to avoid answering questions.

hands for an instant and said in a low tone on which he lived for days and nights:

"Don't you understand that I did not dare to stop you? What you are doing is so mad that it may be quite true. Somehow one can never really manage to be an atheist."

Turnbull stood staring at the sea; but his shoulders showed that he heard, and after one minute he turned his head. But the girl had only brushed Evan's hand with hers and had fled up the dark alley by the lodge gate.

Evan stood rooted upon the road, literally like some heavy statue hewn there in the age of the Druids. It seemed impossible that he should ever move. Turnbull grew restless with this rigidity, and at last, after calling his companion twice or thrice, went up and clapped him impatiently on one of his big shoulders. Evan winced and leapt away from him with a repulsion which was not the hate of an unclean thing nor the dread of a dangerous one, but was a spasm of awe and separation from something from which he was now sundered as by the sword of God. He did not hate the atheist; it is possible that he loved him. But Turnbull was now something more dreadful than an enemy; he was a thing sealed and devoted—a thing now hopelessly doomed to be either a corpse or an executioner.

"What is the matter with you?" asked Turnbull, with his hearty hand still in the air; and yet he knew more about it than his innocent action would allow.

"James," said Evan, speaking like one under strong bodily pain, "I asked for God's answer and I have got it—got it in my vitals. He knows how weak I am, and that I might forget the peril of the faith, forget the face of Our Lady—yes, even with your blow upon her cheek. But the honour of this earth has just this about it, that it can make a man's heart like iron. I am from the Lords of the Isles and I dare not be a mere deserter. Therefore, God has tied me by the chain of my worldly place and word, and there is nothing but fighting now."

"I think I understand you," said Turnbull, "but you say everything tail foremost."

"She wants us to do it," said Evan, in a voice crushed with passion. "She has hurt herself so that we might do it. She has left her good name and her good sleep and all her habits and dignity flung away on the other side of England in the hope that she may hear of us and that we have broken some hole into heaven."

"I thought I knew what you meant," said Turnbull, biting his beard; "it does seem as if we ought to do something after all she has done this night."

"I never liked you so much before," said MacIan, in bitter sorrow.

As he spoke, three solemn footmen came out of the lodge gate and assembled to assist the chauffeur to his room. The mere sight of them made the two wanderers flee as from a too frightful incongruity, and before they knew where they were, they were well upon the grassy ledge of England that overlooks the Channel. Evan said suddenly: "Will they let me see her in heaven once in a thousand ages?" and addressed the remark to the editor of the "Atheist," as one which he would be likely or qualified to answer. But no answer came; a silence sank between the two.

Turnbull strode sturdily to the edge of the cliff and looked out, his companion following, somewhat more shaken by his recent agitation.

"If that's the view you take," said Turnbull, "and I don't say you are wrong, I think I know where we shall be best off for the business. As it happens, I know this part of the south coast pretty well. And unless I am mistaken there's a way down the cliff just here which will land us on a stretch of firm sand where no one is likely to follow us."

The Highlander made a gesture of assent and came also almost to the edge of the precipice. The sunrise, which was broadening over sea and shore, was one of those rare and splendid ones in which there seems to be no mist or doubt, and nothing but a universal clarification more and more complete. All the colours were transparent. It seemed like a triumphant prophecy of some perfect world where everything being innocent will be intelligible; a world where even our bodies, so to speak, may be as of burning glass. Such a world is faintly though fiercely figured in the coloured windows of Christian architecture. The sea that lay before them was like a pavement of emerald, bright and almost brittle; the sky against which its strict horizon hung was almost absolutely white, except that close to the sky line, like scarlet braids on the hem of a garment, lay strings of flaky cloud of so gleaming and gorgeous a red that they seemed cut out of some strange blood-red celestial metal, of which the mere gold of this earth is but a drab yellow imitation.

"The hand of Heaven is still pointing," muttered the man of superstition to himself. "And now it is a blood-red hand."

The cool voice of his companion cut in upon his monologue, calling to him from a little farther along the cliff, to tell him that he had found the ladder of descent. It began as a steep and somewhat greasy path, which then tumbled down twenty or thirty feet in the form of a fall of rough stone steps. After that, there was a rather awkward drop on to a ledge of stone and then the journey was undertaken easily and even elegantly by the remains of an ornamental staircase, such as might have belonged to some long-disused watering-place. All the time that the two travellers sank from stage to stage of this downward journey, there closed over their heads living bridges and caverns of the most varied foliage, all of which grew greener, redder, or more golden, in the growing sunlight of the morning. Life, too, of the more moving sort rose at the sun on every side of them. Birds whirred and fluttered in the undergrowth, as if imprisoned in green cages. Other birds were shaken up in great clouds from the tree-tops, as if they were blossoms detached and scattered up to heaven. Animals which Turnbull was too much of a Londoner and MacIan too much of a Northerner to know, slipped by among the tangle or ran pattering up the tree-trunks. Both the men, according to their several creeds, felt the full thunder of the psalm of life as they had never heard it before; MacIan felt God the Father, benignant in all His energies, and Turnbull that ultimate anonymous energy, that *Natura Naturans*,[86] which is the whole theme of Lucretius.[87] It was down this clamorous ladder of life that they went down to die.

They broke out upon a brown semicircle of sand, so free from human imprint as to justify Turnbull's profession. They strode out upon it,

---

[86] *Natura naturans* means "nature naturing", which was one of the two aspects of nature according to Greek thought: the *passive* reality of our daily experience (*natura naturata*, or "created nature"), and the *active* power that directs and governs life as well as the growth of a work of art (*natura naturans*, or "creating nature").

[87] Titus Lucretius Carus (ca. 99–55 B.C.) was a Roman poet and philosopher and best known for his didactic poem *De rerum natura* ("On the Nature of Things").

stuck their swords in the sand, and had a pause too important for speech. Turnbull eyed the coast curiously for a moment, like one awakening memories of childhood; then he said abruptly, like a man remembering somebody's name: "But, of course, we shall be better off still round the corner of Cragness Point; nobody ever comes there at all." And picking up his sword again, he began striding toward a big bluff of the rocks which stood out upon their left. MacIan followed him round the corner and found himself in what was certainly an even finer fencing court, of flat, firm sand, enclosed on three sides by white walls of rock, and on the fourth by the green wall of the advancing sea.

"We are quite safe here," said Turnbull, and, to the other's surprise, flung himself down, sitting on the brown beach.

"You see, I was brought up near here," he explained. "I was sent from Scotland to stop with my aunt. It is highly probable that I may die here. Do you mind if I light a pipe?"

"Of course, do whatever you like," said MacIan, with a choking voice, and he went and walked alone by himself along the wet, glistening sands.

Ten minutes afterward he came back again, white with his own whirlwind of emotions; Turnbull was quite cheerful and was knocking out the end of his pipe.

"You see, we have to do it," said MacIan. "She tied us to it."

"Of course, my dear fellow," said the other, and leapt up as lightly as a monkey.

They took their places gravely in the very centre of the great square of sand, as if they had thousands of spectators. Before saluting, MacIan, who, being a mystic, was one inch nearer to Nature, cast his eye round the huge framework of their heroic folly. The three walls of rock all leant a little outward, though at various angles; but this impression was exaggerated in the direction of the incredible by the heavy load of living trees and thickets which each wall wore on its top like a huge shock of hair. On all that luxurious crest of life the risen and victorious sun was beating, burnishing it all like gold, and every bird that rose with that sunrise caught a light like a star upon it like the dove of the Holy Spirit. Imaginative life had never so much crowded upon MacIan. He felt that he could write whole books about the feelings of a single bird. He felt that for two centuries he would not tire of being a rabbit. He was in the Palace of Life, of which the very tapestries and curtains were alive. Then he recovered himself, and remembered his affairs. Both men saluted, and iron rang upon iron. It was exactly at the same moment that he realised that his enemy's left ankle was encircled with a ring of salt water that had crept up to his feet.

"What is the matter?" said Turnbull, stopping an instant, for he had grown used to every movement of his extraordinary fellow-traveller's face.

MacIan glanced again at that silver anklet of sea water and then looked beyond at the next promontory round which a deep sea was boiling and leaping. Then he turned and looked back and saw heavy foam being shaken up to heaven about the base of Cragness Point.

"The sea has cut us off," he said, curtly.

"I have noticed it," said Turnbull with equal sobriety. "What view do you take of the development?"

Evan threw away his weapon, and, as his custom was, imprisoned his big head in his hands. Then he let them fall and said: "Yes, I know what it means; and I think it is the fairest thing. It is the finger of God—red as blood—still pointing. But now it points to two graves."

There was a space filled with the sound of the sea, and then MacIan spoke again in a voice pathetically reasonable: "You see, we both saved her—and she told us both to fight—and it would not be just that either should fail and fall alone, while the other——"

"You mean," said Turnbull, in a voice surprisingly soft and gentle, "that there is something fine about fighting in a place where even the conqueror must die?"

"Oh, you have got it right, you have got it right!" cried out Evan, in an extraordinary childish ecstasy. "Oh, I'm sure that you really believe in God!"

Turnbull answered not a word, but only took up his fallen sword.

For the third time Evan MacIan looked at those three sides of English cliff hung with their noisy load of life. He had been at a loss to understand the almost ironical magnificence of all those teeming creatures and tropical colours and smells that smoked happily to heaven. But now he knew that he was in the closed court of death and that all the gates were sealed.

He drank in the last green and the last red and the last gold, those unique and indescribable things of God, as a man drains good wine at the bottom of his glass. Then he turned and saluted his enemy once more, and the two stood up and fought till the foam flowed over their knees.

Then MacIan stepped backward suddenly with a splash and held up his hand. "Turnbull!" he cried; "I can't help it—fair fighting is more even than promises. And this is not fair fighting."

"What the deuce do you mean?" asked the other, staring.

"I've only just thought of it," cried Evan, brokenly. "We're very well matched—it may go on a good time—the tide is coming up fast—and I'm a foot and a half taller. You'll be washed away like seaweed before it's above my breeches. I'll not fight foul for all the girls and angels in the universe."

"Will you oblige me," said Turnbull, with staring grey eyes and a voice of distinct and violent politeness; "will you oblige me by jolly well minding your own business? Just you stand up and fight, and we'll see who will be washed away like seaweed. You wanted to finish this fight and you shall finish it, or I'll denounce you as a coward to the whole of that assembled company."

Evan looked very doubtful and offered a somewhat wavering weapon; but he was quickly brought back to his senses by his opponent's sword-point, which shot past him, shaving his shoulder by a hair. By this time the waves were well up Turnbull's thigh, and what was worse, they were beginning to roll and break heavily around them.

MacIan parried this first lunge perfectly, the next less perfectly; the third in all human probability he would not have parried at all; the Christian champion would have been pinned like a butterfly, and the atheistic champion left to drown like a rat, with such consolation as his view of the cosmos afforded him. But just as Turnbull launched his heaviest stroke, the sea, in which he stood up to his hips, launched a yet heavier one. A wave breaking beyond the others smote him heavily like a hammer of water. One leg gave way, he was swung round and sucked into the retreating sea, still gripping his sword.

MacIan put his sword between his teeth and plunged after his disappearing enemy. He had the sense of having the whole universe on top of him as crest after crest struck him down. It seemed to him quite a cosmic collapse, as if all the seven heavens were falling on him one after the other. But he got hold of the atheist's left leg and he did not let it go.

After some ten minutes of foam and frenzy, in which all the senses at once seemed blasted by the sea, Evan found himself laboriously swimming on a low, green swell, with the sword still in his teeth and the editor of the "Atheist" still under his arm. What he was going to do he had not even the most glimmering idea; so he merely kept his grip and swam somehow with one hand.

He ducked instinctively as there bulked above him a big, black wave, much higher than any that he had seen. Then he saw that it was hardly the shape of any possible wave. Then he saw that it was a fisherman's boat, and, leaping upward, caught hold of the bow. The boat pitched forward with its stern in the air for just as much time as was needed to see that there was nobody in it. After a moment or two of desperate clambering, however, there were two people in it, Mr. Evan MacIan, panting and sweating, and Mr. James Turnbull, uncommonly close to being drowned. After ten minutes' aimless tossing in the empty fishing-boat he recovered, however, stirred, stretched himself, and looked round on the rolling waters. Then, while taking no notice of the streams of salt water that were pouring from his hair, beard, coat, boots, and trousers, he carefully wiped the wet off his sword-blade to preserve it from possibilities of rust.

MacIan found two oars in the bottom of the deserted boat and began somewhat drearily to row.

A rainy twilight was clearing to cold silver over the moaning sea, when the battered boat that had rolled and drifted almost aimlessly all night, came within sight of land, though of land which looked almost as lost and savage as the waves. All night there had been but little lifting in the leaden sea, only now and then the boat had been heaved up, as on a huge shoulder which slipped from under it; such occasional sea-quakes came probably from the swell of some steamer that had passed it in the dark; otherwise the waves were harmless though restless. But it was piercingly cold, and there was, from time to time, a splutter of rain like the splutter of the spray, which seemed almost to freeze as it fell. MacIan, more at home than his companion in this quite barbarous and elemental sort of adventure, had rowed toil-somely with the heavy oars whenever he saw anything that looked like land; but for the most part had trusted with grim transcenden-talism to wind and tide. Among the implements of their first outfit the brandy alone had remained to him, and he gave it to his freezing companion in quantities which greatly alarmed that temperate Lon-doner; but MacIan came from the cold seas and mists where a man can drink a tumbler of raw whiskey in a boat without it making him wink.

When the Highlander began to pull really hard upon the oars, Turn-bull craned his dripping red head out of the boat to see the goal of his exertions. It was a sufficiently uninviting one; nothing so far as could be seen but a steep and shelving bank of shingle, made of loose little pebbles such as children like, but slanting up higher than a house. On the top of the mound, against the sky line, stood up the brown skel-eton of some broken fence or break-water. With the grey and watery dawn crawling up behind it, the fence really seemed to say to our philosophic adventurers that they had come at last to the other end of nowhere.

Bent by necessity to his labour, MacIan managed the heavy boat with real power and skill, and when at length he ran it up on a smoother part of the slope it caught and held so that they could clamber out, not sinking farther than their knees into the water and the shingle. A foot or two farther up their feet found the beach firmer, and a few moments afterward they were leaning on the ragged break-water and looking back at the sea they had escaped.

They had a dreary walk across wastes of grey shingle in the grey dawn before they began to come within hail of human fields or roads; nor had they any notion of what fields or roads they would be. Their boots were beginning to break up and the confusion of stones tried them severely, so that they were glad to lean on their swords, as if they were the staves of pilgrims. MacIan thought vaguely of a weird ballad of his own country which describes the soul in Purgatory as walking on a plain full of sharp stones, and only saved by its own charities upon earth.

> If ever thou gavest hosen and shoon
>   Every night and all,
> Sit thee down and put them on,
>   And Christ receive thy soul.[88]

Turnbull had no such lyrical meditations, but he was in an even worse temper.

At length they came to a pale ribbon of road, edged by a shelf of rough and almost colourless turf; and a few feet up the slope there stood grey and weather-stained, one of those big way-side crucifixes which are seldom seen except in Catholic countries.

MacIan put up his hand to his head and found that his bonnet was not there. Turnbull gave one glance at the crucifix—a glance at once sympathetic and bitter, in which was concentrated the whole of Swinburne's poem on the same occasion.

> O hidden face of man, whereover
>   The years have woven a viewless veil,
> If thou wert verily man's lover
>   What did thy love or blood avail?
> Thy blood the priests mix poison of,
> And in gold shekels coin thy love.[89]

Then, leaving MacIan in his attitude of prayer, Turnbull began to look right and left very sharply, like one looking for something. Suddenly, with a little cry, he saw it and ran forward. A few yards from them along the road a lean and starved sort of hedge came pitifully to an end. Caught upon its prickly angle, however, there was a very small and very dirty scrap of paper that might have hung there for

[88] There are a number of versions of this ballad, called "The Cleveland Lyke-Wake Dirge," that was sung at wakes for the dead. The belief among the common people in Yorkshire was that, after death, the soul of the deceased had to pass over Whinney Moor, a land covered in thorns.

[89] See n. 34, which refers to the same poem.

months, since it escaped from some one tearing up a letter or making
a spill out of a newspaper. Turnbull snatched at it and found it was the
corner of a printed page, very coarsely printed, like a cheap novel-
ette, and just large enough to contain the words: "*et c'est elle qui——*" [90]

"Hurrah!" cried Turnbull, waving his fragment; "we are safe at
last. We are free at last. We are somewhere better than England or
Eden or Paradise. MacIan, we are in the Land of the Duel!"

"Where do you say?" said the other, looking at him heavily and
with knitted brows, like one almost dazed with the grey doubts of
desolate twilight and drifting sea.

"We are in France!" cried Turnbull, with a voice like a trumpet,
"in the land where things really happen—*Tout arrive en France*. We
arrive in France. Look at this little message," and he held out the
scrap of paper. "There's an omen for you superstitious hill folk. *C'est
elle qui—Mais oui, mais oui, c'est elle qui sauvera encore le monde.*"

"France!" repeated MacIan, and his eyes awoke again in his head
like large lamps lighted.

"Yes, France!" said Turnbull, and all the rhetorical part of him
came to the top, his face growing as red as his hair. "France, that has
always been in rebellion for liberty and reason. France, that has always
assailed superstition with the club of Rabelais[91] or the rapier of
Voltaire.[92] France, at whose first council table sits the sublime figure
of Julian the Apostate.[93] France, where a man said only the other
day those splendid unanswerable words"—with a superb gesture—
"'we have extinguished in heaven those lights that men shall never
light again.'"

[90] French translations for this and the phrases that follow are *et c'est elle qui* ("and it
is she who"); *Tout arrive en France* ("all happens in France"); *C'est elle qui—Mais oui,
mais oui, c'est elle qui sauvera encore le monde*" ("It is she who, but yes, but yes, it is she
who will save the world").

[91] François Rabelais (1494?–1553) was a French monk, physician and satirist. He is
famous for his books *Pantagruel* (1532) and *Gargantua* (1534), which are notable for
their racy humor, wit, wisdom and satire.

[92] François Marie Arouet Voltaire (1694–1778) was a French Enlightenment writer
and historian, perhaps best known for his satirical novella *Candide* (1759).

[93] Flavian Claudius Julianus, also known as Julian the Apostate (ca. A.D. 331–363),
was a Roman emperor. After he became Caesar in A.D. 355, he served in the army
overthrowing the Alumni near Strasbourg in what is now France.

"No," said MacIan, in a voice that shook with a controlled passion, "but France, which was taught by St. Bernard[94] and led to war by Joan of Arc.[95] France that made the crusades. France that saved the Church and scattered the heresies by the mouths of Bossuet[96] and Massillon.[97] France, which shows to-day the conquering march of Catholicism, as brain after brain surrenders to it, Brunetière,[98] Coppée,[99] Hauptmann,[100] Barrès,[101] Bourget,[102] Lemaître." [103]

"France!" asserted Turnbull with a sort of rollicking self-exaggeration, very unusual with him, "France, which is one torrent of splendid scepticism from Abelard[104] to Anatole France." [105]

"France," said MacIan, "which is one cataract of clear faith from St. Louis[106] to Our Lady of Lourdes." [107]

---

[94] St. Bernard of Clairvaux (1090–1153) was a French theologian and reformer who founded over seventy monasteries.

[95] Jeanne d'Arc (ca. 1412–1431) was a French patriot and martyr; she was not canonized until 1920, some years after this book was written.

[96] Jacques Bénigne Bossuet (1627–1704) was a French churchman and writer, credited by many as the first person to attempt a philosophy of history. He wrote *The History of the Variations in Protestant Churches* (1688).

[97] Jean Baptiste Massillon (1663–1742), French churchman and Bishop of Clermont (1717), pronounced funeral orations for a variety of notables, including Louis XIV. He is best known for his sermons; the first edition of his works appeared in 1745.

[98] Vincent de Paul Marie Ferdinand Brunetière (1849–1906) was a French critic, professor and essayist and convert to Catholicism.

[99] François Coppée (1842–1908) was a French poet and convert to Catholicism.

[100] Gerhart Johann Robert Hauptmann (1862–1946) was a German dramatist and Nobel prize winner.

[101] Auguste Maurice Barrès (1862–1923) was a French novelist and politician.

[102] Paul Bourget (1852–1935) was a French poet, essayist and novelist.

[103] Jules Lemaître (1853–1914) was a French playwright and critic and convert to Catholicism.

[104] Peter Abelard (1079–1142) was a French philosopher and scholar condemned for heresy by the Catholic Church (1121).

[105] Anatole France, pseudonym of Anatole François Thibault (1844–1924), was a French writer and Nobel prize winner known for satirical and sceptical works in which he was an opponent of both church and state.

[106] St. Louis (1214–1270) was a king of France (Louis IX) canonized in 1297.

[107] Our Lady of Lourdes is the title given the Blessed Virgin Mary following the eighteen apparitions to St. Bernadette (Bernadette Soubirous, 1844–1879, who was canonized 1933) in Lourdes, France, now a well-known place of pilgrimage and healings.

"France at least," cried Turnbull, throwing up his sword in school-boy triumph, "in which these things are thought about and fought about. France, where reason and religion clash in one continual tour-nament. France, above all, where men understand the pride and pas-sion which have plucked our blades from their scabbards. Here, at least, we shall not be chased and spied on by sickly parsons and greasy policemen, because we wish to put our lives on the game. Courage, my friend, we have come to the country of honour."

MacIan did not even notice the incongruous phrase "my friend," but nodding again and again, drew his sword and flung the scabbard far behind him in the road.

"Yes," he cried, in a voice of thunder, "we will fight here and *He* shall look on at it."

Turnbull glanced at the crucifix with a sort of scowling good-humour and then said: "He may look and see His cross defeated."

"The cross cannot be defeated," said MacIan, "for it is Defeat."

A second afterward the two bright, bloodthirsty weapons made the sign of the cross in horrible parody upon each other.

They had not touched each other twice, however, when upon the hill, above the crucifix, there appeared another horrible parody of its shape; the figure of a man who appeared for an instant waving his outspread arms. He had vanished in an instant; but MacIan, whose fighting face was set that way, had seen the shape momentarily but quite photographically. And while it was like a comic repetition of the cross, it was also, in that place and hour, something more incred-ible. It had been only instantaneously on the retina of his eye; but unless his eye and mind were going mad together, the figure was that of an ordinary London policeman.

He tried to concentrate his senses on the sword-play; but one half of his brain was wrestling with the puzzle; the apocalyptic and almost seraphic apparition of a stout constable out of Clapham on top of a dreary and deserted hill in France. He did not, however, have to puzzle long. Before the duellists had exchanged half a dozen passes, the big, blue policeman appeared once more on the top of the hill, a palpable monstrosity in the eye of heaven. He was waving only one arm now and seemed to be shouting directions. At the same moment a mass of blue blocked the corner of the road behind the small, smart figure of Turnbull, and a small company of policemen in the English uniform came up at a kind of half-military double.

Turnbull saw the stare of consternation in his enemy's face and swung round to share its cause. When he saw it, cool as he was, he staggered back.

"What the devil are you doing here?" he called out in a high, shrill voice of authority, like one who finds a tramp in his own larder.

"Well, sir," said the serjeant in command, with that sort of heavy civility shown only to the evidently guilty, "seems to me we might ask what are you doing here?"

"We are having an affair of honour," said Turnbull, as if it were the most rational thing in the world. "If the French police like to interfere, let them interfere. But why the blue blazes should you interfere, you great blue blundering sausages?"

"I'm afraid, sir," said the serjeant with restraint, "I'm afraid I don't quite follow you."

"I mean, why don't the French police take this up if it's got to be taken up? I always heard that they were spry enough in their own way."

"Well, sir," said the serjeant, reflectively, "you see, sir, the French police don't take this up—well, because you see, sir, this ain't France. This is His Majesty's dominions, same as 'Amp-stead 'eath." [108]

"Not France?" repeated Turnbull, with a sort of dull incredulity.

"No, sir," said the serjeant; "though most of the people talk French. This is the island called St. Loup, sir, an island in the Channel. We've been sent down specially from London, as you were such specially distinguished criminals, if you'll allow me to say so. Which reminds me to warn you that anything you say may be used against you at your trial."

---

[108] This turn of events, arriving back in one's own country instead of somewhere else one thinks one has arrived, is a theme that appears often in Chesterton's writings. In *Orthodoxy* and in *Man Alive* it is sometimes necessary to head out on a voyage in order to see "home" for the first time as it should be seen.

"Quite so," said Turnbull, and lurched suddenly against the serjeant, so as to tip him over the edge of the road with a crash into the
shingle below. Then leaving MacIan and the policemen equally and
instantaneously nailed to the road, he ran a little way along it, leapt
off on to a part of the beach, which he had found in his journey to be
firmer, and went across it with a clatter of pebbles. His sudden calculation was successful; the police, unacquainted with the various levels of the loose beach, tried to overtake him by the shorter cut and
found themselves, being heavy men, almost up to their knees in shoals
of slippery shingle. Two who had been slower with their bodies were
quicker with their minds, and seeing Turnbull's trick, ran along the
edge of the road after him. Then MacIan finally awoke, and leaving
half his sleeve in the grip of the only man who tried to hold him,
took the two policemen in the small of their backs with the impetus
of a cannon-ball and, sending them also flat among the stones, went
tearing after his twin defier of the law.

As they were both good runners, the start they had gained was
decisive. They dropped over a high break-water farther on upon the
beach, turned sharply, and scrambled up a line of ribbed rocks,
crowned with a thicket, crawled through it, scratching their hands
and faces, and dropped into another road; and there found that they
could slacken their speed into a steady trot. In all this desperate dart
and scramble, they still kept hold of their drawn swords, which now,
indeed, in the vigorous phrase of Bunyan,[109] seemed almost to grow
out of their hands.

They had run another half mile or so when it became apparent that
they were entering a sort of scattered village. One or two whitewashed cottages and even a shop had appeared along the side of the
road. Then, for the first time, Turnbull twisted round his red beard to
get a glimpse of his companion, who was a foot or two behind, and
remarked abruptly: "Mr. MacIan, we've been going the wrong way to
work all along. We're traced everywhere, because everybody knows

[109] John Bunyan (1628–1688) was an English writer and Nonconformist preacher.
Bunyan's most famous book is *Pilgrim's Progress*, the first part of which was published in
1678, and it is likely the exchanges between Christian (a pilgrim) and various figures
representing challenges to the religious life, to which the reference points.

about us. It's as if one went about with Kruger's[110] beard on Mafeking Night."[111]

"What do you mean?" said MacIan, innocently.

"I mean," said Turnbull, with steady conviction, "that what we
want is a little diplomacy, and I am going to buy some in a shop."

[110] Paul Kruger (1825–1904) was a South African politician who governed the second Boer War (1899–1902); when the tide turned against the Boers, he went to Europe
to seek (in vain) alliances against the British. He was a distinctive figure known for a
striking beard.

[111] Mafeking Night, May 18, 1900, commemorates the successful defense by a British force led by Robert Baden-Powell (who later founded the Boy Scouts) of a town
called Mafeking in the Cape of South Africa. The Boers seiged the town for over two
hundred days. When the British forces were eventually relieved and news of this reached
England, there was an immense public celebration in Britain.

XI

A SCANDAL IN THE VILLAGE

In the little hamlet of Haroc, in the Isle of St. Loup, there lived a man who—though living under the English flag—was absolutely typical of the French tradition. He was quite unnoticeable, but that was exactly where he was quite himself. He was not even extraordinarily French; but then it is against the French tradition to be extraordinarily French. Ordinary Englishmen would only have thought him a little old-fashioned; imperialistic Englishmen would really have mistaken him for the old John Bull of the caricatures. He was stout; he was quite undistinguished; and he had side whiskers, worn just a little longer than John Bull's. He was by name Pierre Durand; he was by trade a wine merchant; he was by politics a conservative republican; he had been brought up a Catholic, had always thought and acted as an agnostic, and was very mildly returning to the Church in his later years. He had a genius (if one can even use so wild a word in connection with so tame a person) a genius for saying the conventional thing on every conceivable subject; or rather what we in England would call the conventional thing. For it was not convention with him, but solid and manly conviction. Convention implies cant or affectation, and he had not the faintest smell of either. He was simply an ordinary citizen with ordinary views; and if you had told him so he would have taken it as an ordinary compliment. If you had asked him about women, he would have said that one must preserve their domesticity and decorum; he would have used the stalest words, but he would have in reserve the strongest arguments. If you had asked him about government, he would have said that all citizens were free and equal, but he would have meant what he said. If you had asked him about education, he would have said that the young must be trained up in habits of industry and of respect for their parents. Still he would have set them the example of industry, and he would have been one of the parents whom they could respect. A state of mind so hopelessly central is depressing to the English instinct. But then in England a man announcing these platitudes is generally a fool and a frightened fool, announcing them out of mere social servility. But Durand was anything but a fool; he had read all the eighteenth century, and could have defended his platitudes round every angle of eighteenth-century argument. And certainly he was anything but a coward: swollen and sedentary as he was, he could have hit any man back who touched him with the instant violence of an automatic machine; and dying in a uniform would have seemed to him only the sort of thing that sometimes happens. I am afraid it is impossible to explain this monster amid the exaggerative sects and the eccentric clubs of my country. He was merely a man.

He lived in a little villa which was furnished well with comfortable chairs and tables and highly uncomfortable classical pictures and medallions. The art in his home contained nothing between the two extremes of hard, meagre designs of Greek heads and Roman togas, and on the other side a few very vulgar Catholic images in the crudest colours; these were mostly in his daughter's room. He had recently lost his wife, whom he had loved heartily and rather heavily in complete silence, and upon whose grave he was constantly in the habit of placing hideous little wreaths, made out of a sort of black-and-white beads. To his only daughter he was equally devoted, though he restricted her a good deal under a sort of theoretic alarm about her innocence; an alarm which was peculiarly unnecessary, first, because she was an exceptionally reticent and religious girl, and secondly, because there was hardly anybody else in the place.

Madeleine Durand was physically a sleepy young woman, and might easily have been supposed to be morally a lazy one. It is, however, certain that the work of her house was done somehow, and it is even more rapidly ascertainable that nobody else did it. The logician is, therefore, driven back upon the assumption that she did it; and that lends a sort of mysterious interest to her personality at the beginning. She had very broad, low, and level brows, which seemed even lower because her warm yellow hair clustered down to her eyebrows; and she had a face just plump enough not to look as powerful as it was. Anything that was heavy in all this was abruptly lightened by two large, light china-blue eyes, lightened all of a sudden as if it had been lifted into the air by two big blue butterflies. The rest of her was less than middle-sized, and was of a casual and comfortable sort; and she had this difference from such girls as the girl in the motor-car, that one did not incline to take in her figure at all, but only her broad and leonine and innocent head.

Both the father and the daughter were of the sort that would normally have avoided all observation; that is, all observation in that extraordinary modern world which calls out everything except strength. Both of them had strength below the surface; they were like quiet peasants owning enormous and unquarried mines. The father with his square face and gray side whiskers, the daughter with her square face and golden fringe of hair, were both stronger than they knew; stronger than any one knew. The father believed in civilisation, in the storied tower we have erected to affront nature; that is, the father believed in Man. The daughter believed in God; and was even stronger. They neither of them believed in themselves; for that is a decadent weakness.

The daughter was called a devotee. She left upon ordinary people the impression—the somewhat irritating impression—produced by such a person; it can only be described as the sense of strong water being perpetually poured into some abyss. She did her housework easily; she achieved her social relations sweetly; she was never neglectful and never unkind. This accounted for all that was soft in her, but not for all that was hard. She trod firmly as if going somewhere; she flung her face back as if defying something; she hardly spoke a cross word, yet there was often battle in her eyes. The modern man asked doubtfully where all this silent energy went to. He would have stared still more doubtfully if he had been told that it all went into her prayers.

The conventions of the Isle of St. Loup were necessarily a compromise or confusion between those of France and England; and it was vaguely possible for a respectable young lady to have half-attached lovers, in a way that would be impossible in the bourgeoisie of France. One man in particular had made himself an unmistakable figure in the track of this girl as she went to church. He was a short, prosperous-looking man, whose long, bushy black beard and clumsy black umbrella made him seem both shorter and older than he really was; but whose big, bold eyes, and step that spurned the ground, gave him an instant character of youth.

His name was Camille Bert, and he was a commercial traveller who had only been in the island an idle week before he began to hover in the tracks of Madeleine Durand. Since every one knows every one in so small a place, Madeleine certainly knew him to speak to; but it is not very evident that she ever spoke. He haunted her, however; especially at church, which was, indeed, one of the few certain places for finding her. In her home she had a habit of being invisible, sometimes through insatiable domesticity, sometimes through an equally insatiable solitude. M. Bert did not give the impression of a pious man, though he did give, especially with his eyes, the impression of an honest one. But he went to Mass with a simple exactitude that could not be mistaken for a pose, or even for a vulgar fascination. It was perhaps this religious regularity which eventually drew Madeleine into recognition of him. At least it is certain that she twice spoke to him with her square and open smile in the porch of the church; and there was human nature enough in the hamlet to turn even that into gossip.

But the real interest arose suddenly as a squall arises with the extraordinary affair that occurred about five days after. There was about a third of a mile beyond the village of Haroc a large but lonely hotel upon the London or Paris model, but commonly almost entirely empty. Among the accidental group of guests who had come to it at this season was a man whose nationality no one could fix and who bore the non-committal name of Count Gregory. He treated everybody with complete civility and almost in complete silence. On the few occasions when he spoke, he spoke either French, English, or once (to the priest) Latin; and the general opinion was that he spoke them all wrong. He was a large, lean man, with the stoop of an aged eagle, and even the eagle's nose to complete it; he had old-fashioned military whiskers and moustache dyed with a garish and highly incredible yellow. He had the dress of a showy gentleman and the manners of a decayed gentleman; he seemed (as with a sort of simplicity) to be trying to be a dandy when he was too old even to know that he was old. Yet he was decidedly a handsome figure with his curled yellow hair and lean fastidious face; and he wore a peculiar frock-coat of bright turquoise blue, with an unknown order pinned to it, and he carried a huge and heavy cane. Despite his silence and his dandified dress and whiskers, the island might never have heard of him but for the extraordinary event of which I have spoken, which fell about in the following way:

In such casual atmospheres only the enthusiastic go to Benediction; and as the warm blue twilight closed over the little candle-lit church and village, the line of worshippers who went home from the former to the latter thinned out until it broke. On one such evening at least no one was in church except the quiet, unconquerable Madeleine, four old women, one fisherman, and, of course, the irrepressible M. Camille Bert. The others seemed to melt away afterward into the peacock colours of the dim green grass and the dark blue sky. Even Durand was invisible instead of being merely reverentially remote; and Madeleine set forth through the patch of black forest alone. She was not in the least afraid of loneliness, because she was not afraid of devils. I think they were afraid of her.

In a clearing of the wood, however, which was lit up with a last patch of the perishing sunlight, there advanced upon her suddenly one who was more startling than a devil. The incomprehensible Count Gregory, with his yellow hair like flame and his face like the white ashes of the flame, was advancing bareheaded toward her, flinging out his arms and his long fingers with a frantic gesture.

"We are alone here," he cried, "and you would be at my mercy, only that I am at yours."

Then his frantic hands fell by his sides and he looked up under his brows with an expression that went well with his hard breathing. Madeleine Durand had come to a halt at first in childish wonder, and now, with more than masculine self-control, "I fancy I know your face, sir," she said, as if to gain time.

"I know I shall not forget yours," said the other, and extended once more his ungainly arms in an unnatural gesture. Then of a sudden there came out of him a spout of wild and yet pompous phrases. "It is as well that you should know the worst and the best. I am a man who knows no limit; I am the most callous of criminals, the most unrepentant of sinners. There is no man in my dominions so vile as I.

But my dominions stretch from the olives of Italy to the fir-woods of Denmark, and there is no nook of all of them in which I have not done a sin. But when I bear you away I shall be doing my first sacrilege, and also my first act of virtue." He seized her suddenly by the elbow; and she did not scream but only pulled and tugged. Yet though she had not screamed, some one astray in the woods seemed to have heard the struggle. A short but nimble figure came along the woodland path like a humming bullet and had caught Count Gregory a crack across the face before his own could be recognised. When it was recognised it was that of Camille, with the black elderly beard and the young ardent eyes.

Up to the moment when Camille had hit the Count, Madeleine had entertained no doubt that the Count was merely a madman. Now she was startled with a new sanity; for the tall man in the yellow whiskers and yellow moustache first returned the blow of Bert, as if it were a sort of duty, and then stepped back with a slight bow and an easy smile.

"This need go no further here, M. Bert," he said. "I need not remind you how far it should go elsewhere."

"Certainly, you need remind me of nothing," answered Camille, stolidly. "I am glad that you are just not too much of a scoundrel for a gentleman to fight."

"We are detaining the lady," said Count Gregory, with politeness; and, making a gesture suggesting that he would have taken off his hat if he had had one, he strode away up the avenue of trees and eventually disappeared. He was so complete an aristocrat that he could offer his back to them all the way up that avenue; and his back never once looked uncomfortable.

"You must allow me to see you home," said Bert to the girl, in a gruff and almost stifled voice; "I think we have only a little way to go."

"Only a little way," she said, and smiled once more that night, in spite of fatigue and fear and the world and the flesh and the devil. The glowing and transparent blue of twilight had long been covered by the opaque and slatelike blue of night, when he handed her into the lamplit interior of her home. He went out himself into the darkness, walking sturdily, but tearing at his black beard.

All the French or semi-French gentry of the district considered this a case in which a duel was natural and inevitable, and neither party had any difficulty in finding seconds, strangers as they were in the place. Two small landowners, who were careful, practising Catholics, willingly undertook to represent that strict church-goer Camille Bert; while the profligate but apparently powerful Count Gregory found friends in an energetic local doctor who was ready for social promotion and an accidental Californian tourist who was ready for anything. As no particular purpose could be served by delay, it was arranged that the affair should fall out three days afterward. And when this was settled the whole community, as it were, turned over again in bed and thought no more about the matter. At least there was only one member of it who seemed to be restless, and that was she who was commonly most restful. On the next night Madeleine Durand went to church as usual; and as usual the stricken Camille was there also. What was not so usual was that when they were a bow-shot from the church Madeleine turned round and walked back to him. "Sir," she began, "it is not wrong of me to speak to you," and the very words gave him a jar of unexpected truth; for in all the novels he had ever read she would have begun: "It is wrong of me to speak to you." She went on with wide and serious eyes like an animal's: "It is not wrong of me to speak to you, because your soul, or anybody's soul, matters so much more than what the world says about anybody. I want to talk to you about what you are going to do."

Bert saw in front of him the inevitable heroine of the novels trying to prevent bloodshed; and his pale firm face became implacable.

"I would do anything but that for you," he said; "but no man can be called less than a man."

She looked at him for a moment with a face openly puzzled, and then broke into an odd and beautiful half smile.

"Oh, I don't mean that," she said; "I don't talk about what I don't understand. No one has ever hit me; and if they had I should not feel as a man may. I am sure it is not the best thing to fight. It would be better to forgive—if one could really forgive. But when people dine with my father and say that fighting a duel is mere murder—of course I can see that is not just. It's all so different—having a reason—and

letting the other man know—and using the same guns and things—
and doing it in front of your friends. I'm awfully stupid, but I know
that men like you aren't murderers. But it wasn't that that I meant."

"What did you mean?" asked the other, looking broodingly at the
earth.

"Don't you know," she said, "there is only one more celebration?
I thought that as you always go to church—I thought you would
communicate this morning."

Bert stepped backward with a sort of action she had never seen in
him before. It seemed to alter his whole body.

"You may be right or wrong to risk dying," said the girl, simply;
"the poor women in our village risk it whenever they have a baby.
You men are the other half of the world. I know nothing about when
you ought to die. But surely if you are daring to try and find God
beyond the grave and appeal to Him—you ought to let Him find you
when He comes and stands there every morning in our little church."

And placid as she was, she made a little gesture of argument, of
which the pathos wrung the heart.

M. Camille Bert was by no means placid. Before that incomplete
gesture and frankly pleading face he retreated as if from the jaws of a
dragon. His dark black hair and beard looked utterly unnatural against
the startling pallor of his face. When at last he said something it was:
"O God! I can't stand this!" He did not say it in French. Nor did he,
strictly speaking, say it in English. The truth (interesting only to anthro-
pologists) is that he said it in Scotch.

"There will be another mass in a matter of eight hours," said
Madeleine, with a sort of business eagerness and energy, "and you can
do it then before the fighting. You must forgive me, but I was so
frightened that you would not do it at all."

Bert seemed to crush his teeth together until they broke, and managed to say between them: "And why should you suppose that I
shouldn't do as you say—I mean not do it at all?"

"You always go to Mass," answered the girl, opening her wide blue
eyes, "and the Mass is very long and tiresome unless one loves God."

Then it was that Bert exploded with a brutality which might have
come from Count Gregory, his criminal opponent. He advanced upon

Madeleine with flaming eyes, and almost took her by the two shoulders. "I do not love God," he cried, speaking French with the broadest Scotch accent; "I do not want to find Him; I do not think He is there to be found. I must burst up the show; I must and will say everything. You are the happiest and honestest thing I ever saw in this godless universe. And I am the dirtiest and most dishonest."

Madeleine looked at him doubtfully for an instant, and then said with a sudden simplicity and cheerfulness: "Oh, but if you are really sorry it is all right. If you are horribly sorry it is all the better. You have only to go and tell the priest so and he will give you God out of his own hands."

"I hate your priest and I deny your God!" cried the man, "and I tell you God is a lie and a fable and a mask. And for the first time in my life I do not feel superior to God."

"What can it all mean?" said Madeleine, in massive wonder.

"Because I am a fable also and a mask," said the man. He had been plucking fiercely at his black beard and hair all the time; now he suddenly plucked them off and flung them like moulted feathers in the mire. This extraordinary spoliation left in the sunlight the same face, but a much younger head—a head with close chestnut curls and a short chestnut beard.

"Now you know the truth," he answered, with hard eyes. "I am a cad who has played a crooked trick on a quiet village and a decent woman for a private reason of his own. I might have played it successfully on any other woman; I have hit the one woman on whom it cannot be played. It's just like my damned luck. The plain truth is," and here when he came to the plain truth he boggled and blundered as Evan had done in telling it to the girl in the motor-car.

"The plain truth is," he said at last, "that I am James Turnbull the atheist. The police are after me; not for atheism but for being ready to fight for it."

"I saw something about you in a newspaper," said the girl, with a simplicity which even surprise could never throw off its balance.

"Evan MacIan said there was a God," went on the other, stubbornly, "and I say there isn't. And I have come to fight for the fact that there is no God; it is for that that I have seen this cursed island and your blessed face."

"You want me really to believe," said Madeleine, with parted lips, "that you think——"

"I want you to hate me!" cried Turnbull, in agony. "I want you to be sick when you think of my name. I am sure there is no God."

"But there is," said Madeline, quite quietly, and rather with the air of one telling children about an elephant. "Why, I touched His body only this morning."

"You touched a bit of bread," said Turnbull, biting his knuckles. "Oh, I will say anything that can madden you!"

"You think it is only a bit of bread," said the girl, and her lips tightened ever so little.

"I know it is only a bit of bread," said Turnbull, with violence.

She flung back her open face and smiled. "Then why did you refuse to eat it?" she said.

James Turnbull made a little step backward, and for the first time in his life there seemed to break out and blaze in his head thoughts that were not his own.

"Why, how silly of them," cried out Madeleine, with quite a schoolgirl gaiety, "why, how silly of them to call *you* a blasphemer! Why, you have wrecked your whole business because you would not commit blasphemy."

The man stood, a somewhat comic figure in his tragic bewilderment, with the honest red head of James Turnbull sticking out of the rich and fictitious garments of Camille Bert. But the startled pain of his face was strong enough to obliterate the oddity.

"You come down here," continued the lady, with that female emphasis which is so pulverising in conversation and so feeble at a public meeting, "you and your MacIan come down here and put on false beards or noses in order to fight. You pretend to be a Catholic commercial traveller from France. Poor Mr. MacIan has to pretend to be a dissolute nobleman from nowhere. Your scheme succeeds; you pick a quite convincing quarrel; you arrange a quite respectable duel; the duel you have planned so long will come off to-morrow with absolute certainty and safety. And then you throw off your wig and throw up your scheme and throw over your colleague, because I ask you to go into a building and eat a bit of bread. And *then* you dare to tell me that you are sure there is nothing watching us. Then you say you know there is nothing on the very altar you run away from. You know——"

"I only know," said Turnbull, "that I must run away from you. This has got beyond any talking." And he plunged along into the village, leaving his black wig and beard lying behind him on the road.

As the market-place opened before him he saw Count Gregory, that distinguished foreigner, standing and smoking in elegant meditation at the corner of the local café. He immediately made his way rapidly toward him, considering that a consultation was urgent. But he had hardly crossed half of that stony quadrangle when a window burst open above him and a head was thrust out, shouting. The man was in his woollen undershirt, but Turnbull knew the energetic, apoplectic head of the serjeant of police. He pointed furiously at Turnbull and shouted his name. A policeman ran excitedly from under an archway and tried to collar him. Two men selling vegetables dropped their baskets and joined in the chase. Turnbull dodged the constable, upset one of the men into his own basket, and bounding toward the distinguished foreign Count, called to him clamorously: "Come on, MacIan, the hunt is up again."

The prompt reply of Count Gregory was to pull off his large yellow whiskers and scatter them on the breeze with an air of considerable relief. Then he joined the flight of Turnbull, and even as he did so, with one wrench of his powerful hands rent and split the strange, thick stick that he carried. Inside it was a naked old-fashioned rapier. The two got a good start up the road before the whole town was awakened behind them; and half way up it a similar transformation was seen to take place in Mr. Turnbull's singular umbrella.

The two had a long race for the harbour; but the English police were heavy and the French inhabitants were indifferent. In any case, they got used to the notion of the road being clear; and just as they had come to the cliffs MacIan banged into another gentleman with unmistakable surprise. How he knew he was another gentleman merely by banging into him, must remain a mystery. MacIan was a very poor and very sober Scotch gentleman. The other was a very drunk and very wealthy English gentleman. But there was something in

the staggered and openly embarrassed apologies that made them understand each other as readily and as quickly and as much as two men
talking French in the middle of China. The nearest expression of
the type is that it either hits or apologises; and in this case both
apologised.

"You seem to be in a hurry," said the unknown Englishman, falling
back a step or two in order to laugh with an unnatural heartiness.
"What's it all about, eh?" Then before MacIan could get past his sprawling and staggering figure he ran forward again and said with a sort of
shouting and ear-shattering whisper: "I say, my name is Wilkinson.
You know—Wilkinson's Entire was my grandfather. Can't drink beer
myself. Liver." And he shook his head with extraordinary sagacity.

"We really are in a hurry, as you say," said MacIan, summoning a
sufficiently pleasant smile, "so if you will let us pass——"

"I'll tell you what, you fellows," said the sprawling gentleman, confidentially, while Evan's agonised ears heard behind him the first paces
of the pursuit, "if you really are, as you say, in a hurry, I know what
it is to be in a hurry—Lord, what a hurry I was in when we all came
out of Cartwright's rooms—if you really are in a hurry——" and he
seemed to steady his voice into a sort of solemnity—"if you are in a
hurry, there's nothing like a good yacht for a man in a hurry."

"No doubt you're right," said MacIan, and dashed past him in
despair. The head of the pursuing host was just showing over the top
of the hill behind him. Turnbull had already ducked under the intoxicated gentleman's elbow and fled far in front.

"No, but look here," said Mr. Wilkinson, enthusiastically running
after MacIan and catching him by the sleeve of his coat. "If you want
to hurry you should take a yacht, and if——" he said, with a burst of
rationality, like one leaping to a further point in logic—"if you want
a yacht—you can have mine."

Evan pulled up abruptly and looked back at him. "We are really in
the devil of a hurry," he said, "and if you really have a yacht, the truth
is that we would give our ears for it."

"You'll find it in harbour," said Wilkinson, struggling with his
speech. "Left side of harbour—called *Gibson Girl*—can't think why,
old fellow, I never lent it you before."

With these words the benevolent Mr. Wilkinson fell flat on his face in the road, but continued to laugh softly, and turned toward his flying companion a face of peculiar peace and benignity. Evan's mind went through a crisis of instantaneous casuistry, in which it may be that he decided wrongly; but about how he decided his biographer can profess no doubt. Two minutes afterward he had overtaken Turnbull and told the tale; ten minutes afterward he and Turnbull had somehow tumbled into the yacht called the *Gibson Girl* and had somehow pushed off from the Isle of St. Loup.

XII

THE DESERT ISLAND

Those who happen to hold the view (and Mr. Evan MacIan, now alive and comfortable, is among the number) that something supernatural, some eccentric kindness from god or fairy had guided our adventurers through all their absurd perils, might have found his strongest argument perhaps in their management or mismanagement of Mr. Wilkinson's yacht. Neither of them had the smallest qualification for managing such a vessel; but MacIan had a practical knowledge of the sea in much smaller and quite different boats, while Turnbull had an abstract knowledge of science and some of its applications to navigation, which was worse. The presence of the god or fairy can only be deduced from the fact that they never definitely ran into anything, either a boat, a rock, a quicksand, or a man-of-war. Apart from this negative description, their voyage would be difficult to describe. It took at least a fortnight, and MacIan, who was certainly the shrewder sailor of the two, realised that they were sailing west into the Atlantic and were probably by this time past the Scilly Isles.[112] How much farther they stood out into the western sea it was impossible to conjecture. But they felt certain, at least, that they were far enough into that awful gulf between us and America to make it unlikely that they would soon see land again. It was therefore with legitimate excitement that one rainy morning after daybreak they saw the distinct shape of a solitary island standing up against that encircling strip of silver which ran round the skyline and separated the gray and green of the billows from the gray and mauve of the morning clouds.

"What can it be?" cried MacIan, in a dry-throated excitement. "I didn't know there were any Atlantic islands so far beyond the Scillies— Good Lord, it can't be Madeira,[113] yet?"

---

[112] The Isles of Scilly are a cluster of about three hundred small granite islands set in the Atlantic Ocean some twenty-eight miles southwest of Land's End in the United Kingdom. Only five of the islands are inhabited.

[113] Madeira is an island and the largest of the Madeira Islands, an autonomous region of Portugal and located in the Atlantic Ocean off Northwest Africa.

"I thought you were fond of legends and lies and fables," said Turn-bull, grimly. "Perhaps it's Atlantis."

"Of course, it might be," answered the other, quite innocently and gravely; "but I never thought the story about Atlantis[114] was very solidly established."

"Whatever it is, we are running on to it," said Turnbull, equably, "and we shall be shipwrecked twice, at any rate."

The naked looking nose of land projecting from the unknown island was, indeed, growing larger and larger, like the trunk of some terrible and advancing elephant. There seemed to be nothing in particular, at least on this side of the island, except shoals of shell-fish lying so thick as almost to make it look like one of those toy grottos that the children make. In one place, however, the coast offered a soft, smooth bay of sand, and even the rudimentary inge-nuity of the two amateur mariners managed to run up the little ship with her prow well on shore and her bowsprit pointing upward, as in a sort of idiotic triumph.

They tumbled on shore and began to unload the vessel, setting the stores out in rows upon the sand with something of the solemnity of boys playing at pirates. There were Mr. Wilkinson's cigar-boxes and Mr. Wilkinson's dozen of champagne and Mr. Wilkinson's tinned salmon and Mr. Wilkinson's tinned tongue and Mr. Wilkinson's tinned sardines, and every sort of preserved thing that could be seen at the Army and Navy stores. Then MacIan stopped with a jar of pickles in his hand and said abruptly:

"I don't know why we're doing all this; I suppose we ought really to fall to and get it over."

Then he added more thoughtfully: "Of course this island seems rather bare and the survivor——"

"The question is," said Turnbull, with cheerful speculation, "whether the survivor will be in a proper frame of mind for potted prawns."

MacIan looked down at the rows of tins and bottles, and the cloud of doubt still lowered upon his face.

---

[114] As described by Plato (ca. 428–ca. 348 B.C.) in the *Timaeus*, Atlantis is a fabled island in the ocean west of the Pillars of Hercules.

"You will permit me two liberties, my dear sir," said Turnbull at last: "The first is to break open this box and light one of Mr. Wilkinson's excellent cigars, which will, I am sure, assist my meditations; the second is to offer a penny for your thoughts; or rather to convulse the already complex finances of this island by betting a penny that I know them."

"What on earth are you talking about?" asked MacIan, listlessly, in the manner of an inattentive child.

"I know what you are really thinking, MacIan," repeated Turnbull, laughing. "I know what I am thinking, anyhow. And I rather fancy it's the same."

"What are you thinking?" asked Evan.

"I am thinking and you are thinking," said Turnbull, "that it is damned silly to waste all that champagne."

Something like the spectre of a smile appeared on the unsmiling visage of the Gael; and he made at least no movement of dissent.

"We could drink all the wine and smoke all the cigars easily in a week," said Turnbull; "and that would be to die feasting like heroes."

"Yes, and there is something else," said MacIan, with slight hesitation. "You see, we are on an almost unknown rock, lost in the Atlantic. The police will never catch us; but then neither may the public ever hear of us; and that was one of the things we wanted." Then, after a pause, he said, drawing in the sand with his sword-point: "She may never hear of it at all."

"Well?" inquired the other, puffing at his cigar.

"Well," said MacIan, "we might occupy a day or two in drawing up a thorough and complete statement of what we did and why we did it, and all about both our points of view. Then we could leave one copy on the island whatever happens to us and put another in an empty bottle and send it out to sea, as they do in the books."

"A good idea," said Turnbull, "and now let us finish unpacking."

As MacIan, a tall, almost ghostly figure, paced along the edge of sand that ran round the islet, the purple but cloudy poetry which was his native element was piled up at its thickest upon his soul. The unique island and the endless sea emphasised the thing solely as an epic. There were no ladies or policemen here to give him a hint either of its farce or its tragedy.

"Perhaps when the morning stars were made," he said to himself, "God built this island up from the bottom of the world to be a tower and a theatre for the fight between yea and nay."

Then he wandered up to the highest level of the rock, where there was a roof or plateau of level stone. Half an hour afterward, Turnbull found him clearing away the loose sand from this table-land and making it smooth and even.

"We will fight up here, Turnbull," said MacIan, "when the time comes. And till the time comes this place shall be sacred."

"I thought of having lunch up here," said Turnbull, who had a bottle of champagne in his hand.

"No, no—not up here," said MacIan, and came down from the height quite hastily. Before he descended, however, he fixed the two swords upright, one at each end of the platform, as if they were human sentinels to guard it under the stars.

Then they came down and lunched plentifully in a nest of loose rocks. In the same place that night they supped more plentifully still. The smoke of Mr. Wilkinson's cigars went up ceaseless and strong smelling, like a pagan sacrifice; the golden glories of Mr. Wilkinson's champagne rose to their heads and poured out of them in fancies and philosophies. And occasionally they would look up at the starlight and the rock and see the space guarded by the two cross-hilted swords, which looked like two black crosses at either end of a grave.

In this primitive and Homeric truce the week passed by; it consisted almost entirely of eating, drinking, smoking, talking, and occasionally singing. They wrote their records and cast loose their bottle. They never ascended to the ominous plateau; they had never stood there save for that single embarrassed minute when they had had no time to take stock of the seascape or the shape of the land. They did not even explore the island; for MacIan was partly concerned in prayer and Turnbull entirely concerned with tobacco; and both these forms of inspiration can be enjoyed by the secluded and even the sedentary. It was on a golden afternoon, the sun sinking over the sea, rayed like the very head of Apollo, when Turnbull tossed off the last half pint from the emptied Wilkinsonian bottle, hurled the bottle into the sea with objectless energy, and went up to where his sword stood waiting

for him on the hill. MacIan was already standing heavily by his with
bent head and eyes reading the ground. He had not even troubled to
throw a glance round the island or the horizon. But Turnbull being
of a more active and birdlike type of mind did throw a glance round
the scene. The consequence of which was that he nearly fell off the
rock.

On three sides of this shelly and sandy islet the sea stretched blue
and infinite without a speck of land or sail; the same as Turnbull had
first seen it, except that the tide being out it showed a few yards more
of slanting sand under the roots of the rocks. But on the fourth side
the island exhibited a more extraordinary feature. In fact, it exhibited
the extraordinary feature of not being an island at all. A long, curving
neck of sand, as smooth and wet as the neck of the sea-serpent, ran
out into the sea and joined their rock to a line of low, billowing and
glistening sand-hills, which the sinking sea had just bared to the sun.
Whether they were firm sand or quicksand it was difficult to guess;
but there was at least no doubt that they lay on the edge of some
larger land; for colourless hills appeared faintly behind them and no
sea could be seen beyond.

"Sakes alive!" cried Turnbull, with rolling eyes; "this ain't an island
in the Atlantic. We've butted the bally continent of America."

MacIan turned his head, and his face, already pale, grew a shade
paler. He was by this time walking in a world of omens and hieroglyphics, and he could not read anything but what was baffling or
menacing in this brown gigantic arm of the earth stretched out into
the sea to seize him.

"MacIan," said Turnbull, in his temperate way, "whatever our eternal interrupted tête-à-têtes have taught us or not taught us, at least
we need not fear the charge of fear. If it is essential to your emotions,
I will cheerfully finish the fight here and now; but I must confess that
if you kill me here I shall die with my curiosity highly excited and
unsatisfied upon a minor point of geography."

"I do not want to stop now," said the other, in his elephantine
simplicity, "but we must stop for a moment, because it is a sign—
perhaps it is a miracle. We must see what is at the end of the road of
sand; it may be a bridge built across the gulf by God."

"So long as you gratify my query," said Turnbull, laughing and letting back his blade into the sheath, "I do not care for what reason you choose to stop."

They clambered down the rocky peninsula and trudged along the sandy isthmus with the plodding resolution of men who seemed almost to have made up their minds to be wanderers on the face of the earth. Despite Turnbull's air of scientific eagerness, he was really the less impatient of the two; and the Highlander went on well ahead of him with passionate strides. By the time they had walked for about half an hour in the ups and downs of those dreary sands, the distance between the two had lengthened and MacIan was only a tall figure silhouetted for an instant upon the crest of some sand dune and then disappearing behind it. This rather increased the Robinson Crusoe feeling in Mr. Turnbull, and he looked about almost disconsolately for some sign of life. What sort of life he expected it to be if it appeared, he did not very clearly know. He has since confessed that he thinks that in his subconsciousness he expected an alligator.

The first sign of life that he did see, however, was something more extraordinary than the largest alligator. It was nothing less than the notorious Mr. Evan MacIan coming bounding back across the sand heaps breathless, without his cap and keeping the sword in his hand only by a habit now quite hardened.

"Take care, Turnbull," he cried out from a good distance as he ran, "I've seen a native."

"A native?" repeated his companion, whose scenery had of late been chiefly of shell-fish, "what the deuce! Do you mean an oyster?"

"No," said MacIan, stopping and breathing hard, "I mean a savage. A black man."

"Why, where did you see him?" asked the staring editor.

"Over there—behind that hill," said the gasping MacIan. "He put up his black head and grinned at me."

Turnbull thrust his hands through his red hair like one who gives up the world as a bad riddle. "Lord love a duck," said he, "can it be Jamaica?"

Then glancing at his companion with a small frown, as of one slightly suspicious, he said: "I say, don't think me rude—but you're a visionary kind of fellow—and then we drank a great deal. Do you mind waiting here while I go and see for myself?"

"Shout if you get into trouble," said the Celt, with composure; "you will find it is as I say."

Turnbull ran off ahead with a rapidity now far greater than his rival's, and soon vanished over the disputed sand-hill. Then five minutes passed, and then seven minutes; and MacIan bit his lip and swung his sword, and the other did not reappear. Finally, with a Gaelic oath, Evan started forward to the rescue, and almost at the same moment the small figure of the missing man appeared on the ridge against the sky.

Even at that distance, however, there was something odd about his attitude; so odd that MacIan continued to make his way in that direction. It looked as if he were wounded; or, still more, as if he were ill. He wavered as he came down the slope and seemed flinging himself into peculiar postures. But it was only when he came within three feet of MacIan's face, that that observer of mankind fully realised that Mr. James Turnbull was roaring with laughter.

"You are quite right," sobbed that wholly demoralised journalist. "He's black, oh, there's no doubt the black's all right—as far as it goes." And he went off again into convulsions of his humourous ailment.

"What ever is the matter with you?" asked MacIan, with stern impatience. "Did you see the nigger——"

"I saw the nigger," gasped Turnbull. "I saw the splendid barbarian Chief. I saw the Emperor of Ethiopia—oh, I saw him all right. The nigger's hands and face are a lovely colour—and the nigger—" And he was overtaken once more.

"Well, well, well," said Evan, stamping each monosyllable on the sand, "what about the nigger?"

"Well, the truth is," said Turnbull, suddenly and startlingly, becoming quite grave and precise, "the truth is, the nigger is a Margate nigger, and we are now on the edge of the Isle of Thanet, a few miles from Margate."

Then he had a momentary return of his hysteria and said: "I say, old boy, I should like to see a chart of our fortnight's cruise in Wilkinson's yacht."

MacIan had no smile in answer, but his eager lips opened as if parched for the truth. "You mean to say," he began——

"Yes, I mean to say," said Turnbull, "and I mean to say something funnier still. I have learnt everything I wanted to know from the partially black musician over there, who has taken a run in his war-paint to meet a friend in a quiet pub. along the coast—the noble savage has told me all about it. The bottle containing our declarations, doctrines, and dying sentiments was washed up on Margate beach yesterday in the presence of one alderman, two bathing-machine men, three policemen, seven doctors, and a hundred and thirteen London clerks on a holiday, to all of whom, whether directly or indirectly, our composition gave enormous literary pleasure. Buck up, old man, this story of ours is a switchback. I have begun to understand the pulse and the time of it; now we are up in a cathedral and then we are down in a theatre, where they only play farces. Come, I am quite reconciled—let us enjoy the farce."

But MacIan said nothing, and an instant afterward Turnbull himself called out in an entirely changed voice: "Oh, this is damnable! This is not to be borne!"

MacIan followed his eye along the sand-hills. He saw what looked like the momentary and waving figure of the nigger minstrel, and then he saw a heavy running policeman take the turn of the sand-hill with the smooth solemnity of a railway train.

XIII

THE GARDEN OF PEACE

Up to this instant Evan MacIan had really understood nothing; but when he saw the policeman he saw everything. He saw his enemies, all the powers and princes of the earth. He was suddenly altered from a staring statue to a leaping man of the mountains.

"We must break away from him here," he cried, briefly, and went like a whirlwind over the sand ridge in a straight line and at a particular angle. When the policeman had finished his admirable railway curve, he found a wall of failing sand between him and the pursued. By the time he had scaled it thrice, slid down twice, and crested it in the third effort, the two flying figures were far in front. They found the sand harder farther on; it began to be crusted with scraps of turf and in a few moments they were flying easily over an open common of rank sea-grass. They had no easy business, however; for the bottle which they had so innocently sent into the chief gate of Thanet had called to life the police of half a county on their trail. From every side across the gray-green common figures could be seen running and closing in; and it was only when MacIan with his big body broke down the tangled barrier of a little wood, as men break down a door with the shoulder; it was only when they vanished crashing into the under world of the black wood, that their hunters were even instantaneously thrown off the scent.

At the risk of struggling a little longer like flies in that black web of twigs and trunks, Evan (who had an instinct of the hunter or the hunted) took an incalculable course through the forest, which let them out at last by a forest opening—quite forgotten by the leaders of the chase. They ran a mile or two farther along the edge of the wood until they reached another and somewhat similar opening. Then MacIan stood utterly still and listened, as animals listen, for every sound in the universe. Then he said: "We are quit of them." And Turnbull said: "Where shall we go now?"

MacIan looked at the silver sunset that was closing in, barred by plumy lines of purple cloud; he looked at the high tree-tops that caught the last light and at the birds going heavily homeward, just as if all these things were bits of written advice that he could read.

Then he said: "The best place we can go to is to bed. If we can get some sleep in this wood, now every one has cleared out of it, it will be worth a handicap of two hundred yards tomorrow."

Turnbull, who was exceptionally lively and laughing in his demeanour, kicked his legs about like a schoolboy and said he did not want to go to sleep. He walked incessantly and talked very brilliantly. And when at last he lay down on the hard earth, sleep struck him senseless like a hammer.

Indeed, he needed the strongest sleep he could get; for the earth was still full of darkness and a kind of morning fog when his fellow-fugitive shook him awake.

"No more sleep, I'm afraid," said Evan, in a heavy, almost submissive, voice of apology. "They've gone on past us right enough for a good thirty miles; but now they've found out their mistake, and they're coming back."

"Are you sure?" said Turnbull, sitting up and rubbing his red eyebrows with his hand.

The next moment, however, he had jumped up alive and leaping like a man struck with a shock of cold water, and he was plunging after MacIan along the woodland path. The shape of their old friend the constable had appeared against the pearl and pink of the sunrise. Somehow, it always looked a very funny shape when seen against the sunrise.

A wash of weary daylight was breaking over the country side, and the fields and roads were full of white mist—the kind of white mist that clings in corners like cotton wool. The empty road, along which the chase had taken its turn, was overshadowed on one side by a very high discoloured wall, stained, and streaked green, as with seaweed—evidently the high-shouldered sentinel of some great gentleman's estate. A yard or two from the wall ran parallel to it a linked and tangled line of lime-trees, forming a kind of cloister along the side of the road. It was under this branching colonnade that the two fugitives fled, almost

concealed from their pursuers by the twilight, the mist and the leaping zoetrope of shadows. Their feet, though beating the ground furiously, made but a faint noise; for they had kicked away their boots in
the wood; their long, antiquated weapons made no jingle or clatter,
for they had strapped them across their backs like guitars. They had
all the advantages that invisibility and silence can add to speed.

A hundred and fifty yards behind them down the centre of the
empty road the first of their pursuers came pounding and panting—a
fat but powerful policeman who had distanced all the rest. He came
on at a splendid pace for so portly a figure; but, like all heavy bodies
in motion, he gave the impression that it would be easier for him to
increase his pace than to slacken it suddenly. Nothing short of a brick
wall could have abruptly brought him up. Turnbull turned his head
slightly and found breath to say something to MacIan. MacIan nodded.

Pursuer and pursued were fixed in their distance as they fled, for
some quarter of a mile, when they came to a place where two or
three of the trees grew twistedly together, making a special obscurity.
Past this place the pursuing policeman went thundering without
thought or hesitation. But he was pursuing his shadow or the wind;
for Turnbull had put one foot in a crack of the tree and gone up it as
quickly and softly as a cat. Somewhat more laboriously but in equal
silence the long legs of the Highlander had followed; and crouching
in crucial silence in the cloud of leaves, they saw the whole posse of
their pursuers go by and die into the dust and mists of the distance.

The white vapour lay, as it often does, in lean and palpable layers;
and even the head of the tree was above it in the half daylight, like a
green ship swinging on a sea of foam. But higher yet behind them,
and readier to catch the first coming of the sun, ran the rampart of
the top of the wall, which in their excitement of escape looked at
once indispensable and unattainable, like the wall of heaven. Here,
however, it was MacIan's turn to have the advantage; for, though less
light-limbed and feline, he was longer and stronger in the arms. In
two seconds he had tugged up his chin over the wall like a horizontal
bar; the next he sat astride of it, like a horse of stone. With his assistance Turnbull vaulted to the same perch, and the two began cautiously to shift along the wall in the direction by which they had

come, doubling on their tracks to throw off the last pursuit. MacIan could not rid himself of the fancy of bestriding a steed; the long, gray coping of the wall shot out in front of him, like the long, gray neck of some nightmare Rosinante.[115] He had the quaint thought that he and Turnbull were the two knights on one steed on the old shield of the Templars.[116]

The nightmare of the stone horse was increased by the white fog, which seemed thicker inside the wall than outside. They could make nothing of the enclosure upon which they were partial trespassers, except that the green and crooked branches of a big apple-tree came crawling at them out of the mist, like the tentacles of some green cuttlefish. Anything would serve, however, that was likely to confuse their trail, so they both decided without need of words to use this tree also as a ladder—a ladder of descent. When they dropped from the lowest branch to the ground their stockinged feet felt hard gravel beneath them.

They had alighted in the middle of a very broad garden-path, and the clearing mist permitted them to see the edge of a well-clipped lawn. Though the white vapour was still a veil, it was like the gauzy veil of a transformation scene in a pantomime; for through it there glowed shapeless masses of colour, masses which might be clouds of sunrise or mosaics of gold and crimson, or ladies robed in ruby and emerald draperies. As it thinned yet further they saw that it was only flowers; but flowers in such insolent mass and magnificence as can seldom be seen out of the tropics. Purple and crimson rhododendrons rose arrogantly, like rampant heraldic animals against their burning background of laburnum gold. The roses were red hot; the clematis was, so to speak, blue hot. And yet the mere whiteness of the syringa seemed the most violent colour of all. As the golden sunlight gradually conquered the mists, it had really something of the sensational

[115]"Rosinante" was the name of Don Quixote's horse in Miguel Cervantes' (1547–1616) classic satire on chivalric romances, *Don Quixote* (1605).

[116] The Knights Templars were a military and religious order founded in 1118 to protect pilgrims from bandits in the Holy Land. The order was suppressed in 1312, and its rival group, the Knights Hospitallers or Sovereign Military Order of Malta (eleventh century), continues to this day as the oldest order of chivalry in existence.

sweetness of the slow opening of the gates of Eden. MacIan, whose mind was always haunted with such seraphic or titanic parallels, made some such remark to his companion. But Turnbull only cursed and said that it was the back garden of some damnable rich man.

When the last haze had faded from the ordered paths, the open lawns, and the flaming flower-beds, the two realised, not without an abrupt re-examination of their position, that they were not alone in the garden.

Down the centre of the central garden-path, preceded by a blue cloud from a cigarette, was walking a gentleman who evidently understood all the relish of a garden in the very early morning. He was a slim yet satisfied figure, clad in a suit of pale-gray tweed, so subdued that the pattern was imperceptible—a costume that was casual but not by any means careless. His face, which was reflective and somewhat overrefined, was the face of a quite elderly man, though his stringy hair and moustache were still quite yellow. A double eyeglass, with a broad, black ribbon, drooped from his aquiline nose, and he smiled, as he communed with himself, with a self-content which was rare and almost irritating. The straw panama on his head was many shades shabbier than his clothes, as if he had caught it up by accident.

It needed the full shock of the huge shadow of MacIan, falling across his sunlit path, to rouse him from his smiling reverie. When this had fallen on him he lifted his head a little and blinked at the intruders with short-sighted benevolence, but with far less surprise than might have been expected. He was a gentleman; that is, he had social presence of mind, whether for kindness or for insolence.

"Can I do anything for you?" he said, at last.

MacIan bowed. "You can extend to us your pardon," he said, for he also came of a whole race of gentlemen—of gentlemen without shirts to their backs. "I am afraid we are trespassing. We have just come over the wall."

"Over the wall?" repeated the smiling old gentleman, still without letting his surprise come uppermost.

"I suppose I am not wrong, sir," continued MacIan, "in supposing that these grounds inside the wall belong to you?"

The man in the panama looked at the ground and smoked thought-fully for a few moments, after which he said, with a sort of matured conviction:

"Yes, certainly; the grounds inside the wall really belong to me, and the grounds outside the wall, too."

"A large proprietor, I imagine," said Turnbull, with a truculent eye.

"Yes," answered the old gentleman, looking at him with a steady smile. "A large proprietor."

Turnbull's eye grew even more offensive, and he began biting his red beard; but MacIan seemed to recognise a type with which he could deal and continued quite easily:

"I am sure that a man like you will not need to be told that one sees and does a good many things that do not get into the newspapers. Things which, on the whole, had better not get into the newspapers."

The smile of the large proprietor broadened for a moment under his loose, light moustache, and the other continued with increased confidence:

"One sometimes wants to have it out with another man. The police won't allow it in the streets—and then there's the County Council—and in the fields even nothing's allowed but posters of pills. But in a gentleman's garden, now——"

The strange gentleman smiled again and said, easily enough: "Do you want to fight? What do you want to fight about?"

MacIan had understood his man pretty well up to that point; an instinct common to all men with the aristocratic tradition of Europe had guided him. He knew that the kind of man who in his own back garden wears good clothes and spoils them with a bad hat is not the kind of man who has an abstract horror of illegal actions or violence or the evasion of the police. But a man may understand ragging and yet be very far from understanding religious ragging. This seeming host of theirs might comprehend a quarrel of husband and lover or a difficulty at cards or even escape from a pursuing tailor; but it still remained doubtful whether he would feel the earth fail under him in that earthquake instant when the Virgin is compared to a goddess of Mesopotamia. Even MacIan, therefore (whose tact was far from being his strong point), felt the necessity for some compromise in the mode of approach. At last he said, and even then with hesitation:

"We are fighting about God; there can be nothing so important as that."

The tilted eyeglasses of the old gentleman fell abruptly from his nose, and he thrust his aristocratic chin so far forward that his lean neck seemed to shoot out longer like a telescope.

"About God?" he queried, in a key completely new.

"Look here!" cried Turnbull, taking his turn roughly, "I'll tell you what it's all about. I think that there's no God. I take it that it's nobody's business but mine—or God's, if there is one. This young gentleman from the Highlands happens to think that it's his business. In consequence, he first takes a walking-stick and smashes my shop; then he takes the same walking-stick and tries to smash me. To this I naturally object. I suggest that if it comes to that we should both have sticks. He improves on the suggestion and proposes that we should both have steel-pointed sticks. The police (with characteristic unreasonableness) will not accept either of our proposals; the result is that we run about dodging the police and have jumped over your garden-wall into your magnificent garden to throw ourselves on your magnificent hospitality."

The face of the old gentleman had grown redder and redder during this address, but it was still smiling; and when he broke out it was with a kind of guffaw.

"So you really want to fight with drawn swords in my garden," he asked, "about whether there is really a God?"

"Why not?" said MacIan, with his simple monstrosity of speech; "all man's worship began when the Garden of Eden was founded."

"Yes, by——!" said Turnbull, with an oath, "and ended when the Zoölogical Gardens were founded."

"In this garden! In my presence!" cried the stranger, stamping up and down the gravel and choking with laughter. "Whether there is a God!" And he went stamping up and down the garden, making it echo with his unintelligible laughter. Then he came back to them more composed and wiping his eyes.

"Why, how small the world is!" he cried at last. "I can settle the whole matter. Why, I am God!"

And he suddenly began to kick and wave his well-clad legs about the lawn.

"You are what?" repeated Turnbull, in a tone which is beyond description.

"Why, God, of course!" answered the other, thoroughly amused. "How funny it is to think that you have tumbled over a garden-wall and fallen exactly on the right person! You might have gone floundering about in all sorts of churches and chapels and colleges and schools of philosophy looking for some evidence of the existence of God. Why, there is no evidence, except seeing him. And now you've seen him. You've seen him dance!"

And the obliging old gentleman instantly stood on one leg without relaxing at all the grave and cultured benignity of his expression.

"I understood that this garden——" began the bewildered MacIan.

"Quite so! Quite so!" said the man on one leg, nodding gravely. "I said this garden belonged to me and the land outside it. So they do. So does the country beyond that and the sea beyond that and all the rest of the earth. So does the moon. So do the sun and stars." And he added, with a smile of apology: "You see, I'm God."

Turnbull and MacIan looked at him for one moment with a sort of notion that perhaps he was not too old to be merely playing the fool. But after staring steadily for an instant Turnbull saw the hard and horrible earnestness in the man's eyes behind all his empty animation. Then Turnbull looked very gravely at the strict gravel walks and the gay flower-beds and the long rectangular red-brick building, which the mist had left evident beyond them. Then he looked at MacIan.

Almost at the same moment another man came walking quickly round the regal clump of rhododendrons. He had the look of a prosperous banker, wore a good tall silk hat, was almost stout enough to burst the buttons of a fine frock-coat; but he was talking to himself, and one of his elbows had a singular outward jerk as he went by.

XIV

A MUSEUM OF SOULS

The man with the good hat and the jumping elbow went by very quickly; yet the man with the bad hat, who thought he was God, overtook him. He ran after him and jumped over a bed of geraniums to catch him.

"I beg your Majesty's pardon," he said, with mock humility, "but here is a quarrel which you ought really to judge."

Then as he led the heavy, silk-hatted man back toward the group, he caught MacIan's ear in order to whisper: "This poor gentleman is mad; he thinks he is Edward VII." At this the self-appointed Creator slightly winked. "Of course you won't trust him much; come to me for everything. But in my position one has to meet so many people. One has to be broadminded."

The big banker in the black frock-coat and hat was standing quite grave and dignified on the lawn, save for his slight twitch of one limb, and he did not seem by any means unworthy of the part which the other promptly forced upon him.

"My dear fellow," said the man in the straw hat, "these two gentlemen are going to fight a duel of the utmost importance. Your own royal position and my much humbler one surely indicate us as the proper seconds. Seconds—yes, seconds—" and here the speaker was once more shaken with his old malady of laughter.

"Yes, you and I are both seconds—and these two gentlemen can obviously fight in front of us. You, he-he, are the king. I am God; really, they could hardly have better supporters. They have come to the right place."

Then Turnbull, who had been staring with a frown at the fresh turf, burst out with a rather bitter laugh and cried, throwing his red head in the air:

"Yes, by God, MacIan, I think we have come to the right place!" And MacIan answered, with an adamantine stupidity:

"Any place is the right place where they will let us do it."

There was a long stillness, and their eyes involuntarily took in the landscape, as they had taken in all the landscapes of their everlasting combat; the bright, square garden behind the shop; the whole lift and leaning of the side of Hampstead Heath; the little garden of the decadent choked with flowers; the square of sand beside the sea at sunrise. They both felt at the same moment all the breadth and blossoming beauty of that paradise, the coloured trees, the natural and restful nooks and also the great wall of stone—more awful than the wall of China—from which no flesh could flee.

Turnbull was moodily balancing his sword in his hand as the other spoke; then he started, for a mouth whispered quite close to his ear. With a softness incredible in any cat, the huge, heavy man in the black hat and frock-coat had crept across the lawn from his own side and was saying in his ear: "Don't trust that second of yours. He's mad and not so mad, either; for he's frightfully cunning and sharp. Don't believe the story he tells you about why I hate him. I know the story he'll tell; I overheard it when the housekeeper was talking to the postman. It's too long to talk about now, and I expect we're watched, but——"

Something in Turnbull made him want suddenly to be sick on the grass; the mere healthy and heathen horror of the unclean; the mere inhumane hatred of the inhuman state of madness. He seemed to hear all round him the hateful whispers of that place, innumerable as leaves whispering in the wind, and each of them telling eagerly some evil that had not happened or some terrific secret which was not true. All the rationalist and plain man revolted within him against bowing down for a moment in that forest of deception and egotistical darkness. He wanted to blow up that palace of delusions with dynamite; and in some wild way, which I will not defend, he tried to do it.

He looked across at MacIan and said: "Oh, I can't stand this!"

"Can't stand what?" asked his opponent, eyeing him doubtfully.

"Shall we say the atmosphere?" replied Turnbull; "one can't use uncivil expressions even to a—deity. The fact is, I don't like having God for my second."

"Sir!" said that being in a state of great offence, "in my position I am not used to having my favours refused. Do you know who I am?"

The editor of "The Atheist" turned upon him like one who has lost all patience, and exploded: "Yes, you are God, aren't you?" he said, abruptly, "why do we have two sets of teeth?"

"Teeth?" spluttered the genteel lunatic; "teeth?"

"Yes," cried Turnbull, advancing on him swiftly and with animated gestures, "why does teething hurt? Why do growing pains hurt? Why are measles catching? Why does a rose have thorns? Why do rhinoceroses have horns? Why is the horn on the top of the nose? Why haven't I a horn on the top of my nose, eh?" And he struck the bridge of his nose smartly with his forefinger to indicate the place of the omission and then wagged the finger menacingly at the Creator.

"I've often wanted to meet you," he resumed, sternly, after a pause, "to hold you accountable for all the idiocy and cruelty of this muddled and meaningless world of yours. You make a hundred seeds and only one bears fruit. You make a million worlds and only one seems inhabited. What do you mean by it, eh? What do you mean by it?"

The unhappy lunatic had fallen back before this quite novel form of attack, and lifted his burnt-out cigarette almost like one warding off a blow. Turnbull went on like a torrent.

"A man died yesterday in Ealing. You murdered him. A girl had the toothache in Croydon. You gave it her. Fifty sailors were drowned off Selsey Bill.[117] You scuttled their ship. What have you got to say for yourself, eh?"

The representative of omnipotence looked as if he had left most of these things to his subordinates; he passed a hand over his wrinkling brow and said in a voice much saner than any he had yet used:

"Well, if you dislike my assistance, of course—perhaps the other gentleman——"

"The other gentleman," cried Turnbull, scornfully, "is a submissive and loyal and obedient gentleman. He likes the people who wear crowns, whether of diamonds or of stars. He believes in the divine right of kings, and it is appropriate enough that he should have the king for his second. But it is not appropriate to me that I should have God for my second. God is not good enough. I dislike and I deny the divine right of kings. But I dislike more and I deny more the divine right of divinity."

---

[117]Selsey Bill is a small town in East Sussex, England.

Then after a pause in which he swallowed his passion, he said to MacIan: "You have got the right second, anyhow."

The Highlander did not answer, but stood as if thunderstruck with one long and heavy thought. Then at last he turned abruptly to his second in the silk hat and said: "Who are you?"

The man in the silk hat blinked and bridled in affected surprise, like one who was in truth accustomed to be doubted.

"I am King Edward VII," [118] he said, with shaky arrogance. "Do you doubt my word?"

"I do not doubt it in the least," answered MacIan.

"Then, why," said the large man in the silk hat, trembling from head to foot, "why do you wear your hat before the king?"

"Why should I take it off," retorted MacIan, with equal heat, "before a usurper?"

Turnbull swung round on his heel. "Well, really," he said, "I thought at least you were a loyal subject."

"I am the only loyal subject," answered the Gael. "For nearly thirty years I have walked these islands and have not found another."

"You are always hard to follow," remarked Turnbull, genially, "and sometimes so much so as to be hardly worth following."

"I alone am loyal," insisted MacIan; "for I alone am in rebellion. I am ready at any instant to restore the Stuarts. I am ready at any instant to defy the Hanoverian brood[119]—and I defy it now even when face to face with the actual ruler of the enormous British Empire!"

And folding his arms and throwing back his lean, hawklike face, he haughtily confronted the man with the formal frock-coat and the eccentric elbow.

"What right had you stunted German squires," he cried, "to interfere in a quarrel between Scotch and English and Irish gentlemen? Who made you, whose fathers could not splutter English while they

[118] Edward VII (1841–1910) was king of Great Britain and Ireland and the eldest son of Queen Victoria and Prince Albert. He was crowned in 1902.

[119] "The Hanoverian brood" and "German squires" (in the following second paragraph) refer to the House of Hanover (see nn. 11 and 16).

walked in Whitehall,[120] who made you the judge between the republic of Sidney[121] and the monarchy of Montrose?[122] What had your
sires to do with England that they should have the foul offering of the
blood of Derwentwater[123] and the heart of Jimmy Dawson?[124] Where
are the corpses of Culloden?[125] Where is the blood of Lochiel?"[126]
MacIan advanced upon his opponent with a bony and pointed finger,
as if indicating the exact pocket in which the blood of that Cameron
was probably kept; and Edward VII fell back a few paces in considerable confusion.

"What good have you ever done to us?" he continued in harsher
and harsher accents, forcing the other back toward the flower-beds.
"What good have you ever done, you race of German sausages? Yards
of barbarian etiquette, to throttle the freedom of aristocracy! Gas of
northern metaphysics to blow up Broad Church bishops like balloons. Bad pictures and bad manners and pantheism and the Albert
Memorial. Go back to Hanover, you humbug! Go to———"

[120] Whitehall is the street in London that runs from Trafalgar Square to the palace of
Westminster and the site of the palace of Whitehall, which was seized from Cardinal
Wolsey by King Henry VIII in 1529. From the eighteenth century on, Whitehall has
become the seat of many departments of state, and the word "Whitehall" now serves
as a generic term for the civil service and the working of the departments of state.

[121] Sir Henry Sidney (1529–1586), administrator and statesman, was lord deputy of
Ireland in 1565.

[122] James Graham, marquis of Montrose (1612–1650) and a Scottish general, was
made lord lieutenant and captain general of Scotland by King Charles I. After much
fighting, he was defeated and, after a time on the continent, pledged to avenge the
death of the king; he invaded Scotland (1650) and tried in vain to raise the clans but
was captured and hanged at Edinburgh.

[123] James Radcliffe, or Radclyffe, 3rd Earl of Derwentwater (1689–1716), was an
English Jacobite and a companion of James Francis Edward Stuart, "the Old Pretender". After the failure of the Jacobite rising at the battle of Culloden (see n. 12), he
was taken prisoner in England and beheaded on Tower Hill.

[124] James Dawson (1717–1746), English Jacobite, served Charles Edward Stuart, "the
Young Pretender"; he was captured, hanged, drawn and quartered on Kensington Green.

[125] Culloden: see n. 12.

[126] Donald Cameron of Lochiel (ca.1695–1748), Scottish Highland chieftain, supported the "Young Pretender" and was seriously wounded at the battle of Culloden in
1745. He was subsequently executed in 1753, the last man to be executed for the
Jacobite cause.

Before the end of this tirade the arrogance of the monarch had entirely given way; he had fairly turned tail and was trundling away down the path. MacIan strode after him still preaching and flourishing his large, lean hands. The other two remained in the centre of the lawn—Turnbull in convulsions of laughter, the lunatic in convulsions of disgust. Almost at the same moment a third figure came stepping swiftly across the lawn.

The advancing figure walked with a stoop, and yet somehow flung his forked and narrow beard forward. That carefully cut and pointed yellow beard was, indeed, the most emphatic thing about him. When he clasped his hands behind him, under the tails of his coat, he would wag his beard at a man like a big forefinger. It performed almost all his gestures; it was more important than the glittering eyeglasses through which he looked or the beautiful bleating voice in which he spoke. His face and neck were of a lusty red, but lean and stringy; he always wore his expensive gold-rim eyeglasses slightly askew upon his aquiline nose; and he always showed two gleaming foreteeth under his moustache, in a smile so perpetual as to earn the reputation of a sneer. But for the crooked glasses his dress was always exquisite; and but for the smile he was perfectly and perennially depressed.

"Don't you think," said the new-comer, with a sort of supercilious entreaty, "that we had better all come into breakfast? It is such a mistake to wait for breakfast. It spoils one's temper so much."

"Quite so," replied Turnbull, seriously.

"There seems almost to have been a little quarrelling here," said the man with the goatish beard.

"It is rather a long story," said Turnbull, smiling. "Originally it might be called a phase in the quarrel between science and religion."

The new-comer started slightly, and Turnbull replied to the question on his face.

"Oh, yes," he said, "I am science!"

"I congratulate you heartily," answered the other, "I am Doctor Quayle."

Turnbull's eyes did not move, but he realised that the man in the panama hat had lost all his ease of a landed proprietor and had withdrawn to a distance of thirty yards, where he stood glaring with all the contraction of fear and hatred that can stiffen a cat.

MacIan was sitting somewhat disconsolately on a stump of tree, his large black head half buried in his large brown hands, when Turnbull strode up to him chewing a cigarette. He did not look up, but his comrade and enemy addressed him like one who must free himself of his feelings.

"Well, I hope, at any rate," he said, "that you like your precious religion now. I hope you like the society of this poor devil whom your damned tracts and hymns and priests have driven out of his wits. Five men in this place, they tell me, five men in this place who might have been fathers of families, and every one of them thinks he is God the Father. Oh! you may talk about the ugliness of science, but there is no one here who thinks he is Protoplasm."

"They naturally prefer a bright part," said MacIan, wearily. "Protoplasm is not worth going mad about."

"At least," said Turnbull, savagely, "it was your Jesus Christ who started all this bosh about being God."

For one instant MacIan opened the eyes of battle; then his tightened lips took a crooked smile and he said, quite calmly:

"No, the idea is older; it was Satan who first said that he was God."

"Then, what," asked Turnbull, very slowly, as he softly picked a flower, "what is the difference between Christ and Satan?"

"It is quite simple," replied the Highlander. "Christ descended into hell; Satan fell into it."

"Does it make much odds?" asked the free-thinker.

"It makes all the odds," said the other. "One of them wanted to go up and went down; the other wanted to go down and went up. A god can be humble, a devil can only be humbled."

"Why are you always wanting to humble a man?" asked Turnbull, knitting his brows. "It affects me as ungenerous."

"Why were you wanting to humble a god when you found him in this garden?" asked MacIan.

"That was an extreme case of impudence," said MacIan.[127]

---

[127] This is an error in the text, hitherto uncorrected in any edition. The response to MacIan should be by Turnbull.

"Granting the man his almighty pretensions, I think he was very modest," said MacIan. "It is we who are arrogant, who know we are only men. The ordinary man in the street is more of a monster than that poor fellow; for the man in the street treats himself as God Almighty when he knows he isn't. He expects the universe to turn round him, though he knows he isn't the centre."

"Well," said Turnbull, sitting down on the grass, "this is a digression, anyhow. What I want to point out is, that your faith does end in asylums and my science doesn't."

"Doesn't it, by George!" cried MacIan, scornfully. "There are a few men here who are mad on God and a few who are mad on the Bible. But I bet there are many more who are simply mad on madness."

"Do you really believe it?" asked the other.

"Scores of them, I should say," answered MacIan. "Fellows who have read medical books or fellows whose fathers and uncles had something hereditary in their heads—the whole air they breathe is mad."

"All the same," said Turnbull, shrewdly, "I bet you haven't found a madman of that sort."

"I bet I have!" cried Evan, with unusual animation. "I've been walking about the garden talking to a poor chap all the morning. He's simply been broken down and driven raving by your damned science. Talk about believing one is God—why, it's quite an old, comfortable, fireside fancy compared with the sort of things this fellow believes. He believes that there is a God, but that he is better than God. He says God will be afraid to face him. He says one is always progressing beyond the best. He put his arm in mine and whispered in my ear, as if it were the apocalypse: 'Never trust a God that you can't improve on.' "

"What can he have meant?" said the atheist, with all his logic awake. "Obviously one should not trust any God that one can improve on."

"It is the way he talks," said MacIan, almost indifferently; "but he says rummier things than that. He says that a man's doctor ought to decide what woman he marries; and he says that children ought not to be brought up by their parents, because a physical partiality will then distort the judgment of the educator."

"Oh, dear!" said Turnbull, laughing, "you have certainly come across a pretty bad case, and incidentally proved your own. I suppose some men do lose their wits through science as through love and other good things."

"And he says," went on MacIan, monotonously, "that he cannot see why any one should suppose that a triangle is a three-sided figure. He says that on some higher plane——"

Turnbull leapt to his feet as by an electric shock. "I never could have believed," he cried, "that you had humour enough to tell a lie. You've gone a bit too far, old man, with your little joke. Even in a lunatic asylum there can't be anybody who, having thought about the matter, thinks that a triangle has not got three sides. If he exists he must be a new era in human psychology. But he doesn't exist."

"I will go and fetch him," said MacIan, calmly; "I left the poor fellow wandering about by the nasturtium bed."

MacIan vanished, and in a few moments returned, trailing with him his own discovery among lunatics, who was a slender man with a fixed smile and an unfixed and rolling head. He had a goatlike beard just long enough to be shaken in a strong wind. Turnbull sprang to his feet and was like one who is speechless through choking a sudden shout of laughter.

"Why, you great donkey," he shouted, in an ear-shattering whisper, "that's not one of the patients at all. That's one of the doctors."

Evan looked back at the leering head with the long-pointed beard and repeated the word inquiringly: "One of the doctors?"

"Oh, you know what I mean," said Turnbull, impatiently. "The medical authorities of the place."

Evan was still staring back curiously at the beaming and bearded creature behind him.

"The mad doctors," said Turnbull, shortly.

"Quite so," said MacIan.

After a rather restless silence Turnbull plucked MacIan by the elbow and pulled him aside.

"For goodness sake," he said, "don't offend this fellow; he may be as mad as ten hatters, if you like, but he has us between his finger and thumb. This is the very time he appointed to talk with us about our—well, our exeat."

"But what can it matter?" asked the wondering MacIan. "He can't keep us in the asylum. We're not mad."

"Jackass!" said Turnbull, heartily, "of course we're not mad. Of course, if we are medically examined and the thing is thrashed out, they will find we are not mad. But don't you see that if the thing is thrashed out it will mean letters to this reference and telegrams to that; and at the first word of who we are, we shall be taken out of a madhouse, where we may smoke, to a gaol, where we mayn't. No, if we manage this very quietly, he may merely let us out at the front door as stray revellers. If there's half an hour of inquiry, we are cooked."

MacIan looked at the grass frowningly for a few seconds, and then said in a new, small and childish voice: "I am awfully stupid, Mr. Turnbull; you must be patient with me."

Turnbull caught Evan's elbow again with quite another gesture. "Come," he cried, with the harsh voice of one who hides emotion, "come and let us be tactful in chorus."

The doctor with the pointed beard was already slanting it forward at a more than usually acute angle, with the smile that expressed expectancy.

"I hope I do not hurry you, gentlemen," he said, with the faintest suggestion of a sneer at their hurried consultation, "but I believe you wanted to see me at half-past eleven."

"I am most awfully sorry, doctor," said Turnbull, with ready amiability; "I never meant to keep you waiting; but the silly accident that has landed us in your garden may have some rather serious consequences to our friends elsewhere, and my friend here was just drawing my attention to some of them."

"Quite so! Quite so!" said the doctor, hurriedly. "If you really want to put anything before me, I can give you a few moments in my consulting room."

He led them rapidly into a small but imposing apartment, which seemed to be built and furnished entirely in red varnished wood. There was one desk occupied with carefully docketed papers; and there were several chairs of the red varnished wood—though of different shape. All along the wall ran something that might have been a bookcase, only that it was not filled with books, but with flat, oblong slabs or cases of the same polished dark-red consistency. What those flat wooden cases were they could form no conception.

The doctor sat down with a polite impatience on his professional perch; MacIan remained standing, but Turnbull threw himself almost with luxury into a hard wooden arm-chair.

"This is a most absurd business, doctor," he said, "and I am ashamed to take up the time of busy professional men with such pranks from outside. The plain fact is, that he and I and a pack of silly men and girls have organised a game across this part of the country—a sort of combination of hare and hounds and hide and seek—I daresay you've heard of it. We are the hares, and, seeing your high wall look so inviting, we tumbled over it, and naturally were a little startled with what we found on the other side."

"Quite so!" said the doctor, mildly. "I can understand that you were startled."

Turnbull had expected him to ask what place was the headquarters of the new exhilarating game, and who were the male and female enthusiasts who had brought it to such perfection; in fact, Turnbull was busy making up these personal and topographical particulars. As the doctor did not ask the question, he grew slightly uneasy, and risked the question: "I hope you will accept my assurance that the thing was an accident and that no intrusion was meant,"

"Oh, yes, sir," replied the doctor, smiling, "I accept everything that you say."

"In that case," said Turnbull, rising genially, "we must not further interrupt your important duties. I suppose there will be some one to let us out?"

"No," said the doctor, still smiling steadily and pleasantly, "there will be no one to let you out."

"Can we let ourselves out, then?" asked Turnbull, in some surprise.

"Why, of course not," said the beaming scientist; "think how dangerous that would be in a place like this."

"Then, how the devil are we to get out?" cried Turnbull, losing his manners for the first time.

"It is a question of time, of receptivity, and treatment," said the doctor, arching his eyebrows indifferently. "I do not regard either of your cases as incurable."

And with that the man of the world was struck dumb, and, as in all intolerable moments, the word was with the unworldly.

MacIan took one stride to the table, leant across it, and said: "We can't stop here, we're not mad people!"

"We don't use the crude phrase," said the doctor, smiling at his patent-leather boots.

"But you *can't* think us mad," thundered MacIan. "You never saw us before. You know nothing about us. You haven't even examined us."

The doctor threw back his head and beard. "Oh, yes," he said, "very thoroughly."

"But you can't shut a man up on your mere impressions without documents or certificates or anything?"

The doctor got languidly to his feet. "Quite so," he said. "You certainly ought to see the documents."

He went across to the curious mock bookshelves and took down one of the flat mahogany cases. This he opened with a curious key at his watch-chain, and laying back a flap revealed a quire of foolscap covered with close but quite clear writing. The first three words were in such large copy-book hand that they caught the eye even at a distance. They were: "MacIan, Evan Stuart."

Evan bent his angry eagle face over it; yet something blurred it and he could never swear he saw it distinctly. He saw something that began: "Prenatal influences predisposing to mania. Grandfather believed in return of the Stuarts. Mother carried bone of St. Eulalia[128] with which she touched children in sickness. Marked religious mania at early age——"

Evan fell back and fought for his speech. "Oh!" he burst out at last "Oh! if all this world I have walked in had been as sane as my mother was."

---

[128] St. Eulalia of Barcelona (ca. 290–ca. 304) was tortured and burnt alive during the persecutions of Emperor Diocletian. St. Eulalia (her name means "victory" in Celtic) is the patron saint of, amongst other things, runaways, seafarers and torture victims.

Then he compressed his temples with his hands, as if to crush them. And then lifted suddenly a face that looked fresh and young, as if he had dipped and washed it in some holy well.

"Very well," he cried; "I will take the sour with the sweet. I will pay the penalty of having enjoyed God in this monstrous modern earth that cannot enjoy man or beast. I will die happy in your madhouse, only because I know what I know. Let it be granted, then—MacIan is a mystic; MacIan is a maniac. But this honest shopkeeper and editor whom I have dragged on my inhuman escapades, you cannot keep him. He will go free, thank God, he is not down in any damned document. His ancestor, I am certain, did not die at Culloden. His mother, I swear, had no relics. Let my friend out of your front door, and as for me——"

The doctor had already gone across to the laden shelves, and after a few minutes' shortsighted peering, had pulled down another parallelogram of dark-red wood.

This also he unlocked on the table, and with the same unerring egotistic eye one of the company saw the words, written in large letters: "Turnbull, James."

Hitherto Turnbull himself had somewhat scornfully surrendered his part in the whole business; but he was too honest and unaffected not to start at his own name. After the name, the inscription appeared to run: "Unique case of Eleutheromania.[129] Parentage, as so often in such cases, prosaic and healthy. Eleutheromaniac signs occurred early, however, leading him to attach himself to the individualist Bradlaugh.[130] Recent outbreak of pure anarchy——"

Turnbull slammed the case to, almost smashing it, and said with a burst of savage laughter: "Oh! come along, MacIan; I don't care so much, even about getting out of the madhouse, if only we get out of this room. You were right enough, MacIan, when you spoke about—about mad doctors."

Somehow they found themselves outside in the cool, green garden, and then, after a stunned silence, Turnbull said: "There is one thing that was puzzling me all the time, and I understand it now."

[129] "Eleutheromania" is a noun meaning "a strong desire for freedom".
[130] Bradlaugh: see n. 54, above.

"What do you mean?" asked Evan.

"No man by will or wit," answered Turnbull, "can get out of this garden; and yet we got into it merely by jumping over a garden-wall. The whole thing explains itself easily enough. That undefended wall was an open trap. It was a trap laid for the two celebrated lunatics. They saw us get in right enough. And they will see that we do not get out."

Evan gazed at the garden-wall, gravely for more than a minute, and then he nodded without a word.

XV

THE DREAM OF MACIAN

The system of espionage in the asylum was so effective and complete that in practice the patients could often enjoy a sense of almost complete solitude. They could stray up so near to the wall in an apparently unwatched garden as to find it easy to jump over it. They would only have found the error of their calculations if they had tried to jump.

Under this insulting liberty, in this artificial loneliness, Evan MacIan was in the habit of creeping out into the garden after dark—especially upon moonlight nights. The moon, indeed, was for him always a positive magnet in a manner somewhat hard to explain to those of a robuster attitude. Evidently, Apollo[131] is to the full as poetical as Diana;[132] but it is not a question of poetry in the matured and intellectual sense of the word. It is a question of a certain solid and childish fancy. The sun is in the strict and literal sense invisible; that is to say, that by our bodily eyes it cannot properly be seen. But the moon is a much simpler thing; a naked and nursery sort of thing. It hangs in the sky quite solid and quite silver and quite useless; it is one huge celestial snowball. It was at least some such infantile facts and fancies which led Evan again and again during his dehumanised imprisonment to go out as if to shoot the moon.

He was out in the garden on one such luminous and ghostly night, when the steady moonshine toned down all the colours of the garden until almost the strongest tints to be seen were the strong soft blue of the sky and the large lemon moon. He was walking with his face turned up to it in that rather half-witted fashion which might have excused the error of his keepers; and as he gazed he became aware of something little and lustrous flying close to the lustrous orb, like a bright chip knocked

[131] Apollo, in Greek mythology, was a god and the son of Zeus and Leto, who was presented as the ideal type of manly beauty and, in later poetry, associated with the sun, musical inspiration, medicine and pastoral life.

[132] Diana, in Roman mythology, was the goddess anciently identified with Artemis, the huntress, and associated with hunting, virginity and the moon.

off the moon. At first he thought it was a mere sparkle or refraction in his own eyesight; he blinked and cleared his eyes. Then he thought it was a falling star; only it did not fall. It jerked awkwardly up and down in a way unknown among meteors and strangely reminiscent of the works of man. The next moment the thing drove right across the moon, and from being silver upon blue, suddenly became black upon silver; then although it passed the field of light in a flash its outline was unmistakable though eccentric. It was a flying ship.

The vessel took one long and sweeping curve across the sky and came nearer and nearer to MacIan, like a steam-engine coming round a bend. It was of pure white steel, and in the moon it gleamed like the armour of Sir Galahad. The simile of such virginity is not inappropriate; for, as it grew larger and larger and lower and lower, Evan saw that the only figure in it was robed in white from head to foot and crowned with snow-white hair, on which the moonshine lay like a benediction. The figure stood so still that he could easily have supposed it to be a statue. Indeed, he thought it was until it spoke.

"Evan," said the voice, and it spoke with the simple authority of some forgotten father re-visiting his children, "you have remained here long enough, and your sword is wanted elsewhere."

"Wanted for what?" asked the young man, accepting the monstrous event with a queer and clumsy naturalness; "what is my sword wanted for?"

"For all that you hold dear," said the man standing in the moonlight; "for the thrones of authority and for all ancient loyalty to law."

Evan looked up at the lunar orb again as if in irrational appeal—a moon calf bleating to his mother the moon. But the face of Luna seemed as witless as his own; there is no help in nature against the supernatural; and he looked again at the tall marble figure that might have been made out of solid moonlight.

Then he said in a loud voice: "Who are you?" and the next moment was seized by a sort of choking terror lest his question should be answered. But the unknown preserved an impenetrable silence for a long space and then only answered: "I must not say who I am until the end of the world; but I may say what I am. I am the law."

And he lifted his head so that the moon smote full upon his beautiful and ancient face.

The face was the face of a Greek god grown old, but not grown either weak or ugly; there was nothing to break its regularity except a rather long chin with a cleft in it, and this rather added distinction than lessened beauty. His strong, well-opened eyes were very brilliant but quite colourless like steel.

MacIan was one of those to whom a reverence and self-submission in ritual come quite easy, and are ordinary things. It was not artificial in him to bend slightly to this solemn apparition or to lower his voice when he said: "Do you bring me some message?"

"I do bring you a message," answered the man of moon and marble. "The king has returned."

Evan did not ask for or require any explanation. "I suppose you can take me to the war," he said, and the silent silver figure only bowed its head again. MacIan clambered into the silver boat, and it rose upward to the stars.

To say that it rose to the stars is no mere metaphor, for the sky had cleared to that occasional and astonishing transparency in which one can see plainly both stars and moon.

As the white-robed figure went upward in his white chariot, he said quite quietly to Evan: "There is an answer to all the folly talked about equality. Some stars are big and some small; some stand still and some circle round them as they stand. They can be orderly, but they cannot be equal."

"They are all very beautiful," said Evan, as if in doubt.

"They are all beautiful," answered the other, "because each is in his place and owns his superior. And now England will be beautiful after the same fashion. The earth will be as beautiful as the heavens, because our kings have come back to us."

"The Stuart——" began Evan, earnestly.

"Yes," answered the old man, "that which has returned is Stuart and yet older than Stuart. It is Capet[133] and Plantagenet[134] and

[133] Hugo Capet (ca. 938–996) was a king of France. The Capetian dynasty he founded ruled France until 1328.

[134] "The Plantagenets" is the name conventionally given to the English royal family descending from Henry II (1133–1189). The legitimate male line ended (1499) with the execution of Edward, Earl of Warwick, grandson of Richard Duke of York.

Pendragon.[135] It is all that good old time of which proverbs tell, that golden reign of Saturn[136] against which gods and men were rebels. It is all that was ever lost by insolence and overwhelmed in rebellion. It is your own forefather, MacIan with the broken sword, bleeding without hope at Culloden. It is Charles[137] refusing to answer the questions of the rebel court. It is Mary[138] of the magic face confronting the gloomy and grasping peers and the boorish moralities of Knox.[139] It is Richard,[140] the last Plantagenet, giving his crown to Bolingbroke as to a common brigand. It is Arthur[141], over-whelmed in Lyonesse by heathen armies and dying in the mist, doubtful if ever he shall return."

"But now——" said Evan, in a low voice.

"But now!" said the old man; "he has returned."

"Is the war still raging?" asked MacIan.

"It rages like the pit itself beyond the sea whither I am taking you," answered the other. "But in England the king enjoys his own again. The people are once more taught and ruled as is best; they are happy knights, happy squires, happy servants, happy serfs, if you will; but free at last of that load of vexation and lonely vanity which was called being a citizen."

"Is England, indeed, so secure?" asked Evan.

---

[135] "Pendragon" is the name given to an ancient British or Welsh prince, often as a title.

[136] Saturn was, in Roman mythology, the ancient god of agriculture.

[137] Charles I (1600–1649) was a king of Great Britain and Ireland. Placed on trial after the second of the British civil wars (1648), Charles refused to plead, which was interpreted as a silent confession, so he was beheaded.

[138] Mary, Queen of Scots (1542–1567), was a queen of Scotland (1542–1567) who enjoyed great beauty and personal accomplishments, including a knowledge of six languages. She was eventually executed at the behest of Queen Elizabeth I, who suspected she wished to be made queen of England.

[139] John Knox (ca. 1513–1572) was a Scottish Protestant revolutionary and founder of the Church of Scotland.

[140] Richard II (1367–1400), king of England, was coerced into abdicating in 1399, then imprisoned and eventually murdered by Henry IV (1366–1413), king of England and known as Bolingbroke, the Lancashire town in which he was born.

[141] Arthur was an early sixth-century legendary king of the Britons.

"Look out and see," said the guide. "I fancy you have seen this place before."

They were driving through the air toward one region of the sky where the hollow of night seemed darkest and which was quite without stars. But against this black background there sprang up, picked out in glittering silver, a dome and a cross. It seemed that it was really newly covered with silver, which in the strong moonlight was like white flame. But, however, covered or painted, Evan had no difficulty in knowing the place again. He saw the great thoroughfare that sloped upward to the base of its huge pedestal of steps. And he wondered whether the little shop was still by the side of it and whether its window had been mended.

As the flying ship swept round the dome he observed other alterations. The dome had been redecorated so as to give it a more solemn and somewhat more ecclesiastical note; the ball was draped or destroyed, and round the gallery, under the cross, ran what looked like a ring of silver statues, like the little leaden images that stood round the hat of Louis XI.[142] Round the second gallery, at the base of the dome, ran a second rank of such images, and Evan thought there was another round the steps below. When they came closer he saw that they were figures in complete armour of steel or silver, each with a naked sword, point upward; and then he saw one of the swords move. These were not statues but an armed order of chivalry thrown in three circles round the cross. MacIan drew in his breath, as children do at anything they think utterly beautiful. For he could imagine nothing that so echoed his own visions of pontifical or chivalric art as this white dome sitting like a vast silver tiara over London, ringed with a triple crown of swords.

As they went sailing down Ludgate Hill, Evan saw that the state of the streets fully answered his companion's claim about the reintroduction of order. All the old black-coated bustle with its cockney vivacity and vulgarity had disappeared. Groups of labourers, quietly but picturesquely clad, were passing up and down in sufficiently large numbers; but it required but a few mounted men to keep the streets in order. The mounted men were not common policemen, but knights with spur

---

[142] Louis XI (1423–1483) was a king of France.

and plume whose smooth and splendid armour glittered like diamond rather than steel. Only in one place—at the corner of Bouverie Street—did there appear to be a moment's confusion, and that was due to hurry rather than resistance. But one old grumbling man did not get out of the way quick enough, and the man on horseback struck him, not severely, across the shoulders with the flat of his sword.

"The soldier had no business to do that," said MacIan, sharply. "The old man was moving as quickly as he could."

"We attach great importance to discipline in the streets," said the man in white, with a slight smile.

"Discipline is not so important as justice," said MacIan.

The other did not answer.

Then after a swift silence that took them out across St. James's Park,[143] he said: "The people must be taught to obey; they must learn their own ignorance. And I am not sure," he continued, turning his back on Evan and looking out of the prow of the ship into the darkness, "I am not sure that I agree with your little maxim about justice. Discipline for the whole society is surely more important than justice to an individual."

Evan, who was also leaning over the edge, swung round with startling suddenness and stared at the other's back.

"Discipline for society—" he repeated, very staccato, "more important—justice to individual?"

Then after a long silence he called out: "Who and what are you?"

"I am an angel," said the white-robed figure, without turning round.

"You are not a Catholic," said MacIan.

The other seemed to take no notice, but reverted to the main topic.

"In our armies up in heaven we learn to put a wholesome fear into subordinates."

MacIan sat craning his neck forward with an extraordinary and unaccountable eagerness.

"Go on!" he cried, twisting and untwisting his long, bony fingers, "go on!"

---

[143] St. James's Park is a park in central London a short distance from Westminster Abbey and the Houses of Parliament.

"Besides," continued he, in the prow, "you must allow for a certain high spirit and haughtiness in the superior type."

"Go on!" said Evan, with burning eyes.

"Just as the sight of sin offends God," said the unknown, "so does the sight of ugliness offend Apollo. The beautiful and princely must, of necessity, be impatient with the squalid and——"

"Why, you great fool!" cried MacIan, rising to the top of his tremendous stature, "did you think I would have doubted only for that rap with a sword? I know that noble orders have bad knights, that good knights have bad tempers, that the Church has rough priests and coarse cardinals; I have known it ever since I was born. You fool! you had only to say, 'Yes, it is rather a shame,' and I should have forgotten the affair. But I saw on your mouth the twitch of your infernal sophistry; I knew that something was wrong with you and your cathedrals. Something is wrong; everything is wrong. You are not an angel. That is not a church. It is not the rightful king who has come home."

"That is unfortunate," said the other, in a quiet but hard voice, "because you are going to see his Majesty."

"No," said MacIan, "I am going to jump over the side."

"Do you desire death?"

"No," said Evan, quite composedly, "I desire a miracle."

"From whom do you ask it? To whom do you appeal?" said his companion, sternly. "You have betrayed the king, renounced the cross on the cathedral, and insulted an archangel."

"I appeal to God," said Evan, and sprang up and stood upon the edge of the swaying ship.

The being in the prow turned slowly round; he looked at Evan with eyes which were like two suns, and put his hand to his mouth just too late to hide an awful smile.

"And how do you know," he said, "how do you know that I am not God?"

MacIan screamed. "Ah!" he cried. "Now I know who you really are. You are not God. You are not one of God's angels. But you were once."

The being's hand dropped from his mouth and Evan dropped out of the car.

XVI

THE DREAM OF TURNBULL

Turnbull was walking rather rampantly up and down the garden on a gusty evening chewing his cigar and in that mood when every man suppresses an instinct to spit. He was not, as a rule, a man much acquainted with moods; and the storms and sunbursts of MacIan's soul passed before him as an impressive but unmeaning panorama, like the anarchy of Highland scenery. Turnbull was one of those men in whom a continuous appetite and industry of the intellect leave the emotions very simple and steady. His heart was in the right place; but he was quite content to leave it there. It was his head that was his hobby. His mornings and evenings were marked not by impulses or thirsty desires, not by hope or by heart-break; they were filled with the fallacies he had detected, the problems he had made plain, the adverse theories he had wrestled with and thrown, the grand gener-alisations he had justified. But even the cheerful inner life of a logi-cian may be upset by a lunatic asylum, to say nothing of whiffs of memory from a lady in Jersey, and the little red-bearded man on this windy evening was in a dangerous frame of mind.

Plain and positive as he was, the influence of earth and sky may have been greater on him than he imagined; and the weather that walked the world at that moment was as red and angry as Turnbull. Long strips and swirls of tattered and tawny cloud were dragged down-ward to the west exactly as torn red raiment would be dragged. And so strong and pitiless was the wind that it whipped away fragments of red-flowering bushes or of copper beech, and drove them also across the garden, a drift of red leaves, like the leaves of autumn, as in parody of the red and driven rags of cloud.

There was a sense in earth and heaven as of everything breaking up, and all the revolutionist in Turnbull rejoiced that it was breaking up. The trees were breaking up under the wind, even in the tall strength of their bloom: the clouds were breaking up and losing even their large heraldic shapes. Shards and shreds of copper cloud split off continually and floated by themselves, and for some reason the truculent eye of Turnbull was attracted to one of these careering cloudlets, which seemed to him to career in an exaggerated manner. Also it kept its shape, which is unusual with clouds shaken off; also its shape was of an odd sort.

Turnbull continued to stare at it, and in a little time occurred that crucial instant when a thing, however incredible, is accepted as a fact. The copper cloud was tumbling down toward the earth, like some gigantic leaf from the copper beeches. And as it came nearer it was evident, first, that it was not a cloud, and, second, that it was not itself of the colour of copper; only, being burnished like a mirror, it had reflected the red-brown colours of the burning clouds. As the thing whirled like a wind-swept leaf down toward the wall of the garden it was clear that it was some sort of air-ship made of metal, and slapping the air with big broad fins of steel. When it came about a hundred feet above the garden, a shaggy, lean figure leapt up in it, almost black against the bronze and scarlet of the west, and, flinging out a kind of hook or anchor, caught on to the green apple-tree just under the wall; and from that fixed holding ground the ship swung in the red tempest like a captive balloon.

While our friend stood frozen for an instant by his astonishment, the queer figure in the airy car tipped the vehicle almost upside down by leaping over the side of it, seemed to slide or drop down the rope like a monkey, and alighted (with impossible precision and placidity) seated on the edge of the wall, over which he kicked and dangled his legs as he grinned at Turnbull. The wind roared in the trees yet more ruinous and desolate, the red tails of the sunset were dragged downward like red dragons sucked down to death, and still on the top of the asylum wall sat the sinister figure with the grimace, swinging his feet in tune with the tempest; while above him, at the end of its tossing or tightened cord, the enormous iron air-ship floated as light and as little noticed as a baby's balloon upon its string.

Turnbull's first movement after sixty motionless seconds was to turn round and look at the large, luxuriant parallelogram of the garden and the long, low rectangular building beyond. There was not a soul or a stir of life within sight. And he had a quite meaningless sensation, as if there never really had been any one else there except he since the foundation of the world.

Stiffening in himself the masculine but mirthless courage of the atheist, he drew a little nearer to the wall and, catching the man at a slightly different angle of the evening light, could see his face and figure quite plain. Two facts about him stood out in the picked colours of some piratical schoolboy's story. The first was that his lean brown body was bare to the belt of his loose white trousers; the other that through hygiene, affectation, or whatever other cause, he had a scarlet handkerchief tied tightly but somewhat aslant across his brow. After these two facts had become emphatic, others appeared sufficiently important. One was that under the scarlet rag the hair was plentiful, but white as with the last snows of mortality. Another was that under the mop of white and senile hair the face was strong, handsome, and smiling, with a well-cut profile and a long cloven chin. The length of this lower part of the face and the strange cleft in it (which gave the man, in quite another sense from the common one, a double chin) faintly spoilt the claim of the face to absolute regularity, but it greatly assisted it in wearing the expression of half-smiling and half-sneering arrogance with which it was staring at all the stones, all the flowers, but especially at the solitary man.

"What do you want?" shouted Turnbull.

"I want you, Jimmy," said the eccentric man on the wall, and with the very word he had let himself down with a leap on to the centre of the lawn, where he bounded once literally like an India-rubber ball and then stood grinning with his legs astride. The only three facts that Turnbull could now add to his inventory were that the man had an ugly-looking knife swinging at his trousers belt, that his brown feet were as bare as his bronzed trunk and arms, and that his eyes had a singular bleak brilliancy which was of no particular colour.

"Excuse my not being in evening dress," said the new-comer with an urbane smile. "We scientific men, you know—I have to work my own engines—Electrical engineer—very hot work."

"Look here," said Turnbull, sturdily clenching his fists in his trousers pockets, "I am bound to expect lunatics inside these four walls; but I do bar their coming from outside, bang out of the sunset clouds."

"And yet you came from the outside, too, Jim," said the stranger in a voice almost affectionate.

"What do you want?" asked Turnbull, with an explosion of temper as sudden as a pistol shot.

"I have already told you," said the man, lowering his voice and speaking with evident sincerity; "I want you."

"What do you want with me?"

"I want exactly what you want," said the new-comer with a new gravity. "I want the Revolution."

Turnbull looked at the fire-swept sky and the wind-stricken woodlands, and kept on repeating the word voicelessly to himself—the word that did indeed so thoroughly express his mood of rage as it had been among those red clouds and rocking tree-tops. "Revolution!" he said to himself. "The Revolution—Yes, that is what I want right enough—anything, so long as it is a Revolution."

To some cause he could never explain he found himself completing the sentence on the top of the wall, having automatically followed the stranger so far. But when the stranger silently indicated the rope that led to the machine, he found himself pausing and saying: "I can't leave MacIan behind in this den."

"We are going to destroy the Pope and all the kings," said the new-comer. "Would it be wiser to take him with us?"

Somehow the muttering Turnbull found himself in the flying ship also, and it swung up into the sunset.

"All the great rebels have been very little rebels," said the man with the red scarf. "They have been like fourth-form boys[144] who sometimes venture to hit a fifth-form boy. That was all the worth of their French Revolution and regicide. The boys never really dared to defy the schoolmaster."

"Whom do you mean by the schoolmaster?" asked Turnbull.

"You know whom I mean," answered the strange man, as he lay back on cushions and looked up into the angry sky.

They seemed rising into stronger and stronger sunlight, as if it were sunrise rather than sunset. But when they looked down at the earth

---

[144]In British schools students are divided not into grades but into "forms".

they saw it growing darker and darker. The lunatic asylum in its large rectangular grounds spread below them in a foreshortened and infantile plan, and looked for the first time the grotesque thing that it was. But the clear colours of the plan were growing darker every moment. The masses of rose or rhododendron deepened from crimson to violet. The maze of gravel pathways faded from gold to brown. By the time they had risen a few hundred feet higher nothing could be seen of that darkening landscape except the lines of lighted windows, each one of which, at least, was the light of one lost intelligence. But on them as they swept upward better and braver winds seemed to blow, and on them the ruby light of evening seemed struck, and splashed like red spurts from the grapes of Dionysus. Below them the fallen lights were literally the fallen stars of servitude. And above them all the red and raging clouds were like the leaping flags of liberty.

The man with the cloven chin seemed to have a singular power of understanding thoughts; for, as Turnbull felt the whole universe tilt and turn over his head, the stranger said exactly the right thing.

"Doesn't it seem as if everything were being upset?" said he; "and if once everything is upset, He will be upset on top of it."

Then, as Turnbull made no answer, his host continued:

"That is the really fine thing about space. It is topsy-turvy. You have only to climb far enough toward the morning star to feel that you are coming down to it. You have only to dive deep enough into the abyss to feel that you are rising. That is the only glory of this universe—it is a giddy universe."

Then, as Turnbull was still silent, he added:

"The heavens are full of revolution—of the real sort of revolution. All the high things sinking low and all the big things looking small. All the people who think they are aspiring find they are falling head foremost. And all the people who think they are condescending find they are climbing up a precipice. That is the intoxication of space. That is the only joy of eternity—doubt. There is only one pleasure the angels can possibly have in flying, and that is, that they do not know whether they are on their head or their heels."

Then, finding his companion still mute, he fell himself into a smiling and motionless meditation, at the end of which he said suddenly:

"So MacIan converted you?"

Turnbull sprang up as if spurning the steel car from under his feet. "Converted me!" he cried. "What the devil do you mean? I have known him for a month, and I have not retracted a single——"

"This Catholicism is a curious thing," said the man of the cloven chin in uninterrupted reflectiveness, leaning his elegant elbows over the edge of the vessel; "it soaks and weakens men without their knowing it, just as I fear it has soaked and weakened you."

Turnbull stood in an attitude which might well have meant pitching the other man out of the flying ship.

"I am an atheist," he said, in a stifled voice. "I have always been an atheist. I am still an atheist." Then, addressing the other's indolent and indifferent back, he cried: "In God's name what do you mean?"

And the other answered without turning round:

"I mean nothing in God's name."

Turnbull spat over the edge of the car and fell back furiously into his seat.

The other continued still unruffled, and staring over the edge idly as an angler stares down at a stream.

"The truth is that we never thought that you could have been caught," he said; "we counted on you as the one red-hot revolutionary left in the world. But, of course, these men like MacIan are awfully clever, especially when they pretend to be stupid."

Turnbull leapt up again in a living fury and cried: "What have I got to do with MacIan? I believe all I ever believed, and disbelieve all I ever disbelieved. What does all this mean, and what do you want with me here?"

Then for the first time the other lifted himself from the edge of the car and faced him.

"I have brought you here," he answered, "to take part in the last war of the world."

"The last war!" repeated Turnbull, even in his dazed state a little touchy about such a dogma; "how do you know it will be the last?"

The man laid himself back in his reposeful attitude, and said:

"It is the last war, because if it does not cure the world forever, it will destroy it."

"What do you mean?"

"I only mean what you mean," answered the unknown in a temperate voice. "What was it that you always meant on those million and one nights when you walked outside your Ludgate Hill shop and shook your hand in the air?"

"Still I do not see," said Turnbull, stubbornly.

"You will soon," said the other, and abruptly bent downward one iron handle of his huge machine. The engine stopped, stooped, and dived almost as deliberately as a man bathing; in their downward rush they swept within fifty yards of a big bulk of stone that Turnbull knew only too well. The last red anger of the sunset was ended; the dome of heaven was dark; the lanes of flaring light in the streets below hardly lit up the base of the building. But he saw that it was St. Paul's Cathedral, and he saw that on the top of it the ball was still standing erect, but the cross was stricken and had fallen sideways. Then only he cared to look down into the streets, and saw that they were inflamed with uproar and tossing passions.

"We arrive at a happy moment," said the man steering the ship. "The insurgents are bombarding the city, and a cannon-ball has just hit the cross. Many of the insurgents are simple people, and they naturally regard it as a happy omen."

"Quite so," said Turnbull, in a rather colourless voice.

"Yes," replied the other. "I thought you would be glad to see your prayer answered. Of course I apologise for the word prayer."

"Don't mention it," said Turnbull.

The flying ship had come down upon a sort of curve, and was now rising again. The higher and higher it rose the broader and broader became the scenes of flame and desolation underneath.

Ludgate Hill indeed had been an uncaptured and comparatively quiet height, altered only by the startling coincidence of the cross fallen awry. All the other thoroughfares on all sides of that hill were full of the pulsation and the pain of battle, full of shaking torches and shouting faces. When at length they had risen high enough to have a bird's-eye view of the whole campaign, Turnbull was already intoxicated. He had smelt gunpowder, which was the incense of his own revolutionary religion.

"Have the people really risen?" he asked, breathlessly. "What are they fighting about?"

"The programme is rather elaborate," said his entertainer with some indifference. "I think Dr. Hertz drew it up."

Turnbull wrinkled his forehead. "Are all the poor people with the Revolution?" he asked.

The other shrugged his shoulders. "All the instructed and class-conscious part of them without exception," he replied. "There were certainly a few districts; in fact, we are passing over them just now——"

Turnbull looked down and saw that the polished car was literally lit up from underneath by the far-flung fires from below. Underneath whole squares and solid districts were in flames, like prairies or forests on fire.

"Dr. Hertz has convinced everybody," said Turnbull's cicerone[145] in a smooth voice, "that nothing can really be done with the real slums. His celebrated maxim has been quite adopted. I mean the three celebrated sentences: 'No man should be unemployed. Employ the employables. Destroy the unemployables.'"

There was a silence, and then Turnbull said in a rather strained voice: "And do I understand that this good work is going on under here?"

"Going on splendidly," replied his companion in the heartiest voice. "You see, these people were much too tired and weak even to join the social war. They were a definite hindrance to it."

"And so you are simply burning them out?"

"It *does* seem absurdly simple," said the man, with a beaming smile, "when one thinks of all the worry and talk about helping a hopeless slave population, when the future obviously was only crying to be rid of them. There are happy babes unborn ready to burst the doors when these drivellers are swept away."

"Will you permit me to say," said Turnbull, after reflection, "that I don't like all this?"

"And will you permit me to say," said the other, with a snap, "that I don't like Mr. Evan MacIan?"

Somewhat to the speaker's surprise this did not inflame the sensitive sceptic; he had the air of thinking thoroughly, and then he said: "No, I

---

[145] A cicerone is a guide who gives information about antiquities and places of interest to sightseers.

don't think it's my friend MacIan that taught me that. I think I should always have said that I don't like this. These people have rights."

"Rights!" repeated the unknown in a tone quite indescribable. Then he added with a more open sneer: "Perhaps they also have souls."

"They have lives!" said Turnbull, sternly; "that is quite enough for me. I understood you to say that you thought life sacred."

"Yes, indeed!" cried his mentor with a sort of idealistic animation. "Yes, indeed! Life is sacred—but lives are not sacred. We are improving Life by removing lives. Can you, as a free-thinker, find any fault in that?"

"Yes," said Turnbull with brevity.

"Yet you applaud tyrannicide," said the stranger with rationalistic gaiety. "How inconsistent! It really comes to this: You approve of taking away life from those to whom it is a triumph and a pleasure. But you will not take away life from those to whom it is a burden and a toil."

Turnbull rose to his feet in the car with considerable deliberation, but his face seemed oddly pale. The other went on with enthusiasm.

"Life, yes, Life is indeed sacred!" he cried; "but new lives for old! Good lives for bad! On that very place where now there sprawls one drunken wastrel of a pavement artist more or less wishing he were dead—on that very spot there shall in the future be living pictures; there shall be golden girls and boys leaping in the sun."

Turnbull, still standing up, opened his lips. "Will you put me down, please?" he said, quite calmly, like one stopping an omnibus.

"Put you down—what do you mean?" cried his leader. "I am taking you to the front of the revolutionary war, where you will be one of the first of the revolutionary leaders."

"Thank you," replied Turnbull with the same painful constraint. "I have heard about your revolutionary war, and I think on the whole that I would rather be anywhere else."

"Do you want to be taken to a monastery," snarled the other, "with MacIan and his winking Madonnas?"

"I want to be taken to a madhouse," said Turnbull distinctly, giving the direction with a sort of precision. "I want to go back to exactly the same lunatic asylum from which I came."

"Why?" asked the unknown.

"Because I want a little sane and wholesome society," answered Turnbull.

There was a long and peculiar silence, and then the man driving the flying machine said quite coolly: "I won't take you back."

And then Turnbull said equally coolly: "Then I'll jump out of the car."

The unknown rose to his full height, and the expression in his eyes seemed to be made of ironies behind ironies, as two mirrors infinitely reflect each other. At last he said, very gravely: "Do you think I am the devil?"

"Yes," said Turnbull, violently. "For I think the devil is a dream, and so are you. I don't believe in you or your flying ship or your last fight of the world. It is all a nightmare. I say as a fact of dogma and faith that it is all a nightmare. And I will be a martyr for my faith as much as St. Catherine, for I will jump out of this ship and risk waking up safe in bed."

After swaying twice with the swaying vessel he dived over the side as one dives into the sea. For some incredible moments stars and space and planets seemed to shoot up past him as the sparks fly upward; and yet in that sickening descent he was full of some unnatural happiness. He could connect it with no idea except one that half escaped him— what Evan had said of the difference between Christ and Satan; that it was by Christ's own choice that He descended into hell.

When he again realised anything, he was lying on his elbow on the lawn of the lunatic asylum, and the last red of the sunset had not yet disappeared.

XVII

THE IDIOT

Evan MacIan was standing a few yards off looking at him in absolute silence.

He had not the moral courage to ask MacIan if there had been anything astounding in the manner of his coming there, nor did MacIan seem to have any question to ask, or perhaps any need to ask it. The two men came slowly toward each other, and found the same expression on each other's faces. Then, for the first time in all their acquaintance, they shook hands.

Almost as if this were a kind of unconscious signal, it brought Dr. Quayle bounding out of a door and running across the lawn.

"Oh, there you are!" he exclaimed with a relieved giggle. "Will you come inside, please? I want to speak to you both."

They followed him into his shiny wooden office where their damning record was kept. Dr. Quayle sat down on a swivel chair and swung round to face them. His carved smile had suddenly disappeared.

"I will be plain with you gentlemen," he said, abruptly; "you know quite well we do our best for everybody here. Your cases have been under special consideration, and the Master himself has decided that you ought to be treated specially and er—under somewhat simpler conditions."

"You mean treated worse, I suppose," said Turnbull, gruffly.

The doctor did not reply, and MacIan said: "I expected this." His eyes had begun to glow.

The doctor answered, looking at his desk and playing with a key: "Well, in certain cases that give anxiety—it is often better——"

"Give anxiety," said Turnbull, fiercely. "Confound your impudence! What do you mean? You imprison two perfectly sane men in a madhouse because you have made up a long word. They take it in good temper, walk and talk in your garden like monks who have found a vocation, are civil even to you, you damned druggists' hack! Behave not only more sanely than any of your patients, but more sanely than half the sane men outside, and you have the soul-stifling cheek to say that they give anxiety."

"The head of the asylum has settled it all," said Dr. Quayle, still looking down.

MacIan took one of his immense strides forward and stood over the doctor with flaming eyes.

"If the head has settled it let the head announce it," he said. "I won't take it from you. I believe you to be a low, gibbering degenerate. Let us see the head of the asylum."

"See the head of the asylum," repeated Dr. Quayle. "Certainly not."

The tall Highlander, bending over him, put one hand on his shoulder with fatherly interest.

"You don't seem to appreciate the peculiar advantages of my position as a lunatic," he said. "I could kill you with my left hand before such a rat as you could so much as squeak. And I wouldn't be hanged for it."

"I certainly agree with Mr. MacIan," said Turnbull with sobriety and perfect respectfulness, "that you had better let us see the head of the institution."

Dr. Quayle got to his feet in a mixture of sudden hysteria and clumsy presence of mind.

"Oh, certainly," he said with a weak laugh. "You can see the head of the asylum if you particularly want to." He almost ran out of the room, and the two followed swiftly on his flying coat tails. He knocked at an ordinary varnished door in the corridor. When a voice said, "Come in," MacIan's breath went hissing back through his teeth into his chest. Turnbull was more impetuous, and opened the door.

It was a neat and well-appointed room entirely lined with a medical library. At the other end of it was a ponderous and polished desk with an incandescent lamp on it, the light of which was just sufficient to show a slender, well-bred figure in an ordinary medical black frock-coat, whose head, quite silvered with age, was bent over neat piles of notes. This gentleman looked up for an instant as they entered, and the lamplight fell on his glittering spectacles and long, clean-shaven face—a face which would have been simply like an aristocrat's but that a certain lion poise of the head and long cleft in the chin made it look more like a very handsome actor's. It was only for a flash that his face was thus lifted. Then he bent his silver head over his notes once more, and said, without looking up again:

"I told you, Dr. Quayle, that these men were to go to cells B and C."

Turnbull and MacIan looked at each other, and said more than they could ever say with tongues or swords. Among other things they said that to that particular Head of the institution it was waste of time to appeal, and they followed Dr. Quayle out of the room.

The instant they stepped out into the corridor four sturdy figures stepped from four sides, pinioned them, and ran them along the galleries. They might very likely have thrown their captors right and left had they been inclined to resist, but for some nameless reason they were more inclined to laugh. A mixture of mad irony with childish curiosity made them feel quite inclined to see what next twist would be taken by their imbecile luck. They were dragged down countless cold avenues lined with glazed tiles, different only in being of different lengths and set at different angles. They were so many and so monotonous that to escape back by them would have been far harder than fleeing from the Hampton Court maze.[146] Only the fact that windows grew fewer, coming at longer intervals, and the fact that when the windows did come they seemed shadowed and let in less light, showed that they were winding into the core or belly of some enormous building. After a little time the glazed corridors began to be lit by electricity.

At last, when they had walked nearly a mile in those white and polished tunnels, they came with quite a shock to the futile finality of a cul-de-sac. All that white and weary journey ended suddenly in an oblong space and a blank white wall. But in the white wall there were

---

[146]Hampton Court is a palace on the north bank of the Thames River in London. It was built by Cardinal Wolsey (ca. 1474–1530). The gardens, rebuilt by Christopher Wren (1632–1723), contain a famous maze. Chesterton once said that discovering the Catholic Church was like discovering the center of the maze at Hampton Court: "When one is at the centre, one does not *think* one is at the centre, one *knows* one is at the centre."

two iron doors painted white on which were written, respectively, in neat black capitals B and C.

"You go in here, sir," said the leader of the officials, quite respectfully, "and you in here."

But before the doors had clanged upon their dazed victims, MacIan had been able to say to Turnbull with a strange drawl of significance: "I wonder who A is."

Turnbull made an automatic struggle before he allowed himself to be thrown into the cell. Hence it happened that he was the last to enter, and was still full of the exhilaration of the adventures for at least five minutes after the echo of the clanging door had died away.

Then, when silence had sunk deep and nothing happened for two and a half hours, it suddenly occurred to him that this was the end of his life. He was hidden and sealed up in this little crack of stone until the flesh should fall off his bones. He was dead, and the world had won.

His cell was of an oblong shape, but very long in comparison with its width. It was just wide enough to permit the arms to be fully extended with the dumb-bells, which were hung up on the left wall, very dusty. It was, however, long enough for a man to walk one thirty-fifth part of a mile if he traversed it entirely. On the same principle a row of fixed holes, quite close together, let in to the cells by pipes what was alleged to be the freshest air. For these great scientific organisers insisted that a man should be healthy even if he was miserable. They provided a walk long enough to give him exercise and holes large enough to give him oxygen. There their interest in human nature suddenly ceased. It seemed never to have occurred to them that the benefit of exercise belongs partly to the benefit of liberty. They had not entertained the suggestion that the open air is only one of the advantages of the open sky. They administered air in secret, but in sufficient doses, as if it were a medicine. They suggested walking, as if no man had ever felt inclined to walk. Above all, the asylum authorities insisted on their own extraordinary cleanliness. Every morning, while Turnbull was still half asleep on his iron bedstead which was lifted half-way up the wall and clamped to it with iron, four sluices or metal mouths opened above him at the four corners of the chamber and washed it white of any defilement. Turnbull's solitary soul surged up against this sickening daily solemnity.

"I am buried alive!" he cried, bitterly; "they have hidden me under mountains. I shall be here till I rot. Why the blazes should it matter to them whether I am dirty or clean."

Every morning and evening an iron hatchway opened in his oblong cell, and a brown hairy hand or two thrust in a plate of perfectly cooked lentils and a big bowl of cocoa. He was not underfed any more than he was underexercised or asphyxiated. He had ample walking space, ample air, ample and even filling food. The only objection was that he had nothing to walk toward, nothing to feast about, and no reason whatever for drawing the breath of life.

Even the shape of his cell especially irritated him. It was a long, narrow parallelogram, which had a flat wall at one end and ought to have had a flat wall at the other; but that end was broken by a wedge or angle of space, like the prow of a ship. After three days of silence and cocoa, this angle at the end began to infuriate Turnbull. It maddened him to think that two lines came together and pointed at nothing. After the fifth day he was reckless, and poked his head into the corner. After twenty-five days he almost broke his head against it. Then he became quite cool and stupid again, and began to examine it like a sort of Robinson Crusoe.

Almost unconsciously it was his instinct to examine outlets, and he found himself paying particular attention to the row of holes which let in the air into his last house of life. He soon discovered that these air-holes were all the ends and mouths of long leaden tubes which doubtless carried air from some remote watering-place near Margate. One evening while he was engaged in the fifth investigation he noticed something like twilight in one of these dumb mouths, as compared with the darkness of the others. Thrusting his finger in as far as it would go, he found a hole and flapping edge in the tube. This he rent open and instantly saw a light behind; it was at least certain that he had struck some other cell.

It is a characteristic of all things now called "efficient," which means mechanical and calculated, that if they go wrong at all they go entirely wrong. There is no power of retrieving a defeat, as in simpler and more living organisms. A strong gun can conquer a strong elephant, but a wounded elephant can easily conquer a broken gun. Thus the Prussian monarchy in the eighteenth century, or now, can make a strong army merely by making the men afraid. But it does it with the permanent possibility that the men may some day be more afraid of their enemies than of their officers. Thus the drainage in our cities so long as it is quite solid means a general safety, but if there is one leak it means concentrated poison—an explosion of deathly germs like dynamite, a spirit of stink. Thus, indeed, all that excellent machinery which is the swiftest thing on earth in saving human labour is also the slowest thing on earth in resisting human interference. It may be easier to get chocolate for nothing out of a shopkeeper than out an automatic machine. But if you did manage to steal the chocolate, the automatic machine would be much less likely to run after you.

Turnbull was not long in discovering this truth in connection with the cold and colossal machinery of this great asylum. He had been shaken by many spiritual states since the instant when he was pitched head foremost into that private cell which was to be his private room till death. He had felt a high fit of pride and poetry, which had ebbed away and left him deadly cold. He had known a period of mere scientific curiosity, in the course of which he examined all the tiles of his cell, with the gratifying conclusion that they were all the same shape and size; but was greatly puzzled about the angle in the wall at the end, and also about an iron peg or spike that stood out from the wall, the object of which he does not know to this day. Then he had a period of mere madness not to be written of by decent men, but only by those few dirty novelists hallooed on by the infernal huntsman to hunt down and humiliate human nature. This also passed, but left behind it a feverish distaste for many of the mere objects around him. Long after he had returned to sanity and such hopeless cheerfulness as a man might have on a desert island, he disliked the regular squares of the pattern of wall and floor and the triangle that terminated his corridor. Above all, he had a hatred, deep as the hell he did not-believe in, for the objectless iron peg in the wall.

But in all his moods, sane or insane, intolerant or stoical, he never really doubted this: that the machine held him as light and as hopelessly as he had from his birth been held by the hopeless cosmos of his own creed. He knew well the ruthless and inexhaustible resources of our scientific civilisation. He no more expected rescue from a medical certificate than rescue from the solar system. In many of his Robinson Crusoe moods he thought kindly of MacIan as of some quarrelsome school-fellow who had long been dead. He thought of leaving in the cell when he died a rigid record of his opinions, and when he began to write them down on scraps of envelope in his pocket, he was startled to discover how much they had changed. Then he remembered the Beauchamp Tower,[147] and tried to write his blazing scepticism on the wall, and discovered that it was all shiny tiles on which nothing could be either drawn or carved. Then for an instant there hung and broke above him like a high wave the whole horror of scientific imprisonment, which manages to deny a man not only liberty, but every accidental comfort of bondage. In the old filthy dungeons men could carve their prayers or protests in the rock. Here the white and slippery walls escaped even from bearing witness. The old prisoners could make a pet of a mouse or a beetle strayed out of a hole. Here the unpierceable walls were washed every morning by an automatic sluice. There was no natural corruption and no merciful decay by which a living thing could enter in. Then James Turnbull looked up and saw the high invincible hatefulness of the society in which he lived, and saw the hatefulness of something else also, which he told himself again and again was not the cosmos in which he believed. But all the time he had never once doubted that the five sides of his cell were for him the wall of the world henceforward, and it gave him a shock of surprise even to discover the faint light through the aperture in the ventilation tube. But he had forgotten how close efficiency has to pack everything together and how easily, therefore, a pipe here or there may leak.

[147] The Beauchamp Tower was built at the Tower of London during the time of Edward I (1239–1307) . The tower takes its name from Thomas Beauchamp (Earl of Warwick). It was used often for prisoners of high rank, many of whom would subsequently have been executed, and it contains some interesting wall carvings left by prisoners.

Turnbull thrust his first finger down the aperture, and at last managed to make a slight further fissure in the piping. The light that came from beyond was very faint, and apparently indirect; it seemed to fall from some hole or window higher up. As he was screwing his eye to peer at this gray and greasy twilight he was astonished to see another human finger very long and lean come down from above toward the broken pipe and hook it up to something higher. The lighted aperture was abruptly blackened and blocked, presumably by a face and mouth, for something human spoke down the tube, though the words were not clear.

"Who is that?" asked Turnbull, trembling with excitement, yet wary and quite resolved not to spoil any chance.

After a few indistinct sounds the voice came down with a strong Argyleshire accent:

"I say, Turnbull, we couldn't fight through this tube, could we?"

Sentiments beyond speech surged up in Turnbull and silenced him for a space just long enough to be painful. Then he said with his old gaiety: "I vote we talk a little first; I don't want to murder the first man I have met for ten million years."

"I know what you mean," answered the other. "It has been awful. For a mortal month I have been alone with God."

Turnbull started, and it was on the tip of his tongue to answer: "Alone with God! Then you do not know what loneliness is."

But he answered, after all, in his old defiant style: "Alone with God, were you? And I suppose you found his Majesty's society rather monotonous?"

"Oh, no," said MacIan, and his voice shuddered; "it was a great deal too exciting."

After a very long silence the voice of MacIan said: "What do you really hate most in your place?"

"You'd think I was really mad if I told you," answered Turnbull, bitterly.

"Then I expect it's the same as mine," said the other voice.

"I am sure it's not the same as anybody's," said Turnbull, "for it has no rhyme or reason. Perhaps my brain really has gone, but I detest that iron spike in the left wall more than the damned desolation or the damned cocoa. Have you got one in your cell?"

"Not now," replied MacIan with serenity. "I've pulled it out."

His fellow-prisoner could only repeat the words.

"I pulled it out the other day when I was off my head," continued the tranquil Highland voice. "It looked so unnecessary."

"You must be ghastly strong," said Turnbull.

"One is, when one is mad," was the careless reply, "and it had worn a little loose in the socket. Even now I've got it out I can't discover what it was for. But I've found out something a long sight funnier."

"What do you mean?" asked Turnbull.

"I have found out where A is," said the other.

Three weeks afterward MacIan had managed to open up communications which made his meaning plain. By that time the two captives had fully discovered and demonstrated that weakness in the very nature of modern machinery to which we have already referred. The very fact that they were isolated from all companions meant that they were free from all spies, and as there were no gaolers to be bribed, so there were none to be baffled. Machinery brought them their cocoa and cleaned their cells; that machinery was as helpless as it was pitiless.[148] A little patient violence, conducted day after day amid constant mutual suggestion, opened an irregular hole in the wall, large enough to let in a small man, in the exact place where there had been before the tiny ventilation holes. Turnbull tumbled somehow into MacIan's apartment, and his first glance found out that the iron spike was indeed plucked from its socket, and left, moreover, another ragged hole into some hollow place behind. But for this MacIan's cell was the duplicate of Turnbull's—a long oblong ending in a wedge and lined with cold and lustrous tiles. The small hole from which the peg had been displaced was in that short oblique wall at the end nearest to Turnbull's. That individual looked at it with a puzzled face.

"What is in there?" he asked.

MacIan answered briefly: "Another cell."

"But where can the door of it be?" said his companion, even more puzzled; "the doors of our cells are at the other end."

---

[148] On page 220, above, it is "a brown hairy hand or two" that introduced the food into the cells. There is no explanation for the inconsistency.

"It has no door," said Evan.

In the pause of perplexity that followed, an eerie and sinister feeling crept over Turnbull's stubborn soul in spite of himself. The notion of the doorless room chilled him with that sense of half-witted curiosity which one has when something horrible is half understood.

"James Turnbull," said MacIan, in a low and shaken voice, "these people hate us more than Nero hated Christians, and fear us more than any man feared Nero.[149] They have filled England with frenzy and galloping in order to capture us and wipe us out—in order to kill us. And they have killed us, for you and I have only made a hole in our coffins. But though this hatred that they felt for us is bigger than they felt for Bonaparte,[150] and more plain and practical than they would feel for Jack the Ripper,[151] yet it is not we whom the people of this place hate most."

A cold and quivering impatience continued to crawl up Turnbull's spine; he had never felt so near to superstition and supernaturalism, and it was not a pretty sort of superstition either.

"There is another man more fearful and hateful," went on MacIan, in his low monotone voice, "and they have buried him even deeper. God knows how they did it, for he was let in by neither door nor window, nor lowered through any opening above. I expect these iron handles that we both hate have been part of some damned machinery for walling him up. He is there. I have looked through the hole at him; but I cannot stand looking at him long, because his face is turned away from me and he does not move."

All Turnbull's unnatural and uncompleted feelings found their outlet in rushing to the aperture and looking into the unknown room.

It was a third oblong cell exactly like the other two except that it was doorless, and except that on one of the walls was painted a large

---

[149] Nero (A.D. 37–68) was a Roman emperor. In July 64 two-thirds of Rome was destroyed by fire. Nero was said to have been responsible and found, in the Christians, a convenient scapegoat; he persecuted them harshly, putting many to death in savage ways.

[150] Napoleon Bonaparte (1769–1821) was an emperor of France.

[151] Jack the Ripper was the name given to an unidentified murderer who, between August and November 1888, killed and mutilated six prostitutes in the East End of London, causing much public alarm.

black A like the B and C outside their own doors. The letter in this case was not painted outside, because this prison had no outside.

On the same kind of tiled floor, of which the monotonous squares had maddened Turnbull's eye and brain, was sitting a figure which was startlingly short even for the sitting posture. Indeed, it had something of the look of a child, only that the enormous head was ringed with hair of a frosty gray. The figure was draped, both insecurely and insufficiently, in what looked like the remains of a brown flannel dressing-gown; an emptied cup of cocoa stood on the floor beside it, and the creature had his big gray head cocked at a particular angle of inquiry or attention which amid all that gathering gloom and mystery struck one as comic if not cocksure.

After six still seconds Turnbull could stand it no longer, but called out to the dwarfish thing—in what words heaven knows. The thing got up with the promptitude of an animal, and turning round offered the spectacle of two owlish eyes and a huge gray-and-white beard not unlike the plumage of an owl. This extraordinary beard covered him literally to his feet (not that that was very far), and perhaps it was as well that it did, for portions of his remaining clothing seemed to fall off whenever he moved. One talks trivially of a face like parchment, but this old man's face was so wrinkled that it was like a parchment loaded with hieroglyphics. The lines of his face were so deep and complex that one could see five or ten different faces besides the real one, as one can see them in an elaborate wall-paper. And yet while his face seemed like a scripture older than the gods, his eyes were quite bright, blue, and startled like those of a baby. They looked as if they had only an instant before been fitted into his head.

Everything depended so obviously upon whether this buried monster spoke that Turnbull did not know or care whether he himself had spoken. He said something or nothing. And then he waited for this dwarfish voice that had been hidden under the mountains of the world. At last it did speak, and spoke in English, with a foreign accent that was neither Latin nor Teutonic. He suddenly stretched out a long and very dirty forefinger, and cried in a voice of clear recognition, like a child's: "That's a hole."

He digested the discovery for some seconds, sucking his finger, and then he cried, with a crow of laughter: "And that's a head come through it."

The hilarious energy in this idiot attitude gave Turnbull another sick turn. He had grown to tolerate those dreary and mumbling madmen who trailed themselves about the beautiful asylum gardens. But there was something new and subversive of the universe in the combination of so much cheerful decision with a body without a brain.

"Why did they put you in such a place?" he asked at last with embarrassment.

"Good place. Yes," said the old man, nodding a great many times and beaming like a flattered landlord. "Good shape. Long and narrow, with a point. Like this," and he made lovingly with his hands a map of the room in the air.

"But that's not the best," he added, confidentially. "Squares very good; I have a nice long holiday, and can count them. But that not the best."

"What is the best?" asked Turnbull in great distress.

"Spike is the best," said the old man, opening his blue eyes blazing; "it sticks out."

The words Turnbull spoke broke out of him in pure pity. "Can't we do anything for you?" he said.

"I am very happy," said the other, alphabetically. "You are a good man. Can I help you?"

"No, I don't think you can, sir," said Turnbull with rough pathos; "I am glad you are contented at least."

The weird old person opened his broad blue eyes and fixed Turnbull with a stare extraordinarily severe. "You are quite sure," he said, "I cannot help you?"

"Quite sure, thank you," said Turnbull with broken brevity. "Good-day."

Then he turned to MacIan who was standing close behind him, and whose face, now familiar in all its moods, told him easily that Evan had heard the whole of the strange dialogue.

"Curse those cruel beasts!" cried Turnbull. "They've turned him to an imbecile just by burying him alive. His brain's like a pin-point now."

"You are sure he is a lunatic?" said Evan, slowly.

"Not a lunatic," said Turnbull, "an idiot. He just points to things and says that they stick out."

"He had a notion that he could help us," said MacIan, moodily, and began to pace toward the other end of his cell.

"Yes, it was a bit pathetic," assented Turnbull; "such a Thing offering help, and besides—Hallo! Hallo! What's the matter?"

"God Almighty guide us all!" said MacIan.

He was standing heavy and still at the other end of the room and staring quietly at the door which for thirty days had sealed them up from the sun. Turnbull, following the other's eye, stared at the door likewise, and then he also uttered an exclamation. The iron door was standing about an inch and a half open.

"He said—" began Evan, in a trembling voice— "he offered——"

"Come along, you fool!" shouted Turnbull with a sudden and furious energy. "I see it all now, and it's the best stroke of luck in the world. You pulled out that iron handle that had screwed up his cell, and it somehow altered the machinery and opened all the doors."

Seizing MacIan by the elbow he bundled him bodily out into the open corridor and ran him on till they saw daylight through a half-darkened window.

"All the same," said Evan, like one answering in an ordinary conversation, "he did ask you whether he could help you."

All this wilderness of windowless passages was so built into the heart of that fortress of fear that it seemed more than an hour before the fugitives had any good glimpse of the outer world. They did not even know what hour of the day it was; and when, turning a corner, they saw the bare tunnel of the corridor end abruptly in a shining square of garden, the grass burning in that strong evening sunshine which makes it burnished gold rather than green, the abrupt opening on to the earth seemed like a hole knocked in the wall of heaven. Only once or twice in life is it permitted to a man thus to see the very universe from outside, and feel existence itself as an adorable adventure not yet begun. As they found this shining escape out of that hellish labyrinth they both had simultaneously the sensation of being babes unborn, of being asked by God if they would like to live upon the earth. They were looking in at one of the seven gates of Eden.

Turnbull was the first to leap into the garden, with an earth-spurning leap like that of one who could really spread his wings and fly. MacIan, who came an instant after, was less full of mere animal gusto and fuller of a more fearful and quivering pleasure in the clear and innocent flower colours and the high and holy trees. With one bound they were in that cool and cleared landscape, and they found just outside the door the black-clad gentleman with the cloven chin smilingly regarding them; and his chin seemed to grow longer and longer as he smiled.

XVIII

A RIDDLE OF FACES

Just behind him stood two other doctors: one, the familiar Dr. Quayle, of the blinking eyes and bleating voice; the other, a more commonplace but much more forcible figure, a stout young doctor with short, well-brushed hair and a round but resolute face. At the sight of the escape these two subordinates uttered a cry and sprang forward, but their superior remained motionless and smiling, and somehow the lack of his support seemed to arrest and freeze them in the very gesture of pursuit.

"Let them be," he cried in a voice that cut like a blade of ice; and not only of ice, but of some awful primordial ice that had never been water.

"I want no devoted champions," said the cutting voice; "even the folly of one's friends bores one at last. You don't suppose I should have let these lunatics out of their cells without good reason. I have the best and fullest reason. They can be let out of their cell to-day, because to-day the whole world has become their cell. I will have no more mediæval mummery of chains and doors. Let them wander about the earth as they wandered about this garden, and I shall still be their easy master. Let them take the wings of the morning and abide in the uttermost parts of the sea—I am there. Whither shall they go from my presence and whither shall they flee from my spirit? Courage, Dr. Quayle, and do not be downhearted; the real days of tyranny are only beginning on this earth." [152]

And with that the Master laughed and swung away from them, almost as if his laugh was a bad thing for people to see.

"Might I speak to you a moment?" said Turnbull, stepping forward with a respectful resolution. But the shoulders of the Master only seemed to take on a new and unexpected angle of mockery as he strode away.

[152]The "Master" here quotes several passages from the Scriptures with himself placed in the position of God in each case: Gen 2:15; Ps 139:7–10; Jn 14:1; Mk 13:8.

Turnbull swung round with great abruptness to the other two doctors, and said, harshly: "What in snakes does he mean—and who are you?"

"My name is Hutton," said the short, stout man, "and I am—well, one of those whose business it is to uphold this establishment."

"My name is Turnbull," said the other; "I am one of those whose business it is to tear it to the ground."

The small doctor smiled, and Turnbull's anger seemed suddenly to steady him.

"But I don't want to talk about that," he said, calmly; "I only want to know what the master of this asylum really means."

Dr. Hutton's smile broke into a laugh which, short as it was, had the suspicion of a shake in it. "I suppose you think that quite a simple question," he said.

"I think it a plain question," said Turnbull, "and one that deserves a plain answer. Why did the Master lock us up in a couple of cupboards like jars of pickles for a mortal month, and why does he now let us walk free in the garden again?"

"I understand," said Hutton, with arched eyebrows, "that your complaint is that you are now free to walk in the garden."

"My complaint is," said Turnbull, stubbornly, "that if I am fit to walk freely now, I have been as fit for the last month. No one has examined me, no one has come near me. Your chief says that I am only free because he has made other arrangements. What are those arrangements?"

The young man with the round face looked down for a little while and smoked reflectively. The other and elder doctor had gone pacing nervously by himself upon the lawn. At length the round face was lifted again, and showed two round blue eyes with a certain frankness in them.

"Well, I don't see that it can do any harm to tell you now," he said. "You were shut up just then because it was just during that month that the Master was bringing off his big scheme. He was getting his bill through Parliament, and organising the new medical police. But of course you haven't heard of all that; in fact, you weren't meant to."

"Heard of all what?" asked the impatient inquirer.

"There's a new law now, and the asylum powers are greatly extended. Even if you did escape now, any policeman would take you up in the next town if you couldn't show a certificate of sanity from us."

"Well," continued Dr. Hutton, "the Master described before both Houses of Parliament the real scientific objection to all existing legislation about lunacy. As he very truly said, the mistake was in supposing insanity to be merely an exception or an extreme. Insanity, like forgetfulness, is simply a quality which enters more or less into all human beings; and for practical purposes it is more necessary to know whose mind is really trustworthy than whose has some accidental taint. We have therefore reversed the existing method, and people now have to prove that they are sane. In the first village you entered, the village constable would notice that you were not wearing on the left lapel of your coat the small pewter S which is now necessary to any one who walks about beyond asylum bounds or outside asylum hours."

"You mean to say," said Turnbull, "that this was what the Master of the asylum urged before the House of Commons?"

Dr. Hutton nodded with gravity.

"And you mean to say," cried Turnbull, with a vibrant snort, "that that proposal was passed in an assembly that calls itself democratic?"

The doctor showed his whole row of teeth in a smile. "Oh, the assembly calls itself Socialist now," he said, "but we explained to them that this was a question for men of science."

Turnbull gave one stamp upon the gravel, then pulled himself together, and resumed: "But why should your infernal head medicine-man lock us up in separate cells while he was turning England into a madhouse? I'm not the Prime Minister; we're not the House of Lords."

"He wasn't afraid of the Prime Minister," replied Dr. Hutton; "he isn't afraid of the House of Lords. But——"

"Well?" inquired Turnbull, stamping again.

"He is afraid of you," said Hutton, simply. "Why, didn't you know?"

MacIan, who had not spoken yet, made one stride forward and stood with shaking limbs and shining eyes.

"He was afraid I" began Evan, thickly. "You mean to say that we——"

"I mean to say the plain truth now that the danger is over," said Hutton, calmly; "most certainly you two were the only people he ever was afraid of." Then he added in a low but not inaudible voice: "Except one—whom he feared worse, and has buried deeper."

"Come away," cried MacIan, "this has to be thought about."

Turnbull followed him in silence as he strode away, but just before he vanished, turned and spoke again to the doctors.

"But what has got hold of people?" he asked, abruptly. "Why should all England have gone dotty on the mere subject of dottiness?"

Dr. Hutton smiled his open smile once more and bowed slightly. "As to that also," he replied, "I don't want to make you vain."

Turnbull swung round without a word, and he and his companion were lost in the lustrous leafage of the garden. They noticed nothing special about the scene, except that the garden seemed more exquisite than ever in the deepening sunset, and that there seemed to be many more people, whether patients or attendants, walking about in it.

From behind the two black-coated doctors as they stood on the lawn another figure somewhat similarly dressed strode hurriedly past them, having also grizzled hair and an open flapping frock-coat. Both his decisive step and dapper black array marked him out as another medical man, or at least a man in authority, and as he passed Turnbull the latter was aroused by a strong impression of having seen the man somewhere before. It was no one that he knew well, yet he was certain that it was some one at whom he had at some time or other looked steadily. It was neither the face of a friend nor of an enemy; it aroused neither irritation nor tenderness, yet it was a face which had for some reason been of great importance in his life. Turning and returning, and making detours about the garden, he managed to study the man's face again and again—a moustached, somewhat military face with a monocle, the sort of face that is aristocratic without being distinguished. Turnbull could not remember any particular doctors in his decidedly healthy existence. Was the man a long-lost uncle, or was he only somebody who had sat opposite him regularly in a railway train? At that moment the man knocked down his own eye-glass with a gesture of annoyance; Turnbull remembered the gesture, and the truth sprang up solid in front of him. The man with the moustaches was Cumberland Vane, the London police magistrate before whom he and MacIan had once stood on their trial. The magistrate must have been transferred to some other official duties—to something connected with the inspection of asylums.

Turnbull's heart gave a leap of excitement which was half hope. As a magistrate Mr. Cumberland Vane had been somewhat careless and shallow, but certainly kindly, and not inaccessible to common-sense so long as it was put to him in strictly conventional language. He was at least an authority of a more human and refreshing sort than the crank with the wagging beard or the fiend with the forked chin.

He went straight up to the magistrate, and said: "Good-evening, Mr. Vane; I doubt if you remember me."

Cumberland Vane screwed the eye-glass into his scowling face for an instant, and then said curtly but not uncivilly: "Yes, I remember you, sir; assault or battery, wasn't it?—a fellow broke your window. A tall fellow—McSomething—case made rather a noise afterward."

"MacIan is the name, sir," said Turnbull, respectfully; "I have him here with me."

"Eh!" said Vane very sharply. "Confound him! Has he got anything to do with this game?"

"Mr. Vane," said Turnbull, pacifically, "I will not pretend that either he or I acted quite decorously on that occasion. You were very lenient with us, and did not treat us as criminals when you very well might. So I am sure you will give us your testimony that, even if we were criminals, we are not lunatics in any legal or medical sense whatever. I am sure you will use your influence for us."

"My influence!" repeated the magistrate, with a slight start. "I don't quite understand you."

"I don't know in what capacity you are here," continued Turnbull, gravely, "but a legal authority of your distinction must certainly be here in an important one. Whether you are visiting and inspecting the place, or attached to it as some kind of permanent legal adviser, your opinion must still——"

Cumberland Vane exploded with a detonation of oaths; his face was transfigured with fury and contempt, and yet in some odd way he did not seem specially angry with Turnbull.

"But Lord bless us and save us!" [153] he gasped, at length; "I'm not here as an official at all. I'm here as a patient. The cursed pack of rat-catching chemists all say that I've lost my wits."

"You!" cried Turnbull with terrible emphasis. "You! Lost your wits!"

In the rush of his real astonishment at this towering unreality Turnbull almost added: "Why, you haven't got any to lose." But he fortunately remembered the remains of his desperate diplomacy.

"This can't go on," he said, positively. "Men like MacIan and I may suffer unjustly all our lives, but a man like you must have influence."

"There is only one man who has any influence in England now," said Vane, and his high voice fell to a sudden and convincing quietude.

"Whom do you mean?" asked Turnbull.

"I mean that cursed fellow with the long split chin," said the other.

"Is it really true," asked Turnbull, "that he has been allowed to buy up and control such a lot? What put the country into such a state?"

Mr. Cumberland Vane laughed outright. "What put the country into such a state?" he asked. "Why, you did. When you were fool enough to agree to fight MacIan, after all, everybody was ready to believe that the Bank of England might paint itself pink with white spots."

"I don't understand," answered Turnbull. "Why should you be surprised at my fighting? I hope I have always fought."

"Well," said Cumberland Vane, airily, "you didn't believe in religion, you see—so we thought you were safe at any rate. You went further in your language than most of us wanted to go; no good in just hurting one's mother's feelings, I think. But of course we all knew you were right, and, really, we relied on you."

"Did you?" said the editor of the "Atheist" with a bursting heart. "I am sorry you did not tell me so at the time."

He walked away very rapidly and flung himself on a garden-seat, and for some six minutes his own wrongs hid from him the huge and hilarious fact that Cumberland Vane had been locked up as a lunatic.

[153] The first American edition has this expression as: "God blast my soul and body!" and the English first-edition publisher, shortly later, went to the expense of cancelling and replacing the entire page for what seems a rather minor change. No details of why this happened have been located.

The garden of the madhouse was so perfectly planned, and answered so exquisitely to every hour of daylight, that one could almost fancy that the sunlight was caught there tangled in its tinted trees, as the wise men of Gotham[154] tried to chain the spring to a bush. Or it seemed as if this ironic paradise still kept its unique dawn or its special sunset while the rest of the earthly globe rolled through its ordinary hours. There was one evening, or late afternoon, in particular, which Evan MacIan will remember in the last moments of death. It was what artists call a daffodil sky, but it is coarsened even by reference to a daffodil. It was of that innocent lonely yellow which has never heard of orange, though it might turn quite unconsciously into green. Against it the tops, one might say the turrets, of the clipt and ordered trees were outlined in that shade of veiled violet which tints the tops of lavender. A white early moon was hardly traceable upon that delicate yellow. MacIan, I say, will remember this tender and transparent evening, partly because of its virgin gold and silver, and partly because he passed beneath it through the most horrible instant of his life.

Turnbull was sitting on his seat on the lawn, and the golden evening impressed even his positive nature, as indeed it might have impressed the oxen in a field. He was shocked out of his idle mood of awe by seeing MacIan break from behind the bushes and run across the lawn with an action he had never seen in the man before, with all his experience of the eccentric humours of this Celt. MacIan fell on the bench, shaking it so that it rattled, and gripped it with his knees like one in dreadful pain of body. That particular run and tumble is typical only of a man who has been hit by some sudden and incurable evil, who is bitten by a viper or condemned to be hung. Turnbull looked up in the white face of his friend and enemy, and almost turned cold at what he saw there. He had seen the blue but gloomy eyes of the western Highlander troubled by as many

---

[154] The "wise men of Gotham" is the name for a group of approximately twenty English folk tales dating back before the sixteenth century that deal with a variety of events supposedly involving the citizens of the town of Gotham in Nottinghamshire. Each of the stories deals with various incidents, many of them humourous, intended to convey some truth or wisdom often turning on the supposed foolishness of the locals.

tempests as his own west Highland seas, but there had always been a fixed star of faith behind the storms. Now the star had gone out, and there was only misery.

Yet MacIan had the strength to answer the question where Turnbull, taken by surprise, had not the strength to ask it.

"They are right, they are right!" he cried. "O my God! they are right, Turnbull. I ought to be here!"

He went on with shapeless fluency as if he no longer had the heart to choose or check his speech. "I suppose I ought to have guessed long ago—all my big dreams and schemes—and every one being against us—but I was stuck up, you know."

"Do tell me about it, really," cried the atheist, and, faced with the furnace of the other's pain, he did not notice that he spoke with the affection of a father.

"I am mad, Turnbull," said Evan, with a dead clearness of speech, and leant back against the garden-seat.

"Nonsense," said the other, clutching at the obvious cue of benevolent brutality, "this is one of your silly moods."

MacIan shook his head. "I know enough about myself," he said, "to allow for any mood, though it opened heaven or hell. But to see things—to see them walking solid in the sun—things that can't be there—real mystics never do that, Turnbull."

"What things?" asked the other, incredulously.

MacIan lowered his voice. "I saw *her*," he said, "three minutes ago—walking here in this hell yard."

Between trying to look scornful and really looking startled, Turnbull's face was confused enough to emit no speech, and Evan went on in monotonous sincerity:

"I saw her walk behind those blessed trees against that holy sky of gold as plain as I can see her whenever I shut my eyes. I did shut them, and opened them again, and she was still there—that is, of course, she wasn't—She still had a little fur round her neck, but her dress was a shade brighter than when I really saw her."

"My dear fellow," cried Turnbull, rallying a hearty laugh, "the fancies have really got hold of you. You mistook some other poor girl here for her."

"Mistook some other——" said MacIan, and words failed him altogether.

They sat for some moments in the mellow silence of the evening garden, a silence that was stifling for the sceptic, but utterly empty and final for the man of faith. At last he broke out again with the words: "Well, anyhow, if I'm mad, I'm glad I'm mad on that."

Turnbull murmured some clumsy deprecation, and sat stolidly smoking to collect his thoughts; the next instant he had all his nerves engaged in the mere effort to sit still.

Across the clear space of cold silver and a pale lemon sky which was left by the gap in the ilex-trees[155] there passed a slim, dark figure, a profile and the poise of a dark head like a bird's, which really pinned him to his seat with the point of coincidence. With an effort he got to his feet, and said with a voice of affected insouciance: "By George! MacIan, she is uncommonly like——"

"What!" cried MacIan, with a leap of eagerness that was heart-breaking, "do you see her, too?" And the blaze came back into the centre of his eyes.

Turnbull's tawny eyebrows were pulled together with a peculiar frown of curiosity, and all at once he walked quickly across the lawn. MacIan sat rigid, but peered after him with open and parched lips. He saw the sight which either proved him sane or proved the whole universe half-witted; he saw the man of flesh approach that beautiful phantom, saw their gestures of recognition, and saw them against the sunset joining hands.

He could stand it no longer, but ran across to the path, turned the corner and saw standing quite palpable in the evening sunlight, talking with a casual grace to Turnbull, the face and figure which had filled his midnights with frightfully vivid or desperately half-forgotten features. She advanced quite pleasantly and coolly, and put out her hand. The moment that he touched it he knew that he was sane even if the solar system was crazy.

She was entirely elegant and unembarrassed. That is the awful thing about women—they refuse to be emotional at emotional moments,

---

[155] The ilex is the common holly tree.

upon some such ludicrous pretext as there being some one else there. But MacIan was in a condition of criticism much less than the average masculine one, being in fact merely overturned by the rushing riddle of the events.

Evan does not know to this day of what particular question he asked, but he vividly remembers that she answered, and every line or fluctuation of her face as she said it.

"Oh, don't you know?" she said, smiling, and suddenly lifting her level brown eyebrows. "Haven't you heard the news? I'm a lunatic."

Then she added after a short pause, and with a sort of pride: "I've got a certificate."

Her manner, by the matchless social stoicism of her sex, was entirely suited to a drawing-room, but Evan's reply fell somewhat far short of such a standard, as he only said: "What the devil in hell does all this nonsense mean?"

"Really," said the young lady, and laughed.

"I beg your pardon," said the unhappy young man, rather wildly, "but what I mean is, why are you here in an asylum?"

The young woman broke again into one of the maddening and mysterious laughs of femininity. Then she composed her features, and replied with equal dignity: "Well, if it comes to that, why are you?"

The fact that Turnbull had strolled away and was investigating rhododendrons may have been due to Evan's successful prayers to the other world, or possibly to his own pretty successful experience of this one. But though they two were as isolated as a new Adam and Eve in a pretty ornamental Eden, the lady did not relax by an inch the rigour of her badinage.

"I am locked up in the madhouse," said Evan, with a sort of stiff pride, "because I tried to keep my promise to you."

"Quite so," answered the inexplicable lady, nodding with a perfectly blazing smile, "and I am locked up because it was to me you promised."

"It is outrageous!" cried Evan; "it is impossible!"

"Oh, you can see my certificate if you like," she replied with some hauteur.

MacIan stared at her and then at his boots, and then at the sky and then at her again. He was quite sure now that he himself was not mad, and the fact rather added to his perplexity.

Then he drew nearer to her, and said in a dry and dreadful voice: "Oh, don't condescend to play the fool with such a fool as me. Are you really locked up here as a patient—because you helped us to escape?"

"Yes," said she, still smiling, but her steady voice had a shake in it.

Evan flung his big elbow across his forehead and burst into tears.

The pure lemon of the sky faded into purer white as the great sunset silently collapsed. The birds settled back into the trees; the moon began to glow with its own light. Mr. James Turnbull continued his botanical researches into the structure of the rhododendron. But the lady did not move an inch until Evan had flung up his face again; and when he did he saw by the last gleam of sunlight that it was not only his face that was wet.

Mr. James Turnbull had all his life professed a profound interest in physical science, and the phenomena of a good garden were really a pleasure to him; but after three-quarters of an hour or so even the apostle of science began to find rhododendrus a bore, and was somewhat relieved when an unexpected development of events obliged him to transfer his researches to the equally interesting subject of hollyhocks, which grew some fifty feet farther along the path. The ostensible cause of his removal was the unexpected reappearance of his two other acquaintances walking and talking laboriously along the way, with the black head bent close to the brown one. Even hollyhocks detained Turnbull but a short time. Having rapidly absorbed all the important principles affecting the growth of those vegetables, he jumped over a flower-bed and walked back into the building. The other two came up along the slow course of the path talking and talking. No one but God knows what they said (for they certainly have forgotten), and if I remembered it I would not repeat it. When they parted at the head of the walk she put out her hand again in the same well-bred way, although it trembled; he seemed to restrain a gesture as he let it fall.

"If it is really always to be like this," he said, thickly, "it would not matter if we were here for ever."

"You tried to kill yourself four times for me," she said, unsteadily, "and I have been chained up as a madwoman for you. I really think that after that——"

"Yes, I know," said Evan in a low voice, looking down. "After that we belong to each other. We are sort of sold to each other—until the stars fall." Then he looked up suddenly, and said: "By the way, what is your name?"

"My name is Beatrice Drake," she replied with complete gravity. "You can see it on my certificate of lunacy."

XIX

THE LAST PARLEY

Turnbull walked away, wildly trying to explain to himself the presence of two personal acquaintances so different as Vane and the girl. As he skirted a low hedge of laurel, an enormously tall young man leapt over it, stood in front of him, and almost fell on his neck as if seeking to embrace him.

"Don't you know me?" almost sobbed the young man, who was in the highest spirits. "Ain't I written on your heart, old boy? I say, what did you do with my yacht?"

"Take your arms off my neck," said Turnbull, irritably. "Are you mad?"

The young man sat down on the gravel-path and went into ecstasies of laughter. "No, that's just the fun of it—I'm not mad," he replied. "They've shut me up in this place, and I'm not mad." And he went off again into mirth as innocent as wedding-bells.

Turnbull, whose powers of surprise were exhausted, rolled his round gray eyes and said, "Mr. Wilkinson, I think," because he could not think of anything else to say.

The tall man sitting on the gravel bowed with urbanity, and said: "Quite at your service. Not to be confused with the Wilkinsons of Cumberland; and as I say, old boy, what have you done with my yacht? You see, they've locked me up here—in this garden—and a yacht would be a sort of occupation for an unmarried man."

"I am really horribly sorry," began Turnbull, in the last stage of bated bewilderment and exasperation, "but really——"

"Oh, I can see you can't have it on you at the moment," said Mr. Wilkinson with much intellectual magnanimity.

"Well, the fact is——" began Turnbull again, and then the phrase was frozen on his mouth, for round the corner came the goatlike face and gleaming eye-glasses of Dr. Quayle.

"Ah, my dear Mr. Wilkinson," said the doctor, as if delighted at a coincidence; "and Mr. Turnbull, too. Why, I want to speak to Mr. Turnbull."

Mr. Turnbull made some movement rather of surrender than assent, and the doctor caught it up exquisitely, showing even more of his two front teeth. "I am sure Mr. Wilkinson will excuse us a moment." And with flying frock-coat he led Turnbull rapidly round the corner of a path.

"My dear sir," he said, in a quite affectionate manner, "I do not mind telling you—you are such a very hopeful case—you understand so well the scientific point of view; and I don't like to see you bothered by the really hopeless cases. They are monotonous and maddening. The man you have just been talking to, poor fellow, is one of the strongest cases of pure *idée fixe*[156] that we have. It's very sad, and I'm afraid utterly incurable. He keeps on telling everybody"—and the doctor lowered his voice confidentially—"he tells everybody that two people have taken his yacht. His account of how he lost it is quite incoherent."

Turnbull stamped his foot on the gravel-path, and called out: "Oh, I can't stand this. Really——"

"I know, I know," said the psychologist, mournfully; "it is a most melancholy case, and also fortunately a very rare one. It is so rare, in fact, that in one classification of these maladies it is entered under a heading by itself—Perdinavititis, mental inflammation creating the impression that one has lost a ship. Really," he added, with a kind of half-embarrassed guilt, "it's rather a feather in my cap. I discovered the only existing case of perdinavititis." [157]

"But this won't do, doctor," said Turnbull, almost tearing his hair, "this really won't do. The man really did lose a ship. Indeed, not to put too fine a point on it, I took his ship."

Dr. Quayle swung round for an instant so that his silk-lined overcoat rustled, and stared singularly at Turnbull. Then he said with hurried amiability: "Why, of course you did. Quite so, quite so," and

[156] An *idée fixe* is a French term for "an idea that dominates the mind" or "an obsession".

[157] This word and the ones following, and the mental conditions supposedly associated with them, appear to have been invented by Chesterton.

with courteous gestures went striding up the garden-path. Under the first laburnum-tree he stopped, however, and pulling out his pencil and note-book wrote down feverishly: "Singular development in the Elentheromaniac, Turnbull. Sudden manifestation of Rapinavititis—the delusion that one has stolen a ship. First case ever recorded."

Turnbull stood for an instant staggered into stillness. Then he ran raging round the garden to find MacIan, just as a husband, even a bad husband, will run raging to find his wife if he is full of a furious query. He found MacIan stalking moodily about the half-lit garden, after his extraordinary meeting with Beatrice. No one who saw his slouching stride and sunken head could have known that his soul was in the seventh heaven of ecstasy. He did not think; he did not even very definitely desire. He merely wallowed in memories, chiefly in material memories; words said with a certain cadence or trivial turns of the neck or wrist. Into the middle of his stationary and senseless enjoyment were thrust abruptly the projecting elbow and the projecting red beard of Turnbull. MacIan stepped back a little, and the soul in his eyes came very slowly to its windows. When James Turnbull had the glittering sword-point planted upon his breast he was in far less danger. For three pulsating seconds after the interruption MacIan was in a mood to have murdered his father.

And yet his whole emotional anger fell from him when he saw Turnbull's face, in which the eyes seemed to be bursting from the head like bullets. All the fire and fragrance even of young and honourable love faded for a moment before that stiff agony of interrogation.

"Are you hurt, Turnbull?" he asked, anxiously.

"I am dying," answered the other quite calmly. "I am in the quite literal sense of the words dying to know something. I want to know what all this can possibly mean."

MacIan did not answer, and he continued with asperity: "You are still thinking about that girl, but I tell you the whole thing is incredible. She's not the only person here. I've met that fellow Wilkinson, whose yacht we lost. I've met the very magistrate you were hauled up to when you broke my window. What can it mean—meeting all these old people again? One never meets such old friends again except in a dream."

Then after a silence he cried with a rending sincerity: "Are you really there, Evan? Have you ever been really there? Am I simply dreaming?"

MacIan had been listening with a living silence to every word, and now his face flamed with one of his rare revelations of life.

"No, you good atheist," he cried; "no, you clean, courteous, reverent, pious old blasphemer. No, you are not dreaming—you are waking up."

"What do you mean?"

"There are two states where one meets so many old friends," said MacIan; "one is a dream, the other is the end of the world."

"And you say——"

"I say this is not a dream," said Evan in a ringing voice.

"You really mean to suggest—" began Turnbull.

"Be silent! or I shall say it all wrong," said MacIan, breathing hard. "It's hard to explain, anyhow. An apocalypse is the opposite of a dream. A dream is falser than the outer life. But the end of the world is more actual than the world it ends. I don't say this is really the end of the world, but it's something like that—it's the end of something. All the people are crowding into one corner. Everything is coming to a point."

"What is the point?" asked Turnbull.

"I can't see it," said Evan; "it is too large and plain."

Then after a silence he said: "I can't see it—and yet I will try to describe it. Turnbull, three days ago I saw quite suddenly that our duel was not right, after all."

"Three days ago!" repeated Turnbull. "When and why did this illumination occur?"

"I knew I was not quite right," answered Evan, "the moment I saw the round eyes of that old man in the cell."

"Old man in the cell!" repeated his wondering companion. "Do you mean the poor old idiot who likes spikes to stick out?"

"Yes," said MacIan, after a slight pause, "I mean the poor old idiot who likes spikes to stick out. When I saw his eyes and heard his old croaking accent, I knew that it would not really have been right to kill you. It would have been a venial sin."

"I am much obliged," said Turnbull, gruffly.

"You must give me time," said MacIan, quite patiently, "for I am try-ing to tell the whole truth. I am trying to tell more of it than I know."

"So you see I confess"—he went on with laborious distinctness—"I confess that all the people who called our duel mad were right in a way. I would confess it to old Cumberland Vane and his eye-glass. I would confess it even to that old ass in brown flannel who talked to us about Love. Yes, they are right in a way. I am a little mad."

He stopped and wiped his brow as if he were literally doing heavy labour. Then he went on:

"I am a little mad; but, after all, it is only a little madness. When hundreds of high-minded men had fought duels about a jostle with the elbow or the ace of spades, the whole world need not have gone wild over my one little wildness. Plenty of other people have killed themselves between then and now. But all England has gone into captivity in order to take us captive. All England has turned into a lunatic asylum in order to prove us lunatics. Compared with the gen-eral public, I might positively be called sane."

He stopped again, and went on with the same air of travailing with the truth:

"When I saw that, I saw everything; I saw the Church and the world. The Church in its earthly action has really touched morbid things—tortures and bleeding visions and blasts of extermination. The Church has had her madnesses, and I am one of them. I am the massacre of St. Bartholomew.[158] I am the Inquisition of Spain.[159] I do not say that we have never gone mad, but I say that we are fit to act as keepers to our enemies. Massacre is wicked even with a provocation, as in the Bar-tholomew. But your modern Nietzsche will tell you that massacre would be glorious without a provocation. Torture should be violently stopped, though the Church is doing it. But your modern Tolstoy will tell you that it ought not to be violently stopped whoever is doing it. In the long run, which is most mad—the Church or the world? Which is madder, the Spanish priest who permitted tyranny, or the Prussian sophist who

---

[158] The St. Bartholomew's Day Massacre: see n. 63.

[159] The Inquisition of Spain was a tribunal for prosecuting heresy founded in the fifteenth century and abolished in 1834.

admired it? Which is madder, the Russian priest who discourages righteous rebellion, or the Russian novelist who forbids it? That is the final and the blasting test. The world left to itself grows wilder than any creed. A few days ago you and I were the maddest people in England. Now, by God! I believe we are the sanest. That is the only real question—whether the Church is really madder than the world. Let the rationalists run their own race, and let us see where *they* end. If the world has some healthy balance other than God, let the world find it. Does the world find it? Cut the world loose," he cried with a savage gesture. "Does the world stand on its own end? Does it stand, or does it stagger?"

Turnbull remained silent, and MacIan said to him, looking once more at the earth: "It staggers, Turnbull. It cannot stand by itself; you know it cannot. It has been the sorrow of your life. Turnbull, this garden is not a dream, but an apocalyptic fulfilment. This garden is the world gone mad."

Turnbull did not move his head, and he had been listening all the time; yet, somehow, the other knew that for the first time he was listening seriously.

"The world has gone mad," said MacIan, "and it has gone mad about Us. The world takes the trouble to make a big mistake about every little mistake made by the Church. That is why they have turned ten counties to a madhouse; that is why crowds of kindly people are poured into this filthy melting-pot. Now is the judgment of this world. The Prince of this World is judged, and he is judged exactly because he is judging. There is at last one simple solution to the quarrel between the ball and the cross——"

Turnbull for the first time started.

"The ball and——" he repeated.

"What is the matter with you?" asked MacIan.

"I had a dream," said Turnbull, thickly and obscurely, "in which I saw the cross struck crooked and the ball secure——"

"I had a dream," said MacIan, "in which I saw the cross erect and the ball invisible. They were both dreams from hell. There must be some round earth to plant the cross upon. But here is the awful difference—that the round world will not consent even to continue round. The astronomers are always telling us that it is shaped like an orange, or like an egg, or like a German sausage. They beat the old world about like a bladder and thump it into a thousand shapeless shapes. Turnbull, we cannot trust the ball to be always a ball; we cannot trust reason to be reasonable. In the end the great terrestrial globe will go quite lop-sided, and only the cross will stand upright."

There was a long silence, and then Turnbull said, hesitatingly: "Has it occurred to you that since—since those two dreams, or whatever they were——"

"Well?" murmured MacIan.

"Since then," went on Turnbull, in the same low voice, "since then we have never even looked for our swords."

"You are right," answered Evan almost inaudibly. "We have found something which we both hate more than we ever hated each other, and I think I know its name."

Turnbull seemed to frown and flinch for a moment. "It does not much matter what you call it," he said, "so long as you keep out of its way."

The bushes broke and snapped abruptly behind them, and a very tall figure towered above Turnbull with an arrogant stoop and a projecting chin, a chin of which the shape showed queerly even in its shadow upon the path.

"You see that is not so easy," said MacIan between his teeth.

They looked up into the eyes of the Master, but looked only for a moment. The eyes were full of a frozen and icy wrath, a kind of utterly heartless hatred. His voice was for the first time devoid of irony. There was no more sarcasm in it than there is in an iron club.

"You will be inside the building in three minutes," he said, with pulverising precision, "or you will be fired on by the artillery at all the windows. There is too much talking in this garden; we intend to close it. You will be accommodated indoors."

"Ah!" said MacIan, with a long and satisfied sigh, "then I was right."

And he turned his back and walked obediently toward the building. Turnbull seemed to canvass for a few minutes the notion of knocking the Master down, and then fell under the same almost fairy fatalism as his companion. In some strange way it did seem that the more smoothly they yielded, the more swiftly would events sweep on to some great collision.

XX

DIES IRÆ

As they advanced toward the asylum they looked up at its rows on rows of windows, and understood the Master's material threat. By means of that complex but concealed machinery which ran like a network of nerves over the whole fabric, there had been shot out under every window-ledge rows and rows of polished-steel cylinders, the cold miracles of modern gunnery. They commanded the whole garden and the whole country side, and could have blown to pieces an army corps.

This silent declaration of war had evidently had its complete effect. As MacIan and Turnbull walked steadily but slowly toward the entrance hall of the institution, they could see that most, or at least many, of the patients had already gathered there as well as the staff of doctors and the whole regiment of keepers and assistants. But when they entered the lamp-lit hall, and the high iron door was clashed to and locked behind them, yet a new amazement leapt into their eyes, and the stalwart Turnbull almost fell. For he saw a sight which was indeed, as MacIan had said—either the Day of Judgment or a dream.

Within a few feet of him at one corner of the square of standing people stood the girl he had known in Jersey, Madeleine Durand. She looked straight at him with a steady smile which lit up that scene of darkness and unreason like the light of some honest fireside. Her square face and throat were thrown back, as her habit was, and there was something almost sleepy in the geniality of her eyes. He saw her first, and for a few seconds saw her only; then the outer edge of his eyesight took in all the other staring faces, and he saw all the faces he had ever seen for weeks and months past. There was the Tolstoyan in Jaeger flannel, with the yellow beard that went backward and the foolish nose and eyes that went forward, with the

The term *dies irae* (Latin for "day of wrath") is both scriptural (Rev 6:17) and liturgical, appearing in the Mass settings for the burial of the dead.

curiosity of a crank. He was talking eagerly to Mr. Gordon, the corpulent Jew shopkeeper whom they had once gagged in his own shop. There was the tipsy old Hertfordshire rustic; he was talking energetically to himself. There was not only Mr. Vane the magistrate, but the clerk of Mr. Vane, the magistrate. There was not only Miss Drake of the motor-car, but also Miss Drake's chauffeur. Nothing wild or unfamiliar could have produced upon Turnbull such a nightmare impression as that ring of familiar faces. Yet he had one intellectual shock which was greater than all the others. He stepped impulsively forward toward Madeleine, and then wavered with a kind of wild humility. As he did so he caught sight of another square face behind Madeleine's, a face with long gray whiskers and an austere stare. It was old Durand, the girl's father; and when Turnbull saw him he saw the last and worst marvel of that monstrous night. He remembered Durand; he remembered his monotonous, everlasting lucidity, his stupefyingly sensible views of everything, his colossal contentment with truisms merely because they were true. "Confound it all!" cried Turnbull to himself, "if *he* is in the asylum, there can't be any one outside." He drew nearer to Madeleine, but still doubtfully and all the more so because she still smiled at him. MacIan had already gone across to Beatrice with an air of right.

Then all these bewildered but partly amicable recognitions were cloven by a cruel voice which always made all human blood turn bitter. The Master was standing in the middle of the room surveying the scene like a great artist looking at a completed picture. Handsome as he looked, they had never seen so clearly what was really hateful in his face; and even then they could only express it by saying that the arched brows and the long emphatic chin gave it always a look of being lit from below, like the face of some infernal actor.

"This is indeed a cosy party," he said with glittering eyes.

The Master evidently meant to say more, but before he could say anything M. Durand had stepped right up to him and was speaking.

He was speaking exactly as a French bourgeois speaks to the manager of a restaurant. That is, he spoke with rattling and breathless rapidity, but with no incoherence, and therefore with no emotion. It was a steady, monotonous vivacity, which came not seemingly from passion, but merely from the reason having been sent off at a gallop. He was saying something like this:

"You refuse me my half-bottle of Médoc, the drink the most wholesome and the most customary. You refuse me the company and obedience of my daughter, which Nature herself indicates. You refuse me the beef and mutton, without pretence that it is a fast of the Church. You now forbid me the promenade, a thing necessary to a person of my age. It is useless to tell me that you do all this by law. Law rests upon the social contract. If the citizen finds himself despoiled of such pleasures and powers as he would have had even in the savage state, the social contract is annulled."

"It's no good chattering away, Monsieur," said Hutton, for the Master was silent. "The place is covered with machine guns. We've got to obey our orders, and so have you."

"The machinery is of the most perfect," assented Durand, somewhat irrelevantly; "worked by petroleum, I believe. I only ask you to admit that if such things fall below the comfort of barbarism, the social contract is annulled. It is a pretty little point of theory."

"Oh! I daresay," said Hutton.

Durand bowed quite civilly and withdrew.

"A cosy party," resumed the Master, scornfully, "and yet I believe some of you are in doubt about how we all came together. I will explain it, ladies and gentlemen; I will explain everything. To whom shall I specially address myself? To Mr. James Turnbull. He has a scientific mind."

Turnbull seemed to choke with sudden protest. The Master seemed only to cough out of pure politeness and proceeded: "Mr. Turnbull will agree with me," he said, "when I say that we long felt in scientific circles that great harm was done by such a legend as that of the Crucifixion."

Turnbull growled something which was presumably assent.

The Master went on smoothly: "It was in vain for us to urge that the incident was irrelevant; that there were many such fanatics, many such executions. We were forced to take the thing thoroughly in hand, to investigate it in the spirit of scientific history, and with the assistance of Mr. Turnbull and others we were happy in being able to announce that this alleged Crucifixion never occurred at all."

MacIan lifted his head and looked at the Master steadily, but Turnbull did not look up.

"This, we found, was the only way with all superstitions," continued the speaker; "it was necessary to deny them historically, and we have done it with great success in the case of miracles and such things. Now within our own time there arose an unfortunate fuss which threatened (as Mr. Turnbull would say) to galvanise the corpse of Christianity into a fictitious life—the alleged case of a Highland eccentric who wanted to fight for the Virgin."

MacIan, quite white, made a step forward, but the speaker did not alter his easy attitude or his flow of words. "Again we urged that this duel was not to be admired, that it was a mere brawl, but the people were ignorant and romantic. There were signs of treating this alleged Highlander and his alleged opponent as heroes. We tried all other means of arresting this reactionary hero worship. Working men who betted on the duel were imprisoned for gambling. Working men who drank the health of a duellist were imprisoned for drunkenness. But the popular excitement about the alleged duel continued, and we had to fall back on our old historical method. We investigated, on scientific principles, the story of MacIan's challenge, and we are happy to be able to inform you that the whole story of the attempted duel is a fable. There never was any challenge. There never was any man named MacIan. It is a melodramatic myth, like Calvary."

Not a soul moved save Turnbull, who lifted his head; yet there was the sense of a silent explosion.

"The whole story of the MacIan challenge," went on the Master, beaming at them all with a sinister benignity, "has been found to originate in the obsessions of a few pathological types, who are now all fortunately in our care. There is, for instance, a person here of the name of Gordon, formerly the keeper of a curiosity shop. He is a victim of the disease called Vinculomania—the impression that one has been bound or tied up. We have also a case of Fugacity (Mr. Whimpey), who imagines that he was chased by two men."

The indignant faces of the Jew shopkeeper and the Magdalen Don started out of the crowd in their indignation, but the speaker continued:

"One poor woman we have with us," he said, in a compassionate voice, "believes she was in a motor-car with two such men; this is the well-known illusion of speed on which I need not dwell. Another wretched woman has the simple egotistic mania that she has caused the duel. Madeleine Durand actually professes to have been the subject of the fight between MacIan and his enemy, a fight which, if it occurred at all, certainly began long before. But it never occurred at all. We have taken in hand every person who professed to have seen such a thing, and proved them all to be unbalanced. That is why they are here."

The Master looked round the room, just showing his perfect teeth with the perfection of artistic cruelty, exalted for a moment in the enormous simplicity of his success, and then walked across the hall and vanished through an inner door. His two lieutenants, Quayle and Hutton, were left standing at the head of the great army of servants and keepers.

"I hope we shall have no more trouble," said Dr. Quayle pleasantly enough, and addressing Turnbull, who was leaning heavily upon the back of a chair.

Still looking down, Turnbull lifted the chair an inch or two from the ground. Then he suddenly swung it above his head and sent it at the inquiring doctor with an awful crash which sent one of its wooden legs loose along the floor and crammed the doctor gasping into a corner. MacIan gave a great shout, snatched up the loose chair-leg, and, rushing on the other doctor, felled him with a blow. Twenty attendants rushed to capture the rebels; MacIan flung back three of them and Turnbull went over on top of one, when from behind them all came a shriek as of something quite fresh and frightful.

Two of the three passages leading out of the hall were choked with blue smoke. Another instant and the hall was full of the fog of it, and red sparks began to swarm like scarlet bees.

"The place is on fire!" cried Quayle with a scream of indecent terror. "Oh, who can have done it? How can it have happened?"

A light had come into Turnbull's eyes, "How did the French Revolution happen?" he asked.

"Oh, how should I know!" wailed the other.

"Then I will tell you," said Turnbull; "it happened because some people fancied that a French grocer was as respectable as he looked."

Even as he spoke, as if by confirmation, old Mr. Durand re-entered the smoky room quite placidly, wiping the petroleum from his hands with a handkerchief. He had set fire to the building in accordance with the strict principles of the social contract.

But MacIan had taken a stride forward and stood there shaken and terrible. "Now," he cried, panting, "now is the judgment of this world. The doctors will leave this place; the keepers will leave this place. They will leave us in charge of the machinery and the machine guns at the windows. But we, the lunatics, will wait to be burned alive if only we may see them go."

"How do you know we shall go?" asked Hutton, fiercely.

"You believe nothing," said MacIan, simply, "and you are insupportably afraid of death."

"So this is suicide," sneered the doctor; "a somewhat doubtful sign of sanity."

"Not at all—this is vengeance," answered Turnbull, quite calmly; "a thing which is completely healthy."

"You think the doctors will go," said Hutton, savagely.

"The keepers have gone already," said Turnbull.

Even as they spoke the main doors were burst open in mere brutal panic, and all the officers and subordinates of the asylum rushed away across the garden pursued by the smoke. But among the ticketed maniacs not a man or woman moved.

"We hate dying," said Turnbull, with composure, "but we hate you even more. This is a successful revolution."

In the roof above their heads a panel shot back, showing a strip of star-lit sky and a huge thing made of white metal, with the shape and fins of a fish, swinging as if at anchor. At the same moment a steel ladder slid down from the opening and struck the floor, and the cleft chin of the mysterious Master was thrust into the opening. "Quayle,

Hutton," he said, "you will escape with me." And they went up the ladder like automata of lead.

Long after they had clambered into the car, the creature with the cloven face continued to leer down upon the smoke-stung crowd below. Then at last he said in a silken voice and with a smile of final satisfaction:

"By the way, I fear I am very absent minded. There is one man specially whom, somehow, I always forget. I always leave him lying about. Once I mislaid him on the Cross of St. Paul's. So silly of me; and now I've forgotten him in one of those little cells where your fire is burning. Very unfortunate—especially for him." And nodding genially, he climbed into his flying ship.

MacIan stood motionless for two minutes, and then rushed down one of the suffocating corridors till he found the flames. Turnbull looked once at Madeleine, and followed.

MacIan, with singed hair, smoking garments, and smarting hands and face, had already broken far enough through the first barriers of burning timber to come within cry of the cells he had once known. It was impossible, however, to see the spot where the old man lay dead or alive; not now through darkness, but through scorching and aching light. The site of the old half-wit's cell was now the heart of a standing forest of fire—the flames as thick and yellow as a corn field. Their incessant shrieking and crackling was like a mob shouting against an orator. Yet through all that deafening density MacIan thought he heard a small and separate sound. When he heard it he rushed forward as if to plunge into that furnace, but Turnbull arrested him by an elbow.

"Let me go!" cried Evan, in agony; "it's the poor old beggar's voice—he's still alive, and shouting for help."

"Listen!" said Turnbull, and lifted one finger from his clenched hand.

"Or else he is shrieking with pain," protested MacIan. "I will not endure it."

"Listen!" repeated Turnbull, grimly. "Did you ever hear any one shout for help or shriek with pain in that voice?"

The small shrill sounds which came through the crash of the conflagration were indeed of an odd sort, and MacIan turned a face of puzzled inquiry to his companion.

"He is singing," said Turnbull, simply.

A remaining rampart fell, crushing the fire, and through the diminished din of it the voice of the little old lunatic came clearer. In the heart of that white-hot hell he was singing like a bird. What he was singing it was not very easy to follow, but it seemed to be something about playing in the golden hay.

"Good Lord!" said Turnbull, bitterly, "there seem to be some advantages in really being an idiot." Then advancing to the fringe of the fire he called out on chance to the invisible singer: "Can you come out? Are you cut off?"

"God help us all!" said MacIan, with a shudder; "he's laughing now."

At whatever stage of being burned alive the invisible now found himself, he was now shaking out peals of silvery and hilarious laughter. As he listened, MacIan's two eyes began to glow, as if a strange thought had come into his head.

"Fool, come out and save yourself!" shouted Turnbull.

"No, by Heaven! that is not the way," cried Evan, suddenly. "Father," he shouted, "come out and save us all!"

The fire, though it had dropped in one or two places, was, upon the whole, higher and more unconquerable than ever. Separate tall flames shot up and spread out above them like the fiery cloisters of some infernal cathedral, or like a grove of red tropical trees in the garden of the devil. Higher yet in the purple hollow of the night the topmost flames leapt again and again fruitlessly at the stars, like golden dragons chained but struggling. The towers and domes of the oppressive smoke seemed high and far enough to drown distant planets in a London fog. But if we exhausted all frantic similes for that frantic scene, the main impression about the fire would still be its ranked upstanding rigidity and a sort of roaring stillness. It was literally a wall of fire.

"Father," cried MacIan, once more, "come out of it and save us all!" Turnbull was staring at him as he cried.

The tall and steady forest of fire must have been already a portent visible to the whole circle of land and sea. The red flush of it lit up the long sides of white ships far out in the German Ocean, and picked out like piercing rubies the windows in the villages on the distant heights. If any villagers or sailors were looking toward it they must have seen a strange sight as MacIan cried out for the third time.

That forest of fire wavered, and was cloven in the centre; and then the whole of one half of it leaned one way as a corn field leans all one way under the load of the wind. Indeed, it looked as if a great wind had sprung up and driven the great fire aslant. Its smoke was no longer sent up to choke the stars, but was trailed and dragged across county after county like one dreadful banner of defeat.

But it was not the wind; or, if it was the wind, it was two winds blowing in opposite directions. For while one half of the huge fire sloped one way toward the inland heights, the other half, at exactly the same angle, sloped out eastward toward the sea. So that earth and ocean could behold, where there had been a mere fiery mass, a thing divided like a V—a cloven tongue of flame. But if it were a prodigy for those distant, it was something beyond speech for those quite near. As the echoes of Evan's last appeal rang and died in the universal uproar, the fiery vault over his head opened down the middle, and, reeling back in two great golden billows, hung on each side as huge and harmless as two sloping hills lie on each side of a valley. Down the centre of this trough, or chasm, a little path ran, cleared of all but ashes, and down this little path was walking a little old man singing as if he were alone in a wood in spring.

When James Turnbull saw this he suddenly put out a hand and seemed to support himself on the strong shoulder of Madeleine Durand. Then after a moment's hesitation he put his other hand on the shoulder of MacIan. His blue eyes looked extraordinarily brilliant and beautiful. In many sceptical papers and magazines afterward he was sadly or sternly rebuked for having abandoned the certainties of materialism. All his life up to that moment he had been most honestly certain that materialism was a fact. But he was unlike the writers in the magazines precisely in this—that he preferred a fact even to materialism.

As the little singing figure came nearer and nearer, Evan fell on his knees, and after an instant Beatrice followed; then Madeleine fell on her; knees, and after a longer instant Turnbull followed. Then the little old man went past them singing down that corridor of flames. They had not looked at his face.

When he had passed they looked up. While the first light of the fire had shot east and west, painting the sides of ships with fire-light or striking red sparks out of windowed houses, it had not hitherto struck upward, for there was above it the ponderous and rococo cavern of its own monstrous coloured smoke. But now the fire was turned to left and right like a woman's hair parted in the middle, and now the shafts of its light could shoot up into empty heavens and strike anything, either bird or cloud. But it struck something that was neither cloud nor bird. Far, far away up in those huge hollows of space something was flying swiftly and shining brightly, something that shone too bright and flew too fast to be any of the fowls of the air, though the red light lit it from underneath like the breast of a bird. Every one knew it was a flying ship, and every one knew whose.

As they stared upward the little speck of light seemed slightly tilted, and two black dots dropped from the edge of it. All the eager, upturned faces watched the two dots as they grew bigger and bigger in their downward rush. Then some one screamed, and no one looked up any more. For the two bodies, larger every second flying, spread out and sprawling in the fire-light, were the dead bodies of the two doctors whom Professor Lucifer had carried with him—the weak and sneering Quayle, the cold and clumsy Hutton. They went with a crash into the thick of the fire.

"They are gone!" screamed Beatrice, hiding her head. "O God! They are lost!"

Evan put his arm about her, and remembered his own vision.

"No, they are not lost," he said. "They are saved. He has taken away no souls with him, after all."

He looked vaguely about at the fire that was already fading, and there among the ashes lay two shining things that had survived the fire, his sword and Turnbull's, fallen haphazard in the pattern of a cross.

MANALIVE

1912

PART I

THE ENIGMAS OF
INNOCENT SMITH

I

HOW THE GREAT WIND CAME
TO BEACON HOUSE

A wind sprang high in the west, like a wave of unreasonable happiness, and tore eastward across England, trailing with it the frosty scent of forests and the cold intoxication of the sea. In a million holes and corners it refreshed a man like a flagon, and astonished him like a blow. In the inmost chambers of intricate and embowered houses it woke like a domestic explosion, littering the floor with some professor's papers till they seemed as precious as fugitive, or blowing out the candle by which a boy read "Treasure Island" and wrapping him in roaring dark. But everywhere it bore drama into undramatic lives, and carried the trump of crisis across the world. Many a harassed mother in a mean backyard had looked at five dwarfish shirts on the clothes-line as at some small, sick tragedy; it was as if she had hanged her five children. The wind came, and they were full and kicking as if five fat imps had sprung into them; and far down in her oppressed subconsciousness she half remembered those coarse comedies of her fathers when the elves still dwelt in the homes of men. Many an unnoticed girl in a dank walled garden had tossed herself into the hammock with the same intolerant gesture with which she might have tossed herself into the Thames; and that wind rent the waving wall of woods and lifted the hammock like a balloon, and showed her shapes of quaint cloud far beyond, and pictures of bright villages far below, as if she rode heaven in a fairy boat. Many a dusty clerk or curate, plodding a telescopic road of poplars, thought for the hundredth time that they were like the plumes of a hearse; when this invisible energy caught and swung and clashed them round his head like a wreath or salutation of seraphic wings. There was in it something more inspired and authoritative even than the old wind of the proverb; for this was the good wind that blows nobody harm.

The flying blast struck London just where it scales the northern heights, terrace above terrace, as precipitous as Edinburgh. It was round about this place that some poet, probably drunk, looked up astonished at all those streets gone skywards, and (thinking vaguely of glaciers and roped mountaineers) gave it the name of Swiss Cottage, which it has never been able to shake off. At some stage of those heights a terrace of tall gray houses, mostly empty and almost as desolate as the Grampians, curved round at the western end, so that the last building, a boarding establishment called "Beacon House," offered abruptly to the sunset its high, narrow, and towering termination, like the prow of some deserted ship.

The ship, however, was not wholly deserted. The proprietor of the boarding-house, a Mrs. Duke, was one of those helpless persons upon whom fate wars in vain; she smiled vaguely both before and after all her calamities; she was too soft to be hurt. But by the aid (or rather under the orders) of a strenuous niece she always kept the remains of a clientele, mostly of young but listless folks. And there were actually five inmates standing disconsolately about the garden when the great gale broke at the base of the terminal tower behind them, as the sea bursts against the base of an outstanding cliff.

All day that hill of houses over London had been domed and sealed up with cold cloud. Yet three men and two girls had at last found even the gray and chilly garden more tolerable than the black and cheerless interior. When the wind came it split the sky and shouldered the cloudland left and right, unbarring great clear furnaces of evening gold. The burst of light released and the burst of air blowing seemed to come almost simultaneously; and the wind especially caught everything in a throttling violence. The bright short grass lay all one way like brushed hair. Every shrub in the garden tugged at its roots like a dog at the collar, and strained every leaping leaf after the hunting and exterminating element. Now and again a twig would snap and fly like a bolt from an arbalist. The three men stood stiffly and aslant against the wind, as if leaning against a wall. The two ladies disappeared into the house; rather, to speak truly, they were blown into the house. Their two frocks, blue and white, looked like two big broken flowers, driving and drifting upon the gale. Nor is such a poetic fancy inappropriate, for there was something oddly romantic about this inrush of air and light after a long, leaden, and unlifting day. Grass and garden trees seemed glittering with something at once good and unnatural, like a fire from fairyland. It seemed like a strange sunrise at the wrong end of the day.

The girl in white dived in quickly enough, for she wore a white hat of the proportions of a parachute, which might have wafted her away into the coloured clouds of evening. She was their one splash of splendour, and irradiated wealth in that impecunious place (staying there temporarily with a friend), an heiress in a small way, by name Rosamund Hunt, brown-eyed, round-faced, but resolute and rather boisterous. On top of her wealth she was good-humoured and rather good-looking; but she had not married, perhaps because there was always a crowd of men round her. She was not fast (though some might have called her vulgar), but she gave irresolute youths an impression of being at once popular and inaccessible. A man felt as if he had fallen in love with Cleopatra, or as if he were asking for a great actress at the stage door. Indeed, some theatrical spangles seemed to cling about Miss Hunt: she played the guitar and the mandoline; she always wanted charades; and with that great rending of the sky by sun and storm, she felt a girlish melodrama swell again within her. To the crashing orchestration of the air the clouds rose like the curtain of some long-expected pantomime.

Nor, oddly enough, was the girl in blue entirely unimpressed by this apocalypse in a private garden; though she was one of the most prosaic and practical creatures alive. She was, indeed, no other than the strenuous niece whose strength alone upheld that mansion of decay. But as the gale swung and swelled the blue and white skirts till they took on the monstrous mushroom contours of Victorian crinolines, a sunken memory stirred in her that was almost romance—a memory of a dusty volume of *Punch*[1] in an aunt's house in infancy: pictures of crinoline hoops and croquet hoops and some pretty story, of which perhaps they were a part. This half-perceptible fragrance in her thoughts faded almost instantly, and Diana Duke entered the house even more

[1] *Punch* was an English humor and social commentary magazine famed for its clever illustrations and cartoons. Founded in 1841 it eventually ceased publication in June 2002.

promptly than her companion. Tall, slim, aquiline, and dark, she seemed made for such swiftness. In body she was of the breed of those birds and beasts that are at once long and alert, like greyhounds or herons or even like an innocent snake. The whole house revolved on her as on a rod of steel. It would be wrong to say that she commanded; for her own efficiency was so impatient that she obeyed herself before any one else obeyed her. Before electricians could mend a bell or locksmiths open a door, before dentists could pluck a loose tooth or butlers draw a tight cork, it was done already with the silent violence of her slim hands. She was light; but there was nothing leaping about her lightness. She spurned the ground, and she meant to spurn it. People talk of the pathos and failure of plain women; but it is a more terrible thing that a beautiful woman may succeed in everything but womanhood.

"It's enough to blow your head off," said the young woman in white, going to the looking-glass.

The young woman in blue made no reply, but put away her gardening gloves, and then went to the sideboard and began to spread out an afternoon cloth for tea.

"Enough to blow your head off, I say," said Miss Rosamund Hunt, with the unruffled cheeriness of one whose songs and speeches had always been safe for an encore.

"Only your hat, I think," said Diana Duke; "but I dare say that is sometimes more important."

Rosamund's face showed for an instant the offence of a spoilt child, and then the humour of a very healthy person. She broke into a laugh and said, "Well, it would have to be a big wind to blow your head off."

There was another silence; and the sunset breaking more and more from the sundering clouds, filled the room with soft fire and painted the dull walls with ruby and gold.

"Somebody once told me," said Rosamund Hunt, "that it's easier to keep one's head when one has lost one's heart."

"Oh, don't talk about such rubbish," said Diana with savage sharpness.

Outside, the garden was clad in a golden splendour; but the wind was still stiffly blowing, and the three men who stood their ground might also have considered the problem of hats and heads. And, indeed, their position, touching hats, was somewhat typical of them. The tallest of the three abode the blast in a high silk hat, which the wind seemed to charge as vainly as that other sullen tower, the house behind him. The second man tried to hold on a stiff straw hat at all angles, and ultimately held it in his hand. The third had no hat, and, by his attitude, seemed never to have had one in his life. Perhaps this wind was a kind of fairy wand to test men and women, for there was much of the three men in this difference.

The man in the solid silk hat was the embodiment of silkiness and solidity. He was a big, bland, bored, and (as some said) boring man, with flat fair hair and handsome heavy features; a prosperous young doctor by the name of Warner. But if his blondness and blandness seemed at first a little fatuous, it is certain that he was no fool. If Rosamund Hunt was the only person there with much money, he was the only person who had as yet found any kind of fame. His treatise on "The Probable Existence of Pain in the Lowest Organisms" had been universally hailed by the scientific world as at once solid and daring. In short, he undoubtedly had brains; and perhaps it was not his fault if they were the kind of brains that most men desire to analyze with a poker.

The young man who put his hat off and on was a scientific amateur in a small way, and worshipped the great Warner with a solemn freshness. It was, in fact, at his invitation that the distinguished doctor was present; for Warner lived in no such ramshackle lodging-house, but in a professional palace in Harley Street. This young man was really the youngest and best looking of the three. But he was one of those persons, both male and female, who seem doomed to be good-looking and insignificant. Brown-haired, high-coloured, and shy, he seemed to lose the delicacy of his features in a sort of blur of brown and red as he stood blushing and blinking against the wind. He was one of those obvious unnoticeable people: every one knew that he was Arthur Inglewood, unmarried, moral, decidedly intelligent, living on a little money of his own, and hiding himself in the two hobbies of photography and cycling. Everybody knew him and forgot him; even as he stood there in the glare of golden sunset there was something about him indistinct, like one of his own red-brown amateur photographs.

The third man had no hat; he was lean, in light, vaguely sporting clothes, and the large pipe in his mouth made him look all the leaner. He had a long ironical face, blue-black hair, the blue eyes of an Irishman, and the blue chin of an actor. An Irishman he was, an actor he was not, except in the old days of Miss Hunt's charades, being, as a matter of fact, an obscure and flippant journalist named Michael Moon. He had once been hazily supposed to be reading for the Bar; but (as Warner would say with his rather elephantine wit) it was mostly at another kind of bar that his friends found him. Moon, however, did not drink, nor even frequently get drunk; he simply was a gentleman who liked low company. This was partly because company is quieter than society: and if he enjoyed talking to a barmaid (as apparently he did), it was chiefly because the barmaid did the talking. Moreover he would often bring other talent to assist her. He shared that strange trick of all men of his type, intellectual and without ambition—the trick of going about with his mental inferiors. There was a small resilient Jew named Moses Gould in the same boarding-house, a little man whose negro vitality and vulgarity amused Michael so much that he went round with him from bar to bar, like the owner of a performing monkey.

The colossal clearance which the wind had made of that cloudy sky grew clearer and clearer; chamber within chamber seemed to open in heaven. One felt one might at last find something lighter than light. In the fullness of this silent effulgence all things collected their colours again: the gray trunks turned silver, and the drab gravel gold. One bird fluttered like a loosened leaf from one tree to another, and his brown feathers were brushed with fire.

"Inglewood," said Michael Moon, with his blue eye on the bird, "have you any friends?"

Dr. Warner mistook the person addressed, and turning a broad beaming face, said,—

"Oh yes, I go out a great deal."

Michael Moon gave a tragic grin, and waited for his real informant, who spoke a moment after in a voice curiously cool, fresh and young, as coming out of that brown and even dusty exterior.

"Really," answered Inglewood, "I'm afraid I've lost touch with my old friends. The greatest friend I ever had was at school, a fellow named Smith. It's odd you should mention it, because I was thinking of him to-day, though I haven't seen him for seven or eight years. He was on the science side with me at school—a clever fellow though queer; and he went up to Oxford when I went to Germany. The fact is, it's rather a sad story. I often asked him to come and see me, and when I heard nothing I made inquiries, you know. I was shocked to learn that poor Smith had gone off his head. The accounts were a bit cloudy, of course, some saying he had recovered again; but they always say that. About a year ago I got a telegram from him myself. The telegram, I'm sorry to say, put the matter beyond a doubt."

"Quite so," assented Dr. Warner stolidly; "insanity is generally incurable."

"So is sanity," said the Irishman, and studied him with a dreary eye.

"Symptoms?" asked the doctor. "What was this telegram?"

"It's a shame to joke about such things," said Inglewood, in his honest, embarrassed way; "the telegram was Smith's illness, not Smith. The actual words were, 'Man found alive with two legs.' "

"Alive with two legs," repeated Michael, frowning. "Perhaps a version of alive and kicking? I don't know much about people out of their senses; but I suppose they ought to be kicking."

"And people in their senses?" asked Warner, smiling.

"Oh, they ought to be kicked," said Michael with sudden heartiness.

"The message is clearly insane," continued the impenetrable Warner. "The best test is a reference to the undeveloped normal type. Even a baby does not expect to find a man with three legs."

"Three legs," said Michael Moon, "would be very convenient in this wind."

A fresh eruption of the atmosphere had indeed almost thrown them off their balance and broken the blackened trees in the garden. Beyond, all sorts of accidental objects could be seen scouring the wind-scoured sky—straws, sticks, rags, papers, and, in the distance, a disappearing hat. Its disappearance, however, was not final; after an interval of minutes they saw it again, much larger and closer, a white panama, towering up into the heavens like a balloon, staggering to and fro for an instant like a stricken kite, and then settling in the centre of their own lawn as falteringly as a fallen leaf.

"Somebody's lost a good hat," said Dr. Warner shortly.

Almost as he spoke, another object came over the garden wall, flying after the fluttering panama. It was a big green umbrella. After that came hurtling a huge yellow Gladstone bag, and after that came a figure like a flying wheel of legs, as in the shield of the Isle of Man.

But though for a flash it seemed to have five or six legs, it alighted upon two, like the man in the queer telegram. It took the form of a large light-haired man in gay green holiday clothes. He had bright blonde hair that the wind brushed back like a German's, a flushed eager face like a cherub's, and a prominent pointing nose, a little like a dog's. His head, however, was by no means cherubic in the sense of being without a body. On the contrary, on his vast shoulders and shape generally gigantesque, his head looked oddly and unnaturally small. This gave rise to a scientific theory (which his conduct fully supported) that he was an idiot.

Inglewood had a politeness instinctive and yet awkward. His life was full of arrested half gestures of assistance. And even this prodigy of a big man in green, leaping the wall like a bright green grasshopper, did not paralyze that small altruism of his habits in such a matter as a lost hat. He was stepping forward to recover the green gentleman's head-gear, when he was struck rigid with a roar like a bull's.

"Unsportsmanlike!" bellowed the big man. "Give it fair play, give it fair play!" And he came after his own hat quickly but cautiously, with burning eyes. The hat had seemed at first to droop and dawdle as in ostentatious languor on the sunny lawn; but the wind again freshening and rising, it went dancing down the garden with the devilry of a *pas de quatre*.[2] The eccentric went bounding after it with kangaroo leaps and bursts of breathless speech, of which it was not always easy to pick up the thread: "Fair play, fair play . . . sport of kings . . . chase their crowns . . . quite humane . . . tramontana . . . cardinals chase red hats . . . old English hunting . . . started a hat in Bramber Combe . . . hat at bay . . . mangled hounds. . . . Got him!"

[2] A *pas de quatre* is a dance for four persons.

As the wind rose out of a roar into a shriek, he leapt into the sky on his strong, fantastic legs, snatched at the vanishing hat, missed it, and pitched sprawling face foremost on the grass. The hat rose over him like a bird in triumph. But its triumph was premature; for the lunatic, flung forward on his hands, threw up his boots behind, waved his two legs in the air like symbolic ensigns (so that they thought again of the telegram), and actually caught the hat with his feet. A prolonged and piercing yell of wind split the welkin from end to end. The eyes of all the men were blinded by the invisible blast, as by a strange, clear cataract of transparency rushing between them and all objects about them. But as the large man fell back in a sitting posture and solemnly crowned himself with the hat, Michael found, to his incredulous surprise, that he had been holding his breath, like a man watching a duel.

While that tall wind was at the top of its sky-scraping energy, another short cry was heard, beginning very querulous, but ending very quick, swallowed in abrupt silence. The shiny black cylinder of Dr. Warner's official hat sailed off his head in the long, smooth parabola of an airship, and in almost cresting a garden tree was caught in the topmost branches. Another hat was gone. Those in that garden felt themselves caught in an unaccustomed eddy of things happening; no one seemed to know what would blow away next. Before they could speculate, the cheering and hallooing hat-hunter was already halfway up the tree, swinging himself from fork to fork with his strong, bent, grasshopper legs, and still giving forth his gasping, mysterious comments.

"Tree of life ... Ygdrasil[3] ... climb for centuries perhaps ... owls nesting in the hat ... remotest generations of owls ... still usurpers ... gone to heaven ... man in the moon wears it ... brigand ... not yours ... belongs to depressed medical man ... in garden ... give it up ... give it up!"

The tree swung and swept and thrashed to and fro in the thundering wind like a thistle, and flamed in the full sunshine like a bonfire. The green, fantastic human figure, vivid against its autumn red and gold, was already among its highest and craziest branches, which by

---

[3] In Norse mythology, Ygdrasil is the great ash tree whose roots and branches hold together the universe.

bare luck did not break with the weight of his big body. He was up there among the last tossing leaves and the first twinkling stars of evening, still talking to himself cheerfully, reasoningly, half apologetically, in little gasps. He might well be out of breath, for his whole preposterous raid had gone with one rush; he had bounded the wall once like a football, swept down the garden like a slide, and shot up the tree like a rocket. The other three men seemed buried under incident piled on incident—a wild world where one thing began before another thing left off. All three had the first thought. The tree had been there for the five years they had known the boarding-house. Each one of them was active and strong. No one of them had even thought of climbing it. Beyond that, Inglewood felt first the mere fact of colour. The bright brisk leaves, the bleak blue sky, the wild green arms and legs, reminded him irrationally of something glowing in his infancy, something akin to a gaudy man on a golden tree; perhaps it was only a painted monkey on a stick. Oddly enough, Michael Moon, though more of a humorist, was touched on a tenderer nerve, half remembered the old, young theatricals with Rosamund, and was amused to find himself almost quoting Shakespeare—

> "For valour. Is not love a Hercules,
>   Still climbing trees in the Hesperides?"[4]

Even the immovable man of science had a bright, bewildered sensation that the Time Machine had given a great jerk, and gone forward with rather rattling rapidity.

He was not, however, wholly prepared for what happened next. The man in green, riding the frail topmost bough like a witch on a very risky broomstick, reached up and rent the black hat from its airy nest of twigs. It had been broken across a heavy bough in the first burst of its passage, a tangle of branches had torn and scored and scratched it in every direction, a clap of wind and foliage had flattened it like a concertina; nor can it be said that the obliging gentleman with the sharp nose showed any adequate tenderness for

---

[4] The quoted lines come from William Shakespeare's play *Love's Labour's Lost* (1595), act 4, scene 3, line 340.

its structure when he finally unhooked it from its place. When he had found it, however, his proceedings were by some counted singular. He waved it with a loud whoop of triumph, and then immediately appeared to fall backwards off the tree, to which, however, he remained attached by his long strong legs, like a monkey swung by his tail. Hanging thus head downwards above the un-helmed Warner, he gravely proceeded to drop the battered silk cylinder upon his brows. "Every man a king," explained the inverted philosopher; "every hat [consequently] a crown. But this is a crown out of heaven."

And he again attempted the coronation of Warner, who, however, moved away with great abruptness from the hovering diadem; not seeming, strangely enough, to wish for his former decoration in its present state.

"Wrong, wrong!" cried the obliging person hilariously. "Always wear uniform, even if it's shabby uniform! Ritualists may always be untidy. Go to a dance with soot on your shirt-front; but go with a shirt-front. Huntsman wears old coat, but old pink coat. Wear a top-per, even if it's got no top. It's the symbol that counts, old cock. Take your hat, because it is your hat after all; its nap rubbed all off by the bark, dears, and its brim not the least bit curled; but for old sakes' sake it is still, dears, the nobbiest tile in the world."

Speaking thus, with a wild comfortableness, he settled or smashed the shapeless silk hat over the face of the disturbed physician, and fell on his feet among the other men, still talking, beaming and breathless.

"Why don't they make more games out of the wind?" he asked in some excitement. "Kites are all right, but why should it only be kites? Why, I thought of three other games for a windy day while I was climbing that tree. Here's one of them: you take a lot of pepper——"

"I think," interposed Moon, with a sardonic mildness, "that your games are already sufficiently interesting. Are you, may I ask, a professional acrobat on a tour, or a travelling advertisement of Sunny Jim? How and why do you display all this energy for clearing walls and climbing trees in our melancholy, but at least rational, suburbs?"

The stranger, so far as so loud a person was capable of it, appeared to grow confidential.

"Well, it's a trick of my own," he confessed candidly. "I do it by having two legs."

Arthur Inglewood, who had sunk into the background of this scene of folly, started and stared at the newcomer with his short-sighted eyes screwed up and his high colour slightly heightened.

"Why, I believe you're Smith," he cried with his fresh, almost boyish voice; and then after an instant's stare, "and yet I'm not sure."

"I have a card, I think," said the unknown, with baffling solemnity—"a card with my real name, my titles, offices, and true purpose on this earth."

He drew out slowly from an upper waist-coat pocket a scarlet card-case, and as slowly produced a very large card. Even in the instant of its production, they fancied it was of a queer shape, unlike the cards of ordinary gentlemen. But it was there only for an instant; for as it passed from his fingers to Arthur's, one or other slipped his hold. The strident, tearing gale in that garden carried away the stranger's card to join the wild waste paper of the universe; and that great western wind shook the whole house and passed.

II

THE LUGGAGE OF AN OPTIMIST

We all remember the fairy tales of science in our infancy, which played with the supposition that large animals could jump in the proportion of small ones. If an elephant were as strong as a grasshopper, he could (I suppose) spring clean out of the Zoological Gardens and alight trumpeting upon Primrose Hill. If a whale could leap from the water like a trout, perhaps men might look up and see one soaring above Yarmouth like the winged island of Laputa.[5] Such natural energy, though sublime, might certainly be inconvenient, and much of this inconvenience attended the gaiety and good intentions of the man in green. He was too large for everything, because he was lively as well as large. By a fortunate physical provision, most very substantial creatures are also reposeful; and middle-class boarding-houses in the lesser parts of London are not built for a man as big as a bull and as excitable as a kitten.

When Inglewood followed the stranger into the boarding-house, he found him talking earnestly (and in his own opinion privately) to the helpless Mrs. Duke. That fat, faint lady could only goggle up like a dying fish at the enormous new gentleman, who politely offered himself as lodger, with vast gestures of the wide white hat in one hand and the yellow Gladstone bag in the other. Fortunately, Mrs. Duke's more efficient niece and partner was there to complete the contract; for, indeed, all the people of the house had somehow collected in the room. This fact, in truth, was typical of the whole episode. The visitor created an atmosphere of comic crisis; and from the time he came into the house to the time he left it, he somehow got the company to gather and even follow (though in derision), as children gather and follow a Punch and

---

[5] The winged island of Laputa is the flying island visited by Lemuel Gulliver on one of his voyages in the fantastic novel *Gulliver's Travels*, written by Anglo-Irish poet and satirist Jonathan Swift (1667–1745).

Judy.[6] An hour ago, and for four years previously, these people had avoided each other, even when they really liked each other. They had slid in and out of dismal and deserted rooms in search of particular newspapers or private needlework. Even now they all came casually, as with varying interests; but they all came. There was the embarrassed Inglewood, still a sort of red shadow; there also the unembarrassed Warner, a pallid but solid substance. There was Michael Moon offering like a riddle the contrast of the horsy crudeness of his clothes and the sombre sagacity of his visage. He was now joined by his yet more comic crony, Moses Gould. Swaggering on short legs with a prosperous purple tie, he was the gayest of godless little dogs; but like a dog also in this, that however he danced and wagged with delight, the two dark eyes on each side of his protuberant nose glistened gloomily like black buttons. There was Miss Rosamund Hunt, still with the fine white hat framing her square, good-humoured face, and still with her native air of being dressed for some party that never came off. She also, like Mr. Moon, had a new companion, new so far as this narrative goes, but in reality an old friend and protégée. This was a slight young woman in dark gray, and in no way notable but for a load of dull red hair, of which the shape somehow gave her pale face that triangular, almost peaked, appearance which was given by the lowering headdress and deep rich ruff of the Elizabethan beauties. Her surname seemed to be Gray, and Miss Hunt called her Mary, in that indescribable tone applied to an old dependent who has practically become a friend. She wore a small silver cross on her very business-like gray clothes, and was the only member of the party who went to church. Last, but the reverse of least, there was Diana Duke, studying the newcomer with eyes of steel, and listening carefully to every idiotic word he said. As for Mrs. Duke, she smiled up at him, but never dreamed of listening to him. She had never really listened to any one in her life; which, some said, was why she had survived.

---

[6] "Punch and Judy" was an English puppet show probably introduced from Europe in the seventeenth century and set up frequently in public parks, where crowds (usually children) would gather to watch the show.

Nevertheless, Mrs. Duke was pleased with her new guest's concentration of courtesy upon herself; for no one ever spoke seriously to her any more than she listened seriously to any one. And she almost beamed as the stranger, with yet wider and almost whirling gestures of explanation with his huge hat and bag, apologized for having entered by the wall instead of the front door. He was understood to put it down to an unfortunate family tradition of neatness and care of his clothes.

"My mother was rather strict about it, to tell the truth," he said, lowering his voice, to Mrs. Duke. "She never liked me to lose my cap at school. And when a man's been taught to be tidy and neat it sticks to him."

Mrs. Duke weakly gasped that she was sure he must have had a good mother; but her niece seemed inclined to probe the matter further.

"You've got a funny idea of neatness," she said, "if it's jumping garden walls and clambering up garden trees. A man can't very well climb a tree tidily."

"He can clear a wall neatly," said Michael Moon; "I saw him do it."

Smith seemed to be regarding the girl with genuine astonishment. "My dear young lady," he said, "I was tidying the tree. You don't want last year's hats there, do you, any more than last year's leaves? The wind takes off the leaves, but it couldn't manage the hat; that wind, I suppose, has tidied whole forests to-day. Rum idea this is, that tidiness is a timid, quiet sort of thing; why, tidiness is a toil for giants. You can't tidy anything without untidying yourself; just look at my trousers. Don't you know that? Haven't you ever had a spring cleaning?"

"Oh yes, sir," said Mrs. Duke, almost eagerly. "You will find everything of that sort quite nice." For the first time she had heard two words that she could understand.

Miss Diana Duke seemed to be studying the stranger in a sort of spasm of calculation; then her black eyes snapped with decision, and she said that he could have a particular bedroom on the top floor if he liked: and the silent and sensitive Inglewood, who had been on the rack through these cross-purposes, eagerly offered to show him up to the room. Smith went up the stairs four at a time, and when he bumped his head against the ultimate ceiling, Inglewood had an odd sensation that the tall house was much shorter than it used to be.

Arthur Inglewood followed his old friend—or his new friend, for he did not very clearly know which he was. The face looked very like his old schoolfellow's at one second and very unlike at another. And when Inglewood broke through his native politeness so far as to say suddenly, "Is your name Smith?" he received only the unenlightening reply, "Quite right; quite right. Very good. Excellent!" Which appeared to Inglewood, on reflection, rather the speech of a new-born babe accepting a name than of a grown-up man admitting one.

Despite these doubts about identity, the hapless Inglewood watched the other unpack, and stood about his bedroom in all the impotent attitudes of the male friend. Mr. Smith unpacked with the same kind of whirling accuracy with which he climbed a tree—throwing things out of his bag as if they were rubbish, yet managing to distribute quite a regular pattern all round him on the floor.

As he did so he continued to talk in the same somewhat gasping manner (he had come upstairs four steps at a time, but even without this his style of speech was breathless and fragmentary), and his remarks were still a string of more or less significant but often separate pictures.

"Like the day of judgment," he said, throwing a bottle so that it somehow settled, rocking on its right end. "People say vast universe ... infinity and astronomy; not sure ... I think things are too close together ... packed up; for travelling ... stars too close really ... why, the sun's a star, too close to be seen properly; the earth's a star, too close to be seen at all ... too many pebbles on the beach; ought all to be put in rings; too many blades of grass to study ... feathers on a bird make the brain reel; wait till the big bag is unpacked ... may all be put in our right places then."

Here he stopped, literally for breath—throwing a shirt to the other end of the room, and then a bottle of ink so that it fell quite neatly beyond it. Inglewood looked round on this strange, half-symmetrical disorder with an increasing doubt.

In fact, the more one explored Mr. Smith's holiday luggage, the less one could make anything of it. One peculiarity of it was that almost everything seemed to be there for the wrong reason; what is secondary with every one else was primary with him. He would wrap up a pot or pan in brown paper; and the unthinking assistant would discover that the pot was valueless or even unnecessary, and that it was the brown paper that was truly precious. He produced two or three boxes of cigars, and explained with plain and perplexing sincerity that he was no smoker, but that cigar-box wood was by far the best for fretwork. He also exhibited about six small bottles of wine, white and red; and Inglewood, happening to note a Volnay[7] which he knew to be excellent, supposed at first that the stranger was an epicure in vintages. He was therefore surprised to find that the next bottle was a vile sham claret from the colonies, which even colonials (to do them justice) do not drink. It was only then that he observed that all six bottles had those bright metallic seals of various tints, and seemed to have been chosen solely because they gave the three primary and three secondary colours: red, blue, and yellow; green, violet, and orange. There grew upon Inglewood an almost creepy sense of the real child-ishness of this creature. For Smith was really, so far as human psychol-ogy can be, innocent. He had the sensualities of innocence: he loved the stickiness of gum, and he cut white wood greedily as if he were cutting a cake. To this man wine was not a doubtful thing to be defended or denounced; it was a quaintly-coloured syrup, such as a child sees in a shop window. He talked dominantly and rushed the social situation; but he was not asserting himself, like a superman in a modern play. He was simply forgetting himself, like a little boy at a party. He had somehow made a giant stride from babyhood to man-hood, and missed that crisis in youth when most of us grow old.

As he shunted his big bag, Arthur observed the initials I. S. printed on one side of it, and remembered that Smith had been called Inno-cent Smith at school, though whether as a formal Christian name or a moral description he could not remember. He was just about to venture another question, when there was a knock at the door, and the short figure of Mr. Gould offered itself, with the melancholy Moon, standing like his tall crooked shadow, behind him. They had drifted

[7] Volnay is a highly regarded red wine from the Burgundy region of France.

up the stairs after the other two men with the wandering gregarious-
ness of the male.

"Hope there's no intrusion," said the beaming Moses with a glow
of good nature, but not the airiest tinge of apology.

"The truth is," said Michael Moon with comparative courtesy, "we
thought we might see if they had made you comfortable. Miss Duke
is rather——"

"I know," cried the stranger, looking up radiantly from his bag;
"magnificent, isn't she? Go close to her—hear military music going
by, like Joan of Arc."

Inglewood started and stared at the speaker like one who has just
heard a wild fairy tale, which nevertheless contains one small and
forgotten fact. For he remembered how he had himself thought of
Jeanne d'Arc years ago, when, hardly more than a schoolboy, he had
first come to the boarding-house. Long since the pulverizing rationalism of his friend Dr. Warner had crushed such youthful ignorances
and disproportionate dreams. Under the Warnerian scepticism and
science of hopeless human types, Inglewood had long come to regard
himself as a timid, insufficient, and "weak" type, who would never
marry; to regard Diana Duke as a materialistic maidservant; and to
regard his first fancy for her as the small, dull farce of a collegian
kissing his landlady's daughter. And yet the phrase about military music
moved him queerly, as if he had heard those distant drums.

"She has to keep things pretty tight, as is only natural," said Moon,
glancing round the rather dwarfish room, with its wedge of slanted
ceiling, like the conical hood of a dwarf.

"Rather a small box for you, sir," said the waggish Mr. Gould.

"Splendid room, though," answered Mr. Smith enthusiastically, with
his head inside his Gladstone bag, "I love these pointed sorts of rooms,
like Gothic. By the way," he cried out, pointing in quite a startling
way, "where does that door lead to?"

"To certain death, I should say," answered Michael Moon, staring
up at a dust-stained and disused trapdoor in the sloping roof of the
attic. "I don't think there's a loft there; and I don't know what else it
could lead to." Long before he had finished his sentence the man
with the strong green legs had leapt at the door in the ceiling, swung

himself somehow on to the ledge beneath it, wrenched it open after a struggle, and clambered through it. For a moment they saw the two symbolic legs standing like a truncated statue; then they vanished. Through the hole thus burst in the roof appeared the empty and lucid sky of evening, with one great many-coloured cloud sailing across it like a whole county upside down.

"Hullo, you fellows!" came the far cry of Innocent Smith, apparently from some remote pinnacle. "Come up here; and bring some of my things to eat and drink. It's just the spot for a picnic."

With a sudden impulse Michael snatched two of the small wine bottles, one in each solid fist; and Arthur Inglewood, as if mesmerized, groped for a biscuit tin and a big jar of ginger. The enormous hand of Innocent Smith appearing through the aperture, like a giant's in a fairy tale, received these tributes and bore them off to the eyrie; then they both hoisted themselves out of the window. They were both athletic, and even gymnastic; Inglewood through his concern for hygiene, and Moon through his concern for sport, which was not quite so idle and inactive as that of the average sportsman. Also they both had a lightheaded celestial sensation when the door was burst in the roof, as if a door had been burst in the sky, and they could climb on to the very roof of the universe. They were both men who had long been unconsciously imprisoned in the commonplace, though one took it comically, and the other seriously. They were both men, nevertheless, in whom sentiment had never died. But Mr. Moses Gould had an equal contempt for their suicidal athletics and their subconscious transcendentalism, and he stood and laughed at the thing with the shameless rationality of another race.

When the singular Smith, astride of a chimney-pot, learnt that Gould was not following, his infantile officiousness and good nature forced him to dive back into the attic to comfort or persuade; and Inglewood and Moon were left alone on the long gray-green ridge of the slate roof, with their feet against gutters and their backs against chimney-pots, looking agnostically at each other. Their first feeling was that they had come out into eternity, and that eternity was very like topsy-turvydom. One definition occurred to one of them—that he had come out into the light of that lucid and radiant ignorance in which all beliefs had begun. The sky above them was full of mythology. Heaven seemed deep enough to hold all the gods. The round of the ether turned from green to yellow gradually like a great unripe fruit. All around the sunken sun it was like a lemon; round all the east it was a sort of golden green, more suggestive of a greengage; but the whole had still the emptiness of daylight and none of the secrecy of dusk. Tumbled here and there across this gold and pale green were shards and shattered masses of inky purple cloud, which seemed falling towards the earth in every kind of colossal perspective. One of them really had the character of some many-mitred, many-bearded, many-winged Assyrian image, huge head downwards, hurled out of heaven—a sort of false Jehovah, who was perhaps Satan. All the other clouds had preposterous pinnacled shapes, as if the god's palaces had been flung after him.

And yet, while the empty heaven was full of silent catastrophe, the height of human buildings above which they sat held here and there a tiny and trivial noise that was the exact antithesis; and they heard some six streets below a newsboy calling, and a bell bidding to chapel. They could also hear talk out of the garden below; and realized that the irrepressible Smith must have followed Gould downstairs, for his eager and pleading accents could be heard, followed by the half-humorous protests of Miss Duke and the full and very youthful laughter of Rosamund Hunt. The air had that cold kindness that comes after a storm. Michael Moon drank it in with as serious a relish as he had drunk the little bottle of cheap claret, which he had emptied almost at a draught. Inglewood went on eating ginger very slowly and with a solemnity unfathomable as the sky above him. There was still enough stir in the freshness of the atmosphere to make them almost fancy they could smell the garden soil and the last roses of the autumn. Suddenly there came from the darkening garden a silvery ping and pong which told them that Rosamund had brought out the long-neglected mandoline. After the first few notes there was more of the distant bell-like laughter.

"Inglewood," said Michael Moon, "have you ever heard that I am a blackguard?" [8]

---

[8] A blackguard was a villain, a scoundrel and a low and worthless character usually given to criminal activity.

"I haven't heard it, and I don't believe it," answered Inglewood, after an odd pause. "But I have heard you were—what they call rather wild."

"If you have heard that I am wild, you can contradict the rumour," said Moon, with an extraordinary calm: "I am tame. I am quite tame; I am about the tamest beast that crawls. I drink too much of the same kind of whisky at the same time every night. I even drink about the same amount too much. I go to the same number of public-houses. I meet the same damned women with mauve faces. I hear the same number of dirty stories—generally the same dirty stories. You may reassure my friends, Inglewood, you see before you a person whom civilization has thoroughly tamed."

Arthur Inglewood was staring with feelings that made him nearly fall off the roof, for indeed the Irishman's face, always sinister, was now almost demoniacal.

"Christ confound it!" cried out Moon, suddenly clutching the empty claret bottle; "this is about the thinnest and filthiest wine I ever uncorked, and it's the only drink I have really enjoyed for nine years. I was never wild until just ten minutes ago." And he sent the bottle whizzing, a wheel of glass, far away beyond the garden into the road, where, in the profound evening silence, they could even hear it break and part upon the stones.

"Moon," said Arthur Inglewood, rather huskily, "you mustn't be so bitter about it. Everybody has to take the world as he finds it; of course one often finds it a bit dull——"

"That fellow doesn't," said Michael decisively; "I mean that fellow Smith. I have a fancy there's some method in his madness. It looks as if he could turn into a sort of wonderland any minute by taking one step out of the plain road. Who would have thought of that trapdoor? Who would have thought that this cursed colonial claret could taste quite nice among the chimney-pots? Perhaps that is the real key of fairyland. Perhaps Nosey Gould's beastly little Empire Cigarettes ought only to be smoked on stilts, or something of that sort. Perhaps Mrs. Duke's cold leg of mutton would seem quite appetizing at the top of a tree. Perhaps—even my damned, dirty, monotonous drizzle of Old Bill Whisky——"

"Don't be rough on yourself," said Inglewood, in serious distress. "The dullness isn't your fault or the whisky's. Fellows who don't— fellows like me I mean—have just the same feeling that it's all rather flat and a failure. But the world's made like that; it's all survival. Some people are made to get on, like Warner; and some people are made to stick quiet, like me. You can't help your temperament. I know you're much cleverer than I am; but you can't help having all the loose ways of a poor literary chap, and I can't help having all the doubts and helplessness of a small scientific chap, any more than a fish can help floating or a fern help curling up. Humanity, as Warner said so well in that lecture, really consists of quite different tribes of animals all disguised as men."

In the dim garden below the buzz of talk was suddenly broken by Miss Hunt's musical instrument banging with the abruptness of artillery into a vulgar but spirited tune.

Rosamund's voice came up rich and strong in the words of some fatuous, fashionable coon song:—

> "Darkies sing a song on the old plantation,
>   Sing it as we sang it in the days long since gone by."

Inglewood's brown eyes softened and saddened still more as he continued his monologue of resignation to such a rollicking and romantic tune. But the blue eyes of Michael Moon brightened and hardened with a light that Inglewood did not understand. Many centuries, and many villages and valleys, would have been happier if Inglewood or Inglewood's countrymen had ever understood that light, or guessed at the first blink that it was the battle star of Ireland.

"Nothing can ever alter it; it's in the wheels of the universe," went on Inglewood, in a low voice: "some men are weak and some strong, and the only thing we can do is to know that we are weak. I have been in love lots of times, but I could not do anything, for I remembered my own fickleness. I have formed opinions, but I haven't the cheek to push them, because I've so often changed them. That's the upshot, old fellow. We can't trust ourselves—and we can't help it."

Michael had risen to his feet, and stood poised in a perilous position at the end of the roof, like some dark statue hung above its gable.

Behind him, huge clouds of an almost impossible purple turned slowly topsy-turvy in the silent anarchy of heaven. Their gyration made the dark figure seem yet dizzier.

"Let us ..." he said, and was suddenly silent.

"Let us what?" asked Arthur Inglewood, rising equally quick though somewhat more cautiously, for his friend seemed to find some difficulty in speech.

"Let us go and do some of these things we can't do," said Michael.

At the same moment there burst out of the trapdoor below them the cockatoo hair and flushed face of Innocent Smith, calling to them that they must come down as the "concert" was in full swing, and Mr. Moses Gould about to recite "Young Lochinvar." [9]

As they dropped into Innocent's attic they nearly tumbled over its entertaining impedimenta again. Inglewood, staring at the littered floor, thought instinctively of the littered floor of a nursery. He was therefore the more moved, and even shocked, when his eye fell on a large well-polished American revolver.

"Hullo!" he cried, stepping back from the steely glitter as men step back from a serpent; "are you afraid of burglars? or when and why do you deal death out of that machine gun?"

"Oh, that!" said Smith, throwing it a single glance; "I deal life out of that," and he went bounding down the stairs.

---

[9] "Young Lochinvar" is from the long narrative poem *Marmion: a Tale of Flodden Field*, (1808) canto 5, stanza 12, by Sir Walter Scott (1771–1832).

III

THE BANNER OF BEACON

All next day at Beacon House there was a crazy sense that it was everybody's birthday. It is the fashion to talk of institutions as cold and cramping things. The truth is that when people are in exceptionally high spirits, really wild with freedom and invention, they always must, and they always do, create institutions. When men are weary they fall into anarchy; but while they are gay and vigorous they invariably make rules. This, which is true of all the churches and republics of history, is also true of the most trivial parlour game or the most unsophisticated meadow romp. We are never free until some institution frees us, and liberty cannot exist till it is declared by authority. Even the wild authority of the harlequin Smith was still authority, because it produced everywhere a crop of crazy regulations and conditions. He filled every one with his own half-lunatic life; but it was not expressed in destruction, but rather in a dizzy and toppling construction. Each person with a hobby found it turning into an institution. Rosamund's songs seemed to coalesce into a kind of opera; Michael's jests and paragraphs into a magazine. His pipe and her mandoline seemed between them to make a sort of smoking concert. The bashful and bewildered Arthur Inglewood almost struggled against his own growing importance. He felt as if, in spite of him, his photographs were turning into a picture gallery, and his bicycle into a gymkhana. But no one had any time to criticize these impromptu estates and offices, for they followed each other in wild succession like the topics of a rambling talker.

Existence with such a man was an obstacle race made of pleasant obstacles. Out of any homely and trivial object he could drag reels of exaggeration, like a conjurer. Nothing could be more shy and impersonal than poor Arthur's photography. Yet the preposterous Smith was seen assisting him eagerly through sunny morning hours, and an indefensible sequence described as "Moral Photography" began to unroll itself about the boarding-house. It was only a version of the old photographer's joke which produces the same figure twice on one plate, making a man play chess with himself, dine with himself, and so on. But these plates were more mystical and ambitious—as, "Miss Hunt forgets Herself," showing that lady answering her own too rapturous recognition with a most appalling stare of ignorance; or "Mr. Moon questions Himself," in which Mr. Moon appeared as one driven to madness under his own legal cross-examination, which was conducted with a long forefinger and an air of ferocious waggery. One highly successful trilogy—representing Inglewood recognizing Inglewood, Inglewood prostrating himself before Inglewood, and Inglewood severely beating Inglewood with an umbrella—Innocent Smith wanted to have enlarged and put up in the hall, like a sort of fresco, with the inscription,—

> "Self-reverence, self-knowledge, self-control—
> These three alone will make a man a prig."
> TENNYSON[10]

Nothing, again, could be more prosaic and impenetrable than the domestic energies of Miss Diana Duke. But Innocent had somehow blundered on the discovery that her thrifty dressmaking went with a considerable feminine care for dress—the one feminine thing that had never failed her solitary self-respect. In consequence Smith pestered her with a theory (which he really seemed to take seriously) that ladies might combine economy with magnificence if they would draw light chalk patterns on a plain dress and then dust them off again. He set up "Smith's Lightning Dressmaking Company" with two screens, a cardboard placard, and box of bright soft crayons; and Miss Diana actually threw him an abandoned black overall or working dress on which to exercise the talents of a modiste. He promptly produced for her a garment aflame with red and gold sunflowers; she held it up an instant to her shoulders, and looked like an empress. And Arthur Inglewood, some hours afterwards cleaning his bicycle (with his usual air of being inextricably hidden in it), glanced up; and his hot face grew

---

[10]Chesterton appears here to be deliberately misquoting Alfred Lord Tennyson (1809–1892), who, in his poem Œone, wrote, "Self-reverence, self-knowledge, self-control,— These three alone lead life to sovereign power."

hotter, for Diana stood laughing for one flash in the doorway, and her dark robe was rich with the green and purple of great decorative peacocks, like a secret garden in the "Arabian Nights." [11] A pang too swift to be named pain or pleasure went through his heart like an old-world rapier. He remembered how pretty he thought her years ago, when he was ready to fall in love with anybody; but it was like remembering a worship of some Babylonian princess in some previous existence. At his next glimpse of her (and he caught himself awaiting it) the purple and green chalk was dusted off, and she went by quickly in her working clothes.

As for Mrs. Duke, none who knew that matron could conceive her as actively resisting this invasion that had turned her house upside down. But among the most exact observers it was seriously believed that she liked it. For she was one of those women who at bottom regard all men as equally mad, wild animals of some utterly separate species. And it is doubtful if she really saw anything more eccentric or inexplicable in Smith's chimney-pot picnics or crimson sunflowers than she had in the chemicals of Inglewood or the sardonic speeches of Moon. Courtesy, on the other hand, is a thing that any one can understand, and Smith's manners were as courteous as they were unconventional. She said he was "a real gentleman," by which she simply meant a kind-hearted man, which is a very different thing. She would sit at the head of the table with fat, folded hands and a fat, folded smile for hours and hours, while every one else was talking at once. At least, the only other exception was Rosamund's companion, Mary Gray, whose silence was of a much more eager sort. Though she never spoke she always looked as if she might speak any minute. Perhaps this is the very definition of a companion. Innocent Smith seemed to throw himself, as into other adventures, into the adventure of making her talk. He never succeeded, yet he was never snubbed; if he achieved anything, it was only to draw attention to this quiet figure, and to turn her, by ever so little, from a modesty to a mystery. But if she was

[11] *The Arabian Nights* is a collection of Arabic stories variously published as *The Thousand and One Nights* or *Arabian Night's Entertainment*. The stories were translated into French and other languages in the eighteenth century. These well-known tales include *Aladdin* and *Sinbad the Sailor*.

a riddle, every one recognized that she was a fresh and unspoilt riddle, like the riddle of the sky and the woods in spring. Indeed, though she was rather older than the other two girls, she had an early morning ardour, a fresh earnestness of youth, which Rosamund seemed to have lost in the mere spending of money, and Diana in the mere guarding of it. Smith looked at her again and again. Her eyes and mouth were set in her face the wrong way—which was really the right way. She had the knack of saying everything with her face: her silence was a sort of steady applause.

But among the hilarious experiments of that holiday (which seemed more like a week's holiday than a day's) one experiment towers supreme, not because it was any sillier or more successful than the others, but because out of this particular folly flowed all the odd events that were to follow. All the other practical jokes exploded of themselves, and left vacancy; all the other fictions returned upon themselves, and were finished like a song. But the string of solid and startling events— which were to include a hansom cab, a detective, a pistol, and a marriage licence—were all made primarily possible by the joke about the High Court of Beacon.

It had originated, not with Innocent Smith, but with Michael Moon. He was in a strange glow and pressure of spirits, and talked incessantly; yet he had never been more sarcastic, and even inhuman. He used his old useless knowledge as a barrister to talk entertainingly of a tribunal that was a parody on the pompous anomalies of English law. The High Court of Beacon, he declared, was a splendid example of our free and sensible constitution. It had been founded by King John in defiance of Magna Carta, and now held absolute power over windmills, wine and spirit licences, ladies travelling in Turkey, revision of sentences for dog-stealing and parricide, as well as anything whatever that happened in the town of Market Bosworth. The whole hundred and nine seneschals of the High Court of Beacon met once in every four centuries; but in the intervals (as Mr. Moon explained) the whole powers of the institution were vested in Mrs. Duke. Tossed about among the rest of the company, however, the High Court did not retain its historical and legal seriousness, but was used somewhat unscrupulously in a riot of domestic detail. If somebody spilt the

Worcester Sauce on the tablecloth, he was quite sure it was a rite without which the sittings and findings of the Court would be invalid; or if somebody wanted a window to remain shut, he would suddenly remember that none but the third son of the lord of the manor of Penge had the right to open it. They even went the length of making arrests and conducting criminal inquiries. The proposed trial of Moses Gould for patriotism was rather above the heads of the company, especially of the criminal; but the trial of Inglewood on a charge of photographic libel, and his triumphant acquittal upon a plea of insanity, were admitted to be in the best traditions of the Court.

But when Smith was in wild spirits he grew more and more serious, not more and more flippant like Michael Moon. This proposal of a private court of justice, which Moon had thrown off with the detachment of a political humorist, Smith really caught hold of with the eagerness of an abstract philosopher. It was by far the best thing they could do, he declared, to claim sovereign powers even for the individual household.

"You believe in Home Rule for Ireland; I believe in Home Rule for homes," he cried eagerly to Michael. "It would be better if every father *could* kill his son, as with the old Romans; it would be better, because nobody would be killed. Let's issue a Declaration of Independence from Beacon House. We could grow enough greens in that garden to support us, and when the tax-collector comes let's tell him we're self-supporting, and play on him with the hose.... Well, perhaps, as you say, we couldn't very well have a hose, as that comes from the main; but we could sink a well in this chalk, and a lot could be done with water-jugs.... Let this be really Beacon House. Let's light a bonfire of independence on the roof, and see house after house answering it across the valley of the Thames! Let us begin the League of the Free Families! Away with Local Government! A fig for Local Patriotism! Let every house be a sovereign state as this is, and judge its own children by its own law, as we do by the Court of Beacon. Let us cut the painter, and begin to be happy together, as if we were on a desert island."

"I know that desert island," said Michael Moon; "it only exists in the 'Swiss Family Robinson.' A man feels a strange desire for some sort of vegetable milk, and crash comes down some unexpected cocoa-nut from some undiscovered monkey. A literary man feels inclined to pen a sonnet, and at once an officious porcupine rushes out of a thicket and shoots out one of his quills."

"Don't you say a word against the 'Swiss Family Robinson,' " [12] cried Innocent with great warmth. "It mayn't be exact science, but it's dead accurate philosophy. When you're really shipwrecked, you do really find what you want. When you're really on a desert island, you never find it a desert. If we were really besieged in this garden, we'd find a hundred English birds and English berries that we never knew were here. If we were snowed up in this room, we'd be the better for reading scores of books in that book-case that we don't even know are there; we'd have talks with each other, good, terrible talks, that we shall go to the grave without guessing; we'd find materials for everything—christening, mar-riage, or funeral; yes, even for a coronation—if we didn't decide to be a republic."

"A coronation on 'Swiss Family' lines, I suppose," said Michael, laughing. "Oh, I know you would find everything in that atmo-sphere. If we wanted such a simple thing, for instance, as a Corona-tion Canopy, we should walk down beyond the geraniums and find the Canopy Tree in full bloom. If we wanted such a trifle as a crown of gold, why, we should be digging up dandelions, and we should find a gold mine under the lawn. And when we wanted oil for the ceremony, why, I suppose a great storm would wash everything on shore, and we should find there was a Whale on the premises."

"And so there *is* a Whale on the premises for all you know," asseverated Smith, striking the table with passion. "I bet you've never examined the premises! I bet you've never been round at the back as I was this morning—for I found the very thing you say could only grow on a tree. There's an old sort of square tent up against the dustbin; it's got three holes in the canvas, and a pole's broken, so it's not much good as a tent, but as a Canopy——" And his voice quite

[12] *Swiss Family Robinson* is a popular children's story by the Swiss writer Johan David Wyss (1743–1818). The story involves the adventures and ingenuity of a family that is shipwrecked.

failed him to express its shining adequacy; then he went on with controversial eagerness: "You see I take every challenge as you make it. I believe every blessed thing you say couldn't be here has been here all the time. You say you want a whale washed up for oil. Why, there's oil in that cruet-stand at your elbow; and I don't believe anybody has touched it or thought of it for years. And for your gold crown, we're none of us wealthy here, but we could collect enough ten-shilling bits from our own pockets to string round a man's head for half an hour; or one of Miss Hunt's gold bangles is nearly big enough to——"

The good-humoured Rosamund was almost choking with laughter. "All is not gold that glitters," she said; "and besides——"

"What a mistake that is!" cried Innocent Smith, leaping up in great excitement. "All is gold that glitters—especially now we are a Sovereign State. What's the good of a Sovereign State if you can't define a sovereign? We can make anything a precious metal, as men could in the morning of the world. They didn't choose gold because it was rare; your scientists can tell you twenty sorts of slime much rarer. They chose gold because it was bright—because it was a thing hard to find, but pretty when you've found it. You can't fight with golden swords or eat golden biscuits; you can only look at it—and you can look at it out here."

With one of his incalculable motions he sprang back and burst open the doors into the garden. At the same time also, with one of his gestures that never seemed at the instant so unconventional as they were, he stretched out his hand to Mary Gray, and led her out on to the lawn as if for a dance.

The French windows, thus flung open, let in an evening even lovelier than that of the day before. The west was swimming with sanguine colours, and a sort of sleepy flame lay along the lawn. The twisted shadows of the one or two garden trees showed upon this sheen, not gray or black, as in common daylight, but like arabesques written in vivid violet ink on some page of Eastern gold. The sunset was one of those festive and yet mysterious conflagrations in which common things by their colours remind us of costly or curious things. The slates upon the sloping roof burned like the plumes of a vast peacock, in every mysterious blend of blue and green. The red-brown bricks of the wall glowed with all the October tints of strong ruby and tawny wines. The sun seemed to set each object alight with a different coloured flame, like a man lighting fireworks; and even Innocent's hair, which was of a rather colourless fairness, seemed to have a flame of pagan gold on it as he strode across the lawn towards the one tall ridge of rockery.

"What would be the good of gold," he was saying, "if it did not glitter? Why should we care for a black sovereign any more than a black sun at noon? A black button would do just as well. Don't you see that everything in this yard looks like a jewel? And will you kindly tell me what the deuce is the good of a jewel except that it looks like a jewel? Leave off buying and selling, and start looking! Open your eyes, and you'll wake up in the New Jerusalem.

> "All is gold that glitters—
>   Tree and tower of brass;
> Rolls the golden evening air
>   Down the golden grass.
> Kick the cry to Jericho,
>   How yellow mud is sold;
> All is gold that glitters,
>   For the glitter is the gold."

"And who wrote that?" asked Rosamund, amused.

"No one will ever write it," answered Smith, and cleared the rockery with a flying leap.

"Really," said Rosamund to Michael Moon, "he ought to be sent to an asylum. Don't you think so?"

"I beg your pardon," inquired Michael, rather sombrely; his long, swarthy head was dark against the sunset, and, either by accident or mood, he had the look of something isolated and even hostile amid the social extravagance of the garden.

"I only said Mr. Smith ought to go to an asylum," repeated the lady.

The lean face seemed to grow longer and longer, for Moon was unmistakably sneering. "No," he said; "I don't think it's at all necessary."

"What do you mean?" asked Rosamund quickly. "Why not?"

"Because he is in one now," answered Michael Moon, in a quiet but ugly voice. "Why, didn't you know?"

"What?" cried the girl, and there was a break in her voice; for the Irishman's face and voice were really almost creepy. With his dark figure and dark sayings in all that sunshine he looked like the devil in paradise.

"I'm sorry," he continued, with a sort of harsh humility. "Of course we don't talk about it much ... but I thought we all really knew."

"Knew what?"

"Well," answered Moon, "that Beacon House is a certain rather singular sort of house—a house with the tiles loose, shall we say? Innocent Smith is only the doctor that visits us; hadn't you come when he called before? As most of our maladies are melancholic, of course he has to be extra cheery. Sanity, of course, seems a very bumptious eccentric thing to us. Jumping over a wall, climbing a tree—that's his bedside manner."

"You daren't say such a thing!" cried Rosamund in a rage. "You daren't suggest that I——"

"Not more than I am," said Michael soothingly; "not more than the rest of us. Haven't you ever noticed that Miss Duke never sits still—a notorious sign? Haven't you ever observed that Inglewood is always washing his hands—a known mark of mental disease? I, of course, am a dipsomaniac."

"I don't believe you," broke out his companion, not without agitation. "I've heard you had some bad habits——"

"All habits are bad habits," said Michael, with deadly calm. "Madness does not come by breaking out, but by giving in; by settling down in some dirty, little, self-repeating circle of ideas; by being tamed. *You* went mad about money, because you're an heiress."

"It's a lie," cried Rosamund furiously. "I never was mean about money."

"You were worse," said Michael, in a low voice and yet violently. "You thought that other people were. You thought every man who came near you must be a fortune-hunter; you would not let yourself go and be sane; and now you're mad and I'm mad, and serve us right."

"You brute!" said Rosamund, quite white. "And is this true?"

With an intellectual cruelty of which the Celt is capable when his abysses are in revolt, Michael was silent for some seconds, and then stepped back with an ironical bow. "Not literally true, of course," he said; "only really true. An allegory, shall we say? a social satire."

"And I hate and despise your satires," cried Rosamund Hunt, letting loose her whole forcible female personality like a cyclone, and speaking every word to wound. "I despise it as I despise your rank tobacco, and your nasty, loungy ways, and your snarling, and your Radicalism, and your old clothes, and your potty little newspaper, and your rotten failure at everything. I don't care whether you call it snobbishness or not, I like life and success, and jolly things to look at, and action. You won't frighten me with Diogenes;[13] I prefer Alexander." [14]

"*Victrix causa deæ*—" [15] said Michael gloomily; and this angered her more, as, not knowing what it meant, she imagined it to be witty.

"Oh, I dare say you know Greek," she said, with cheerful inaccuracy; "you haven't done much with that either." And she crosssed the garden, pursuing the vanished Innocent and Mary.

In doing so she passed Inglewood, who was returning to the house slowly, and with a thought-clouded brow. He was one of those men who are quite clever, but quite the reverse of quick. As he came back out of the sunset garden into the twilight parlour, Diana Duke slipped swiftly to her feet and began putting away the tea things. But it was not before Inglewood had seen an instantaneous picture so unique that he might well have snapshotted it with his everlasting camera. For Diana had been sitting in front of her unfinished work with her chin on her hand, looking straight out of the window in pure thoughtless thought.

[13] Diogenes was a Greek cynic philosopher (ca. 412–323 B.C.) who rejected social convention and lived in a tub; he once went through the streets holding a lantern "looking for an honest man".

[14] Alexander the Great (356–323 B.C.) was a king of Macedon and a soldier; he once reputed to have met Diogenes and to have said, "If I were not Alexander, I would be Diogenes." Legend relates that when he met Diogenes he asked the philosopher if he lacked anything. Diogenes said, "Yes, that I do: that you stand out of my sun a little."

[15] *Victrix causa deæ*: the proper line from the Roman poet Lucan (A.D. 39–65), is in Latin, not as Rosamund says, in Greek and is "Victrix causa deis placuit", meaning, "the winning cause pleased the gods" (from *Pharsalia*, bk. 1, line 128).

"You are busy," said Arthur, oddly embarrassed with what he had seen, and wishing to ignore it.

"There's no time for dreaming in this world," answered the young lady with her back to him.

"I have been thinking lately," said Inglewood in a low voice, "that there's no time for waking up."

She did not reply, and he walked to the window and looked out on the garden.

"I don't smoke or drink, you know," he said irrelevantly, "because I think they're drugs. And yet I fancy all hobbies, like my camera and bicycle, are drugs too. Getting under a black hood, getting into a dark room—getting into a hole anyhow. Drugging myself with speed, and sunshine, and fatigue, and fresh air. Pedalling the machine so fast that I turn into a machine myself. That's the matter with all of us. We're too busy to wake up."

"Well," said the girl solidly, "what is there to wake up to?"

"There must be!" cried Inglewood, turning round in a singular excitement—"there must be something to wake up to! All we do is preparations—your cleanliness, and my healthiness, and Warner's scientific appliances. We're always preparing for something—something that never comes off. I ventilate the house, and you sweep the house; but what is going *to happen* in the house?"

She was looking at him quietly, but with very bright eyes, and seemed to be searching for some form of words which she could not find.

Before she could speak the door burst open, and the boisterous Rosamund Hunt, in her flamboyant white hat, boa, and parasol, stood framed in the doorway. She was in a breathing heat, and on her open face was an expression of the most infantile astonishment.

"Well, here's a fine game!" she said, panting. "What am I to do now, I wonder? I've wired for Dr. Warner; that's all I can think of doing."

"What is the matter?" asked Diana, rather sharply, but moving forward like one used to be called upon for assistance.

"It's Mary," said the heiress, "my companion Mary Gray: that cracked friend of yours called Smith has proposed to her in the garden, after ten hours' acquaintance, and he wants to go off with her now for a special licence."

Arthur Inglewood walked to the open French windows and looked out on the garden, still golden with evening light. Nothing moved there but a bird or two hopping and twittering; but beyond the hedge and railings, in the road outside the garden gate, a hansom cab was waiting, with the yellow Gladstone bag on top of it.

IV

THE GARDEN OF THE GOD

Diana Duke seemed inexplicably irritated at the abrupt entrance and utterance of the other girl.

"Well," she said shortly, "I suppose Miss Gray can decline him if she doesn't want to marry him."

"But she *does* want to marry him!" cried Rosamund in exasperation. "She's a wild, wicked fool, and I won't be parted from her."

"Perhaps," said Diana icily; "but I really don't see what we can do."

"But the man's balmy, Diana," reasoned her friend angrily. "I can't let my nice governess marry a man that's balmy! You or somebody *must* stop it!—Mr. Inglewood, you're a man; go and tell them they simply can't."

"Unfortunately, it seems to me they simply can," said Inglewood, with a depressed air. "I have far less right of intervention than Miss Duke, besides having, of course, far less moral force than she."

"You haven't either of you got much," cried Rosamund, the last stays of her formidable temper giving way; "I think I'll go somewhere else for a little sense and pluck. I think I know some one who will help me more than you do, at any rate ... he's a cantankerous beast, but he's a man, and has a mind, and knows it...." And she flung out into the garden, with checks aflame, and the parasol whirling like a Catherine wheel.

She found Michael Moon standing under the garden tree, looking over the hedge; hunched like a bird of prey, with his large pipe hanging down his long blue chin. The very hardness of his expression pleased her, after the nonsense of the new engagement and the shilly-shallying of her other friends.

"I am sorry I was cross, Mr. Moon," she said frankly. "I hated you for being a cynic; but I've been well punished, for I want a cynic just now. I've had my fill of sentiment—I'm fed up with it. The world's gone mad, Mr. Moon—all except the cynics, I think. That maniac

Smith wants to marry my old friend Mary, and she—and she—doesn't seem to mind."

Seeing his attentive face still undisturbedly smoking, she added smartly, "I'm not joking; that's Mr. Smith's cab outside. He swears he'll take her off now to his aunt's, and go for a special licence. Do give me some practical advice, Mr. Moon."

Mr. Moon took his pipe out of his mouth, held it in his hand for an instant reflectively, and then tossed it to the other side of the garden. "My practical advice to you is this," he said: "Let him go for his special licence, and ask him to get another one for you and me."

"Is that one of your jokes?" asked the young lady. "Do say what you really mean."

"I mean that Innocent Smith is a man of business," said Moon with ponderous precision—"a plain, practical man; a man of affairs; a man of facts and the daylight. He has let down twenty ton of good building bricks suddenly on my head, and I am glad to say they have woken me up. We went to sleep a little while ago on this very lawn, in this very sunlight. We have had a little nap for five years or so, but now we're going to be married, Rosamund, and I can't see why that cab . . ."

"Really," said Rosamund stoutly, "I don't know what you mean."

"What a lie!" cried Michael, advancing on her with brightening eyes. "I'm all for lies in an ordinary way; but don't you see that to-night they won't do? We've wandered into a world of facts, old girl. That grass growing, and that sun going down, and that cab at the door, are facts. You used to torment and excuse yourself by saying I was after your money, and didn't really love you. But if I stood here now and told you I didn't love you—you wouldn't believe me: for truth is in this garden to-night."

"Really, Mr. Moon . . ." said Rosamund, rather more faintly.

He kept two big blue magnetic eyes fixed on her face. "Is my name Moon?" he asked. "Is your name Hunt? On my honour, they sound to me as quaint and distant as Red Indian names. It's as if your name was 'Swim' and my name was 'Sunrise.' But our real names are Husband and Wife, as they were when we fell asleep."

"It is no good," said Rosamund, with real tears in her eyes; "one can never go back."

"I can go where I damn please," said Michael, "and I can carry you on my shoulder."

"But really, Michael, really, you must stop and think!" cried the girl earnestly. "You could carry me off my feet, I dare say, soul and body, but it may be bitter bad business for all that. These things done in that romantic rush, like Mr. Smith's, they—they do attract women, I don't deny it. As you say, we're all telling the truth to-night. They've attracted poor Mary, for one. They attract me, Michael. But the cold fact remains: imprudent marriages do lead to long unhappiness and disappointment—you've got used to your drinks and things—I shan't be pretty much longer——"

"Imprudent marriages!" roared Michael. "And pray where in earth or heaven are there any prudent marriages? Might as well talk about prudent suicides. You and I have dawdled round each other long enough, and are we any safer than Smith and Mary Gray, who met last night? You never know a husband till you marry him. Unhappy! of course you'll be unhappy. Who the devil are you that you shouldn't be unhappy, like the mother that bore you? Disappointed! of course we'll be disappointed. I, for one, don't expect till I die to be so good a man as I am at this minute, for just now I'm fifty thousand feet high—a tower with all the trumpets shouting."

"You see all this," said Rosamund, with a grand sincerity in her solid face, "and do you really want to marry me?"

"My darling, what else is there to do?" reasoned the Irishman. "What other occupation is there for an active man on this earth, except to marry you? What's the alternative to marriage, barring sleep? It's not liberty, Rosamund. Unless you marry God, as our nuns do in Ireland, you must marry Man—that is Me. The only third thing is to marry yourself—to live with yourself—yourself, yourself, yourself—the only companion that is never satisfied—and never satisfactory."

"Michael," said Miss Hunt, in a very soft voice, "if you won't talk so much, I'll marry you."

"It's no time for talking," cried Michael Moon; "singing is the only thing. Can't you find that mandoline of yours, Rosamund?"

"Go and fetch it for me," said Rosamund, with crisp and sharp authority.

The lounging Mr. Moon stood for one split second astonished; then he shot away across the lawn, as if shod with the feathered shoes out of the Greek fairy tale. He cleared three yards and fifteen daisies at a leap, out of mere bodily levity; but when he came within a yard or two of the open parlour windows, his flying feet fell in their old manner like lead; he twisted round and came back slowly, whistling. The events of that enchanted evening were not at an end.

Inside the dark sitting-room of which Moon had caught a glimpse a curious thing had happened, almost an instant after the intemperate exit of Rosamund. It was something which, occurring in that obscure parlour, seemed to Arthur Inglewood like heaven and earth turning head over heels, the sea being the ceiling and the stars the floor. No words can express how it astonished him, as it astonishes all simple men when it happens. Yet the stiffest female stoicism seems separated from it only by a sheet of paper or a sheet of steel. It indicates no surrender, far less any sympathy. The most rigid and ruthless woman can begin to cry, just as the most effeminate man can grow a beard. It is a separate sexual power, and proves nothing one way or the other about force of character. But to young men ignorant of women, like Arthur Inglewood, to see Diana Duke crying was like seeing a motor-car shedding tears of petrol.

He could never have given (even if his really manly modesty had permitted it) any vaguest vision of what he did when he saw that portent. He acted as men do when a theatre catches fire—very differently from how they would have conceived themselves as acting, whether for better or worse. He had a faint memory of certain half-stifled explanations, that the heiress was the one really paying guest, and she would go, and the bailiffs (in consequence) would come; but after that he knew nothing of his own conduct except by the protests it evoked.

"Leave me alone, Mr. Inglewood—leave me alone; that's not the way to help."

"But I can help you," said Arthur, with grinding certainty; "I can, I can, I can...."

"Why, you said," cried the girl, "that you were much weaker than me."

"So I am weaker than you," said Arthur, in a voice that went vibrating through everything, "but not just now."

"Let go my hands!" cried Diana. "I won't be bullied."

In one element he was much stronger than she—the matter of humour. This leapt up in him suddenly, and he laughed, saying: "Well, you are mean. You know quite well you'll bully me all the rest of my life. You might allow a man the one minute of his life when he's allowed to bully."

It was as extraordinary for him to laugh as for her to cry, and for the first time since her childhood Diana was entirely off her guard.

"Do you mean you want to marry me?" she said.

"Why, there's a cab at the door!" cried Inglewood, springing up with an unconscious energy and bursting open the glass doors that led into the garden.

As he led her out by the hand they realized somehow for the first time that the house and garden were on a steep height over London. And yet, though they felt the place to be uplifted, they felt it also to be secret: it was like some round walled garden on the top of one of the turrets of heaven.

Inglewood looked around dreamily, his brown eyes devouring all sorts of details with a senseless delight. He noticed for the first time that the railings of the gate beyond the garden bushes were moulded like little spearheads and painted blue. He noticed that one of the blue spears was loosened in its place, and hung sideways; and this almost made him laugh. He thought it somehow exquisitely harmless and funny that the railing should be crooked; he thought he should like to know how it happened, who did it, and how the man was getting on.

When they were gone a few feet across that fiery grass they realized that they were not alone. Rosamund Hunt and the eccentric Mr. Moon, both of whom they had last seen in the blackest temper of detachment, were standing together on the lawn. They were standing in quite an ordinary manner, and yet they looked somehow like people in a book.

"Oh," said Diana, "what lovely air!"

"I know," called out Rosamund, with a pleasure so positive that it rang out like a complaint. "It's just like that horrid, beastly, fizzy stuff they gave me that made me feel happy."

"Oh, it isn't like anything but itself!" answered Diana, breathing deeply. "Why, it's all cold, and yet it feels like fire."

"Balmy is the word we use in Fleet Street," said Mr. Moon. "Balmy—especially on the crumpet." And he fanned himself quite unnecessarily with his straw hat. They were all full of little leaps and pulsations of objectless and airy energy. Diana stirred and stretched her long arms rigidly, as if crucified, in a sort of excruciating restfulness; Michael stood still for long intervals, with gathered muscles, then spun round like a teetotum, and stood still again; Rosamund did not trip, for women never trip, except when they fall on their noses, but she struck the ground with her foot as she moved, as if to some inaudible dance tune; and Inglewood, leaning quite quietly against a tree, had unconsciously clutched a branch and shaken it with a creative violence. Those giant gestures of Man, that make the high statues and the strokes of war, tossed and tormented all their limbs. Silently as they strolled and stood they were bursting like batteries with an animal magnetism.

"And now," cried Moon quite suddenly, stretching out a hand on each side, "let's dance round that bush!"

"Why, what bush do you mean?" asked Rosamund, looking round with a sort of radiant rudeness.

"The bush that isn't there," said Michael—"the Mulberry Bush." [16]

They had taken each other's hands, half laughing and quite ritually; and before they could disconnect again Michael spun them all round, like a demon spinning the world for a top. Diana felt, as the circle of the horizon flew instantaneously around her, a far aerial sense of the ring of heights beyond London and corners where she had climbed as a child; she seemed almost to hear the rooks cawing about the old pines on Highgate, or to see the glowworms gathering and kindling in the woods of Box Hill.

The circle broke—as all such perfect circles of levity must break—and sent its author, Michael, flying, as by centrifugal force, far away against the blue rails of the gate. When reeling there he suddenly raised shout after shout of a new and quite dramatic character.

[16]"The Mulberry Bush" is a reference to a children's game in which the players join hands and dance in a circle while singing, "Here we go round the mulberry bush!"

"Why, it's Warner!" he shouted, waving his arms. "It's jolly old Warner—with a new silk hat and the old silk moustache!"

"Is that Dr. Warner?" cried Rosamund, bounding forward in a burst of memory, amusement, and distress. "Oh, I'm so sorry! Oh, do tell him it's all right!"

"Let's take hands and tell him," said Michael Moon. For indeed, while they were talking, another hansom had dashed up behind the one already waiting, and Dr. Herbert Warner, leaving a companion in the cab, had carefully deposited himself on the pavement.

Now, when you are an eminent physician and are wired for by an heiress to come to a case of dangerous mania, and when, as you come in through the garden to the house, the heiress and her landlady and two of the gentlemen boarders join hands and dance round you in a ring, calling out, "It's all right! it's all right!" you are apt to be flustered and even displeased. Dr. Warner was a placid but hardly a placable person. The two things are by no means the same; and even when Moon explained to him that he, Warner, with his high hat and tall, solid figure, was just such a classic column as *ought* to be danced round by a ring of laughing maidens on some old golden Greek seashore—even then he seemed to miss the point of the general rejoicing.

"Inglewood!" cried Dr. Warner, fixing his former disciple with a stare, "are you mad?"

Arthur flushed to the roots of his brown hair, but he answered, easily and quietly enough, "Not now. The truth is, Warner, I've just made a rather important medical discovery—quite in your line."

"What do you mean?" asked the great doctor stiffly—"what discovery?"

"I've discovered that health really is catching, like disease," answered Arthur.

"Yes; sanity has broken out, and is spreading," said Michael, performing a *pas seul*[17] with a thoughtful expression. "Twenty thousand more cases taken to the hospitals; nurses employed night and day."

---

[17] A *pas seul* is a solo dance.

Dr. Warner studied Michael's grave face and lightly moving legs with an unfathomed wonder. "And is *this*, may I ask," he said, "the sanity that is spreading?"

"You must forgive me, Dr. Warner," cried Rosamund Hunt heartily. "I know I've treated you badly; but indeed it was all a mistake. I was in a frightfully bad temper when I sent for you, but now it all seems like a dream—and—and Mr. Smith is the sweetest, most sensible, most delightful old thing that ever existed, and he may marry any one he likes—except me."

"I should suggest Mrs. Duke," said Michael.

The gravity of Dr. Warner's face increased. He took a slip of pink paper from his waistcoat pocket, with his pale blue eyes quietly fixed on Rosamund's face all the time. He spoke with a not inexcusable frigidity.

"Really, Miss Hunt," he said, "you are not yet very reassuring. You sent me this wire only half an hour ago: 'Come at once, if possible, with another doctor. Man—Innocent Smith—gone mad on premises, and doing dreadful things. Do you know anything of him?' I went round at once to a distinguished colleague of mine, a doctor who is also a private detective and an authority on criminal lunacy; he has come round with me, and is waiting in the cab. Now you calmly tell me that this criminal madman is a highly sweet and sane old thing, with accompaniments that set me speculating on your own definitions of sanity. I hardly comprehend the change."

"Oh, how can one explain a change in sun and moon and everybody's soul?" cried Rosamund, in despair. "Must I confess we had got so morbid as to think him mad merely because he wanted to get married; and that we didn't even know it was only because we wanted to get married ourselves? We'll humiliate ourselves, if you like, doctor; we're happy enough."

"Where is Mr. Smith?" asked Warner of Inglewood very sharply.

Arthur started; he had forgotten all about the central figure of their farce, who had not been visible for an hour or more.

"I—I think he's on the other side of the house, by the dustbin," he said.

"He may be on the road to Russia," said Warner; "but he must be found." And he strode away and disappeared round a corner of the house by the sunflowers.

"I hope," said Rosamund, "he won't really interfere with Mr. Smith."

"Interfere with the daisies!" said Michael with a snort. "A man can't be locked up for falling in love—at least I hope not."

"No; I think even a doctor couldn't make a disease out of him. He'd throw off the doctor like the disease, don't you know? I believe it's a case of a sort of holy well. I believe Innocent Smith is simply innocent, and that is why he is so extraordinary."

It was Rosamund who spoke, restlessly tracing circles in the grass with the point of her white shoe.

"I think," said Inglewood, "that Smith is not extraordinary at all. He's comic just because he's so startlingly commonplace. Don't you know what it is to be in all one family circle, with aunts and uncles, when a schoolboy comes home for the holidays? That bag there on the cab is only a schoolboy's hamper. This tree here in the garden is only the sort of tree that any schoolboy would have climbed. Yes, that's the thing that has haunted us all about him, the thing we could never fit a word to. Whether he is my old schoolfellow or no, at least he is all my old schoolfellows. He is the endless bun-eating, ball-throwing animal that we have all been."

"That is only you absurd boys," said Diana. "I don't believe any girl was ever so silly, and I'm sure no girl was ever so happy, except—" and she stopped.

"I will tell you the truth about Innocent Smith," said Michael Moon in a low voice. "Dr. Warner has gone to look for him in vain. He is not there. Haven't you noticed that we never saw him since we found ourselves? He was an astral baby born of all four of us; he was only our own youth returned. Long before poor old Warner had clambered out of his cab, the thing we called Smith had dissolved into dew and light on this lawn. Once or twice more, by the mercy of God, we may feel the thing, but the man we shall never see. In a spring garden before breakfast we shall smell the smell called Smith. In the snapping of brisk twigs in tiny fires we shall hear a noise named Smith. Everything insatiable and innocent in the grasses that gobble up the earth like babies at a bun feast, in the white mornings that split the sky as a boy splits up white firwood, we may feel for one instant the presence of an impetuous purity; but his innocence was too close to the unconsciousness of inanimate things not to melt back at a mere touch into the mild hedges and heavens; he——"

He was interrupted from behind the house by a bang like that of a bomb. Almost at the same instant the stranger in the cab sprang out of it, leaving it rocking upon the stones of the road. He clutched the blue railings of the garden, and peered eagerly over them in the direction of the noise. He was a small, loose, yet alert man, very thin, with a face that seemed made out of fish bones, and a silk hat quite as rigid and resplendent as Warner's, but thrust back recklessly on the hinder part of his head.

"Murder!" he shrieked, in a high and feminine but very penetrating voice. "Stop that murderer there!"

Even as he shrieked a second shot shook the lower windows of the house, and with the noise of it Dr. Herbert Warner came flying round the corner like a leaping rabbit. Yet before he had reached the group a third discharge had deafened them, and they saw with their own eyes two spots of white sky drilled through the second of the unhappy Herbert's high hats. The next moment the fugitive physician fell over a flowerpot, and came down on all fours, staring like a cow. The hat with the two shot-holes in it rolled upon the gravel path before him, and Innocent Smith came round the corner like a railway train. He was looking twice his proper size—a giant clad in green, the big revolver still smoking in his hand, his face sanguine and in shadow, his eyes blazing like stars, and his yellow hair standing out all ways like Struwelpeter's.[18]

Though this startling scene hung but an instant in stillness, Inglewood had time to feel once more what he had felt when he saw the other lovers standing on the lawn—the sensation of a certain cut and coloured clearness that belongs rather to the things of art than to the

---

[18] Struwelpeter is a character in a collection of children's stories by Henrich Hoffman (1809–1904). The character is identified by long hair and extremely long fingernails. The name in German means "shock-headed Peter".

things of experience. The broken flowerpot with its red-hot geraniums, the green bulk of Smith and the black bulk of Warner, the blue-spiked railings behind, clutched by the stranger's yellow vulture claws and peered over by his long vulture neck, the silk hat on the gravel, and the little cloudlet of smoke floating across the garden as innocently as the puff of a cigarette—all these seemed unnaturally distinct and definite. They existed, like symbols, in an ecstasy of separation. Indeed, every object grew more and more particular and precious because the whole picture was breaking up. Things look so bright just before they burst.

Long before his fancies had begun, let alone ceased, Arthur had stepped across and taken one of Smith's arms. Simultaneously the little stranger had run up the steps and taken the other. Smith went into peals of laughter, and surrendered his pistol with perfect willingness. Moon raised the doctor to his feet, and then went and leaned sullenly on the garden gate. The girls were quiet and vigilant, as good women mostly are in instants of catastrophe, but their faces showed that, somehow or other, a light had been dashed out of their sky. The doctor himself, when he had risen, collected his hat and wits, and dusting himself down with an air of great disgust, turned to them in brief apology. He was very white with his recent panic, but he spoke with perfect self-control.

"You will excuse us, ladies," he said; "my friend and Mr. Inglewood are both scientists in their several ways. I think we had better all take Mr. Smith indoors, and communicate with you later."

And under the guard of the three natural philosophers the disarmed Smith was led tactfully into the house, still roaring with laughter.

From time to time during the next twenty minutes his distant boom of mirth could again be heard through the half-open window; but there came no echo of the quiet voices of the physicians. The girls walked about the garden together, rubbing up each other's spirits as best they might; Michael Moon still hung heavily against the gate. Somewhere about the expiration of that time Dr. Warner came out of the house again with a face less pale but even more stern, and the little man with the fish-bone face advanced gravely in his rear. And if the face of Warner in the sunlight was that of a hanging judge, the face of the little man behind was more like a death's-head.

"Miss Hunt," said Dr. Herbert Warner, "I only wish to offer you my warm thanks and admiration. By your prompt courage and wisdom in sending for us by wire this evening, you have enabled us to capture and put out of mischief one of the most cruel and terrible of the enemies of humanity—a criminal whose plausibility and pitilessness have never been before combined in flesh."

Rosamund looked across at him with a white, blank face and blinking eyes. "What do you mean?" she asked. "You can't mean Mr. Smith?"

"He has gone by many other names," said the doctor gravely, "and not one he did not leave to be cursed behind him. That man, Miss Hunt, has left a track of blood and tears across the world. Whether he is mad as well as wicked, we are trying, in the interests of science, to discover. In any case, we shall have to take him before a magistrate first, even if only on the road to a lunatic asylum. But the lunatic asylum in which he is confined will have to be sealed with wall within wall, and ringed with guns like a fortress, or he will break out again to bring forth carnage and darkness on the earth."

Rosamund looked at the two doctors, her face growing paler and paler. Then her eyes strayed to Michael, who was leaning on the gate; but he continued to lean on it without moving, with his face turned away towards the darkening road.

V

THE ALLEGORICAL PRACTICAL JOKER

The criminal specialist who had come with Dr. Warner was a some-what more urbane and even dapper figure on closer inspection than he had appeared when clutching the railings and craning his neck into the garden. He even looked comparatively young when he took his hat off, having fair hair parted in the middle and carefully curled on each side, and lively movements, especially of the hands. He had a dandified monocle slung round his neck by a broad black ribbon, and a big bow tie, as if a big American moth had alighted on him. His dress and gestures were bright enough for a boy's; it was only when you looked at the fish-bone face itself that you beheld some-thing acrid and old. His manners were excellent, though hardly English, and he had two half-conscious tricks by which people who only met him once remembered him. One was a trick of closing his eyes when he wished to be particularly polite; the other was one of lifting his joined thumb and forefinger in the air as if holding a pinch of snuff, when he was hesitating or hovering over a word. But those who were longer in his company tended to forget these odd-ities in the stream of his quaint and solemn conversation and really singular views.

"Miss Hunt," said Dr. Warner, "this is Dr. Cyras Pym."

Dr. Cyrus Pym shut his eyes during the introduction, rather as if he were "playing fair" in some child's game, and gave a prompt little bow which somehow suddenly revealed him as a citizen of the United States.

"Dr. Cyrus Pym," continued Warner (Dr. Pym shut his eyes again), "is perhaps the first criminological expert of America. We are very fortunate to be able to consult with him in this extraordinary case——"

"I can't make head or tail of anything," said Rosamund. "How can poor Mr. Smith be so dreadful as he is by your account?"

"Or by your telegram," said Herbert Warner, smiling.

"Oh, you don't understand," cried the girl impatiently. "Why, he's done us all more good than going to church."

"I think I can explain to the young lady," said Dr. Cyrus Pym. "This criminal or maniac Smith is a very genius of evil, and has a method of his own, a method of the most daring ingenuity. He is popular wherever he goes, for he invades every house as an uproarious child. People are getting suspicious of all the respectable disguises for a scoundrel; so he always uses the disguise of—what shall I say— the Bohemian, the blameless Bohemian. He always carries people off their feet. People are used to the mask of conventional good conduct. He goes in for eccentric good-nature. You expect a Don Juan[19] to dress up as a solemn and solid Spanish merchant; but you're not prepared for Don Juan when he dresses up as Don Quixote. You expect a humbug to behave like Sir Charles Grandison;[20] because (with all respect, Miss Hunt, for the deep, tear-moving tenderness of Samuel Richardson) Sir Charles Grandison so often behaved like a humbug. But no real red-blooded citizen is quite ready for a humbug that models himself not on Sir Charles Grandison but on Sir Roger de Coverley.[21] Setting up to be a good man a little cracked is a new criminal incognito, Miss Hunt. It's been a great notion, and commonly successful; but its success just makes it mighty cruel. I can forgive Dick Turpin[22] if he impersonates Dr. Busby;[23] I can't forgive him when he

[19] Don Juan was a legendary Spanish nobleman famous for seducing women. Don Quixote was a hero of a romance of the same name by Spanish writer Miguel Cervantes (1547–1616). Don Juan was as calculating and debauched as Don Quixote was innocent and naive.

[20] Sir Charles Grandison is a character in a novel of the same name by English writer Samuel Richardson (1689–1761) described as a fine gentleman but, by Scottish novelist Sir Walter Scott, as "the faultless monster that the world ne'er saw".

[21] Sir Roger de Coverley is a fictional member of the famous Club described in the *Spectator* essays of Richard Steele (1672–1729) and Joseph Addison (1672–1719). Sir Roger was a country squire, aged and lovable but politically incompetent.

[22] Dick Turpin (1705–1739) was an Essex butcher turned highwayman; he worked around the south of London. He was eventually captured in York, where he was tried and executed.

[23] Dr. Richard Busby (1606–1695) was an English clergyman and headmaster of Westminster School; traditionally he was a severe disciplinarian.

impersonates Dr. Johnson.[24] The saint with a tile loose is a bit too sacred, I guess, to be parodied."

"But how do you know," cried Rosamund desperately, "that Mr. Smith is a known criminal?"

"I collated all the documents," said the American, "when my friend Warner knocked me up on receipt of your cable. It is my professional affair to know these facts, Miss Hunt; and there's no more doubt about them than about the Bradshaw down at the depôt. This man has hitherto escaped the law, through his admirable affectations of infancy or insanity. But I myself, as a specialist, have privately authenticated notes of some eighteen or twenty crimes attempted or achieved in this manner. He comes to houses as he has to this, and gets a grand popularity. He makes things go. They do go; when he's gone the things are gone. Gone, Miss Hunt, gone, a man's life or a man's spoons, or more often a woman. I assure you I have all the memoranda."

"I have seen them," said Warner solidly. "I can assure you this is all correct."

"The most unmanly aspect, according to my feelings," went on the American doctor, "is this perpetual deception of innocent women by a wild simulation of innocence. From almost every house where this great imaginative devil has been, he has taken some poor girl away with him; some say he's got a hypnotic eye with his other queer features, and that they go like automata. What's become of all those poor girls nobody knows. Murdered, I dare say; for we've lots of instances, besides this one, of his turning his hand to murder, though none ever brought him under the law. Anyhow, our most modern methods of research can't find any trace of the wretched women. It's when I think of them that I am real moved, Miss Hunt. And I've really nothing else to say just now except what Dr. Warner has said."

[24] Dr. Samuel Johnson (1709–1784) was a writer, critic and lexicographer much loved for his wit, learning and wisdom. Chesterton was often compared to Dr. Johnson and liked to dress up as him for fancy dress events. Chesterton even wrote a play entitled *The Judgment of Dr. Johnson* (1927).

"Quite so," said Warner, with a smile that seemed moulded in marble—"that we all have to thank you very much for that telegram."

The little Yankee scientist had been speaking with such evident sincerity that one forgot the tricks of his voice and manner—the falling eyelids, the rising intonation, and the poised finger and thumb—which were at other times a little comic. It was not so much that he was cleverer than Warner; perhaps he was not so clever, though he was more celebrated. But he had what Warner never had, a fresh and unaffected seriousness—the great American virtue of simplicity. Rosamund knitted her brows and looked gloomily towards the darkening house that contained the dark prodigy.

Broad daylight still endured; but it had already changed from gold to silver, and was changing from silver to gray. The long plumy shadows of the one or two trees in the garden faded more and more upon a dead background of dusk. In the sharpest and deepest shadow, which was the entrance to the house by the big French windows, Rosamund could watch a hurried consultation between Inglewood (who was still left in charge of the mysterious captive) and Diana, who had moved to his assistance from without. After a few sentences and gestures they went inside, shutting the glass doors upon the garden; and the garden seemed to grow grayer still.

The American gentleman named Pym seemed to be turning and on the move in the same direction; but before he started he spoke to Rosamund with a flash of that guileless tact which redeemed much of his childish vanity, and with something of that spontaneous poetry which made it difficult, pedantic as he was, to call him a pedant.

"I'm vurry sorry, Miss Hunt," he said; "but Dr. Warner and I, as two quali-*fied* practitioners, had better take Mr. Smith away in that cab, and the less said about it the better. Don't you agitate yourself, Miss Hunt. You've just got to think that we're taking away a monstrosity, something that oughtn't to be at all—something like one of those gods in your Britannic Museum, all wings, and beards, and legs, and eyes, and no shape. That's what Smith is, and you shall soon be quit of him."

He had already taken a step towards the house, and Warner was about to follow him, when the glass doors were opened again and

Diana Duke came out with more than her usual quickness across the lawn. Her face was aquiver with worry and excitement, and her dark earnest eyes fixed only on the other girl.

"Rosamund," she cried in despair, "what shall I do with her?"

"With her?" cried Miss Hunt, with a violent jump. "O lord, he isn't a woman too, is he?"

"No, no, no," said Dr. Pym soothingly, as if in common fairness. "A woman? no, really, he is not so bad as that."

"I mean your friend Mary Gray," retorted Diana with equal tartness. "What on earth am I to do with her?"

"How can we tell her about Smith, you mean," answered Rosamund, her face at once clouding and softening. "Yes, it will be pretty painful."

"But I *have* told her," exploded Diana, with more than her congenital exasperation. "I have told her, and she doesn't seem to mind. She still says she's going away with Smith in that cab."

"But it's impossible!" ejaculated Rosamund. "Why, Mary is really religious. She——"

She stopped in time to realize that Mary Gray was comparatively close to her on the lawn. Her quiet companion had come down very quietly into the garden, but dressed very decisively for travel. She had a neat but very ancient blue-gray tam-o'-shanter on her head, and was pulling some rather threadbare gray gloves on to her hands. Yet the two tints fitted excellently with her heavy copper-coloured hair; the more excellently for the touch of shabbiness: for a woman's clothes never suit her so well as when they seem to suit her by accident.

But in this case the woman had a quality yet more unique and attractive. In such gray hours, when the sun is sunk and the skies are already sad, it will often happen that one reflection at some occasional angle will cause to linger the last of the light. A scrap of window, a scrap of water, a scrap of looking-glass, will be full of the fire that is lost to all the rest of the earth. The quaint, almost triangular face of Mary Gray was like some triangular piece of mirror that could still repeat the splendour of hours before. Mary, though she was always graceful, could never have properly been called beautiful; and yet her happiness amid all that misery was so beautiful as to make a man catch his breath.

"O Diana," cried Rosamund in a lower voice and altering her phrase; "but how did you tell her?"

"It is quite easy to tell her," answered Diana sombrely; "it makes no impression at all."

"I'm afraid I've kept everything waiting," said Mary Gray apologetically, "and now we must really say good-bye. Innocent is taking me to his aunt's over at Hampstead, and I'm afraid she goes to bed early."

Her words were quite casual and practical, but there was a sort of sleepy light in her eyes that was more baffling than darkness; she was like one speaking absently with her eye on some very distant object.

"Mary, Mary," cried Rosamund, almost breaking down, "I'm so sorry about it, but the thing can't be at all. We—we have found out all about Mr. Smith."

"All?" repeated Mary, with a low and curious intonation; "why, that must be awfully exciting."

There was no noise for an instant and no motion except that the silent Michael Moon, leaning on the gate, lifted his head, as it might be to listen. Then Rosamund remaining speechless, Dr. Pym came to her rescue in his definite way.

"To begin with," he said, "this man Smith is constantly attempting murder. The Warden of Brakespeare College——"

"I know," said Mary, with a vague but radiant smile; "Innocent told me."

"I can't say what he told you," replied Pym quickly, "but I'm very much afraid it wasn't true. The plain truth is that the man's stained with every known human crime. I assure you I have all the documents. I have evidence of his committing burglary, signed by a most eminent English curate. I have——"

"Oh, but there were two curates," cried Mary, with a certain gentle eagerness; "that was what made it so much funnier."

The darkened glass doors of the house opened once more, and Inglewood appeared for an instant, making a sort of signal. The American doctor bowed, the English doctor did not, but they both set out stolidly towards the house. No one else moved, not even Michael hanging on the gate; but the back of his head and shoulders had still an indescribable indication that he was listening to every word.

"But don't you understand, Mary," cried Rosamund in despair; "don't you know that awful things have happened even before our very eyes. I should have thought you would have heard the revolver shots upstairs."

"Yes, I heard the shots," said Mary almost brightly; "but I was busy packing just then. And Innocent had told me he was going to shoot at Dr. Warner; so it wasn't worth while to come down."

"Oh, I don't understand what you mean," cried Rosamund Hunt, stamping, "but you must and shall understand what I mean. I don't care how cruelly I put it, if only I can save you. I mean that your Innocent Smith is the most awfully wicked man in the world. He has sent bullets at lots of other men and gone off in cabs with lots of other women. And he seems to have killed the women too, for nobody can find them."

"He is really rather naughty sometimes," said Mary Gray, laughing softly as she buttoned her old gray gloves.

"Oh, this is really mesmerism, or something," said Rosamund, and burst into tears.

At the same moment the two black-clad doctors appeared out of the house with their great green-clad captive between them. He made no resistance, but was still laughing in a groggy and half-witted style. Arthur Inglewood followed in the rear, a dark and red study in the last shades of distress and shame. In this black, funereal, and painfully realistic style the exit from Beacon House was made by the man whose entrance a day before had been effected by the happy leaping of a wall and the hilarious climbing of a tree. No one moved of the groups in the garden except Mary Gray, who stepped forward quite naturally, calling out, "Are you ready, Innocent? Our cab's been waiting such a long time."

"Ladies and gentlemen," said Dr. Warner firmly, "I must insist on asking this lady to stand aside. We shall have trouble enough as it is, with the three of us in a cab."

"But it *is* our cab," persisted Mary. "Why, there's Innocent's yellow bag on the top of it."

"Stand aside," repeated Warner roughly. "And you, Mr. Moon, please be so obliging as to move a moment. Come, come! the sooner this ugly business is over the better—and how can we open the gate if you will keep leaning on it?"

Michael Moon looked at his long lean forefinger, and seemed to consider and reconsider this argument. "Yes," he said at last; "but how can I lean on this gate if you keep on opening it?"

"Oh, get out of the way!" cried Warner, almost good-humouredly. "You can lean on the gate any time."

"No," said Moon reflectively. "Seldom the time and the place and the blue gate altogether; and it all depends whether you come of an old country family. My ancestors leaned on gates before any one had discovered how to open them."

"Michael!" cried Arthur Inglewood in a kind of agony, "are you going to get out of the way?"

"Why, no; I think not," said Michael, after some meditation, and swung himself slowly round, so that he confronted the company, while still, in a lounging attitude, occupying the path.

"Hullo!" he called out suddenly; "what are you doing to Mr. Smith?"

"Taking him away," answered Warner shortly, "to be examined."

"Matriculation?" asked Moon brightly.

"By a magistrate," said the other curtly.

"And what other magistrate," cried Michael, raising his voice, "dares to try what befell on this free soil, save only the ancient and independent Dukes of Beacon? What other court dares to try one of our company, save only the High Court of Beacon? Have you forgotten that only this afternoon we flew the flag of independence and severed ourselves from all the nations of the earth?"

"Michael," cried Rosamund, wringing her hands, "how can you stand there talking nonsense? Why, you saw the dreadful thing yourself. You were there when he went mad. It was you that helped the doctor up when he fell over the flower-pot."

"And the High Court of Beacon," replied Moon with hauteur, "has special powers in all cases concerning lunatics, flower-pots, and doctors who fall down in gardens. It's in our very first charter from Edward I.: 'Si medicus quisquam in horto prostratus—'"[25]

"Out of the way!" cried Warner with sudden fury, "or we will force you out of it."

"What!" cried Michael Moon, with a cry of hilarious fierceness. "Shall I die in defence of this sacred pale? Will you paint these blue railings red with my gore?" and he laid hold of one of the blue spikes behind him. As Arthur Inglewood had noticed earlier in the evening, the railing was loose and crooked at this place, and the painted iron staff and spearhead came away in Michael's hand as he shook it.

"See!" he cried, brandishing this broken javelin in the air, "the very lances round Beacon Tower leap from their places to defend it. Ah, in such a place and hour it is a fine thing to die alone!" And in a voice like a drum he rolled the noble lines of Ronsard—

> "Ou pour l'honneur de Dieu, ou pour le droit de mon prince,
> Navré, poitrine ouverte, au bord de mon province."[26]

"Sakes alive!" said the American gentleman, almost in an awed tone. Then he added, "Are there two maniacs here?"

"No; there are five," thundered Moon. "Smith and I are the only sane people left."

"Michael!" cried Rosamund; "Michael, what does it mean?"

"It means bosh!" roared Michael, and slung his painted spear hurtling to the other end of the garden. "It means that doctors are bosh, and criminology is bosh, and Americans are bosh—much more bosh than our Court of Beacon. It means, you fat-heads, that Innocent Smith is no more mad or bad than the bird on that tree."

[25] Edward I (1239–1307) was a king of England (1272–1307). It was not he, but King John (1167–1216) who sealed *Magna Carta* (1215), which is considered the fundamental statement of English liberties. The Latin phrase *Si medicus quisquam in horto prostratus*, literally translated, means "any doctor lying on the ground in a garden". This would not likely be a phrase in the document referred to even if there were such a document.

[26] Pierre Ronsard was a French poet (1524–1585). The passage quoted is the last two lines of "Hynne de la Mort" ("Hymn of the Dead") and can be translated as "either for the honour of God or for the right of my Prince, Sadly, open-hearted, on the borders of my homeland".

"But, my dear Moon," began Inglewood in his modest manner, "these gentlemen——"

"On the word of two doctors," exploded Moon again, without listening to anybody else, "shut up in a private hell on the word of two doctors! And such doctors! Oh, my hat! Look at 'em!—do just look at 'em! Would you read a book, or buy a dog, or go to a hotel on the advice of twenty such? My people came from Ireland, and were Catholics. What would you say if I called a man wicked on the word of two priests?"

"But it isn't only their word, Michael," reasoned Rosamund; "they've got evidence too."

"Have you looked at it?" asked Moon.

"No," said Rosamund, with a sort of faint surprise; "these gentlemen are in charge of it."

"And of everything else, it seems to me," said Michael. "Why, you haven't even had the decency to consult Mrs. Duke."

"Oh, that's no use," said Diana in an undertone to Rosamund; "Auntie couldn't say 'Bo!' to a goose."

"I am glad to hear it," answered Michael, "for with such a flock of geese to say it to, the horrid expletive might be constantly on her lips. For my part, I simply refuse to let things be done in this light and airy style. I appeal to Mrs. Duke—it's her house."

"Mrs. Duke?" repeated Inglewood doubtfully.

"Yes, Mrs. Duke," said Michael firmly, "commonly called the Iron Duke."

"If you ask Auntie," said Diana quietly, "she'll only be for doing nothing at all. Her only idea is to hush things up or to let things slide. That just suits her."

"Yes," replied Michael Moon; "and, as it happens, it just suits all of us. You are impatient with your elders, Miss Duke; but when you are as old yourself you will know what Napoleon knew—that half one's letters answer themselves if you can only refrain from the fleshly appetite of answering them."

He was still lounging in the same absurd attitude, with his elbow on the gate, but his voice had altered abruptly for the third time; just as it had changed from the mock heroic to the humanly indignant, it now changed to the airy incisiveness of a lawyer giving good legal advice.

"It isn't only your aunt who wants to keep this quiet if she can," he said; "we all want to keep it quiet if we can. Look at the large facts— the big bones of the case. I believe these scientific gentlemen have made a highly scientific mistake. I believe Smith is as blameless as a buttercup. I admit buttercups don't often let off loaded pistols in private houses; I admit there is something demanding explanation. But I am morally certain there's some blunder, or some joke, or some allegory, or some accident behind all this. Well, suppose I'm wrong. We've disarmed him; we're five men to hold him; he may as well go to a lock-up later on as now. But suppose there's even a chance of my being right. Is it anybody's interest here to wash this linen in public?"

"Come, I'll take each of you in order. Once take Smith outside that gate, and you take him into the front page of the evening papers. I know; I've written the front page myself. Miss Duke, do you or your aunt want a sort of notice stuck up over your boarding-house— 'Doctors shot here'? No, no—doctors are rubbish, as I said; but you don't want the rubbish shot here. Arthur, suppose I am right, or suppose I am wrong. Smith has appeared as an old schoolfellow of yours. Mark my words, if he's proved guilty, the Organs of Public Opinion will say you introduced him. If he's proved innocent, they will say you helped to collar him. Rosamund, my dear, suppose I am right or wrong. If he's proved guilty, they'll say you engaged your companion to him. If he's proved innocent, they'll print that telegram. I know the Organs, damn them."

He stopped an instant; for this rapid rationalism left him more breathless than had either his theatrical or his real denunciation. But he was plainly in earnest, as well as positive and lucid; as was proved by his proceeding quickly the moment he had found his breath.

"It is just the same," he cried, "with our medical friends. You will say that Dr. Warner has a grievance. I agree. But does he want specially to be snap-shotted by all the journalists *prostratus in horto?*[27] It was no fault of his, but the scene was not very dignified even for him.

---

[27] See n. 25, p. 318 above, regarding this playful Latin tag.

He must have justice; but does he want to ask for justice, not only on his knees but on his hands and knees? Does he want to enter the court of justice on all fours? Doctors are not allowed to advertise; and I'm sure no doctor wants to advertise himself as looking like that. And even for our American guest the interest is the same. Let us suppose that he has conclusive documents. Let as assume that he has revelations really worth reading. Well, in a legal inquiry (or a medical inquiry, for that matter) ten to one he won't be allowed to read them. He'll be tripped up every two or three minutes with some tangle of old rules. A man can't tell the truth in public nowadays. But he can still tell it in private; he can tell it inside that house."

"It is quite true," said Dr. Cyrus Pym, who had listened throughout the speech with a seriousness which only an American could have retained through such a scene. "It is quite true that I have been per-ceptibly less hampered in private inquiries."

"Dr. Pym!" cried Warner in a sort of sudden anger. "Dr. Pym! you aren't surely going to admit——"

"Smith may be mad," went on the melancholy Moon in a mono-logue that seemed as heavy as a hatchet, "but there was something after all in what he said about Home Rule for every home. Yes, there is something, when all's said and done, in the High Court of Beacon. It is really true that human beings might often get some sort of domes-tic justice where just now they can only get legal injustice—oh, I am a lawyer too, and I know that as well. It is true that there's too much official and indirect power. Often and often the thing a whole nation can't settle is just the thing a family could settle. Scores of young criminals have been fined and sent to jail when they ought to have been thrashed and sent to bed. Scores of men, I am sure, have had a lifetime at Hanwell when they only wanted a week at Brighton.[28] There *is* something in Smith's notion of domestic self-government; and I propose that we put it in practice. You have the prisoner; you have the documents. Come, we are a company of free, white, Chris-tian people, such as might be besieged in a town or cast up on a desert

[28] Hanwell is the best known London lunatic asylum. Brighton, a town on the English south coast, is famous as a holiday resort.

island. Let us do this thing ourselves. Let us go into that house there and sit down and find out with our own eyes and ears whether this thing is true or not; whether this Smith is a man or a monster. If we can't do a little thing like that, what right have we to put crosses on ballot papers?"

Inglewood and Pym exchanged a glance; and Warner, who was no fool, saw in that glance that Moon was gaining ground. The motives that led Arthur to think of surrender were indeed very different from those which affected Dr. Cyrus Pym. All Arthur's instincts were on the side of privacy and a polite settlement; he was very English and would often endure wrongs rather than right them by scenes and serious rhetoric. To play at once the buffoon and the knight-errant, like his Irish friend, would have been absolute torture to him; but even the semi-official part he had played that afternoon was very painful. He was not likely to be reluctant if any one could convince him that his duty was to let sleeping dogs lie.

On the other hand, Cyrus Pym belonged to a country in which things are possible that seem crazy to the English. Regulations and authorities exactly like one of Innocent's pranks or one of Michael's satires really exist, propped by placid policemen and imposed on bustling business men. Pym knew whole States which are vast and yet secret and fanciful; each is as big as a nation yet as private as a lost village, and as unexpected as an apple-pie bed.[29] States where no man may have a cigarette, States where any man may have ten wives, very strict prohibition States, very lax divorce States—all these large local vagaries had prepared Cyrus Pym's mind for small local vagaries in a smaller country. Infinitely more remote from England than any Russian or Italian, utterly incapable even of conceiving what English conventions are, he could not see the social impossibility of the Court of Beacon. It is firmly believed by those who shared the experiment, that to the very end Pym believed in that phantasmal court and supposed it to be some Britannic institution.

---

[29] An apple-pie bed is a bed made as a joke with the sheets folded short so that the legs cannot be inserted between them.

Towards the synod thus somewhat at a standstill there approached through the growing haze and gloaming a short dark figure with a walk apparently founded on the imperfect repression of a negro breakdown. Something at once in the familiarity and the incongruity of this being moved Michael to even heartier outbursts of a healthy and humane flippancy.

"Why, here's little Nosey Gould," he exclaimed. "Isn't the mere sight of him enough to banish all your morbid reflections?"

"Really," replied Dr. Warner, "I really fail to see how Mr. Gould affects the question; and I once more demand——"

"Hello! what's the funeral, gents?" inquired the newcomer with the air of an uproarious umpire. "Doctor demandin' something? Always the way at a boarding-house, you know. Always lots of demand. No supply."

As delicately and impartially as he could, Michael restated his position, and indicated generally that Smith had been guilty of certain dangerous and dubious acts, and that there had even arisen an allegation that he was insane.

"Well, of course he is," said Moses Gould equably; "it don't need old 'Olmes to see that. The 'awk-like face of 'Olmes," he added with abstract relish, "showed a shide of disappointment, the sleuth-like Gould 'avin' got there before 'im."

"If he is mad," began Inglewood.

"Well," said Moses, "when a cove gets out on the tiles the first night there's generally a tile loose."

"You never objected before," said Diana Duke rather stiffly, "and you're generally pretty free with your complaints."

"I don't compline of him," said Moses magnanimously, "the poor chap's 'armless enough; you might tie 'im up in the garden here and 'e'd make noises at the burglars."

"Moses," said Moon with solemn fervour, "you are the incarnation of Common Sense. You think Mr. Innocent is mad. Let me introduce you to the incarnation of Scientific Theory. He also thinks Mr. Innocent is mad.—Doctor, this is my friend Mr. Gould.—Moses, this is the celebrated Dr. Cyrus Pym." The celebrated Dr. Cyrus Pym closed his eyes and bowed. He also murmured his national war-cry in a low voice, which sounded like "Pleased to meet you."

"Now you two people," said Michael cheerfully, "who both think our poor friend mad, shall jolly well go into that house over there and prove him mad. What could be more powerful than the combination of Scientific Theory with Common Sense? United you stand; divided you fall. I will not be so uncivil as to suggest that Dr. Pym has no common sense; I confine myself to recording the chronological accident that he has not shown us any so far. I take the freedom of an old friend in staking my shirt that Moses has no scientific theory. Yet against this strong coalition I am ready to appear, armed with nothing but an intuition—which is American for a guess."

"Distinguished by Mr. Gould's assistance," said Pym, opening his eyes suddenly. "I gather that though he and I are identical in primary di-agnosis there is yet between us something that cannot be called a disagreement, something which we may perhaps call a——" He put the points of thumb and forefinger together, spreading the other fingers exquisitely in the air, and seemed to be waiting for somebody else to tell him what to say.

"Catchin' flies?" inquired the affable Moses.

"A divergence," said Dr. Pym, with a refined sigh of relief; "a divergence. Granted that the man in question is deranged, he would not necessarily be all that science requires in a homicidal maniac——"

"Has it occurred to you," observed Moon, who was leaning on the gate again, and did not turn round, "that if he were a homicidal maniac he might have killed us all here while we were talking."

Something exploded silently underneath all their minds, like sealed dynamite in some forgotten cellars. They all remembered for the first time for some hour or two that the monster of whom they were talking was standing quite silently among them. They had left him in the garden like a garden statue; there might have been a dolphin coiling round his legs, or a fountain pouring out of his mouth, for all the notice they had taken of Innocent Smith. He stood with his crest of blonde, blown hair thrust somewhat forward, his fresh-coloured, rather short-sighted face looking patiently downwards at nothing in particular, his huge shoulders humped, and his hands in his trousers pockets. So far as they could guess he had not moved at all. His green coat might have been cut out of the green turf on which he stood. In his shadow Pym had expounded and Rosamund expostulated, Michael had ranted and Moses had ragged. He had remained like a thing graven; the god of the garden. A sparrow had perched on one of his heavy shoulders; and then, after correcting its costume of feathers, had flown away.

"Why," cried Michael, with a shout of laughter, "the Court of Beacon has opened—and shut up again too. You all know now I am right. Your buried common sense has told you just what my buried common sense has told me. Smith might have fired off a hundred cannons instead of a pistol, and you would still know he was harmless as I know he is harmless. Back we all go to the house and clear a room for discussion. For the High Court of Beacon, which has already arrived at its decision, is just about to begin its inquiry."

"Just a goin' to begin!" cried little Mr. Moses in an extraordinary sort of disinterested excitement, like that of an animal during music or a thunderstorm. "Follow on to the 'Igh Court of Eggs and Bacon; 'ave a kipper from the old firm! 'Is Lordship complimented Mr. Gould on the 'igh professional delicacy 'e had shown, and which was worthy of the best traditions of the Saloon Bar—and three of Scotch hot, miss! Oh, chase me, girls!"

The girls betraying no temptation to chase him, he went away in a sort of waddling dance of pure excitement; and had made a circuit of the garden before he reappeared, breathless but still beaming. Moon had known his man when he realized that no people presented to Moses Gould could be quite serious, even if they were quite furious. The glass doors stood open on the side nearest to Mr. Moses Gould; and as the feet of that festive idiot were evidently turned in the same direction, everybody else went that way with the unanimity of some uproarious procession. Only Diana Duke retained enough rigidity to say the thing that had been boiling at her fierce feminine lips for the last few hours. Under the shadow of tragedy she had kept it back as unsympathetic. "In that case," she said sharply, "these cabs can be sent away."

"Well, Innocent must have his bag, you know," said Mary with a smile. "I dare say the cabman would get it down for us."

"I'll get the bag," said Smith, speaking for the first time for hours; his voice sounded remote and rude, like the voice of a statue.

Those who had so long danced and disputed round his immobility were left breathless by his precipitance. With a run and spring he was out of the garden into the street; with a spring and one quivering kick he was actually on the roof of the cab. The cabman happened to be standing by the horse's head, having just removed its emptied nose-bag. Smith seemed for an instant to be rolling about on the cab's back in the embraces of his own Gladstone bag. The next instant, however, he had rolled, as if by a royal luck, into the high seat behind, and with a shriek of piercing and appalling suddenness had sent the horse flying and scampering far away down the street.

His evanescence was so violent and swift, that this time it was all the other people who were turned into garden statues. Mr. Moses Gould, however, being ill-adapted both physically and morally for the purposes of permanent sculpture, came to life some time before the rest, and, turning to Moon, remarked, like a man starting chattily with a stranger on an omnibus, "Tile loose, eh? Cab loose anyhow." There followed a fatal silence; and then Dr. Warner said, with a sneer like a club of stone,—

"This is what comes of the Court of Beacon, Mr. Moon. You have let loose a maniac on the whole metropolis."

Beacon House stood, as has been said, at the end of a long crescent of continuous houses. The little garden that shut it in ran out into a sharp point like a green cape pushed out into the sea of two streets. Smith and his cab shot up one side of the triangle, and certainly most of those standing inside it never expected to see him again. At the apex, however, he turned the horse sharply round and drove with equal violence up the other side of the garden, visible to all the group. With a common impulse the little crowd ran across the lawn as if to stop him, but they soon had reason to duck and recoil. Even as he vanished up street for the second time, he let the big yellow bag fly from his hand, so that it fell in the centre of the garden, scattering the company like a bomb, and nearly damaging Dr. Warner's hat for the third time. Long before they had collected themselves, the cab had shot away with a shriek that went into a whisper.

"Well," said Michael Moon, with a very queer note in his voice, "you may as well all go inside anyhow; it's getting rather dark and cold. We've got two relics of Mr. Smith at least; his fiancée and his trunk."

"Why do you want us to go inside?" asked Arthur Inglewood, in whose red brow and rough brown hair botheration seemed to have reached its limit.

"I want the rest to go in," said Michael in a clear voice, "because I want the whole of this garden in which to talk to you."

There was an atmosphere of irrational doubt; it was really getting colder, and a night wind had begun to wave the one or two trees in the twilight. Dr. Warner, however, spoke in a voice devoid of indecision.

"I refuse to listen to any such proposal," he said; "you have lost this ruffian, and I must find him."

"I don't ask you to listen to any proposal," answered Moon quietly; "I only ask you to listen."

He made a silencing movement with his hand, and immediately the whistling noise that had been lost in the dark streets on one side of the house could be heard from quite a new quarter on the other side. Through the night-maze of streets the noise increased with incredible rapidity, and the next moment the flying hoofs and flashing wheels had swept up to the blue-railed gate at which they originally stood. Mr. Smith got down from his perch with an air of absent-mindedness, and coming back into the garden stood in the same in an elephantine attitude as before.

"Get inside! get inside!" cried Moon hilariously, with the air of one shooing a company of cats. "Come, come, be quick about it! Didn't I tell you I wanted to talk to Inglewood?"

How they were all really driven into the house again it would have been difficult afterwards to say. They had reached the point of being exhausted with incongruities, as people at a farce are ill with laughing, and the brisk growth of the storm among the trees seemed like a final gesture of things in general. Inglewood lingered behind them, saying with a certain amicable exasperation, "I say, do you really want to speak to me?"

"I do," said Michael, "very much."

Night had come as it generally does, quicker than the twilight had seemed to promise. While the human eye still felt the sky as light gray, a very large and lustrous moon appearing abruptly above a bulk of roofs and trees, proved by contrast that the sky was already a very dark gray indeed. A drift of barren leaves across the lawn, a drift of riven clouds across the sky, seemed to be lifted on the same strong and yet laborious wind.

"Arthur," said Michael, "I began with an intuition; but now I am sure. You and I are going to defend this friend of yours before the blessed Court of Beacon, and to clear him too—clear him both of crime and lunacy. Just listen to me while I preach to you for a bit." They walked up and down the darkening garden together as Michael Moon went on.

"Can you," asked Michael, "shut your eyes and see some of those queer old hieroglyphics they stuck up on white walls in the old hot countries. How stiff they were in shape and yet how gaudy in colour. Think of some alphabet of arbitrary figures picked out in black and red, or white and green, with some old Semitic crowd of Nosey Gould's ancestors staring at it, and try to think why the people put it up at all."

Inglewood's first instinct was to think that his perplexing friend had really gone off his head at last; there seemed so reckless a flight of irrelevancy from the tropic-pictured walls he was asked to imagine to the gray, wind-swept, and somewhat chilly suburban garden in which he was actually kicking his heels. How he could be more happy in one by imagining the other he could not conceive. Both (in themselves) were unpleasant.

"Why does everybody repeat riddles," went on Moon abruptly, "even if they've forgotten the answers? Riddles are easy to remember because they are hard to guess. So were those stiff old symbols in black, red, or green easy to remember because they had been hard to guess. Their colours were plain. Their shapes were plain. Everything was plain except the meaning."

Inglewood was about to open his mouth in an amiable protest, but Moon went on, plunging quicker and quicker up and down the garden and smoking faster and faster. "Dances, too," he said; "dances were not frivolous. Dances were harder to understand than inscriptions and texts. The old dances were stiff, ceremonial, highly coloured but silent. Have you noticed anything odd about Smith?"

"Well, really," cried Inglewood, left behind in a collapse of humour, "have I noticed anything else about him?"

"Have you noticed this about him," asked Moon, with unshaken persistency, "that he has done so much and said so very little? When first he came he talked, but in a gasping, irregular sort of way, as if he wasn't used to it. All he really did was actions—painting red flowers on black gowns or throwing yellow bags on to the grass. I tell you that big green figure is figurative—like any green figure capering on some white Eastern wall."

"My dear Michael," cried Inglewood, in a rising irritation which increased with the rising wind, "you are getting absurdly fanciful."

"I think of what has just happened," said Michael steadily. "The man has not spoken for hours; and yet he has been speaking all the time. He fired three shots from a six-shooter and then gave it up to us, when he might have shot us dead in our boots. How could he express his trust in us better than that? He wanted to be tried by us. How could he have shown it better than by standing quite still and letting us discuss it? He wanted to show that he stood there willingly, and could escape if he liked. How could he have shown it better than by escaping in the cab and coming back again? Innocent Smith is not a madman—he is a ritualist. He wants to express himself, not with his tongue, but with his arms and legs—with my body I thee worship, as it says in the marriage service. I begin to understand the old plays and pageants. I see why the mutes at a funeral were mute. I see why the mummers were mum. They *meant* something; and Smith means something too. All other jokes have to be noisy—like little Nosey Gould's jokes, for instance. The only silent jokes are the practical jokes. Poor Smith, properly considered, is an allegorical practical joker. What he has really done in this house has been as frantic as a war-dance, but as silent as a picture."

"I suppose you mean," said the other dubiously, "that we have got to find out what all these crimes meant, as if they were so many coloured picture-puzzles. But even supposing that they do mean something—why, Lord bless my soul!——"

Taking the turn of the garden quite naturally, he had lifted his eyes to the moon, by this time risen big and luminous, and had seen a huge, half-human figure sitting on the garden wall. It was outlined so sharply against the moon that for the first flash it was hard to be certain even that it was human: the hunched shoulders and outstanding hair had rather the air of a colossal cat. It resembled a cat also in the fact that when first startled it sprang up and ran with easy activity along the top of the wall. As it ran, however, its heavy shoulders and small stooping head rather suggested a baboon. The instant it came within reach of a tree it made an ape-like leap and was lost in the branches. The gale, which by this time was shaking every shrub in the garden, made the identification yet more difficult, since it melted the moving limbs of the fugitive in the multitudinous moving limbs of the tree.

"Who is there?" shouted Arthur. "Who are you? Are you Innocent?"

"Not quite," answered an obscure voice among the leaves. "I cheated you once about a penknife."

The wind in the garden had gathered strength, and was throwing the tree backwards and forwards with the man in the thick of it, just as it had on the gay and golden afternoon when he had first arrived.

"But are you Smith?" asked Inglewood, as in an agony.

"Very nearly," said the voice out of the tossing tree.

"But you must have some real names," shrieked Inglewood in despair. "You must call yourself something."

"Call myself something," thundered the obscure, shaking the tree so that all its ten thousand leaves seemed to be talking at once. "I call myself Roland Oliver Isaiah Charlemagne Arthur Hildebrand Homer Danton Michaelangelo Shakespeare Brakespeare——"

"But, manalive!" began Inglewood in exasperation.

"That's right! that's right!" came with a roar out of the rocking tree; "that's my real name." And he broke a branch, and one or two autumn leaves fluttered away across the moon.

PART II

THE EXPLANATIONS
OF INNOCENT SMITH

I

THE EYE OF DEATH;
OR, THE MURDER CHARGE

The dining-room of the Dukes had been set out for the Court of
Beacon with a certain impromptu pomposity that seemed somehow
to increase its cosiness. The big room was, as it were, cut up into
small rooms, with walls only waist high—the sort of separations that
children make when they are playing at shops. This had been done by
Moses Gould and Michael Moon (the two most active members of
this remarkable inquiry) with the ordinary furniture of the place. At
one end of the long mahogany table was set the one enormous garden
chair, which was surmounted by the old torn tent or umbrella which
Smith himself had suggested as a coronation canopy. Inside this erection could be perceived the dumpy form of Mrs. Duke, with cushions and a form of countenance that already threatened slumber. At
the other end sat the accused Smith, in a kind of dock; for he was
carefully fenced in with a quadrilateral of light bedroom chairs, any of
which he could have tossed out of the window with his big toe. He
had been provided with pens and paper, out of the latter of which he
made paper boats, paper darts, and paper dolls contentedly through
the whole proceedings. He never spoke or even looked up, but seemed
as unconscious as a child on the floor of an empty nursery.

On a row of chairs raised high on the top of a long settee sat the
three young ladies with their backs up against the window, and Mary
Gray in the middle; it was something between a jury box and the stall
of the Queen of Beauty at a tournament. Down the centre of the
long table Moon had built a low barrier out of eight bound volumes
of "Good Words" [30] to express the moral wall that divided the con-
flicting parties. On the right side sat the two advocates of the prosecution, Dr. Pym and Mr. Gould; behind, a barricade of books and
documents, chiefly (in the case of Dr. Pym) solid volumes of

---

[30] *Good Words* was a popular Victorian Journal that ran from 1860 to 1906.

criminology. On the other side, Moon and Inglewood, for the defence, were also fortified with books and papers; but as these included several old yellow volumes by Ouida[31] and Wilkie Collins,[32] the hand of Mr. Moon seemed to have been somewhat careless and comprehensive. As for the victim and prosecutor, Dr. Warner, Moon wanted at first to have him kept entirely behind a high screen in the corner, urging the indelicacy of his appearance in court, but privately assuring him of an unofficial permission to peep over the top now and then. Dr. Warner, however, failed to rise to the chivalry of such a course, and after some little disturbance and discussion he was accommodated with a seat on the right side of the table in a line with his legal advisers.

It was before this solidly-established tribunal that Dr. Cyrus Pym, after passing a hand through the honey-coloured hair over each ear, rose to open the case. His statement was clear and even restrained, and such flights of imagery as occurred in it only attracted attention by a certain indescribable abruptness, not uncommon in the flowers of American speech.

He planted the points of his ten frail fingers on the mahogany, closed his eyes, and opened his mouth. "The time has gone by," he said, "when murder could be regarded as a moral and individual act, important perhaps to the murderer, perhaps to the murdered. Science has profoundly ..." here he paused, poising his compressed finger and thumb in the air as if he were holding an elusive idea very tight by its tail, then he screwed up his eyes and said "modified," and let it go—"has profoundly Modified our view of death. In superstitious ages it was regarded as the termination of life, catastrophic, and even tragic, and was often surrounded with solemnity. Brighter days, however, have dawned, and we now see death as universal and inevitable, as part of that great soul-stirring and heart-upholding average which we call for convenience the order of nature. In the same way we have

[31] "Ouida" is a pseudonym of Marie Louise de la Ramee (1839–1908), English-born writer of "hot-house" romances, ridiculed for their improbable plots and outrageous heroes.
[32] Wilkie Collins (1824–1889) was an English novelist best noted for mystery, suspense and crime writing, including the first full-length detective stories in English.

come to consider murder *socially*. Rising above the mere private feelings of a man while being forcibly deprived of life, we are privileged to behold murder as a mighty whole, to see the rich rotation of the cosmos, bringing, as it brings the golden harvests and the golden-bearded harvesters, the return for ever of the slayers and the slain."

He looked down, somewhat affected with his own eloquence, coughed slightly, putting up four of his pointed fingers with the excellent manners of Boston, and continued: "There is but one result of this happier and humaner outlook which concerns the wretched man before us. It is that thoroughly elucidated by a Milwaukee doctor, our great secret-guessing Sonnenschein, in his great work, 'The Destructive Type.' We do not denounce Smith as a murderer, but rather as a murderous man. The type is such that its very life—I might say its very health—is in killing. Some hold that it is not properly an aberration, but a newer and even a higher creature. My dear old friend Dr. Bulger, who kept ferrets—" (here Moon suddenly ejaculated a loud "hurrah!" but so instantaneously resumed his tragic expression that Mrs. Duke looked everywhere else for the origin of the sound); Dr. Pym continued somewhat sternly—"who, in the interests of knowledge, kept ferrets, held that the creature's ferocity is not utilitarian, but absolutely an end in itself. However this may be with ferrets, it is certainly so with the prisoner. In his other iniquities you may find the cunning of the maniac; but his acts of blood have almost the simplicity of sanity. But it is the awful sanity of the sun and the elements—a cruel, an evil sanity. As soon stay the iris-leapt cataracts of our virgin West as stay the natural force that sends him forth to slay. No environment, however scientific, could have softened him. Place that man in the silver-silent purity of the palest cloister, and there will be some deed of violence done with the crozier or the alb. Rear him in a happy nursery, amid our brave-browed Anglo-Saxon infancy, and he will find some way to strangle with the skipping-rope or to brain with the brick. Circumstances may be favourable, training may be admirable, hopes may be high, but the huge elemental hunger of Innocent Smith for blood will in its appointed season burst like a well-timed bomb."

Arthur Inglewood glanced curiously for an instant at the huge creature at the foot of the table, who was fitting a paper figure with a paper cocked hat, and then looked back at Dr. Pym, who was concluding in a quieter tone.

"It only remains for us," he said, "to bring forward actual evidence of his previous attempts. By an agreement already made with the Court and the leaders of the defence, we are permitted to put in evidence authentic letters from witnesses to these scenes, which the defence is free to examine. Out of several cases of such outrages we have decided to select one—the clearest and most scandalous. I will therefore, without further delay, call on my junior, Mr. Gould, to read two letters—one from the Sub-Warden and the other from the porter of Brakespeare College, in Cambridge University." [33]

Gould jumped up with a jerk like a jack-in-the-box, an academic-looking paper in his hand and a fever of importance on his face. He began in a loud, high, cockney voice that was as abrupt as cock-crow:—

"Sir,—Hi am the Sub-Warden of Brikespeare College, Cambridge——"

"Lord have mercy on us," muttered Moon, making a backward movement as men do when a gun goes off.

"Hi am the Sub-Warden of Brikespeare College, Cambridge," proclaimed the uncompromising Moses, "and I can endorse the description you give of the conduct of the un'appy Smith. It was not alone my unfortunate duty to rebuke many of the lesser violences of his undergraduate period, but I was actually a witness to the last iniquity which terminated that period. Hi happened to be passing under the house of my friend the Warden of Brikespeare, which is semi-detached from the College and connected with it by two or three very ancient arches or props, like bridges, across a small strip of water connected with the river. To my grive astonishment I be'eld my eminent friend suspended in mid-air and clinging to one of these pieces

---

[33] Breakspeare College, Cambridge: though a few say otherwise, Cambridge (founded in the thirteenth century) is generally regarded as England's premier university. There is no college by this name at Cambridge University though the description given, however, could well describe St. John's College. See comments in the introduction regarding Chesterton's references to Cambridge and Oxford in these novels.

of masonry, his appearance and attitude indicatin' that he suffered from the grivest apprehensions. After a short time I heard two very loud shots, and distinctly perceived the unfortunate undergraduate Smith leaning far out of the Warden's window and aiming at the Warden repeatedly with a revolver. Upon seeing me, Smith burst into a loud laugh (in which impertinence was mingled with insanity), and appeared to desist. I sent the college porter for a ladder, and he succeeded in detaching the Warden from his painful position. Smith was sent down. The photograph I enclose is from the group of the University Rifle Club prizemen, and represents him as he was when at the College.—Hi am, your obedient servant, AMOS BOULTER.

"The other letter," continued Gould in a glow of triumph, "is from the porter, and won't take long to read.

"DEAR SIR,—It is quite true that I am the porter of Brikespeare College, and that I 'elped the Warden down when the young man was shooting at him, as Mr. Boulter has said in his letter. The young man who was shooting was Mr. Smith, the same that is in the photograph Mr. Boulter sends.—Yours respectfully, SAMUEL BARKER."

Gould handed the two letters across to Moon, who examined them. But for the vocal divergences in the matter of h's and a's, the Sub-Warden's letter was exactly as Gould had rendered it; and both that and the porter's letter were plainly genuine. Moon handed them to Inglewood, who handed them back in silence to Moses Gould.

"So far as this first charge of continual attempted murder is concerned," said Dr. Pym, standing up for the last time, "that is my case."

Michael Moon rose for the defence with an air of depression which gave little hope at the outset to the sympathizers with the prisoner. He did not, he said, propose to follow the doctor into the abstract questions. "I do not know enough to be an agnostic," he said, rather wearily, "and I can only master the known and admitted elements in such controversies. As for science and religion, the known and admitted facts are few and plain enough. All that the parsons say is unproved. All that the doctors say is disproved. That's the only difference between

science and religion there's ever been, or will be. Yet these new discoveries touch me, somehow," he said, looking down sorrowfully at
his boots. "They remind me of a dear old great-aunt of mine who
used to enjoy them in her youth. It brings tears to my eyes. I can see
the old bucket by the garden fence and the line of shimmering poplars behind——"

"Hi! here, stop the 'bus a bit," cried Mr. Moses Gould, rising in a
sort of perspiration. "We want to give the defence a fair run—like
gents, you know; but any gent would draw the line at shimmering
poplars."

"Well, hang it all," said Moon, in an injured manner, "if Dr. Pym
may have an old friend with ferrets, why mayn't I have an old aunt
with poplars?"

"I am sure," said Mrs. Duke, bridling, with something almost like
a shaky authority, "Mr. Moon may have what aunts he likes."

"Why, as to liking her," began Moon, "I—but perhaps, as you say,
she is scarcely the core of the question. I repeat that I do not mean to
follow the abstract speculations. For, indeed, my answer to Dr. Pym is
simple and severely concrete. Dr. Pym has only treated one side of the
psychology of murder. If it be true that there is a kind of man who has
a natural tendency to murder, is it not equally true"—here he lowered
his voice and spoke with a crushing quietude and earnestness—"is it not
equally true that there is a kind of man who has a natural tendency to
get murdered? Is it not at least a hypothesis holding the field that Dr.
Warner is such a man? I do not speak without the book, any more than
my learned friend. The whole matter is expounded in Dr. Moonen-
schein's monumental work, 'The Destructible Doctor,' with diagrams,
showing the various ways in which such a person as Dr. Warner may be
resolved into his elements. In the light of these facts——"

"Hi, stop the 'bus! stop the 'bus!" cried Moses, jumping up and
gesticulating in great excitement, "My principal's got something to
say! My principal wants to do a bit of talkin'."

Dr. Pym was indeed on his feet, looking pallid and rather vicious.
"I have strictly *con*-fined myself," he said nasally, "to books to which
immediate reference can be made, I have Sonnenschein's 'Destructive
Type' here on the table, if the defence wish to see it. Where is this

wonderful work on Destructibility Mr. Moon is talking about? Does it exist? Can he produce it?"

"Produce it!" cried the Irishman with a rich scorn. "I'll produce it in a week if you'll pay for the ink and paper."

"Would it have much authority?" asked Pym, sitting down.

"Oh, authority!" said Moon lightly; "that depends on a fellow's religion."

Dr. Pym jumped up again. "Our authority is based on masses of accurate detail," he said. "It deals with a region in which things can be handled and tested. My opponent will at least admit that death is a fact of experience."

"Not of mine," said Moon mournfully, shaking his head. "I've never experienced such a thing in all my life."

"Well, really," said Dr. Pym, and sat down sharply amid a crackle of papers.

"So we see," resumed Moon, in the same melancholy voice, "that a man like Dr. Warner is, in the mysterious workings of evolution, doomed to such attacks. My client's onslaught, even if it occurred, was not unique. I have in my hand letters from more than one acquaintance of Dr. Warner whom that remarkable man has affected in the same way. Following the example of my learned friends I will read only two of them. The first is from an honest and laborious matron living off the Harrow Road.

"MR. MOON, SIR,—Yes, I did throw a sorsepan at him. Wot then? It was all I had to throw, all the soft things being porned, and if your Docter Warner doesn't like having sorsepans thrown at him, don't let him were his hat in a respectable woman's parler, and tell him to leave orf smiling or tell us the joke.—Yours respectfully,

"HANNAH MILES.

"The other letter is from a physician of some note in Dublin, with whom Dr. Warner was once engaged in consultation. He writes as follows:—

"DEAR SIR,—The incident to which you refer is one which I regret, and which, moreover, I have never been able to explain. My own branch of medicine is not mental; and I should be glad to have the view of a mental specialist on my singular momentary and indeed almost automatic action. To say that I 'pulled Dr. Warner's nose' is, however, inaccurate in a respect that strikes me as important. That I punched his nose I must cheerfully admit (I need not say with what regret); but pulling seems to me to imply a precision of handling and an exactitude of objective with which I cannot reproach myself. In comparison with this, the act of punching was an outward, instantaneous, and even natural gesture.—Believe me, yours faithfully,

"BURTON LESTRANGE.

"I have numberless other letters," continued Moon, "all bearing witness to this widespread feeling about my eminent friend; and I therefore think that Dr. Pym should have admitted this side of the question into his survey. We are in the presence, as Dr. Pym so truly says, of a natural force. As soon stay the cataracts of the London water-works as stay the great tendency of Dr. Warner to be assassinated by somebody. Place that man in a Quakers' meeting, among the most peaceful of Christians, and he will immediately be beaten to death with sticks of chocolate. Place him among the angels of the New Jerusalem, and he will be stoned to death with precious stones. Circumstances may be beautiful and wonderful, the average may be heart-upholding, the harvester may be golden-bearded, the doctor may be secret-guessing, the cataract may be iris-leapt, the Anglo-Saxon infant may be brave-browed, but against and above all these prodigies the grand simple tendency of Dr. Warner to get murdered will still pursue its way until it happily and triumphantly succeeds at last."

He pronounced this peroration with an appearance of strong emotion. But even stronger emotions were manifesting themselves on the other side of the table. Dr. Warner had leaned his large body quite across the little figure of Moses Gould and was talking in excited whispers to Dr. Pym. That expert nodded a great many times and finally started to his feet with a sincere expression of sternness.

"Ladies and gentlemen," he cried indignantly, "as my colleague has said, we should be delighted to give any latitude to the defence—if there were a defence. But Mr. Moon seems to think he is there to make jokes—very good jokes I dare say, but not at all adapted to assist his client. He picks holes in science. He picks holes in my client's social popularity. He picks holes in my literary style, which doesn't seem to suit his high-toned European taste. But how does this picking of holes affect the issue? This Smith has picked two holes in my client's hat, and with an inch better aim would have picked two holes in his head. All the jokes in the world won't unpick those holes or be any use for the defence."

Inglewood looked down in some embarrassment, as if shaken by the evident fairness of this, but Moon still gazed at his opponent in a dreamy way. "The defence?" he said vaguely—"oh, I haven't begun that yet."

"You certainly have not," said Pym warmly, amid a murmur of applause from his side, which the other side found it impossible to answer. "Perhaps, if you have any defence, which has been doubtful from the very beginning——"

"While you're standing up," said Moon, in the same almost sleepy style, "perhaps I might ask you a question."

"A question? Certainly," said Pym stiffly. "It was distinctly arranged between us that as we could not cross-examine the witnesses, we might vicariously cross-examine each other. We are in a position to invite all such inquiry."

"I think you said," observed Moon absently, "that none of the prisoner's shots really hit the doctor."

"For the cause of science," cried the complacent Pym, "fortunately not."

"Yet they were fired from a few feet away."

"Yes; about four feet."

"And no shots hit the Warden, though they were fired quite close to him too?" asked Moon.

"That is so," said the witness gravely.

"I think," said Moon, suppressing a slight yawn, "that your Sub-Warden mentioned that Smith was one of the University's record men for shooting."

"Why, as to that——" began Pym, after an instant of stillness.

"A second question," continued Moon, comparatively curtly. "You said there were other cases of the accused trying to kill people. Why have you not got evidence of them?"

The American planted the points of his fingers on the table again. "In those cases," he said precisely, "there was no evidence from outsiders, as in the Cambridge case, but only the evidence of the actual victims."

"Why didn't you get their evidence?"

"In the case of the actual victims," said Pym, "there was some difficulty and reluctance, and——"

"Do you mean," asked Moon, "that none of the actual victims would appear against the prisoner?"

"That would be exaggerative," began the other.

"A third question," said Moon, so sharply that every one jumped. "You've got the evidence of the Sub-Warden who heard some shots; where's the evidence of the Warden himself who was shot at? The Warden of Brakespeare lives, a prosperous gentleman."

"We did ask for a statement from him," said Pym a little nervously; "but it was so eccentrically expressed that we suppressed it out of deference to an old gentleman whose past services to science have been great."

Moon leaned forward. "You mean, I suppose," he said, "that his statement was favourable to the prisoner."

"It might be understood so," replied the American doctor; "but, really, it was difficult to understand at all. In fact, we sent it back to him."

"You have no longer, then, any statement signed by the Warden of Brakespeare."

"No."

"I only ask," said Michael quietly, "because we have. To conclude my case I will ask my junior, Mr. Inglewood, to read a statement of the true story—a statement attested as true by the signature of the warden himself."

Arthur Inglewood rose with several papers in his hand, and though he looked somewhat refined and self-effacing, as he always did, the spectators were surprised to feel that his presence was, upon the whole, more efficient and sufficing than his leader's. He was, in truth, one of those modest men who cannot speak until they are told to speak; and then can speak well. Moon was entirely the opposite. His own impudences amused him in private, but they slightly embarrassed him in public: he felt a fool while he was speaking, whereas Inglewood felt a fool only because he could not speak. The moment he had anything to say he could speak; and the moment he could speak speaking seemed quite natural. Nothing in this universe seemed quite natural to Michael Moon.

"As my colleague has just explained," said Inglewood, "there are two enigmas or inconsistencies on which we base the defence. The first is a plain physical fact. By the admission of everybody, by the very evidence adduced by the prosecution, it is clear that the accused was celebrated as a specially good shot. Yet on both the occasions complained of he shot at a man from a distance of four or five feet, and shot at him four or five times, and never hit him once. That is the first startling circumstance on which we base our argument. The second, as my colleague has urged, is the curious fact that we cannot find a single victim of these alleged outrages to speak for himself. Subordinates speak for him. Porters climb up ladders to him. But he himself is silent. Ladies and gentlemen, I propose to explain on the spot both the riddle of the shots and the riddle of the silence. I will first of all read the covering letter in which the true account of the Cambridge incident is contained, and then that document itself. When you have heard both, there will be no doubt about your decision. The covering letter runs as follows:—

"Dear Sir,—The following is a very exact and even vivid account of the incident as it really happened at Brakespeare College. We, the undersigned, do not see any particular reason why we should refer it to any isolated authorship. The truth is, it has been a composite production; and we have even had some difference of opinion about the adjectives. But every word of it is true.—We are, yours faithfully,

"Wilfred Emerson Eames,
"Warden of Brakespeare College, Cambridge.
"Innocent Smith.

"The enclosed statement" continued Inglewood, "runs as follows:—

"A celebrated English university backs so abruptly on the river, that it has, so to speak, to be propped up and patched with all sorts of bridges and semi-detached buildings. The river splits itself into several small streams and canals, so that in one or two corners the place has almost the look of Venice. It was so specially in the case with which we are concerned, in which a few flying buttresses or airy ribs of stone sprang across a strip of water to connect Brakespeare College with the house of the Warden of Brakespeare.

"The country around these colleges is flat; but it does not seem flat when one is thus in the midst of the colleges. For in these flat fens there are always wandering lakes and lingering rivers of water. And these always change what might have been a scheme of horizontal lines into a scheme of vertical lines. Wherever there is water the height of high buildings is doubled, and a British brick house becomes a Babylonian tower. In that shining unshaken surface the houses hang head downwards exactly to their highest or lowest chimney. The coral-coloured cloud seen in that abyss is as far below the world as its original appears above it. Every scrap of water is not only a window but a skylight. Earth splits under men's feet into precipitous aerial perspectives, into which a bird could as easily wing its way as——"

Dr. Cyrus Pym rose in protest. The documents he had put in evidence had been confined to cold affirmations of fact. The defence, in a general way, had an indubitable right to put their case in their own way, but all this landscape gardening seemed to him (Dr. Cyrus Pym) to be not up to the business. "Will the leader of the defence tell me," he asked, "how it can possibly affect this case, that a cloud was cor'l-coloured, or that the river was unshaken and shiny, or that a bird could have winged itself anywhere?"

"Oh, I don't know," said Michael, lifting himself lazily; "you see, you don't know yet what our defence is. Till you know that, don't you see, anything may be relevant. Why, suppose," he said suddenly, as if an idea had struck him, "suppose we wanted to prove the old Warden colour-blind. Suppose he was shot by a black man with white hair, when he thought he was being shot by a white man with yellow hair! To ascertain if that cloud was really and truly coral-coloured might be of the most massive importance."

He paused with a seriousness which was hardly generally shared, and continued with the same fluency: "Or suppose we wanted to maintain that the Warden committed suicide—that he just got Smith to hold the pistol as Brutus's slave held the sword.[34] Why, it would make all the difference whether the Warden could see himself plain in still water. Still water has made hundreds of suicides: one sees oneself so very—well, so very plain."

"Do you, perhaps," inquired Pym with austere irony, "maintain that your client was a bird of some sort—say, a flamingo?"

"In the matter of his being a flamingo," said Moon with sudden severity, "my client reserves his defence."

No one quite knowing what to make of this, Mr. Moon resumed his seat with an air of great sternness, and Inglewood resumed the reading of his document:—

"There is something pleasing to a mystic in such a land of mirrors. For a mystic is one who holds that two worlds are better than one. In the highest sense, indeed, all thought is reflection.

"This is the real truth, in the saying that second thoughts are best. Animals have no second thoughts: man alone is able to see his own thought double, as a drunkard sees a lamp-post; man alone is able to see his own thought upside down as one sees a house in a puddle. This duplication of mentality, as in a mirror, is (we repeat) the inmost thing of human philosophy. There is a mystical, even a monstrous truth, in the statement that two heads are better than one. But they ought both to grow on the same body."

"I know it's a little transcendental at first," interposed Inglewood, beaming round with a broad apology, "but you see this document was written in collaboration by a don and a——"

[34] "Brutus' slave held the sword" is a reference to Marcus Junius Brutus (85–42 B.C.), Roman politician and conspirator who committed suicide by throwing himself upon his sword as it was being held by his slave. The event was dramatized in Shakespeare's *Julius Ceasar* (1599), act v, scene 5, lines 47–48.

"Drunkard, eh?" suggested Moses Gould, beginning to enjoy himself.

"I rather think," proceeded Inglewood with an unruffled and critical air, "that this part was written by the don. I merely warn the Court that the statement, though indubitably accurate, bears here and there the trace of coming from two authors."

"In that case," said Dr. Pym, leaning back and sniffing, "I cannot agree with them that two heads are better than one."

"The undersigned persons think it needless to touch on a kindred problem so often discussed at committees for University Reform: the question of whether dons see double because they are drunk, or get drunk because they see double. It is enough for them (the undersigned persons) if they are able to pursue their own peculiar and profitable theme—which is puddles. What (the undersigned persons ask themselves) is a puddle? A puddle repeats infinity, and is full of light; nevertheless, if analyzed objectively, a puddle is a piece of dirty water spread very thin on mud. The two great historic universities of England have all this large and level and reflective brilliance. They repeat infinity. They are full of light. Nevertheless, or, rather, on the other hand, they are puddles—puddles, puddles, puddles, puddles. The undersigned persons ask you to excuse an emphasis inseparable from strong conviction."

Inglewood ignored a somewhat wild expression on the faces of some present, and continued with eminent cheerfulness:—

"Such were the thoughts that failed to cross the mind of the undergraduate Smith as he picked his way among the stripes of canal and the glittering rainy gutters into which the water broke up round the back of Brakespeare College. Had these thoughts crossed his mind he would have been very much happier than he was. Unfortunately he did not know that his puzzles were puddles. He did not know that the academic mind reflects infinity and is full of light by the simple process of being shallow and standing still. In his case, therefore, there was something solemn, and even evil about the infinity implied. It was half-way through a starry night of bewildering brilliancy; stars were both above and below. To young Smith's sullen fancy the skies below seemed even hollower than the skies above: he had a horrible idea that if he counted the stars he would find one too many in the pool.

"In crossing the little paths and bridges he felt like one stepping on the black and slender ribs of some cosmic Eiffel Tower. For to him, and nearly all the educated youth of that epoch, the stars were cruel things. Though they glowed in the great dome every night, they were an enormous and ugly secret; they uncovered the nakedness of nature; they were a glimpse of the iron wheels and pulleys behind the scenes. For the young men of that sad time thought that the god always came from the machine. They did not know that in reality the machine only comes from the god. In short, they were all pessimists, and star-light was atrocious to them—atrocious because it was true. All their universe was black with white spots.

"Smith looked up with relief from the glittering pools below to the glittering skies and the great black bulk of the college. The only light other than stars glowed through one peacock-green curtain in the upper part of the building, marking where Dr. Emerson Eames always worked till morning and received his friends and favourite pupils at any hour of the night. Indeed, it was to his rooms that the melancholy Smith was bound. Smith had been at Dr. Eames's lecture for the first half of the morning, and at pistol practice and fencing in a saloon for the second half. He had been sculling madly for the first half of the afternoon and thinking idly (and still more madly) for the second half. He had gone to a supper where he was uproarious, and on to a debating club where he was perfectly insufferable, and the melancholy Smith was melancholy still. Then, as he was going home to his diggings he remembered the eccentricity of his friend and master, the Warden of Brakespeare, and resolved desperately to turn in to that gentleman's private house.

"Emerson Eames was an eccentric in many ways, but his throne in philosophy and metaphysics was of international eminence; the university could hardly have afforded to lose him, and, moreover, a don has only to continue any of his bad habits long enough to make them a part of the British Constitution. The bad habits of Emerson Eames were to sit up all night and to be a student of

Schopenhauer.[35] Personally, he was a lean, lounging sort of man, with a blond pointed beard, not so very much older than his pupil Smith in the matter of mere years, but older by centuries in the two essential respects of having a European reputation and a bald head.

"'I came, against the rules, at this unearthly hour,' said Smith, who was nothing to the eye except a very big man trying to make himself small, 'because I am coming to the conclusion that existence is really too rotten. I know all the arguments of the thinkers that think otherwise—bishops, and agnostics, and those sort of people. And knowing you were the greatest living authority on the pessimist thinkers——'

"'All thinkers,' said Eames, 'are pessimist thinkers.'

"After a patch of pause, not the first—for this depressing conversation had gone on for some hours with alternations of cynicism and silence—the Warden continued with his air of weary brilliancy: 'It's all a question of wrong calculation. The moth flies into the candle because he doesn't happen to know that the game is not worth the candle. The wasp gets into the jam in hearty and hopeful efforts to get the jam into him. In the same way the vulgar people want to enjoy life just as they want to enjoy gin—because they are too stupid to see that they are paying too big a price for it. That they never find happiness——that they don't even know how to look for it—is proved by the paralyzing clumsiness and ugliness of everything they do. Their discordant colours are cries of pain. Look at the brick villas beyond the college on this side of the river. There's one with spotted blinds; look at it! just go and look at it!'

"'Of course,' he went on dreamily, 'one or two men see the sober fact a long way off—they go mad. Do you notice that maniacs mostly try either to destroy other things, or (if they are thoughtful) to destroy themselves? The madman is the man behind the scenes, like the man

[35] Arthur Schopenhauer (1788–1860) was a German philosopher for whom the complete silencing of the will was the ideal for human beings. Inspired by Buddhism and influential to, amongst others, Tolstoy, whom Chesterton elsewhere criticized as being part of a "cult of simplicity", this philosophy was one Chesterton rejected and takes on in all three novels in this volume in various ways.

that wanders about the *coulisse* of a theatre.[36] He has only opened the wrong door and come into the right place. He sees things at the right angle. But the common world——'

"'Oh, hang the world!' said the sullen Smith, letting his fist fall on the table in an idle despair.

"'Let's give it a bad name first,' said the Professor calmly, 'and then hang it. A puppy with hydrophobia would probably struggle for life while we killed it; but if we were kind we should kill it. So an omniscient god would put us out of our pain. He would strike us dead.'

"'Why doesn't he strike us dead?' asked the undergraduate abstractedly, plunging his hands into his pockets.

"'He is dead himself,' said the philosopher; 'that is where he is really enviable.'

"'To any one who thinks,' proceeded Eames, 'the pleasures of life, trivial and soon tasteless, are bribes to bring us into a torture chamber. We all see that for any thinking man mere extinction is the ... What are you doing? ... Are you mad? ... Put that thing down.'

"Dr. Eames had turned his tired but still talkative head over his shoulder, and had found himself looking into a small round black hole, rimmed by a six-sided circlet of steel, with a sort of spike standing up on the top. It fixed him like an iron eye. Through those eternal instants during which the reason is stunned he did not even know what it was. Then he saw behind it the chambered barrel and cocked hammer of a revolver, and behind that the flushed and rather heavy face of Smith, apparently quite unchanged, or even more mild than before.

"'I'll help you out of your hole, old man,' said Smith, with rough tenderness. 'I'll put the puppy out of his pain.'

"Emerson Eames retreated towards the window. 'Do you mean to kill me?' he cried.

"'It's not a thing I'd do for every one,' said Smith with emotion; 'but you and I seem to have got so intimate to-night, somehow. I know all your troubles now, and the only cure, old chap.'

"'Put that thing down,' shouted the Warden.

---

[36] The *coulisse* of a theatre is a piece of side scenery or the space between two of these.

"'It'll soon be over, you know,' said Smith with the air of a sympathetic dentist. And as the Warden made a run for the window and balcony, his benefactor followed him with a firm step and a compassionate expression.

"Both men were perhaps surprised to see that the gray and white of early daybreak had already come. One of them, however, had emotions calculated to swallow up surprise. Brakespeare College was one of the few that retained real traces of Gothic ornament, and just beneath Dr. Eames's balcony there ran out what had perhaps been a flying buttress, still shapelessly shaped into gray beasts and devils, but blinded with mosses and washed out with rains. With an ungainly and most courageous leap, Eames sprang out on this antique bridge, as the only possible mode of escape from the maniac. He sat astride of it, still in his academic gown, dangling his long thin legs, and considering further chances of flight. The whitening daylight opened under as well as over him that impression of vertical infinity already remarked about the little lakes round Brakespeare. Looking down and seeing the spires and chimneys pendent in the pools, they felt alone in space. They felt as if they were peering over the edge from the North Pole and seeing the South Pole below.

"'Hang the world, we said,' observed Smith, 'and the world is hanged. "He has hanged the world upon nothing," says the Bible. Do you like being hanged upon nothing? I'm going to be hanged on something myself. I'm going to swing for you ... Dear, tender old phrase,' he murmured; 'never true till this moment. I am going to swing for you. For you, dear friend. For your sake. At your express desire.'

"'Help!' cried the Warden of Brakespeare College; 'help!'

"'The puppy struggles,' said the undergraduate, with an eye of pity; 'the poor little puppy struggles. How fortunate it is that I am wiser and kinder than he,' and he sighted his weapon so as exactly to cover the upper part of Eames's bald head.

"'Smith,' said the philosopher with a sudden change to a sort of ghastly lucidity, 'I shall go mad.'

"'And so look at things from the right angle,' observed Smith, sighing gently. 'Ah, but madness is only a palliative at best, a drug. The only cure is an operation—an operation that is always successful: death.'

"As he spoke the sun rose. It seemed to put colour into everything, with the rapidity of a lightning artist. A fleet of little clouds sailing across the sky changed from pigeon-gray to pink. All over the little academic town the tops of different buildings took on different tints: here the sun would pick out the green enamel on a pinnacle, there the scarlet tiles of a villa; here the copper ornament on some artistic shop, and there the sea-blue slates of some old and steep church roof. All these coloured crests seemed to have something oddly individual and significant about them, like crests of famous knights pointed out in a pageant or a battlefield: they each arrested the eye, especially the rolling eye of Emerson Eames as he looked round on the morning and accepted it as his last. Through a narrow chink between a black timber tavern and a big gray college he could see a clock with gilt hands which the sunshine set on fire. He stared at it as though hypnotized; and suddenly the clock began to strike, as if in personal reply. As if at a signal, clock after clock took up the cry: all the churches awoke like chickens at cockcrow. The birds were already noisy in the trees behind the college. The sun rose, gathering glory that seemed too full for the deep skies to hold, and the shallow waters beneath them seemed golden and brimming and deep enough for the thirst of the gods. Just round the corner of the College, and visible from his crazy perch, were the brightest specks on that bright landscape, the villa with the spotted blinds which he had made his text that night. He wondered for the first time what people lived in them.

"Suddenly he called out with mere querulous authority, as he might have called to a student to shut a door.

"'Let me come off this place,' he cried; 'I can't bear it,'

"'I rather doubt if it will bear you,' said Smith critically; 'but before you break your neck, or I blow out your brains, or let you back into this room (on which complex points I am undecided), I want the metaphysical point cleared up. Do I understand that you want to get back to life?'

"'I'd give anything to get back,' replied the unhappy professor.

"'Give anything!' cried Smith; 'then, blast your impudence, give us a song!'

"'What do you mean?' demanded the exasperated Eames; 'what song?'

"'A hymn, I think, would be most appropriate,' answered the other gravely. 'I'll let you off if you'll repeat after me the words—

"'I thank the goodness and the grace
        That on my birth have smiled,
    And perched me on this curious place,
        A happy English child.'[37]

"Dr. Emerson Eames having briefly complied, his persecutor abruptly told him to hold his hands up in the air. Vaguely connecting this proceeding with the usual conduct of brigands and bushrangers, Mr. Eames held them up, very stiffly, but without marked surprise. A bird alighting on his stone seat took no more notice of him than of a comic statue.

"'You are now engaged in public worship,' remarked Smith severely, 'and before I have done with you, you shall thank God for the very ducks on the pond.'

"The celebrated pessimist half articulately expressed his perfect readiness to thank God for the ducks on the pond.

"'Not forgetting the drakes,' said Smith sternly. (Eames weakly conceded the drakes.) 'Not forgetting anything, please. You shall thank heaven for churches and chapels and villas and vulgar people and puddles and pots and pans and sticks and rags and bones and spotted blinds.'

"'All right, all right,' repeated the victim in despair; 'sticks and rags and bones and blinds.'

"'Spotted blinds, I think we said,' remarked Smith with a roguish ruthlessness, and wagging the pistol-barrel at him like a long metallic finger.

"'Spotted blinds,' said Emerson Eames faintly.

"'You can't say fairer than that,' admitted the younger man, 'and now I'll just tell you this to wind up with. If you really were what you profess to be, I don't see that it would matter to snail or seraph if you

[37] "I thank the goodness and the grace / That on my birth have smiled" comes from a popular hymn entitled "A Child's Hymn of Praise". It was written by Jane Taylor (1783–1824).

broke your impious stiff neck and dashed out all your drivelling devil-worshipping brains. But in strict biographical fact you are a very nice fellow, addicted to talking putrid nonsense, and I love you like a brother. I shall therefore fire off all my cartridges round your head so as not to hit you (I am a good shot, you may be glad to hear), and then we will go in and have some breakfast.'

"He let off two barrels in the air, which the Professor endured with singular firmness, and then said, 'But don't fire them all off.'

"'Why not?' asked the other buoyantly.

"'Keep them,' answered his companion, 'for the next man you meet who talks as we were talking.'

"It was at this moment that Smith, looking down, perceived apopletic terror upon the face of the Sub-Warden, and heard the refined shriek with which he summoned the porter and the ladder.

"It took Dr. Eames some little time to disentangle himself from the ladder, and some little time longer to disentangle himself from the Sub-Warden. But as soon as he could do so unobtrusively, he rejoined his companion in the late extraordinary scene. He was astonished to find the gigantic Smith heavily shaken, and sitting with his shaggy head on his hands. When addressed, he lifted a very pale face.

"'Why, what is the matter?' asked Eames, whose own nerves had by this time twittered themselves quiet, like the morning birds.

"'I must ask your indulgence,' said Smith, rather brokenly. 'I must ask you to realize that I have just had an escape from death.'

"'You have had an escape from death?' repeated the Professor in not unpardonable irritation. 'Well, of all the cheek——'

"'Oh, don't you understand, don't you understand?' cried the pale young man impatiently. 'I had to do it, Eames; I had to prove you wrong or die. When a man's young, he nearly always has some one whom he thinks the top-water mark of the mind of man—some one who knows all about it, if anybody knows.

"'Well, you were that to me; you spoke with authority, and not as the scribes. Nobody could comfort me if you said there was no comfort. If you really thought there was nothing anywhere, it was because you had been there to see. Don't you see that I had to prove you didn't really mean it?—or else drown myself in the canal.'

"'Well,' said Eames hesitatingly, 'I think perhaps you confuse——'

"'Oh, don't tell me that!' cried Smith with the sudden clairvoyance of mental pain; 'don't tell me that I confuse enjoyment of existence with the Will to Live! That's German, and German is High Dutch, and High Dutch is Double Dutch. The thing I saw shining in your eyes when you dangled on that bridge was enjoyment of life and not "the Will to Live." What you knew when you sat on that damned gargoyle was that the world, when all is said and done, is a wonderful and beautiful place; I know it, because I knew it at the same minute. I saw the gray clouds turn pink, and the little gilt clock in the crack between the houses. It was *those* things you hated leaving, not Life, whatever that is. Eames, we've been to the brink of death together; won't you admit I am right?'

"'Yes,' said Eames very slowly, 'I think you are right. You shall have a First!'[38]

"'Right!' cried Smith, springing up reanimated. 'I've passed with honours, and now let me go and see about being sent down.'[39]

"'You needn't be sent down,' said Eames with the quiet confidence of twelve years of intrigue. 'Everything with us comes from the man on top to the people just round him: I am the man on top, and I shall tell the people round me the truth.'

"The massive Mr. Smith rose and went slowly to the window, but he spoke with equal firmness. 'I must be sent down,' he said, 'and the people must not be told the truth.'

"'And why not?' asked the other.

"'Because I mean to follow your advice,' answered the massive youth, in heavy meditation. 'I mean to keep the remaining shots for people in the shameful state you and I were in last night—I wish we could even plead drunkenness. I mean to keep those bullets for pessimists—pills for pale people. And in this way I want to walk the world like a wonderful surprise—to float as idly as the thistledown, and come as silently as the sunrise; not to be expected any more

---

[38] A First is the highest of the four levels of degree awarded at Cambridge and most British universities.

[39] Being "sent down" is the traditional expression at Oxford and Cambridge for being expelled.

than the thunderbolt, not to be recalled any more than the dying breeze. I don't want people to anticipate me as a well-known practical joke. I want both my gifts to come virgin and violent, the death and the life after death. I am going to hold a pistol to the head of the Modern Man. But I shall not use it to kill him—only to bring him to life. I begin to see a new meaning in being the skeleton at the feast.'

"'You can scarcely be called a skeleton,' said Dr. Eames, smiling.

"'That comes of being so much at the feast,' answered the massive youth. 'No skeleton can keep his figure if he is always dining out.[40] But that is not quite what I meant: what I mean is that I caught a kind of glimpse of the meaning of death and all that—the skull and crossbones, the *memento mori*.[41] It isn't only meant to remind us of a future life, but to remind us of a present life too. With our weak spirits we should grow old in eternity if we were not kept young by death. Providence has to cut immortality into lengths for us, as nurses cut the bread and butter into fingers.'

"Then he added suddenly in a voice of unnatural actuality, 'But I know something now, Eames. I knew it when the clouds turned pink.'

"'What do you mean?' asked Eames. 'What did you know?'

"'I knew for the first time that murder is really wrong.'

"He gripped Dr. Eames's hand and groped his way somewhat unsteadily to the door. Before he had vanished through it he had added, 'It's very dangerous, though, when a man thinks for a split second that he understands death.'

"Dr. Eames remained in repose and rumination some hours after his late assailant had left. Then he rose, took his hat and umbrella, and went for a brisk if rotatory walk. Several times, however, he stood outside the villa with the spotted blinds, studying them intently with his head slightly on one side. Some took him for a lunatic and some for an intending purchaser. He is not yet sure that the two characters would be widely different.

---

[40] "Skeleton at the feast" is something that spoils ones' pleasure.

[41] *Memento mori* is Latin for "remember you too must die" and may refer to an object, such as a skull, intended to remind people of death.

"The above narrative has been constructed on a principle which is, in the opinion of the undersigned persons, new in the art of letters. Each of the two actors is described as he appeared to the other. But the undersigned persons absolutely guarantee the exactitude of the story; and if their version of the thing be questioned, they, the undersigned persons, would deucedly well like to know who does know about it if they don't.

"The undersigned persons will now adjourn to 'The Spotted Dog' for beer. Farewell.

"(*Signed*) JAMES EMERSON EAMES,
"Warden of Brakespeare College, Cambridge.
"INNOCENT SMITH."

II

THE TWO CURATES;
OR, THE BURGLARY CHARGE

Arthur Inglewood handed the document he had just read to the leaders of the prosecution, who examined it with their heads together. Both the Jew and the American were of sensitive and excitable stocks, and they revealed by the jumpings and bumpings of the black head and the yellow that nothing could be done in the way of denial of the document. The letter from the Warden was as authentic as the letter from the Sub-Warden, however regrettably different in dignity and social tone.

"Very few words," said Inglewood, "are required to conclude our case in this matter. Surely it is now plain that our client carried his pistol about with the eccentric but innocent purpose of giving a wholesome scare to those whom he regarded as blasphemers. In each case the scare was so wholesome that the victim himself has dated from it as from a new birth. Smith, so far from being a madman, is rather a mad doctor—he walks the world curing frenzies and not distributing them. That is the answer to the two unanswerable questions which I put to the prosecutors. That is why they dared not produce a line by any one who had actually confronted the pistol. All who had actually confronted the pistol confessed that they had profited by it. That was why Smith, though a good shot, never hit anybody. He never hit anybody because he was a good shot. His mind was as clear of murder as his hands are of blood. This, I say, is the only possible explanation of these facts and of all the other facts. No one can possibly explain the Warden's conduct except by believing the Warden's story. Even Dr. Pym, who is a very factory of ingenious theories, could find no other theory to cover the case."

"There are promising per-spectives in hypnotism and dual personality," said Dr. Cyrus Pym dreamily; "the science of criminology is in its infancy, and——"

"Infancy!" cried Moon, jerking his red pencil in the air with a gesture of enlightenment; "why, that explains it!"

"I repeat," proceeded Inglewood, "that neither Dr. Pym nor any one else can account on any other theory but ours for the Warden's signature, for the shots missed and the witnesses missing."

The little Yankee had slipped to his feet with some return of a cock-fighting coolness. "The defence," he said, "omits a coldly colossal fact. They say we produce none of the actual victims. Wal, here is one victim—England's celebrated and stricken Warner. I reckon he is pretty well produced. And they suggest that all the outrages were followed by reconciliations. Wal, there's no flies on England's Warner; and he isn't reconciliated much."

"My learned friend," said Moon, getting elaborately to his feet, "must remember that the science of shooting Dr. Warner is in its infancy. Dr. Warner would strike the idlest eye as one specially difficult to startle into any recognition of the glory of God. We admit that our client, in this one instance, failed, and that the operation was not successful. But I am empowered to offer, on behalf of my client, a proposal for operating on Dr. Warner again, at his earliest convenience, and without further fees."

" 'Ang it all, Michael," cried Gould, quite serious for the first time in his life, "you might give us a bit of bally sense for a chinge."

"What was Dr. Warner talking about just before the first shot?" asked Moon sharply.

"The creature," said Dr. Warner superciliously, "asked me, with characteristic rationality, whether it was my birthday."

"And you answered, with characteristic swank," cried Moon, shooting out a long lean finger, as rigid and arresting as the pistol of Smith, "that you didn't keep your birthday."

"Something like that," assented the doctor.

"Then," continued Moon, "he asked you why not, and you said it was because you didn't see that birth was anything to rejoice over. Agreed? Now, is there any one who doubts that our tale is true?"

There was a cold crash of stillness in the room; and Moon said, "*Pax populi vox Dei*;[42] it is the silence of the people that is the voice

---

[42] *Pax Populi vox Dei*, literally, "the peace of the people is the voice of God", is a wordplay on the usual formulation, *vox populi vox Dei*, "the voice of the people is the voice of God".

of God. Or in Dr. Pym's more civilized language, it is up to him to open the next charge. On this we claim an acquittal."

It was about an hour later. Dr. Cyrus Pym had remained for an unprecedented time with his eyes closed and his thumb and finger in the air. It almost seemed as if he had been "struck so," as the nurses say; and in the deathly silence Michael Moon felt forced to relieve the strain with some remark. For the last half-hour or so the eminent criminologist had been explaining that science took the same view of offences against property as it did of offences against life. "Most murder," he had said, "is a variation of homicidal mania, and in the same way most theft is a version of kleptomania. I cannot entertain any doubt that my learned friends opposite adequately con-ceive how this must involve a scheme of punishment more tol'rant and humane than the cruel methods of ancient codes. They will doubtless exhibit consciousness of a chasm so eminently yawning, so thought-arresting, so——" It was here that he paused and indulged in the delicate gesture to which allusion has been made; and Michael could bear it no longer.

"Yes, yes," he said impatiently, "we admit the chasm. The old cruel codes accused a man of theft and sent him to prison for ten years. The tolerant and humane ticket accuses him of nothing and sends him to prison for ever. We pass the chasm."

It was characteristic of the eminent Pym, in one of his trances of verbal fastidiousness, that he went on, unconscious not only of his opponent's interruption, but even of his own pause.

"So stock-improving," continued Dr. Cyrus Pym, "so fraught with real high hopes of the future. Science therefore regards thieves, in the abstract, just as it regards murderers. It regards them not as sinners to be punished for an arbitrary period, but as patients to be detained and cared for" (his two first digits closed again as he hesitated)—"in short, for the required period. But there is something special in the case we investigate here. Kleptomania commonly con-joins itself——"

"I beg pardon," said Michael; "I did not ask just now because, to tell the truth, I really thought Dr. Pym, though seemingly vertical, was enjoying well-earned slumber, with a pinch in his fingers of scentless and delicate dust. But now that things are moving a little more, there is something I should really like to know. I have hung on Dr. Pym's lips, of course, with an interest that it were weak to call rapture, but I have so far been unable to form any conjecture about what the accused, in the present instance, is supposed to have been and gone and done."

"If Mr. Moon will have patience," said Pym with dignity, "he will find that this was the very point to which my exposition was di-rected. Kleptomania, I say, exhibits itself as a kind of physical attraction to certain defined materials; and it has been held (by no less a man than Harris) that this is the ultimate explanation of the strict specialism and vurry narrow professional outlook of most criminals. One will have an irresistible physical impulsion towards pearl sleeve-links, while he passes over the most elegant and celebrated diamond sleeve-links, placed about in the most con-spicuous locations. Another will impede his flight with no less than forty-seven buttoned boots, while elastic-sided boots leave him cold, and even sarcastic. The specialism of the criminal, I repeat, is a mark rather of insanity than of any brightness of business habits; but there is one kind of depredator to whom this principle is at first sight hard to apply. I allude to our fellow-citizen the housebreaker.

"It has been maintained by some of our boldest young truth-seekers, that the eye of a burglar beyond the back-garden wall could hardly be caught and hypnotized by a fork that is insulated in a locked box under the butler's bed. They have thrown down the gauntlet to American science on this point. They declare that diamond links are not left about in conspicuous locations in the haunts of the lower classes, as they were in the great test experiment of Calypso College. We hope this experiment here will be an answer to that young ring-ing challenge, and will bring the burglar once more into line and union with his fellow-criminals."

Moon, whose face had gone through every phase of black bewil-derment for five minutes past, suddenly lifted his hand and struck the table in explosive enlightenment.

"Oh, I see!" he cried; "you mean that Smith is a burglar."

"I thought I made it quite ad'quately lucid," said Mr. Pym, folding up his eyelids. It was typical of this topsy-turvy private trial that all the eloquent extras, all the rhetoric or digression on either side, was exasperating and unintelligible to the other. Moon could not make head or tail of the solemnity of a new civilization. Pym could not make head or tail of the gaiety of an old one.

"All the cases in which Smith has figured as an expropriator," continued the American doctor, "are cases of burglary. Pursuing the same course as in the previous case, we select the indubitable instance from the rest, and we take the most correct cast-iron evidence. I will now call on my colleague, Mr. Gould, to read a letter we have received from the earnest, unspotted Canon of Durham, Canon Hawkins."

Mr. Moses Gould leapt up with his usual alacrity to read the letter from the earnest and unspotted Hawkins. Moses Gould could imitate a farmyard well, Sir Henry Irving[43] not so well, Marie Lloyd to a point of excellence, and the new motor horns in a manner that put him upon the platform of great artists. But his imitation of a Canon of Durham was not convincing; indeed, the sense of the letter was so much obscured by the extraordinary leaps and gasps of his pronunciation that it is perhaps better to print it here as Moon read it when, a little later, it was handed across the table.

"DEAR SIR,—I can scarcely feel surprise that the incident you mention, private as it was, should have filtered through our omnivorous journals to the mere populace; for the position I have since attained makes me, I conceive, a public character, and this was certainly the most extraordinary incident in a not uneventful and perhaps not an unimportant career. I am by no means without experience in scenes of civil tumult. I have faced many a political crisis in the old Primrose League[44] days at Herne Bay,[45] and, before I broke with the wilder

[43] Sir Henry Irving was an English actor (1838–1905) famed for his roles in *Hamlet* and *Macbeth* and considered the greatest actor of his time. Marie Lloyd (1870–1922) was an English music-hall entertainer famed for her witty portrayals of working-class Londoners.

[44] The Primrose League was founded in 1883 to commemorate Prime Minister Benjamin Disraeli's politics and promote the principles of Tory Democracy. It became a conservative political organization.

[45] Herne Bay is a popular Evangelical holiday site and lovers' trysting place in Kent near Canterbury, England.

set, have spent many a night at the Christian Social Union. But this other experience was quite inconceivable. I can only describe it as the letting loose of a place which it is not for me, as a clergyman, to mention.

"It occurred in the days when I was, for a short period, a curate at Hoxton; and the other curate, then my colleague, induced me to attend a meeting which he described, I must say profanely described, as calculated to promote the kingdom of God. I found, on the contrary, that it consisted entirely of men in corduroys and greasy clothes whose manners were coarse and their opinions extreme.

"Of my colleague in question I wish to speak with the fullest respect and friendliness, and I will therefore say little. No one can be more convinced than I of the evil of politics in the pulpit; and I never offer my congregation any advice about voting except in cases in which I feel strongly that they are likely to make an erroneous selection. But, while I do not mean to touch at all upon political or social problems, I must say that for a clergyman to countenance, even in jest, such discredited nostrums of dissipated demagogues as Socialism or Radicalism partakes of the character of the betrayal of a sacred trust. Far be it from me to say a word against the Reverend Raymond Percy, the colleague in question. He was brilliant, I suppose, and to some apparently fascinating; but a clergyman who talks like a Socialist, wears his hair like a pianist, and behaves like an intoxicated person, will never rise in his profession, or even obtain the admiration of the good and wise. Nor is it for me to utter my personal judgments of the appearance of the people in the hall. Yet a glance round the room, revealing ranks of debased and envious faces——"

"Adopting," said Moon explosively, for he was getting restive—"adopting the reverend gentleman's favourite figure of logic, may I say that while tortures would not tear from me a whisper about his intellect, he is a blasted old jackass."

"Really!" said Dr Pym; "I protest."

"You must keep quiet, Michael," said Inglewood; "they have a right to read their story."

"Chair! Chair! Chair!" cried Gould, rolling about exuberantly in his own; and Pym glanced for a moment towards the canopy which covered all the authority of the Court of Beacon.

"Oh, don't wake the old lady," said Moon, lowering his own voice in a moody good-humour. "I apologize. I won't interrupt again."

Before the little eddy of interruption was ended the reading of the clergyman's letter was already continuing.

"The proceedings opened with a speech from my colleague, of which I will say nothing. It was deplorable. Many of the audience were Irish, and showed the weakness of that impetuous people. When gathered together into gangs and conspiracies they seem to lose altogether that lovable good-nature and readiness to accept anything one tells them which distinguishes them as individuals."

With a slight start, Michael rose to his feet, bowed solemnly, and sat down again.

"These persons, if not silent, were at least applausive during the speech of Mr. Percy. He descended to their level with witticisms about rent and a reserve of labour. Confiscation, expropriation, arbitration, and such words with which I cannot soil my lips, recurred constantly. Some hours afterwards the storm broke. I had been addressing the meeting for some time, pointing out the lack of thrift in the working classes, their insufficient attendance at evening service, their neglect of the Harvest Festival, and of many other things that might materially help them to improve their lot. It was, I think, about this time that an extraordinary interruption occurred. An enormous, powerful man, partly concealed with white plaster, arose in the middle of the hall, and offered (in a loud, roaring voice, like a bull's) some observations which seemed to be in a foreign language. Mr. Raymond Percy, my colleague, descended to his level by entering into a duel of repartee, in which he appeared to be the victor. The meeting began to behave more respectfully for a little; yet before I had said twelve sentences more the rush was made for the platform. The enormous plasterer, in particular, plunged towards us, shaking the earth like an elephant; and I really do not know what would have happened if a man equally large, but not quite so ill-dressed, had not jumped up also and held him away. This other big man shouted a sort of speech to the mob as he was shoving them back. I don't know what he said, but, what with shouting and shoving and such horseplay, he got us out at a back door, while the wretched people went roaring down another passage.

"Then follows the truly extraordinary part of my story. When he had got us outside, in a mean backyard of blistered grass leading into a lane with a very lonely-looking lamp-post, this giant addressed us as follows: 'You're well out of that, sir; now you'd better come along with me. I want you to help me in an act of social justice, such as we've all been talking about. Come along!' And turning his big back abruptly, he led us down the lean old lane with the one lean old lamp-post, we scarcely knowing what to do but to follow him. He had certainly helped us in a most difficult situation, and, as a gentleman, I could not treat such a benefactor with suspicion without grave grounds. Such also was the view of my Socialistic colleague, who (with all his dreadful talk of arbitration) is a gentleman also. In fact, he comes of the Staffordshire Percys, a branch of the old house, and has the black hair and pale, clear-cut face of the whole family. I cannot but refer it to vanity that he should heighten his personal advantages with black velvet or a red cross of considerable ostentation, and certainly—but I digress.

"A fog was coming up the street, and that last lost lamp-post faded behind us in a way that certainly depressed the mind. The large man in front of us looked larger and larger in the haze. He did not turn round, but he said with his huge back to us, 'All that talking's no good; we want a little practical Socialism.'

"'I quite agree,' said Percy; 'but I always like to understand things in theory before I put them into practice.'

"'Oh, you leave it to me,' said the practical Socialist, or whatever he was, with the most terrifying vagueness. 'I have a way with me. I'm a Permeator.'

"I could not imagine what he meant, but my companion laughed, so I was sufficiently reassured to continue the unaccountable journey for the present. It led us through most singular ways; out of the lane, where we were already rather cramped, into a paved passage, at the end of which we passed through a wooden gate left open. We then found ourselves, in the increasing darkness and vapour, crossing what appeared to be a beaten path across a kitchen garden. I called out to the enormous person going on in front, but he answered obscurely that it was a short cut.

"I was just repeating my very natural doubt to my clerical companion when I was brought up against a short ladder, apparently leading to a higher level of road. My thoughtless colleague ran up it so quickly that I could not do otherwise than follow as best I could. The path on which I then planted my feet was quite unprecedentedly narrow. I had never had to walk along a thoroughfare so exiguous. Along one side of it grew what, in the dark and density of air, I first took to be some short, strong thicket of shrubs. Then I saw that they were not short shrubs; they were the tops of tall trees. I, an English gentleman and clergyman of the Church of England—I was walking along the top of a garden wall like a torn cat.

"I am glad to say that I stopped within my first five steps, and let loose my just reprobation, balancing myself as best I could all the time.

" 'It's a right-of-way,' declared my indefensible informant. 'It's closed to traffic once in a hundred years.'

" 'Mr. Percy, Mr. Percy!' I called out; 'you are not going on with this blackguard?'

" 'Why, I think so,' answered my unhappy colleague flippantly. 'I think you and I are bigger blackguards than he is, whatever he is.'

" 'I am a burglar,' explained the big creature quite calmly. 'I am a member of the Fabian Society. I take back the wealth stolen by the capitalist, not by sweeping civil war and revolution, but by reform fitted to the special occasion—here a little and there a little. Do you see that fifth house along the terrace with the flat roof? I'm permeating that one to-night.'

" 'Whether this is a crime or a joke,' I cried, 'I desire to be quit of it.'

" 'The ladder is just behind you,' answered the creature with horrible courtesy; 'and, before you go, do let me give you my card.'

"If I had had the presence of mind to show any proper spirit I should have flung it away, though any adequate gesture of the kind would have gravely affected my equilibrium upon the wall. As it was, in the wildness of the moment, I put it in my waistcoat pocket, and, picking my way back by wall and ladder, landed in the respectable streets once more. Not before, however, I had seen with my own eyes the two awful and lamentable facts—that the burglar was climbing up a slanting roof towards the chimneys, and that Raymond Percy (a priest of God and, what was worse, a gentleman) was crawling up after him. I have never seen either of them since that day.

"In consequence of this soul-searching experience I severed my connection with the wild set. I am far from saying that every member of the Christian Social Union must necessarily be a burglar. I have no right to bring any such charge. But it gave me a hint of what such courses may lead to in many cases; and I saw them no more."

"I have only to add that the photograph you enclose, taken by a Mr. Inglewood, is undoubtedly that of the burglar in question. When I got home that night I looked at his card, and he was inscribed there under the name of Innocent Smith.—Yours faithfully,

"JOHN CLEMENT HAWKINS."

Moon merely went through the form of glancing at the paper. He knew that the prosecutors could not have invented so heavy a document; that Moses Gould (for one) could no more write like a canon than he could read like one. After handing it back he rose to open the defence on the burglary charge.

"We wish," said Michael, "to give all reasonable facilities to the prosecution; especially as it will save the time of the whole court. The latter object I shall once again pursue by passing over all those points of theory which are so dear to Dr. Pym. I know how they are made. Perjury is a variety of aphasia, leading a man to say one thing instead of another. Forgery is a kind of writer's cramp, forcing a man to write his uncle's name instead of his own. Piracy on the high seas is probably a form of sea-sickness. But it is unnecessary for us to inquire into the causes of a fact which we deny. Innocent Smith never did commit burglary at all.

"I should like to claim the power permitted by our previous arrangement, and ask the prosecution two or three questions."

Dr. Cyrus Pym closed his eyes to indicate a courteous assent.

"In the first place," continued Moon, "have you the date of Canon Hawkins's last glimpse of Smith and Percy climbing up the walls and roofs?"

"Ho, yuss!" called out Gould smartly. "November thirteen, eighteen ninety-one."

"Have you," continued Moon, "identified the houses in Hoxton up which they climbed?"

"Must have been Ladysmith Terrace out of the highroad," answered Gould with the same clockwork readiness.

"Well," said Michael, cocking an eyebrow at him, "was there any burglary in that terrace that night? Surely you could find that out."

"There may well have been," said the doctor primly, after a pause, "an unsuccessful one that led to no legalities."

"Another question," proceeded Michael. "Canon Hawkins, in his blood-and-thunder boyish way, left off at the exciting moment. Why don't you produce the evidence of the other clergyman, who actually followed the burglar and presumably was present at the crime?"

Dr. Pym rose and planted the points of his fingers on the table, as he did when he was specially confident of the clearness of his reply.

"We have entirely failed," he said, "to track the other clergyman, who seems to have melted into the ether after Canon Hawkins had seen him as-cending the gutters and the leads. I am fully aware that this may strike many as sing'lar; yet, upon reflection, I think it will appear pretty natural to a bright thinker. This Mr. Raymond Percy is admittedly, by the canon's evidence, a minister of eccentric ways. His con-nection with England's proudest and fairest does not seemingly prevent a taste for the society of the real low-down. On the other hand, the prisoner Smith is, by general agreement, a man of irr'sistible fascination. I entertain no doubt that Smith led the Reverend Percy into the crime and forced him to hide his head in the real crim'nal class. That would fully account for his nonappearance, and the failure of all attempts to trace him."

"It is impossible, then, to trace him?" asked Moon.

"Impossible," repeated the specialist, shutting his eyes.

"You are sure it is impossible?"

"Oh dry up, Michael," cried Gould, irritably. "We'd 'ave found 'im if we could, for you bet 'e saw the burglary. Don't *you* start looking for 'im. Look for your own 'ead in the dustbin. You'll find that—after a bit," and his voice died away in grumbling.

"Arthur," directed Michael Moon, sitting down, "kindly read Mr. Raymond Percy's letter to the court."

"Wishing, as Mr. Moon has said, to shorten the proceedings as much as possible," began Inglewood, "I will not read the first part of the letter sent to us. It is only fair to the prosecution to admit the account given by the second clergyman fully ratifies, as far as facts are concerned, that given by the first clergyman. We concede, then, the canon's story so far as it goes. This must necessarily be valuable to the prosecutor and also convenient to the court. I begin Mr. Percy's letter, then, at the point when all three men were standing on the garden wall:—

"As I watched Hawkins wavering on the wall, I made up my own mind not to waver. A cloud of wrath was on my brain, like the cloud of copper fog on the houses and gardens round. My decision was violent and simple; yet the thoughts that led up to it were so complicated and contradictory that I could not retrace them now. I knew Hawkins was a kind, innocent gentleman; and I would have given ten pounds for the pleasure of kicking him down the road. That God should allow good people to be as bestially stupid as that—rose against me like a towering blasphemy.

"At Oxford, I fear, I had the artistic temperament rather badly; and artists love to be limited. I liked the church as a pretty pattern; discipline was mere decoration. I delighted in mere divisions of time; I liked eating fish on Friday. But then I like fish; and the fast was made for men who like meat. Then I came to Hoxton and found men who had fasted for five hundred years; men who had to gnaw fish because they could not get meat—and fish-bones when they could not get fish. As too many British officers treat the army as a review, so I had treated the Church Militant as if it were the Church Pageant. Hoxton cures that. Then I realized that for eighteen hundred years the Church Militant had been not a pageant, but a riot—and a suppressed riot.

There, still living patiently in Hoxton, were the people to whom the tremendous promises had been made. In the face of that I had to become revolutionary if I was to continue to be religious. In Hoxton one cannot be a conservative without being also an atheist—and a pessimist. Nobody but the devil could want to conserve Hoxton.

"On the top of all this comes Hawkins. If he had cursed all the Hoxton men, excommunicated them and told them they were going to hell, I should have rather admired him. If he had ordered them all to be burned in the market-place, I should still have had that patience that all good Christians have with the wrongs inflicted on other people. But there is no priestcraft about Hawkins—nor any other kind of craft. He is as perfectly incapable of being a priest as he is of being a carpenter or a cabman or a gardener or a plasterer. He is a perfect gentleman; that is his complaint. He does not impose his creed, but simply his class. He never said a word of religion in the whole of his damnable address. He simply said all the things his brother, the major, would have said. A voice from heaven assures me that he has a brother, and that this brother is a major.

"When this helpless aristocrat had praised cleanliness in the body and convention in the soul to people who could hardly keep body and soul together, the stampede against our platform began. I took part in his undeserved rescue, I followed his obscure deliverer, until (as I have said) we stood together on the wall above the dim gardens, already clouding with fog. Then I looked at the curate and at the burglar, and decided, in a spasm of inspiration, that the burglar was the better man of the two. The burglar seemed quite as kind and human as the curate was—and he was also brave and self-reliant, which the curate was not. I knew there was no virtue in the upper class, for I belong to it myself; I knew there was not so very much in the lower class, for I had lived with it a long time. Many old texts about the despised and persecuted came back to my mind, and I thought that the saints might well be hidden in the criminal class. About the time Hawkins let himself down the ladder I was crawling up a low, sloping, blue-slate roof after the large man, who went leaping in front of me like a gorilla.

"This upward scramble was short, and we soon found ourselves tramping along a broad road of flat roofs, broader than many big thoroughfares, with chimney-pots here and there that seemed in the haze as bulky as small forts. The asphyxiation of the fog seemed to increase the somewhat swollen and morbid anger under which my brain and body laboured. The sky and all those things that are commonly clear seemed overpowered by sinister spirits. Tall spectres with turbans of vapour seemed to stand higher than sun or moon, eclipsing both. I thought dimly of illustrations to the 'Arabian Nights' on brown paper with rich but sombre tints, showing genii gathering round the Seal of Solomon. By the way, what was the Seal of Solomon?[46] Nothing to do with sealing-wax really, I suppose; but my muddled fancy felt the thick clouds as being of that heavy and clinging substance, of strong opaque colour, poured out of boiling pots and stamped into monstrous emblems.

"The first effect of the tall turbaned vapours was that discoloured look of pea-soup or coffee brown of which Londoners commonly speak. But the scene grew subtler with familiarity. We stood above the average of the housetops and saw something of that thing called smoke, which in great cities creates the strange thing called fog. Beneath us rose a forest of chimneypots. And there stood in every chimney-pot, as if it were a flower-pot, a brief shrub or a tall tree of coloured vapour. The colours of the smoke were various; for some chimneys were from firesides and some from factories, and some again from mere rubbish heaps. And yet, though the tints were all varied, they all seemed unnatural, like fumes from a witch's pot. It was as if the shameful and ugly shapes growing shapeless in the cauldron sent up each its separate spurt of steam, coloured according to the fish or flesh consumed. Here, aglow from underneath, were dark red clouds, such as might drift from dark jars of sacrificial blood; there the vapour was dark indigo gray, like the long hair of witches steeped in the hell-broth. In another place the smoke was of an awful opaque ivory yellow, such as might be the disembodiment of one of their old, leprous, waxen images. But right across it ran a line of bright, sinister, sulphurous green, as clear and crooked as Arabic——"

[46] Solomon was the son of David and a king of Israel (ca. 970–ca. 930 B.C.); the "seal" is a figure like the Star of David.

Mr. Moses Gould once more attempted the arrest of the 'bus. He was understood to suggest that the reader should shorten the proceedings by leaving out all the adjectives. Mrs. Duke, who had woken up, observed that she was sure it was all very nice, and the decision was duly noted down by Moses with a blue, and by Michael with a red, pencil. Inglewood then resumed the reading of the document.

"Then I read the writing of the smoke. Smoke was like the modern city that makes it; it is not always dull or ugly, but it is always wicked and vain.

"Modern England was like a cloud of smoke; it could carry all colours, but it could leave nothing but a stain. It was our weakness and not our strength that put a rich refuse in the sky. These were the rivers of our vanity pouring into the void. We had taken the sacred circle of the whirlwind, and looked down on it, and seen it as a whirlpool. And then we had used it as a sink. It was a good symbol of the mutiny in my own mind. Only our worst things were going to heaven. Only our criminals could still ascend like angels.

"As my brain was blinded with such emotions, my guide stopped by one of the big chimney-pots that stood at regular intervals like lamp-posts along that uplifted and aerial highway. He put his heavy hand upon it, and for the moment I thought he was merely leaning on it, tired with his steep scramble and long tramp along the top of the terrace. So far as I could guess from the abysses, full of fog on either side, and the veiled lights of red brown and old gold glowing through them now and again, we were on the top of one of those long, consecutive, and genteel rows of houses which are still to be found lifting their heads above poorer districts, the remains of some rage of optimism in earlier speculative builders. Probably enough, they were entirely untenanted, or tenanted only by such small clans of the poor as gather also in the old emptied palaces of Italy. Indeed, some time later, when the fog had lifted a little, I discovered that we were walking round a semicircle of crescent which fell away below us into one flat square or wide street below another, like a giant stairway, in a manner not unknown in the eccentric building of London, and looking like the last ledges of the land. But a cloud sealed the giant stairway as yet.

"My speculations about the sullen sky-scape, however, were interrupted by something as unexpected as the moon fallen from the sky. Instead of my burglar lifting his hand from the chimney he leaned on, he leaned on it a little more heavily, and the whole chimney-pot turned over like the opening top of an inkstand. I remembered the short ladder leaning against the low wall, and felt sure he had arranged his criminal approach long before.

"The collapse of the big chimney-pot ought to have been the culmination of my chaotic feelings; but, to tell the truth, it produced a sudden sense of comedy and even of comfort. I could not recall what connected this abrupt bit of housebreaking with some quaint but still kindly fancies. Then I remembered the delightful and uproarious scenes of roofs and chimneys in the harlequinades of my childhood, and was darkly and quite irrationally comforted by a sense of unsubstantiality in the scene, as if the houses were of lath and paint and paste-board, and were only meant to be tumbled in and out of by policemen and pantaloons. The law-breaking of my companion seemed not only seriously excusable, but even comically excusable. Who were all these pompous preposterous people with their footmen and their footscrapers, their chimney-pots and their chimney-pot hats, that they should prevent a poor clown from getting sausages if he wanted them? One would suppose that property was a serious thing. I had reached, as it were, a higher level of that mountain of vaporous visions, the heaven of a higher levity.

"My guide had jumped down into the dark cavity revealed by the displaced chimney-pot. He must have landed at a level considerably lower, for, tall as he was, nothing but his weirdly tousled head remained visible. Something again far off, and yet familiar, pleased me about this way of invading the houses of men. I thought of little chimney-sweeps, and 'The Water Babies;' [47] but I decided that it was not that. Then I remembered what it was that made me connect such topsy-turvy trespass with ideas quite opposite to the idea of crime. Christmas Eve, of course, and Santa Claus coming down the chimney.

[47] *The Water Babies* is a children's classic written in 1863 by Charles Kingsley (1819–1875).

"Almost at the same instant the hairy head disappeared into the black hole; but I heard a voice calling to me from below. A second or two afterwards, the hairy head reappeared; it was dark against the more fiery part of the fog, and nothing could be spelt of its expression, but its voice called on me to follow with that enthusiastic impatience, proper only among old friends. I jumped into the gulf, and as blindly as Curtius,[48] for I was still thinking of Santa Claus and the traditional virtue of such vertical entrance.

"In every well-appointed gentleman's house, I reflected, there was the front door for the gentlemen, and the side door for the tradesmen; but there was also the top door for the gods. The chimney is, so to speak, the underground passage between earth and heaven. By this starry tunnel Santa Claus manages—like the skylark—to be true to the kindred points of heaven and home. Nay, owing to certain conventions, and a widely distributed lack of courage for climbing, this door was, perhaps, little used. But Santa Claus's door was really the front door: it was the door fronting the universe.

"I thought this as I groped my way across the black garret, or loft below the roof, and scrambled down the squat ladder that let us down into a yet larger loft below. Yet it was not till I was half-way down the ladder that I suddenly stood still, and thought for an instant of retracing all my steps, as my companion had retraced them from the beginning of the garden wall. The name of Santa Claus had suddenly brought me back to my senses. I remembered why Santa Claus came, and why he was welcome.

"I was brought up in the propertied classes, and with all their horror of offences against property. I had heard all the regular denunciations of robbery, both right and wrong; I had read the Ten Commandments in church a thousand times. And then and there, at the age of thirty-four, half-way down a ladder in a dark room in the bodily act of burglary, I saw suddenly for the first time that theft, after all, is really wrong.

---

[48] Curtius Mettus or Mettius (fourth century B.C.) was a Roman hero; the story goes that he leapt on horseback into a chasm, which an earthquake had caused to open through the Forum. A soothsayer had proclaimed that it could be closed only by the sacrifice of Rome's greatest treasure; Curtius, considering that this must be a brave man, sacrificed himself and thereby closed the chasm.

"It was too late to turn back, however, and I followed the strangely soft footsteps of my huge companion across the lower and larger loft, till he knelt down on a part of the bare flooring and, after a few fumbling efforts, lifted a sort of trapdoor. This released a light from below, and we found ourselves looking down into a lamp-lit sitting-room, of the sort that in large houses often leads out of a bedroom, and is an adjunct to it. Light thus breaking from beneath our feet like a soundless explosion, showed that the trapdoor just lifted was clogged with dust and rust, and had doubtless been long disused until the advent of my enterprising friend. But I did not look at this long, for the sight of the shining room underneath us had an almost unnatural attractiveness. To enter a modern interior at so strange an angle, by so forgotten a door, was an epoch in one's psychology. It was like having found a fourth dimension.

"My companion dropped from the aperture into the room so suddenly and soundlessly, that I could do nothing but follow him; though, through lack of practice in crime, I was by no means soundless. Before the echo of my boots had died away, the big burglar had gone quickly to the door, half opened it, and stood looking down the staircase and listening. Then, leaving the door still half open, he came back into the middle of the room, and ran his roving blue eye round its furniture and ornament. The room was comfortably lined with books in that rich and human way that makes the walls seem alive; it was a deep and full, but slovenly, bookcase, of the sort that is constantly ransacked for the purposes of reading in bed. One of those stunted German stoves that look like red goblins stood in a corner, and a sideboard of walnut wood with closed doors in its lower part. There were three windows, high but narrow. After another glance round, my house-breaker plucked the walnut doors open and rummaged inside. He found nothing there, apparently, except an extremely handsome cut-glass decanter, containing what looked like port. Somehow the sight of the thief returning with this ridiculous little luxury in his hand woke within me once more all the revelation and revulsion I had felt above.

"'Don't do it!' I cried quite incoherently. 'Santa Claus——'

"'Ah,' said the burglar, as he put the decanter on the table and stood looking at me, 'you've thought about that, too.'

"'I can't express a millionth part of what I've thought of,' I cried, 'but it's something like this ... oh, can't you see it? Why are children not afraid of Santa Claus, though he comes like a thief in the night? He is permitted secrecy, trespass, almost treachery—because there are more toys where he has been. What should we feel if there were less? Down what chimney from hell would come the goblin that should take away the children's balls and dolls while they slept? Could a Greek tragedy be more gray and cruel than that daybreak and awakening? Dog-stealer, horse-stealer, man-stealer—can you think of anything so base as a toy-stealer?'

"The burglar, as if absently, took a large revolver from his pocket and laid it on the table beside the decanter, but still kept his blue reflective eyes fixed on my face.

"'Man!' I said, 'all stealing is toy-stealing. That's why it's really wrong. The goods of the unhappy children of men should be respected because of their worthlessness. I know Naboth's vineyard is as painted as Noah's Ark. I know Nathan's ewe-lamb is really a woolly baa-lamb on a wooden stand. That is why I could not take them away. I did not mind so much, as long as I thought of men's things as their valuables; but I dare not put a hand upon their vanities.'

"After a moment I added abruptly, 'Only saints and sages ought to be robbed. They may be stripped and pillaged; but not the poor little worldly people of the things that are their poor little pride.'

"He set out two wineglasses from the cupboard, filled them both, and lifted one of them with a salutation towards his lips.

"'Don't do it!' I cried. 'It might be the last bottle of some rotten vintage or other. The master of this house may be proud of it. Don't you see there's something sacred in the silliness of such things?'

"'It's not the last bottle,' answered my criminal calmly; 'there's plenty more in the cellar.'

"'You know the house, then?' I said.

"'Too well,' he answered, with a sadness so strange as to have something eerie about it. 'I am always trying to forget what I know—and to find what I don't know.' He drained his glass. 'Besides,' he added, 'it will do him good.'

"'What will do him good?'

"'The wine I'm drinking,' said the strange person.

"'Does he drink too much, then?' I inquired.

"'No,' he answered; 'not unless I do.'

"'Do you mean,' I demanded, 'that the owner of this house approves of all you do?'

"'God forbid,' he answered; 'but he has to do the same.'

"The dead face of the fog looking in at all the three windows unreasonably increased a sense of riddle, and even terror, about this tall, narrow house we had entered out of the sky. I had once more the notion about the gigantic genii—I fancied that enormous Egyptian faces, of the dead reds and yellows of Egypt, were staring in at each window of our little lamp-lit room as at a lighted stage of marionettes. My companion went on playing with the pistol in front of him, and talking with the same rather creepy confidentialness.

"'I am always trying to find him—to catch him unawares. I come in through skylights and trapdoors to find him; but whenever I find him—he is doing what I am doing.'

"I sprang to my feet with a thrill of fear. 'There is some one coming,' I cried, and my cry had something of a shriek in it.

"Not from the stairs below, but along the passage from the inner bedchamber (which seemed somehow to make it more alarming), footsteps were coming nearer. I am quite unable to say what mystery, or monster, or double, I expected to see when the door was pushed open from within. I am only quite certain that I did not expect to see what I did see,

"Framed in the open doorway stood, with an air of great serenity, a rather tall young woman, definitely though indefinably artistic— her dress the colour of spring and her hair of autumn leaves, with a face which, though still comparatively young, conveyed experience as well as intelligence. All she said was, 'I didn't hear you come in.'

"'I came in another way,' said the Permeator, somewhat vaguely. 'I'd left my latchkey at home.'

"I got to my feet in a mixture of politeness and mania. 'I'm really very sorry,' I cried. 'I know my position is irregular. Would you be so obliging as to tell me whose house this is?'

"'Mine,' said the burglar. 'May I present you to my wife?'

"I doubtfully, and somewhat slowly, resumed my seat; and I did not get out of it till nearly morning. Mrs. Smith (such was the prosaic name of this far from prosaic household) lingered a little, talking slightly and pleasantly. She left on my mind the impression of a certain odd mixture of shyness and sharpness; as if she knew the world well, but was still a little harmlessly afraid of it. Perhaps the possession of so jumpy and incalculable a husband had left her a little nervous. Anyhow, when she had retired to the inner chamber once more, that extraordinary man poured forth his apologia and autobiography over the dwindling wine.

"He had been sent to Cambridge with a view to a mathematical and scientific, rather than a classical or literary, career. A starless nihilism was then the philosophy of the schools; and it bred in him a war between the members and the spirit, but one in which the members were right. While his brain accepted the black creed, his very body rebelled against it. As he put it, his right hand taught him terrible things.[49] As the authorities of Cambridge University put it, unfortunately, it had taken the form of his right hand flourishing a loaded firearm in the very face of a distinguished don, and driving him to climb out of the window and cling to a waterspout. He had done it solely because the poor don had professed in theory a preference for non-existence. For this very unacademic type of argument he had been sent down. Vomiting as he was with revulsion, from the pessimism that had quailed under his pistol, he made himself a kind of fanatic of the joy of life. He cut across all the associations of serious-minded men. He was gay, but by no means careless. His practical jokes were more in earnest than verbal ones. Though not an optimist in the absurd sense of maintaining that life is all beer and skittles,[50] he did really seem to maintain that beer and skittles are the most serious part of it. 'What is more immortal,' he would cry, 'than

[49] "Right hand taught him terrible things" is a reference to Psalm 45:4 in the King James Version.

[50] "Life isn't all beer and skittles" was a popular mid-nineteenth-century proverb. Chesterton was well known for his advocacy of the pleasures of pubs and games. Innocent Smith here represents Chesterton's insight that serious intent and amusement can go together.

love and war? Type of all desire and joy—beer. Type of all battle and conquest—skittles.'

"There was something in him of what the old world called the solemnity of revels—when they spoke of 'solemnizing' a mere masquerade or wedding banquet. Nevertheless, he was not a mere pagan any more than he was a mere practical joker. His eccentricities sprang from a static fact of faith, in itself mystical, and even childlike and Christian.

"'I don't deny,' he said, 'that there should be priests to remind men that they will one day die. I only say that at certain strange epochs it is necessary to have another kind of priests, called poets, actually to remind men that they are not dead yet. The intellectuals among whom I moved were not even alive enough to fear death. They hadn't blood enough in them to be cowards. Until a pistol barrel was poked under their very noses they never even knew they had been born. For ages looking up an eternal perspective it might be true that life is a learning to die. But for these little white rats it was just as true that death was their only chance of learning to live.'

"His creed of wonder was Christian by this absolute test; that he felt it continually slipping from himself as much as from others. He had the same pistol for himself, as Brutus said of the dagger. He continually ran preposterous risks of high precipice or headlong speed to keep alive the mere conviction that he was alive. He treasured up trivial and yet insane details that had once reminded him of the awful subconscious reality. When the don had hung on the stone gutter, the sight of his long dangling legs, vibrating in the void like wings, somehow awoke the naked satire of the old definition of man as a two-legged animal without feathers.[51] The wretched professor had been brought into peril by his head, which he had so elaborately cultivated, and only saved by his legs, which he had treated with coldness and neglect. Smith could think of no other way of announcing or recording this, except to send a telegram to an old school friend (by this time a total stranger) to say that he had just seen a man with two legs; and that the man was alive.

[51] The "old definition of man as a two-legged animal without feathers" is Plato's *bipes et implumis* from Aristotle's *Politics*.

"The uprush of his released optimism burst into stars like a rocket when he suddenly fell in love. He happened to be shooting a high and very headlong weir in a canoe, by way of proving to himself that he was alive; and he soon found himself involved in some doubt about the continuance of the fact. What was worse, he found he had equally jeopardized a harmless lady alone in a rowing-boat, and one who had provoked death by no professions of philosophic negation. He apologized in wild gasps through all his wild wet labours to bring her to the shore, and when he had done so at last, he seems to have proposed to her on the bank. Anyhow, with the same impetuosity with which he had nearly murdered her, he completely married her; and she was the lady in green to whom I had recently said 'good-night.'

"They had settled down in these high narrow houses near Highbury. Perhaps, indeed, that is hardly the word. One could strictly say that Smith was married, that he was very happily married, that he not only did not care for any woman but his wife, but did not seem to care for any place but his home; but perhaps one could hardly say that he had settled down. 'I am a very domestic fellow,' he explained with gravity, 'and I have often come in through a broken window rather than be late for tea.'

"He lashed his soul with laughter to prevent it falling asleep. He lost his wife a series of excellent servants by knocking at the door as a total stranger, and asking if Mr. Smith lived there and what kind of a man he was. The London general servant is not used to the master indulging in such transcendental ironies. And it was found impossible to explain to her that he did it in order to feel the same interest in his own affairs that he always felt in other people's.

"'I know there's a fellow called Smith,' he said in his rather weird way, 'living in one of the tall houses in this terrace. I know he is really happy, and yet I can never catch him at it.'

"Sometimes he would, of a sudden, treat his wife with a kind of paralyzed politeness, like a young stranger struck with love at first sight. Sometimes he would extend this poetic fear to the very furniture; would seem to apologize to the chair he sat on, and climb the staircase as cautiously as a cragsman, to renew in himself the sense of their skeleton of reality. Every stair is a ladder and every stool a leg, he said. And at other times he would play the stranger exactly in the opposite sense, and would enter by another way, so as to feel like a thief and a robber. He would break and violate his own home, as he had done with me that night. It was nearly morning before I could tear myself from this queer confidence of the Man Who Would Not Die, and as I shook hands with him on the doorstep the last load of fog was lifting, and rifts of day-light revealed the stairway of irregular street levels that looked like the end of the world.

"It will be enough for many to say that I had passed a night with a maniac. What other term, it will be said, could be applied to such a being? A man who reminds himself that he is married by pretending not to be married! A man who tries to covet his own goods instead of his neighbour's! On this I have but one word to say, and I feel it of my honour to say it, though no one understands. I believe the maniac was one of those who do not merely come, but are sent; sent like a great gale upon ships by Him who made His angels winds and His messengers a flaming fire. This, at least, I know for certain. Whether such men have laughed or wept, we have laughed at their laughter as much as at their weeping. Whether they cursed or blessed the world, they have never fitted it. It is true that men have shrunk from the sting of a great satirist as if from the sting of an adder. But it is equally true that men flee from the embrace of a great optimist as from the embrace of a bear. Nothing brings down more curses than a real benediction. For the goodness of good things, like the badness of bad things, is a prodigy past speech; it is to be pictured rather than spoken. We shall have gone deeper than the deeps of heaven and grown older than the oldest angels before we feel, even in its first faint vibrations, the everlasting violence of that double passion with which God hates and loves the world.—I am, yours faithfully,

"RAYMOND PERCY."

"Oh, 'oly, 'oly, 'oly!" said Mr. Moses Gould.

The instant he had spoken all the rest knew they had been in an almost religious state of submission and assent. Something had bound them all together; something in the sacred tradition of the last two words of the letter; something also in the touching and boyish embarrassment with which Inglewood had read them—for he had all the thin-skinned reverence of the agnostic. Moses Gould was as good a fellow in his way as ever lived; far kinder to his family than more refined men of pleasure, simple and steadfast in his admirations, a thoroughly wholesome animal and a thoroughly genuine character. But wherever there is conflict, crises come in which any soul, personal or racial, unconsciously turns on the world the most hateful of its hundred faces. English reverence, Irish mysticism, American idealism, looked up and saw on the face of Moses a certain smile. It was that smile of the Cynic Triumphant, which has been the tocsin for many a cruel riot in Russian villages or mediæval towns.

"Oh, 'oly, 'oly, 'oly!" said Moses Gould.

Finding that this was not well received, he explained further, exuberance deepening on his dark exuberant features.

"Always fun to see a bloke swallow a wasp when 'e's corfin' up a fly," he said pleasantly. "Don't you see you've bunged up old Smith anyhow. If this parson's tale's O.K.—why, Smith is 'ot. 'E's pretty 'ot. We find him elopin' with Miss Gray (best respects!) in a cab. Well, what abart this Mrs. Smith the curate talks of, with her blarsted shyness—transmigogrified into a blighted sharpness? Miss Gray ain't been very sharp, but I reckon she'll be pretty shy."

"Don't be a brute," growled Michael Moon.

None could lift their eyes to look at Mary; but Inglewood sent a glance along the table at Innocent Smith. He was still bowed above his paper toys, and a wrinkle was on his forehead that might have been worry or shame. He carefully plucked out one corner of a complicated paper ship and tucked it in elsewhere; then the wrinkle vanished and he looked relieved.

III

THE ROUND ROAD;
OR, THE DESERTION CHARGE

Pym rose with sincere embarrassment; for he was an American, and his respect for ladies was real, and not at all scientific.

"Ignoring," he said, "the delicate and considerably knightly protests that have been called forth by my colleague's native sense of oration, and apologizing to all for whom our wild search for truth seems unsuitable to the grand ruins of a feudal land, I still think my colleague's question by no means devoid of rel'vancy. The last charge against the accused was one of burglary; the next charge on the paper is of bigamy and desertion. It does without question appear that the defence, in aspiring to rebut the last charge, have really admitted the next. Either Innocent Smith is still under a charge of attempted burglary, or else that is exploded; but he is pretty well fixed for attempted bigamy. It all depends what view we take of the alleged letter from Curate Percy. Under these conditions I feel justified in claiming my right to questions. May I ask how the defence got hold of the letter from Curate Percy? Did it come direct from the prisoner?"

"We have had nothing direct from the prisoner," said Moon quietly. "The few documents which the defence guarantees came to us from another quarter."

"From what quarter?" asked Dr. Pym.

"If you insist," answered Moon, "we had them from Miss Gray."

Dr. Cyrus Pym quite forgot to close his eyes, and, instead, opened them very wide.

"Do you really mean to say," he said, "that Miss Gray was in possession of this document testifying to a previous Mrs. Smith?"

"Quite so," said Inglewood, and sat down.

The doctor said something about infatuation in a low and painful voice, and then with visible difficulty continued his opening remarks.

"Unfortunately the tragic truth revealed by Curate Percy's narrative is only too crushingly confirmed by other and shocking documents in our own possession. Of these the principal and most certain is the testimony of Innocent Smith's gardener, who was present at the most dramatic and eye-opening of his many acts of marital infidelity. Mr. Gould, the gardener, please."

Mr. Gould, with his tireless cheerfulness, arose to present the gardener. That functionary explained that he had served Mr. and Mrs. Innocent Smith when they had a little house on the edge of Croydon. From the gardener's tale, with its many small allusions, Inglewood grew certain that he had seen the place. It was one of those corners of town or country that one does not forget, for it looked like a frontier. The garden hung very high above the lane, and its end was steep and sharp, like a fortress. Beyond was a roll of real country, with a white path sprawling across it, and the roots, boles, and branches of great gray trees writhing and twisting against the sky. But as if to assert that the lane itself was suburban, were sharply relieved against that gray and tossing upland a lamp-post painted a peculiar yellow-green and a red pillar-box that stood exactly at the corner. Inglewood was sure of the place; he had passed it twenty times in his constitutionals on the bicycle; he had always dimly felt it was a place where something might occur. But it gave him quite a shiver to feel that the face of his frightful friend or enemy Smith might at any time have appeared over the garden bushes above. The gardener's account, unlike the curate's, was quite free from decorative adjectives, however many he may have uttered privately while writing it. He simply said that on a particular morning Mr. Smith came out and began to play about with a rake, as he often did. Sometimes he would tickle the nose of his eldest child (he had two children); sometimes he would hook the rake on to the branch of a tree, and hoist himself up with horrible gymnastic jerks, like those of a giant frog in its final agony. Never, apparently, did he think of putting the rake to any of its proper uses, and the gardener, in consequence, treated his actions with coldness and brevity. But the gardener was certain that on one particular morning in October he (the gardener) had come round the corner of the house carrying the hose, had seen Mr. Smith standing on the lawn in a striped red and white jacket (which might have been his smoking jacket, but was quite as like a part of his pyjamas), and had heard him then and there call out to his wife, who was looking out of the bedroom window on to the garden, these decisive and very loud expressions—

"I won't stay here any longer. I've got another wife and much better children a long way from here. My other wife's got redder hair than yours, and my other garden's got a much finer situation; and I'm going off to them."

With these words, apparently, he sent the rake flying far up into the sky, higher than many could have shot an arrow, and caught it again. Then he cleared the hedge at a leap, and alighted on his feet down in the lane below, and set off up the road without even a hat. Much of the picture was doubtless supplied by Inglewood's accidental memory of the place. He could see with his mind's eye that big bare-headed figure with the ragged rake swaggering up the crooked woodland road, and leaving lamp-post and pillar-box behind. But the gardener, on his own account, was quite prepared to swear to the public confession of bigamy, to the temporary disappearance of the rake in the sky, and the final disappearance of the man up the road. Moreover, being a local man, he could swear that, beyond some local rumours that Smith had embarked on the south-eastern coast, nothing was known of him again.

This impression was somewhat curiously clinched by Michael Moon in the few but clear phrases in which he opened the defence upon the third charge. So far from denying that Smith had fled from Croydon and disappeared upon the Continent, he seemed prepared to prove all this on his own account. "I hope you are not so insular," he said, "that you will not respect the word of a French innkeeper as much as that of an English gardener. By Mr Inglewood's favour we will hear the French innkeeper."

Before the company had decided the delicate point Inglewood was already reading out the account in question. It was in French. It seemed to them to run something like this:—

"Sir,—Yes; I am Durobin of Durobin's Café on the sea-front at Gras, rather north of Dunquerque. I am willing to write all I know of the stranger out of the sea.

"I have no sympathy with eccentrics or poets. A man of sense looks for beauty in things deliberately intended to be beautiful, such as a trim flower-bed or an ivory statuette. One does not permit beauty to pervade one's whole life, just as one does not pave all the roads with ivory or cover all the fields with geraniums. My faith, but we should miss the onions!

"But whether I read things backwards through my memory, or whether there are indeed atmospheres of psychology which the eye of science cannot as yet pierce, it is the humiliating fact that on that particular evening I felt like a poet—like any little rascal of a poet who drinks absinthe in the mad Montmartre.[52]

"Positively the sea itself looked like absinthe, green and bitter and poisonous. I had never known it look unfamiliar before. In the sky was that early and stormy darkness that is so depressing to the mind, and the wind blew shrilly round the little lonely coloured kiosk where they sell the newspapers, and along the sand-hills by the shore. Then I saw a fishing-boat with a brown sail standing in silently from the sea. It was already quite close, and out of it clambered a man of monstrous stature, who came wading to shore with the water not up to his knees, though it would have reached the hips of many men. He leaned on a long rake or forked pole, which looked like a trident, and made him look like a Triton. Wet as he was, and with strips of seaweed clinging to him, he walked across to my café, and, sitting down at a table outside, asked for cherry brandy, a liqueur which I keep, but is seldom demanded. Then the monster, with great politeness, invited me to partake of a vermouth before my dinner, and we fell into conversation. He had apparently crossed from Kent by a small boat got at a private bargain because of some odd fancy he had for passing promptly in an easterly direction, and not waiting for any of the official boats. He was, he somewhat vaguely explained, looking for a house. When I naturally asked where the house was, he answered that he did not know; it was on an island; it

---

[52]Absinthe is an extremely strong, bitter (and some said addictive) alcoholic drink containing wormwood and flavoured with aniseed. It was banned by law in France in 1915. Montmartre is an area of Paris frequented by artists of all sorts.

was somewhere to the east; or, as he expressed it with a hazy and yet impatient gesture, 'over there.'

"I asked him how, if he did not know the place, he would know it when he saw it. Here he suddenly ceased to be hazy, and became alarmingly minute. He gave a description of the house detailed enough for an auctioneer. I have forgotten nearly all the details except the last two, which were that the lamp-post was painted green, and that there was a red pillar-box at the corner.

"'A red pillar-box!' I cried in astonishment. 'Why, the place must be in England!'

"'I had forgotten,' he said, nodding heavily. 'That is the island's name.'

"'But, *nom du nom.*' I cried testily, 'you've just come from England, my boy.'

"'They *said* it was England,' said my imbecile, conspiratorally. 'They said it was Kent. But those Kentish men are such liars one can't believe anything they say.'

"'Monsieur,' I said, 'you must pardon me. I am elderly, and the *fumisteries*[53] of the young men are beyond me. I go by common sense or, at the largest, by that extension of applied common sense called science.'

"'Science!' cried the stranger. 'There is only one good thing science ever discovered—a good thing, good tidings of great joy—that the world is round.'

"I told him with civility that his words conveyed no impression to my intelligence. 'I mean,' he said, 'that going right round the world is the shortest way to where you are already.'

"'Is it not even shorter,' I asked, 'to stop where you are?'

"'No, no, no!' he cried emphatically. 'That way is very long and very weary. At the end of the world, at the back of the dawn, I shall find the wife I really married and the house that is really mine. And that house will have a greener lamp-post and a redder pillar-box. Do you,' he asked with a sudden intensity, 'do you never want to rush out of your house in order to find it?'

---

[53] *Fumisteries* is French for "jokes" or "joking".

"'No, I think not,' I replied; 'reason tells a man from the first to adapt his desires to the probable supply of life. I remain here, content to fulfil the life of man. All my interests are here, and most of my friends, and——'

"'And yet,' he cried, starting to his almost terrific height, 'you made the French Revolution!'

"'Pardon me,' I said, 'I am not quite so elderly. A relative perhaps.'

"'I mean your sort did!' exclaimed this personage. 'Yes, your damned smug, settled, sensible sort made the French Revolution. Oh! I know some say it was no good, and you're just back where you were before. Why, blast it all, that's just where we all want to be—back where we were before! That is revolution—going right round. Every revolution, like every repentance, is a return.'

"He was so excited that I waited till he had taken his seat again, and then said something indifferent and soothing; but he struck the tiny table with his colossal fist and went on.

"'I am going to have a revolution, not a French Revolution, but an English Revolution. God has given to each tribe its own type of mutiny. The Frenchmen march against the citadel of the city together; the Englishman marches to the outskirts of the city, and alone. But I am going to turn the world upside down too. I'm going to turn myself upside down. I'm going to walk upside down in the cursed upside-downland of the Antipodes, where trees and men hang head downward in the sky. But my revolution, like yours, like the earth's, will end up in the holy, happy place—the celestial, incredible place—the place where we were before.'

"With these remarks, which can scarcely be reconciled with reason, he leapt from the seat and strode away into the twilight, swinging his pole and leaving behind him an excessive payment, which also pointed to some loss of mental balance. This is all I know of the episode of the man landed from the fishing-boat, and I hope it may serve the interests of justice.—Accept, Sir, the assurances of the very high consideration, with which I have the honour to be your obedient servant,

"JULES DUROBIN."

"The next document in our dossier," continued Inglewood, "comes from the town of Crazok, in the central plains of Russia, and runs as follows:—

"Sɪʀ,—My name is Paul Nickolaiovitch: I am the stationmaster at the station near Crazok. The great trains go by across the plains taking people to China, but very few people get down at the platform where I have to watch. This makes my life rather lonely, and I am thrown back much upon the books I have. But I cannot discuss these very much with my neighbours, for enlightened ideas have not spread in this part of Russia so much as in other parts. Many of the peasants round here have never heard of Bernard Shaw.[54]

"I am a Liberal, and do my best to spread Liberal ideas; but since the failure of the revolution this has been even more difficult. The revolutionists committed many acts contrary to the pure principles of humanitarianism, with which indeed, owing to the scarcity of books, they were ill acquainted. I did not approve of these cruel acts, though provoked by the tyranny of the government; but now there is a tendency to reproach all Intelligents with the memory of them. This is very unfortunate for Intelligents.

"It was when the railway strike was almost over, and a few trains came through at long intervals, that I stood one day watching a train that had come in. Only one person got out of the train, far away up at the other end of it, for it was a very long train. It was evening, with a cold, greenish sky. A little snow had fallen, but not enough to whiten the plain, which stretched away a sort of sad purple in all directions, save where the flat tops of some distant tablelands caught the evening light like lakes. As the solitary man came stamping along on the thin snow by the train he grew larger and larger; I thought I had never seen so large a man. But he looked even taller than he was, I think, because his shoulders were very big and his head comparatively little. From the big shoulders hung a tattered old jacket, striped dull red and dirty white, very thin for the winter, and one

---

[54] Bernard Shaw (1856–1950) was an Irish dramatist and critic. Chesterton is here poking fun at his friend and debating opponent who, being a socialist and on the trendy cutting edge of things "left", would like to have been known in Russia—and everywhere else.

hand rested on a huge pole such as peasants rake in weeds with to burn them.

"Before he had traversed the full length of the train he was entangled in one of those knots of rowdies that were the embers of the extinct revolution, though they mostly disgraced themselves upon the government side. I was just moving to his assistance, when he whirled up his rake and laid out to left and right with such energy that he came through them without scathe and strode right up to me, leaving them staggered and really astonished.

"Yet when he reached me, after so abrupt an assertion of his aim, he could only say rather dubiously in French that he wanted a house.

"'There are not many houses to be had round here,' I answered in the same language, 'the district has been very disturbed. A revolution, as you know, has recently been suppressed. Any further building——'

"'Oh! I don't mean that,' he cried; 'I mean a real house—a live house. It really is a live house, for it runs away from me.'

"I am ashamed to say that something in his phrase or gesture moved me profoundly. We Russians are brought up in an atmosphere of folklore, and its unfortunate effects can still be seen in the bright colours of the children's dolls and of the ikons. For an instant the idea of a house running away from a man gave me pleasure, for the enlightenment of man moves slowly.

"'Have you no other house of your own?' I asked.

"'I have left it,' he said very sadly. 'It was not the house that grew dull, but I that grew dull in it. My wife was better than all women, and yet I could not feel it.'

"'And so,' I said with sympathy, 'you walked straight out of the front door, like a masculine Nora.' [55]

"'Nora?' he inquired politely, apparently supposing it to be a Russian word.

"'I mean Nora in *The Doll's House*,' I replied.

[55] "Like a masculine Nora" is a reference to the heroine in a play by the man generally considered to be the father of modern drama, Norwegian dramatist Henrik Ibsen (1828–1906). In *The Doll's House*, the heroine, Nora Helmer, slams the door on her marriage and family at the end of the play.

"At this he looked very much astonished, and I knew he was an Englishman; for Englishmen always think that Russians study nothing but 'ukases.' [56]

"'*The Doll's House!*' he cried vehemently; 'why, that is just where Ibsen was so wrong! Why, the whole aim of a house is to be a doll's house. Don't you remember, when you were a child, how those little windows *were* windows, while the big windows weren't. A child has a doll's house, and shrieks when a front door opens inwards. A banker has a real house, yet how numerous are the bankers who fail to emit the faintest shriek when their real front doors open inwards.'

"Something from the folk-lore of my infancy still kept me foolishly silent; and before I could speak, the Englishman had leaned over and was saying in a sort of loud whisper, 'I have found out how to make a big thing small. I have found out how to turn a house into a doll's house. Get a long way off it: God lets us turn all things into toys by his great gift of distance. Once let me see my old brick house standing up quite little against the horizon, and I shall want to go back to it again. I shall see the funny little toy lamp-post painted green outside the gate, and all the dear little people like dolls looking out of the window. For the windows really open in my doll's house.'

"'But why?' I asked, 'should you wish to return to that particular doll's house? Having taken, like Nora, the bold step against convention, having made yourself in the conventional sense disreputable, having dared to be free, why should you not take advantage of your freedom? As the greatest modern writers have pointed out, what you called your marriage was only your mood. You have a right to leave it all behind, like the clippings of your hair or the parings of your nails. Having once escaped, you have the world before you. Though the words may seem strange to you, you are free in Russia.'

"He sat with his dreamy eyes on the dark circles of the plains, where the only moving thing was the long and labouring trail of smoke out of the railway engine, violet in tint, volcanic in outline, the one hot and heavy cloud of that cold clear evening of pale green.

[56] Ukase is an edict of the Russian government.

"'Yes,' he said with a huge sigh, 'I am free in Russia. You are right. I could really walk into that town over there and have love all over again, and perhaps marry some beautiful woman and begin again, and nobody could ever find me. Yes, you have certainly convinced me of something.'

"His tone was so queer and mystical that I felt impelled to ask him what he meant, and of what exactly I had convinced him.

"'You have convinced me,' he said with the same dreamy eye, 'why it is really wicked and dangerous for a man to run away from his wife.'

"'And why is it dangerous?' I inquired.

"'Why, because nobody can find him,' answered this odd person, 'and we all want to be found.'

"'The most original modern thinkers,' I remarked, 'Ibsen, Gorki,[57] Nietzsche,[58] Shaw, would all say rather that what we want most is to be lost: to find ourselves in untrodden paths, and to do unprecedented things; to break with the past and belong to the future.'

"He rose to his whole height somewhat sleepily, and looked round on what was, I confess, a somewhat desolate scene—the dark purple plains, the neglected railroad, the few ragged knots of the malcontents. 'I shall not find the house here,' he said. 'It is still eastward—further and further eastward.'

"Then he turned upon me with something like fury, and struck the foot of his pole upon the frozen earth.

"'And if I do go back to my country,' he cried, 'I may be locked up in a madhouse before I reach my own house. I have been a bit unconventional in my time! Why, Nietzsche stood in a row of ramrods in the silly old Prussian army, and Shaw takes temperance beverages in the suburbs; but the things I do are unprecedented things. This round road I am treading is an untrodden path. I do believe in breaking out; I am a revolutionist. But don't you see that all these real leaps and destructions and escapes are only attempts to get back to

[57] Maxim Gorki, pseudonym of Aleksei Maksimovich Peshkov (1868–1936), was a Russian novelist, dramatist and supporter of the Soviet regime.

[58] Friedrich Wilhelm Nietzsche (1844–1900) was a German philosopher and writer. The general themes of his work are a repudiation of Christian and liberal ethics, a detestation of democratic ideals and a celebration of "the will to power" working through the imposition of self-defined "values".

Eden—to something we have had, to something at least we have heard of? Don't you see one only breaks the fence or shoots the moon in order to get *home*?'

"'No,' I answered after due reflection, 'I don't think I should accept that.'

"'Ah,' he said with a sort of sigh, 'then you have explained a second thing to me.'

"'What do you mean?' I asked; 'what thing?'

"'Why your revolution has failed,' [59] he said; and walking across quite suddenly to the train he got into it just as it was steaming away at last. And I saw the long snaky tail of it disappear along the darkening flats.

"I saw no more of him. But though his views were adverse to the best advanced thought, he struck me as an interesting person: I should like to find out if he has produced any literary works.—Yours, etc.,

"PAUL NICKOLAIOVITCH."

There was something in this odd set of glimpses into foreign lives which kept the absurd tribunal quieter than it had hitherto been, and it was again without interruption that Inglewood opened another paper upon his pile. "The Court will be indulgent," he said, "if the next note lacks the special ceremonies of our letter-writing. It is ceremonious enough in its own way:—

"The Celestial Principles are permanent: Greeting.—I am Wong-Hi, and I tend the temple of all the ancestors of my family in the forest of Fu. The man that broke through the sky and came to me said that it must be very dull, but I showed him the wrongness of his thought. I am indeed in one place, for my uncle took me to this temple when I was a boy, and in this I shall doubtless die. But if a man remain in one place he shall see that the place changes. The pagoda of my temple stands up silently out of all the trees, like a yellow pagoda above many green pagodas. But the skies are sometimes blue like por-

---

[59] Here Chesterton, through Innocent Smith, anticipates the eventual failure of the Russian Revolution (which officially began in 1917, five years after this novel was published).

celain, and sometimes green like jade, and sometimes red like garnet. But the night is always ebony and always returns, said the Emperor Ho.

"The sky-breaker came at evening very suddenly, for I had hardly seen any stirring in the tops of the green trees over which I look as over a sea, when I go to the top of the temple at morning. And yet when he came, it was as if an elephant had strayed from the armies of the great kings of India. For palms snapped, and bamboos broke, and there came forth in the sunshine before the temple one taller than the sons of men.

"Strips of red and white hung about him like ribbons of a carnival, and he carried a pole with a row of teeth on it like the teeth of a dragon. His face was white and discomposed, after the fashion of the foreigners, so that they look like dead men filled with devils; and he spoke our speech brokenly.

"He said to me, 'This is only a temple; I am trying to find a house.' And then he told me with indelicate haste that the lamp outside his house was green, and that there was a red post at the corner of it.

"'I have not seen your house or any houses,' I answered. 'I dwell in this temple and serve the gods.'

"'Do you believe in the gods?' he asked with hunger in his eyes, like the hunger of dogs. And this seemed to me a strange question to ask, for what should a man do except what men have done?

"'My Lord,' I said, 'it must be good for men to hold up their hands even if the skies are empty. For if there are gods, they will be pleased, and if there are none, then there are none to be displeased. Sometimes the skies are gold and sometimes porphyry and sometimes ebony, but the trees and the temple stand still under all. So the great Confucius taught us that if we do always the same things with our hands and our feet as do the wise beasts and birds, with our heads we may think many things: yes, my Lord, and doubt many things. So long as men offer rice at the right season, and kindle lanterns at the right hour, it matters little whether there be gods or no. For these things are not to appease gods, but to appease men.'

"He came yet closer to me, so that he seemed enormous; yet his look was very gentle.

"'Break your temple,' he said, 'and your gods will be freed.'

"And I, smiling at his simplicity, answered: 'And so, if there be no gods, I shall have nothing but a broken temple.'

"And at this, that giant from whom the light of reason was withheld threw out his mighty arms and asked me to forgive him. And when I asked him for what he should be forgiven he answered: 'For being right.'

"'Your idols and emperors are so old and wise and satisfying,' he cried, 'it is a shame that they should be wrong. We are so vulgar and violent, we have done you so many iniquities—it is a shame that we should be right after all.'

"And I, still enduring his harmlessness, asked him why he thought that he and his people were right.

"And he answered: 'We are right because we are bound where men should be bound, and free where men should be free. We are right because we doubt and destroy laws and customs—but we do not doubt our own right to destroy them. For you live by customs, but we by creeds. Behold me! In my country I am called Smip. My country is abandoned, my name is defiled, because I pursue across the world what really belongs to me. You are steadfast as the trees because you do not believe. I am as fickle as the tempest because I do believe. I do believe in my own house, which I shall find again. And at the last remaineth the green lantern and the red post.'

"I said to him: 'At the last remaineth only wisdom.'

"But even as I said the word he uttered a horrible shout, and rushing forward disappeared among the trees. I have not seen this man again nor any other man. The virtues of the wise are of fine brass.

"WONG-HI."

"The next letter I have to read," proceeded Arthur Inglewood, "will probably make clear the nature of our client's curious but innocent experiment. It is dated from a mountain village in California, and runs as follows:—

"SIR,—A person answering to the rather extraordinary description required certainly went, some time ago, over the high pass of the Sierras on which I live and of which I am probably the sole stationary inhabitant. I keep a rudimentary tavern, rather ruder than a hut, on the very top of this specially steep and threatening pass. My name is Louis Hara, and the very name may puzzle you about my nationality. Well, it puzzles me a great deal. When one has been for fifteen years without society it is hard to have patriotism; and where there is not even a hamlet it is difficult to invent a nation. My father was an Irishman of the fiercest and most free-shooting of the old Californian kind. My mother was a Spaniard, proud of descent from the old Spanish families round San Francisco, yet accused for all that of some admixture of Red Indian blood. I was well educated and fond of music and books. But, like many other hybrids, I was too bad or too good for the world; and after attempting many things I was glad enough to get a sufficient though a lonely living in this little cabaret in the mountains. In my solitude I fell into many of the ways of a savage. Like an Eskimo, I was shapeless in winter; like a Red Indian, I wore in hot summers nothing but a pair of leather trousers, with a great straw hat as big as a parasol to defend me from the sun. I had a bowie knife at my belt and a long gun under my arm; and I dare say I produced a pretty wild impression on the few peaceable travellers that could climb up to my place. But I promise you I never looked as mad as that man did. Compared to him I was Fifth Avenue.[60]

"I dare say that living under the very tops of the Sierras has an odd effect on the mind; one tends to think of those lonely rocks not as peaks coming to a point, but rather as pillars holding up heaven itself. Straight cliffs sail up and away beyond the hope of the eagles; cliffs so tall that they seem to attract the stars and collect them as sea-crags collect a mere glitter of phosphorous. These terraces and towers of rock do not, like smaller crests, seem to be the end of the world. Rather they seem to be its awful beginning: its huge foundations. We could almost fancy the mountain branching out above us like a tree of stone, and carrying all those cosmic lights like a candelabrum. For just as the peaks failed us, soaring impossibly far, so the stars crowded us (as it seemed), coming impossibly near. The spheres burst about us

---

[60] Fifth Avenue is one of the principal avenues in Manhattan, New York City. It contains many first-class clothing establishments, tobacco shops and, on the upper East side, runs alongside Central Park and the Metropolitan Museum of Art.

more like thunderbolts hurled at the earth than planets circling placidly about it.

"All this may have driven me mad: I am not sure. I know there is
one angle of the road down the pass where the rock leans out a little,
and on windy nights I seem to hear it clashing overhead with other
rocks—yes, city against city and citadel against citadel, far up into the
night. It was on such an evening that the strange man struggled up
the pass. Broadly speaking, only strange men did struggle up the pass.
But I had never seen one like this one before.

"He carried (I cannot conceive why) a long, dilapidated garden
rake, all bearded and bedraggled with grasses, so that it looked like
the ensign of some old barbarian tribe. His hair, which was as long
and rank as the grass, hung down below his huge shoulders; and such
clothes as clung about him were rags and tongues of red and yellow,
so that he had the air of being dressed like an Indian in feathers or
autumn leaves. The rake or pitchfork, or whatever it was, he used
sometimes as an alpenstock, sometimes (I was told) as a weapon. I do
not know why he should have used it as a weapon, for he had, and
afterwards showed me, an excellent six-shooter in his pocket. 'But
that,' he said, 'I use only for peaceful purposes.' I have no notion
what he meant.

"He sat down on the rough bench outside my inn and drank some
wine from the vineyards below, sighing with ecstasy over it like one
who had travelled long among alien, cruel things and found at last
something that he knew. Then he sat staring rather foolishly at the
rude lantern of lead and coloured glass that hangs over my door. It is
old, but of no value; my grandmother gave it me long ago: she was
devout, and it happens that the glass is painted with a crude picture of
Bethlehem and the Wise Men and the Star. He seemed so mesmerized with the transparent glow of Our Lady's blue gown and the big
gold star behind, that he led me also to look at the thing, which I had
not done for fourteen years.

"Then he slowly withdrew his eyes from this and looked out eastward where the road fell away below us. The sunset sky was a vault of
rich violet, fading away into mauve and silver round the edges of the
dark mountain amphitheatre; and between us and the ravine below

rose up out of the deeps and went up into the heights the straight solitary rock we call Green Finger. Of a queer volcanic colour, and wrinkled all over with what looks undecipherable writing, it hung there like a Babylonian pillar or needle.

"The man silently stretched out his rake in that direction, and before he spoke I knew what he meant. Beyond the great green rock in the purple sky hung a single star.

"'A star in the east,' he said in a strange hoarse voice like one of our ancient eagles. 'The wise men followed the star and found the house. But if I followed the star, should I find the house?'

"'It depends perhaps,' I said, smiling, 'on whether you are a wise man.' I refrained from adding that he certainly didn't look it.

"'You may judge for yourself,' he answered. 'I am a man who left his own house because he could no longer bear to be away from it.'

"'It certainly sounds paradoxical,' I said.

"'I heard my wife and children talking and saw them moving about the room,' he continued, 'and all the time I knew they were walking and talking in another house thousands of miles away, under the light of different skies, and beyond the series of the seas. I loved them with a devouring love, because they seemed not only distant but unattainable. Never did human creatures seem so dear and so desirable: but I seemed like a cold ghost. I loved them intolerably; therefore I cast off their dust from my feet for a testimony. Nay, I did more. I spurned the world under my feet so that it swung full circle like a treadmill.'

"'Do you really mean,' I cried, 'that you have come right round the world? Your speech is English, yet you are coming from the west.'

"'My pilgrimage is not yet accomplished,' he replied sadly. 'I have become a pilgrim to cure myself of being an exile.'

"Something in the word 'pilgrim' awoke down in the roots of my ruinous experience memories of what my fathers had felt about the world, and of something from whence I came. I looked again at the little pictured lantern at which I had not looked for fourteen years.

"'My grandmother,' I said in a low tone, 'would have said that we were all in exile, and that no earthly house could cure the holy homesickness that forbids us rest.'

"He was silent a long while, and watched a single eagle drift out beyond the Green Finger into the darkening void.

"Then he said: 'I think your grandmother was right,' and stood up leaning on his grassy pole. 'I think that must be the reason,' he said— 'the secret of this life of man, so ecstatic and so unappeased. But I think there is more to be said. I think God has given us the love of special places, of a hearth and of a native land, for a good reason.'

"'I dare say,' I said. 'What reason?'

"'Because otherwise,' he said, pointing his pole out at the sky and the abyss, 'we might worship that.'

"'What do you mean?' I demanded.

"'Eternity,' he said in his harsh voice, 'the largest of the idols—the mightiest of the rivals of God.'

"'You mean pantheism and infinity and all that,' I suggested.

"'I mean,' he said with increasing vehemence, 'that if there be a house for me in heaven it will either have a green lamp-post and a hedge, or something quite as positive and personal as a green lamp-post and a hedge. I mean that God bade me love one spot and serve it, and do all things however wild in praise of it, so that this one spot might be a witness against all the infinities and the sophistries, that Paradise is somewhere and not anywhere, is something and not anything. And I would not be so very much surprised if the house in heaven had a real green lamp-post after all.'

"With which he shouldered his pole and went striding down the perilous paths below, and left me alone with the eagles. But since he went a fever of homelessness will often shake me. I am troubled by rainy meadows and mud cabins I have never seen; and I wonder whether America will endure.—Yours faithfully,   LOUIS HARA."

After a short silence Inglewood said: "And, finally, we desire to put in as evidence the following document:—

"This is to say that I am Ruth Davis, and have been housemaid to Mrs. I. Smith at 'The Laurels' in Croydon for the last six months. When I came the lady was alone, with two children; she was not a widow, but her husband was away. She was left with plenty of money and did not seem disturbed about him, though she often hoped he would be back soon. She said he was rather eccentric and a little change did him good. One evening last week I was bringing the tea-things out on to the lawn when I nearly dropped them. The end of a long rake was suddenly stuck over the hedge, and planted like a jumping-pole; and over the hedge, just like a monkey on a stick, came a huge, horrible man, all hairy and ragged like Robinson Crusoe. I screamed out, but my mistress didn't even get out of her chair, but smiled and said he wanted shaving. Then he sat down quite calmly at the garden table and took a cup of tea, and then I realized that this must be Mr. Smith himself. He has stopped here ever since and does not really give much trouble, though I sometimes fancy he is a little weak in his head.

"RUTH DAVIS.

"P.S.—I forgot to say that he looked round at the garden and said, very loud and strong: 'Oh, what a lovely place you've got;' just as if he'd never seen it before."

The room had been growing dark and drowsy; the afternoon sun sent one heavy shaft of powdered gold across it, which fell with an intangible solemnity upon the empty seat of Mary Gray, for the younger women had left the court before the more recent of the investigations. Mrs. Duke was still asleep, and Innocent Smith, looking like a huge hunchback in the twilight, was bending closer and closer to his paper toys. But the five men really engaged in the controversy, and concerned not to convince the tribunal but to convince each other, still sat round the table like the Committee of Public Safety.

Suddenly Moses Gould banged one big scientific book on top of another, cocked his little legs up against the table, tipped his chair backwards so far as to be in direct danger of falling over, emitted a startling and prolonged whistle like a steam engine, and asserted that it was all his eye.

When asked by Moon what was all his eye, he banged down behind the books again and answered with considerable excitement, throwing his papers about. "All those fairy-tales you've been reading out," he said. "Oh! don't talk to me! I ain't littery and that, but I know fairy-tales when I hear 'em. I got a bit stumped in some of the philosophical bits and felt inclined to go out for a B. and S.[61] But we're living in West 'Ampstead and not in 'Ell; and the long and the short of it is that some things 'appen and some things don't 'appen. Those are the things that don't 'appen."

"I thought," said Moon gravely, "that we quite clearly explained——"

"Oh yes, old chap, you quite clearly explained," assented Mr. Gould with extraordinary volubility. "You'd explain an elephant off the doorstep, you would. I ain't a clever chap like you; but I ain't a born natural, Michael Moon, and when there's an elephant on my doorstep I don't listen to no explanations. 'It's got a trunk,' I says.—'My trunk,' you says: 'I'm fond of travellin', and a change does me good.'— 'But the blasted thing's got tusks,' I says.—'Don't look a gift 'orse in the mouth,' you says, 'but thank the goodness and the graice that on your birth 'as smiled.'—'But it's nearly as big as the 'ouse,' I says.— 'That's the bloomin' perspective,' you says, 'and the saicred magic of distance.'—'Why, the elephant's trumpetin' like the Day of Judgment,' I says.—'That's your own conscience a-talking to you, Moses Gould,' you says in a grive and tender voice. Well, I 'ave got a conscience as much as you. I don't believe most of the things they tell you in church on Sundays; and I don't believe these 'ere things any more because you goes on about 'em as if you was in church. I believe an elephant's a great big ugly dingerous beast—and I believe Smith's another."

"Do you mean to say," asked Inglewood, "that you still doubt the evidence of exculpation we have brought forward?"

"Yes, I do still doubt it," said Gould warmly. "It's all a bit too far-fetched, and some of it a bit too far off. 'Ow can we test all those tales? 'Ow can we drop in and buy the 'Pink 'Un' at the railway station at Kosky Wosky or whatever it was? 'Ow can we go and do a gargle at that saloon-bar on top of the Sierra Mountains? But anybody can go and see Bunting's boarding-house at Worthing."

Moon regarded him with an expression of real or assumed surprise.

----

[61] "B. and S." is the abbreviated form for a "brandy and soda", a popular drink in England in Chesterton's time.

"Any one," continued Gould, "can call on Mr. Trip."

"It is a comforting thought," replied Michael with restraint; "but why should any one call on Mr. Trip?"

"For just exactly the sime reason," cried the excited Moses, hammering on the table with both hands, "for just exactly the sime reason that he should communicate with Messrs. 'Anbury and Bootle of Paternoster Row and with Miss Gridley's 'igh class Academy at 'Endon, and with old Lady Bullingdon who lives at Penge."

"Again, to go at once to the moral roots of life," said Michael, "why is it among the duties of man to communicate with old Lady Bullingdon who lives at Penge?"

"It ain't one of the duties of man," said Gould, "nor one of his pleasures either, I can tell you. She takes the crumpet, does Lady Bullingdon at Penge. But it's one of the duties of a prosecutor pursuin' the innocent, blameless butterfly career of your friend Smith, and it's the sime with all the others I mentioned."

"But why do you bring in these people here?" asked Inglewood.

"Why! Because we've got proof enough to sink a steamboat," roared Moses; "because I've got the papers in my very 'and; because your precious Innocent is a blackguard and 'ome smasher, and these are the 'omes he's smashed. I don't set up for an 'oly man; but I wouldn't 'ave all those poor girls on my conscience for something. And I think a chap that's capable of deserting and perhaps killing 'em all is about capable of cracking a crib or shootin' an old schoolmaster—so I don't care much about the other yarns one way or another."

"I think," said Dr. Cyrus Pym with a refined cough, "that we are approaching this matter rather irregularly. This is really the fourth charge on the charge sheet, and perhaps I had better put it before you in an ordered and scientific manner."

Nothing but a faint groan from Michael broke the silence of the darkening room.

IV

THE WILD WEDDINGS;
OR, THE POLYGAMY CHARGE

"A modern man," said Dr. Cyrus Pym, "must, if he be thoughtful, approach the problem of marriage with some caution. Marriage is a stage—doubtless a suitable stage—in the long advance of mankind towards a goal which we cannot as yet conceive; which we are not, perhaps, yet fitted even to desire. What, gentlemen, is now the ethical position of marriage? Have we outlived it?"

"Outlived it?" broke out Moon; "why, nobody's ever survived it! Look at all the people married since Adam and Eve—and all as dead as mutton."

"This is no doubt an inter-pellation joc'lar in its character," said Dr. Pym frigidly. "I cannot tell what may be Mr. Moon's matured and ethical view of marriage——"

"I can tell," said Michael savagely, out of the gloom. "Marriage is a duel to the death, which no man of honour should decline."

"Michael," said Arthur Inglewood in a low voice, "you *must* keep quiet."

"Mr. Moon," said Pym with exquisite good temper, "probably regards the institution in a more antiquated manner. Probably he would make it stringent and uniform. He would treat divorce in some great soul of steel—the divorce of a Julius Cæsar[62] or of a Salt Ring Robinson—exactly as he would treat some no-account tramp or labourer who scoots from his wife. Science has views broader and more humane. Just as murder for the scientist is a thirst for absolute destruction, just as theft for the scientist is a hunger for monotonous acquisition, so polygamy for the scientist is an extreme development of the instinct for variety. A man thus afflicted is incapable of con-

---

[62]Julius Caesar (100 or 102–44 B.C.) divorced his second wife, Pompeia, because, according to Plutarch, the wife of Caesar "must be above suspicion". No reference for Salt Ring Robinson (much less his divorce) has been found.

stancy. Doubtless there is a physical cause for this flitting from flower to flower—as there is, doubtless, for the intermittent groaning which appears to afflict Mr. Moon at the present moment. Our own world-scorning Winterbottom has even dared to say, 'For a certain rare and fine physical type free polygamy is but the realization of the variety of females, as comradeship is the realization of the variety of males.' In any case, the type that tends to variety is recognized by all authoritative inquirers. Such a type, if the widower of a negress, does in many ascertained cases espouse *en seconde noces*[63] an albino; such a type, when freed from the gigantic embraces of a female Patagonian, will often evolve from its own imaginative instinct the consoling figure of an Eskimo. To such a type there can be no doubt that the prisoner belongs. If blind doom and unbearable temptation constitute any slight excuse for a man, there is no doubt that he has these excuses.

"Earlier in the inquiry the defence showed real chivalric ideality in admitting half of our story without further dispute. We should like to acknowledge and imitate so eminently large-hearted a style by conceding also that the story told by Curate Percy about the canoe, the weir, and the young wife seems to be substantially true. Apparently Smith did marry a young woman he had nearly run down in a boat; it only remains to be considered whether it would not have been kinder of him to have murdered her instead of marrying her. In confirmation of this fact I can now con-cede to the defence an unquestionable record of such a marriage."

So saying, he handed across to Michael a cutting from the *Maidenhead Gazette* which distinctly recorded the marriage of the daughter of a "coach," a tutor well known in the place, to Mr. Innocent Smith, late of Brakespeare College, Cambridge.

When Dr. Pym resumed it was realized that his face had grown at once both tragic and triumphant.

"I pause upon this pre-liminary fact," he said seriously, "because this fact alone would give us the victory, were we aspiring after victory and not after truth. As far as the personal and domestic problem

---

[63] *En second noces* is French for "in second marriage".

holds us, that problem is solved. Dr. Warner and I entered this house at an instant of highly emotional diff'culty. England's Warner has entered many houses to save human kind from sickness; this time he entered to save an innocent lady from a walking pestilence. Smith was just about to carry away a young girl from this house; his cab and bag were at the very door. He had told her she was going to await the marriage licence at the house of his aunt. That aunt," continued Cyrus Pym, his face darkening grandly—"that visionary aunt had been the dancing will-o'-the-wisp who had led many a high-souled maiden to her doom. Into how many virginal ears has he whispered that holy word? When he said 'aunt' there glowed about her all the merriment and high morality of the Anglo-Saxon home. Kettles began to hum, pussy cats to purr, in that very wild cab that was being driven to destruction."

Inglewood looked up, to find, to his astonishment (as many another denizen of the eastern hemisphere has found), that the American was not only perfectly serious, but was really eloquent and affecting—when the difference of the hemispheres was adjusted.

"It is therefore atrociously evident that the man Smith has at least represented himself to one innocent female of this house as an eligible bachelor, being, in fact, a married man. I agree with my colleague, Mr. Gould, that no other crime could approximate to this. As to whether what our ancestors called purity has any ultimate ethical value indeed, science hesitates with a high, proud hesitation. But what hesitation can there be about the baseness of a citizen who ventures, by brutal experiments upon living females, to anticipate the verdict of science on such a point?

"The woman mentioned by Curate Percy as living with Smith in Highbury may or may not be the same as the lady he married in Maidenhead. If one short sweet spell of constancy and heart repose interrupted the plunging torrent of his profligate life, we will not deprive him of that long past possibility. After that conjectural date, alas, he seems to have plunged deeper and deeper into the shaking quagmires of infidelity and shame."

Dr. Pym closed his eyes, but the unfortunate fact that there was no more light left this familiar signal without its full and proper moral effect. After a pause, which almost partook of the character of prayer, he continued.

"The first instance of the accused's repeated and irregular nuptials," he exclaimed, "comes from Lady Bullingdon, who expresses herself with the high haughtiness which must be excused in those who look out upon all mankind from the turrets of a Norman and ancestral keep. The communication she has sent to us runs as follows:—

"Lady Bullingdon recalls the painful incident to which reference is made, and has no desire to deal with it in detail. The girl Polly Green was a perfectly adequate dressmaker, and lived in the village for about two years. Her unattached condition was bad for her as well as for the general morality of the village. Lady Bullingdon, therefore, allowed it to be understood that she favoured the marriage of the young woman. The villagers, naturally wishing to oblige Lady Bullingdon, came forward in several cases; and all would have been well had it not been for the deplorable eccentricity or depravity of the girl Green herself. Lady Bullingdon supposes that where there is a village there must be a village idiot, and in her village, it seems, there was one of these wretched creatures. Lady Bullingdon only saw him once, and she is quite aware that it is really difficult to distinguish between actual idiots and the ordinary heavy type of the rural lower classes. She noticed, however, the startling smallness of his head in comparison to the rest of his body; and, indeed, the fact of his having appeared upon election day wearing the rosette of both the two opposing parties appears to Lady Bullingdon to put the matter beyond a doubt. Lady Bullingdon was astounded to learn that this afflicted being had put himself forward as one of the suitors of the girl in question. Lady Bullingdon's nephew interviewed the wretch upon the point, telling him that he was a 'donkey' to dream of such a thing, and actually received, along with an imbecile grin, the answer that donkeys generally go after carrots. But Lady Bullingdon was yet further amazed to find the unhappy girl inclined to accept this monstrous proposal, though she was actually asked in marriage by Garth, the undertaker, a man in a far superior position to her own. Lady Bullingdon could not, of course, countenance such an arrangement for a moment, and the two unhappy persons escaped for a clandestine marriage. Lady Bullingdon cannot exactly recall the man's name, but thinks it was Smith. He was always called in the village the Innocent. Later, Lady Bullingdon believes he murdered Green in a mental outbreak."

"The next communication," proceeded Pym, "is more conspicuous for brevity, but I am of opinion that it will adequately convey its upshot. It is dated from the offices of Messrs. Hanbury and Bootle, publishers, and is as follows:—

"SIR,—Yrs. rcd. and conts. noted. Rumour *re* typewriter possibly refers to a Miss Blake or similar name, left here nine years ago to marry an organ-grinder. Case was undoubtedly curious, and attracted police attention. Girl worked excellently till about Oct. 1907, when apparently went mad. Record was written at the time, part of which I enclose.—Yrs., etc., W. TRIP."

"The fuller statement runs as follows:—

"On October 12 a letter was sent from this office to Messrs. Bernard and Juke, bookbinders. Opened by Mr. Juke, it was found to contain the following: 'Sir, our Mr. Trip will call at 3, as we wish to know whether it is really decided 00000073*bb* ! ! ! ! ! *xy*.' To this Mr. Juke, a person of a playful mind, returned the answer: 'Sir, after consulting all the members of the firm, I am in a position to give it as my most decided opinion that it is not really decided that 00000073*bb* ! ! ! ! ! *xy*.—Yrs. etc.,

'J. JUKE.'

"On receiving this extraordinary reply, our Mr. Trip asked for the original letter sent from him, and found that the typewriter had indeed substituted these demented hieroglyphics for the sentences really dictated to her. Our Mr. Trip interviewed the girl, fearing that she was in an unbalanced state, and was not much reassured when she merely remarked that she always went like that when she heard the barrel organ. Becoming yet more hysterical and extravagant, she made a series of most improbable statements—as, that she was engaged to the barrel-organ man, that he was in the habit of serenading her on that instrument, that she was in the habit of playing back to him upon the typewriter (in the style of King Richard and Blondel),[64] and that the organ man's musical ear was so exquisite and his adoration of herself so ardent that he could detect the note of the different letters on the machine, and was enraptured by them as by a melody. To all these statements of course our Mr. Trip and the rest of us only paid that sort of assent that is paid to persons who must as quickly as possible be put in the charge of their relations. But on our conducting the lady downstairs, her story received the most startling and even exasperating confirmation; for the organ-grinder, an enormous man with a small head and manifestly a fellow-lunatic, had pushed his barrel organ in at the office doors like a battering-ram, and was boisterously demanding his alleged *fiancée*. When I myself came on the scene he was flinging his great, ape-like arms about and reciting a poem to her. But we were used to lunatics coming and reciting poems in our office, and we were not quite prepared for what followed. The actual verse he uttered began, I think,

> 'O vivid, inviolate head,
> Ringed—'

but he never got any further. Mr. Trip made a sharp movement towards him, and the next moment the giant picked up the poor lady typewriter like a doll, sat her on top of the organ, ran it with a crash out of the office doors, and raced away down the street like a flying wheelbarrow. I put the police upon the matter; but no trace of the amazing pair could ever be found. I was sorry myself; for the lady was not only pleasant but unusually cultivated for her position. As I am leaving the service of Messrs. Hanbury and Bootle, I put these things in a record and leave it with them. (*Signed*) AUBREY CLARKE,
Publishers' Reader.

"And the last document," said Dr. Pym complacently, "is from one of those high-souled women who have in this age introduced your

---

[64] Blondel, also called Blondel de Nesle, was a twelfth-century French troubadour who accompanied King Richard I, Coeur de Lion (1157–1199), king of England, to Palestine on the Crusades. There is a legend that Blondel discovered the king in captivity in the Austrian castle of Düerrenstein (1193) by virtue of a song they had jointly composed.

English girlhood to hockey, the higher mathematics, and every form of ideality.

"DEAR SIR (she writes),—I have no objection to telling you the facts about the absurd incident you mention; though I would ask you to communicate them with some caution, for such things, however entertaining in the abstract, are not always auxiliary to the success of a girls' school. The truth is this: I wanted some one to deliver a lecture on a philological or historical question—a lecture which, while containing solid educational matter, should be a little more popular and entertaining than usual, as it was the last lecture of the term. I remembered that a Mr. Smith of Cambridge had written somewhere or other an amusing essay about his own somewhat ubiquitous name—an essay which showed considerable real knowledge of genealogy and topography. I wrote to him, asking if he would come and give us a bright address upon English surnames; and he did. It was very bright, almost too bright. To put the matter otherwise, by the time that he was halfway through it became apparent to the other mistresses and myself that the man was totally and entirely off his head. He began rationally enough by dealing with the two departments of place names and trade names, and he said (quite rightly, I dare say) that the loss of all significance in names was an instance of the deadening of civilization. But he then went on calmly to maintain that every man who had a place name ought to go to live in that place, and that every man who had a trade name ought instantly to adopt that trade; that people named after colours should always dress in those colours, and that people named after trees or plants (such as Beech or Rose) ought to surround and decorate themselves with these vegetables. In a slight discussion that arose afterwards among the elder girls the difficulties of the proposal were clearly, and even eagerly, pointed out. It was urged, for instance, by Miss Younghusband that it was substantially impossible for her to play the part assigned to her; Miss Mann was in a similar dilemma, from which no modern views on the sexes could apparently extricate her; and some young ladies, whose surnames happened to be Low, Coward, and Craven, were quite enthusiastic against the idea. But all this happened afterwards. What happened at the crucial moment was that the lecturer produced several horseshoes and a large iron hammer from his bag, announced his immediate intention of setting up a smithy in the neighbourhood, and called on every one to rise in the same cause as for a heroic revolution. The other mistresses and I attempted to stop the wretched man, but I must confess that by an accident this very intercession produced the worst explosion of his insanity. He was waving the hammer, and wildly demanding the names of everybody; and it so happened that Miss Brown, one of the younger teachers, was wearing a brown dress—a reddish-brown dress that went quietly enough with the warmer colour of her hair, as well she knew. She was a nice girl, and nice girls do know about those things. But when our maniac discovered that we really had a Miss Brown who *was* brown, his *idée fixe* blew up like a powder magazine, and there, in the presence of all the mistresses and girls, he publicly proposed to the lady in the red-brown dress. You can imagine the effect of such a scene at a girls' school. At least, if you fail to imagine it, I certainly fail to describe it.

"Of course the anarchy died down in a week or two, and I can think of it now as a joke. There was only one curious detail, which I will tell you, as you say your inquiry is vital; but I should desire you to consider it a little more confidential than the rest. Miss Brown, who was an excellent girl in every way, did quite suddenly and surreptitiously leave us only a day or two afterwards. I should never have thought that her head would be the one to be really turned by so absurd an excitement.—Believe me, yours faithfully, ADA GRIDLEY.

"I think," said Pym, with a really convincing simplicity and seriousness, "that these letters speak for themselves."

Mr. Moon rose for the last time in a darkness that gave no hint of whether his native gravity was mixed with his native irony.

"Throughout this inquiry," he said, "but especially in this its closing phase, the prosecution has perpetually relied on one argument; I mean the fact that no one knows what has become of all the unhappy women apparently seduced by Smith. There is no sort of proof that they were murdered, but that implication is perpetually made when the question is asked as to how they died. Now I am not interested in how they died, or when they died, or whether they died. But I am interested in another analogous question—that of how they were born, and when they were born, and whether they were born. Do not misunderstand me. I do not dispute the existence of these women, or the veracity of those who have witnessed to them. I merely remark on the notable fact that only one of these victims, the Maidenhead girl, is described as having any home or parents. All the rest are boarders or birds of passage—a guest, a solitary dressmaker, a bachelor-girl doing typewriting. Lady Ballingdon, looking from her turrets, which she bought from the Whartons with the old soap-boiler's money when she jumped at marrying an unsuccessful gentleman from Ulster— Lady Ballingdon, looking out from those turrets, did really see an object which she describes as Green. Mr. Trip, of Hanbury and Bootle, really did have a typewriter betrothed to Smith. Miss Gridley, though idealistic, is absolutely honest. She did house, feed, and teach a young woman whom Smith succeeded in decoying away. We admit that all these women really lived. But we still ask whether they were ever born?"

"Oh, crikey!" said Moses Gould, stifled with amusement.

"There could hardly," interposed Pym with a quiet smile, "be a better instance of the neglect of true scientific processes. The scientist, when once convinced of the fact of vitality and consciousness, would infer from these the previous processes of generation."

"If these gals," said Gould impatiently—"if these gals were all alive (all alive O!), I'd chance a fiver they were all born."

"You'd lose your fiver," said Michael, speaking gravely out of the gloom. "All those admirable ladies were alive. They were more alive for having come into contact with Smith. They were all quite definitely alive, but only one of them was ever born."

"Are you asking us to believe—" began Dr. Pym.

"I am asking you a second question," said Moon sternly. "Can the court now sitting throw any light on a truly singular circumstance? Dr. Pym, in his interesting lecture on what are called, I believe, the relations of the sexes, said that Smith was the slave of a lust for variety which would lead a man first to a negress and then to an albino, first to a Patagonian giantess and then to a tiny Eskimo. But is there any evidence of such variety here? Is there any trace of a gigantic Patagonian in the story? Was the typewriter an Eskimo? So picturesque a circumstance would not surely have escaped remark. Was Lady Bullingdon's dressmaker a negress? A voice in my bosom answers, 'No!' Lady Bullingdon, I am sure, would think a negress so conspicuous as to be almost Socialistic, and would feel something a little rakish even about an albino.

"But was there in Smith's taste any such variety as the learned doctor describes? So far as our slight materials go, the very opposite seems to be the case. We have only one actual description of any of the prisoner's wives—the short but highly poetic account by the æsthetic curate. 'Her dress was the colour of spring, and her hair of autumn leaves.' Autumn leaves, of course, are of various colours, some of which would be rather startling in hair (green, for instance); but I think such an expression would be most naturally used of the shades from red-brown to red, especially as ladies with their coppery-coloured hair do frequently wear light artistic greens. Now when we come to the next wife, we find the eccentric lover, when told he is a donkey, answering that donkeys always go after carrots; a remark which Lady Bullingdon evidently regarded as pointless and part of the natural table-talk of a village idiot, but which has an obvious meaning if we suppose that Polly's hair was red. Passing to the next wife, the one he took from the girls' school, we find Miss Gridley noticing that the schoolgirl in question wore 'a reddish-brown dress, that went quietly enough with the warmer colour of her hair.' In other words, the colour of the girl's hair was something redder than red-brown. Lastly, the romantic organ-grinder declaimed in the office some poetry that only got as far as the words,—

> 'O vivid, inviolate head,
> Ringed—'

But I think a wide study of the worst modern poets will enable us to guess that 'ringed with a glory of red,' or 'ringed with its passionate red,' was the line that rhymed to 'head.' In this case once more, therefore, there is good reason to suppose that Smith fell in love with a girl with some sort of auburn or darkish-red hair—rather," he said, looking down at the table, "rather like Miss Gray's hair."

Cyrus Pym was leaning forward with lowered eyelids, ready with one of his more pedantic interpellations; but Moses Gould suddenly struck his forefinger on his nose, with an expression of extreme astonishment and intelligence in his brilliant eyes.

"Mr. Moon's contention at present," interposed Pym, "is not, even if veracious, inconsistent with the lunatico-criminal view of I. Smith, which we have nailed to the mast. Science has long anticipated such a complication. An incurable attraction to a particular type of physical woman is one of the commonest of criminal per-versities, and when not considered narrowly, but in the light of induction and evolution——"

"At this late stage," said Michael Moon very quietly, "I may perhaps relieve myself of a simple emotion that has been pressing me throughout the proceedings, by saying that induction and evolution may go and boil themselves. The Missing Link and all that is well enough for kids, but I'm talking about things we know. All we know of the Missing Link is that he is missing—and he won't be missed either. I know all about his human head and his horrid tail; they belong to a very old game called 'Heads I win, tails you lose.' If you do find a fellow's bones, it proves he lived a long while ago; if you don't find his bones, it proves how long ago he lived. That is the game you've been playing with this Smith affair. Because Smith's head is small for his shoulders you call him microcephalous; if it had been large, you'd have called it water-on-the-brain. As long as poor old Smith's seraglio seemed pretty various, variety was the sign of madness: now, because it's turning out to be a bit monochrome—now monotony is the sign of madness. I suffer from all the disadvantages of being a grown-up person, and I'm jolly well going to get some of the advantages too; and with all politeness I propose not to be bullied with long words instead of short reasons, or consider your business a triumphant progress merely because you're always finding out that you were wrong. Having relieved myself of these feelings, I have merely to add that I regard Dr. Pym as an ornament to the world far more beautiful than the Parthenon, or the monument on Bunker's Hill, and that I propose to resume and conclude my remarks on the many marriages of Mr. Innocent Smith.

"Besides this red hair, there is another unifying thread that runs through these scattered incidents. There is something very peculiar and suggestive about the names of these women. Mr. Trip, you will remember, said he thought the typewriter's name was Blake, but could not remember exactly. I suggest that it might very well have been Black, and in that case we have a curious series: Miss Green in Lady Bullingdon's village; Miss Brown at the Hendon School; Miss Black at the publishers. A chord of colour, as it were, which ends up with Miss Gray at Beacon House, West Hampstead."

Amid a dead silence Moon continued his exposition. "What is the meaning of this queer coincidence about colours? Personally I cannot doubt for a moment that these names are purely arbitrary names, assumed as part of some general scheme or joke. I think it very probable that they were taken from a series of costumes—that Polly Green only meant Polly (or Mary) when in green, and that Mary Gray only means Mary (or Polly) when in gray. This would explain——"

Cyrus Pym was standing up rigid and almost pallid. "Do you actually mean to suggest——" he cried.

"Yes," said Michael; "I do mean to suggest that. Innocent Smith has had many wooings, and many weddings for all I know; but he has had only one wife. She was sitting on that chair an hour ago, and is now talking to Miss Duke in the garden.

"Yes, Innocent Smith has behaved here, as he has on hundreds of other occasions, upon a plain and perfectly blameless principle. It is odd and extravagant in the modern world, but not more than any other principle plainly applied in the modern world would be. His principle can be quite simply stated: he refuses to die while he is still alive. He seeks to remind himself, by every electric shock to the intellect, that he is still a man alive, walking on two legs about the world. For this reason he fires bullets at his best friends; for this reason he arranges ladders and collapsible chimneys to steal his own property; for this reason he goes plodding round a whole planet to get back to his own home; and for this reason he has been in the habit of taking the woman whom he loved with a permanent loyalty, and leaving her about (so to speak) at schools, boarding-houses, and places of business, so that he might recover her again and again with a raid and a romantic elopement. He seriously sought by a perpetual recapture of his bride to keep alive the sense of her perpetual value, and the perils that should be run for her sake.

"So far his motives are clear enough; but perhaps his convictions are not quite so clear. I think Innocent Smith has an idea at the bottom of all this. I am by no means sure that I believe it myself, but I am quite sure that it is worth a man's uttering and defending.

"The idea that Smith is attacking is this. Living in an entangled civilization, we have come to think certain things wrong which are not wrong at all. We have come to think outbreak and exuberance, banging and barging, rotting and wrecking, wrong. In themselves they are not merely pardonable; they are unimpeachable. There is nothing wicked about firing off a pistol even at a friend, so long as you do not mean to hit him and know you won't. It is no more wrong than throwing a pebble at the sea—less, for you do occasionally hit the sea. There is nothing wrong in bashing down a chimney-pot and breaking through a roof, so long as you are not injuring the life or property of other men. It is no more wrong to choose to enter a house from the top than to choose to open a packing-case from the bottom. There is nothing wicked about walking round the world and coming back to your own house; it is no more wicked than walking round the garden and coming back to your own house. And there is nothing wicked about picking up your wife here, there, and everywhere, if, forsaking all others, you keep only to her so long as you both shall live. It is as innocent as playing a game of hide-and-seek in the garden. You associate such acts with blackguardism by a mere snobbish association, as you think there is something vaguely vile about going (or being seen going) into a pawnbroker's or a public-house. You think there is something squalid and common-place about such a connection. You are mistaken.

"This man's spiritual power has been precisely this, that he has distinguished between custom and creed. He has broken the conventions, but he has kept the commandments. It is as if a man were found gambling wildly in a gambling hell, and you found that he only played for trouser buttons. It is as if you found a man making a clandestine appointment with a lady at a Covent Garden ball, and then you found it was his grandmother. Everything is ugly and discreditable, except the facts; everything is wrong about him, except that he has done no wrong.

"It will then be asked, 'Why does Innocent Smith continue far into his middle age a farcical existence, that exposes him to so many false charges?' To this I merely answer that he does it because he really is happy, because he really is hilarious, because he really is a man and alive. He is so young that climbing garden trees and playing silly practical jokes are still to him what they once were to us all. And if you ask me yet again why he alone among men should be fed with such inexhaustible follies, I have a very simple answer to that, though it is one that will not be approved.

"There is but one answer, and I am sorry if you don't like it. If Innocent is happy, it is because he *is* innocent. If he can defy the conventions, it is just because he can keep the commandments. It is just because be does not want to kill but to excite to life that a pistol is still as exciting to him as it is to a schoolboy. It is just because he does not want to steal, because he does not covet his neighbour's goods, that he has captured the trick (oh, how we all long for it!), the trick of coveting his own goods. It is just because he does not want to commit adultery that he achieves the romance of sex; it is just because he loves one wife that he has a hundred honeymoons. If he had really murdered a man, if he had really deserted a woman, he would not be able to feel that a pistol or a love-letter was like a song—at least, not a comic song."

"Do not imagine, please, that any such attitude is easy to me or appeals in any particular way to my sympathies. I am an Irishman, and a certain sorrow is in my bones, bred either of the persecutions of my creed, or of my creed itself. Speaking singly, I feel as if man was tied to tragedy, and there was no way out of the trap of old age and doubt. But if there is a way out, then, by Christ and St. Patrick, this is the way out. If one could keep as happy as a child or a dog, it would be by being as innocent as a child, or as sinless as a dog. Barely and brutally to be good—that may be the road, and he may have found it. Well, well, well, I see a look of scepticism on the face of my old friend Moses. Mr. Gould does not believe that being perfectly good in all respects would make a man merry."

"No," said Gould, with an unusual and convincing gravity; "I do not believe that being perfectly good in all respects would make a man merry."

"Well," said Michael quietly, "will you tell me one thing? Which of us has ever tried it?"

A silence ensued, rather like the silence of some long geological epoch which awaits the emergence of some unexpected type; for there rose at last in the stillness a massive figure that the other men had almost completely forgotten.

"Well, gentlemen," said Dr. Warner cheerfully, "I've been pretty well entertained with all this pointless and incompetent tomfoolery for a couple of days; but it seems to be wearing rather thin, and I'm engaged for a city dinner. Among the hundred flowers of futility on both sides I was unable to detect any sort of reason why a lunatic should be allowed to shoot me in the back garden."

He had settled his silk hat on his head and gone out sailing placidly to the garden gate, while the almost wailing voice of Pym still followed him: "But really the bullet missed you by several feet." And another voice added: "The bullet missed him by several years."

There was a long and mainly unmeaning silence, and then Moon said suddenly, "We have been sitting with a ghost. Dr. Herbert Warner died years ago."

V

HOW THE GREAT WIND WENT
FROM BEACON HOUSE

Mary was walking between Diana and Rosamund slowly up and down the garden; they were silent, and the sun had set. Such spaces of daylight as remained open in the west were of a warm-tinted white, which can be compared to nothing but a cream cheese; and the lines of plumy cloud that ran across them had a soft but vivid violet bloom, like a violet smoke. All the rest of the scene swept and faded away into a dove-like gray, and seemed to melt and mount into Mary's dark-gray figure until she seemed clothed with the garden and the skies. There was something in these last quiet colours that gave her a setting and a supremacy; and the twilight, which concealed Diana's statelier figure and Rosamund's braver array, exhibited and emphasized her, leaving her the lady of the garden, and alone.

When they spoke at last it was evident that a conversation long fallen silent was being suddenly revived.

"But where is your husband taking you?" asked Diana in her practical voice.

"To an aunt," said Mary; "that's just the joke. There really is an aunt, and we left the children with her when I arranged to be turned out of the other boarding-house down the road. We never take more than a week of this kind of holiday, but sometimes we take two of them together."

"Does the aunt mind much?" asked Rosamund innocently. "Of course, I dare say it's very narrow-minded and—what's that other word?—you know, what Goliath was—but I've known many aunts who would think it—well, silly."

"Silly?" cried Mary with great heartiness. "Oh, my Sunday hat! I should think it was silly! But what do you expect? He really is a good man, and it might have been snakes or something."

"Snakes?" inquired Rosamund, with a slightly puzzled interest.

"Uncle Harry kept snakes, and said they loved him," replied Mary with perfect simplicity. "Auntie let him have them in his pockets, but not in the bedroom."

"And you—" began Diana, knitting her dark brows a little.

"Oh, I do as auntie did," said Mary: "as long as we're not away from the children more than a fortnight together I play the game. He calls me 'Manalive;' and you must write it all in one word, or he's quite flustered."

"But if men want things like that," began Diana.

"Oh, what's the good of talking about men?" cried Mary impatiently; "why, one might as well be a lady novelist or some horrid thing. There aren't any men. There are no such people. There's a man; and whoever he is he's quite different."

"So there's no safety," said Diana in a low voice.

"Oh, I don't know," answered Mary, lightly enough; "there's only two things generally true of them. At certain curious times they're just fit to take care of us, and they're never fit to take care of themselves."

"There is a gale getting up," said Rosamund suddenly. "Look at those trees over there, a long way off, and the clouds going quicker."

"I know what you're thinking about," said Mary; "and don't you be silly fools. Don't you listen to the lady novelists. You go down the king's highway; for God's truth, it is God's. Yes, my dear Michael will often be extremely untidy. Arthur Inglewood will be worse—he'll be tidy. But what else are all the trees and clouds for, you silly kittens?"

"The clouds and trees are all waving about," said Rosamund. "There is a storm coming, and it makes me feel quite excited, somehow. Michael is really rather like a storm: he frightens me and makes me happy."

"Don't you be frightened," said Mary. "All over, these men have one advantage: they are the sort that go out."

A sudden thrust of wind through the trees drifted the dying leaves along the path, and they could hear the far-off trees roaring faintly.

"I mean," said Mary, "they are the kind that look outwards and get interested in the world. It doesn't matter a bit whether it's arguing, or bicycling, or breaking down the ends of the earth as poor old Innocent does. Stick to the man who looks out of the window and tries to understand the world. Keep clear of the man who looks in at the window and tries to understand you. When poor old Adam had gone out gardening (Arthur will go out gardening), the other sort came along and wormed himself in, nasty old snake."

"You agree with your aunt," said Rosamund, smiling: "no snakes in the bedroom."

"I didn't agree with my aunt very much," replied Mary simply, "but I think she was right to let Uncle Harry collect dragons and griffins, so long as it got him out of the house."

Almost at the same moment lights sprang up inside the darkened house, turning the two glass doors into the garden into gates of beaten gold. The golden gates were burst open, and the enormous Smith, who had sat like a clumsy statue for so many hours, came flying and turning cart-wheels down the lawn and shouting, "Acquitted! acquitted!" Echoing the cry, Michael scampered across to Rosamund and wildly swung her into a few steps of what was supposed to be a waltz. But the company knew Innocent and Michael by this time, and their extravagances were gaily taken for granted; it was far more extraordinary that Arthur Inglewood walked straight up to Diana and kissed her as if it had been his sister's birthday. Even Dr. Pym, though he refrained from dancing, looked on with real benevolence; for indeed the whole of the absurd revelation had disturbed him less than the others; he half supposed that such irresponsible tribunals and insane discussions were part of the mediæval mummeries of the Old Land.

While the tempest tore the sky as with trumpets, window after window was lighted up in the house within; and before the company, broken with laughter and the buffeting of the wind, had groped their way to the house again, they saw that the great apish figure of Innocent Smith had clambered out of his own attic window, and roaring again and again, "Beacon House!" whirled round his head a huge log or trunk from the wood fire below, of which the river of crimson flame and purple smoke drove out on the deafening air.

He was evident enough to have been seen from three counties; but when the wind died down, and the party, at the top of their evening's merriment, looked again for Mary and for him, they were not to be found.

THE FLYING INN

1914

I

A SERMON ON INNS

The sea was a pale elfin green and the afternoon had already felt the fairy touch of evening, as a young woman with dark hair, dressed in a crinkly copper-coloured sort of dress of the artistic order, was walking rather listlessly along the parade of Pebblewick-on-Sea, trailing a parasol and looking out upon the sea's horizon. She had a reason for looking instinctively out at the sea-line: a reason that many young women have had in the history of the world. But there was no sail in sight.

On the beach below the parade were a succession of small crowds surrounding the usual orators of the seaside; whether niggers or Socialists, whether clowns or clergymen. Here would stand a man doing something or other with paper boxes; and the holiday-makers would watch him for hours in the hope of some time knowing what it was he was doing with them. Next to him would be a man in a top-hat with a very big Bible and a very small wife, who stood silently beside him, while he fought with his clenched fist against the heresy of Milnian Sublapsarianism, so widespread in fashionable watering-places. It was not easy to follow him, he was so very much excited, but every now and then the words "our Sublapsarian friends" would recur with a kind of wailing sneer. Next was a young man talking of nobody knew what (least of all himself), but apparently relying for public favour mainly on having a ring of carrots round his hat. He had more money lying in front of him than the others. Next were niggers. Next was a children's service conducted by a man with a long neck who beat time with a little wooden spade. Further along there was an atheist in a towering rage, who pointed every now and then at the children's service; and spoke of Nature's fairest things being corrupted with the secrets of the Spanish Inquisition—by the man with the little spade, of course. The atheist (who wore a red rosette) was very withering to his own audience as well. "Hypocrites!" he would say; and then they would throw him money. "Dupes and dastards!" and then they would throw him more money. But between the atheist and the children's service was a little owlish old man in a red fez, weakly waving a green gamp umbrella. His face was brown and wrinkled like a walnut, his nose was of the sort we associate with Judæa, his beard was the sort of black wedge we associate rather with Persia. The young woman had never seen him before; he was a new exhibit in the now familiar museum of cranks and quacks. The young woman was one of those people in whom a real sense of humour is always at issue with a certain temperamental tendency to boredom or melancholia: and she lingered a moment, and leaned on the rail to listen.

It was fully four minutes before she could understand a word the man was saying: he spoke English with so extraordinary an accent that she supposed at first that he was talking in his own Oriental tongue. All the noises of that articulation were odd; the most marked was an extreme prolongation of the short "u" into "oo" as in "poo-oot" for "put." Gradually the girl got used to the dialect; and began to understand the words; though some time elapsed even then before she could form any conjecture of their subject-matter. Eventually it appeared to her that he had some fad about English civilization having been founded by the Turks; or perhaps by the Saracens after their victory in the Crusades. He also seemed to think that Englishmen would soon return to this way of thinking; and seemed to be urging the spread of teetotalism as an evidence of it. The girl was the only person listening to him.

"Loo-ook," he said, wagging a curled brown finger, "loo-ook at your own inns" (which he pronounced as "ince"). "Your inns of which you write in your boo-ooks! Those inns were not poo-oot up in the beginning to sell ze alcoholic Christian drink. They were put up to sell ze non-alcoholic Islamic drink. You can see this in the names of your inns. They are Eastern names, Asiatic names. You have a famous public-house to which your omnibuses go on the pilgrimage. It is called 'The Elephant and Castle.' That is not an English name. It is an Asiatic name. You will say there are Castles in England, and I will agree with you. There is the Windsor Castle. But where," he cried sternly, shaking his green umbrella at the girl in an angry oratorical triumph, "where is the Windsor Elephant? They have searched all Windsor Park. No elephant."

The girl with the dark hair smiled; and began to think that this man was better than any of the others. In accordance with the strange system of concurrent religious endowment which prevails at watering-places, she dropped a two-shilling piece into the round copper tray beside him. With honourable and disinterested eagerness, the old gentleman in the red fez took no notice of this, but went on warmly, if obscurely, with his argument.

"Then you have a place of drink in this town which you call 'The Bool.'"

"We generally call it 'The Bull,'" said the interested young lady, with a very melodious voice.

"You have a place of drink which you call 'The Bool,'" he reiterated in a sort of abstract fury, "and surely you see that this is all vary ridiculous!"

"No, no," said the girl softly, and in deprecation.

"Why should there be a Bull," he cried, prolonging the word in his own way. "Why should there be a Bull in connexion with a festive locality? Who thinks about a Bull in gardens of delight? What need is there of a Bull when we watch the tulip-tinted maidens dance or pour the sparkling sherbet? You yourselves, my friends"—and he looked around radiantly, as if addressing an enormous mob—"you yourselves have a proverb, 'It is not calculated to promote prosperity to have a Bull in a china-shop.' Equally, my friends, it would not be calculated to promote prosperity to have a Bull in a wine-shop. All this is clear."

He stuck his umbrella upright in the sand and struck one finger against another, like a man getting to business at last.

"It iss as clear as the sun at noon," he said solemnly. "It is as clear as the sun at noon that this word 'Bull,' which is devoid of restful and pleasurable associations, is but the corruption of another word, which possesses restful and pleasurable associations. The word is not Bull; it is the Bul-Bul!" His voice rose suddenly like a trumpet and he spread abroad his hands like the fans of a tropic palm-tree.

After this great effect he was a little more subdued and leaned gravely on his umbrella. "You will find the same trace of Asiatic nomenclature in the names of all your English inns," he went on. "Nay, you will find it, I am almost certain, in all your terms in any way connected with your revelries and your reposes. Why, my good friends, the very name of that insidious spirit by which you make strong your drinks is an Arabic word: alcohol. It is obvious, is it not, that this is the Arabic article 'Al' as in Alhambra, as in Algebra; and we need not pause here to pursue its many appearances in connexion with your festive institutions, as in your Alsop's beer, your Ally Sloper,[1] and your partly joyous institution of the Albert Memorial.[2] Above all, in your greatest feasting day, in your Christmas Day which you so erroneously suppose to be connected with your religion. What do you say, then? Do you say the names of the Christian nations? Do you say, 'I will have a little France. I will have a little Ireland. I will have a little Scotland. I will have a little Spain?' No-o." And the noise of the negative seemed to waggle as does the bleating of a sheep. "You say, 'I will have a little Turkey'; which is your name for the country of the servants of the Prophet!"

And once more he stretched out his arms sublimely to the east and west and appealed to earth and heaven. The young lady, looking at the sea-green horizon with a smile, clapped her grey gloved hands softly together as if at a peroration. But the little old man with the fez was far from exhausted yet.

"In reply to this you will object——" he began.

"Oh no, no," breathed the young lady, in a sort of dreamy rapture. "I don't object. I don't object the littlest bit!"

"In reply to this you will object," proceeded her preceptor, "that some inns are actually named after the symbols of your national superstitions. You will hasten to point out to me that the Golden Cross is situated opposite Charing Cross; and you will expatiate at length on King's Cross, Gerrard's Cross, and the many crosses that are to be found in or near London. But you must not forget"—and here he wagged his green umbrella roguishly at the girl, as if he was going to

---

[1] "The presence of Ally Sloper" was a clue as to the readership of a magazine or comic. It first appeared in *Judy* in 1867, and a periodical appeared in 1884 called *Ally Sloper's Half Holiday*. He was named after the tendency to slip off when the rent man came to stay.

[2] The Albert Memorial was erected in Kensington Gardens, London, in 1871 to honour Prince Albert (1819–1861), consort to Queen Victoria.

poke her with it—"none of you, my friends, must forget, what a large number of Crescents there are in London! Denmark Crescent, Mornington Crescent, St. Mark's Crescent, St. George's Crescent, Grosvenor Crescent, Regent's Park Crescent! Nay, Royal Crescent! And why should we forget Pelham Crescent? Why indeed? Everywhere, I say, homage paid to the holy symbol of the religion of the Prophet! Compare with this network and pattern of crescents, this city almost consisting of crescents, the meagre array of crosses, which remain to attest the ephemeral superstition to which you were, for one weak moment, inclined."

The crowds on the beach were rapidly thinning as tea-time drew nearer. The west grew clearer and clearer with the evening, till the sunshine seemed to have got behind the pale sea and to be shining through, as through a wall of thin green glass. The very transparency of sky and sea might have to this girl, for whom the sea was the romance and the tragedy, the hint of a sort of radiant hopelessness. The flood made of a million emeralds was ebbing as slowly as the sun was sinking; but the river of human nonsense flowed on for ever.

"I will not for one moment maintain," said the old gentleman, "that there are no difficulties in my case; or that all the examples are as obviously true as those that I have just demonstrated. No-o. It is obvious, let us say, that 'The Saracen's Head' is a corruption of the historic truth 'The Saracen is Ahead.' I am far from saying it is equally obvious that 'The Green Dragon' was originally 'The Agreeing Dragoman'; though I hope to prove in my book that it is so. I will only say here that it is su-urely more probable that one poo-ooting himself forward to attract the wayfarer in the desert, would compare himself to a friendly and persuadable guide or courier, rather than to a voracious monster. Sometimes the true origin is very hard to trace; as in the inn that commemorates our great Moslem warrior, Amir Ali Ben Bhoze, whom you have so quaintly abbreviated into Admiral Benbow. Sometimes it is even more difficult for the seeker after truth. There is a place of drink near to here called 'The Old Ship'——"

The eyes of the girl remained on the ring of the horizon as rigid as the ring itself: but her whole face had coloured and altered. The sands were almost emptied by now: the atheist was as non-existent as his

God; and those who had hoped to know what was being done to the paper boxes had gone away to their tea without knowing it. But the young woman still leaned on the railing. Her face was suddenly alive; and it looked as if her body could not move.

"It shood be admitted," bleated the old man with the green umbrella, "that there is no literally self-evident trace of the Asiatic nomenclature in the old words 'The Old Ship.' But even here the see-eeker after truth can poot himself in touch with facts. I questioned the proprietor of 'The Old Ship,' who is, according to such notes as I have kept, a Mr. Pumph."

The girl's lip trembled.

"Poor old Hump!" she said. "Why, I'd forgotten about him. He must be very nearly as worried as I am! I hope this man won't be too silly about this! I'd rather it weren't about this!"

"And Mr. Pumph to-old me the inn was named by a vary intimate friend of his, an Irishman who had been a Captain in the Britannic Royal Navy, but had resigned his po-ost in anger at the treatment of Ireland. Though quitting the service, he retained joost enough of the superstition of your Western sailors to wish his friend's inn to be named after his old ship. But as the name of the ship was *The United Kingdom*——"

His female pupil, if she could not exactly be said to be sitting at his feet, was undoubtedly leaning out very eagerly above his head. Amid the solitude of the sands she called out, in a loud and clear voice, "Can you tell me the Captain's name?"

The old gentleman jumped, blinked and stared like a startled owl. Having been talking for hours as if he had an audience of thousands, he seemed suddenly very much embarrassed to find that he had even an audience of one. By this time they seemed to be almost the only human creatures along the shore; almost the only living creatures, except the seagulls. The sun, in dropping finally, seemed to have broken as a blood orange might break; and lines of blood-red light were spilt along the split, low, level skies. This abrupt and belated brilliancy took all the colour out of the man's red cap and green umbrella; but his dark figure, distinct against the sea and the sunset, remained the same, save that it was more agitated than before.

"The name," he said, "the Captain's name. I—I understood it was Dalroy. But what I wish to indicate, what I wish to expound, is that here again the seeker after truth can find the connexion of his ideas. It was explained to me by Mr. Pumph that he was rearranging the place of festivity, in no inconsiderable proportion because of the anticipated return of the Captain in question, who had, as it appeared, taken service in some not very large navy, but had left it and was coming home. Now mark, all of you, my friends," he said to the seagulls, "that even here the chain of logic holds."

He said it to the seagulls because the young lady, after staring at him with starry eyes for a moment and leaning heavily on the railing, had turned her back and disappeared rapidly into the twilight After her hasty steps had fallen silent there was no other noise than the faint but powerful purring of the now distant sea, the occasional shriek of a sea-bird, and the continuous sound of a soliloquy.

"Mark, all of you," continued the man, flourishing his green umbrella so furiously that it almost flew open like a green flag unfurled, and then striking it deep in the sand, in the sand in which his fighting fathers had so often struck their tents. "Mark, all of you, this marvellous fact! That when, being for a time astonished—embarrassed— brought up, as you would say, short—by the absence of any absolute evidence of Eastern influence in the phrase 'The Old Ship,' I inquired from what country the Captain was returning, Mr. Pumph said to me in solemnity, 'From Turkey.' From Turkey! From the nearest country of the Religion! I know men say it is not our country. What does it matter where we come from, if we carry a message from Paradise? With a great galloping of horses we carry it, and have no time to stop in places. But what we bring is the only creed that has regarded what you will call in your great words the virginity of a man's reason, that has put no man higher than a prophet, and has respected the solitude of God."

And again he spread his arms out, as if addressing a mass meeting of millions, all alone on the dark sea-shore.

THE END OF OLIVE ISLAND

The great sea-dragon of the changing colours that wriggles round the world like a chameleon was pale green as it washed on Pebbleswick but strong blue where it broke on the Ionian Isles. One of the innumerable islets, hardly more than a flat white rock in the azure expanse, was celebrated as the Isle of Olives; not because it was rich in such vegetation, but because, by some freak of soil or climate, two or three olives grew there to an unparalleled height. Even in the full heat of the South it is very unusual for an olive-tree to grow up any taller than a small pear-tree; but the three olives that stood up, signals on this sterile place, might well be mistaken, except for the shape, for moderate-sized pines or larches of the North. It was also connected with some ancient Greek legend about Pallas, the patroness of the olive; for all that sea was alive with the first fairyland of Hellas; and from the platform of marble under the olive-tree could be seen the grey outline of Ithaca.

On the island and under the trees was a table set in the open air and covered with papers and inkstands. At the table were sitting four men, two in uniforms, and two in plain black clothes. Aides-de-camp, equerries, and such persons stood in a group in the background; and behind them a string of two or three silent battleships lay along the sea. For peace was being given to Europe.

There had just come to an end the long agony of one of the many unsuccessful efforts to break the strength of Turkey and save the small Christian tribes. There had been many other such meetings in the later phases of the matter as, one after another, the smaller nations gave up the struggle, or the greater nations came in to coerce them. But the interested parties had now dwindled to these four. For the Powers of Europe, being entirely agreed on the necessity for peace on a Turkish basis, were content to leave the last negotiations to England and Germany, who could be trusted to enforce it; there was a representative of the Sultan, of course; and there was a representative of the only enemy of the Sultan who had not hitherto come to terms.

For one tiny power had alone carried on the war month after month and with a tenacity and temporary success that was a new nine days' marvel every morning. An obscure and scarcely recognized prince, calling himself the "King of Ithaca," had filled the Eastern Mediterranean with exploits that were not unworthy of the audacious parallel that the name of his island suggested. Poets could not help asking if it were Odysseus come again; patriotic Greeks, even if they themselves had been forced to lay down their arms, could not help feeling curious as to what Greek race or name was boasted by the new heroic royal house. It was therefore with some amusement that the world at last discovered that the descendant of Ulysses was a cheeky Irish adventurer named Patrick Dalroy; who had once been in the English Navy, had got into a quarrel through his Fenian sympathies and resigned his commission. Since then he had seen many adventures in many uniforms; and always got himself or some one else into hot water with an extraordinary mixture of cynicism and quixotry. In his fantastic little kingdom, of course, he had been his own General, his own Admiral, his own Foreign Secretary, and his own Ambassador; but he was always careful to follow the wishes of his people in the essentials of peace and war; and it was at their direction that he had come to lay down his sword at last. Besides his professional skill, he was chiefly famous for his enormous bodily strength and stature. It is the custom in newspapers nowadays to say that mere barbaric muscular power is valueless in modern military actions; but this view may be as much exaggerated as its opposite. In such wars as these of the Near East, where whole populations are slightly armed and personal assault is common, a leader who can defend his head often has a real advantage; and it is not true, even in a general way, that strength is of no use. This was admitted by Lord Ivywood, the English Minister, who was pointing out in detail to King Patrick the hopeless superiority of the light pattern of Turkish field gun; and the King of Ithaca, remarking that he was quite convinced, said he would take it with him, and ran away with it under his arm. It would be conceded by the greatest of the Turkish warriors, the terrifying Oman Pasha, equally famous for his courage in war and his cruelty in peace; but who carried on his brow a scar from Patrick's sword, taken after three hours' mortal combat—

and taken without spite or shame, be it said, for the Turk is always at his best in that game. Nor would the quality be doubted by Mr. Hart, a financial friend of the German Minister, whom Patrick Dalroy, after asking him which of his front windows he would prefer to be thrown into, threw into his bedroom window on the first floor with so considerate an exactitude that he alighted on the bed where he was in a position to receive any medical attention. But, when all is said, one muscular Irish gentleman on an island cannot fight all Europe for ever, and he came, with a kind of gloomy good-humour, to offer the terms now dictated to him by his adopted country. He could not even knock all the diplomatists down (for which he possessed both the power and the inclination), for he realized, with the juster part of his mind, that they were only obeying orders, as he was. So he sat heavily and sleepily at the little table; in the green and white uniform of the navy of Ithaca (invented by himself); a big bull of a man, monstrously young for his size, with a bull neck and two blue bull's eyes for eyes, and red hair rising so steadily off his scalp that it looked as if his head had caught fire: as some said it had.

The most dominant person present was the great Oman Pasha himself, with his strong face starved by the asceticism of war, his hair and moustache seeming rather blasted with lightning than blanched with age; a red fez on his head, and between the red fez and the moustache a scar at which the King of Ithaca did not look. His eyes had an awful lack of expression.

Lord Ivywood, the English Minister, was probably the handsomest man in England; save that he was almost colourless both in hair and complexion. Against that blue marble sea he might almost have been one of its old marble statues that are faultless in line but show nothing but shades of grey or white. It seemed a mere matter of the luck of lighting whether his hair looked dull silver or pale brown; and his splendid mask never changed in colour or expression. He was one of the last of the old Parliamentary orators; and yet he was probably a comparatively young man: he could make anything he had to mention blossom into verbal beauty: yet his face remained dead while his lips were alive. He had little old-fashioned ways, as out of older Parliaments; for instance, he would always stand up, as in a senate, to speak to those three other men, alone on a rock in the ocean.

In all this he perhaps appeared more personal in contrast to the man sitting next to him, who never spoke at all but whose face seemed to speak for him. This man was Dr. Gluck, the German Minister, whose face had nothing German about it; neither the German vision nor the German sleep. His face was as vivid as a highly coloured photograph and altered like a cinema: but his scarlet lips never moved in speech. His almond eyes seemed to shine with all the shifting fires of the opal; his small curled black moustache seemed sometimes almost to twist itself afresh, like a live black snake: but there came from him no sound. He put a paper in front of Lord Ivywood. Lord Ivywood took a pair of eyeglasses to read it, and looked ten years older by the act.

It was merely a statement of agenda; of the few last things to be settled at this last conference. The first item ran:

"The Ithacan Ambassador asks that the girls taken to harems after the capture of Pylos be restored to their families. This cannot be granted." Lord Ivywood rose. The mere beauty of his voice startled every one who had not heard it before.

"Your Excellencies and gentlemen," he said, "a statesman to whose policy I by no means assent, but to whose historic status I could not conceivably aspire, has familiarized you with a phrase about peace with honour. But when we have to celebrate a peace between such historic soldiers as Oman Pasha and His Majesty the King of Ithaca, I think we may say that it is peace with glory."

He paused for half an instant; yet even the silence of sea and rock seemed full of multitudinous applause, so perfectly had the words been spoken.

"I think there is but one thought among us, whatever our many just objections through these long and harassing months of negotiation—I think there is but one thought now. That the peace may be as full as the war—that the peace may be as fearless as the war."

Once more he paused an instant; and felt a phantom clapping, as it were, not from the hands but the heads of men. He went on:

"If we are to leave off fighting, we may surely leave off haggling. A statute of limitations or, if you will, an amnesty, is surely proper when so sublime a peace seals so sublime a struggle. And if there be anything in which an old diplomatist may advise you, I would most strongly say this: that there should be no new disturbance of whatever amicable or domestic ties have been formed during this disturbed time. I will admit I am sufficiently old-fashioned to think any interference with the interior life of the family a precedent of no little peril. Nor will I be so illiberal as not to extend to the ancient customs of Islam what I would extend to the ancient customs of Christianity. A suggestion has been brought before us that we should enter into a renewed war or recrimination as to whether certain women have left their homes with or without their own consent. I can conceive no controversy more perilous to begin or more impossible to conclude. I will venture to say that I express all your thoughts when I say that, whatever wrongs may have been wrought on either side, the homes, the marriages, the family arrangements of this great Ottoman Empire shall remain as they are to-day."

No one moved except Patrick Dalroy, who put his hand on his sword-hilt for a moment and looked at them all with bursting eyes: then his hand fell and he laughed out loud and sudden.

Lord Ivywood took no notice, but picked up the agenda paper again, and again fitted on the glasses that made him look older. He read the second item—needless to say, not aloud. The German Minister with the far from German face had written this note for him:

"Both Coote and the Bernsteins insist there must be Chinese for the marble. Greeks cannot be trusted in the quarries just now."

"But while," continued Lord Ivywood, "we desire these fundamental institutions, such as the Moslem family, to remain as they are even at this moment, we do not assent to social stagnation. Nor do we say for one moment that the great tradition of Islam is capable alone of sustaining the necessities of the Near East. But I would seriously ask your Excellencies, why should we be so vain as to suppose that the only cure for the Near East is of necessity the Near West? If new ideas are needed, if new blood is needed, would it not be more natural to appeal to those most living, those most laborious, civilizations which form the vast reserve of the Orient. Asia in Europe, if my friend Oman Pasha will allow me the criticism, has hitherto been Asia in arms. May we not yet see Asia in Europe and yet Asia in peace? These at least are the reasons which lead me to consent to a scheme of colonization."

Patrick Dalroy sprang erect, pulling himself out of his seat by clutching at an olive-branch above his head. He steadied himself by putting one hand on the trunk of the tree; and simply stared at them all. There fell on him the huge helplessness of mere physical power. He could throw them into the sea; but what good would that do? More men on the wrong side would be accredited to the diplomatic campaign; and the only man on the right side would be discredited for anything. He shook the branching olive-tree above him in his fury. But he did not for one moment disturb Lord Ivywood, who had just read the third item on his private agenda ("Oman Pasha insists on the destruction of the vineyards"), and was by this time engaged in a peroration which afterwards became famous and may be found in many rhetorical text-books and primers. He was well into the middle of it before Dalroy's rage and wonder allowed him to follow the words.

". . . do we indeed owe nothing," the diplomatist was saying, "to that gesture of high refusal in which, so many centuries ago, the great Arabian mystic put the wine-cup from his lips? Do we owe nothing to the long vigil of a valiant race, the long fast by which they have testified against the venomous beauty of the vine? Ours is an age when men come more and more to see that the creeds hold treasures for each other, that each religion has a secret for its neighbour, that faith unto faith uttereth speech and church unto church showeth knowledge. If it be true, and I claim again the indulgence of Oman Pasha when I say I think it is true, that we of the West have brought some light to Islam in the matter of the preciousness of peace and of civil order, may we not say that Islam, in answer, shall give us peace in a thousand homes, and encourage us to cut down that curse that has done so much to thwart and madden the virtues of Western Christendom? Already in my own country the orgies that made horrible the nights of the noblest families are no more. Already the legislature takes more and more sweeping action to deliver the populace from the bondage of the all-destroying drug. Surely the Prophet of Mecca is reaping his harvest; the cession of the disputed vineyards to the greatest of his champions is of all acts the most appropriate to this day; to this happy day that may yet deliver the East from the curse of war and the West from the curse of wine. The gallant prince who meets us here at last, to offer an olive-branch even more glorious than his sword, may well have our sympathy if he himself views the cession with some sentimental regret; but I have little doubt that he also will live to rejoice in it at last. And I would remind you that it is not the vine alone that has been the sign of the glory of the South. There is another sacred tree unstained by loose and violent memories, guiltless of the blood of Pentheus or of Orpheus[3] and the broken lyre. We shall pass from this place in a little while as all things pass and perish:

> " 'Far called, our navies melt away,
>   On dune and headland sinks the fire,
>   And all our pomp of yesterday
>   Is one with Nineveh and Tyre.'

But so long as sun can shine and soil can nourish, happier men and women after us shall look on this lonely islet and it shall tell its own story: for they shall see these three holy olive-trees lifted in everlasting benediction, over the humble spot out of which came the peace of the world."

The other two men were staring at Patrick Dalroy; his hand had tightened on the tree, and a giant billow of effort went over his broad breast. A small stone jerked itself out of the ground at the foot of the tree, as if it were a grasshopper jumping: and then the coiled roots of the olive-tree rose very slowly out of the earth like the limbs of a dragon lifting itself from sleep.

"I offer an olive-branch," said the King of Ithaca, totteringly leaning out the loose tree so that its vast shadow, much larger than itself,

---

[3]Pentheus and Orpheus were characters in Greek mythology. Pentheus, king of Thebes, was torn apart by the Maenads, frenzied women who followed Dionysius. Orpheus was a poet who sang and played his lyre so wonderfully that even wild beasts were spellbound by his music. Failing to honor Dionysius, he too was torn apart by Maenads.

fell across the whole council. "An olive-branch," he gasped, "more glorious than my sword. Also heavier."

Then he made another effort and tossed it into the sea below. The German who was no German had put his arm up in apprehension when the shadow fell across him. Now he got up and edged away from the table; seeing that the wild Irishman was tearing up the second tree. This one came out more easily; and before he flung it after the first, he stood with it a moment; looking like a man juggling with a tower.

Lord Ivywood showed more firmness; but he rose in tremendous remonstrance. Only the Turkish Pasha still sat with blank eyes, immovable. Dalroy rent out the last tree and hurled it, leaving the island bare.

"There!" said Dalroy, when the third and last olive had splashed in the tide. "Now I will go. I have seen something to-day that is worse than death: and the name of it is Peace."

Oman Pasha rose and held out his hand.

"You are right," he said in French, "and I hope we meet again in the only life that is a good life. Where are you going now?"

"I am going," said Dalroy dreamily, "to 'The Old Ship'."

"Do you mean," asked the Turk, "that you are going back to the warships of the English King?"

"No," answered the other. "I am going back to 'The Old Ship' that is behind apple-trees by Pebbleswick; where the Ule flows among the trees. I fear I shall never see you there."

After an instant's hesitation he wrung the red hand of the great tyrant and walked to his boat without a glance at the diplomatists.

III

THE SIGN OF "THE OLD SHIP"

Upon few of the children of men has the surname of Pump fallen, and of these few have been maddened into naming a child Humphrey in addition to it. To such extremity, however, had the parents of the innkeeper at "The Old Ship" proceeded; that their son might come at last to be called "Hump" by his dearest friends and "Pumph" by an aged Turk with a green umbrella. All this, or all he knew of it, he endured with a sour smile; for he was of a stoical temper.

Mr. Humphrey Pump stood outside his inn, which was almost on the sea-shore, screened only by one line of apple-trees, dwarfed, twisted, and salted by the sea air; but in front of it was a highly banked bowling green; and beside it the land sank abruptly; so that one very steep, sweeping road vanished into the depth and mystery of taller trees. Mr. Pump was standing immediately under his inn sign: which stood erect in the turf; a wooden pole painted white and suspending a square wooden board, also painted white, but further decorated with a highly grotesque blue ship, such as a child might draw, but into which Mr. Pump's patriotism had insinuated a disproportionately large red St. George's cross.

Mr. Humphrey Pump was a man of middle size, with very broad shoulders, wearing a sort of shooting suit with gaiters. Indeed, he was engaged at the moment in cleaning and reloading a double-barrelled gun, a short but powerful weapon which he had invented, or at least improved, himself; and which, though eccentric enough as compared with latest scientific arms, was neither clumsy nor necessarily out of date. For Pump was one of those handy men who seem to have a hundred hands, like Briareus: he made nearly everything for himself, and everything in his house was slightly different from the same thing in any one else's house. He was also as cunning as Pan or a poacher in everything affecting every bird or fish, every leaf or berry in the woods. His mind was a rich soil of subconscious memories and traditions; and he had a curious kind of gossip so allusive as to almost amount to reticence; for he always took it for granted that every one knew his county and its tales as intimately as he did; so he would mention the most mysterious and amazing things without relaxing a muscle of his face, which seemed to be made of knotted wood. His dark brown hair ended in two rudimentary side-whiskers, giving him a slightly horsy look, but in the old-fashioned sportsman's style. His smile was rather wry and crabbed, but his brown eyes were kindly and soft. He was very English.

As a rule his movements, though quick, were cool; but on this occasion he put down the gun on the table outside the inn in a rather hurried manner and came forward dusting his hands in an unusual degree of animation and even deference. Beyond the goblin green apple-trees and against the sea had appeared the tall, slight figure of a girl in a dress about the colour of copper and a large shady hat. Under the hat her face was grave and beautiful, though rather swarthy. She shook hands with Mr. Pump; then he very ceremoniously put a chair for her and called her "Lady Joan."

"I thought I would like a look at the old place," she said. "We have had some happy times here when we were boys and girls. I suppose you hardly see any of your old friends now."

"Very little," answered Pump, rubbing his short whisker reflectively. "Lord Ivywood's become quite a Methody parson, you know, since he took the Place; he's pulling down beershops right and left. And Mr. Charles was sent to Australia for lying down flat at the funeral. Pretty stiff, I call it; but the old lady was a terror."

"Do you ever hear," asked Lady Joan Brett carelessly, "of that Irishman, Captain Dalroy?"

"Yes, more often than from the rest," answered the innkeeper. "He seems to have done wonders in this Greek business. Ah! He was a sad loss to the Navy!"

"They insulted his country," said the girl, looking at the sea with a heightened colour. "After all, Ireland was his country; and he had a right to resent its being spoken of like that."

"And when they found he'd painted him green," went on Mr. Pump.

"Painted him what?" asked Lady Joan.

"Painted Captain Dawson green," continued Mr. Pump in colourless tones. "Captain Dawson said green was the colour of Irish traitors, so Dalroy painted him green. It was a great temptation, no doubt, with this fence being painted at the same time and the pail of stuff there: but of course it had a very prejudicial effect on his professional career."

"What an extraordinary story!" said the staring Lady Joan, breaking into a rather joyless laugh. "It must go down among your county legends. I never heard that version before. Why, it might be the origin of 'The Green Man' over there by the town."

"Oh no," said Pump simply. "That's been there since before Waterloo times. Poor old Noyle had it until they put him away. You remember old Noyle, Lady Joan? Still alive, I hear, and still writing love-letters to Queen Victoria. Only of course they aren't posted now."

"Have you heard from your Irish friend lately?" asked the girl, keeping a steady eye on the sky-line.

"Yes, I had a letter last week," answered the innkeeper. "It seems not impossible that he may return to England. He's been acting for one of these Greek places, and the negotiations seem to be concluded. It's a queer thing that his lordship himself was the English Minister in charge of them."

"You mean Lord Ivywood," said Lady Joan rather coldly. "Yes, he has a great career before him, evidently."

"I wish he hadn't got his knife into us so much," chuckled Pump. "I don't believe there'll be an inn left in England. But the Ivywoods were always cranky. It's only fair to him to remember his grandfather."

"I think it's very ungallant on your part," said Lady Joan, with a mournful smile, "to ask a lady to remember his grandfather."

"You know what I mean, Lady Joan," said he, most good-humouredly. "And I never was hard on the case myself; we all have our little ways. I shouldn't like it done to my pig; but I don't see why a man shouldn't have his own pig in his own pew with him if he likes it. It wasn't a free seat. It was the family pew."

Lady Joan broke out laughing again. "What horrible things you do seem to have heard of," she said. "Well, I must be going, Mr. Hump—I mean Mr. Pump—I used to call you Hump ... Oh, Hump, do you think any of us will ever be happy again?"

"I suppose it rests with Providence," he said, looking at the sea.

"Oh, do say Providence again!" cried the girl. "It's as good as 'Masterman Ready.' " [4]

With which inconsequent words she betook herself again to the path by the apple-trees and walked back by the sea-front to Pebbleswick.

The inn of "The Old Ship" lay a little beyond the old fishing village of Pebbleswick; and that again was separated by an empty half-mile or so from the new watering-place of Pebbleswick-on-Sea. But the dark-haired lady walked steadily along the sea-front, on a sort of parade which had been stretched out to east and west in the insane optimism of watering-places, and as she approached the more crowded part looked more and more carefully at the groups on the beach. Most of them were much the same as she had seen more than a month before. The seekers after truth (as the man in the fez would say) who assembled daily to find out what the man was doing with the paper boxes, had not found out yet; neither had they wearied of their intellectual pilgrimage. Pennies were still thrown to the thundering atheist in acknowledgment of his incessant abuse; and this was all the more mysterious because the crowd was obviously indifferent, and the atheist was obviously sincere. The man with the long neck who led Low Church hymns with a little wooden spade had indeed disappeared, for children's services of this kind are generally a moving feast; but the man whose only claim consisted of carrots round his hat was still there; and seemed to have even more money than before. But Lady Joan could see no sign of the little old man in the fez. She could only suppose that he had failed entirely; and, being in a bitter mood, she told herself bitterly that he had sunk out of sight precisely because there was in his rubbish a touch of unearthly and insane clear-headedness of which all these vulgar idiots were incapable. She did not confess to herself consciously that what had made both the man in the fez and the man at the inn interesting was the subject of which they had spoken.

As she walked on rather wearily along the parade she caught sight of a girl in black with faint fair hair and a tremulous intelligent face which she was sure she had seen before. Pulling together all her

---

[4] *Masterman Ready* was a children's novel (1841) by Captain Frederick Marryat (1792–1848).

aristocratic training for the remembering of middle-class people, she managed to remember that this was a Miss Browning who had done typewriting work for her a year or two before; and immediately went forward to greet her, partly out of genuine good-nature and partly as a relief from her own rather dreary thoughts. Her tone was so seriously frank and friendly that the lady in black summoned the social courage to say:

"I've so often wanted to introduce you to my sister, who's much cleverer than I am, though she does live at home; which I suppose is very old-fashioned. She knows all sorts of intellectual people. She is talking to one of them, now; this Prophet of the Moon that every one's talking about. Do let me introduce you."

Lady Joan Brett had met many prophets of the moon and of other things. But she had the spontaneous courtesy which redeems the vices of her class, and she followed Miss Browning to a seat on the parade. She greeted Miss Browning's sister with glowing politeness; and this may really be counted to her credit; for she had great difficulty in looking at Miss Browning's sister at all. For on the seat beside her, still in a red fez but in a brilliantly new black frock-coat and every appearance of prosperity, sat the old gentleman who had lectured on the sands about the inns of England.

"He lectured at our Ethical Society," whispered Miss Browning, "on the word 'alcohol.' Just on the word 'alcohol.' He was perfectly thrilling. All about Arabia and Algebra, you know, and how everything comes from the East. You really would be interested."

"I am interested," said Lady Joan.

"Poot it to yourselfs," the man in the fez was saying to Miss Browning's sister, "joost what zort of meaning the names of your ince can have if they do not commemorate the unlimitable influence of Islam. There is a vary populous inn in London, one of the most distinguished, one of the most of the centre, and it is called 'The Horseshoe.' Now, my friends, why should any one commemorate a horseshoe? It iss but an appendage to a creature more interesting than itself. I have already demonstrated to you that the very fact that you have in your town a place of drink called 'The Bool'——"

"I should like to ask——" began Lady Joan suddenly.

"A place of drink called 'The Bool,' went on the man in the fez, deaf to all distractions, "and I have urged that the Bool is a disturbing thought, while the Bulbul is a reassuring thought. But even you, my friends, would not name a place after the ring in the Bool's nose and not after the Bool. Why then name an equivalent place after the shoo, the mere shoo, upon a horse's hoof, and not after the noble horse? Surely it is clear, surely it is evident, that the term 'horseshoe' is a cryptic term, an esoteric term, a term made during the days when the ancient Moslem faith of this English country was oppressed by the passing superstition of the Galilaeans. That bent shape, that duplex curving shape, which you call 'Horseshoe,' is it not clearly the Crescent?"—and he cast his arms wide as he had done on the sands— "the Crescent of the Prophet of the only God?"

"I should like to ask," began Lady Joan again, "how you would explain the name of the inn called 'The Green Man' just behind that row of houses."

"Exactly! exactly!" cried the Prophet of the Moon, in almost insane excitement. "The seeker after truth could not at all probably find a more perfect example of these principles. My friendss, how could there be a green man? You are acquainted with green grass, with green leaves, with green cheese, with green chartreusse. I ask if any of you, however wide her social circle, has ever been acquainted with a green man. Surely, surely, it is evident, my friendss, that this is an imperfect version, an abbreviated version, of the original words. What can be clearer than that the original expression, the reasonable expression, the highly historical expression, was 'the green-turban'd man,' in allusion to the well-known uniform of the descendants of the Prophet? 'Turban'd' surely is just the sort of word, exactly the sort of foreign and unfamiliar word, that might easily be slurred over and ultimately suppressed."

"There is a legend in these parts," said Lady Joan steadily, "that a great hero, hearing the colour that was sacred to his holy island insulted, really poured it over his enemy for a reply."

"A legend! A fable!" cried the man in the fez, with another radiant and rational expansion of the hands. "Is it not evident that no such thing can have really happened."

"Oh yes—it really happened," said the young lady softly. "There is not much to comfort one in this world; but there are some things. Oh, it really happened."

And taking a graceful farewell of the group, she resumed her rather listless walk along the parade.

IV

THE INN FINDS WINGS

Mr. Humphrey Pump stood in front of his inn once more; the cleaned and loaded gun lay on the table, and the white sign of the Ship still swung in the slight sea-breeze over his head; but his leatherish features were knotted over a new problem. He held two letters in his hand, letters of a very different sort, but letters that pointed to the same difficult problem. The first ran:

"DEAR HUMP,

"I am so bothered that I simply must call you by the old name again. You understand I've got to keep in with my people: Lord Ivywood is a sort of cousin of mine, and for that and some other reasons, my poor old mother would just die if I offended him. You know her heart is weak; you know everything there is to know in this county. Well, I only write to warn you that something is going to be done against your dear old inn. I don't know what this country's coming to. Only a month or two ago I saw a shabby old pantaloon on the beach with a green gamp, talking the craziest stuff you ever heard in your life. Three weeks ago I heard he was lecturing at Ethical Societies—whatever they are—for a handsome salary. Well, when I was last at Ivywood—I must go because Mamma likes it—there was the living lunatic again, in evening dress, and talked about by people who really *know*. I mean who know better.

"Lord Ivywood is entirely under his influence and thinks him the greatest prophet the world has ever seen. And Lord Ivywood is not a fool; one can't help admiring him. Mamma, I think, wants me to do more than admire him. I am telling you everything, Hump, because I think perhaps this is the last honest letter I shall ever write in the world. And I warn you seriously that Lord Ivywood is *sincere*, which is perfectly terrible. He will be the biggest English statesman, and he does really mean to ruin—the old ships. If ever you see me here again taking part in such work, I hope you may forgive me.

"Somebody we mentioned, whom I shall never see again, I leave to your friendship. It is the second best thing I can give, and I am not sure it may not be better than the first would have been. Good-bye.

"J. B."

This letter seemed to distress Mr. Pump rather than puzzle him. The second letter seemed to puzzle him more than it distressed him. It ran as follows:

"SIR,

"The Committee of the Imperial Commission of Liquor Control is directed to draw your attention to the fact that you have disregarded the Committee's communications under section 5A of the Act for the Regulation of Places of Public Entertainment; and that you are now under section 47C of the Act amending the Act for the Regulation of Places of Public Entertainment aforesaid. The charges on which prosecution will be founded are as follows:

"(1) Violation of sub-section 23f of the Act, which enacts that no pictorial signs shall be exhibited before premises of less than the rateable value of £400 per annum.

"(2) Violation of sub-section 113d of the Act, which enacts that no liquor containing alcohol shall be sold in any inn, hotel, tavern, or public-house, except when demanded under a medical certificate from one of the doctors licensed by the State Medical Council, or in the specially excepted cases of Claridge's Hotel and the Criterion Bar, where urgency has already been proved.

"As you have failed to acknowledge previous communications on this subject, this is to warn you that legal steps will be taken immediately.

"We are yours truly,

"IVYWOOD, President.

"J. LEVESON, Secretary."

Mr. Humphrey Pump sat down at the table outside his inn and whistled in a way which, combined with his little whiskers, made him for the moment seem literally like an ostler. Then the very real wit and learning he had returned slowly into his face, and with his warm brown eyes he considered the cold grey sea. There was not much to be got out of the sea. Humphrey Pump might drown himself in the sea; which would be better for Humphrey Pump than being finally separated from "The Old Ship." England might be sunk under the sea; which would be better for England than never again having such places as "The Old Ship." But these were not serious remedies nor rationally attainable; and Pump could only feel that the sea had simply warped him as it had warped his apple-trees. The sea was a dreary business altogether. There was only one figure walking on the sands. It was only when the figure drew nearer and nearer and grew to more than human size, that he sprang to his feet with a cry. Also the level light of morning lit the man's hair, and it was red.

The late King of Ithaca came casually and slowly up the slope of the beach that led to "The Old Ship." He had landed in a boat from a battleship that could still be seen near the horizon, and he still wore the astounding uniform of sea-green and silver which he had himself invented as that of a navy that had never existed very much, and which now did not exist at all. He had a straight naval sword at his side; for the terms of his capitulation had never required him to surrender it; and inside the uniform and beside the sword there was what there always had been, a big and rather bewildered man with rough red hair, whose misfortune was that he had good brains, but that his bodily strength and bodily passions were a little too strong for his brains.

He had flung his crashing weight on the chair outside the inn before the innkeeper could find words to express his astounded pleasure in seeing him. His first words were, "Have you got any rum?"

Then, as if feeling that his attitude needed explanation, he added, "I suppose I shall never be a sailor again after to-night. So I must have some rum."

Humphrey Pump had a talent for friendship and understood his old friend. He went into the inn without a word; and came back idly pushing or rolling with an alternate foot (as if he were playing football with two footballs at once) two objects that rolled very easily. One was a big keg or barrel of rum and the other a great solid drum of a cheese. Among his thousand other technical tricks he had a way of tapping a cask without a tap, or anything that could impair its revolutionary or revolving qualities. He was feeling for the instrument with which he solved such questions in his pocket, when his Irish friend suddenly sat bolt upright, as one startled out of sleep, and spoke with his strongest and most unusual brogue.

"Oh, thank you, Hump, a thousand times; and I don't think I really want anything to drink at arl. Now I know I can have it I don't seem to want it at arl. But hwhat I do want"—and he suddenly dashed his big fist on the little table so that one of its legs leapt and nearly snapped—"hwhat I do want is some sort of account of what's happening in this England of yours that shan't be just obviously rubbish."

"Ah," said Pump, fingering the two letters thoughtfully. "And what do you mean by rubbish?"

"I carl it rubbish," cried Patrick Dalroy, "when ye put the Koran into the Bible and not the Apocrypha; and I carl it rubbish when a mad person's allowed to propose to put a crescent on St. Paul's Cathedral. I know the Turks are our allies now; but they often were before, and I never heard that Palmerston or Colin Campbell had any truck with such trash."

"Lord Ivywood is very enthusiastic, I know," said Pump, with a restrained amusement "He was saying only the other day at the Flower Show here that the time had come for a full unity between Christianity and Islam."

"Something called Chrislam perhaps," said the Irishman, with a moody eye. He was gazing across the grey and purple woodlands that stretched below them at the back of the inn; and into which the steep white road swept downwards and disappeared. The steep road looked like the beginning of an adventure; and he was an adventurer.

"But you exaggerate, you know," went on Pump, polishing his gun, "about the crescent on St. Paul's. It wasn't exactly that. What Dr. Moole suggested, I think, was some sort of double emblem, you know combining cross and crescent——"

"And called the Croscent," muttered Dalroy.

"And you can't call Dr. Moole a parson either," went on Mr. Humphrey Pump, polishing industriously. "Why, they say he's a sort of atheist, or what they call an agnostic, like Squire Brunton who used to bite elm-trees by Marley. The grand folks have these fashions, Captain, but they've never lasted long that I know of."

"I think it's serious this time," said his friend, shaking his big red head. "This is the last inn on this coast, and will soon be the last inn in England. Do you remember 'The Saracen's Head,' Plumlea, along the shore there?"

"I know," assented the innkeeper. "My aunt was there when he hanged his mother; but it's a charming place."

"I passed there just now; and it has been destroyed," said Dalroy.

"Destroyed by fire?" asked Pump, pausing in his gun-scrubbing.

"No," said Dalroy, "destroyed by lemonade. They've taken away its licence, or whatever you call it. I made a song about it, which I'll sing to you now." And with an astounding air of suddenly revived spirits he roared in a voice like thunder the following verses, to a simple but spirited tune of his own invention.

> "'The Saracen's Head' looks down the lane,
> Where we shall never drink wine again,
> For the wicked old women who feel well-bred
> Have turned to a tea-shop 'The Saracen's Head.'
>
> 'The Saracen's Head' out of Araby came,
> King Richard riding in arms like flame,
> And where he established his folk to be fed
> He set up a spear—and the Saracen's Head.
>
> But 'The Saracen's Head' outlived the Kings,
> It thought and it thought of most horrible things,
> Of Health and of Soap and of Standard Bread,
> And of Saracen drinks at 'The Saracen's Head.'"

"Hullo!" cried Pump, with another low whistle. "Why, here comes his lordship. And I suppose that young man in the goggles is a Committee or something."

"Let him come," said Dalroy, and continued in a yet more earthquake bellow:

> "So 'The Saracen's Head' fulfils its name,
> They drink no wine—a ridiculous game—
> And I shall wonder until I'm dead,
> How it ever came into the Saracen's Head."

As the last echo of this lyrical roar rolled away among the apple-trees, and down the steep white road into the woods, Captain Dalroy leaned back in his chair and nodded good-humouredly to Lord Ivywood, who was standing on the lawn with his usual cold air, but with slightly compressed lips. Behind him was a dark young man with double eyeglasses, and a number of printed papers in his hand; presumably J. Leveson, Secretary. In the road outside stood a group of three which struck Pump as strangely incongruous, like a group in a three-act farce. The first was a police inspector in uniform; the second was a workman in a leather apron, more or less like a carpenter, and the third was an old man in a scarlet Turkish fez, but otherwise dressed in very fashionable English clothes in which he did not seem very comfortable. He was explaining something about the inn to the policeman and the carpenter, who appeared to be restraining their amusement.

"Fine song that, my lord," said Dalroy, with cheerful egotism. "I'll sing you another." And he cleared his throat.

"Mr. Pump," said Lord Ivywood, in his bell-like and beautiful voice, "I thought I would come in person, if only to make it clear that every indulgence has been shown you. The mere date of this inn brings it within the statute of 1909; it was erected when my great-grandfather was Lord of the Manor here, though I believe it then bore a different name, and——"

"Ah, my lord," broke in Pump, with a sigh, "I'd rather deal with your great-grandfather, I would, though he married a hundred negresses instead of one, than see a gentleman of your family taking away a poor man's livelihood."

"The Act is specially designed in the interests of the relief of poverty," proceeded Lord Ivywood in an unruffled manner, "and its final advantages will accrue to all citizens alike." He turned for an instant to the dark Secretary, saying, "You have that second report"; and receiving a folded paper in answer.

"It is here fully explained," said Lord Ivywood, putting on his elderly eyeglasses, "that the purpose of the Act is largely to protect the savings of the more humble and necessitous classes. I find in paragraph three, 'We strongly advise that the deleterious element of alcohol be made illegal, save in such few places as the Government may specially exempt for Parliamentary or other public reasons, and that the provocative and demoralizing display on inn signs be strictly forbidden except in the case thus specially exempted; the absence of such temptations will, in our opinion, do much to improve the precarious financial conditions of the working class.' That disposes, I think, of any such suggestion as Mr. Pump's that our inevitable acts of social reform are in any sense oppressive. To Mr. Pump's prejudice it may appear for the moment to bear hardly upon him; but" (and here Lord Ivywood's voice took one of its moving oratorical turns) "what better proof could we desire of the insidiousness of the sleepy poison we denounce, what better evidence could we offer of the civic corruption that we seek to cure, than the very fact that good and worthy men of established repute in the country can, by living in such places as these, become so stagnant and sodden and unsocial, whether through the fumes of wine or through meditations as maudlin about the past, that they consider the case solely as their own case, and laugh at the long agony of the poor?"

Captain Dalroy had been studying Ivywood with a very bright blue eye; and he spoke now much more quietly than he generally did.

"Excuse me one moment, my lord," he said. "But there was one point in your important explanation which I am not sure I have got right. Do I understand you to say that, though sign-boards are to be abolished, yet where, if anywhere, they are retained, the right to sell fermented liquor will be retained also? In other words, though an Englishman may at last find only one inn and sign in England, yet if the place has an inn sign, it will also have your gracious permission to be really an inn?"

Lord Ivywood had an admirable command of temper, which had helped him much in his career as a statesman. He did not waste time in wrangling about the Captain's *locus standi*[5] in the matter; he replied quite simply:

"Yes. Your statement of facts is correct."

---

[5] *Locus standi* means a "recognized or identifiable status" and usually refers to "standing to bring a legal action."

"Wherever I find an inn sign permitted by the police, I may go in and ask for a glass of beer—also permitted by the police."

"If you find any such, yes," answered Ivywood, quite temperately. "But we hope soon to have removed them altogether."

Captain Patrick Dalroy rose enormously from his seat, with a sort of stretch and yawn.

"Well, Hump," he said to his friend, "the best thing, it seems to me, is to take the important things with us."

With two sight-staggering kicks he sent the keg of rum and the round cheese flying over the fence, in such a direction that they bounded on the descending road and rolled more and more rapidly down towards the dark woods into which the path disappeared. Then he gripped the pole of the inn sign, shook it twice, and plucked it out of the turf like a tuft of grass.

It had all happened before any one could move, but as he strode out into the road the policeman ran forward. Dalroy smote him flat across face and chest with the wooden sign-board, so as to send him flying into the ditch on the other side of the road. Then turning on the man in the fez, he poked him with the end of the pole so sharply in his new white waistcoat and watch-chain as to cause him to sit down suddenly in the road, looking very serious and thoughtful.

The dark Secretary made a movement of rescue, but Humphrey Pump, with a cry, caught up his gun from the table and pointed it at him; which so alarmed J. Leveson, Secretary, as to cause him almost to double up with his emotions. The next moment Pump, with his gun under his arm, was scampering down the hill after the Captain, who was scampering after the barrel and the cheese.

Before the policeman had struggled out of the ditch, they had all disappeared into the darkness of the forest. Lord Ivywood, who had remained firm through the scene, without a sign of fear or impatience (or, I will add, amusement) held up his hand and stopped the policeman in his pursuit.

"We should only make ourselves and the law ridiculous," he said, "by pursuing those ludicrous rowdies now. They can't escape or do any real harm in the state of modern communications. What is far more important, gentlemen, is to destroy their stores and their base.

Under the Act of 1911 we have a right to confiscate and destroy any property in an inn where the law has been violated."

And he stood for hours on the lawn, watching the smashing of bottles and the breaking up of casks, and feeding on fanatical pleasure: the pleasure which his strange, cold, courageous nature could not get from food or wine or woman.

V

THE ASTONISHMENT OF THE AGENT

Lord Ivywood shared the mental weakness of most men who have fed on books; he ignored, not the value but the very existence of other forms of information. Thus Humphrey Pump was perfectly aware that Lord Ivywood considered him an ignorant man who carried a volume of "Pickwick" and could not be got to read any other book. But Lord Ivywood was quite unaware that Humphrey never looked at him without thinking that he could be most successfully hidden in a wood of small beeches, as his grey-brown hair and sallow ashen face exactly reproduced the three predominant tints of such a sylvan twilight. Mr. Pump, I fear, had sometimes partaken of partridge or pheasant, in his early youth, under circumstances in which Lord Ivywood was not only unconscious of the hospitality he was dispensing, but would have sworn that it was physically impossible for any one to elude the vigilance of his efficient system of gamekeeping. But it is very unwise in one who counts himself superior to physical things to talk about physical impossibility.

Lord Ivywood was in error, therefore, when he said that the fugitives could not possibly escape in modern England. You can do a great many things in modern England if you have noticed some things in fact which others know by pictures or current speech: if you know, for instance, that most roadside hedges are taller and denser than they look, and that even the largest man lying just behind them takes up far less room than you would suppose; if you know that many natural sounds are much more like each other than the enlightened ear can believe, as in the case of wind in leaves and of the sea; if you know that it is easier to walk in socks than in boots if you know how to take hold of the ground; if you know that the proportion of dogs who will bite a man under any circumstances is rather less than the proportion of men who will murder you in a railway carriage; if you know that you need not be drowned even in a river, unless the tide is very strong, and unless you practise putting yourself into the special attitudes of a suicide; if you know that country stations have objectless extra waiting-rooms that nobody ever goes into; and if you know that country folk will forget you if you speak to them, but talk about you all day if you don't.

By the exercise of these and other arts and sciences Humphrey Pump was able to guide his friend across country, mostly in the character of trespasser and occasionally in that of something like housebreaker, and eventually, with sign, keg, cheese and all, to step out of a black pine-wood on to a white road in a part of the county where they would not be sought for the present.

Opposite them was a cornfield and on their right, in the shades of the pine-trees, a cottage, a very tumbledown cottage that seemed to have collapsed under its own thatch. The red-haired Irishman's face wore a curious smile. He stuck the inn sign erect in the road and went and hammered on the door.

It was opened tremulously by an old man with a face so wrinkled that the wrinkles seemed more distinctly graven than the features themselves, which seemed lost in the labyrinth of them. He might have crawled out of the hole in a gnarled tree and he might have been a thousand years old.

He did not seem to notice the sign-board, which stood rather to the left of the door; and what life remained in his eyes seemed to awake in wonder at Dalroy's stature and strange uniform and the sword at his side. "I beg your pardon," said the Captain courteously. "I fear my uniform startles you. It is Lord Ivywood's livery. All his servants are to dress like this. In fact, I understand the tenants also and even yourself perhaps ... excuse my sword. Lord Ivywood is very particular that every man should have a sword. You know his beautiful eloquent way of putting his views. 'How can we profess,' he was saying to me yesterday while I was brushing his trousers,—'how can we profess that all men are brothers while we refuse to them the symbol of manhood; or with what assurance can we claim it as a movement of modern emancipation to deny the citizen that which has in all ages marked the difference between the free man and the slave? Nor need we anticipate any such barbaric abuses as my honourable friend who is cleaning the knives has prophesied, for this gift is a sublime act of confidence in your universal passion for the severe splendours of Peace; and he that has the right to strike is he who has learnt to spare.'"

Talking all this nonsense with extreme rapidity and vast oratorical flourishes of the hand, Captain Dalroy proceeded to trundle both the big cheese and the cask of rum into the house of the astonished cottager: Mr. Pump following with a grim placidity and his gun under his arm.

"Lord Ivywood," said Dalroy, setting the rum cask with a bump on the plain deal table, "wishes to take wine with you. Or, more strictly speaking, rum. Don't you run away, my friend, with any of these stories about Lord Ivywood being opposed to drink. Three-bottle Ivywood, we call him in the kitchen. But it must be rum: nothing but rum for the Ivywoods. 'Wine may be a mocker,' he was saying the other day (and I particularly noted the phrasing, which seemed to be very happy even for his lordship; he was standing at the top of the steps, and I stopped cleaning them to make a note of it),—'wine may be a mocker; strong drink may be raging, but nowhere in the sacred pages will you find one word of censure of the sweeter spirit sacred to them that go down to the sea in ships; no tongue of priest and prophet was ever lifted to break the sacred silence of Holy Writ about rum.' He then explained to me," went on Dalroy, signing to Pump to tap the cask according to his own technical secret, "that the great tip for avoiding any bad results that a cask or two of rum might have on young and inexperienced people was to eat cheese with it, particularly this kind of cheese that I have here. I've forgotten its name."

"Cheddar," said Pump quite gravely.

"But mind you!" continued the Captain almost ferociously, shaking his big finger in warning at the aged man. "Mind you, no *bread* with the cheese. All the devastating ruin wrought by cheese and the once happy homes of this country, has been due to the reckless and insane experiment of eating bread with it. You'll get no bread from me, my friend. Indeed, Lord Ivywood has given directions that the allusion to this ignorant and depraved habit shall be eliminated from the Lord's Prayer. Have a drink."

He had already poured out a little of the spirit into two thick tumblers and a broken teacup, which he had induced the aged man to produce; and now solemnly pledged him.

"Thank ye kindly, sir," said the old man, using his cracked voice for the first time. Then he drank; and his old face changed as if it were an old horn lantern in which the flame began to rise.

"Ar," he said. "My son be a sailor."

"I wish him a happy voyage," said the Captain. "And I'll sing you a song about the first sailor there ever was in the world; and who (as Lord Ivywood acutely observes) lived before the time of rum."

He sat down on a wooden chair and lifted his loud voice once more, beating on the table with the broken teacup.

"Old Noah he had an ostrich farm and fowls on the largest scale,
He ate his egg with a ladle in an egg-cup big as a pail,
And the soup he took was Elephant Soup and the fish he took was Whale,
But they all were small to the cellar he took when he set out to sail,
And Noah he often said to his wife when he sat down to dine,
'I don't care where the water goes if it doesn't get into the wine.'

The cataract of the cliff of heaven fell blinding off the brink
As if it would wash the stars away as suds go down a sink,
The seven heavens came roaring down for the throats of hell to drink,
And Noah he cocked his eye and said, 'It looks like rain, I think,
The water has drowned the Matterhorn as deep as a Mendip mine,
But I don't care where the water goes if it doesn't get into the wine.'

But Noah he sinned, and we have sinned; on tipsy feet we trod,
Till a great big black teetotaller was sent to us for a rod,
And you can't get wine at a P.S.A., or chapel, or Eisteddfod,
For the Curse of Water has come again because of the wrath of God,
And water is on the Bishop's board and the Higher Thinker's shrine,
But I don't care where the water goes if it doesn't get into the wine."

"Lord Ivywood's favourite song," concluded Mr. Patrick Dalroy, drinking. "Sing us a song yourself."

Rather to the surprise of the two humorists, the old gentleman actually began in a quavering voice to chant:

"King George that lives in London Town,
I hope they will defend his crown,
And Bonyparte be quite put down,
    On Christmas Day in the morning.

Old Squire is gone to the Meet to-day,
All in his——"

It is perhaps fortunate for the rapidity of this narrative that the old
gentleman's favourite song, which consists of forty-seven verses, was
interrupted by a curious incident. The door of the cottage opened,
and a sheepish-looking man in corduroys stood silently in the room
for a few seconds and then said, without preface or further explanation:

"Four ale."

"I beg your pardon?" inquired the polite Captain.

"Four ale," said the man, with solidity; then catching sight of
Humphrey seemed to find a few more words in his vocabulary.

"Morning, Mr. Pump. Didn't know as how you'd moved 'The Old
Ship.'"

Mr. Pump, with a twist of a smile, pointed to the old man whose
song had been interrupted.

"Mr. Marne's seeing after it now, Mr. Gowl," said Pump, with the
strict etiquette of the country-side. "But he's got nothing but this
rum in stock as yet."

"Better'nowt," said the laconic Mr. Gowl; and put down some
money in front of the aged Marne, who eyed it wonderingly. As he
was turning with a farewell and wiping his mouth with the back of
his hand, the door once more moved, letting in white sunlight and a
man with a red neckerchief.

"Morning, Mr. Marne. Morning, Mr. Pump. Morning, Mr. Gowl,"
said the man in the red neckerchief.

"Morning, Mr. Coote," said the other three, one after another.

"Have some rum, Mr. Coote?" asked Humphrey Pump genially.
"That's all Mr. Marne's got just now."

Mr. Coote also had a little rum; and also laid a little money under
the rather vague gaze of the venerable cottager. Mr. Coote was just
proceeding to explain that these were bad times, but if you saw a sign
you were all right still; a lawyer up at Grunton Abbot had told him
so; when the company was increased and greatly excited by the arrival
of a boisterous and popular tinker, who ordered glasses all round and
said he had his donkey and cart outside. A prolonged, rich, and confused

conversation about his donkey and cart then ensued, in which the most varied views were taken of their merits; and it gradually began to dawn on Dalroy that the tinker was trying to sell them.

An idea suited to the romantic opportunism of his present absurd career suddenly swept over his mind, and he rushed out to look at the cart and donkey. The next moment he was back again, asking the tinker what his price was, and almost in the same breath offering a much bigger price than the tinker would have dreamed of asking. This was considered, however, as a lunacy specially allowed to gentlemen; the tinker had some more rum on the strength of the payment, and then Dalroy, offering his excuses, sealed up the cask and took it and the cheese to be stowed in the bottom of the cart. The money, however, he still left lying in shining silver and copper before the silver beard of old Marne.

No one acquainted with the quaint and often wordless *camaraderie* of the English poor will require to be told that they all went out and stared at him as he loaded the cart and saw to the harness of the donkey—all except the old cottager, who sat as if hypnotized by the sight of the money. While they were standing there they saw, coming down the white hot road where it curled over the hill, a figure that gave them no pleasure, even when it was a mere marching black spot in the distance. It was a Mr. Bullrose, the agent of Lord Ivywood's estates.

Mr. Bullrose was a short square man with a broad square head with ridges of close black curls on it, with a heavy, frog-like face, and starting, suspicious eyes; a man with a good silk hat but a square business jacket. Mr. Bullrose was not a nice man. The agent on that sort of estate hardly ever is a nice man. The landlord often is; and even Lord Ivywood had an arctic magnanimity of his own, which made most people want, if possible, to see him personally. But Mr. Bullrose was petty. Every really practical tyrant must be petty.

He evidently failed to understand the commotion in front of Mr. Marne's partly collapsed cottage, but he felt there must be something wrong about it. He wanted to get rid of the cottage altogether, and had not, of course, the faintest intention of giving the cottager any compensation for it. He hoped the old man would die; but in any case he could easily clear him out if it became suddenly necessary, for he could not possibly pay the rent for this week. The rent was not very much; but it was immeasurably too much for the old man, who had no conceivable way of borrowing or earning it. That is where the chivalry of our aristocratic land system comes in.

"Good-bye, my friends," the enormous man in the fantastic uniform was saying. "All roads lead to Rum, as Lord Ivywood said at the Church Congress, and we hope to be back soon, establishing the first-class hotel here, of which prospectuses will soon be sent out."

The heavy, frog-like face of Mr. Bullrose the agent grew uglier with astonishment; and the eyes stood out more like a snail's than a frog's. The indefensible allusion to Lord Ivywood would in any case have caused a choleric intervention, if it had not been swallowed up in the earthquake suggestion of an unlicensed hotel on the estate. This again would have effected the explosion, if that and everything else had not been struck still and rigid by the sight of a solid wooden sign-post already erected outside old Marne's miserable cottage.

"I've got him now," muttered Mr. Bullrose. "He can't possibly pay; and out he shall go." And he walked swiftly towards the door of the cottage, almost at the same moment that Dalroy went to the donkey's head, as if to lead it off along the road.

"Look here, my man," burst out Bullrose the instant he was inside the cottage. "You've cooked yourself this time. His lordship has been a great deal too indulgent with you; but this is going to be the end of it. The insolence of what you've done outside, especially when you know his lordship's wishes in such things, has just put the lid on." He stopped a moment and sneered. "So unless you happen to have the exact rent down to a farthing or two about you, out you go. We're sick of your sort."

In a very awkward and fumbling manner the old man pushed a heap of coins across the table. Mr. Bullrose sat down suddenly on the wooden chair with his silk hat on, and began counting them furiously. He counted them once; he counted them twice; and he counted them again. Then he stared at them more steadily than the cottager had done.

"Where did you get this money?" he asked in a thick, gross voice. "Did you steal it?"

"I ain't very spry for stealin'," said the old man in quavering comedy.

Bullrose looked at him and then at the money; and remembered with fury that Ivywood was a just though cold magistrate on the bench.

"Well, anyhow," he cried, in a hot, heady way. "We've got enough against you to turn you out of this. Haven't you broken the law, my man, to say nothing of the regulations for tenants, in sticking up that fancy sign of yours outside the cottage? Eh?"

The tenant was silent.

"Eh?" reiterated the agent.

"Ar," replied the tenant.

"Have you or have you not a sign-board outside this house?" shouted Bullrose, hammering the table.

The tenant looked at him for a long time with a patient and venerable face, and then said, "Mubbe, yes. Mubbe, no."

"I'll mubbe you," cried Mr. Bullrose, springing up and sticking his silk hat on the back of his head. "I don't know whether you people are too drunk to see anything, but I saw the thing with my own eyes out in the road. Come out, and deny it if you dare!"

"Ar," said Mr. Marne dubiously.

He tottered after the agent, who flung open the door with a business-like fury, and stood outside on the threshold. He stood there quite a long time. And he did not speak. Deep in the hardened mud of his materialist mind there had stirred two things that were its ancient enemies: the old fairy tale in which everything can be believed; the new scepticism in which nothing can be believed—not even one's own eyes. There was no sign, nor sign of a sign, in the landscape.

On the withered face of the old man Marne there was a faint renewal of that laughter that has slept since the Middle Ages.

VI

THE HOLE IN HEAVEN

That delicate ruby light which is one of the rarest but one of the most exquisite of evening effects warmed the land, sky, and seas as if the whole world were washed in wine: and dyed almost scarlet the strong red head of Patrick Dalroy as he stood on the waste of furze and bracken, where he and his friends had halted. One of his friends was re-examining a short gun, rather like a double-barrelled carbine, the other was eating thistles.

Dalroy himself was idle and ruminant, with his hands in his pockets and his eye on the horizon. Landwards the hills, plains, and woods lay bathed in the rose-red light; but it changed somewhat to purple, to cloud and something like storm over the distant violet strip of sea. It was towards the sea that he was staring.

Suddenly he woke up; and seemed almost to rub his eyes, or at any rate to rub his red eyebrow.

"Why, we're on the road back to Pebbleswick!" he said. "That's the damned little tin chapel by the beach."

"I know," answered his friend and guide. "We've done the old hare trick; doubled, you know. Nine times out of ten it's the best. Parson Whitelady used to do it when they were after him for dog-stealing. I've pretty much followed his trail; you can't do better than stick to the best examples. They tell you in London that Dick Turpin[6] rode to York. Well, I know he didn't; for my old grandfather up at Cobble's End knew the Turpins intimately—threw one of them into the river on a Christmas Day: but I think I can guess what he did do and how the tale got about. If Dick was wise, he went flying up the old North Road, shouting 'York! York!' or what not, before people recognized him: then if he did the thing properly, he might half an hour afterwards walk down the Strand

---

[6]Dick Turpin (1705–1739) was an Essex butcher turned highwayman who worked around the south of London. He was eventually captured in York, where he was tried and executed.

with a pipe in his mouth. They say old Boney said, 'Go where you aren't expected,' and I suppose as a soldier he was right. But for a gentleman dodging the police like yourself, it isn't exactly the right way of putting it. I should say, 'Go where you ought to be expected'—and you'll generally find your fellow-creatures don't do what they ought about expecting any more than about anything else."

"Well, this bit between here and the sea," said the Captain, in a brown study; "I know it so well—so well that—that I rather wish I'd never seen it again. Do you know," he asked, suddenly pointing to a patch and pit of sand that showed white in the dusky heath a hundred yards away,—"do you know what makes that spot so famous in history?"

"Yes," answered Mr. Pump; "that's where old Mother Grouch shot the Methodist."

"You are in error," said the Captain. "Such an incident as you describe would in no case call for special comment or regret. No, that spot is famous, because a very badly brought-up girl once lost a ribbon off a plait of black hair and somebody helped her to find it."

"Has the other person been well brought up?" asked Pump, with a faint smile.

"No," said Dalroy, staring at the sea. "He has been brought down." Then, rousing himself again, he made a gesture towards a further part of the heath. "Do you know the remarkable history of that old wall, the one beyond the last gorge over there?"

"No," replied the other, "unless you mean Dead Man's Circus; and that happened further along."

"I do not mean Dead Man's Circus," said the Captain. "The remarkable history of that wall is that somebody's shadow once fell on it: and that shadow was more desirable than the substance of all other living things. It is *this*," he cried, almost violently resuming his flippant tone. "It is this circumstance, Hump, and not the trivial and everyday incident of a dead man going to a circus to which you have presumed to compare it; it is *this* historical event which Lord Ivywood is about to commemorate by rebuilding the wall with solid gold and Greek marbles stolen by the Turks from the grave of Socrates, enclosing a column of solid gold four hundred feet high and surmounted by a colossal equestrian statue of a bankrupt Irishman riding backwards on a donkey."

He lifted one of his long legs over the animal, as if about to pose for the group; then swung back on both feet again and again looked at the purple limit of the sea.

"Do you know, Hump," he said, "I think modern people have somehow got their minds all wrong about human life. They seem to expect what Nature has never promised; and then try to ruin all that Nature has really given. At all those atheist chapels of Ivywood's they're always talking of Peace, Perfect Peace, and Utter Trust, and Universal Joy and souls that beat as one. But they don't look any more cheerful than any one else: and the next thing they do is to start smashing a thousand good jokes and good stories and good songs and good friendships by pulling down 'The Old Ship.' " He gave a glance at the loose sign-post lying on the heath beside him, almost as if to reassure himself that it was not stolen. "Now, it seems to me," he went on, "that this is asking for too much and getting too little. I don't know whether God means a man to have happiness in that All in All and Utterly Utter sense of happiness. But God does mean man to have a little Fun; and I mean to go on having it. If I mustn't satisfy my heart, I can gratify my humour. The cynical fellows who think themselves so damned clever have a sort of saying, 'Be good and you will be happy; but you will not have a jolly time.' The cynical fellows are quite wrong, as they generally are. They have got hold of the exact opposite of the truth. God knows I don't set up to be good; but even a rascal sometimes has to fight the world in the same way as a saint. I think I have fought the world; *et militavi non sine*[7]—what's the Latin for having a lark? I can't pretend to Peace and Joy, and all the rest of it, particularly in this original briar-patch. I haven't been happy, Hump; but I have had a jolly time."

The sunset stillness settled down again, save for the cropping of the donkey in the undergrowth; and Pump said nothing sympathetically; and it was Dalroy once more who took up his parable.

"So I think there's too much of this playing on our emotions, Hump; as this place is certainly playing the cat and banjo with mine. Damn it

[7] *Et militavi non sine* is from *Horace*, bk. 3, ode 26. The lines in which this latin phrase occurs have been translated in many ways including, "Experienced in your wars,/ Not long ago I was a not inglorious soldier."

all, there are other things to do with the rest of one's life! I don't like all this fuss about feeling things—it only makes people miserable. In my present frame of mind I'm in favour of doing things. All of which, Hump," he said, with a sudden lift of the voice that always went in him with a rushing irrational return of merely animal spirits,—"all of which I have put into a Song Against Songs, that I will now sing you."

"I shouldn't sing it here," said Humphrey Pump, picking up his gun and putting it under his arm. "You look large in this open place; and you sound large. But I'll take you to the Hole in Heaven you've been talking about so much, and hide you as I used to hide you from that tutor—I couldn't catch his name—man who could only get drunk on Greek wine at Squire Wimpole's."

"Hump!" cried the Captain. "I abdicate the throne of Ithaca. You are far wiser than Ulysses. Here I have had my heart torn with temptations to ten thousand things between suicide and abduction, and all by the mere sight of that hole in the heath, where we used to have picnics. And all that time I'd forgotten we used to call it the Hole in Heaven. And, by God, what a good name—in both senses!"

"I thought you'd have remembered it, Captain," said the innkeeper, "from the joke young Mr. Matthews made."

"In the heat of some savage hand-to-hand struggle in Albania," said Mr. Dalroy sadly, passing his palm across his brow, "I must have forgotten for one fatal instant the joke young Mr. Matthews made."

"It wasn't very good," said Mr. Pump simply. "Ah, his aunt was the one for things like that. She went too far with old Gudgeon, though."

With these words he jumped and seemed to be swallowed up by the earth. But they had merely strolled the few yards needed to bring them to the edge of the sand-pit on the heath of which they had been speaking. And it is one of the truths concealed by Heaven from Lord Ivywood, and revealed by Heaven to Mr. Pump, that a hiding-place can be covered when you are close to it; and yet be open and visible from some spot of vantage far off. From the side by which he approached it, the sudden hollow of sand, a kind of collapsed chamber in the heath, seemed covered with a natural curve of fern and furze, and he flashed out of sight like a fairy.

"It's all right," he called out from under a floor or roof of leaves. "You'll remember it all when you get here. This is the place to sing your song, Captain. Lord bless me, Captain, don't I remember your singing that Irish song you made up at college—bellowing it like a bull of Bashan—all about hearts and sleeves, or some such things— and her ladyship and the tutor never heard a breath, because that bank of sand breaks everything? It's worth knowing all this, you know. It's a pity it's not part of a young gentleman's education. Now you shall sing me the song in favour of having no feelings, or whatever you call it."

Dalroy was staring about him at the cavern of his old picnics, so forgotten and so startlingly familiar. He seemed to have lost all thought of singing anything, and simply to be groping in the dark house of his own boyhood. There was a slight trickle from a natural spring, in sandstone just under the ferns, and he remembered they used to try to boil the water in a kettle. He remembered a quarrel about who had upset the kettle which, in the morbidity of first love, had given him for days the tortures of the damned. When the energetic Pump broke once more through the rather thorny roof, on an impulse to accumulate their other eccentric possessions, Patrick remembered about a thorn in a finger, that made his heart stop with something that was pain and perfect music. When Pump returned with the rum-keg and the cheese, and rolled them with a kick down the shelving sandy side of the hole, he remembered, with almost wrathful laughter, that in the old days he had rolled down that slope himself, and thought it rather a fine thing to do. He felt then as if he were rolling down a smooth side of the Matterhorn. He observed now that the height was rather less than that of the second story of one of the stunted cottages he had noted on his return. He suddenly understood he had grown bigger; bigger in a bodily sense. He had doubts about any other.

"The Hole in Heaven!" he said. "What a good name! What a good poet I was in those days! The Hole in Heaven! But does it let one in, or let one out?"

In the last level shafts of the fallen sun the fantastic shadow of the long-eared quadruped, whom Pump had now tethered to a new and nearer pasture, fell across the last sunlit scrap of sand. Dalroy looked at the long, exaggerated shadow of the ass: and laughed that short explosive laugh he had uttered when the doors of the harems had been closed after the Turkish war. He was normally a man much too loquacious; but he never explained those laughs.

Humphrey Pump plunged down again into the sunken nest, and began to broach the cask of rum in his own secret style, saying:

"We can get something else somehow to-morrow. For to-night we can eat cheese and drink rum, especially as there's water on tap, so to speak. And now, Captain, sing us the song against songs."

Patrick Dalroy drank a little rum out of a small medicine-glass which the generally unaccountable Mr. Pump unaccountably produced from his waistcoat pocket; but Patrick's colour had risen, his brow was almost as red as his hair; and he was evidently reluctant.

"I don't see why I should sing all the songs," he said. "Why the divil don't you sing a song yourself? And now I come to think of it," he cried, with an accumulating brogue not, perhaps, wholly unaffected by the rum, which he had not in fact drunk for years,—"and now I come to think of it, what about that song of yours? All me youth's coming back in this blest and cursed place; and I remember that song of yours, that never existed nor ever will. Don't ye remember now, Humphrey Pump, that night when I sang ye no less than seventeen songs of me own composition?"

"I remember it very well," answered the Englishman, with restraint.

"And don't ye remember," went on the exhilarated Irishman, with solemnity, "that unless ye could produce a poetic lyric of your own, written and sung by your self, I threatened to——"

"To sing again," said the impenetrable Pump. "Yes, I know."

He calmly proceeded to take out of his pockets, which were, alas! more like those of a poacher than an innkeeper, a folded and faded piece of paper.

"I wrote it when you asked me," he said simply. "I have never tried to sing it. But I'll sing it myself, when you've sung your song against anybody singing at all."

"All right!" cried the somewhat excited Captain. "To hear a song from you—why, I'll sing anything. This is the Song against Songs, Hump."

And again he let his voice out in a bellow against the evening silence.

"The song of the sorrow of Melisande is a weary song and a dreary song,
The glory of Mariana's grange had got into great decay,
The song of the Raven Never More has never been called a cheery song,
And the brightest things in Baudelaire are anything else but gay.

But who will write us a riding song
Or a hunting song or a drinking song,
Fit for them that arose and rode
When day and the wine were red?
But bring me a quart of claret out,
And I will write you a clinking song,
A song of war and a song of wine
And a song to wake the dead.

The song of the fury of Fragolette is a florid song and a torrid song,
The song of the sorrow of Tara is sung to a harp unstrung,
The song of the cheerful Shropshire Lad I consider a perfectly horrid song,
And the song of the happy Futurist is a song that can't be sung.

But who will write us a riding song
Or a fighting song or a drinking song,
Fit for the fathers of you and me,
That knew how to think and thrive?
But the song of Beauty and Art and Love
Is simply an utterly stinking song,
To double you up and drag you down
And damn your soul alive."

"Take some more rum," concluded the Irish officer affably; "and let's hear your song at last."

With gravity inseparable from the deep conventionality of country people, Mr. Pump unfolded the paper on which he had recorded the only antagonistic emotion that was strong enough in him to screw his infinite English tolerance to the pitch of song. He read out the title very carefully and in full.

"Song Against Grocers, by Humphrey Pump, sole Proprietor of 'The Old Ship,' Pebbleswick. Good Accommodation for Man and

Beast. Celebrated as the House at which both Queen Charlotte and
Jonathan Wilde put up on different occasions; and where the chim-
panzee man was mistaken for Bonaparte. This song is written against
Grocers.

"God made the wicked Grocer
For a mystery and a sign,
That men might shun the awful shops
And go to inns to dine;
Where the bacon's on the rafter
And the wine is in the wood,
And God that made good laughter
Has seen that they are good.

The evil-hearted Grocer
Would call his mother 'Ma'am,'
And bow at her and bob at her,
Her aged soul to damn,
And rub his horrid hands and ask
What article was next,
Though *mortis in articulo*
Should be her proper text.

His props are not his children,
But pert lads underpaid,
Who call out 'Cash!' and bang about
To work his wicked trade;
He keeps a lady in a cage
Most cruelly all day,
And makes her count and calls her 'Miss'
Until she fades away.

The righteous minds of innkeepers
Induce them now and then
To crack a bottle with a friend
Or treat unmoneyed men,
But who hath seen the Grocer
Treat housemaids to his teas
Or crack a bottle of fish-sauce
Or stand a man a cheese?

He sells us sands of Araby
As sugar for cash down;
He sweeps his shop and sells the dust
The purest salt in town,
He crams with cans of poisoned meat
Poor subjects of the King,
And when they die by thousands
Why, he laughs like anything.

The wicked Grocer groces
In spirits and in wine,
Not frankly and in fellowship
As men in inns do dine;
But packed with soap and sardines
And carried off by grooms,
For to be snatched by Duchesses
And drunk in dressing-rooms.

The hell-instructed Grocer
Has a temple made of tin,
And the ruin of good innkeepers
Is loudly urged therein;
But now the sands are running out
From sugar of a sort,
The Grocer trembles; for his time,
Just like his weight, is short."

Captain Dalroy was getting considerably heated with his nautical liquor, and his appreciation of Pump's song was not merely noisy but active. He leapt to his feet and waved his glass. "Ye ought to be Poet Laureate, Hump—ye're right, ye're right; well stand all this no longer!"

He dashed wildly up the sand slope and pointed with the sign-post towards the darkening shore, where the low shed of corrugated iron stood almost isolated.

"There's your tin temple!" he said. "Let's burn it!"

They were some way along the coast from the large watering-place of Pebbleswick, and between the gathering twilight and the rolling country it could not be clearly seen. Nothing was now in sight but the corrugated iron hall by the beach and three half-built red brick villas.

Dalroy appeared to regard the hall and the empty houses with great malevolence.

"Look at it!" he said. "Babylon!"

He brandished the inn sign in the air like a banner, and began to stride towards the place, showering curses.

"In forty days," he cried, "shall Pebbleswick be destroyed. Dogs shall lap the blood of J. Leveson, Secretary, and Unicorns——"

"Come back, Pat!" cried Humphrey. "You've had too much rum."

"Lions shall howl in its high places!" vociferated the Captain.

"Donkeys will howl anyhow," said Pump. "But I suppose the other donkey must follow."

And loading and untethering the quadruped, he began to lead him along.

VII

THE SOCIETY OF SIMPLE SOULS

Under a sunset, at once softer and more sombre, under which the leaden sea took on a Lenten purple, a tint appropriate to tragedy, Lady Joan Brett was once more drifting moodily along the sea-front. The evening had been rainy and lowering; the watering-place season was nearly over; and she was almost alone on the shore; but she had fallen into the habit of restlessly pacing the place, and it seemed to satisfy some subconscious hunger in her rather mixed psychology. Through all her brooding her animal senses always remained abnormally active: she could *smell* the sea when it had ebbed almost to the horizon; and in the same way she heard, through every whisper of waves or wind, the swish or flutter of another woman's skirt behind her. There is, she felt, something unmistakable about the movements of a lady who is generally very dignified and rather slow, and who happens to be in a hurry.

She turned to look at the lady who was thus hastening to overtake her; lifted her eyebrows a little and held out her hand. The interruption was known to her as Lady Enid Wimpole, cousin of Lord Ivywood; a tall and graceful lady who unbalanced her own elegance by a fashionable costume that was at once funereal and fantastic; her fair hair was pale but plentiful; her face was not only handsome and fastidious in the aquiline style, but when considered seriously was sensitive, modest, and even pathetic, but her wan blue eyes seemed slightly prominent, with that expression of cold eagerness that is seen in the eyes of ladies who ask questions at public meetings.

Joan Brett was herself, as she had said, a connexion of the Ivywood family; but Lady Enid was Ivywood's first cousin, and for all practical purposes his sister. For she kept house for him and his mother; who was now so incredibly old that she only survived to satisfy conventional opinion in the character of a speechless and useless chaperon. And Ivywood was not the sort who would be likely to call out any activity in an old lady exercising that office. Nor, for that matter, was

Lady Enid Wimpole; there seemed to shine on her face the same kind of inhuman, absent-minded common sense that shone on her cousin's.

"Oh, I'm so glad I've caught you up," she said to Joan. "Lady Ivywood wants you *so* much to come to us for the week-end or so, while Philip is still there. He always admired your sonnet on Cyprus so much, and he wants to talk to you about this policy of his in Turkey. Of course he's awfully busy; but I shall be seeing him to-night after the meeting."

"No living creature," said Lady Joan, with a smile, "ever saw him except before or after a meeting."

"Are you a Simple Soul?" asked Lady Enid carelessly.

"Am I a simple soul?" asked Joan, drawing her black brows together. "Merciful Heaven—no! What can you mean?"

"Their meeting's on to-night at the small Universal Hall, and Philip's taking the chair," explained the other lady. "He's very annoyed that he has to leave early to get up to the House; but Mr. Leveson can take the chair for the last bit. They've got Misysra Ammon."

"Got Mrs. who?" asked Joan, in honest doubt.

"You make game of everything," said Lady Enid, in cheerless amiability. "It's the man every one's talking about—*you* know as well as I do. It's really his influence that has *made* the Simple Souls."

"Oh!" said Lady Joan Brett.

Then, after a long silence, she added, "Who are the Simple Souls? I should be interested in them, if I could meet any." And she turned her dark brooding face on the darkening purple sea.

"Do you mean to say, my dear," asked Lady Enid Wimpole, "that you haven't met any of them yet?"

"No," said Joan, looking at the last dark line of sea. "I never met but one simple soul in my life."

"But you must come to the meeting!" cried Lady Enid, with frosty and sparkling gaiety. "You must come at once! Philip is certain to be eloquent on a subject like this. And of course Misysra Ammon is *always* so wonderful."

Without any very distinct idea of where she was going or why she was going there, Joan allowed herself to be piloted to a low iron or tin shed, beyond the last straggling hotels; out of the echoing shell of which she could prematurely hear a voice that she thought she recognized. When she came in Lord Ivywood was on his feet, in exquisite evening dress, but with a light overcoat thrown over the seat behind him. Beside him, in less tasteful but more obvious evening dress, was the little old man she had heard on the beach.

No one else was on the platform; but just under it, rather to Joan's surprise, sat Miss Browning, her old typewriting friend in her old black dress, industriously taking down Lord Ivywood's words in shorthand. A yard or two off, even more to her surprise, sat Miss Browning's more domestic sister, also taking down the same words in shorthand.

"That is Misysra Ammon," whispered Lady Enid earnestly, pointing a delicate finger at the little old man beside the chairman.

"Where's the umbrella?" said Joan. "He can't *really* do it without the umbrella."

". . . at least evident," Lord Ivywood was saying, "that one of those ancestral impossibilities is no longer impossible. The East and the West are one. The East is no longer East nor the West West; for a small isthmus has been broken; and the Atlantic and Pacific are a single sea. No man assuredly has done more of this mighty work of unity than the brilliant and distinguished philosopher to whom you will have the pleasure of listening to-night; and I profoundly wish that affairs more practical, for I will not call them more important, did not prevent my remaining to enjoy his eloquence as I have so often enjoyed it before. Mr. Leveson has kindly consented to take my place; and I can do no more than express my deep sympathy with the aims and ideals which will be developed before you to-night. I have long been increasingly convinced that underneath a certain mask of stiffness which the Mahomedan religion has worn through certain centuries, as a somewhat similar mask has been worn by the religion of the Jews, Islam has in it the potentialities of being the most progressive of all religions; so that a century or two to come we may see the cause of peace, of science, and of reform everywhere supported by Islam as it is everywhere supported by Israel. Not in vain, I think, is the symbol of that faith the Crescent, the growing thing. While other creeds carry emblems implying more or less of finality, for this great creed of hope its very imperfection is its pride; and men shall walk fearlessly in new and wonderful paths, following the increasing curve which contains and holds up before them the eternal promise of the orb."

It was characteristic of Lord Ivywood that, though he was really in a hurry, he sat down slowly and gravely amid the outburst of applause. The quiet resumption of the speaker's seat, like the applause itself, was an artistic part of the peroration. When the last clap or stamp had subsided, he sprang up alertly, his light great-coat over his arm, shook hands with the lecturer, bowed to the audience, and slid quickly out of the hall. Mr. Leveson, the swarthy young man with the drooping double eyeglass, came rather bashfully to the front, took the empty seat on the platform, and in a few words presented the eminent Turkish mystic, Misysra Ammon, sometimes called the Prophet of the Moon.

Lady Joan found the Prophet's English accent somewhat improved by good society; but he still elongated the letter "u" in the same bleating manner; and his remarks had exactly the same rabidly wrong-headed ingenuity as his lecture upon English inns. It appeared that he was speaking on the Higher Polygamy; but he began with a sort of general defence of the Moslem civilization, especially against the charges of sterility and worldly ineffectiveness.

"It iss joost in the practical tings," he was saying, "it iss joost in the practical tings, if you could come to consider them in a manner quite equal that our methods are better than your methods. My ancestors invented the curved swords; because one cuts better with a curved sword. Your ancestors possessed the straight swords, out of some romantic fancy of being what you call straight. Or I will take a more plain example, of which I have myself experience. When I first had the honour of meeting Lord Ivywood, I was unused to your various ceremonies; and had a little difficulty, joost a little difficulty, in entering Mr. Claridge's hotel, where his lordship had invited me. A servant of the hotel was standing joost beside me on the doorstep. I stoo-ooped down to take off my boo-oots; and he asked me what I was dooing. I said to him, 'My friend, I am taking off my boo-oots.' "

A smothered sound came from Lady Joan Brett; but the lecturer did not notice it, and went on with a beautiful simplicity:

"I told him that in my country, when showing respect for any spot, we do not take off our hats; we take off our boo-oots. And because I would keep on my hat and take off my boo-oots, he suggested to me that I had been afflicted by Allah in the head. Now was not that foony?"

"Very," said Lady Joan inside her handkerchief; for she was choking with laughter. Something like a faint smile passed over the earnest faces of the two or three most intelligent of the Simple Souls; but for the most part the Souls seemed very simple indeed, helpless-looking people, with limp hair and gowns like green curtains; and their dry faces were as dry as ever.

"But I explained to him, I explained to him for a long time, for a carefully occupied time, that it was more practical, more business-like, more altogether for utility, to take off the boo-oots than to remove the hat. 'Let us,' I said to him, 'consider what many complaints are made against the footwear, what few complaints against the head-wear. You complain if in your drawing-rooms is the marching about of muddy boo-oots. Are any of your drawing-rooms marked thus with the marching about of muddy hats? How very many of your husbands kick you with the boo-oot! Yet how few of your husbands on any occasion butt you with the hat?'"

He looked round with a radiant seriousness, which made Lady Joan almost as speechless for sympathy as she was for amusement. With all that was most sound in her too complicated soul, she realized the presence of a man really convinced.

"The man on the doorstep, he would not listen to me," went on Misysra Ammon pathetically. "He said there would be a crowd if I stood on the doorstep, holding in my hand my boo-oots. Well, I do not know why, in your country, you always send the young males to be the first of your crowds. They certainly were making a number of noises, the young males."

Lady Joan Brett stood up suddenly and displayed enormous interest in the rest of the audience in the back parts of the hall. She felt that if she looked for one moment more at the serious face with the Jewish nose and the Persian beard, she would publicly disgrace herself; or, what was quite as bad (for she was the generous sort of aristocrat), publicly insult the lecturer. She had a feeling that the sight of all the Simple Souls in bulk might have a soothing effect. It had. It had what might have been mistaken for a depressing effect. Lady Joan resumed her seat with a controlled countenance.

"Now why," asked the Eastern philosopher, "do I tell so simple a story of your London streets—a thing happening any day? The little mistake had no preju-udicial effect. Lord Ivywood came out, at the end. He made no attempt to explain the true view of so important matters to Mr. Claridge's servant; though Mr. Claridge's servant remained on the door-step. But he commanded Mr. Claridge's servant to restore to me one of my boo-oots, which had fallen down the front steps while I was explaining this harmlessness of the hat in the home. So all was, for me very well. But why do I tell such little tales?"

He spread out his hands again in his fan-like, Eastern style. Then he clapped them together, so suddenly that Joan jumped and looked instinctively for the entrance of five hundred negro slaves laden with jewels. But it was only his emphatic gesture of eloquence. He went on, with an excited thickening of the accent:

"Because, my friends, this is the best example I could give of the wrong and slanderous character of the charge that we fail in our domesticities; that we fail especially in our treatment of the womankind. I appeal to any lady, to any Christian lady. Is not the boo-oot more devastating, more dreaded in the home than the hat? The boot jumps, he bound, he run about, he break things, he leave on the carpet the earths of the garden. The hat, he remain quiet on his hat-peg. Look at him on his hat-peg; how quiet and good he remain! Why not let him remain quiet also on his head?"

Lady Joan applauded warmly, as did several other ladies; and the sage went on, encouraged:

"Can you not therefore trust, dear ladies, this great religion to understand you concerning other things, as it understands you regarding boo-oots? What is the common objection our worthy enemies make against our polygamy? That it is disdainful of the womanhood. But how can this be so, my friends, when it allows the womanhood to be present in so large numbers? When in your House of Commons you put a hundred English members and joost one little Welsh member, you do not say, 'The Welshman is on top; he is our Sultan; may he live for ever!' If your jury contained eleven great large ladies and one leetle man, you would not say, 'This is unfair to the great large ladies.' Why should you shrink, then, ladies, from this great polygamical experiment, which Lord Ivywood himself——"

Joan's dark eyes were still fixed on the wrinkled, patient face of the lecturer; but every word of the rest of the lecture was lost to her. Under her glowing Spanish tint she had turned pale with extraordinary emotions; but she did not stir a hair.

The door of the hall stood open; and occasional sounds came even from that deserted end of the town. Two men seemed to be passing along the distant parade; one of them was singing. It was common enough for workmen to sing going home at night; and the voice, though a loud one, would have been too far off for Joan to hear the words. Only Joan happened to know the words. She could almost see them before her, written in a round, swaggering hand on the pink page of on old school-girl album at home. She knew the words; and the voice.

> "I come from Castlepatrick, and me heart is on me sleeve,
> And any sword or pistol boy can hit ut with me leave,
> It shines there for an epaulette, as golden as a flame,
> As naked as me ancestors, as noble as me name.
> For I come from Castlepatrick and me heart is on me sleeve,
> But a lady stole it from me on St. Gallowglass's Eve."

Startlingly and with strong pain, there rose up before Joan's eyes a patch of broken heath, with a very deep hollow of white sand, blinding in the sun. No words, no name; only the place.

> "The folk that live in Liverpool, their heart is in their boots;
> They go to hell like lambs, they do, because the hooter hoots.
> Where men may not be dancin', though the wheels may dance all day;
> And men may not be smokin'; but only chimneys may.
> But I come from Castlepatrick, and me heart is on me sleeve,
> But a lady stole it from me on St. Poleander's Eve.

The folk that live in black Belfast, their heart is in their mouth,
They see us making murders in the meadows of the South;
They think a plough's a rack, they do, and cattle-calls are creeds,
And they think we're burnin' witches when we're only burnin' weeds;
But I come from Castlepatrick, and me heart is on me sleeve;
But a lady stole it from me on St. Barnabas's Eve."

The voice had stopped suddenly; but the last lines were so much more distinct that it was certain the singer had come nearer, and was not marching away.

It was only after all this, and through a sort of cloud, that Lady Joan heard the indomitable Oriental bringing his whole eloquent address to a conclusion.

". . . And if you do not refu-use the sun that returns and rises in the East with every morning, you will not refu-use either this great social experiment, this great polygamical method which also arose out of the East, and always returns. For this is that Higher Polygamy which always comes like the sun itself, out of the Orient, but is only at its noontide splendour when the sun is high in heaven."

She was but vaguely conscious of Mr. Leveson, the man with the dark face and the eyeglasses, acknowledging the entrancing lecture in suitable terms, and calling on any of the Simple Souls who might have questions to ask, to ask them. It was only when the Simple Souls had displayed their simplicity with the usual parade of well-bred reluctance and fussy self-effacement, that any one addressed the chair. And it was only after somebody had been addressing the chair for some time that Joan gradually awoke to the fact that the address was somewhat unusual.

VIII

VOX POPULI VOX DEI

"I am sure," Mr. Leveson the Secretary had said, with a somewhat constrained smile, "that after the eloquent and epoch-making speech to which we have listened there will be some questions asked; and we hope to have a debate afterwards. I am sure somebody will ask a question." Then he looked interrogatively at one weary-looking gentleman in the fourth row and said, "Mr. Hinch?"

Mr. Hinch shook his head with a pallid passion of refusal wonderful to watch, and said, "I couldn't! I really couldn't!"

"We should be very pleased," said Mr. Leveson, "if any lady would ask a question."

In the silence that followed it was somehow psychologically borne in on the whole audience that one particular great large lady (as the lecturer would say) sitting at the end of the second row was expected to ask a question. Her own wax-work immobility was witness both to the expectation and its disappointment. "Are there any other questions?" asked Mr. Leveson—as if there had been any yet. He seemed to speak with a slight air of relief.

There was a sort of stir at the back of the hall and half-way down one side of it. Choked whispers could be heard of "Now then, Garge!" "Go it, Garge! Is there any questions! Gor!"

Mr. Leveson looked up with an alertness somewhat akin to alarm. He realized for the first time that a few quite common men, in coarse, unclean clothes, had somehow strolled in through the open door. They were not true rustics, but semi-rustic labourers that linger about the limits of the large watering-places. There was no "Mr." among them. There was a general tendency to call everybody George.

Mr. Leveson saw the situation and yielded to it. He modelled himself on Lord Ivywood and did much what he would have done in all cases, but with a timidity Lord Ivywood would not have shown. And the same social training that made him ashamed to be with such men, made him ashamed to own his shame. The same modern spirit that taught him to loathe such rags, also taught him to lie about his loathing.

"I am sure we should be very glad," he said nervously, "if any friends from outside care to join in our inquiry. Of course, we're all Democrats," and he looked round at the grand ladies with a ghastly smile, "and believe in the Voice of the People, and so on. If our friend at the back of the hall will put his question briefly, we need not insist, I think, on his putting it in writing."

There were renewed hoarse encouragements to George (that rightly christened champion), and he wavered forward on legs tied in the middle with string. He did not appear to have had any seat since his arrival, and made his remarks standing half-way down what we may call the central aisle.

"Well, I want to ask the proprietor——" he began.

"Questions," said Mr. Leveson, swiftly seizing a chance for that obstruction of debate which is the main business of a modern chairman, "must be asked of the chair, if they are points of order. If they concern the address, they should be asked of the lecturer."

"Well, I ask the lecturer," said the patient Garge, "whether it ain't right that when you 'ave the thing outside you should 'ave the thing inside?" (Hoarse applause at the back.)

Mr. Leveson was evidently puzzled and already suspicious that something was quite wrong. But the enthusiasm of the Prophet of the Moon sprang up instantly at any sort of question, and swept the chairman along with it.

"But it iss the essence of our who-ole message," he cried, spreading out his arms to embrace the world, "that the outer manifestation should be one with the inner manifestation. My friendss, it iss this very tru-uth our friend has stated, that iss reponsible for our apparent lack of symbolism in Islam! We appear to neglect the symbol because we insist on the satisfactory symbol. My friend in the middle will walk round all our mosques and say loudly, 'Where is the statue of Allah?' But can my friend in the middle really execute a complete and generally approved statue of Allah?"

Misysra Ammon sat down greatly satisfied with his answer; but it was doubted by many whether he had conveyed the satisfaction to his friend in the middle. That seeker after truth wiped his mouth with the back of his hand with an unsatisfied air and said:

"No offence, sir. But ain't it the Law, sir, that if you 'ave that outside we're all right? I came in 'ere as natural as could be. But Gorlumme, I never see a place like this afore." (Hoarse laughter behind)

"No apology is needed, my friend," cried the Eastern sage eagerly; "I can conceive you are not perhaps du-uly conversant with such schools of truth. But the Law is All. The Law is Allah. The inmost u-unity of——"

"Well, ain't it the Law?" repeated the dogged George; and every time he mentioned the Law the poor men who are its chief victims applauded loudly. "I'm not one to make a fuss. I never was one to make a fuss. I'm a law-abidin' man, I am." (More applause.) "Ain't it the Law that if so be such is your sign and such is your profession, you ought to serve us?"

"I fear I not quite follow," cried the eager Turk. "I ought?"

"To serve us," shouted a throng of thick voices from the back of the hall, which was already much more crowded than before.

"Serve you!" cried Misysra, leaping up like a spring released. "The Holy Prophet came from heaven to serve you! The virtue and valour of a thousand years, my friends, has had no hunger but to serve you! We are of all faiths the most the faith of service. Our highest prophet is no more than the servant of God, as I am, as you all are. Even for our symbol we choose a satellite; and honour the Moon because it only serves the Earth, and does not pretend to be the Sun."

"I'm sure," cried Mr. Leveson, jumping up with a tactful grin, "that the lecturer has answered this last point in a most eloquent and effective way; and the motor-cars are waiting for some of the ladies who have come from some distance, and—and I really think the proceedings——"

All the artistic ladies were already getting on their wraps with faces varying from bewilderment to blank terror. Only Lady Joan lingered, trembling with unexplained excitement. The hitherto speechless Hinch had slid up to the chairman's seat and whispered to him:

"You must get all the ladies away. I can't imagine what's up; but something's up."

"Well?" repeated the patient George. "So be it's the Law, where is it?"

"Ladies and gentlemen," said Mr. Leveson, in his most ingratiating manner, "I think we have had a most delightful evening, and——"

"No, we ain't," cried a new and nastier voice from a corner of the room. "Where is it?"

"That's what we got a right to know," said the law-abiding George. "Where is it?"

"Where is what?" cried the nearly demented Secretary in the chair. "What do you want?"

The law-abiding Mr. George made a half-turn and a gesture towards the man in the corner and said:

"What's yours, Jim?"

"I'll 'ave a drop of Scotch," said the man in the corner.

Lady Enid Wimpole, who had lingered a little in loyalty to Joan, the only other lady still left, caught both her wrists, and cried in a thrilling whisper:

"Oh, we must go to the car, dear! They're using the most awful language!"

Away on the wettest edge of the sands by the sea the print of two wheels and four hoofs were being slowly washed away by a slowly rising tide; which was, indeed, the only motive of the man Humphrey Pump, leading the donkey cart, in leading it almost ankle-deep in water.

"I hope you're sober again now," he said, with some seriousness, to his companion, a huge man walking heavily and even humbly with a straight sword swinging to and fro at his hip; "for honestly it was a mug's game to go and stick up the old sign before that tin place. I haven't often spoken to you like this, Captain, but I don't believe any other man in the county could get you out of the hole as I can. But to go down there and frighten the ladies—why, there's been nothing so silly here since Bishop's Folly. You could hear the ladies screaming before we left."

"I heard worse than that long before we left," said the large man, without lifting his head. "I heard one of them laugh.... Christ, do you think I shouldn't hear her laugh?"

There was a silence. "I didn't mean to speak sharp," said Humphrey Pump, with that incorruptible kindliness which was the root of his Englishry, and may yet save the soul of the English, "but it's the truth, I was pretty well bothered about how to get out of this business. You're braver than I am, you see, and I own I was frightened about both of us. If I hadn't known my way to the lost tunnel, I should be fairly frightened still."

"Known your way to what?" asked the Captain, lifting his red head for the first time.

"Oh, you know all about No Nose Ivywood's lost tunnel," said Pump carelessly. "Why, we all used to look for it when we were boys. Only I happened to find it."

"Have mercy on an exile," said Dalroy humbly. "I don't know which hurt him most, the things he forgets or the things he remembers."

Mr. Pump was silent for a little while and then said, more seriously than usual, "Well, the people from London say you must put up placards and statues and subscriptions and epitaphs and the Lord knows what, to the people who've found some new trick and made it come off. But only a man that knows his own land for forty miles round, knows what a lot of people, and clever people too, there were who found new tricks, and had to hide them because they didn't come off. There was Dr. Boone, up by Gill-in-Hugby, who held out against Dr. Collison and the vaccination. His treatment saved sixty patients who had got small-pox; and Dr. Collison's killed ninety-two patients who hadn't got anything. But Boone had to keep it dark: naturally, because all his lady patients grew moustaches. It was a result of the treatment. But it wasn't a result he wishes to dwell on. Then there was old Dean Arthur, who discovered balloons, if ever a man did. He discovered them long before they were discovered. But people were suspicious about such things just then—there was a revival of the witch business in spite of all the parsons—and he had to sign a paper saying where he'd got the notion. Well, it stands to reason, you wouldn't like to sign a paper saying you'd got it from the village idiot when you were both blowing soap-bubbles: and that's all he could have signed; for he was an honest gentleman, the poor old Dean. Then there was Jack Arlingham and the diving-bell—but you remember all about that.

Well, it was just the same with the man that made this tunnel—one of the mad Ivywoods. There's many a man, Captain, that has a statue in the great London squares for helping to make the railway trains. There's many a man has his name in Westminster Abbey for doing something in discovering steamboats. Poor old Ivywood discovered both at once; and had to be put under control. He had a notion that a railway train might be made to rush right into the sea and turn into a steamboat; and it seemed all right, according as he worked it out. But his family were so ashamed of the thing that they didn't like the tunnel even mentioned. I don't think anybody knows where it is but me and Bunchy Robinson. We shall be there in a minute or two. They've thrown the rocks about at this end; and let the thick plantation grow at the other; but I've got a racehorse through before now, to save it from Colonel Chepstow's little games; and I think I can manage this donkey. Honestly, I think it's the only place we'll be safe in after what we've left behind us at Pebbleswick. But it's the best place in the world, there's no doubt, for lying low and starting afresh. Here we are. You think you can't get behind that rock, but you can. In fact, you have."

Dalroy found himself, with some bewilderment, round the corner of a rock, and in a long bore or barrel of blackness that ended in a very dim spot of green. Hearing the hoofs of the ass and the feet of his friend behind him, he turned his head, but could see nothing but the pitch darkness of a closed coal cellar. He turned again to the dim green speck; and marching forward was glad to see it grow larger and brighter, like a big emerald, till he came out on a throng of trees, mostly thin, but growing so thickly and so close to the cavernous entrance of the tunnel that it was quite clear the place was meant to be choked up by forests and forgotten. The light that came glimmering through the trees was so broken and tremulous that it was hard to tell whether it was daybreak or moonrise.

"I know there's water here," said Pump. "They couldn't keep it out of the stone-work when they made the tunnel; and old Ivywood hit the hydraulic engineer with a spirit-level. With the bit of covert here and the sea behind us we ought to be able to get food of one kind or another, when the cheese has given out; and donkeys can eat anything. By the way," he added, with some embarrassment, "you don't mind my saying it, Captain, but I think we'd better keep that rum for rare occasions. It's the best rum in England, and may be the last, if these mad games are going on. It'll do us good to feel it's there, so we can have it when we want it. The cask's still nearly full."

Dalroy put out his hand and shook the other's. "Hump," he said seriously, "you're right. It's a sacred trust for Humanity; and we'll only drink it ourselves to celebrate great victories. In token of which I will take a glass now, to celebrate our glorious victory over Leveson and his tin tabernacle."

He drained one glass and then sat down on the cask, as if to put temptation behind him. His blue ruminant bull's eye seemed to plunge deeper and deeper into the emerald twilight of the trees in front of him; and it was long before he spoke again.

At last he observed, "I think you said, Hump, that a friend of yours—a gentleman named Bunchy Robinson, I think—was also a *habitué* here."

"Yes; he knew the way," answered Pump, leading the donkey to the most suitable patch of pasturage.

"May we, do you think, have the pleasure of a visit from Mr. Robinson?" inquired the Captain.

"Not unless they're jolly careless up in Blackstone Gaol," replied Pump. And he moved the cheese well into the arch of the tunnel. Dalroy still sat with his square chin on his hand, staring at the mystery of the little wood.

"You seem absent-minded, Captain," remarked Humphrey.

"The deepest thoughts are all commonplaces," said Dalroy. "That is why I believe in Democracy; which is more than you do, you foul blood-stained old British Tory. And the deepest commonplace of all is that Vanitas Vanitatem;[8] which is not pessimism but is really the opposite of pessimism. It is man's futility that makes us feel he must be a god. And I think of this tunnel; and how the poor old lunatic walked about on this grass, watching it being built, the soul in him on

_____

[8] *Vanitas Vanitatem* is part of a Scripture quote from Ecclesiastes 1:2; the Latin Vulgate version reads, *vanitas vanitatum dixit Ecclesiastes, vanitas vanitatum et omnia vanitas*, which translated is "Vanity of vanities, said Ecclesiastes. Vanity of vanities, and all is vanity."

fire with the future. And he saw the whole world changed and the seas thronged with his new shipping; and now,"—and Dalroy's voice changed and broke,—"now there is good pasture for the donkey and it is very quiet here."

"Yes," said Pump; in some way that conveyed his knowledge that the Captain was thinking of other things also. The Captain went on dreamily:

"And I think about another Lord Ivywood recorded in history who also had a great vision. For it is a great vision, after all; and though the man is a prig, he is brave. He also wants to drive a tunnel—between East and West—to make the British Empire more Indian; to effect what he calls the orientation of England and I call the ruin of Christendom. And I am wondering just now, whether the clear intellect and courageous will of a madman will be strong enough to burst and drive that tunnel, as everything seems to show at this moment that it will. Or whether there be indeed enough life and growth in your England to leave it at last as this is left, buried in English forests and wasted by an English sea."

The silence fell between them again, and again there was only the slight sound the animal made in eating. As Dalroy had said, it was very quiet there.

But it was not quiet in Pebbleswick that night; when the Riot Act was read; and all the people who had seen the sign-board outside fought all the people who hadn't seen the sign-board outside: or when babies and scientists next morning, seeking for shells and other common objects of the sea-shore, found that their study included fragments of the outer clothing of J. Leveson, and scraps of corrugated iron.

IX

THE HIGHER CRITICISM AND MR. HIBBS

Pebbleswick boasted an enterprising evening paper of its own, called the *Pebbleswick Globe*, and it was the great vaunt of the editor's life that he had got out an edition announcing the mystery of the vanishing sign-board almost simultaneously with its vanishing. In the rows that followed sandwich men found no little protection from the blows indiscriminately given them behind and before, in the large wooden boards they carried inscribed:

THE VANISHING PUB.

PEBBLESWICK'S FAIRY TALE

SPECIAL

And the paper contained a categorical and mainly correct account of what had happened, or what seemed to have happened, to the eyes of the amazed Garge and his crowd of sympathizers. "George Burn, carpenter, of this town, with Samuel Gripes, drayman in the service of Messrs. Jay and Gubbins, brewers, together with a number of other well-known residents, passed by the new building erected on the West Beach for various forms of entertainment and popularly called the small Universal Hall. Seeing outside it one of the old inn signs now so rare, they drew the quite proper inference that the place retained the licence to sell alcoholic liquors, which so many other places in this neighbourhood have recently lost. The persons inside, however, appear to have denied all knowledge of the fact, and when the party (after some regrettable scenes in which no life was lost) came out on the beach again, it was found that the inn sign had been destroyed or stolen. All parties were quite sober; and had indeed obtained no opportunity to be anything else. The mystery is undergoing inquiry."

But this comparatively realistic record was local and spontaneous; and owed not a little to the accidental honesty of the editor. Moreover, evening papers are often more honest than morning papers, because they are written by ill-paid and hard-worked underlings in a great hurry; and there is no time for more timid people to correct them. By the time the morning papers came out next day a faint but perceptible change had passed over the story of the vanishing sign-board. In the daily paper which had the largest circulation and the most influence in that part of the world, the problem was committed to a gentleman known by what seemed to the non-journalistic world the singular name of Hibbs However. It had been affixed to him in jest in connexion with the almost complicated caution with which all his public criticisms were qualified at every turn; so that everything came to depend upon the conjunctions; upon "but" and "yet" and "though" and similar words. As his salary grew larger (for editors and proprietors like that sort of thing) and his old friends fewer (for the most generous of friends cannot but feel faintly acid at a success which has in it nothing of the infectious flavour of glory) he grew more and more to value himself as a diplomatist; a man who always said the right thing. But he was not without his intellectual Nemesis; for at last he became so very diplomatic as to be darkly and densely unintelligible. People who knew him had no difficulty in believing that what he had said was the right thing, the tactful thing, the thing that should save the situation; but they had great difficulty in discovering what it was. In his early days he had had a great talent for one of the worst tricks of modern journalism; the trick of dismissing the important part of a question as if it could wait, and appearing to get to business on the unimportant part of it. Thus, he would say, "Whatever we may think of the rights and wrongs of the vivisection of pauper children, we shall all agree that it should only be done, in any event, by fully qualified practitioners." But in the later and darker days of his diplomacy, he seemed rather to dismiss the important part of a subject, and get to grips with some totally different subject, following some timid and elusive train of associations of his own. In his late bad manner, as they say of painters, he was just as likely to say, "Whatever we may think of the rights and wrongs of the vivisection of pauper children, no progressive mind can doubt that the influence of the Vatican is on the decline." His nickname had stuck to him in honour of a paragraph he was alleged to have written when the American President was wounded by a bullet fired by a lunatic in New Orleans; and which was said to have run: "The President passed a good night and his condition is greatly improved. The assassin is not, however, a German as was at first supposed." Men stared at that mysterious remark till they wanted to go mad and to shoot somebody themselves.

Hibbs However was a long, lank man with straight yellowish hair and a manner that was externally soft and mild but secretly supercilious. He had been when at Cambridge a friend of Leveson, and they had both prided themselves on being moderate politicians. But if you have had your hat smashed over your nose by one who has very recently described himself as a "law-abidin' man," and if you have had to run for your life with one coat-tail, and encouraged to further bodily activity by having irregular pieces of a corrugated iron roof thrown after you by men more energetic than yourself, you will find you emerge with emotions which are not solely those of a moderate politician. Hibbs However had already composed a leaderette on the Pebbleswick incident, which rather pointed to the truth of the story, so far as his articles ever pointed to anything. His motives for veering vaguely in this direction were, as usual, complex. He knew the millionaire who owned the paper had a hobby of Spiritualism; and something might always come out of not suppressing a marvellous story. He knew that two at least of the prosperous artisans or small tradesmen who had attested the tale were staunch supporters of The Party. He knew that Lord Ivywood must be mildly and not effectually checked; for Lord Ivywood was of The Other Party. And there could be no milder or less effectual way of checking him than allowing the paper to lend at least a temporary credit to a well-supported story that came from outside; and certainly had not been (like so many stories) created in the office. Amid all these considerations had Hibbs However steered his way to a more or less confirmatory article, when the sudden apparition of J. Leveson Secretary in the sub-editor's room, with a burst collar and broken eyeglasses, led Mr. Hibbs into a long private conversation with him and a comparative reversal of his plans. But of course he did not write a new article; he was not of that divine order who make all things new. He chopped and changed his original article in such a way that it was something quite beyond the most bewildering article he had written in the past; and is still prized by those highly cultured persons who collect the worst literature of the world.

It began, indeed, with the comparatively familiar formula, "Whether we take the more lax or the more advanced view of the old disputed problem of the morality or immorality of the wooden sign-board as such, we shall all agree that the scenes enacted at Pebbleswick were very discreditable, to most, though not all, concerned." After that, tact degenerated into a riot of irrelevance. It was a wonderful article. The reader could get from it a faint glimpse of Mr. Hibbs's opinion on almost every other subject except the subject of the article. The first half of the next sentence made it quite clear that Mr. Hibbs (had he been present) would not have lent his active assistance to the Massacre of St. Bartholomew or the Massacres of September. But the second half of the sentence suggested with equal clearness that, since these two acts were no longer, as it were, in contemplation, and all attempts to prevent them would probably arrive a little late, he felt the warmest friendship for the French nation. He merely insisted that his friendship should never be mentioned except in the French language. It must be called an "entente" in the language taught to tourists by waiters. It must on no account be called an "understanding," in a language understanded of the people. From the first half of the sentence following it might safely be inferred that Mr. Hibbs had read Milton, or at least the passage about sons of Belial; from the second half that he knew nothing about bad wine, let alone good. The next sentence began with the corruption of the Roman Empire and contrived to end with Dr. Clifford. Then there was a weak plea for Eugenics; and a warm plea against Conscription, which was not True Eugenics. That was all; and it was headed, "The Riot at Pebbleswick."

Yet some injustice would be done to Hibbs However, if we concealed the fact that this chaotic leader was followed by quite a considerable mass of public correspondence. The people who write to newspapers are, it may be supposed, a small eccentric body, like most of those that sway a modern State. But at least, unlike the lawyers, or the financiers, or the members of Parliament, or the men of science, they are people of all kinds scattered all over the country, of all classes, counties, ages, sects, sexes, and stages of insanity. The letters that followed Hibbs's article are still worth looking up in the dusty old files of his paper.

A dear old lady in the densest part of the Midlands wrote to suggest that there might really have been an old ship wrecked on the shore during the proceedings. "Mr. Leveson may have omitted to notice it; or, at that late hour of the evening, it may have been mistaken for a sign-board, especially by a person of defective sight. My own sight has been failing for some time; but I am still a diligent reader of your paper." If Mr. Hibbs's diplomacy had left one nerve in his soul undrugged, he would have laughed, or burst into tears, or got drunk, or gone into a monastery over a letter like that. As it was, he measured it with a pencil, and decided that it was just too long to get into the column.

Then there was a letter from a theorist; and a theorist of the worst sort. There is no great harm in the theorist who makes up a new theory to fit a new event. But the theorist who starts with a false theory and then sees everything as making it come true is the most dangerous enemy of human reason. The letter began like a bullet let loose by the trigger. "Is not the whole question met by Ex. iv. 3? I enclose several pamphlets in which I have proved the point quite plainly; and which none of the Bishops or the so-called Free Church Ministers have attempted to answer. The connexion between the rod or pole, and the snake, so clearly indicated in Scripture, is neglected by the well-paid prostitutors of religion for their own ends. Moses distinctly testifies to a rod or pole turning into a snake. We all know that those following after strong drink are given over to believe a lie; and profess that they behold a snake. It is therefore perfectly natural that these unhappy men should have professed to see a pole. They may have seen it before or after the well-known change which——" The letter went on for nine closely written pages; and this time Mr. Hibbs may be excused for thinking it a little long.

Then there was the scientific correspondent, who said—Might it not be due to the acoustic qualities of the hall? He had never believed in the corrugated iron hall. The very word "hall" itself (he added playfully) was often so sharpened and shortened by the abrupt echoes of those repeated metallic curves, that it had every appearance of being the word "hell"; and had caused many theological entanglements, and some police prosecutions. In the light of these facts, he wished to draw the editor's attention to some very curious details about this supposed presence or absence of an inn sign. It would be noted that many of the witnesses, and especially the most respectable of them, constantly refer to something that is supposed to be outside. The word "outside" occurs at least five times in the depositions of the complaining persons. Surely by all scientific analogy we may infer that the unusual phrase "inn sign" is an acoustic error for "inside." The word "inside" would so naturally occur in any discussion either about the building or the individual, when the debate was of a hygienic character. This letter was signed "Medical Student": and the less intelligent parts of it were selected for publication in the paper.

Then there was a really humorous man, who wrote and said there was nothing at all inexplicable or unusual about the case. He himself (he said) had often seen a sign-board outside a pub. when he went into it; and been quite unable to see it when he came out. This letter (the only one that had any quality of literature) was sternly set aside by Mr. Hibbs.

Then came a cultured gentleman with a light touch, who merely made a suggestion. Had any one read H. G. Wells's story about the kink in space? He contrived indescribably to suggest that no one had even heard of it except himself; or perhaps of Mr. Wells either. The story indicated that men's feet might be in one part of the world and their eyes in another. He offered the suggestion for what it was worth. The particular pile of letters on which Hibbs However threw it, showed only too clearly what it was worth.

Then there was a man, of course, who called it all a plot of frenzied foreigners against Britain's shore. But as he did not make it quite clear whether the chief wickedness of these aliens had lain in sticking the sign up or in pulling it down, his remarks (the remainder of which referred exclusively to the conversational misconduct of an Italian ice-cream man, whose side of the case seemed insufficiently represented) carried the less weight.

And then, last but the reverse of least, there plunged in all the people who think they can solve a problem they cannot understand by abolishing everything that has contributed to it. We all know these people. If a barber has cut his customer's throat because the girl has changed her partner for a dance or donkey-ride on Hampstead Heath, there are always people to protest against the mere institutions that led up to it This would not have happened if barbers were abolished, or if cutlery were abolished, or if the objection felt by girls to imperfectly grown beards were abolished, or if the girls were abolished, or if heaths and open spaces were abolished, or if dancing were abolished, or if donkeys were abolished. But donkeys, I fear, will never be abolished.

There were plenty of such donkeys in the common land of this particular controversy. Some made it an argument against democracy, because poor Garge was a carpenter. Some made it an argument against Alien Immigration, because Misysra Ammon was a Turk. Some proposed that ladies should no longer be admitted to any lectures anywhere; because they had constituted a slight and temporary difficulty at this one, without the faintest fault of their own. Some urged that all holiday resorts should be abolished; some urged that all holidays should be abolished. Some vaguely denounced the seaside; some, still more vaguely, proposed to remove the sea. All said that if this or that, stones or seaweed, or strange visitors, or bad weather, or bathing-machines were swept away with a strong hand, this which had happened would not have happened. They only had one slight weakness, all of them; that they did not seem to have the faintest notion of what *had* happened. And in this they were not inexcusable. Nobody did know what had happened: nobody knows it to this day, of course; or it would be unnecessary to write this story. No one can suppose this story is written from any motive save that of telling the plain, humdrum truth.

That queer, confused cunning which was the only definable quality possessed by Hibbs However had certainly scored a victory so far; for the tone of the weekly papers followed him; with more intelligence and less trepidation: but they followed him. It seemed more and more clear that some kind of light and sceptical explanation was to be given of the whole business; and that the whole business was to be dropped.

The story of the sign-board and the ethical chapel of corrugated iron was discussed and somewhat disparaged in all the more serious and especially in the religious weeklies; though the Low Church papers seemed to reserve their distaste chiefly for the sign-board; and the High Church papers chiefly for the chapel. All agreed that the combination was incongruous; and most treated it as fabulous. The only intellectual organs which seemed to think it might have happened were the Spiritualist papers; and their interpretation had not that solidity which would have satisfied Mr. Garge.

It was not until almost a year after that it was felt in philosophical circles that the last word had been said on the matter. An estimate of the incident and of its bearing on natural and supernatural history occurred in Professor Widge's celebrated "Historicity of the Petro-Piscatorial Phenomena"; which so profoundly affected modern thought when it came out in parts in the *Hibbert Journal*.[9] Every one remembers Professor Widge's main contention; that the modern critic must apply to the thaumaturgics of the Lake of Tiberias the same principle of criticism which Dr. Bunk and others have so successfully applied to the thaumaturgics of the Cana narrative: "Authorities as final as Pink and Toscher," wrote the Professor, "have now shown with an emphasis that no emancipated mind is entitled to question, that the Aqua-Vinic thaumaturgy at Cana is wholly inconsistent with the psychology of the 'master of the feast' as modern research has analysed it; and, indeed, with the whole Judæo-Aramaic psychology at that stage of its development; as well as being painfully incongruous with the elevated ideas of the ethical teacher in question. But as we rise to higher levels of moral achievement it will probably be found necessary to apply the Canaic principle to other and later events in the narrative. This principle has, of course, been mainly expounded by Huscher in the sense that the whole episode is unhistorical; while the

---

[9] *The Hibbert Journal* was a "quarterly review of religion, theology and philosophy" founded in 1902 with the funds established 50 years earlier by the Victorian philanthropist Robert Hibbert (1770–1849).

alternative theory, that the wine was non-alcoholic and was naturally infused into the water, can claim on its side the impressive name of Minns. It is clear that if we apply the same alternative to the so-called Miraculous Draught of Fishes we must either hold with Gilp that the fishes were stuffed representations of fishes artificially placed in the lake (see the Rev. Y. Wyse's 'Christo-Vegetarianism as a World-System,' where this position is forcibly set forth) or we must, on the Huscherian hypothesis, deprive the Piscatorial narrative of all claim to historicity whatever.

"The difficulty felt by the most daring critics (even Pooke) in adopting this entirely destructive attitude, is the alleged improbability of so detailed a narrative being founded on so slight a phrase as the anti-historical critics refer it to. It is urged by Pooke, with characteristic relentless reasoning, that according to Huscher's theory a metaphorical but at least noticeable remark, such as, 'I will make you fishers of men,' was expanded into a realistic chronicle of events; which contains no mention, even in the passages evidently interpolated, of any men actually found in the nets when they were hauled up out of the sea; or, more properly, lagoon.

"It must appear presumptuous or even bad taste for any one in the modern world to differ on any subject from Pooke; but I would venture to suggest that the very academic splendour and unique standing of the venerable professor (whose ninety-seventh birthday was so beautifully celebrated in Chicago last year) may have forbidden him all but intuitive knowledge of how errors arise among the vulgar. I crave pardon for mentioning a modern case known to myself (not indeed by personal presence, but by careful study of all the reports) which presents a curious parallel to such ancient expansions of a text into an incident, in accordance with Huscher's law.

"It occurred at Pebbleswick, in the south of England. The town had long been in a state of dangerous religious excitement. The great religious genius who has since so much altered our whole attitude to the religions of the world, Misysra Ammon, had been lecturing on the sands to thousands of enthusiastic hearers. Their meetings were often interrupted, both by children's services run on the most ruthless lines of orthodoxy; and by the League of the Red Rosette, the formidable atheist and anarchist organization. As if this were not enough to swell the whirlpool of fanaticism, the old popular controversy between the Milnian and the Complete Sablapsarians broke out again on the fated beach. It is natural to conjecture that in the thickening atmosphere of theology in Pebbleswick, some controversialist quoted the text,' An evil and adulterous generation *seek for a sign*. But no sign shall be given it save the sign of the prophet Jonas.' [10]

"A mind like that of Pooke will find it hard to credit, but it seems certain that the effect of this text on the ignorant peasantry of southern England was actually to make them go about looking for a sign, in the sense of those old tavern signs now so happily disappearing. (The 'sign of the prophet Jonas' they somehow translated in their stunted minds into a sign-board of the ship out of which Jonah was thrown. They went about literally looking for 'The Sign of the Ship': and there are some cases of their suffering Smail's Hallucination and actually seeing it. The whole incident is a curious parallel to the Gospel narrative, and a triumphant vindication of Huscher's law."

Lord Ivywood paid a public compliment to Professor Widge, saying that he had rolled back from his country what might have been an ocean of superstitions. But indeed poor Hibbs had struck the first and stunning blow, that scattered the brains of all men.

[10] Mt 12:39; Lk 11:29.

X

THE CHARACTER OF QUOODLE

There lay about in Lord Ivywood's numerous gardens, terraces, out-houses, stable-yards, and similar places, a dog who came to be called by the name of Quoodle. Lord Ivywood did not call him Quoodle. Lord Ivywood was almost physically incapable of articulating such sounds. Lord Ivywood did not care for dogs. He cared for the Cause of Dogs, of course; and he cared still more for his own intellectual self-respect and consistency. He would never have permitted a dog in his house to be physically ill-treated; nor, for that matter, a rat; nor, for that matter, even a man. But if Quoodle was not physically ill-treated, he was at least socially neglected: and Quoodle did not like it. For dogs care for companionship more than for kindness itself.

Lord Ivywood would probably have sold the dog: but he consulted experts (as he did on everything he didn't understand and many things that he did), and the impression he gathered from them was that the dog, technically considered, would fetch very little; mostly, it seemed, because of the mixture of qualities that it possessed. It was a sort of mongrel bull-terrier; but with rather too much of the bull-dog; and this fact seemed to weaken its price as much as it strengthened its jaw. His lordship also gained a hazy impression that the dog might have been valuable as a watch-dog if it had not been able to follow game like a pointer; and that even in the latter walk of life it would always be discredited by an unfortunate talent for swimming as well as a retriever. But Lord Ivywood's impressions may very well have been slightly confused; as he was probably thinking about the Black Stone of Mecca, or some such subject at the moment. The victim of this entanglement of virtues, therefore, still lay about in the sunlight of Ivywood; exhibiting no general result of that entanglement except the most appalling ugliness.

Now Lady Joan Brett did appreciate dogs. It was the whole of her type and a great deal of her tragedy that all that was natural in her was still alive under all that was artificial; and she could smell hawthorn or the sea as far off as a dog can smell his dinner. Like most aristocrats, she would carry cynicism almost to the suburbs of the city of Satan; she was quite as irreligious as Lord Ivywood, or rather more. She could be quite equally frigid or supercilious when she felt inclined; and in the great social talent of being tired, she could beat him any day of the week. But the difference remained in spite of her sophistries and ambitions; that her elemental communications were not cut, and his were. For her the sunrise was still the rising of a sun, and not the turning on of a light by a convenient cosmic servant. For her the Spring was really the Season in the country, and not merely the Season in town. For her cocks and hens were natural appendages to an English house; and not (as Lord Ivywood had proved to her from an encyclopædia) animals of Indian origin, recently imported by Alexander the Great. And so for her a dog was a dog, and not one of the higher animals, nor one of the lower animals, nor something that had the sacredness of life, nor something that ought to be muzzled, nor something that ought not to be vivisected. She knew that in every practical sense proper provision would be made for the dog; as, indeed, provision was made for the yellow dogs in Constantinople by Abdul Hamid; whose life Lord Ivywood was writing for the *Progressive Potentates* series. Nor was she in the least sentimental about the dog or anxious to turn him into a pet. It simply came natural to her in passing to rub all his hair the wrong way and call him something which she instantly forgot.

The man who was mowing the garden lawn looked up for a moment; for he had never seen the dog behave in exactly that way before. Quoodle arose, shook himself, and trotted on in front of the lady, leading her up an iron side staircase, of which, as it happened, she had never made use before. It was then, most probably, that she first took any special notice of him; and her pleasure, like that which she took in the sublime prophet from Turkey, was of a humorous character. For the complex quadruped had retained the bow legs of the bulldog; and seen from behind, reminded her ridiculously of a swaggering little Major waddling down to his club.

The dog and the iron stairway between them led her into a series of long rooms, one opening into the other. They formed part of what she had known in earlier days as the disused wing of Ivywood House; which had been neglected or shut up, probably because it bore some defacements from the fancies of the mad ancestor, the memory of whom the present Lord Ivywood did not think helpful to his own political career. But it seemed to Joan that there were indications of a recent attempt to rehabilitate the place. There was a pail of whitewash in one of the empty rooms; a step-ladder in another, here and there a curtain rod, and at last, in the fourth room, a curtain. It hung all alone on the old wood-work; but it was a very gorgeous curtain, being a kind of orange-gold relieved with wavy bars of crimson, which somehow seemed to suggest the very spirit and presence of serpents; though they had neither eyes nor mouths among them.

In the next of the endless series of rooms she came upon a kind of ottoman, striped with green and silver standing alone on the bare floor. She sat down on it from a mixed motive of fatigue and of impudence; for she dimly remembered a story which she had always thought one of the funniest in the world: about a lady only partly initiated in Theosophy who had been in the habit of resting on a similar object, only to discover afterwards that it was a Mahatma, covered with his eastern garment and prostrate and rigid in ecstasy. She had no hopes of sitting on a Mahatma herself; but the very thought of it made her laugh; because it would make Lord Ivywood look such a fool. She was not sure whether she liked or disliked Lord Ivywood; but she felt quite certain that it would gratify her to make him look a fool. The moment she had sat down on the ottoman, the dog, who had been trotting beside her, sat down also, and on the edge of her skirt.

After a minute or two she rose (and the dog rose), and she looked yet further down that long perspective of large rooms, in which men like Philip Ivywood forget that they are only men. The next was more ornate and the next yet more so; it was plain that the scheme of decoration that was in progress had been started at the other end. She could now see that the long lane ended in rooms that from afar off looked like the end of a kaleidoscope, rooms like nests made only from humming-birds or palaces built of fixed fireworks. Out of this furnace of fragmentary colours, she saw Ivywood advancing towards her, with his black suit and his white face accented by the contrast.

His lips were moving; for he was talking to himself, as many orators do. He did not seem to see her; and she had to strangle a subconscious and utterly senseless cry, "He is blind!"

The next moment he was welcoming her intrusion with the well-bred surprise and rather worldly simplicity suitable to such a case: and Joan fancied she understood why his face had seemed a little bleaker and blinder than usual. It was by contrast. He was carrying clutched to his forefinger, as his ancestors might have carried a falcon clutched to the wrist, a small bright-coloured semi-tropical bird, the expression of whose head, neck, and eye was the very opposite of his own. Joan thought she had never seen a living creature with a head so lively and insulting. Its provocative eye and pointed crest seemed to be offering to fight fifty game-cocks. It was no wonder (she told herself) that by the side of this gaudy gutter-snipe with feathers Ivywood's faint-coloured hair and frigid face looked like the hair and face of a corpse walking.

"You'll never know what this is," said Ivywood, in his most charming manner. "You've heard of him a hundred times and never had a notion of what he was. This is the bulbul."

"I never knew," replied Joan. "I am afraid I never cared. I always thought it was something like a nightingale."

"Ah, yes," answered Ivywood, "but this is the real bulbul peculiar to the East: *Pycnonotus Haemorrhus*. You are thinking of *Daulias Golzii*."

"I suppose I am," replied Lady Joan, with a faint smile. "It is an obsession. When shall I not be thinking of Daulias Galsworthy? Was it Galsworthy?" Then feeling quite touched by the soft austerity of her companion's face, she caressed the gaudy and pugnacious bird with one finger and said, "It's a dear little thing."

The quadruped ultimately called Quoodle did not approve of all this at all. Like most dogs, he liked to be with human beings when they were silent; and he extended a magnificent toleration to them as long as they were talking to each other. But conversational attention paid to any other animal at all remote from a mongrel bull-terrier, wounded Mr. Quoodle in his most sensitive and gentlemanly feelings. He emitted a faint growl. Joan, with all the instincts that were in her, bent down and pulled his hair about once more, and felt the instant necessity of diverting the general admiration from *Pycnonotus Haemorrhus*.[11] She turned it to the decoration at the end of the refurnished wing; for they had already come to the last of the long suite of rooms; which ended in some unfinished but exquisite panelling in white and coloured woods, inlaid in the Oriental manner. At one corner the whole corridor ended by curving into a round turret chamber over-looking the landscape; and which Joan, who had known the house in childhood, was sure was an innovation. On the other hand a black gap still left in the lower left-hand corner of the Oriental woodwork suddenly reminded her of something she had forgotten.

"Surely," she said (after much mere æsthetic ecstasy), "there used to be a staircase there, leading to the old kitchen garden, or the old chapel or something."

Ivywood nodded gravely. "Yes," he said, "it did lead to the ruins of a mediæval chapel, as you say. The truth is it led to several things that I cannot altogether consider a credit to the family in these days. All that scandal and joking about the unsuccessful tunnel (your mother may have told you of it), well, it did us no good in the county, I'm afraid; so as it's a mere scrap of land bordering on the sea, I've fenced it off and let it grow wild. But I'm boarding up the end of the room here for quite another reason. I want you to come and see it."

He led her into the round corner turret in which the new architecture ended; and Joan, with her thirst for the beautiful, could not stifle a certain thrill of beatitude at the prospect. Five open windows of a light and exquisite Saracenic outline looked over the bronze and copper and purple of the Autumn parks and forests to the peacock colours of the sea. There was neither house nor living thing in sight; and familiar as she had been with that coast she knew she was looking out from a new angle of vision on a new landscape of Ivywood.

"You can write sonnets?" said Ivywood, with something more like emotion in his voice than she had ever heard in it. "What comes first into your mind with these open windows?"

"I know what you mean," said Joan, after a silence." 'The same hath oft——' "

---

[11] *Pycnonotus Haemorrhus* appears to be a term of Chesterton's own making.

"Yes," he said. "That is how I felt . . . 'of perilous seas in fairy lands forlorn.' "[12]

There was another silence and the dog sniffed round and round the circular turret chamber.

"I want it to be like that," said Ivywood, in a low and singularly moved intonation. "I want this to be the end of the house. I want this to be the end of the world. Don't you feel that is the real beauty of all this eastern art; that it is coloured like the edges of things; like the little clouds of morning and the islands of the blest? Do you know," and he lowered his voice yet more, "it has the power over me of making me feel as if I were myself absent and distant; some Oriental traveller who was lost and for whom men were looking. When I see that greenish lemon-yellow enamel there let into the white, I feel that I am standing thousands of leagues from where I stand."

"You are right," said Joan, looking at him with some wonder. "I have felt like that myself."

"This art," went on Ivywood as in a dream, "does indeed take the wings of the morning and abide in the uttermost parts of the sea. They say it contains no form of life; but surely we can read its alphabet as easily as the red hieroglyphics of sunrise and sunset, which are on the fringes of the robe of God."

"I never heard you talk like that before," said the lady; and again stroked the vivid violet feathers of the small eastern bird.

Mr. Quoodle could stand it no longer. He had evidently formed a very low opinion of the turret chamber and of Oriental art generally; but seeing Joan's attention once more transferred to his rival, he trotted out into the longer rooms; and finding the gap in the woodwork which was soon to be boarded up, but which still opened on an old dark staircase, he went "galumphing" down the stairs.

Lord Ivywood gently placed the bird on the girl's own finger; and went to one of the open windows, leaning out a little.

[12] "The same hath oft . . . . of perilous seas" is a line taken from John Keats' (1795–1821) "Ode to a Nightingale" and should be "the same that oft-times hath". Chesterton was well known for quoting from memory and for not checking his quotations and then, when errors were pointed out, ignoring them.

"Look here," he said, "doesn't this express what we both feel? Isn't this the sort of fairy-tale house that ought to hang on the last wall of the world?"

And he motioned her to the window-sill, just outside which hung the bird's empty cage, beautifully wrought in brass or some of the yellow metals.

"Why, that is the best of all!" cried Lady Joan. "It makes one feel as if it really were the Arabian Nights. As if this were a tower of the gigantic Genii with turrets up to the moon; and this were an enchanted Prince caged in a golden palace suspended by the evening star."

Something stirred in her dim but teeming subconsciousness; something like a chill or change, like that by which we half know that weather has altered, or distant and unnoticed music suddenly ceased.

"Where is the dog?" she asked suddenly.

Ivywood turned with a mild grey eye.

"Was there a dog here?" he asked.

"Yes," said Lady Joan Brett; and gave him back the bird, which he restored carefully to its cage.

The dog after whom she inquired had in truth trundled down a dark winding staircase and turned into the daylight into a part of the garden he had never seen before; nor, indeed, had anybody else for some time past. It was altogether tangled and overgrown with weeds; and the only trace of human handiwork, the wreck of an old Gothic chapel, stood waist high in numberless nettles and soiled with crawling fungoids. Most of these merely discoloured the grey crumbling stone with shades of bronze or brown; but some of them, particularly on the side farthest from the house, were of orange or purple tints almost bright enough for Lord Ivywood's Oriental decoration. Some fanciful eyes that fell on the place afterwards found something like an allegory in those graven and broken saints or archangels feeding such fiery and ephemeral parasites as those toad-stools like blood or gold. But Mr. Quoodle had never set himself up as an allegorist; and he merely trotted deeper and deeper into the grey-green English jungle. He grumbled very much at the thistles and nettles; much as a City man will grumble at the jostling of a crowd. But he continued to press forward, with his nose near the ground, as if he had already smelt something that interested him. And indeed he had smelt something in which a dog, except on special occasions, is much more interested than he is in dogs. Breaking through a last barrier of high and hoary purple thistles he came out on a semicircle of somewhat clearer ground, dotted with slender trees, and having, by way of back scene, the brown brick arch of an old tunnel. The tunnel was boarded up with a very irregular fence or mask made of motley wooden laths; and looking somehow rather like a pantomime cottage. In front of this a sturdy man in very shabby shooting clothes was standing attending to a battered old frying-pan which he held over a rather irregular flame which, small as it was, smelt strongly of burning rum. In the frying-pan, and also on the top of a cask or barrel that served for a table hard by, were a number of the grey, brown, and even orange fungi which were plastered over the stone angels and dragons of the fallen chapel.

"Hullo, old man," said the person in the shooting jacket, with tranquillity and without looking up from his cooking. "Come to pay us a visit? Come along, then." He flashed one glance at the dog and returned to the frying-pan. "If your tail were two inches shorter, you'd be worth a hundred pounds. Had any breakfast?"

The dog trotted across to him and began nosing and sniffing round his dilapidated leather gaiters. The man did not interrupt his cookery, on which his eyes were fixed and both his hands were busy; but he crooked his knee and foot so as to caress the quadruped in a nerve under the angle of the jaw, the stimulation of which (as some men of science have held) is for a dog what a good cigar is for a man. At the same moment a huge voice like an ogre's came from within the masked tunnel, calling out, "And who are ye talking to?"

A very crooked kind of window in the upper part of the pantomime cottage burst open and an enormous head, with erect, startling and almost scarlet hair and blue eyes as big as a bull frog's, was thrust out above the scene.

"Hump," cried the ogre. "Me moral counsels have been thrown away. In the last week I've sung you fourteen and a half songs of me own composition; instead of which you go about stealing dogs. You're following in the path of Parson Whats-his-name in every way, I'm afraid."

"No," said the man with the frying-pan, impartially. "Parson White-lady struck a very good path for doubling on Pebbleswick, that I was glad to follow. But I think he was quite silly to steal dogs. He was young and brought up pious. I know too much about dogs to steal one."

"Well," asked the large red-haired man, "and how do you get a dog like that?"

"I let him steal me," said the person stirring the pan. And indeed the dog was sitting erect and even arrogant at his feet, as if he was a watch-dog at a high salary, and had been there before the building of the tunnel.

XI

VEGETARIANISM IN THE DRAWING-ROOM

The company that assembled to listen to the Prophet of the Moon on the next occasion of his delivering any formal address, was much more select than the comparatively mixed and middle-class society of the Simple Souls. Miss Browning and her sister, Mrs. Mackintosh, were indeed present; for Lord Ivywood had practically engaged them both as private secretaries; and kept them pretty busy too. There was also Mr. Leveson, because Lord Ivywood believed in his organizing power; and also Mr. Hibbs, because Mr. Leveson believed in his political judgment, whenever he could discover what it was. Mr. Leveson had straight dark hair; and looked nervous. Mr. Hibbs had straight fair hair; and also looked nervous. But the rest of the company were more of Ivywood's own world; or the world of high finance with which it mixes both here and on the Continent. Lord Ivywood welcomed with something approaching to warmth a distinguished foreign diplomatist; who was, indeed, none other than that silent German representative who had sat beside him in that last conference on the Island of the Olives. Dr. Gluck was no longer in his quiet black suit, but wore an ornate diplomatic uniform with a sword, and Prussian, Austrian, or Turkish Orders; for he was going on from Ivywood to a function at Court. But his curl of red lips, his screw of black moustache, and his unanswering almond eyes had no more changed than the face of a wax figure in a barber's shop window.

The Prophet had also effected an improvement in his dress. When he had orated on the sands his costume, except for the fez, was the shabby but respectable costume of any rather unsuccessful English clerk. But now that he had come among aristocrats who petted their souls as they did their senses, there must be no such incongruity. He must be a proper fresh-picked Oriental tulip or lotus. So he wore long flowing robes of white relieved here and there by flame-coloured threads of tracery, and round his head was a turban of a kind of pale golden-green. He had to look as if he had come flying across Europe on the magic carpet; or fallen a moment before from his paradise in the moon.

The ladies of Lord Ivywood's world were much as we have already found them. Lady Enid Wimpole still overwhelmed her earnest and timid face with a tremendous costume, that was more like a procession than a dress. It looked rather like the funeral procession of Aubrey Beardsley.[13] Lady Joan Brett still looked like a very beautiful Spaniard with no illusions left about her castle in Spain. The large and resolute lady who had refused to ask any questions at Misysra's earlier lecture, and who was known as Lady Crump, the distinguished Feminist, still had the air of being so full and bursting with questions fatal to Man as to have passed the speaking and reached the speechless stage of hostility. Throughout the proceedings she contributed nothing but bursting silence and a malevolent eye. And old Lady Ivywood, under the oldest and finest lace and the oldest and finest manners, had a look like death on her, which can often be seen in the parents of pure intellectuals. She had that face of a lost mother that is more pathetic than the face of a lost child.

"And what are you going to delight us with to-day?" Lady Enid was asking of the Prophet.

"My lecture," answered Misysra gravely, "is on the Pig."

It was part of a simplicity really respectable in him that he never saw any incongruity in the arbitrary and isolated texts or symbols out of which he spun his thousand insane theories. Lady Enid endured the impact of this singular subject for debate without losing that expression of wistful sweetness, which she wore on principle when talking to such people.

"The Pig, he is a large subject," continued the Prophet making curves in the air, as if embracing some particularly prize specimen. "He include many subjects. It is to me very strange that the Christians should so laugh and be surprised because we hold ourselves to be defiled by pork; we and also another of the Peoples of the Book.

---

[13] Aubrey Beardsley (1872–1898) was an English artist and illustrator and the chief English representative of the Aesthetic Movement in art, which rejected the notion that art should have social or moral purpose.

But surely you Christians yourselves consider the pig as a manner of pollution; since it is your most usual expression of your despising, of your very great dislike. You say 'swine,' my dear lady; you do not say animals far more unpopular, such as the alligator."

"I see," said the lady; "how wonderful!"

"If you are annoyed," went on the encouraged and excited gentleman,—"if you are annoyed with any one, with a—what you say?—a lady's maid, you do not say to her 'Horse.' You do not say to her 'Camel.' "

"Ah, no," said Lady Enid earnestly.

" 'Pig of a lady's maid' you say in your colloquial English," continued the Prophet triumphantly. "And yet this great and awful Pig, this monster whose very name, when whispered, you think will wither all your enemies, you allow, my dear lady, to approach yet closer to you. You incorporate this great Pig in the substance of your own person."

Lady Enid Wimpole was looking a little dazed at last, at this description of her habits; and Joan gave Lord Ivywood a hint that the lecturer had better be transferred to his legitimate sphere of lecturing. Ivywood led the way into a larger room that was full of ranked chairs, with a sort of lectern at the other end; and flanked on all four sides with tables laden with all kinds of refreshments. It was typical of the strange, half-fictitious enthusiasm and curiosity of that world, that one long table was set out entirely with vegetarian foods, especially of an Eastern sort (like a table spread in the desert for a rather fastidious Indian hermit); but that tables covered with game patties, lobster, and champagne were equally provided; and very much more frequented. Even Mr. Hibbs, who would honestly have thought entering a public-house more disgraceful than entering a brothel, could not connect any conception of disgrace with Lord Ivywood's champagne.

For the purpose of the lecture was not wholly devoted to the great and awful Pig; and the purpose of the meeting even less. Lord Ivywood, the white furnace of whose mind was always full of new fancies hardening into ambitions, wanted to have a debate on the diet of East and West; and felt that Misysra might very appropriately open with an account of the eastern veto on pork or other coarse forms of flesh food. He reserved it to himself to speak second.

The Prophet began indeed with some of his dizziest flights. He informed the company that they, the English, had always gone in hidden terror and loathing of the pig, as a sacred symbol of evil. He proved it by the common English custom of drawing a pig with one's eyes shut. Lady Joan smiled; and yet she asked herself (in a doubt that had been darkening round her about many modern things lately) whether it was really much more fanciful than many things the scientists told her: as, the traces of Marriage by Capture which they found in that ornamental and even frivolous being, the Best Man.

He said that the dawn of greater enlightenment is shown in the use of the word "gammon," which still expresses disgust at "the porcine image" but no longer fear of it, but rather a rational disdain and disbelief. "Rowley," said the Prophet solemnly. And then, after a long pause, "Powley. *Gammon* and spinach." Lady Joan smiled again: but again asked herself if it was much more far-fetched than a history book she had read, which proved the unpopularity of Catholicism in Tudor times from the word "hocus pocus."

He got into a most amazing labyrinth of philology between the red primeval sins of the first pages of Genesis and the common English word "ham." But again Joan wondered whether it was much wilder than the other things she had heard said about Primitive Man, by people who had never seen him.

He suggested that the Irish were set to keep pigs because they were a low and defiled caste, and the serfs of the pig-scorning Saxon. And Joan thought it was about as sensible as what the dear old Archdeacon had said about Ireland years ago; which had caused an Irishman of her acquaintance to play "The Shan Van Voght" and then smash the piano.

Joan Brett had been thoughtful for the last few days. It was partly due to the scene in the turret, where she had struck a sensitive and artistic side of Philip Ivywood she had never seen before; and partly to disturbing news of her mother's health, which, though not menacing, made her feel hypothetically how isolated she was in the world. On all previous occasions she had merely enjoyed the mad lecturer now at the reading-desk. To-day she felt a strange desire to analyse him: and imagine how a man could be so connected and so convinced and yet so wildly wide of the mark. As she listened carefully, looking at the hands in her lap, she began to think she understood.

The lecturer did really try to prove that the "porcine image" had never been used in English history or literature except in contempt. And the lecturer really did know a very great deal about English history and literature: much more than she did: much more than the aristocrats round her did. But she noted that in every case what he knew was a fragmentary fact. In every case what he did not know was the truth behind the fact. What he did not know was the atmosphere. What he did not know was the tradition. She found herself ticking off the cases like counts in an indictment.

Misysra Ammon knew, what next to none of the English present knew, that Richard III was called a "boar" by an eighteenth-century poet and a "hog" by a fifteenth-century poet. What he did not know was the habit of sport and of heraldry. He did not know (what Joan knew instantly, though she had never thought of it before in her life) that beasts courageous and hard to kill are noble beasts, by the law of chivalry. Therefore the boar was a noble beast; and a common crest for great captains. Misysra tried to show that Richard had only been called a pig after he was cold pork at Bosworth.

Misysra Ammon knew, what next to none of the English present knew, that there never was such a person as Lord Bacon. The phrase is a falsification of what should be Lord Verulam or Lord St. Albans.[14] What he did not know was exactly what Joan did know (though it had never crossed her mind till that moment), that when all is said and done, a title is a sort of joke, while a surname is a serious thing. Bacon was a gentleman, and his name was Bacon; whatever titles he took. But Misysra seriously tried to prove that "Bacon" was a term of abuse applied to him during his unpopularity or after his fall.

[14] Lord Francis Bacon (1561–1626), 1st Baron of Verulam and Viscount of St. Albans, was an English statesman, lawyer and philosopher of radical beliefs. His works—particularly the *Novum Organum* (1620), which detached scientific investigation from theological concerns—were influential throughout Europe and in England. His ideas are considered to have influenced Isaac Newton and John Locke and provided a significant force behind the establishment of the Royal Society (1660).

Misysra Ammon knew, what next to none of the English present knew, that the poet Shelley had a friend called Hogg, who treated him on one occasion with grave treachery. He instantly tried to prove that the man was only called "Hogg" because he had treated Shelley with grave treachery. And he actually adduced the fact that another poet, practically contemporary, was called "Hogg" as completing the connexion with Shelley. What he did not know was just what Joan had always known without knowing it: the kind of people concerned; the traditions of aristocrats like the Shelleys or of Borderers like the Ettrick Shepherd.[15]

The lecturer concluded with a passage of impenetrable darkness about pig-iron and pigs of lead, which Joan did not even venture to understand. She could only say that if it did not mean that some day our diet might become so refined that we ate lead and iron, she could form no fancy of what it did mean.

"Can Philip Ivywood believe this kind of thing?" she asked herself; and even as she did so Philip Ivywood rose.

He had, as Pitt and Gladstone had, an impromptu classicism of diction, his words wheeling and deploying into their proper places like a well-disciplined army in its swiftest advance. And it was not long before Joan perceived that the last phase of the lecture, obscure and monstrous as it seemed, gave Ivywood exactly the opening he wanted. Indeed, she felt no doubt that he had arranged for it beforehand.

"It is within my memory," said Lord Ivywood, "though it need in no case have encumbered yours, that when it was my duty to precede the admired lecturer whom I now feel it a privilege even to follow, I submitted a suggestion which, however simple, would appear to many paradoxical. I affirmed or implied the view that the religion of Mahomet was, in a peculiar sense, a religion of progress. This is so contrary, not only to historical convention but to common platitude, that I shall find no ground either of surprise or censure if it takes a perceptible time before it sinks into the mind of the English public. But I

---

[15] "The Ettrick Shepherd" is the nickname for James Hogg (1770–1835), Scottish poet and shepherd in the Ettrick Forest who was "discovered" by Sir Walter Scott.

think, ladies and gentlemen, that this period is notably abbreviated by the remarkable exposition which we have heard to-day. For this question of the attitude of Islam towards food affords as excellent an example of its special mode of progressive purification as the more popular example of its attitude towards drink. For it illustrates that principle which I have ventured to call the principle of the Crescent: the principle of perpetual growth towards an implied and infinite perfection.

"The great religion of Islam does not itself forbid the eating of flesh foods. But in accordance with that principle of growth which is its life, it has pointed the way to a perfection not yet perhaps fully attainable by our nature; it has taken a plain and strong example of the dangers of meat-eating; and hung up the repellent carcass as a warning and a sign. In the gradual emergence of mankind from a gross and sanguinary mode of sustenance, the Semite has led the way. He has laid, as it were, a symbolic embargo upon the beast typical, the beast of beasts. With the instinct of the true mystic, he selected for exemption from such cannibal feasts the creature which appeals to both sides of the higher vegetarian ethic. The pig is at once the creature whose helplessness most moves our pity, and whose ugliness most repels our taste.

"It would be foolish to affirm that no difficulty arises out of the different stages of moral evolution in which the different races find themselves. Thus it is constantly said, and such things are not said without some excuse in document or incident, that followers of the Prophet have specialized in the arts of war, and have come into a contact, not invariably friendly, with those Hindoos of India who have specialized in the arts of peace. In the same way the Hindoos, it must be confessed, have been almost as much in advance of Islam in the question of meat, as Islam is in advance of Christianity in the matter of drink. It must be remembered again and again, ladies and gentlemen, that every allegation we have of any difference between Hindoo and Moslem comes through a Christian channel; and is therefore tainted evidence. But in this matter even, can we not see the perils of disregarding such plain danger-signals as the veto on pork? Did not an Empire nearly slip out of our hands, because our hands were greased with cow-fat? And did not the well of Cawnpore brim with blood instead of water, because we would not listen to the instinct of the Oriental about the shedding of sacred blood?

"But if it be proposed, with whatever graduation, to approach that repudiation of flesh food which Buddhism mainly and Islam partly recommends, it will always be asked by those who hate the very vision of Progress—'Where do you draw the line? May I eat oysters? May I eat eggs? May I drink milk?' You may. You may eat or drink anything essential to your stage of evolution, so long as you are evolving towards a clearer and cleaner ideal of bodily life. If," he said gravely, "I may employ a phrase of flippancy, I would say that you may eat six dozen oysters to-day; but I should strongly advise five dozen oysters to-morrow. For how else has all progress in public or private manners been achieved? Would not the primitive cannibals be surprised at the strange distinction we draw between men and beasts? All historians pay high honour to the Huguenots, and the great Huguenot Prince, Henri Quatre.[16] None need deny that his aspiration that every French-man should have a chicken in his pot was, for his period, a high aspiration. It is no disrespect to him that we, mounting to higher levels, and looking down longer perspectives, consider the chicken. And this august march of discovery passes figures higher than that of Henry of Navarre. I shall always give a high place, as Islam has always given a high place, to that figure, mythical or no, which we find presiding over the foundations of Christianity. I cannot doubt that the fable, incredible and revolting otherwise, which records the rush of swine into the sea, was an allegory of his early realization that a spirit, evil indeed, does reside in all animals in so far as they tempt us to devour them. I cannot doubt that the Prodigal leaving his sins among the swine is another illustration of the great thesis of the Prophet of the Moon. But here also progress and relativity are relentless in their advance; and not a few of us may have risen to-day to the point of regretting that the joyful sounds around the return of the Prodigal should be marred by the moaning of a calf.

[16] Henri Quatre (Henry IV of Navarre, 1553–1610) was the first Bourbon king of France; he was brought up a Calvinist and led the Huguenot army at the Battle of Jarnac (1569). In 1593 he became a Catholic, unifying the country. He was assassinated in Paris by a religious fanatic.

"For the rest, he who asks us whither we go, knows not the meaning of Progress. If we come at last to live on light, as men said of the chameleon, if some cosmic magic closed to us now, as radium was but recently closed, allows us to transmute the very metals into flesh without breaking into the bloody house of life, we shall know these things when we achieve them. It is enough for us now if we have reached a spiritual station, in which at least the living head we lop has not eyes to reproach us; and the herbs we gather cannot cry against our cruelty like the mandrake."

Lord Ivywood resumed his seat, his colourless lips still moving. By some previous arrangement probably, Mr. Leveson rose to move a motion about Vegetarianism. Mr. Leveson was of opinion that the Jewish and Moslem veto on pork had been the origin of Vegetarianism. He thought it was a great step; and showed how progressive the creed could be. He thought the persecution of the Hindoos by Moslems had probably been much exaggerated; he thought our experience in the Indian Mutiny showed we considered the feeling of Easterns too little in such matters. He thought Vegetarianism in some ways an advance on orthodox Christianity. He thought we must be ready for yet further advances; and he sat down. And as he had said precisely, clause by clause, everything that Lord Ivywood had said, it is needless to say that that nobleman afterwards congratulated him on the boldness and originality of his brilliant speech.

At a similar sort of preconcerted signal, Hibbs However rose rather vaguely to his feet to second the motion. He rather prided himself on being a man of few words, in the vocal sense. He was no orator, as Brutus was. It was only with pen in hand, in an office lined with works of reference, that he could feel that sense of confused responsibility that was the one pleasure of his life. But on this occasion he was brighter than usual; partly because he liked being in a lord's house; partly because he had never tasted champagne before, and he felt as if it agreed with him; partly because he saw in the subject of Progress an infinite opportunity of splitting hairs.

"Whatever," said Hibbs with a solemn cough,—"whatever we may think of the old belief that Moslems have differed from Buddhism in a regrettable way, there can be no doubt the responsibility lay with

the Christian Churches. Had the Free Churches put their foot down
and met Messrs. Opalstein's demand, we should have heard nothing
of these old differences between one belief and another." As it was, it
reminded him of Napoleon. He gave his own opinion for what it was
worth; but he was not afraid to say at any cost, even there and in that
company, that this business of Asiatic vegetation had occupied less of
the time of the Wesleyan Conference than it should have done. He
would be the last to say, of course, that any one was in any sense to
blame. They all knew Dr. Coon's qualifications. They all knew as
well as he did that a more strenuous social worker than Charles Chad-
der had never rallied the forces of Progress. But that which was not
really an indiscretion might be represented as an indiscretion; and
perhaps we had had enough of that just lately. It was all very well to
talk about coffee, but it should be remembered, with no disrespect to
those in Canada to whom we owe so much, that all that happened
before 1891. No one had less desire to offend our Ritualist friends
than he had, but he had no hesitation in saying that the question was
a question that could be asked; and though no doubt, from one point
of view, the goats——

Lady Joan moved sharply in her chair, as if gripped by sudden pain.
And indeed she had suddenly felt the chronic and recurrent pain of
her life. She was brave about bodily pain, as are most women, even
luxurious women: but the torment that from time to time returned
and tore her was one to which many philosophical names have been
given: but no name so philosophical as Boredom.

She felt she could not stand a minute more of Mr. Hibbs. She felt
she would die if she heard about the goats—from one or any point of
view. She slipped from her chair and somehow slid round the corner,
in pretence of seeking one of the tables of refreshment in the new
wing. She was soon among the new Oriental apartments, now almost
completed; but she took no refreshments, though attenuated tables
could still be found here and there. She threw herself on an ottoman
and stared towards the empty and elfin turret chamber, in which Ivywood had made her understand that he also could thirst for beauty
and desire to be at peace. He certainly had a poetry of his own, after
all; a poetry that never touched earth; the poetry of Shelley rather

than Shakespeare. His phrase about the fairy turret was true: it did look like the end of the world. It did seem to teach her that there is always some serene limit at last.

She started and half rose on her elbow with a small laugh. A dog of ludicrous but familiar appearance came shuffling towards her and she lifted herself in the act of lifting him. She also lifted her head; and saw something that seemed to her, in a sense more Christian and catastrophic, very like the end of the world.

XII

VEGETARIANISM IN THE FOREST

Humphrey Pump's cooking a fungus in an old frying-pan (which he had found on the beach) was extremely typical of him. He was, indeed, without any pretence of book-learning, a certain kind of scientific man that science has really been unfortunate in losing. He was the old-fashioned English naturalist, like Gilbert White[17] or even Izaak Walton,[18] who learnt things not academically like an American Professor, but actually, like an American Indian. And every truth a man has found out as a man of science is always subtly different from any truth he has found out as a man; because a man's family, friends, habits, and social type have always got well under way before he has thoroughly learnt the theory of anything. For instance, any eminent botanist at a *soirée* of the Royal Society could tell you, of course, that other edible fungi exist as well as mushrooms and truffles. But long before he was a botanist, still less an eminent botanist, he had begun, so to speak, on a basis of mushrooms and truffles. He felt, in a vague way, that these were really edible: that mushrooms were a moderate luxury, proper to the middle classes; while truffles were a much more expensive luxury, more suitable to the Smart Set. But the old English naturalists, of whom Izaak Walton was perhaps the first and Humphrey Pump perhaps the last, had in many cases really begun at the other end; and found by experience (often most disastrous experience) that some fungi are wholesome and some are not; but the wholesome ones are, on the whole, the majority. So a man like Pump was no more afraid of a fungus as such than he was of an animal as such. He no more started with the supposition that a grey or purple growth on

[17] Gilbert White (1720–1793) was an English clergyman and naturalist. He was known for his acute observations of natural history, many of which were published in *The Natural History and Antiquities of Selbourne* (1789).

[18] Izaak Walton (1593–1683) was an English writer most known for his book *The Complete Angler* (1653), which contains practical information on fishing along with some songs and ballads.

a stone must be a poisonous growth than he started with the supposition that the dog who came to him out of the wood must be a mad dog. Most of them he knew; those he did not know he treated with rational caution, but to him, as a whole race, these weird-hued and one-legged goblins of the forests were creatures friendly to man.

"You see," he said to his friend the Captain, "eating vegetables isn't half bad, so long as you know what vegetables there are and eat all of them that you can. But there are two ways where it goes wrong among the gentry. First, they've never had to eat a carrot or a potato because it was all there was in the house; so they've never learnt how to be really hungry for carrots, as that donkey might be. They only know the vegetables that are meant to help the meat. They know you take duck and peas; and when they turn vegetarian they can only think of peas without the duck. They know you take lobster in a salad; and when they turn vegetarian they can only think of the salad without the lobster. But the other reason is worse. There's plenty of good people even round here, and still more in the north, who get meat very seldom. But then, when they do get it, they gobble it up like good 'uns. But the trouble with the gentry is different. The trouble is, the same sort of gentry that don't want to eat meat don't really want to eat anything. The man called a vegetarian who goes to Ivywood House is generally like a cow trying to live on a blade of grass a day. You and I, Captain, have pretty well been vegetarians for some time, so as not to break into the cheese; and we haven't found it so difficult, because we eat as much as we can."

"It's not so difficult as being teetotallers," answered Dalroy, "so as not to break into the cask. But I'll never deny that I feel the better for that too, on the whole. But only because I could leave off being one whenever I chose. And, now I come to think of it," he cried, with one of his odd returns of animal energy, "if I'm to be a vegetarian why shouldn't I drink? Why shouldn't I have a purely vegetarian drink? Why shouldn't I take vegetables in their highest form, so to speak? The modest vegetarians ought obviously to stick to wine or beer, plain vegetarian drinks, instead of filling their goblets with the blood of bulls and elephants, as all conventional meat-eaters do, I suppose. What is the matter?"

"Nothing," answered Pump. "I was looking out for somebody who generally turns up about this time. But I think I'm fast."

"I should never have thought so from the look of you," answered the Captain; "but what I'm saying is that the drinking of decent fermented liquor is just simply the triumph of vegetarianism. Why, it's an inspiring idea! I could write a sort of song about it. As, for instance—

> "You will find me drinking rum,
>   Like a sailor in a slum,
> You will find me drinking beer like a Bavarian.
>   You will find me drinking gin
>   In the lowest kind of inn,
> Because I am a rigid Vegetarian.

"Why, it's a vista of verbal felicity and spiritual edification! It has I don't know how many hundred aspects! Let's see; how could the second verse go? Something like—

> "So I cleared the inn of wine,
>   And I tried to climb the sign,
> And I tried to hail the constable as 'Marion.'
>   But he said I couldn't speak,
>   And he bowled me to the Beak
> Because I was a Happy Vegetarian.

"I really think something instructive to the human race may come out of all this.... Hullo! Is that what you were looking for?"

The quadruped Quoodle came in out of the woods a whole minute later than the usual time and took his seat beside Humphrey's left foot with a preoccupied air.

"Good old boy!" said the Captain. "You seem to have taken quite a fancy to us. I doubt, Hump, if he's properly looked after up at the house. I particularly don't want to talk against Ivywood, Hump. I don't want his soul to be able in all eternity to accuse my soul of a mean detraction. I want to be fair to him, because I hate him like hell, and he has taken from me all for which I lived. But I don't think, with all this in my mind, I don't think I say anything beyond what he would own himself (for his brain is clear) when I say that he could never understand an animal. And so he could never understand the animal side of a man. He doesn't know to this day, Hump, that your sight and hearing are sixty times quicker than his. He doesn't know that I have a better circulation. That explains the extraordinary people he picks up and acts with: he never looks at them as you and I look at that dog. There was a fellow calling himself Gluck who was (mainly by Ivywood's influence, I believe) his colleague on the Turkish conferences, being supposed to represent Germany. My dear Hump, he was a man a great gentleman like Ivywood ought not to have touched with a barge-pole. It's not the race he was—if it was one race—it's the Sort he was. A coarse, common, Levantine nark and eaves-dropper—but you mustn't lose your temper, Hump. I implore you, Hump, to control this tendency to lose your temper, when talking at any length about such people. Have recourse, Hump, to that consoling system of versification which I have already explained to you.

> "Oh, I knew a Doctor Gluck,
> And his nose it had a hook,
> And his attitudes were anything but Aryan;
> So I gave him all the pork
> That I had, upon a fork;
> Because I am myself a Vegetarian."

"If you are," said Humphrey Pump, "you'd better come and eat some vegetables. The White Hat can be eaten cold—or raw, for that matter. But Blood-spots wants some cooking."

"You are right, Hump," said Dalroy, seating himself with every appearance of speechless greed. "I will be silent. As the poet says—

> "I am silent in the Club,
> I am silent in the pub.,
> I am silent on a bally peak in Darien;
> For I stuff away for life
> Shoving peas in with a knife,
> Because I am at heart a Vegetarian."

He fell to his food with great gusto, dispatched a good deal of it in a very short time, threw a glance of gloomy envy at the cask; and then sprang to his feet again. He caught up the inn sign from where it leant against the pantomime cottage, and planted it like a pike in the ground beside him. Then he began to sing again, in an even louder voice than before.

> "O Lord Ivywood may lop,
>   And is also free to top,
> And his privilege is sylvan and riparian.
>   But——"

"Do you know," said Hump, also finishing his lunch, "that I'm rather tired of that particular tune,"

"Tired, is it?" said the indignant Irishman. "Then I'll sing you a longer song, to an even worse tune, about more and more vegetarians; and you shall see me dance as well; and I will dance till you burst into tears and offer me the half of your kingdom; and I shall ask for Mr. Leveson's head on the frying-pan. For this, let me tell you, is a song of Oriental origin, celebrating the caprices of an ancient Babylonian Sultan and should be performed in palaces of ivory with palm-trees and a bulbul accompaniment."

And he began to bellow another and older lyric of his own on vegetarianism.

> "Nebuchadnezzar the King of the Jews
> Suffered from new and original views,
> He crawled on his hands and knees, it's said,
> With grass in his mouth and a crown on his head.
>   With a wowtyiddly, etc.
>
> Those in traditional paths that trod
> Thought the thing was a curse from God,
> But a Pioneer men always abuse
> Like Nebuchadnezzar the King of the Jews."

Dalroy, as he sang this, actually began to dance about like a ballet girl, an enormous and ridiculous figure in the sunlight; waving the wooden sign round his head. Quoodle opened his eyes and pricked up his ears and seemed much interested in these extraordinary evolutions. Suddenly, with one of those startling changes that will transfigure the most sedentary dogs, Quoodle decided that the dance was

a game; and began to bark and bound round the performer, sometimes leaping so far into the air as almost to threaten the man's throat.
But though the sailor naturally knew less about dogs than the coun-
tryman, he knew enough about them (as about many other things)
not to be afraid; and the voice he sang with might have drowned the
baying of a pack.

> "Black Lord Foulon the Frenchman slew
> Thought it a Futurist thing to do.
> He offered them grass instead of bread.
> So they stuffed him with grass when they cut off
>   his head.
>   With a wowtyiddly, etc.
>
> For the pride of his soul he perished then—
> But of course it is always of Pride that men,
> A Man in Advance of his Age accuse,
> Like Nebuchadnezzar the King of the Jews.
>
> Simeon Scudder of Styx, in Maine,
> Thought of the thing and was at it again.
> He gave good grass and water in pails
> To a thousand Irishmen hammering rails.
>   With a wowtyiddly, etc.
>
> Appetites differ; and tied to a stake
> He was tarred and feathered for Conscience' Sake.
> But stoning the prophets is ancient news,
> Like Nebuchadnezzar the King of the Jews."

In an abandon unusual even for him, he had danced his way down
through the thistles into the jungle of weeds risen round the sunken
chapel. And the dog, now fully convinced that it was not only a game
but an expedition, perhaps a hunting expedition, ran barking in front
of him, along the path that his own dog's paws had already burst through
the tangle. Before Patrick Dalroy well knew what he was doing, or
even remembered that he still carried the ridiculous sign-board in his
hand, he found himself outside the open porch of a sort of narrow
tower at the angle of a building which, to the best of his recollection,
he had never seen before. Quoodle instantly ran up four or five steps

in the dark staircase inside, and then, lifting up his ears again, looked back for his companion.

There is perhaps such a thing as asking too much of a man. If there is, it was asking too much of Patrick Dalroy to ask him not to accept so eccentric an invitation. Hurriedly plunging his unwieldy wooden ensign upright, in the thick of thistles and grass, he bent his gigantic neck and shoulders to enter the porch, and proceeded to climb the stair. It was quite dark, and it was only after at least two twists of the stone spiral that he saw light ahead of him; and then it was a sort of rent in the wall that seemed to him as ragged as the mouth of a Cornish cave. It was also so low that he had some difficulty in squeezing his bulk through it; but the dog had jumped through with an air of familiarity, and once more looked back to see him follow.

If he had found himself inside any ordinary domestic interior he would instantly have repented his escapade and gone back. But he found himself in surroundings which he had never seen before or even, in one sense, believed possible.

His first feeling was that he was walking in the most sealed and secret suite of apartments in the castle of a dream. All the chambers had that air of perpetually opening inwards, which is the soul of the "Arabian Nights." And the ornament was of the same tradition; gorgeous and flamboyant yet featureless and stiff. A purple mansion seemed to be built inside a green mansion and a golden mansion inside that. And the quaintly cut doorways or fretted lattices all had wavy lines like a dancing sea; and for some reason (sea-sickness for all he knew) this gave him a feeling as if the place was beautiful, but faintly evil: as if it were bored and twisted for the fallen palace of the Worm.

But, he had also another sensation, which he could not analyse; but it reminded him of being a fly on the ceiling or the wall. Was it the Hanging Gardens of Babylon coming back to his imagination; or the Castle East of the Sun and West of the Moon? [19] Then he remembered that in some boyish illness he had stared at a rather Moorish

---

[19] *East of the Sun and West of the Moon* is a collection of traditional Norse folk tales, the title story of which is a version of *Beauty and the Beast*.

sort of wall-paper, which was like rows and rows of brightly coloured corridors empty and going on for ever. And he remembered that a fly was walking along one of the parallel lines: and it seemed to his childish fancy that the corridors were all dead in front of the fly, but all came to life as he passed.

"By George!" he cried. "I wonder whether that's the real truth about East and West! That the gorgeous East offers everything needed for adventures except the man to enjoy them. It would explain the tradition of the Crusades uncommonly well. Perhaps that's what God meant by Europe and Asia. We dress the characters and they paint the scenery. Well, anyhow, three of the least Asiatic things in the world are lost in this endless Asiatic palace—a good dog, a straight sword, and an Irishman."

But as he went down this telescope of tropical colours he really felt something of that hard fatalistic freedom of the heroes (or should we say villains?) in the "Arabian Nights." He was prepared for any impossibility. He would hardly have been surprised if from under the lid of one of the porcelain pots standing in a corner had come a serpentine string of blue or yellow smoke, as if some wizard's oil were within. He would hardly have been surprised if from under the curtains or closed doors had crawled out a snaky track of blood, or if a dumb negro dressed in white had come out with a bow-string having done his work. He would not have been surprised if he had walked suddenly into the still chamber of some Sultan asleep, whom to wake was a death in torments. And yet he was very much more surprised by what he did see; and when he saw it, he was certain at last that he was only wandering in the labyrinth of his own brain. For what he saw was what was really in the core of all his dreams.

What he saw indeed was more appropriate to that inmost eastern chamber than anything he had imagined. On a divan of blood-red and orange cushions lay a startlingly beautiful woman, with a skin almost swarthy enough for an Arab's; and who might well have been the Princess proper to such an Arabian tale. But in truth it was not her appropriateness to the scene, but rather her inappropriateness, that made his heart bound. It was not her strangeness but her familiarity that made his big feet suddenly stop.

The dog ran on yet more rapidly; and the princess on the sofa welcomed him warmly, lifting him on his short hind legs. Then she looked up; and seemed turned to stone.

"Bismillah," said the Oriental traveller affably, "may your shadow never grow less—or more, as the ladies would say. The Commander of the Faithful has deputed his least competent slave to bring you back a dog. Owing to temporary delay in collecting the fifteen largest diamonds in the moon, he has been compelled to send the animal without any collar. Those responsible for the delay will instantly be beaten to death with the tails of dragons——"

The frightful shock, which had not yet left the lady's face, brought him back to responsible speech.

"In short," he said, "in the name of the Prophet, dog. I say, Joan, I wish this wasn't a dream."

"It isn't," said the girl, speaking for the first time, "and I don't know yet whether I wish it was."

"Well," argued the dreamer rationally, "what are you, any time, if you're not a dream—or a vision? And what are all these rooms, if they aren't a dream—or rather a nightmare?"

"This is the new wing of Ivywood House," said the lady addressed as Joan, speaking with great difficulty. "Lord Ivywood has fitted them up in the eastern style; he is inside conducting a most interesting debate in defence of eastern Vegetarianism. I only came out because the room was rather hot."

"Vegetarian!" cried Dalroy, with abrupt and rather unreasonable exasperation. "That table seems to fall a bit short of Vegetarianism." And he pointed to one of the long, narrow tables, laid somewhere in almost all the central rooms, and loaded with elaborate cold meats and expensive wines.

"He must be liberal-minded," cried Joan, who seemed to be on the verge of something; possibly temper. "He can't expect people suddenly to begin being Vegetarians when they've never been before."

"It has been done," said Dalroy tranquilly, walking across to look at the table. "I say, your ascetical friends seem to have made a pretty good hole in the champagne. You may not believe it, Joan, but I haven't touched what you call alcohol for a month."

With which words he filled with champagne a large tumbler intended for claret-cup, and swallowed it at a draught.

Lady Joan Brett stood up straight but trembling.

"Now that's really wrong, Pat," she cried. "Oh, don't be silly— you know I don't care about the alcohol or all that. But you're in the man's house; uninvited; and he doesn't know. That wasn't like you."

"He shall know all right," said the large man quietly. "I know the exact price of a tumbler of that champagne."

And he scribbled some words in pencil on the back of a bill of fare on the table; and then carefully laid three shillings on top of it.

"And there you do Philip the worst wrong of all," cried Lady Joan, flaming white. "You know as well as I do, anyhow, that he would not take your money."

Patrick Dalroy stood looking at her for some seconds with an expression on his broad and usually open face which she found utterly puzzling.

"Curiously enough," he observed at last, and with absolutely even temper,—"curiously enough, it is you who are doing Philip Ivywood a wrong. I think him quite capable of breaking England or creation. But I do honestly think he would never break his word. And what is more, I think the more arbitrary and literal his word had been, the more he would keep it. You will never understand a man like that till you understand that he can have devotion to a definition; even a new definition. He can really feel about an amendment to an Act of Parliament, inserted at the last moment, as you feel about England or your mother."

"Oh, don't philosophize,"cried Joan suddenly. "Can't you see this has been a shock?"

"I only want you to see the point," he replied. "Lord Ivywood clearly told me, with his own careful lips, that I might go in and pay for fermented liquor in any place displaying a public sign outside. And he won't go back on that definition, or on any definition. If he finds me here, he may quite possibly put me in prison on some other charge, as a thief or a vagabond, or what not. But he will not grudge the champagne. And he will accept the three shillings. And I shall honour him for his glorious consistency."

"I don't understand," said Joan, "one word of what you are talking about. Which way did you come? How can I get you away? You don't seem to grasp that you're in Ivywood House."

"You see, there's a new name outside the gate," observed Patrick conversationally; and led the lady to the end of the corridor by which he had entered, and into its ultimate turret chamber.

Following his indications, Lady Joan peered a little over the edge of the window, where hung the brilliant purple bird in its brilliant golden cage. Almost immediately below, outside the entrance to the half-closed stairway, stood a wooden tavern sign, as solid and still as if it had been there for centuries.

"All back at the sign of 'The Old Ship,' you see," said the Captain. "Can I offer you anything in a lady-like way?"

There was a vast impudence in the slight hospitable movement of his hand that disturbed Lady Joan's features with an emotion other than any that she desired to show.

"Well!" cried Patrick, with a wild geniality, "I've made you laugh again, my dear."

He caught her to him in a whirlwind; and then vanished from the fairy turret like a blast: leaving her standing with her hand up to her wild black hair.

XIII

THE BATTLE OF THE TUNNEL

What Joan Brett really felt as she went back from the second *tête-à-tête* she had experienced in the turret, it is doubtless if any one will ever know. But she was full of the pungent feminine instinct to "drive at practise": and what she did clearly realize was the pencil writing Dalroy had left on the back of Lord Ivywood's *menu*. Heaven alone knew what it was: and (as it pleased her profane temper to tell herself) she was not satisfied with Heaven alone knowing. She went swiftly back with swishing skirts to the table where it had been left. But her skirts fell more softly and her feet trailed slower and more in her usual manner as she came near the table. For standing at it was Lord Ivywood, reading the card with tranquil, lowered eyelids, that set off perfectly the long and perfect oval of his face. He put down the card with a quite natural action; and, seeing Joan, smiled at her in his most sympathetic way.

"So you've come out too," he said. "So have I: it's really too hot for anything. Dr. Gluck is making an uncommonly good speech, but I couldn't stop even for that. Don't you think my Eastern decorations are rather a success after all? A sort of Vegetarianism in design, isn't it?"

He led her up and down the corridors, pointing out lemon-coloured crescents or crimson pomegranates in the scheme or ornament, with such utter detachment that they twice passed the open mouth of the hall of debate; and Joan could distinctly hear the voice of the diplomatic Gluck saying:

"Indeed, we owe our knowledge of the pollution of the pork primarily to the Jewth and not the Mothlemth. I do not thare that prejudithe against the Jewth, which ith too common in my family and all the arithtocratic military Prutthian familieth. I think we Prutthian arithocrats owe everything to the Jewth. The Jewth have given to our old Teutonic rugged virtueth, jutht that touch of refinement, jutht that intellectual thuperiority which——"

And then the voice would die away behind, as Lord Ivywood lectured luxuriantly, and very well, on the peacock tail in decoration, or some more extravagant eastern version of the Greek Key. But the third time they turned, they heard the noise of subdued applause and the breaking up [of] the meeting; and people came pouring forth.

With stillness and swiftness Ivywood pitched on the people he wanted and held them. He button-holed Leveson and was evidently asking him to do something which neither of the two liked doing.

"If your lordship insists," she heard Leveson whispering. "Of course I will go myself. But there is a great deal to be done here with your lordship's immediate matters. And if there were any one else——"

If Philip, Lord Ivywood, had ever looked at a human being in his life, he would have seen that J. Leveson, Secretary, was suffering from a very ancient human malady; excusable in all men, and rather more excusable in one who has had his top-hat smashed over his eyes and has run for his life. As it was, he saw nothing, but merely said: "Oh, well, get some one else. What about your friend Hibbs?"

Leveson ran across to Hibbs, who was drinking another glass of champagne at one of the innumerable buffets.

"Hibbs," said Leveson rather nervously. "Will you do Lord Ivywood a favour? He says you have so much tact. It seems possible that a man may be hanging about the grounds just below that turret there. He is a man it would certainly be Lord Ivywood's public duty to put into the hands of the police, if he is there. But then, again, he is quite capable of not being there at all—I mean of having sent his message from somewhere else and in some other way. Naturally, Lord Ivywood doesn't want to alarm the ladies, and perhaps turn the laugh against himself, by getting up a sort of police raid about nothing. He wants some sensible, tactful friend of his to go down and look round the place—it's a sort of disused garden—and report if there's any one about. I'd go myself, but I'm wanted here,"

Hibbs nodded, and filled another glass.

"But there's a further difficulty," went on Leveson. "He's a clever brute, it seems, 'a remarkable and a dangerous man,' were his lordship's words: and it looks as if he'd spotted a very good hiding-place; a disused tunnel leading to the sands, just beyond the disused garden and chapel. It's a smart choice, you see, for he can bolt into the woods if any one comes from the shore, or on to the shore if any one comes from the woods. But it would take a good time even to get the police here: and it would take ten times longer to get 'em round to the sea end of the tunnel, especially as the sea comes up to the cliffs once or twice between here and Pebbleswick. So we mustn't frighten him away, or he'll get a start. If you meet any one down there, talk to him quite naturally, and come back with the news. We won't send for the police till you come. Talk as if you were just wandering, like himself. His lordship wishes your presence to appear quite accidental."

"Wishes my presence to appear quite accidental," repeated Hibbs gravely.

When the feverish Leveson had flashed off, satisfied, Hibbs took a glass or two more of wine; feeling that he was going on a great diplomatic mission to please a lord. Then he went through the opening, picked his way down the stair, and somehow found his way out into the neglected garden and shrubbery.

It was already evening, and an early moon was brightening over the sunken chapel, with its dragon-coloured scales of fungus. The night breeze was very fresh, and had a marked effect on Mr. Hibbs. He found himself taking a meaningless pleasure in the scene; especially in one fungus that was white with brown spots. He laughed shortly, to think that it should be white with brown spots. Then he said, with carefully accurate articulation: "His lordship wishes my presence to appear quite accidental." Then he tried to remember something else that Leveson had said.

He began to wade through the waves of weed and thorn past the chapel, but he found the soil much more uneven and obstructive than he had supposed.

He slipped, and sought to save himself by throwing one arm round a broken stone angel at a corner of the heap of Gothic fragments; but it was loose and rocked in its socket.

Mr. Hibbs presented for a moment the appearance of waltzing with the angel in the moonlight, in a very amorous and irreverent manner. Then the statue rolled over one way and he rolled over the other; and lay on his face in the grass, making inaudible remarks. He might have lain there for some time, or at least found some difficulty in rising, but for another circumstance. The dog Quoodle, with characteristic officiousness, had followed him down the dark stairs and out of the doorway, and finding him in this unusual posture, began to bark as if the house were on fire.

This brought a heavy human footstep from the more hidden part of the copse; and in a minute or two the large man with the red hair was looking down at him in undisguised wonder. Hibbs said, in a muffled voice which came obscurely from under his hidden face:

"Wish my presence to appear quite accidental."

"It does," said the Captain. "Can I help you up? Are you hurt?"

He gently set the prostrate gentleman on his feet; and looked genuinely concerned. The fall had somewhat sobered Lord Ivywood's representative; and he really had a red graze on the left cheek, that looked more ugly than it was.

"I am so sorry," said Patrick Dalroy cordially. "Come and sit down in our camp. My friend Pump will be back presently; and he's a capital doctor."

His friend Pump may or may not have been a capital doctor, but the Captain himself was certainly a most inefficient one. So small was his talent for diagnosing the nature of a disease at sight, that having given Mr. Hibbs a seat on a fallen tree by the tunnel, he proceeded to give him (in mere automatic hospitality) a glass of rum.

Mr. Hibbs's eyes awoke again when he had sipped it; but they awoke to a new world.

"Wherever may be our invidual pinions," he said; and looked into space with an expression of humorous sagacity.

He then put his hand hazily in his pocket, as if to find some letter he had to deliver. He found nothing but his old journalistic notebook, which he often carried when there was a chance of interviewing anybody. The feel of it under his fingers changed the whole attitude of his mind. He took it out and said:

"And wha' would you say of Vegetarianism, Colonel Pump?"

"I think it palls," replied the recipient of this complex title, staring.

"Sha'we say," asked Hibbs brightly, turning a leaf in his note-book, "sha'we say long been strong veg'tarian by conviction?"

"No; I have only once been convicted," answered Dalroy, with restraint. "And I hope to lead a better life when I come out."

"Hopes lead better life," murmured Hibbs, writing eagerly with the wrong end of his pencil. "And wha' would you shay was best vegable food for really strong veg'tarian by conviction?"

"Thistles," said the Captain wearily. "But I don't know much about it, you know."

"Lord Ivywoo' strong veg'tarian by conviction," said Mr. Hibbs, shaking his head with unction. "Lord Ivywoo' says tact. Talk to him naturally. And so I do. That's what I do. Talk to him naturally."

Humphrey Pump came through the clearer part of the wood leading the donkey, which had just partaken of the diet recommended to a vegetarian by conviction. The dog sprang up and ran to them. Pump was, perhaps, the most naturally polite man in the world, and said nothing. But his eyes had accepted with one snap of surprise the other fact, also not unconnected with diet, which had escaped Dalroy's notice when he administered rum as a restorative,

"Lord Ivywoo' says," murmured the journalistic diplomatist, "Lord Ivywoo' says, 'Talk as if you were just wandering.' That's it. That's tact. That's what I've got to do—talk as if I was just wandering. Long way round to other end tunnel: sea and cliffs. Don' spose they can swim." He seized his note-book again and looked in vain for his pencil. "Good subjec' cosspondence. Can Policem'n Swim?"

"Policemen?" said Dalroy, in a dead silence. The dog looked up; and the innkeeper did not.

"Get to Ivywood one thing," reasoned the diplomatist. "Get policemen beach other end other thing. No good do one thing no' do other thing, no goo' do other thing no' do other thing. Wish my presence appear quite accidental. Haw!"

"I'll harness the donkey," said Pump.

"Will he go through that door?" asked Dalroy, with a gesture towards the entrance of the rough boarding with which they had faced the tunnel, "or shall I smash it all at once?"

"He'll go through all right," answered Pump. "I saw to that when I made it. And I think I'll get him to the safe end of the tunnel before I load him up. The best thing you can do is to pull up one of those saplings to bar the door with. That'll delay them a minute or two; though I think we've got warning in pretty easy time."

He led his donkey to the cart and carefully harnessed the donkey; like all men cunning in the old healthy sense, he knew that the last chance of leisure ought to be leisurely, in order that it may be lucid. Then he led the whole equipment through the temporary wooden door of the tunnel, the inquisitive Quoodle, of course, following at his heels.

"Excuse me if I take a tree," said Dalroy politely to his guest, like a man reaching across another man for a match. And with that he rent up a young tree by its roots, as he had done in the Island of the Olives; and carried it on his shoulder, like the club of Hercules.

Up in Ivywood House, Lord Ivywood had telephoned twice to Pebbleswick. It was a delay he seldom suffered; and though he never expressed impatience in unnecessary words, he expressed it in unnecessary walking. He would not yet send for the police without news from his ambassador, but he thought a preliminary conversation with some police authorities he knew well might advance matters. Seeing Leveson rather shrunk in a corner, he wheeled round in his walk and said abruptly:

"You must go and see what has happened to Hibbs. If you have any other duties here, I authorize you to neglect them. Otherwise I can only say——"

At this moment the telephone rang, and the impatient nobleman rushed for his delayed call with the rapidity he seldom showed. There was simply nothing for Leveson to do except to do as he was told, or be sacked. He walked swiftly towards the staircase, and only stopped once at the table where Hibbs had stood; and gulped down two goblets of the same wine. But let no man attribute to Mr. Leveson the loose and luxurious social motives of Mr. Hibbs. Mr. Leveson did not drink for pleasure; in fact, he hardly knew what he was drinking. His motive was something far more simple and sincere; a sentiment forcibly described in legal phraseology as going in bodily fear.

He was partly nerved, but by no means reconciled to his adventure, when he crept carefully down the stairs and peered about the thicket for any sign of his diplomatic friend. He could find neither sight nor sound to guide him, except a sort of distant singing, which greatly increased in volume of sound as he pursued it. The first words he heard seemed to run something like:

> "No more the milk of cows
> Shall pollute my private house
> Than the milk of the wild mares of the Barbarian;
> I will stick to port and sherry
> For they are so very, very,
> So very, very, very Vegetarian."

Leveson did not know the huge and horrible voice in which these words were shouted. But he had a most strange and even sickening suspicion that he did know the voice, however altered, the quavering and rather refined voice, that joined in the chorus and sang:

> "Because they are so vegy
> So vegy, vegy, very Veretarian."

Terror lit up his wits; and he made a wild guess at what had happened. With a gasp of relief he realized that he had now good excuse for returning to the house with the warning. He ran there like a hare, still hearing the great voice from the woods like the roaring of a lion in his rear.

He found Lord Ivywood in consultation with Dr. Gluck; and also with Mr. Bullrose the agent, whose froglike eyes hardly seemed to have recovered yet from the fairy-tale of the flying sign-board in the English lane; but who, to do him justice, was more plucky and practical than most of Lord Ivywood's present advisers.

"I'm afraid Mr. Hibbs has inadvertently," stammered Leveson. "I'm afraid he has ... I'm afraid the man is making his escape, my lord. You had better send for the police."

Ivywood turned to the agent. "You go and see what's happening," he said simply. "I will come myself when I've rung them up. And get some of the servants up with sticks and things. Fortunately the ladies have gone to bed. Hullo! Is that the Police Station?"

Bullrose went down into the shrubbery, and had, for many reasons, less difficulty in crossing it than the hilarious Hibbs. The moon had increased to an almost unnatural brilliancy, so that the whole scene was like a rather silver daylight. And in this clear medium he beheld a very tall man with erect red hair and a colossal cylinder of cheese carried under one arm, while he employed the other to wag a big forefinger at a dog with whom he was conversing.

It was the agent's duty and desire to hold the man, whom he recognized from the sign-board mystery, in play and conversation; and prevent his final escape. But there are some people who really cannot be courtteous, even when they want to be, and Mr. Bullrose was one of them.

"Lord Ivywood," he said abruptly, "wants to know what you want."

"Do not, however, fall into the common error, Quoodle," Dalroy was saying to the dog, whose unfathomable eyes were fixed on his face, "of supposing that the phrase 'good dog' is used in its absolute sense. A dog is good or bad relatively to a limited scheme of duties created by human civilization——"

"What are you doing here?" asked Mr. Bullrose.

"A dog, my dear Quoodle," continued the Captain, "cannot be either so good or bad as a man. Nay, I should go farther. I would almost say a dog cannot be so stupid as a man. He cannot be utterly wanting as a dog—as some men are as men."

"Answer me, you there!" roared the agent.

"It is all the more pathetic," continued the Captain, to whose monologue Quoodle seemed to listen with magnetized attention, "it is all the more pathetic because this mental insufficiency is sometimes found in the good; though there are, I should imagine, at least an equal number of opposite examples. The person standing a few feet off us, for example, is both stupid *and* wicked. But be very careful, Quoodle, to remember that any disadvantage under which we place him should be based on his *moral* and not his *mental* defects. Should I say to you at any time, 'Go for him, Quoodle,' or 'Hold him, Quoodle,' be certain in your own mind, please, that it is solely because he is *wicked* and not because he is *stupid*, that I am entitled to do so. The fact that he is *stupid* would not justify me in saying 'Hold him, Quoodle,' with the realistic intonation I now employ——"

"Curse you, call him off!" cried Mr. Bullrose, retreating. For Quoodle was coming towards him with the bull-dog part of his pedigree very prominently displayed, like a pennon. "Should Mr. Bullrose find it expedient to climb a tree, or even a sign-post," proceeded Dalroy, (for indeed the agent had already clasped the pole of 'The Old Ship,' which was stouter than the slender trees standing just around it,) "you will keep an eye on him, Quoodle, and, I doubt not, constantly remind him that it is his *wickedness*, and not, as he might hastily be inclined to suppose, his *stupidity*, that has placed him on so conspicuous an elevation."

"Some of you'll wish yourself dead for this," said the agent; who was by this time clinging to the wooden sign like a monkey on a stick, while Quoodle watched him from below with an unsated interest. "Some of you'll see something. Here comes his lordship and the police, I reckon."

"Good morning, my lord," said Dalroy, as Ivywood, paler than ever in the strong moonshine, came through the thicket towards them. It seemed to be his fate that his faultless and hueless face should always be contrasted with richer colours; and even now it was thrown up by the gorgeous diplomatic uniform of Dr. Gluck, who walked just behind him.

"I am glad to see you, my lord," said Dalroy, in a stately manner; "it is always so awkward doing business with an agent. Especially for the agent."

"Captain Dalroy," said Lord Ivywood, with a more serious dignity, "I am sorry we meet again like this, and such things are not of my seeking. It is only right to tell you that the police will be here in a moment."

"Quite time too!" said Dalroy, shaking his head. "I never saw anything so disgraceful in my life. Of course, I am sorry it's a friend of yours; and I hope the police will keep Ivywood House out of the papers. But I won't be a party to one law for the rich and another for the poor; and it would be a great shame if a man in that state got off altogether merely because he had got the stuff at your house."

"I do not understand you," said Ivywood. "What are you talking of?"

"Why, of him," replied the Captain, with a genial gesture towards a fallen tree-trunk that lay a yard or two from the tunnel wall, "the poor chap the police are coming for."

Lord Ivywood looked at the forest log by the tunnel, which he had not glanced at before; and in his pale eyes, perhaps for the first time, stood a simple astonishment.

Above the log appeared two duplicate objects, which, after a prolonged stare, he identified as the soles of a pair of patent leather shoes, offered to his gaze, as if demanding his opinion in the matter of resoling. They were all that was visible of Mr. Hibbs, who had fallen backwards off his woodland seat and seemed contented with his new situation.

His lordship put up the pince-nez that made him look ten years older, and said with a sharp, steely accent, "What is all this?"

The only effect of his voice upon the faithful Hibbs was to cause him to feebly wave his legs in the air, in recognition of a feudal superior. He clearly considered it hopeless to attempt to get up; so Dalroy, striding across to him, lugged him up by his shirt collar and exhibited him, limp and wild-eyed, to the company.

"You won't want many policemen to take him to the station," said the Captain. "I'm sorry, Lord Ivywood, I'm afraid it's no use your asking me to overlook it again. We can't afford it," and he shook his head implacably. "We've always kept a respectable house, Mr. Pump and I. 'The Old Ship' has a reputation all over the country—in quite a lot of different parts, in fact. People in the oddest places have found it a quiet family house. Nothing gad-about in 'The Old Ship.' And if you think you can send all your staggering revellers——"

"Captain Dalroy," said Ivywood simply, "you seem to be under a misapprehension which I think it would be hardly honourable to leave undisturbed. Whatever these extraordinary events may mean, and whatever be fitting in the case of this gentleman, when I spoke of the police coming, I meant they were coming for you and your confederate."

"For me!" cried the Captain, with a stupendous air of surprise. "Why, I have never done anything naughty in my life."

"You have been selling alcohol contrary to Clause V. of the Act of——"

"But I've got a sign," cried Dalroy excitedly; "you told me yourself it was all right if I'd got a sign. Oh, do look at our new sign! The Sign of the Agile Agent."

Mr. Bullrose had remained silent, feeling his position none of the most dignified and hoping his employer would go away. But Lord Ivywood looked up at him; and thought he had wandered into a planet of monsters.

As he slowly recovered himself Patrick Dalroy said briskly, "All quite correct and conventional, you see. You can't run us in for not having a sign: we've rather an extra life-like one. And you can't run us in as rogues and vagabonds either. Visible means of subsistence," and he slapped the huge cheese under his arm with his great flat hand, so that it reverberated like a drum. "Quite visible. Perceptible," he added, holding it out suddenly almost under Lord Ivywood's nose,—"perceptible to the naked eye through your lordship's eyeglasses."

He turned abruptly, burst open the pantomime door behind him, and bowled the big cheese down the tunnel with a noise like thunder, which ended in a cry of acceptation in the distant voice of Mr. Humphrey Pump. It was the last of their belongings left at this end of the tunnel; and Dalroy turned again, a man totally transfigured.

"And now, Ivywood," he said, "what can I be charged with? Well, I have a suggestion to make. I will surrender to the police quite quietly when they come, if you will do me one favour. Let me choose my crime."

"I don't understand you," answered the other coolly; "what crime? What favour?"

Captain Dalroy unsheathed the straight sword that still hung on his now shabby uniform. The slender blade sparkled splendidly in the moonlight as he pointed it straight at Dr. Gluck.

"Take away his sword from the little pawnbroker," he said. "It's about the length of mine; or we'll change if you like. Give me ten minutes on that strip of turf. And then it may be, Ivywood, that I shall be removed from your public path in a way a little worthier of enemies who have once been friends; than if you tripped me up with Bow Street runners, of whose help every ancestor you have would have been ashamed. Or, on the other hand, it may be—that when the police come, there will be something to arrest me for."

There was a long silence; and the elf of irresponsibility peeped out again for an instant in Dalroy's mind.

"Mr. Bullrose will see fair play for you, from a throne above the lists," he said. "I have already put my honour in the hands of Mr. Hibbs."

"I must decline Captain Dalroy's invitation," said Ivywood at last, in a curious tone. "Not so much because——"

Before he could proceed, Leveson came racing across the copse, halloing "The police are here!"

Dalroy, who loved leaving everything to the last instant, tore up the sign, with Bullrose literally hanging to it, shook him off like a ripe fruit; and then plunged into the tunnel, the clamorous Quoodle at his heels. Before even Ivywood (the promptest of his party) could reach the spot, he had clashed to the wood door and bolted it across with his wooden staple. He had not had time even to sheath his sword.

"Break down this door," said Ivywood calmly. "I noticed they haven't finished loading their cart."

Under his directions, and vastly against their will, Bullrose and Leveson lifted the tree-trunk vacated by Hibbs, and swinging it thrice as a battering-ram, burst in the door. Lord Ivywood instantly sprang into the entrance.

A voice called out to him quietly from the other end of the tunnel. There was something touching and yet terrible about a voice so human coming out of that inhuman darkness. If Philip Ivywood had been really a poet, and not rather its opposite, an æsthete, he would have known that all the past and people of England were uttering their oracle out of the cavern. As it was, he only heard a publican wanted by the police. Yet even he paused, and indeed seemed spellbound.

"My lord, I would like a word. I learned my catechism; and never was with the Radicals. I want you to look at what you've done to me. You've stolen a house that was mine, as that one's yours. You've made me a dirty tramp, that was a man respected in church and market. Now you send me where I might have cells or the cat. If I might make so bold, what do you suppose I think of you? Do you think because you go up to London and settle it with lords in Parliament, and bring back a lot of papers and long words, that makes any difference to the man you do it to? By what I can see, you're just a bad and cruel master, like those God punished in the old days; like Squire Varney the weasels killed in Holy Wood. Well, parson always said we might shoot at robbers. And I want to tell your lordship," he ended respectfully, "that I have a gun."

Ivywood instantly stepped into the darkness; and spoke in a voice shaken with some emotion, the nature of which was never certainly known.

"The police are here," he said. "But I'll arrest you myself."

A shot shrieked and rattled through the thousand echoes of the tunnel: Lord Ivywood's legs doubled and twisted under him; and he collapsed on the earth with a bullet above his knee.

Almost at the same instant a shout and a bark announced that the cart had started as a complete equipage. It was even more than complete; for the instant before it moved Mr. Quoodle had sprung into it; and as it was driven off, sat erect in it, looking solemn.

XIV

THE CREATURE THAT MAN FORGETS

Despite the natural hubbub round the wound of Lord Ivywood and the difficulties of the police in finding their way to the shore, the fugitives of The Flying Inn must almost certainly have been captured, but for a curious accident; which also flowed, as it happened, from the great Ivywood debate on Vegetarianism.

The comparatively late hour at which Lord Ivywood had made his discovery had been largely due to a very long speech which Joan had not heard, and which was delivered immediately before the few concluding observations she had heard from Dr. Gluck. The speech was made by an eccentric, of course. Most of those who attended, and nearly all of those who talked, were eccentric in one way or another. But he was an eccentric of great wealth and good family, an M. P., a J. P., a relation of Lady Enid, a man well known in art and letters—in short, a personality who could not be prevented from being anything he chose, from a revolutionist to a bore.

Dorian Wimpole had first become famous outside his own class under the fanciful title of the Poet of the Birds. A volume of verse, expanding the several notes or cries of separate song-birds into fantastic soliloquies of these feathered philosophers, had really contained a great deal of ingenuity and elegance. Unfortunately he was one of those who always tend to take their own fancies seriously; and in whose otherwise legitimate extravagance there is too little of the juice of jest. Hence, in his later works, when he explained "The fable of the Angel" by trying to prove that the fowls of the air were creatures higher than man or the anthropoids, his manner was felt to be too austere. And when he moved an amendment to Lord Ivywood's scheme for the model village called Peaceways, urging that its houses should all follow the more hygienic architecture of nests hung in trees, many regretted that he had lost his light touch. But when he went beyond birds and filled his poems with conjectural psychology about all the Zoological Gardens, his meaning became obscure; and Lady Susan had even described it as his bad period. It was all the more uncomfortable reading because he poured forth the imaginary hymns, love-songs, and war-songs of the lower animals, without a word of previous explanation. Thus if some one seeking for an ordinary drawing-room song came on lines that were headed "A Desert Love Song"; and which began

> "Her head is high against the stars
> Her hump is heaved in pride,"

the compliment to the lady would at first seem startling; until the reader realized that all the characters in the idyll were camels. Or if he began a poem simply entitled "The March of Democracy" and found in the first lines

> "Comrades, marching evermore
> Fix your teeth in floor and door,"

he might be doubtful about such a policy for the masses; until he discovered that it was supposed to be addressed by an eloquent and aspiring rat to the social solidarity of his race. Lord Ivywood had nearly quarrelled with his poetic relative over the uproarious realism of the verses called "A Drinking Song"; until it was carefully explained to him that the drink was water, and that the festive company consisted of bisons. His visions of the perfect husband, as it exists in the feelings of the young female walrus, is thoughtful and suggestive; but would doubtless receive many emendations from any one who had experienced those feelings. And in his sonnet called "Motherhood" he has made the young scorpion consistent and convincing, yet somehow not wholly lovable. In justice to him, however, it should be remembered that he attacked the most difficult cases on principle; declaring that there was no earthly creature that a poet should forget.

He was of the blond type of his cousin, with flowing fair hair and moustache, and a bright blue absent-minded eye; he was very well dressed in the carefully careless manner, with a brown velvet jacket: and the image on his ring of one of those beasts men worshipped in Egypt.

His speech was graceful and well worded and enormously long; and it was all about an oyster. He passionately protested against the suggestion of some humanitarians, who were vegetarians in other respects, but maintained that organisms so simple might fairly be counted as exceptions. Man, he said, even at his miserable best, was always trying to excommunicate some one citizen of the cosmos, to forget some one creature that he should remember. Now, it seemed that creature was the oyster. He gave a long account of the tragedy of the oyster, a really imaginative and picturesque account; full of fantastic fishes; and coral crags crawling and climbing; and bearded creatures streaking the seashore; and the green darkness in the cellars of the sea.

"What a horrid irony it is," he cried, "that this is the only one of the lower creatures whom we call a Native! We speak of him, and of him alone, as if he were a native of the country. Whereas, indeed, he is an exile in the universe. What can be conceived more pitiful than the eternal frenzy of the impotent amphibian? What is more terrible than the tear of an oyster? Nature herself has sealed it with the hard seal of eternity. The creature man forgets bears against him a testimony that cannot be forgotton. For the tears of widows and of captives are wiped away at last like the tears of children. They vanish like the mists of morning or the small pools after a flood. But the tear of the oyster is a pearl."

The Poet of the Birds was so excited with his own speech that, after the meeting, he walked out with a wild eye to the motor-car, which had been long awaiting him, the chauffeur giving some faint signs of relief.

"Towards home, for the present," said the poet, and stared at the moon with an inspired face.

He was very fond of motoring, finding it fed him with inspirations; and he had been doing it from an early hour that morning, having enjoyed a slightly lessened sleep. He had scarcely spoken to anybody until he spoke to the cultured crowd at Ivywood. He did not wish to speak to any one for many hours yet. His ideas were racing. He had thrown on a fur coat over his velvet jacket; but he let it fly open, having long forgotten the coldness in the splendour of the moonstruck night. He realized only two things: the swiftness of his car and the swiftness of his thoughts. He felt, as it were, a fury of omniscience: he seemed flying with every bird that sped or spun above the woods, with every squirrel that had leapt and tumbled within them, with every tree that had swung under and sustained the blast.

Yet in a few moments he leaned forward and tapped the glass frontage of the car; and the chauffeur, suddenly squaring his shoulders, jarringly stopped the wheels. Dorian Wimpole had just seen something in the clear moonlight by the roadside, which appealed both to this and to the other side of his tradition; something that appealed to Wimpole as well as to Dorian.

Two shabby-looking men, one in tattered gaiters and the other in what looked like the remains of fancy dress, with the addition of hair of so wild a red that it looked like a wig, were halted under the hedge, apparently loading a donkey cart. At least two rounded, rudely cylindrical objects, looking more or less like tubs, stood out in the road beside the wheels; along with a sort of loose wooden post that lay along the road beside them. As a matter of fact, the man in the old gaiters had just been feeding and watering the donkey, and was now adjusting its harness more easily. But Dorian Wimpole naturally did not expect that sort of thing from that sort of man. There swelled up in him the sense that his omnipotence went beyond the poetical; that he was a gentleman, a magistrate, an M. P. and J. P., and so on. This callousness or ignorance about animals should not go on while he was a J. P.; especially since Ivywood's last Act. He simply strode across to the stationary cart and said:

"You are overloading that animal; and it is forfeited. And you must come with me to the police station."

Humphrey Pump, who was very considerate to animals, and had always tried to be considerate to gentlemen, in spite of having put a bullet into one of their legs, was simply too astounded and distressed to make any answer at all. He moved a step or two backwards and stared with brown, blinking eyes at the poet, the donkey, the cask, the cheese, and the sign-board lying in the road.

But Captain Dalroy, with the quicker recovery of his national temperament, swept the poet and magistrate a vast fantastic bow and said with agreeable impudence, "Interested in donkeys, no doubt?"

"I am interested in all things men forget," answered the poet, with a fine touch of pride, "but mostly in those like this, that are most easily forgotten."

Somehow from those two first sentences Pump realized that these two eccentric aristocrats had unconsciously recognized each other. The fact that it was unconscious seemed, somehow, to exclude him all the more. He stirred a little the moonlit dust of the road with his rather dilapidated boots, and eventually strolled across to speak to the chauffeur.

"Is the next police station far from here?" he asked.

The chauffeur answered with one syllable of which the nearest literal rendering is "Dno." Other spellings have been attempted; but the sentiment expressed is that of agnosticism.

But something of special brutality of abbreviation made the shrewd, and therefore sensitive, Mr. Pump look at the man's face. And he saw it was not only the moonlight that made it white.

With that dumb delicacy that was so English in him, Pump looked at the man again; and saw he was leaning heavily on the car with one arm; and saw that the arm was shaking. He understood his countrymen enough to know that whatever he said he must say in a careless manner.

"I hope it's nearer to your place. You must be a bit done up."

"Oh, hell!" said the driver, and spat on the road.

Pump was sympathetically silent; and Mr. Wimpole's chauffeur broke out incoherently, as if in another place:

"Blarsted beauties o' dibrike and no breakfast. Blarsted lunch Hivywood and no lunch. Blarsted black everlastin' hours artside while 'e 'as 'is cike an' champine. And then it's a dornkey!"

"You don't mean to say," said Pump, in a very serious voice, "that you've had no food to-day?"

"Ow no!" replied the cockney, with the irony of the deathbed. "Ow, of course not."

Pump strolled back into the road again, picked up the cheese in his left hand, and landed it on the seat beside the driver. Then his right hand went to one of his large, loose equivocal pockets; and the blade of a big jack-knife caught and recaught the steady splendours of the moon.

The driver stared for several instants at the cheese, with the knife shaking in his hand. Then he began to hack it; and in that white witchlike light the happiness of his face was almost horrible.

Pump was wise in all such things; and knew that just as a little food will sometimes prevent sheer intoxication, so a little stimulant will sometimes prevent sudden and dangerous indigestion. It was practically impossible to make the man stop eating cheese. It was far better to give him a very little of the rum; especially as it was very good rum, and better than anything he could find in any of the public-houses that were still permitted. He walked across the road again and picked up the small cask; which he put on the other side of the cheese and from which he filled, in his own manner, the little cup he carried in his pocket.

But at the sight of this the cockney's eyes lit at once with terror and desire.

"But yer cawn't do it," he whispered hoarsely, "it's the pleece. It's gile for that, with no doctor's letter nor sign-board nor nothink."

Mr. Humphrey Pump made yet another march back into the road. When he got there he hesitated for the first time; but it was quite clear from the attitude of the two insane aristocrats who were arguing and posturing in the road that they would notice nothing except each other. He picked the loose post off the road and brought it to the car, humorously propping it erect in the aperture between keg and cheese.

The little glass of rum was wavering in the poor chauffeur's hand exactly as the big knife had done. But when he looked up and actually saw the wooden sign above him, he seemed, not so much to pluck up his courage, but rather to drag up some forgotten courage from the foundations of some unfathomable sea. It was indeed the forgotten courage of the people.

He looked once at the bleak black pine-woods around him and took the mouthful of golden liquid at a gulp, as if it were a fairy potion. He sat silent; and then very slowly a sort of stony glitter began to come into his eyes. The brown and vigilant eyes of Humphrey Pump were studying him with some anxiety or even fear. He did look rather like a man enchanted or turned to stone. But he spoke very suddenly.

"The blighter!" he said; "I'll give 'im 'ell! I'll give 'im bleeding 'ell! I'll give 'im somethink wot 'e don't expect."

"What do you mean?" asked the innkeeper.

"Why," answered the chauffeur, with abrupt composure, "I'll give 'im a little dornkey."

Mr. Pump looked troubled. "Do you think," he observed, affecting to speak lightly, "that he's fit to be trusted even with a little donkey?"

"Ow, yes," said the man. "He's very amiable with dornkeys. And dornkeys we is to be amiable with 'im."

Pump still looked at him doubtfully; appearing or affecting not to follow his meaning. Then he looked equally anxiously across at the other two men: but they were still talking. Different as they were in every other way, they were of the sort who forget everything, class, quarrel, time, place, and physical facts in front of them, in the lust of lucid explanation and equal argument.

Thus, when the Captain began by lightly alluding to the fact that after all it was his donkey, since he had bought it from a tinker for a just price, the police station practically vanished from Wimpole's mind—and I fear the donkey-cart also. Nothing remained but the necessity of dissipating the superstition of personal property.

"I own nothing," said the poet, waving his hands outwards,—"I own nothing save in the sense that I own everything. All depends whether wealth or power be used for or against the higher purposes of the cosmos."

"Indeed," replied Dalroy, "and how does your motor-car serve the higher purposes of the cosmos?"

"It helps me," said Mr. Wimpole, with honourable simplicity, "to produce my poems."

"And if it could be used for some higher purpose (if such a thing could be), if some new purpose had come into his cosmos's head by accident," inquired the other, "I suppose it would cease to be your property?"

"Certainly," replied the dignified Dorian. "I should not complain. Nor have you any title to complain when the donkey ceases to be yours when you depress it in the cosmic scale."

"What makes you think," asked Dalroy, "that I wanted to depress it?"

"It is my firm belief," replied Dorian Wimpole sternly, "that you wanted to ride on it"; (for indeed the Captain had once repeated his playful gesture of putting his large leg across). "Is not that so?"

"No," answered the Captain innocently; "I never ride on a donkey. I'm afraid of it."

"Afraid of a "donkey!" cried Wimpole incredulously.

"Afraid of an historical comparison," said Dalroy.

There was a short pause; and Wimpole said coolly enough, "Oh, well; we've outlived those comparisons."

"Easily," answered the Irish Captain. "It is wonderful how easily one outlives some one else's crucifixion."

"In this case," said the other grimly, "I think it is the donkey's crucifixion."

"Why, you must have drawn that old Roman caricature of the crucified donkey," said Patrick Dalroy, with an air of some wonder. "How well you have worn! Why, you look quite young! Well, of course, if this donkey is crucified, he must be uncrucified. But are you quite sure," he added, very gravely, "that you know how to uncrucify a donkey? I assure you it's one of the rarest of human arts. All a matter of knack. It's like the doctors with the rare diseases, you know; the necessity so seldom arises. Granted that, by the higher purposes of the cosmos, I am unfit to look after this donkey, I must still feel a faint shiver of responsibility in passing him on to you. Will you understand this donkey? He is a delicate-minded donkey. He is a complex donkey. How can I be certain that, on so short an acquaintance, you will understand every shade of his little likes and dislikes?"

The dog Quoodle, who had been sitting as still as the sphinx under the shadow of the pine-trees, waddled out for an instant into the middle of the road and then returned. He ran out when a slight noise as of rotatory grinding was heard; and ran back when it had ceased. But Dorian Wimpole was much too keen on his philosophical discovery to notice either dog or wheel.

"I shall not sit on its back, anyhow," he said proudly, "but if that were all it would be a small matter. It is enough for you that you have left it in the hands of the only person who could really understand it; one who searches the skies and seas so as not to neglect the smallest creature."

"This is a very curious creature," said the Captain anxiously. "He has all sorts of odd antipathies. He can't stand a motor-car, for instance, especially one that throbs like that while it's standing still. He doesn't mind a fur coat so much; but if you wear a brown velvet jacket under it, he bites you. And you must keep him out of the way of a certain kind of people. I don't suppose you've met them; but they always think that anybody with less than two hundred a year is drunk and very cruel, and that anybody with more than two thousand a year is conducting the Day of Judgment. If you will keep our dear donkey from the society of such persons—Hullo! Hullo! Hullo!"

He turned in genuine disturbance; and dashed after the dog, who had dashed after the motor-car and jumped inside. The Captain jumped in after the dog, to pull him out again. But before he could do so he found the car was flying along too fast for any such leap. He looked up and saw the sign of "The Old Ship" erect in the front like a rigid banner; and Pump, with his cask and cheese, sitting stolidly beside the driver.

The thing was more of an earthquake and transformation to him even than to any of the others; but he rose waveringly to his feet and shouted out to Wimpole:

"You've left it in the right hands. I've never been cruel to a motor."

In the moonlight of the magic pine-wood far behind, Dorian and the donkey were left looking at each other.

To the mystical mind, when it is a mind at all (which is by no means always the case), there are no two things more impressive and symbolical than a poet and a donkey. And the donkey was a very genuine donkey. And the poet was a very genuine poet; however lawfully he might be mistaken for the other animal at times. The interest of the donkey in the poet will never be known. The interest of the poet in the donkey was perfectly genuine; and survived even that appalling private interview in the owlish secrecy of the woods.

But I think even the poet would have been enlightened if he had seen the white, set, frantic face of the man on the driver's seat of his vanishing motor. If he had seen it he might have remembered the name, or perhaps even begun to understand the nature, of a certain animal which is neither the donkey nor the oyster; but the creature whom man has always found it easiest to forget, since the hour he forgot God in a garden.

XV

THE SONGS OF THE CAR CLUB

More than once as the car flew through blank and silver fairylands of fir-wood and pine-wood Dalroy put his head out of the side window and remonstrated with the chauffeur without effect. He was reduced at last to asking him where he was going.

"I'm goin' 'ome," said the driver, in an undecipherable voice. "I'm a-goin' 'ome to my mar."

"And where does she live?" asked Dalroy, with something more like diffidence than he had ever shown before in his life.

"Wiles," said the man, "but I ain't seen 'er since I was born. But she'll do."

"You must realize," said Dalroy, with difficulty, "that you may be arrested—it's the man's own car; and he's left behind with nothing to eat, so to speak."

" 'E's got 'is dornkey," grunted the man. "Let the stinker eat 'is dornkey, with thistle sauce. 'E would if 'e was as 'ollow as I was."

Humphrey Pump opened the glass window that separated him from the rear part of the car, and turned to speak to his friend over his square elbow and shoulder.

"I'm afraid," he said, "he won't stop for anything just yet. He's as mad as Moody's aunt, as they say."

"Do they say it?" asked the Captain, with a sort of anxiety. "They never said it in Ithaca."

"Honestly, I think you'd better leave him alone," answered Pump, with his sagacious face. "He'd just run us into a Scotch Express, like Dandy Mutton did, when they said he was driving carelessly. We can send the car back to Ivywood, somehow, later on. And really, I don't think it'll do the gentleman any harm to spend a night with a donkey. The donkey might teach him something, I tell you."

"It's true he denied the Principle of Private Property," said Dalroy reflectively. "But I fancy he was thinking of a plain house fixed on the ground. A house on wheels, such as this, he might perhaps think a more permanent possession. But I never understand it"; and again he passed a weary palm across his open forehead. "Have you ever noticed, Hump, what is really odd about those people?"

The car shot on amid the comfortable silence of Pump; and then the Irishman said again:

"That poet in the pussy-cat clothes wasn't half bad. Lord Ivywood isn't cruel; but he's inhuman. But that man wasn't inhuman. He was ignorant: like most cultured fellows. But what's odd about them is that they try to be simple and never clear away a single thing that's complicated. If they have to choose between beef and pickles, they always abolish the beef. If they have to choose between a meadow and a motor, they forbid the meadow. Shall I tell you the secret? These men only surrender the things that bind them to other men. Go and dine with a temperance millionaire, and you won't find he's abolished the *hors d'œuvres* or the five courses or even the coffee. What he's abolished is the port and sherry; because poor men like that as well as rich. Go a step farther, and you won't find he's abolished the fine silver forks and spoons; but he's abolished the meat: because poor men like meat—when they can get it. Go a step farther; and you won't find he goes without gardens or gorgeous rooms, which poor men can't enjoy at all. But you will find he boasts of early rising; because sleep is a thing poor men can still enjoy. About the only thing they can still enjoy. Nobody ever heard of a modern philanthropist giving up petrol or typewriting or troops of servants. No, no! What he gives up must be some simple and universal thing. He will give up beef or beer or sleep—because these pleasures remind him that he is only a man."

Humphrey Pump nodded, but still answered nothing; and the voice of the sprawling Dalroy took one of its upward turns of a sort of soaring flippancy; which commonly embodied itself in remembering some song he had composed.

"Such," he said, "was the case of the late Mr. Mandragon, so long popular in English aristocratic society as a bluff and simple democrat from the West, until he was unfortunately sand-bagged by six men whose wives he had had shot by private detectives, on his incautiously landing on American soil.

"Mr. Mandragon the Millionaire he wouldn't have wine or wife,
He couldn't endure complexity; he lived the simple life;
He ordered his lunch by megaphone in manly simple tones,
And used all his motors for canvassing voters, and twenty
   telephones;
        Besides a dandy little machine,
        Cunning and neat as ever was seen,
        With a hundred pulleys and cranks between,
        Made of iron and kept quite clean,
To hoist him out of his healthful bed on every day of his life,
And wash him, and brush him, and shave him, and dress him
   to live the Simple Life.

Mr. Mandragon was most refined, and quietly, neatly dressed,
Say all the American newspapers that know refinement best;
Quiet and neat the hair and hat, and the coat quiet and neat,
A trouser worn upon either leg, while boots adorn the feet;
        And not, as any one might expect,
        A Tiger Skin, all striped and specked,
        And a Peacock Hat with the tail erect,
        A scarlet tunic with sunflowers decked,
        —That might have had a more marked effect
And pleased the pride of a weaker man that yearned for wine
   or wife
But fame and the flagon for Mr. Mandragon obscured the
   Simple Life.

Mr. Mandragon the Millionaire, I am happy to say, is dead,
He enjoyed a quiet funeral in a crematorium shed,
And he lies there fluffy and soft and grey, and certainly quite
   refined,
When he might have rotted to flowers and fruit with Adam and
   all mankind.
        Or been eaten by bears that fancy blood,
        Or burnt on a big tall tower of wood,
        In a towering flame as a heathen should,
        Or even sat with us here at food,
Merrily taking twopenny rum and cheese with a pocket-knife;
But these were luxuries lost for him that lived for the Simple
   Life."

Mr. Pump had made many attempts to arrest this song; but they were as vain as all attempts to arrest the car. The angry chauffeur seemed, indeed, rather inspired to further energy by the violent vocal noises behind; and Pump again found it best to fall back on conversation.

"Well, Captain," he said amicably, "I can't quite agree with you about those things. Of course you can trust foreigners too much, as poor Thompson did; but then you can go too far the other way. Aunt Sarah lost a thousand pounds that way. I told her again and again he wasn't a nigger, but she wouldn't believe me. And of course that was just the kind of thing to offend an ambassador, if he *was* an Austrian. It seems to me, Captain, you aren't quite fair to these foreign chaps. Take these Americans now. There were many Americans went by Pebbleswick, you may suppose. But in all the lot there was never a bad lot; never a nasty American, nor a stupid American—nor, well, never an American that I didn't rather like."

"I know," said Dalroy; "you mean there was never an American who did not appreciate 'The Old Ship.'"

"I suppose I do mean that," answered the innkeeper, "and somehow I feel 'The Old Ship' might appreciate the American too."

"You English are an extraordinary lot," said the Irishman, with a sudden and sombre quietude. "I sometimes feel you may pull through after all."

After another silence he said, "You're always right, Hump, and one oughtn't to think of Yankees like that. The rich are the scum of the earth in every country. And a vast proportion of the real Americans are among the most courteous, intelligent, self-respecting people in the world. Some attribute this to the fact that a vast proportion of the real Americans are Irishmen."

Pump was still silent; and the Captain resumed in a moment:

"All the same," he said, "it's very hard for a man, especially a man of a small country like me, to understand how it must feel to be an American; especially in the matter of nationality. I shouldn't like to have to write the American National Anthem; but fortunately there is no great probability of the commission being given. The shameful secret of my inability to write an American patriotic song is one that will die with me."

"Well, what about an English one?" said Pump sturdily. "You might do worse, Captain."

"English, you bloody tyrant!" said Patrick indignantly. "I could no more fancy a song by an Englishman than you could one by that dog."

Mr. Humphrey Pump gravely took the paper from his pocket, on which he had previously inscribed the sin and desolation of grocers; and felt in another of his innumerable pockets for a pencil.

"Hallo," cried Dalroy, "are you going to have a shy at the Ballad of Quoodle?"

Quoodle lifted his ears at his name. Mr. Pump smiled a slight and embarrassed smile. He was secretly proud of Dalroy's admiration for his previous literary attempt, and he had some natural knack for verse as a game, as he had for all games; and his reading, though desultory, had not been merely rustic or low.

"On condition," he said deprecatingly, "that you write a song for the English."

"Oh, very well," said Patrick, with a huge sigh that really indicated the very opposite of reluctance. "We must do something till the thing stops, I suppose, and this seems a blameless parlour game. 'Songs of the Car Club.' Sounds quite aristocratic."

And he began to make marks with a pencil on the fly-leaf of a little book he had in his pocket—Wilson's "Noctes Ambrosianæ." Every now and then, however, he looked up and delayed his own composition by watching Pump and the dog; whose proceedings amused him very much. For the owner of "The Old Ship" sat sucking his pencil and looking at Mr. Quoodle with eyes of fathomless attention. Every now and then he slightly scratched his brown hair with the pencil, and wrote down a word. And the dog Quoodle, with that curious canine power of either understanding, or most brazenly pretending to understand, what is going on, sat erect with his head at an angle, as if he were sitting for his portrait.

Hence it happened that though Pump's poem was a little long, as are often the poems of inexperienced poets, and though Dalroy's poem was very short (being much hurried towards the end) the long poem was finished some time before the short one.

Therefore it was that there was first produced for the world the song more familiarly known as "No Noses"; or more correctly called "The Song of Quoodle." Part of it ran eventually thus:

"They haven't got no noses,
The fallen sons of Eve;
Even the smell of roses
Is not what they supposes;
But more than mind discloses
And more than men believe.

They haven't got no noses,
They cannot even tell
When door and darkness closes
The park a Jew encloses,
Where even the Law of Moses
Will let you steal a smell.

The brilliant smell of water,
The brave smell of a stone,
The smell of dew and thunder,
The old bones buried under,
Are things in which they blunder
And err, if left alone.

The wind from winter forests,
The scent of scentless flowers.
The breath of brides' adorning,
The smell of snare and warning,
The smell of Sunday morning,
God gave to us for ours.

And Quoodle here discloses
All things that Quoodle can,
They haven't got no noses,
They haven't got no noses,
And goodness only knowses
The Noselessness of Man."

This poem also shows traces of haste in its termination; and the present editor (who has no aim save truth) is bound to confess that parts of it were supplied in the criticisms of the Captain; and even enriched (in later and livelier circumstances) by the Poet of the Birds himself. At the actual moment the chief features of this realistic song about dogs was a crashing chorus of "Bow-wow, wow," begun by Mr Patrick Dalroy; but immediately imitated (much more successfully) by Mr. Quoodle. In the face of all this Dalroy suffered some real difficulty in fulfilling the bargain by reading out his much shorter poem about what he imagined an Englishman might feel. Indeed, there was something very rough and vague in his very voice as he read it out; as of one who had not found the key to his problem. The present compiler (who has no aim save truth) must confess that the verses ran as follows:

> "St. George he was for England,
> And before he killed the dragon
> He drank a pint of English ale
> Out of an English flagon.
> For though he fast right readily
> In hair-shirt or in mail,
> It isn't safe to give him cakes
> Unless you give him ale.
>
> St. George he was for England,
> And right gallantly set free
> The lady left for dragon's meat
> And tied up to a tree;
> But since he stood for England
> And knew what England means,
> Unless you give him bacon
> You musn't give him beans.
>
> St. George he is for England,
> And shall wear the shield he wore
> When we go out in armour
> With the battle-cross before.
> But though he is jolly company
> And very pleased to dine,
> It isn't safe to give him nuts
> Unless you give him wine."

"Very philosophical song that," said Dalroy, shaking his head solemnly, "full of deep thought. I really think that is about the truth of the matter, in the case of the Englishman. Your enemies say you're stupid; and you boast of being illogical—which is about the only thing you do that really *is* stupid. As if anybody ever made an Empire or anything else by saying that two and two make five! Or as if any one was ever the stronger for *not* understanding anything—if it were only tip-cat or chemistry. But this *is* true about you, Hump. You English are supremely an artistic people; and therefore you go by associations, as I said in my song. You won't have one thing without the other thing that goes with it. And as you can't imagine a village without a squire and parson, or a college without port and old oak, you get the reputation of a conservative people. But it's because you're sensitive, Hump, not because you're stupid, that you won't part with things. It's lies, lies and flattery, they tell you, Hump, when they tell you you're fond of compromise. I tell ye, Hump, every real revolution is a compromise. D'ye think Wolfe Tone[20] or Charles Stewart Parnell[21] never compromised? But it's just because you're afraid of a compromise that you won't have a revolution. If you really overhauled 'The Old Ship'—or Oxford—you'd have to make up your mind what to take and what to leave. And it would break your heart, Humphrey Pump."

He stared in front of him with a red and ruminant face and at length added, somewhat more gloomily:

"This æsthetic way ye have, Hump, has only two little disadvantages, which I will now explain to you. The first is exactly what has sent us flying in this contraption. When the beautiful, smooth, harmonious thing you've made is worked by a new type, in a new spirit, then I tell you it would be better for you a thousand times to be living

---

[20]Wolfe Tone (1763–1798) was an Irish revolutionist and a founder of the United Irishmen; he asserted Irish independence and wrote a pamphlet promoting union of dissenters with Roman Catholics against the British government (1791).

[21]Charles Stewart Parnell (1846–1891) was an Irish nationalist leader elected to Parliament in 1875 who became leader of the Irish Home Rule faction in 1880. He was noted for, amongst other things, initiating a calculated set of obstructive parliamentary tactics in order to obtain concessions.

under the thousand paper constitutions of Condorcet[22] and Sieyes.[23] When the English oligarchy is run by an Englishman who hasn't got an English mind—then you have Lord Ivywood and all this nightmare, of which God could only guess the end."

The car had beaten some roods of dust behind it, and he ended still more darkly:

"And the other disadvantage, my amiable æsthete, is this. If ever, in blundering about the planet, you come on an island in the Atlantic—Atlantis, let us say—which won't accept *all* your pretty picture—to which you can't give everything—*then*, you will probably decide to give nothing. You will say in your hearts: 'Perhaps they will starve soon': and you will become, for that island, the deafest and the most evil of all the princes of the earth."

It was already daybreak; and Pump, who knew the English boundaries almost by intuition, could tell even through the twilight that the tail of the little town they were leaving behind was of a new sort, the sort to be seen in the western border. The chauffeur's phrase about his mother might merely have been a music-hall joke: but certainly he had driven darkly in that direction.

White morning lay about the grey stony streets like spilt milk. A few proletarian early risers, wearier at morning than most men at night, seemed merely of opinion that it was no use crying over it. The two or three last houses, which looked almost too tired to stand upright, seemed to have moved the Captain into another sleepy explosion.

---

[22] The Marquis de Condorcet (1743–1794) was a French philosopher, mathematician and politician. As a member and president of the Legislative Assembly (1792), he sided with the Girondist Party. Condemned by the Jacobins, he was arrested and died in prison. In his philosophy he proclaimed the idea of progress and the indefinite perfectibility of the human race. Of the former, Chesterton wrote that it was impossible without a standard against which to measure progress, and the latter Chesterton denied absolutely.

[23] Emmanuel Joseph Sieyès (1748–1836), called the Abbe Sieyès, was a French cleric, political theorist and Revolutionary leader. He sympathized with the reform movement preceding the French Revolution and was a prominent Jacobin. He became one of the chief organizers of the coup d'etat, which raised Napoleon to power (1799). He is best known, perhaps, for his answer when asked what he had done during the Revolution: "I survived."

"There are two kinds of idealists, as everybody knows—or must have thought of. There are those who idealize the real and those who (precious seldom) realize the ideal. Artistic and poetical people like the English generally idealize the real. This I have expressed in a song, which——"

"No, really," protested the innkeeper, "really now, Captain——"

"This I have expressed in a song," repeated Dalroy in an adamantine manner, "which I will now sing with every circumstance of leisure, loudness or any other——"

He stopped because the flying universe seemed to stop. Charging hedgerows came to a halt, as if challenged by the bugle. The racing forests stood rigid. The last few tottering houses stood suddenly at attention. For a noise like a pistol-shot from the car itself had stopped all that race, as a pistol-shot might start any other.

The driver clambered out very slowly, and stood about in various tragic attitudes round the car. He opened an unsuspected number of doors and windows in the car, and touched things and twisted things and felt things.

"I must back as best I can to that there garrige, sir," be said, in a heavy and husky tone they had not heard from him before.

Then he looked round on the long woods and the last houses; and seemed to gnaw his lip, like a great general who has made a great mistake. His brow seemed as black as ever; yet his voice, when he spoke again, had fallen many further degrees towards its dull and daily tone.

"Yer see, this is a bit bad," he said. "It'll be a beastly job even at the best plices, if I'm gettin' back at all."

"Getting back," repeated Dalroy, opening the blue eyes of a bull. "Back where?"

"Well, yer see," said the chauffeur reasonably, "I was bloody keen to show 'im it was me drove the car and not 'im. By a bit o' bad luck I done damage to 'is car. Well—if *you* can stick in 'is car——"

Captain Patrick Dalroy sprang out of the car so rapidly that he almost reeled and slipped upon the road. The dog sprang after him, barking furiously.

"Hump," said Patrick quietly, "I've found out everything about you. I know what always bothered me about the Englishman."

Then, after an instant's silence, he said: "That Frenchman was right who said (I forget how he put it) that you march to Trafalgar Square to rid yourself of your temper; not to rid yourself of your tyrant. Our friend was quite ready to rebel, rushing away. To rebel sitting still was too much for him. Do you read *Punch*? I am sure you do. Pump and *Punch* must be almost the only survivors of the Victorian Age. Do you remember an old joke in an excellent picture, representing two ragged Irishmen with guns, waiting behind a stone wall to shoot a landlord? One of the Irishmen says the landlord is late; and adds, 'I hope no accident's happened to the poor gintleman.' Well, it's all perfectly true; I knew that Irishman intimately, but I want to tell you a secret about him. He was an Englishman."

The chauffeur had backed with breathless care to the entrance of the garage; which was next door to a milkman's, or merely separated from it by a black and lean lane, looking no larger than the crack of a door. It must, however, have been larger than it looked; because Captain Dalroy disappeared down it.

He seemed to have beckoned the driver after him: at any rate that functionary instantly followed. The functionary came out again in an almost guilty haste touching his cap and stuffing loose papers into his pocket. Then the functionary returned yet again from what he called the "garrige"; carrying larger and looser things over his arm.

All this did Mr. Humphrey Pump observe, not without interest. The place, remote as it was, was evidently a rendezvous for motorists. Otherwise a very tall motorist, throttled and masked in the most impenetrable degree, would hardly have strolled up to speak to him. Still less would the tall motorist have handed him a similar horrid disguise of wraps and goggles, in a bundle over his arm. Least of all would any motorist, however tall, have said to him from behind the cap and goggles, "Put on these things, Hump, and then we'll go into the milkshop. I'm waiting for the car. Which car, my seeker after truth? Why, the car I'm going to buy for you to drive."

The remorseful chauffeur, after many adventures, did actually find his way back to the little moonlit wood where he had left his master and the donkey. But his master and the donkey had vanished.

XVI

THE SEVEN MOODS OF DORIAN

That timeless clock of all lunatics which was so bright in the sky that night may really have had some elfin luck about it, like a silver penny. Not only had it initiated Mr. Hibbs into the mysteries of Dionysus and Mr. Bullrose into the arboreal habits of his ancestors, but one night of it made a very considerable and rather valuable change in Mr. Dorian Wimpole, the Poet of the Birds. He was a man neither foolish nor evil, any more than Shelley; only a man made sterile by living in a world of indirectness and insincerity; with words rather than with things. He had not had the smallest intention of starving his chauffeur; he did not realize that there was worse spiritual murder in merely forgetting him. But as hour after hour passed over him, alone with the donkey and the moon, he went through a raging and shifting series of frames of mind, such as his cultured friends would have described as moods.

The First Mood, I regret to say, was one of black and grinding hatred. He had no notion of the chauffeur's grievance; and could only suppose he had been bribed or intimidated by the dæmonic donkey-torturers. But Mr. Wimpole was much more capable at that moment of torturing a chauffeur than Mr. Pump had ever been of torturing a donkey: for no sane man can hate an animal. He kicked the stones in the road, sending them flying into the forest; and wished that each one of them was a chauffeur. The bracken by the roadside he tore up by the roots, as representing the hair of the chauffeur; to which it bore no resemblance. He hit with his fist such trees, as (I suppose) seemed in form and expression most reminiscent of the chauffeur; but desisted from this; finding that in this apparently one-sided contest the tree had rather the best of it. But the whole wood and the whole world had become a kind of omnipresent and pantheistic chauffeur, and he hit at him everywhere.

The thoughtful reader will realize that Mr. Wimpole had already taken a considerable upward stride in what he would have called the cosmic scale. The next best thing to really loving a fellow-creature is really hating him: especially when he is a poorer man, separated from you otherwise by mere social stiffness. The desire to murder him is at least an acknowledgment that he is alive. Many a man has owed the first white gleams of the dawn of Democracy in his soul to a desire to find a stick and beat the butler. And we have it on the unimpeachable local authority of Mr. Humphrey Pump that Squire Merriman chased his librarian through three villages with a horse-pistol: and was a Radical ever after.

His rage also did him good merely as a relief; and he soon passed into a second and more positive mood of meditation.

"The damnable monkeys go on like this," he muttered, "and then they call a donkey one of the lower animals. Ride on a donkey, would he? I'd like to see the donkey riding on him for a bit. Good old man."

The patient ass turned mild eyes on him when he patted it, and Dorian Wimpole discovered, with a sort of subconscious surprise, that he really was fond of the donkey. Deeper still in his subliminal self he knew that he had never been fond of an animal before. His poems about fantastic creatures had been quite sincere; and quite cold. When he said he loved a shark, he meant he saw no reason for hating a shark; which was right enough. There is no reason for hating a shark, however much reason there may be for avoiding one. There is no harm in a Craken if you keep it in a tank—or in a sonnet.

But he also realized that his love of creatures had been turned clean round and was working from the other end. The donkey was a companion, and not a monstrosity. It was dear because it was near, not because it was distant. The oyster had attracted him because it was utterly unlike a man; unless it be counted a touch of masculine vanity to grow a beard. The fancy is no idler than that he had himself used, in suggesting a sort of feminine vanity in the permanence of a pearl. But in that maddening vigil among the mystic pines he found himself more and more drawn towards the donkey, because it was more like a man than anything else around him; because it had eyes to see, and ears to hear—the latter even unduly developed.

"He that hath ears to hear, let him hear," he said, scratching those grey, hairy flappers with affection. "Haven't you lifted your ears towards heaven? And will you be the first to hear the Last Trumpet?"

The ass rubbed his nose against him with what seemed almost like a human caress. And Dorian caught himself wondering how a caress from an oyster could be managed. Everything else around him was beautiful but inhuman. Only in the first glory of anger could he really trace in a tall pine-tree the features of an ex-taxi-cabman from Kennington. Trees and ferns had no living ears that they could wag nor mild eyes that they could move. He patted the donkey again.

But the donkey had reconciled him to the landscape; and in his third mood he began to realize how beautiful it was. On a second study, he was not sure it was so inhuman. Rather he felt that its beauty at least was half human; that the aureole of the sinking moon behind the woods was chiefly lovely because it was like the tender-coloured aureole of an early saint; and that the young trees were after all noble because they held up their heads like virgins. Cloudily there crowded into his mind ideas with which it was imperfectly familiar, especially an idea which he had heard called "The Image of God." It seemed to him more and more that all these things, from the donkey to the very docks and ferns by the roadside, were dignified and sanctified by their partial resemblance to something else. It was as if they were baby drawings; the wild, crude sketches of Nature in her first sketch-books of stone.

He had flung himself on a pile of pine-needles to enjoy the gathering darkness of the pine-woods as the moon sank behind them. There is nothing more deep and wonderful than really impenetrable pine-woods, where the nearer trees show against the more shadowy; a tracery of silver upon grey and of grey upon black.

It was, by this time, in pure pleasure and idleness that he picked up a pine-needle to philosophize about it.

"Think of sitting on needles!" he said. "Yet I suppose this is the sort of needle that Eve, in the old legend, used in Eden. Aye, and the old legend was right too! Think of sitting on all the needles in London! Think of sitting on all the needles in Sheffield! Think of sitting on any needles, except on all the needles of Paradise! Oh yes, the old legend was right enough. The very needles of God are softer than the carpets of men."

He took a pleasure in watching the weird little forest animals creeping out from under the green curtains of the wood. He reminded himself that in the old legend they had been as tame as the ass, as well as being as comic. He thought of Adam naming the animals; and said to a beetle, "I should call *you* Budger."

The slugs gave him great entertainment, and so did the worms. He felt a new and realistic interest in them which he had not known before; it was, indeed, the interest that a man feels in a mouse in a dungeon; the interest of any man tied by the leg and forced to see the fascination of small things. Creatures of the wormy kind especially crept out at very long intervals; yet he found himself waiting patiently for hours for the pleasure of their acquaintance. One of them rather specially arrested his eye, because it was a little longer than most worms and seemed to be turning its head in the direction of the donkey's left fore-leg. Also, it had a head to turn, which most worms have not.

Dorian Wimpole did not know much about exact Natural History; except what he had once got up very thoroughly from an encyclopædia for purposes of a sympathetic *vilanelle*. But as this information was entirely concerned with the conjectural causes of laughter in the Hyena, it was not directly helpful in this case. But though he did not know much Natural History, he knew some. He knew enough to know that a worm ought not to have a head; and especially not a squared and flattened head, shaped like a spade or a chisel. He knew enough to know that a creeping thing with a head of that pattern survives in the English countrysides, though it is not common. In short, he knew enough to step across the road and set a sharp and savage boot-heel on the neck and spine of the creature, breaking it into three black bits that writhed once more before they stiffened.

Then he gave out a great explosive sigh. The donkey, whose leg had been in such danger, looked at the dead adder with eyes that had never lost their moony mildness. Even Dorian himself looked at it for a long time, and with feelings he could neither arrest nor understand; before he remembered that he had been comparing the little wood to Eden.

"And even in Eden" he said at last; and then the words of Fitzgerald[24] failed upon his lips.

---

[24]Edward Fitzgerald (1809–1883) was an English scholar and poet most famous for his translated version of *The Rubáiyát of Omar Khayyám* (1859); the passage referred to is from the first edition, line 230: "And who with Eden didst devise the Snake".

And while he was warring with such words and thoughts, something happened about him and behind him, something he had written about a hundred times and read about a thousand; something he had never seen in his life. It flung faintly across the broad foliage a wan and pearly light far more mysterious than the lost moonshine. It seemed to enter through all the doors and windows of the woodland, pale and silent but confident, like men that keep a tryst; soon its white robes had threads of gold and scarlet: and the name of it was morning.

For some time past, loud and in vain, all the birds had been singing to the Poet of the Birds. But when that minstrel actually saw broad daylight breaking over wood and road, the effect on him was somewhat curious. He stood staring at it in gaping astonishment, until it had fulfilled the fullness of its shining fate; and the pinecones and the curling ferns and the live donkey and the dead viper were almost as distinct as they could be at noon, or in a Pre-Raphaelite picture. And then the Fourth Mood fell upon him like a bolt from the blue, and he strode across and took the donkey's bridle, as if to lead it along.

"Damn it all," he cried, in a voice as cheerful as the cock-crow that rang recently from the remote village, "it's not everybody who's killed a snake." Then he added reflectively, "I bet Dr. Gluck never did. Come along, donkey; let's have some adventures."

The finding and fighting of positive evil is the beginning of all fun—and even of all farce. All the wild woodland looked jolly now the snake was killed. It was one of the fallacies of his literary clique to refer all natural emotions to literary names: but it might not untruly be said that he had passed out of the mood of Maeterlinck[25] into the mood of Whitman,[26] and out of the mood of Whitman into the mood

[25] Count Maurice Maeterlinck (1862–1949) was a Belgian poet, dramatist and essayist who published a collection of symbolist poems that reacted against prevailing tendencies of naturalism and realism. His work is characterized by an air of mystery and melancholy.

[26] Walt Whitman (1819–1892) was an American poet most famous for his collection, *Leaves of Grass* (1855), which was much loved by Chesterton. The poems celebrate the liberated spirit in union with nature.

of Stevenson.[27] He had not been a hypocrite when he asked for gilded birds of Asia or purple polypi out of the Southern Seas: he was not a hypocrite now, when he asked for mere comic adventures along a common English road. It was his misfortune and not his fault if his first adventure was his last; and was much too comic to laugh at.

Already the wan morning had warmed into a pale blue and was spotted with those little plump pink clouds which must surely have been the origin of the story that pigs might fly. The insects of the grass chattered so cheerfully that every green tongue seemed to be talking. The skyline on every side was broken only by objects that encouraged such swashbucklering comedy. There was a windmill that Chaucer's Miller[28] might have inhabited, or Cervantes' champion[29] charged. There was an old leaden church spire that might have been climbed by Robert Clive.[30] Away towards Pebbleswick and the sea, there were the two broken stumps of wood which Humphrey Pump declares to this day to have been the stands for an unsuccessful children's swing; but which tourists always accept as the remains of the antique gallows. In the gaiety of such surroundings, it is small wonder if Dorian and the donkey stepped briskly along the road. The donkey reminded him of Sancho Panza.

He did not wake out of this boisterous reverie of the white road and the wind till a motor horn had first hooted and then howled, till the ground had shaken with the shock of a stoppage, and till a human hand fell heavily and tightly on his shoulder. He looked up and saw the complete costume of a police inspector. He did not worry about

[27] Robert Louis Stevenson (1850–1894) was a Scottish novelist, poet and travel writer most famous for his novel *Treasure Island*. Chesterton here moves from the mystical to the increasingly naturalistic and realistic.

[28] "Chaucer's Miller" is a reference to one of the pilgrims in the *Canterbury Tales* of Geoffrey Chaucer (ca. 1342–1400). It is a tale known for its bawdy and riotous humour.

[29] "Cervantes' Champion" is a reference to Spanish novelist and dramatist Miguel de Cervantes' (1547–1626) famous satire on chivalric romances, *Don Quixote*, in which the hero "tilted at windmills" on his trusty steed Rosinante.

[30] Robert Clive, Baron Clive of Plassey (1725–1774) and known as Clive of India, was a British soldier and administrator. The reference is, most likely, to the kind of "daring do" for which Clive was often lauded in *Boys Own*-type stories of the day, though he applies it in an obviously absurd manner.

the face. And there fell on him the Fifth, or Unexpected Mood, which is called by the vulgar Astonishment.

In despair he looked at the motor-car itself that had anchored so abruptly under the opposite hedge. The man at the steering wheel was so erect and unresponsive that Dorian felt sure he was feasting his eyes on yet another policeman. But on the seat behind was a very different figure, a figure that baffled him all the more because he felt certain he had seen it somewhere. The figure was long and slim, with sloping shoulders: and the costume, which was untidy, yet contrived to give the impression that it was tidy on other occasions. The individual had bright yellow hair, one lock of which stuck straight up and was exalted, like the little horn in his favourite scriptures. Another tuft of it, in a bright but blinding manner, fell across and obscured the left optic, as in literal fulfilment of the parable of a beam in the eye. The eyes, with or without beams in them, looked a little bewildered; and the individual was always nervously resettling his necktie. For the individual went by the name of Hibbs, and had only recently recovered from experiences wholly new to him.

"What on earth do you want?" asked Wimpole of the policeman.

His innocent and startled face, and perhaps other things about his appearance, evidently caused the inspector to waver.

"Well, it's about this 'ere donkey, sir," he said.

"Do you think I stole it?" cried the indignant aristocrat. "Well, of all the mad worlds! A pack of thieves steal my Limousine, I save their damned donkey's life at the risk of my own—and *I'm* run in for stealing."

The clothes of the indignant aristocrat probably spoke louder than his tongue; the officer dropped his hand, and after consulting some papers in his hand, walked across to consult with the unkempt gentleman in the car.

"That seems to be a similar cart and donkey," Dorian heard him saying. "But the clothes don't seem to fit your description of the men you saw."

Now Mr. Hibbs had extremely vague and wild recollections of the men he saw. He could not even tell what he had done and what he had merely dreamed. If he had spoken sincerely, he would have described a sort of green nightmare of forests, in which he found himself in the power of an ogre about twelve feet high, with scarlet flames for hair and dressed rather like Robin Hood. But a long course of what is known as "keeping the party together" had made it as unnatural to him to tell any one (even himself) what he really thought about anything, as it would have been to spit—or to sing. He had at present only three motives and strong resolves: (1) not to admit that he had been drunk; (2) not to let any one escape whom Lord Ivywood might possibly want to question; and (3) not to lose his reputation for sagacity and tact.

"This party has a brown velvet suit, you see, and a furred overcoat," the inspector continued. "And in the notes I have from you, you say the man wore a uniform."

"When we say uniform," said Mr. Hibbs, frowning intellectually,—"when we say *uniform*, of course—we must distinguish. Some of our friends who don't quite see eye to eye with us, you know," and he smiled with tender leniency, "some of our friends wouldn't like it called a *uniform*, perhaps. But ... of course ... well, it wasn't a police uniform, for instance. Ha! Ha!"

"I should hope not," said the official shortly.

"So ... in a way ... however," said Hibbs, clutching his verbal talisman at last, "it might be brown velvet in the dark."

The inspector replied to this helpful suggestion with some wonder. "But it was a moon like limelight," he protested.

"Yars, yars," cried Hibbs, in a high tone that can only be described as a hasty drawl. "Yars—discolours everything, of course. The flowers and things——"

"But look here," said the inspector, "you said the principal man's hair was red."

"A blonde type! A blonde type!" said Hibbs, waving his hand with a solemn lightness; "reddish, yellowish brownish sort of hair, you know." Then he shook his head and said with the heaviest solemnity the word was capable of carrying, "Teutonic. Purely Teutonic."

The inspector began to feel some wonder that, even in the confusion following on Lord Ivywood's fall, he had been put under the guidance of this particular guide. The truth was that Leveson, once more masking his own fears under his usual parade of hurry, had found Hibbs at a table by an open window, with wild hair and sleepy eyes, picking himself up with some sort of medicine. Finding him already fairly clear-headed in a dreary way, he had not scrupled to use the remains of his bewilderment to dispatch him with the police in the first pursuit. Even the mind of a semi-recovered drunkard he thought could be trusted to recognize any one so unmistakable as the Captain.

But though the diplomatist's debauch was barely over, his strange, soft fear and cunning were awake. He felt fairly certain the man in the fur coat had something to do with the mystery: as men with fur coats do not commonly wander about with donkeys. He was afraid of offending Lord Ivywood, and at the same time afraid of exposing himself to a policeman.

"You have large discretion," he said gravely. "Very right you should have large discretion in the interests of the public. I think you would be quite authorized, for the present, in preventing the man's escape."

"And the other man?" inquired the officer, with knitted brow. "Do you suppose he has escaped?"

"The *other* man," repeated Hibbs However, regarding the distant windmill through half-closed lids, as if this were a new fine shade introduced into an already delicate question.

"Well, hang it all," said the police officer, "you must know whether there were two men or one."

Gradually it dawned, in a grey dawn of horror, over the brain of Hibbs that this was what he specially couldn't know. He had always heard, and read in comic papers, that a drunken man "sees double" and beholds two lamp-posts, one of which is (as the Higher Critic would have said) purely subjective. For all he knew (being a mere novice) inebriation might produce the impression of the two men of his dream-like adventure, when in truth there had only been one.

"Two men, you know—one man," he said, with a sort of moody carelessness. "Well, we can go into their numbers later: they can't have a very large following." Here he shook his head very firmly.

"Quite impossible. And as the late Lord Goschen[31] used to say, 'You can prove anything by statistics.' "

And here came an interruption from the other side of the road.

"And how long am I to wait here for you and your Goschens, you silly goat?" were the intemperate wood-notes issuing from the Poet of the Birds. "I'm shot if I'll stand this! Come along, donkey, and let's pray for a better adventure next time. These are very inferior specimens of your own race."

And seizing the bridle of the ass again, he strode past them swiftly, and almost as if urging the animal to a gallop.

Unfortunately this disdainful dash for liberty was precisely what was wanting to weigh down the rocking intelligence of the inspector on the wrong side. If Wimpole had stood still a minute or two longer, the official, who was no fool, might have ended in disbelieving Hibbs's story altogether. As it was, there was a scuffle, not without blows on both sides; and eventually the Honourable Dorian Wimpole, donkey and all, was marched off to the village: in which there was a police station; in which was a temporary cell; in which a Sixth Mood was experienced.

His complaints, however, were at once so clamorous and so convincing, and his coat was so unquestionably covered with fur, that after some questioning and cross purposes they agreed to take him in the afternoon to Ivywood House, where there was a magistrate incapacitated by a shot, only recently extracted from his leg.

They found Lord Ivywood lying on a purple ottoman in the midst of his Chinese puzzle of Oriental apartments. He continued to look away as they entered, as if expecting, with Roman calm, the entrance of a recognized enemy. But Lady Enid Wimpole, who was attending to the wants of the invalid, gave a sharp cry of astonishment; and the next moment the three cousins were looking at each other. One could almost have guessed they were cousins, all being (as Mr. Hibbs subtly put it) a blonde type. But two of the blonde type expressed amazement; and one blonde type merely rage.

[31] Lord George Joachim Goschen (1837–1907) was a British statesman, banker and chancellor of the exchequer.

"I am sorry, Dorian," said Ivywood, when he had heard the whole story. "These fanatics are capable of anything, I fear, and you very rightly resent their stealing your car——"

"You are wrong, Philip," answered the poet emphatically. "I do not even faintly resent their stealing my car. What I do resent is the continued existence on God's earth of this Fool" (pointing to the serious Hibbs) "and of that Fool" (pointing to the inspector) "and— yes, by thunder, of *that* Fool too" (and he pointed straight at Lord Ivywood). "And I tell you frankly, Philip, if there really are, as you say, two men who are bent on smashing your schemes and making your life a hell—I am very happy to put my car at their disposal. And now I'm off."

"You'll stop to dinner?" inquired Ivywood, with frigid forgiveness.

"No, thanks," said the disappearing bard; "I'm going up to town."

The Seventh Mood of Dorian Wimpole had a grand finale at the Café Royal: and consisted largely of oysters.

XVII

THE POET IN PARLIAMENT

During the singular entrance and exit of Dorian Wimpole, M. P., J. P., etc., Lady Joan was looking out of the magic casements of that turret room which was now literally, and not only poetically, the last limit of Ivywood House. The old broken hole and black staircase up which the lost dog Quoodle used to come and go, had long ago been sealed up and cemented with a wall of exquisite Eastern workmanship. All through the patterns Lord Ivywood had preserved and repeated the principle that no animal shape must appear. But, like all lucid dogmatists, he perceived all the liberties his dogma allowed him. And he had irradiated this remote end of Ivywood with sun and moon and solar and starry systems, with the Milky Way for a dado and a few comets for comic relief. The thing was well done of its kind (as were all the things that Philip Ivywood got done for him); and if all the windows of the turret were closed with their peacock curtains, a poet with anything like a Hibbsian appreciation of the family champagne might almost fancy he was looking out across the sea on a night crowded with stars. And (what was yet more important) even Misysra (that exact thinker) could not call the moon a live animal without falling into Idolatry.

But Joan, looking out of real windows on a real sky and sea, thought no more about the astronomical wall-paper than about any other wall-paper. She was asking herself in sullen emotionalism, and for the thousandth time, a question she had never been able to decide. It was the final choice between an ambition and a memory. And there was this heavy weight in the scale: that the ambition would probably materialize; and the memory probably wouldn't. It has been the same weight in the same scale a million times, since Satan became the prince of this world. But the evening stars were strengthening over the old seashore: and they also wanted weighing like diamonds.

As once before, at the same stage of brooding, she heard behind her the swish of Lady Enid's skirts, that never came so fast save for serious cause.

"Joan! Please do come! Nobody but you, I do believe, could move him." Joan looked at Lady Enid and realized that the lady was close on crying. She turned a trifle pale and asked quietly for the question. "Philip says he's going to London now, with that leg and all," cried Enid, "and he won't let us say a word."

"But how did it all happen?" asked Joan.

Lady Enid Wimpole was quite incapable of explaining how it all happened, so the task must for the moment devolve on the author. The simple fact was that Ivywood, in the course of turning over magazines on his sofa, happened to look at a paper from the Midlands.

"The Turkish news," said Mr. Leveson, rather nervously, "is on the other side of the page."

But Lord Ivywood continued to look at the side of the paper that did not contain the Turkish news, with the same dignity of lowered eyelids and unconscious brow with which he had looked at the Captain's message when Joan found him by the turret.

On the page covered merely with casual provincial happenings was a paragraph, "Echo of Pebbleswick Mystery. Reported Reappearance of the Vanishing Inn." Underneath was printed in smaller letters:

"An almost incredible report from Wyddington announces that the mysterious 'Sign of the Old Ship' has once more been seen in this country; though it has long been relegated by scientific investigators to the limbo of old rustic superstitions. According to the local version, Mr. Simmons, a dairyman of Wyddington, was serving in his shop, when two motorists entered, one of them asking for a glass of milk. They were in the most impenetrable motoring panoply, with darkened goggles and waterproof collars turned up, so that nothing can be recalled of them personally, except that one was a person of unusual stature. In a few moments this latter individual went out of the shop again and returned with a miserable specimen out of the street, one of the tattered loafers that linger about our most prosperous towns, tramping the streets all night and even begging in defiance of the police. The filth and disease of the creature were so squalid that Mr. Simmons at first refused to serve him with the glass of milk which the taller motorist wished to provide for him. At length, however, Mr. Simmons consented; and was immediately astonished by an incident against which he certainly had a more assured right to protest.

"The taller motorist, saying to the loafer, 'But, man, you're blue in the face'; made a species of sign to the smaller motorist, who there-upon appears to have pierced a sort of cylindrical trunk or chest, that seemed to be his only luggage: and drawn from it a few drops of a yellow liquid, which he deliberately dropped into the ragged crea-ture's milk. It was afterwards discovered to be rum; and the protests of Mr. Simmons may be imagined. The tall motorist, however, warmly defended his action, having apparently some wild idea that he was doing an act of kindness. 'Why, I found the man nearly fainting,' he said. 'If you'd picked him off a raft, he couldn't be more collapsed with cold and sickness. And if you'd picked him off a raft you'd have given him rum—yes, by St. Patrick, if you were a bloody pirate and made him walk the plank afterwards.' Mr. Simmons replied with dig-nity that he did not know how it was with rafts: and could not permit such language in his shop. He added that he would lay himself open to a police prosecution if he permitted the consumption of alcohol in his shop; since he did not display a sign. The motorist then made the amazing reply, 'But you *do* display a sign, you jolly old man. Did you think I couldn't find my way to the sign of "The Old Ship," you sly-boots?' Mr. Simmons was now fully convinced of the intoxication of his visitors; and refusing a glass of rum rather boisterously offered him, went outside his shop to look round for a policeman. To his surprise he found the officer engaged in dispersing a considerable crowd, which was staring up at some object behind him. On looking round (he states in his deposition) he 'saw what was undoubtedly one of the low tavern signs at one time common in England.' He was wholly unable to explain its presence outside his premises, and as it undoubtedly legalized the motorist's action, the police declined to move in the matter.

"*Later.*—The two motorists have apparently left the town un-molested, in a small second-hand two-seater. There is no clue to their destination, except it be indicated by a single incident. It appears that when they were waiting for the second glass of milk, one of them drew attention to a milk-can of a shape seemingly unfamiliar to him;

which was, of course, the Mountain Milk now so much recommended by doctors. The taller motorist (who seemed in every way strangely ignorant of modern science and social life) asked his companion where it came from: receiving, of course, the reply that it is manufactured in the model village of Peaceways, under the personal superintendence of its distinguished and philanthropic inventor, Dr. Meadows. Upon this the taller person, who appeared highly irresponsible, actually bought the whole can; observing, as he tucked it under his arm, that it would help him to remember the address.

"*Later.*—Our readers will be glad to hear that the legend of 'The Old Ship' sign has once more yielded to the wholesome scepticism of science. Our representative reached Wyddington after the practical jokers, or whatever they were, had left; but he searched the whole frontage of Mr. Simmons's shop; and we are in a position to assure the public that there is no trace of the alleged sign."

Lord Ivywood laid down the newspaper and looked at the rich and serpentine embroideries on the wall with the expression that a great general might have if he saw a chance of really ruining his enemy, if he would also ruin all his previous plan of campaign. His pallid and classic profile was as immovable as a cameo: but any one who had known him at all would have known that his brain was going like a motor-car that has broken the speed limit long ago.

Then he turned his head and said, "Please tell Hicks to bring round the long blue car in half an hour; it can be fitted up for a sofa. And ask the gardener to cut a pole of about 4 ft. 9 in., and put a cross-piece for a crutch. I'm going up to London to-night."

Mr. Leveson's lower jaw literally fell with astonishment.

"The doctor said three weeks," he said. "If I may ask, where are you going?"

"St. Stephen's, Westminster," answered Ivywood.

"Surely," said Mr. Leveson, "I could take a message."

"You could take a message," assented Ivywood. "I'm afraid they would not allow you to make a speech."

It was a moment or two afterwards that Enid Wimpole had come into the room; and striven in vain to shake his decision. Then it was that Joan had been brought out of the turret and saw Philip standing sustained upon a crutch of garden timber; and admired him as she had never admired him before. While he was being helped down-stairs; while he was being propped in the car with such limited comfort as was possible, she did really feel in him something worthy of his ancient roots, worthy of such hills and of such a sea. For she felt God's wind from nowhere which is called the Will; and is man's only excuse upon this earth. In the small hoot of the starting motor she could hear a hundred trumpets, such as might have called her ancestors and his to the glories of the Third Crusade.

Such imaginary military honours were not, at least in the strategic sense, undeserved. Lord Ivywood really had seen the whole map of the situation in front of him and swiftly formed a plan to meet it, in a manner not unworthy of Napoleon. The realities of the situation unrolled themselves before him; and his mind was marking them one by one as with a pencil.

First, he knew that Dalroy would probably go to the model village. It was just the sort of place he would go to. He knew Dalroy was almost constitutionally incapable of not kicking up some kind of row in a place of that kind.

Second, he knew that if he missed Dalroy at this address, it was very likely to be his last address: he and Mr. Pump were quite clever enough to leave no more hints behind.

Third, he guessed, by careful consideration of map and clock, that they could not get to so remote a region in so cheap a car under something like two days; nor do anything very conclusive in less than three. Thus, he had just time to turn round in.

Fourth, he realized that ever since that day when Dalroy swung round the sign-board and smote the policeman into the ditch, Dalroy had swung round the Ivywood Act on Lord Ivywood. He (Lord Ivy-wood) had thought, and might well have thought rightly, that by restricting the old sign-posts to a few places so select that they can afford to be eccentric, and forbidding such artistic symbols to all other places, he could sweep fermented liquor for all practical purposes out of the land. The arrangement was exactly that at which all such leg-islation is consciously or unconsciously aiming. A sign-board could be a favour granted by the governing class to itself. If a gentleman wished to claim the liberties of a Bohemian, the path would be open. If a Bohemian wished to claim the liberties of a gentleman, the path would be shut. So gradually, Lord Ivywood had thought, the old signs which can alone sell alcohol will dwindle down to mere curiosities, like rare Tokay or the mead that may still be found in the New Forest. The calculation was by no means unstatesmanlike. But like many other statesmanlike calculations, it did not take into account the idea of dead wood walking about. So long as his flying foes might set up their sign anywhere, it mattered little whether the result was enjoyment or disappointment for the populace. In either case it must mean constant scandal or riot. If there was one thing worse than the appearance of "The Old Ship," it was its disappearance.

He realized that his own law was letting them loose every time: for the local authorities hesitated to act on the spot in defiance of a symbol now so exclusive and therefore impressive. He realized that the law must be altered. Must be altered at once; must be altered, if possible, before the fugitives broke away from the model village of Peaceways.

He realized that it was Thursday. This was the day on which any private member of Parliament could introduce any private Bill of the kind called "non-contentious" and pass it without a division, so long as no particular member made any particular fuss. He realized that it was improbable that any particular member would make any particular fuss about Lord Ivywood's own improvement on Lord Ivywood's own Act

Finally, he realized that the whole case could be met by so slight an improvement as this. Change the words of the Act (which he knew by heart as happier men might know a song), "If such sign be present liquids containing alcohol can be sold on the premises," to these other words, "Liquids containing alcohol can be sold, if previously preserved for three days on the premises"; it was mate in a few moves. Parliament could never reject or even examine so slight an emendation. And the revolution of "The Old Ship" and the late King of Ithaca would be crushed for ever.

It does undoubtedly show, as we have said, something Napoleonic in the man's mind that the whole of this excellent and even successful plan was complete long before he saw the great glowing clock on the towers of Westminster; and knew he was in time.

It was unfortunate, perhaps, that about the same time, or not long after, another gentleman of the same rank, and indirectly of the same family, having left the restaurant in Regent Street and the tangle of Piccadilly, had drifted serenely down Whitehall, and had seen the same great golden goblin's eye on the tall tower of St. Stephen.

The Poet of the Birds, like most æsthetes, had known as little of the real town as he had of the real country. But he had remembered a good place for supper; and as he passed certain great cold clubs built of stone and looking like Assyrian sarcophagi, he remembered that he belonged to many of them. And so when he saw afar off, sitting above the river, what has been very erroneously described as the best club in London, he suddenly remembered that he belonged to that too. He could not at the moment recall what constituency in South England it was that he sat for; but he knew he could walk into the place if he wanted to. He might not so have expressed the matter, but he knew that in an oligarchy things go by respect for persons and not for claims; by visiting-cards and not by voting-cards. He had not been near the place for years, being permanently paired against a famous Patriot who had accepted an important Government appointment in a private madhouse. Even in his silliest days he had never pretended to feel any respect for modern politics; and made all haste to put his "leaders" and the mad Patriot's "leaders" on the well-selected list of the creatures whom man forgets. He had made one really eloquent speech in the House (on the subject of gorillas), and then found he was speaking against his party. It was an indescribable sort of place, anyhow. Even Lord Ivywood did not go to it except to do some business that could be done nowhere else; as was the case that night.

Ivywood was what is called a peer by courtesy; his place was in the Commons and for the time being on the Opposition side. But, though he visited the House but seldom, he knew far too much about it to go into the Chamber itself. He limped into the smoking-room (though he did not smoke), procured a needless cigarette and a much-needed sheet of note-paper; and composed a curt but careful note to the one member of the Government whom he knew must be in the House. Having sent it up to him, he waited.

Outside Mr. Dorian Wimpole also waited, leaning on the parapet of Westminster Bridge and looking down the river. He was becoming one with the oysters in a more solemn and solid sense than he had hitherto conceived possible, and also with a strictly vegetarian beverage which bears the noble and starry name of Nuits. He felt at peace with all things, even in a manner with politics. It was one of those magic hours of evening when the red and golden lights of men are already lit along the river, and look like the lights of goblins, but daylight still lingers in a cold and delicate green. He felt about the river something of that smiling and glorious sadness which two Englishmen have expressed under the figure of the white wood of an old ship fading like a phantom; Turner in painting[32] and Henry Newbolt[33] in poetry. He had come back to earth like a man fallen from the moon; he was at bottom not only a poet but a patriot; and a patriot is always a little sad. Yet his melancholy was mixed up with that immutable yet meaningless faith which few Englishmen, even in modern times, fail to feel at the unexpected sight either of Westminster or of that height on which stands the temple of St. Paul.

> "While flows the sacred river,
> While stands the sacred hill,"

he murmured in some schoolboy echo of the ballad of Lake Regillus.[34]

---

[32] Joseph Mallord William Turner (1775–1851) was an English painter noted for his poetic and dreamlike effects that anticipated the impressionistic schools of painting later in the nineteenth century. The reference here is most likely to his painting "The Fighting Téméraire" (1839). It will be recalled that Chesterton studied at the Slade School of Art in London and wrote books on English artists, some of which are entitled G. F. Watts (1902) and William Blake (1910).

[33] Sir Henry John Newbolt (1862–1938) was an English poet, man of letters and lawyer particularly noted for his poems and ballads on ships and the sea.

[34] The parody is of the ballad "The Battle of Lake Regillus", from Lays of Ancient Rome (1842) by Thomas Babbington Macaulay (1800–1859), English politician, historian and writer. Before beginning his obvious parody, Chesterton begins by incorrectly quoting lines 13 and 14 of the Lay's first stanza which read, "While flows the Yellow River, / While stands the Sacred Hill".

"While flows the sacred river,
While stands the sacred hill,
The proud old pantaloons and nincompoops
Who yawn at the very length of their own lies
in that accursed sanhedrim where
people put each other's hats on in a poisonous room
with no more windows than hell,
Shall have such honour still."

Relieved by this rendering of Macaulay in the style known among his cultured friends as *vers libre*, or poesy set free from the shackles of formal metre, he strolled towards the members' entrance and went in.

Lacking Lord Ivywood's experience, he strolled into the Commons Chamber itself and sat down on a green bench, under the impression that the House was not sitting. He was, however, gradually able to distinguish some six or eight drowsy human forms from the seats on which they sat; and to hear a senile voice with an Essex accent, saying all on one note and without beginning or end, in a manner which it is quite impossible to punctuate:

". . . no wish at all that this proposal should be regarded except in the right way and have tried to put it in the right way and cannot think the honourable member was altogether adding to his reputation in putting it in what those who think with me must of course consider the wrong way and I for one am free to say than if in his desire to settle this great question he takes this hasty course and this revolutionary course about slate pencils he may not be able to prevent the extremists behind him from applying it to lead pencils and while I should be the last to increase the heat and the excitement and the personalities of this debate if I could possibly help it I must confess that in my opinion the honourable gentleman has himself encouraged that heat and personality in a manner that he now doubtless regrets I have no desire to use abusive terms indeed you Mr. Speaker would not allow me of course to use abusive terms but I must tell the honourable member face to face that the perambulators with which he has twitted me cannot be germane to this discussion I should be the last person . . ."

Dorian Wimpole had softly risen to go, when he was arrested by the sight of some one sliding into the House and handing a note to the solitary young man with heavy eyelids who was at that moment governing all England from the Treasury Bench. Seeing him go out, Dorian had a sickening sweetness of hope (as he might have said in his earlier poems) that something intelligible might happen after all, and followed him out almost with alacrity.

The solitary and sleepy governor of Great Britain went down into the lower crypts of its temple of freedom and turned into an apartment where Wimpole was astonished to see his cousin Ivywood sitting at a little table with a large crutch leaning beside him, as serene as Long John Silver. The young man with the heavy eyelids sat down opposite him and they had a conversation, which Wimpole, of course, did not hear. He withdrew into an adjoining room, where he managed to procure coffee and a liqueur; an excellent liqueur which he had forgotten and of which he had more than one glass.

But he had so posted himself that Ivywood could not come out without passing him; and he waited for what might happen with exquisite patience. The only thing that seemed to him queer was that every now and then a bell rang in several rooms at once. And whenever the bell rang, Lord Ivywood nodded; as if he were part of the electrical machinery. And whenever Lord Ivywood nodded the young man turned and sped upstairs like a mountaineer, returning in a short time to resume the conversation. On the third occasion the poet began to observe that many others from the other rooms could be heard running upstairs at the sound of this bell and returning with the slightly less rapid step which expresses relief after a duty done. Yet did he not know that this duty was Representative Government; and that it is thus that the cry of Cumberland or Cornwall can come to the ears of an English king.

Suddenly the sleepy young man sprang erect, uninspired by any bell, and strode out once more. The poet could not help hearing him say as he left the table, jotting down something with a pencil, "Alcohol can be sold if previously preserved for three days on the premises. I think we can do it, but you can't come on for half an hour."

Saying this, he darted upstairs again: and when Dorian saw Ivywood come out laboriously afterwards on his large country crutch, he had exactly the same revulsion in his favour that Joan had had. Jumping up from his table, which was in one of the private dining-rooms, he touched the other on the elbow and said:

"I want to apologize to you, Philip, for my rudeness this afternoon. Honestly, I am sorry. Pine-woods and prison-cells try a man's temper; but I had no rag of excuse for not seeing that neither of them were your fault. I'd no notion you were coming up to town to-night; with your leg and all. You mustn't knock yourself up like this. Do sit down a minute."

It seemed to him that the bleak face of Philip softened a little; how far he really softened will never be known until such men as he are understood by their fellows. It is certain that he carefully unhooked himself from his crutch and sat down opposite his cousin. Whereupon his cousin struck the table so that it rang like a dinner-bell and called out "Waiter!" as if he were in a crowded restaurant. Then, before Lord Ivywood could protest he said:

"It's awfully jolly that we've met. I suppose you've come up to make a speech. I *should* like to hear it. We haven't always agreed; but, by God, if there's anything good left in literature it's your speeches reported in a newspaper. That thing of yours that ended 'death and the last shutting of the iron doors of defeat'—why, you must go back to Strafford's[35] last speech for such English. Do let me hear your speech! I've got a seat upstairs, you know."

"If you wish it," said Ivywood hurriedly, "but I shan't make much of a speech to-night." And he looked at the wall behind Wimpole's head with thunderous wrinkles thickening on his brow. It was essential to his brilliant and rapid scheme, of course, that the Commons should make no comment at all on his little alteration in the law.

An attendant hovered near in response to the demand for a waiter; and was much impressed by the presence and condition of Lord Ivywood. But as that exalted cripple resolutely refused anything in the way of liquor, his cousin was so kind as to have a little more himself, and resumed his remarks.

[35] The reference is to Thomas Wentworth, 1st Earl of Strafford (1593–1641), an English statesman.

"It's about this public-house affair of yours, I suppose. I'd like to hear you speak on that. P'raps I'll speak myself. I've been thinking about it a good deal all day, and a good deal of last night too. Now here's what I should say to the House if I were you. 'To begin with, can you abolish the public-house? Are you *important* enough now to abolish the public-house? Whether it's right or wrong, can you in the long run prevent haymakers having ale any more than you can prevent me having this glass of Chartreuse?'"

The attendant, hearing the word, once more drew near; but heard no further order; or, rather, the orders he heard were such as he was less able to cope with.

"Remember the curate!" said Dorian abstractedly shaking his head at the functionary, "remember the sensible little High Church curate, who when asked for a Temperance Sermon preached on the text 'Suffer us not to be overwhelmed in the water-floods.' Indeed, indeed, Philip, you are in deeper waters than you know. *You* will abolish ale! *You* will make Kent forget hop-poles and Devonshire forget cider! The fate of the Inn is to be settled in that hot little room upstairs! Take care its fate and yours are not settled in the Inn. Take care Englishmen don't sit in judgment on you as they do on many another corpse at an inquest—at a common public-house! Take care that the one tavern that is really neglected and shut up and passed like a house of pestilence, is not the tavern in which I drink to-night; and that merely because it is the worst tavern on the king's highway. Take care this place where we sit does not get a name like any pub where sailors are hocussed or girls debauched. That is what I shall say to them," said he, rising cheerfully, "that's what I shall say. See you to it," he cried, with sudden passion and apparently to the waiter,—"see you to it if the sign that is destroyed is not the sign of 'The Old Ship' but the sign of the Mace and Bauble, and, in the words of a highly historical brewer, if we see a dog bark at your going."

Lord Ivywood was observing him with a deathly quietude; another idea had come into his fertile mind. He knew his cousin, though excited, was not in the least intoxicated; he knew he was quite capable of making a speech and even a good one. He knew that any speech, good or bad, would wreck his whole plan and send the wild inn flying again. But the orator had resumed his seat and drained his glass, passing a hand across his brow. And he remembered that a man who keeps a vigil in a wood all night and drinks wine on the following evening is liable to an accident that is not drunkenness, but something much healthier.

"I suppose your speech will come on pretty soon," said Dorian, looking at the table. "You'll let me know when it does, of course. Really and truly, I don't want to miss it. And I've forgotten all the ways here, and feel pretty tired. You'll let me know?"

"Yes," said Lord Ivywood.

Stillness fell along all the rooms until Lord Ivywood broke it by saying:

"Debate is a most necessary thing: but there are times when it rather impedes than assists parliamentary government."

He received no reply. Dorian still sat as if looking at the table; but his eyelids had lightly fallen; he was asleep. Almost at the same moment the Member of the Government, who was nearly asleep, appeared at the entrance of the long room and made some sort of weary signal.

Philip Ivywood raised himself on his crutch and stood for a moment looking at the sleeping man. Then he and his crutch trailed out of the long room, leaving the sleeping man behind. Nor was that the only thing that he left behind. He also left behind an unlighted cigarette and his honour and all the England of his fathers—everything that could really distinguish that high house beside the river from any tavern for the hocussing of sailors. He went upstairs and did his business in twenty minutes in the only speech he had ever delivered without any trace of eloquence. And from that hour forth he was the naked fanatic; and could feed on nothing but the future.

XVIII

THE REPUBLIC OF PEACEWAYS

In a hamlet round about Windermere, let us say, or somewhere in Wordsworth's country, there could be found a cottage, in which could be found a cottager. So far all is as it should be: and the visitor would first be conscious of a hearty and even noisy elderly man, with an apple face and a short white beard. This person would then loudly proffer to the visitor the opportunity of seeing his father a somewhat more elderly man, with a somewhat longer white beard; but still "up and about." And these two together would then initiate the neophyte into the joys of the society of a grandfather, who was more than a hundred years old, and still very proud of the fact.

The miracle, it seemed, had been worked entirely on milk. The subject of this diet the oldest of the three men continued to discuss in enormous detail. For the rest, it might be said that his pleasures were purely arithmetical. Some men count their years with dismay: and he counted his with a juvenile vanity. Some men collect stamps or coins; and he collected days. Newspaper men interviewed him about the historic times through which he had lived, without eliciting anything whatever; except that he had apparently taken to an exclusive milk diet at about the age when most of us leave it off. Asked if he was alive in 1815, he said that was the very year he found it wasn't any milk, but must be Mountain Milk, like Dr. Meadows says. Nor would his calculating creed of life have allowed him to understand you, if you had said that in a meadowland oversea that lies before the city of Brussels, boys of his old school in that year gained the love of the gods and died young.

It was the philanthropic Dr. Meadows, of course, who discovered this deathless tribe; and erected on it the whole of his great dietic philosophy, to say nothing of the houses and dairies of Peaceways. He attracted many pupils and backers among the wealthy and influential; young men who were, so to speak, training for extreme old age; infant old men; embryo nonagenarians. It would be an exaggeration to say that they watched joyfully for the first white hair as Fascination Fledgeby watched for his first whisker: but it is quite true to say that they seemed to have scorned the beauty of woman and the feasting of friends and above all the old idea of death with glory: in comparison with this vision of the sports of second childhood.

Peaceways was in its essential plan much like what we call a Garden City; a ring of buildings where the workpeople did their work, with a pretty ornamental town in the centre, where they lived in the open country outside. This was no doubt much healthier than the factory system in the great towns and may have partly accounted for the serene expression of Dr. Meadows and his friends, if any part of the credit can be spared from the splendours of Mountain Milk. The place lay far from the common highways of England; and its inhabitants were enabled to enjoy their quiet skies and level woods almost undisturbed, and fully absorb whatever may be valuable in the Meadows method and view; until one day a small and very dirty motor drove into the middle of their town. It stopped beside one of those triangular islets of grass that are common at forked roads: and two men in goggles, one tall and the other short, got out and stood on the central space of grass, as if they were buffoons about to do tricks. As, indeed, they were.

Before entering the town they had stopped by a splendid mountain stream quickening and thickening rapidly into a river; unhelmed and otherwise eased themselves, eaten a little bread bought at Wyddington and drank the water of the widening current which opened on the valley of Peaceways.

"I'm beginning quite to like water," said the taller of the two knights. "I used to think it a most dangerous drink. In theory, of course, it ought only to be given to people who are fainting. It's really good for them, much better than brandy. Besides, think of wasting good brandy on people who are fainting. But I don't go so far as I did: I shouldn't insist on a doctor's prescription before I allowed people water. That was the too severe morality of youth: that was my innocence and goodness. I thought that if I fell once, water-drinking might become a habit. But I do see the good side of water now. How good it is when you're really thirsty; how it glitters and gurgles! How alive it is! After all, it's the best of drinks, after the other. As it says in the song:

"Feast on wine or fast on water,
And your honour shall stand sure,
God Almighty's son and daughter
He the valiant, she the pure;
If an angel out of heaven
Brings you other things to drink,
Thank him for his kind intentions,
Go and pour them down the sink.

Tea is like the East he grows in,
A great yellow Mandarin
With urbanity of manner
And unconsciousness of sin;
All the women, like a harem,
At his pig-tail troop along;
And, like all the East he grows in,
He is Poison when he's strong.

Tea, although an Oriental,
Is a gentleman at least;
Cocoa is a cad and coward,
Cocoa is a vulgar beast,
Cocoa is a dull, disloyal,
Lying, crawling cad and clown,
And may very well be grateful
To the fool that takes him down.

As for all the windy waters,
They were rained like tempests down
When good drink had been dishonoured
By the tipplers of the town;
When red wine had brought red ruin
And the death-dance of our times,
Heaven sent us Soda Water
As a torment for our crimes.

Upon my soul, this water tastes quite nice. I wonder what vintage, now?" and he smacked his lips with solemnity. "It tastes just like the year 1881 tasted."

"You can fancy anything in the tasting way," returned his shorter companion. "Mr. Jack, who was always up to his tricks, did serve plain water in those little glasses they drink liqueurs out of, and every one swore it was a delicious liqueur, and wanted to know where they could get it—all except old Admiral Guffin, who said it tasted too strong of olives. But water's much the best for our game certainly."

Patrick nodded; and then said:

"I doubt if I could do it, if it weren't for the comfort of looking at that," and he kicked the rum-keg, "and feeling we shall have a good swig at it some day. It feels like a fairy-tale, carrying that about—as if rum were a pirates' treasure, as if it were molten gold. Besides, we can have such fun with it with other people—what was that joke I thought of this morning? Oh? I remember! Where's that milk-can of mine?"

For the next twenty minutes he was industriously occupied with his milk-can and the cask; Pump watching him with an interest amounting to anxiety. Lifting his head, however, at the end of that time, he knotted his red brows and said "What's that?"

"What's what?" asked the other traveller.

"That," said Captain Patrick Dalroy, and pointed to a figure approaching on the road parallel to the river. "I mean, what's it for?"

The figure had a longish beard and very long hair falling far below its shoulders. It had a serious and steadfast expression. It was dressed in what the inexperienced Mr. Pump at first took to be its night-gown; but afterwards learned to be its complete goats' hair tunic, unmixed even with a thread of the destructive and deadly wool of the sheep. It had no boots on its feet. It walked very swiftly to a particular turn of the stream and then turned very sharply (since it had accomplished its constitutional) and walked back towards the perfect town of Peaceways.

"I suppose it's somebody from that milk place," said Humphrey Pump indulgently. "They seem to be pretty mad."

"I don't mind that so much," said Dalroy; "I'm mad myself some-times. But a madman has only one merit and last link with God. A madman is always logical. Now what is the logical connexion between living on milk and wearing your hair long? Most of us lived on milk when we had no hair at all. How do they connect it up? Are there any heads even for a synopsis? Is it, say, 'milk—water—shaving-water—shaving—hair?' Is it milk—kindness—unkindness—convicts—hair?'

What is the logical connexion between having too much hair and having far too few boots? What *can* it be? Is it 'hair—hair-trunk—leather-trunk—leather-boots?' Is it 'hair—beard—oysters—seaside—paddling—no boots?' Man is liable to err—especially when every mistake he makes is called a movement—but why should all the lunacies live together?"

"Because all the lunatics should live together," said Humphrey, "and if you'd seen what happened up at Crampton, with the farming-out idea, you'd know. It's all very well, Captain; but if people can prevent a guest of great importance being buried up to the neck in farm manure, they will. They will, really." He coughed almost apologetically. He was about to attempt a resumption of the conversation, when he saw his companion slap the milk-can and keg back into the car; and get into it himself. "You drive," he said,—"drive me where those things live; you know, Hump."

They did not, however, arrive in the civic centre of such things without yet another delay. They left the river and followed the man with the long hair and the goatshair frock; and he stopped, as it happened, at a house on the outskirts of the village. The adventurers stopped also, out of curiosity; and were at first relieved to see the man almost instantly reappear having transacted his business with a quickness that seemed incredible. A second glance showed them it was not the man, but another man dressed exactly like him. A few minutes more of inquisitive delay, showed them many of the milky and goatish sect going in and out of this particular place, each clad in his innocent uniform.

"This must be the temple and chapel," muttered Patrick; "it must be here they sacrifice a glass of milk to a cow, or whatever it is they do. Well, the joke is pretty obvious; but we must wait for a lull in the crowding of the congregation."

When the last long-haired phantom had faded up the road, Dalroy sprang from the car and drove the sign-board deep into the earth with savage violence and then very quietly knocked at the door.

The apparent owner of the place, of whom the two last of the long-haired and bare-footed idealists were taking a rather hurried farewell, was a man curiously ill-fitted for the part he seemed cast for in the only possible plot.

Both Pump and Dalroy thought they had never seen a man look so sullen. His face was of the rubicund sort that does not suggest jollity, but merely a stagnant indigestion in the head. His moustache hung heavy and dark, his brows yet heavier and darker. Dalroy had seen something of the sort on the faces of defeated peoples disgracefully forced into submission; but he could not make head or tail of it in connexion with the priggish perfections of Peaceways. It was all the odder because he was manifestly prosperous: his clothes were smartly cut in something of the sporting manner: and the inside of his house was at least four times grander than the outside.

But what mystified them most was this; that he did not so much exhibit the natural curiosity of a gentleman whose private house is entered by strangers, but rather an embarrassed and restless expectation. During Dalroy's eager apologies and courteous inquiries about the direction and accommodations of Peaceways, the man's eye (which was of the boiled gooseberry order) perpetually wandered from them to the cupboard and then again to the window: and at last he got up and went to look out into the road.

"Oh, yes, sir; very healthy place Peaceways," he said, peering through the lattice. "Very ... dash it, what they mean? ... Very healthy place. Of course they have their little ways."

"Only drink pure milk, don't they?" asked Dalroy.

The householder looked at him with a rather wild eye and grunted.

"Yes; so they say." And he went again to the window.

"I've bought some of it," said Patrick, patting his pet milk-can, which he carried under his arm, as if unable to be separated from Dr. Meadows's discovery. "Have a glass of milk, sir."

The man's boiled eye began to bulge in anger—or some other emotion.

"What you want?" he muttered; "are you 'tecs or what?"

"Agents and distributors of the Meadows Mountain Milk," said the Captain, with simple pride. "Taste it?"

The dazed householder took a glass of the blameless liquid and sipped it: and the change on his face was extraordinary.

"Well, I'm jiggered!" he said, with a broad and rather coarse grin. "That's a queer dodge. You're in the joke, I see." Then he went again restlessly to the window; and added:

"But if we're all friends, why the blazes don't the others come in? I've never known trade so slow before."

"Who are the others?" asked Mr. Pump.

"Oh, the usual Peaceways people," said the other. "They generally come here before work. Dr. Meadows don't work them for very long hours, that wouldn't be healthy or whatever he calls it: but he's particular about their being punctual. I've seen 'em running, with all their pure-minded togs on, when the hooter gave the last call."

Then he abruptly opened the front door and called out impatiently but not loudly:

"Come along in, if you're coming. You'll give the show away if you play the fool out there."

Patrick looked out also and the view of the road outside was certainly rather singular. He was used to crowds, large and small, collecting outside houses which he had honoured with the sign of "The Old Ship"; but they generally stared up at it in unaffected wonder and amusement. But outside this open door, some twenty or thirty persons in what Pump had called their night-gowns were moving to and fro like somnambulists, apparently blind to the presence of the sign; looking at the other side of the road, looking at the horizon, looking at the clouds of morning; and only occasionally stopping to whisper to each other. But when the owner of the house called to one of these ostentatiously abstracted beings and asked him hoarsely what the devil was the matter, it was natural for the milk-fed one to turn his feeble eye towards the sign. The gooseberry eyes followed his; and the face to which they belonged was a study in apoplectic astonishment.

"What the hell have you done to my house?" he demanded. "Of course they can't come in if this thing's here."

"I'll take it down, if you like," said Dalroy, stepping out and picking it up like a flower from the front garden (to the amazement of the men in the road, who thought they had strayed into a nursery fairy-tale), "but I wish, in return, you'd give me some idea of what the blazes all this means."

"Wait till I've served these men," replied his host

The goat-garbed persons went very sheepishly (or goatishly) into the now signless building; and were rapidly served with raw spirits, which Mr. Pump suspected to be of no very superior quality. When the last goat was gone, Captain Dalroy said:

"I mean that all this seems to me topsy-turvy. I understood that as the law stands now, if there's a sign they are allowed to drink and if there isn't they aren't."

"The law!" said the man, in a voice thick with scorn. "Do you think these poor brutes are afraid of the law as they are of the Doctor?"

"Why should they be afraid of the Doctor?" asked Dalroy innocently. "I always heard that Peaceways was a self-governing republic."

"Self-governing be damned!" was the illiberal reply. "Don't he own all the houses and could turn 'em out in a snow-storm? Don't he pay all the wages and could starve 'em stiff in a month? The law!" And he snorted.

A moment after he squared his elbows on the table and began to explain more fully:

"I was a brewer about here and had the biggest brewery in these parts. There were only two houses which didn't belong to me, and the magistrates took away their licences after a time. Ten years ago you could see Hugby's Ales written beside every sign in the county. Then came these cursed Radicals and our leader Lord Ivywood must go over to their side about it; and let this Doctor buy all the land under some new law that there shan't be any pubs. at all. And so my business is ruined so that he can sell his milk. Luckily I'd done pretty well before and had some compensation, of course; and I still do a fair trade on the Q. T., as you see. But of course that don't amount to half the old one, for they're afraid of old Meadows finding out. Snuffling old blighter!"

And the gentleman with the good clothes spat on the carpet.

"I am a Radical myself," said the Irishman rather coldly; "for all information on the Conservative party I must refer you to my friend Mr. Pump, who is, of course, in the inmost secrets of his leaders. But it seems to me very rum sort of Radicalism to eat and drink at the orders of a master who is a madman, merely because he's also a millionaire. O Liberty, what very complicated and even unsatisfactory social developments are committed in thy name! Why don't they kick the old ass round the town a bit? No boots? Is that why they're allowed no boots? Oh, roll him downhill in a milk-can: he can't object to that."

"I don't know," said Pump, in his ruminant way, "Master Christian's aunt did; but ladies are more particular, of course."

"Look here!" cried Dalroy, in some excitement. "If I stick up that sign outside, and stay here to help, will you defy them? You'd be strictly within the law, and any private coercion I can promise you they shall repent. Plant the sign and sell the stuff openly like a man; and you may stand in English history like a deliverer."

Mr. Hugby of Hugby's Ales only looked gloomily at the table. His was not the sort of drinking nor the sort of drink-selling on which the revolutionary sentiment flourishes.

"Well," said the Captain, "will you come with me and say, 'Hear, hear!' and 'How true!'—'What matchless eloquence!' if I make a speech in the market-place? Come along! There's room in our car."

"Well, I'll come with you, if you like," replied Mr. Hugby heavily. "It's true if yours is allowed we might get our trade back too." And putting on a silk hat he followed the Captain and the innkeeper out to their little car. The model village was not an appropriate background for Mr. Hugby's silk hat. Indeed, the hat somehow seemed to bring out by contrast all that was fantastic in the place.

It was a superb morning, some hours after sunrise. The edges of the sky touching the ring of dim woods and distant hills were still jewelled with the tiny transparent clouds of daybreak, delicate red and green or yellow. But above the vault of heaven rose through turquoise into a torrid and solid blue in which the other clouds, the colossal cumuli, tumbled about like a celestial pillow-fight. The bulk of the houses were as white as the clouds, so that it looked (to use another simile) as if some of the whitewashed cottages were flying and falling about the sky. But most of the white houses were picked out here and there with bright colours, here an ornament in orange or there a stripe of lemon-yellow, as if by the brush of a baby giant. The houses had no thatching (thatching is not hygienic) but were mostly covered with a sort of peacock-green tiles bought cheap at a Pre-Raphaelite Bazaar: or less frequently by some still more esoteric sort of terra-cotta bricks. The houses were not English nor homelike nor suited to

the landscape; for the houses had not been built by free men for themselves, but at the fancy of a whimsical lord. But considered as a sort of
elfin city in a pantomime, it was a really picturesque background for
pantomimic proceedings.

I fear Mr. Dalroy's proceedings from the first rather deserved that
name. To begin with he left the sign, the cask, and the keg all wrapped
and concealed in the car, but removed all the wraps of his own disguise, and stood on the central patch of grass in that green uniform
that looked all the more insolent for being as ragged as the grass. Even
that was less ragged than his red hair, which no red jungle of the East
could imitate. Then he took out, almost tenderly, the large milk-can:
and deposited it, almost reverently, on the island of turf. Then he
stood beside it, like Napoleon beside a gun; with an expression of
tremendous seriousness and even severity. Then he drew his sword,
and with that flashing weapon as with a flail lashed and thrashed the
echoing metal can till the din was deafening, and Mr. Hugby hastily
got out of the car and withdrew to a slight distance, stopping his ears.
Mr. Pump sat solidly at the steering wheel, well knowing it might be
necessary to start in some haste.

"Gather, gather, gather, Peaceways!" shouted Patrick, still banging
on the can and lamenting the difficulties of adapting "Macgregor's
Gathering" to the name and occasion. "We're landless, *landless*, Landless, Peaceways!"

Two or three of the goat-clad, recognizing Mr. Hugby with a guilty
look, drew near with great caution; and the Captain shouted at them
as if they were an army covering Salisbury Plain.

"Citizens," he roared, saying anything that came into his head, "try
the only original unadulterated Mountain Milk for which alone Mahomet came to the mountain. The original milk of the land flowing
with milk and honey; the high quality of which could alone have
popularized so unappetizing a combination. Try our milk! None others are genuine! Who can do without milk? Even whales can't do
without milk. If any lady or gentleman keeps a favourite whale at
home, now's their chance! The early whale catches the milk. Just look
at our milk! If you say you can't look at the milk, because it's in the
can—well, look at the can! You must look at the can! You simply

must! When Duty whispers low, 'Thou Must!'" he bellowed at the top of his voice in a highly impromptu peroration,—"when Duty whispers low, 'Thou Must!' the Youth replies, 'I can!'" And with the word "Can" he hit the can with a shocking and shattering noise, like a peal of demoniac bells of steel.

This introductory speech is open to criticism from those who regard it as intended for the study rather than the stage. The present chronicler (who has no aim save truth) is bound to record that for its own unscrupulous purpose it was extremely successful: a great mass of the citizens of Peaceways having been attracted by the noise of one man shouting like a crowd. There are crowds who do not care to revolt; but there are no crowds who do not like some one else to do if for them; a fact which the safest oligarchs may be wise to learn.

But Dalroy's ultimate triumph (I regret to say) consisted in actually handing to a few of the foremost of his audience some samples of his blameless beverage. The fact was certainly striking. Some were paralysed with surprise. Some were abruptly broken double with laughter. Many chuckled. Some cheered. All looked radiantly towards the eccentric orator.

And yet the radiance died quietly and suddenly from their faces. And only because one little old man had joined the group; a little old man in white linen with a white, pointed beard and a white powderpuff of hair like thistledown: a man whom almost every man present could have killed with the left arm.

XIX

THE HOSPITALITY OF THE CAPTAIN

Dr. Moses Meadows, whether that was his name or an Anglicized version of it, had certainly come in the first instance from a little town in Germany, and his first two books were written in German. His first two books were his best: for he began with a genuine enthusiasm for physical science, and this was adulterated with nothing worse than a hatred of what he thought was superstition, and what many of us think is the soul of the State. The first enthusiasm was most notable in the first book, which was concerned to show that the, in the female, not upsprouting of the whiskers was from the therewith increasing arrested mentality derived. In his second book he came more to grips with delusions; and for some time he was held to have proved (to every one who agreed with him already) that the Time Ghost had been walking particularly rapidly lately; and that the Christus Mythus was by the alcoholic mind's trouble explained. Then, unfortunately, he came across the institution called Death, and began to argue with it. Not seeing any rational explanation of this custom of dying, so prevalent among his fellow-citizens, he concluded that it was merely traditional (which he thought meant "effete"), and began to think of nothing but ways of evading or delaying it. This had a rather narrowing effect on him; and he lost much of that acrid ardour which had humanized the atheism of his youth, when he would almost have committed suicide for the pleasure of taunting God with not being there. His later idealism grew more and more materialist; and consisted of his changing hypotheses and discoveries about the healthiest foods. There is no need to detain the reader over what has been called his Oil Period; his Seaweed Period has been authoritatively expounded in Professor Nym's valuable little work; and on the events of his Glue Period it is perhaps not very generous to dwell. It was during his prolonged stay in England that he chanced on the instance of the longevity of milk consumers; and built on it a theory which was, at the beginning at least, sincere. Unfortunately it was also successful:

wealth flowed in to the inventor and proprietor of Mountain Milk; and he began to feel a fourth and last enthusiasm, which also can come late in life and have a narrowing effect on the mind.

In the altercation which naturally followed on his discovery of the antics of Mr. Patrick Dalroy, he was very dignified but naturally not very tolerant; for he was quite unused to anything happening in spite of him, or anything important even happening without him, in the land that lay around. At first he hinted severely that the Captain had stolen the milk-can from the milk-producing premises, and sent several workmen to count the cans in each shed; but Dalroy soon put him right about that.

"I bought it in a shop at Wyddington," he said. "And since then I have used no other. You'll hardly believe me," he said, with some truth, "but when I went into that shop I was quite a little man. I had one glass of your Mountain Milk; and look at me now."

"You have no right to sell the milk here," said Dr. Meadows, with the faintest trace of a German accent. "You are not in my employment. I am not responsible for your methods. You are not a representative of the business."

"I'm an Advertisement," said the Captain. "We advertise you all over England. You see that lean, skimpy little man over there," pointing to the indignant Mr. Pump. "He's Before Taking Meadows' Mountain Milk. I'm After," added Mr. Dalroy, with satisfaction.

"You shall laugh at the magistrate," said the other, with a thickening accent.

"I shall," agreed Patrick. "Well, I'll make a clean breast of it, sir. The truth is, it isn't your milk at all. It has quite a different taste. These gentlemen will tell you so."

A smothered giggle sent all the blood to the eminent capitalist's face.

"Then either you have stolen my can and are a thief," he said, stamping, "or you have introduced inferior substances into my discovery and are an adulterer—er——"

"Try adulteratist," said Dalroy kindly. "Prince Albert always said 'adulteratarian'. Dear old Albert! It seems like yesterday! But it is, of course, to-day. And it's as true as daylight that this stuff tastes different. I can't tell you what the taste is" (subdued guffaws from the out-skirts of the crowd). "It's something between the taste of your first sugar-stick and the fag-end of your father's cigar. It's as innocent as heaven and as hot as hell. It tastes like a paradox. It tastes like a pre-historic inconsistency—I trust I make myself clear. The men who taste it most are the simplest men that God has made, and it always reminds them of the salt; because it is made out of sugar. Have some!"

And with a gesture of staggering hospitality, he shot out his long arm with the little glass at the end of it. The despotic curiosity of the Prussian overcame even his despotic dignity. He took a sip of the liquid; and his eyes stood out from his face.

"You've been mixing something with the milk," were the first words that came to him.

"Yes," answered Dalroy, "and so have you, unless you're a swindler. Why is your milk advertised as different from every one else's milk, if you haven't made the difference? Why does a glass of your milk cost threepence; and a glass of ordinary milk a penny, if you haven't put twopennorth of something into it? Now, look here, Dr. Meadows. The Public Analyst who would judge this happens to be an honest man. I have a list of the twenty-one and a half honest men still employed in such posts. I make you a fair offer. He shall decide what it is I add to the milk, if you let him decide what it is you add to the milk. You must add something to the milk: or what can all these wheels and pumps and pulleys be for? Will you tell me, here and now, what you add to the milk which makes it so exceedingly Mountain?"

There was a long silence, full of the same sense of submerged mirth in the mob. But the philanthropist had fallen into a naked frenzy in the sunlight; and shaking his fists aloft in a way unknown to all the English around him, he cried out:

"Ach! but I know what you add! I know what you add! It is the Alcohol! And you have no sign, and you shall laugh at a magistrate."

Dalroy, with a bow, retired to the car, removed a number of wrap-pings and produced the prodigious wooden sign-post of "The Old Ship," with its blue three-decker and red St. George's cross conspic-uously displayed. This he planted on his narrow territory of turf and looked round serenely.

"In this old oak-panelled inn of mine," he said, "I will laugh at a million magistrates. Not that there's anything unhygienic about this inn. No low ceilings or stuffiness here. Windows open everywhere, except in the floor. And as I hear some are saying there ought always to be food sold with fermented liquor, why, my dear Dr. Meadows, I've got a cheese here that will make another man of you. At least, we'll hope so. We can but try."

But Dr. Meadows was long past being merely angry. The exhibition of the sign had put him into a serious difficulty. Like most sceptics, like even the most genuine sceptics such as Bradlaugh,[36] he was as legal as he was sceptical. He had a profound fear, which also had in it something better than fear, of being ultimately found in the wrong in a police-court or a public inquiry. And he also suffered the tragedy of all such men living in modern England; that he must always be certain to respect the law, while never being certain of what it was. He could only remember generally that Lord Ivywood, when introducing or defending the great Ivywood Act on this matter, had dwelt very strongly on the unique and significant nature of the sign. And he could not be certain that if he disregarded it altogether, he might not eventually be cast in heavy damages—or even go to prison, in spite of his success in business. Of course he knew quite well that he had a thousand answers to such nonsense: that a patch of grass in the road couldn't be an inn; that the sign wasn't even produced when the Captain began to hand round the rum. But he also knew quite well that in the black peril we call British law, that is not the point. He had heard points quite as obvious urged to a judge, and urged in vain. At the bottom of his mind he found this fact. Rich as he was, Lord Ivywood had made him—and on which side would Lord Ivywood be?

"Captain," said Humphrey Pump, speaking for the first time, "we'd better be getting away. I feel it in my bones."

"Inhospitable innkeeper!" cried the Captain indignantly. "And after I have gone out of the way to license your premises! Why, this is the

---

[36]Charles Bradlaugh (1833–1891) was an English politician, radical secularist and religious sceptic. He was an advocate of birth control and published a pamphlet on this subject for which he was prosecuted, unsuccessfully, for obscenity.

dawn of peace in the great city of Peaceways. I don't despair of Dr. Meadows tossing off another bumper before we've done. For the moment, Brother Hugby will engage."

As he spoke, he served out milk and rum at random; and still the Doctor had too much terror of our legal technicalities to make a final interference. But when Mr. Hugby of Hugby's Ales heard his name called, he first of all jumped so as almost to dislodge the silk hat: then he stood quite still. Then he accepted a glass of the new Mountain Milk: and then his very face became full of speech, before he had spoken a word.

"There's a motor coming along the road from the far hills," said Humphrey quietly. "It'll be across the last bridge down-stream in ten minutes and come up on this side."

"Well," said the Captain impatiently, "I suppose you've seen a motor before."

"Not in this valley all this morning," answered Pump.

"Mr. Chairman," said Mr. Hugby, feeling a dim disposition to say "Mr. Vice," in memory of old commercial banquets. "I'm sure we're all law-abiding people here; and wish to remain friends, especially with our good friend the Doctor: may he never want a friend or a bottle—that is, in short, anything he wants. As we go up the hill of prosperity and so on. But as our friend here with the sign-board seems to be within his rights, well, I think the time's come when we can look at these things more broadly, so to speak. Now I know it's quite true those dirty little pubs. do a lot of harm to a property, and you get a lot of ignorant people there who are just like pigs; and I don't say our friend the Doctor hasn't done good by clearing 'em away. But a big, well-managed business with plenty of capital behind it is quite another thing. Well, friends, you all know that I was originally in the Trade; though I have, of course, left off selling under the new regulations." Here the goats looked rather guiltily at their cloven hooves. "But I've got my little bit and I wouldn't mind putting it into this 'Old Ship' here, if our friend would allow it to be run on business lines. And especially if he'd enlarge the premises a bit. Ha! Ha! And if our good friend the Doctor——"

"You rascal fellow!" spluttered Meadows, "your goot friend the Doctor will make you dance before a magistrate."

"Now, don't be unbusinesslike," reasoned the brewer. "It won't hurt your sales. It's quite a different public don't you see? Do talk like a business man."

"I am not a business man," said the scientist, with a fiery eye. "I am a servant of humanity."

"Then," said Dalroy, "why do you never do what your master tells you?"

"The motor has crossed the river," said Humphrey Pump.

"You would undo all my works," cried the Doctor, with sincere passion. "When I have built this town myself, when I have made it sober and healthful myself, when I am awake and about before any one in the town myself, watching over its interests—you would ruin all to sell your barbaric and fundamentally beastly beer. And then you call me a goot friend. I am not a goot friend!"

"That I can't say," growled Hugby. "But if it comes to that—aren't you trying to sell——"

A motor-car drove up with a white explosion of dust; and about six very dusty people got out of it. Even through the densest disguise of the swift motorist Pump perceived in many of them the peculiar style and bodily carriage of the police. The most evident exception was a long and more slender figure, which, on removing its cap and goggles, disclosed the dark and drooping features of J. Leveson, Secretary. He walked across to the little old millionaire, who instantly recognized him and shook hands. They confabulated for some little time, turning over some official documents. Dr. Meadows cleared his throat and said to the whole crowd:

"I am very glad to be able to announce to you all that this extraordinary outrage has been too late attempted. Lord Ivywood, with the promptitude he so invariably shows, has immediately communicated to places of importance such as this a most just and right alteration of the law, which exactly meets the present case."

"We shall sleep in jail to-night," said Humphrey Pump. "I knew it in my bones."

"It is enough to say," proceeded the millionaire, "that by the law as it now stands any innkeeper, even if he display a sign, is subject to imprisonment if he sells alcohol on premises where it has not been previously kept for three days."

"I thought it would be something like that," muttered Pump. "Shall we give up, Captain, or shall we try a bolt for it?"

Even the impudence of Dalroy appeared for the instant dazed and stilled. He was staring forlornly up into the abyss of sky above him; as if, like Shelley, he could get inspiration from the last and purest clouds and the perfect hues of the ends of heaven.

At last he said in a soft and meditative voice, the single syllable: "Sells!"

Pump looked at him sharply, with a remarkable expression growing on his grim face. But the Doctor was far too rapidly rejoicing in his triumph to understand the Captain's meaning.

"Sells alcohol are the exact words," he insisted, brandishing the blue oblong of the new Act of Parliament.

"So far as I am concerned they are inexact words," said Captain Dalroy, with polite indifference. "I have not been selling alcohol; I have been giving it away. Has anybody here paid me money? Has anybody here seen anybody else pay me money? I'm a philanthropist just like Dr. Meadows. I'm his living image."

Mr. Leveson and Dr. Meadows looked across at each other, and on the face of the first was consternation and of the second a full return of all his terrors of the complicated law.

"I shall remain here for several weeks," continued the Captain, leaning elegantly on the can, "and shall give away gratis such supplies of this excellent drink as may be demanded by the citizens. It appears that there is no such supply at present in this district; and I feel sure that no person present can object to so strictly legal and highly charitable an arrangement."

In this he was apparently in error; for several persons present seemed to object to it. But curiously enough it was not the withered and fanatical face of the philanthropist Meadows, nor the dark and equine face of the official Leveson, which stood out most vividly as a picture of protest. The face most strangely unsympathetic with this form of charity was that of the ex-proprietor of Hugby's Ales. His gooseberry eyes were almost dropping from his head and his words sprang from his lips before he could stop them.

"And you blooming well think you can come here like a big buffoon, you beast, and take away all my trade——"

Old Meadows turned on him with the swiftness of an adder.

"And what is your trade, Mr. Hugby?" he asked.

The brewer bubbled with a sort of bursting anger. The goats all looked at the ground as is, according to a Roman poet, the habit of the lower animals. Man (in the character of Mr. Patrick Dalroy) taking advantage of a free but fine translation of the Latin passage, "looked aloft and with uplifted eyes, beheld his own hereditary skies."

"Well, all I can say is," roared Mr. Hugby, "if the police come all this way and can't lock up a dirty loafer whose coat's all in rags, there's an end of me paying these fat infernal taxes and——"

"Yes," said Dalroy, in a voice that fell like an axe, "there is an end of you, please God. It's brewers like you that have made the inns stink with poison, till even good men asked for no inns at all. And you are worse than the teetotallers, for you perverted what they never knew. And as for you, eminent man of science, great philanthropist, idealist and destroyer of inns, let me give one cold fact for your information. You are not respected. You are obeyed. Why should I or any one respect you particularly? You say you built this town and get up at daybreak to watch this town. You built it for money and you watch it for more money. Why should I respect you because you are fastidious about food, that your poor old digestion may outlive the hearts of better men? Why should you be the god of this valley, whose god is your belly, merely because you do not even love your god, but only fear him? Go home to your prayers, old man; for all men shall die. Read the Bible, if you like, as they do in your German home; and I suppose you once read it to pick texts, as you now read it to pick holes. I don't read it myself, I'm afraid, but I remember some words in old Mulligan's translation; and I leave them with you. 'Unless God'"—and he made a movement with his arm, so natural and yet so vast that for an instant the town really looked like a toy of bright-coloured cardboard at the feet of the giant,—"'unless God build the city, their labour is but lost that build it; unless God keep the city, the watchman watcheth in vain. It is lost labour that you rise up early in the morning and eat the bread of carefulness; for He giveth His beloved sleep.' Try and understand what that means; and never mind whether it's Elohistic. And now, Hump, we'll away and away. I'm tired of the green tiles over there. Come, fill up my cup," and he banged down the cask in the car. "Come, fill up my can!" and he banged down the can.

> "Come, saddle my horses and call out my men.
> And tremble, gay goats, in the midst of your glee;
> For you've no' seen the last of my milk-can and me."

This song was joyously borne away with Mr. Dalroy in the disappearing car; and the motorists were miles beyond pursuit from Peaceways before they thought of halting again. But they were still beside the bank of that noble and enlarging river; and in a place of deep fern and fairy-ribboned birches with the glooming and gleaming water behind them, Patrick asked his friend to stop the car.

"By the way," said Humphrey suddenly, "there was one thing I didn't understand. Why was he so afraid of the Public Analyst? What poison and chemicals does he put in the milk?"

"H_2O," answered the Captain, "I take it without milk myself."

And he bent over as if to drink of the stream, as he had done at daybreak.

XX

THE TURK AND THE FUTURISTS

Mr. Adrian Crooke was a successful chemist whose shop was in the neighbourhood of Victoria; but his face expressed more than is generally required in a successful chemist. It was a curious face, prematurely old and like parchment, but acute and decisive, with real headwork in every line of it. Nor was his conversation, when he did converse, out of keeping with this: he had lived in many countries, and had a rich store of anecdote about the more quaint and sometimes the more sinister side of his work, visions of the vapour of Eastern drugs or guesses at the ingredients of Renaissance poisons. He himself, it need hardly be said, was a most respectable and reliable apothecary, or he would not have had the custom of families, especially among the upper classes; but he enjoyed as a hobby the study of the dark days and lands where his science had lain sometimes on the borders of magic and sometimes upon the borders of murder. Hence it often happened that persons who in their serious senses were well aware of his harmless and useful habits, would leave his shop on some murky and foggy night, with their heads so full of wild tales of the eating of hemp or the poisoning of roses, they could hardly help fancying that the shop, with its glowing moon of crimson or saffron, like bowls of blood and sulphur, was really a house of the Black Art.

It was doubtless for such conversational pleasures in part that Hibbs However entered the shop; as well as for a small glass of the same restorative medicine which he had been taking when Leveson found him by the open window. But this did not prevent Hibbs from expressing considerable surprise and some embarrassment when Leveson entered the same chemist's and asked for the same chemical. Indeed Leveson looked harassed and weary enough to want it.

"You've been out of town, haven't you?" said Leveson. "No luck. They got away again on some quibble. The police wouldn't make the arrest; and even old Meadows thought it might be illegal. I'm sick of it. Where are you going?"

"I thought," said Mr. Hibbs, "of dropping in at this Post-Futurist exhibition. I believe Lord Ivywood will be there; he is showing it to the Prophet. I don't pretend to know much about art; but I hear it's very fine."

There was a long silence and Mr. Leveson said, "People always prejudiced against new ideas."

Then there was another long silence, and Mr. Hibbs said, "After all, they said the same of Whistler."

Refreshed by this ritual, Mr. Leveson became conscious of the existence of Crooke and said to him cheerfully, "That's so in your department too, isn't it? I suppose the greatest pioneers in chemistry were unpopular in their own time."

"Look at the Borgias," said Mr. Crooke. "They got themselves quite disliked."

"You're very flippant, you know," said Leveson, in a fatigued way. "Well, so long. Are you coming, Hibbs?"

And the two gentlemen, who were both attired in high hats and afternoon caller's coats, betook themselves down the street. It was a fine sunny day, the twin of the day before that had shone so brightly on the white town of Peaceways; and their walk was a pleasant one, along a handsome street with high houses and small trees that overlooked the river all the way. For the pictures were exhibited in a small but famous gallery, a rather rococo building of which the entrance steps almost descended upon the Thames. The building was girt on both sides and behind with gaudy flower-beds, and on the top of the steps in front of the Byzantine doorway stood their old friend Misysra Ammon smiling broadly and in an unusually sumptuous costume. But even the sight of that fragrant Eastern flower did not seem to revive altogether the spirits of the drooping Secretary.

"You have coome," said the beaming Prophet, "to see the decoration? It is approo-ooved. I haf approo-ooved it."

"We came to see the Post-Futurist pictures," began Hibbs: but Leveson was silent.

"There are no pictures," said the Turk simply. "If there had been I could not haf approo-ooved. For those of our Religion pictures are not goo-ood; they are Idols, my friendss. Loo-ook in there," and he turned and darted a solemn forefinger just under his nose towards the gates of the gallery. "Loo-ook in there, and you will find no Idols. No Idols at all. I have most carefully loo-ooked into every one of the frames. Every one I have approo-ooved. No trace of ze Man form. No trace of ze Animal form. All decoration as goo-ood as the goo-oodest of carpets: it harms not. Lord Ivywood smile of happiness; for I tell him Islam indeed progresses. Ze old Moslems allow to draw the picture of the vegetable. Here I hunt even for the vegetable. And there is no vegetable."

Hibbs, whose trade was tact, naturally did not think it wise that the eminent Misysra should go on lecturing from a tall flight of steps to the whole street and river; so he had slipped past with a general proposal to go in and see. The Prophet and the Secretary followed; and all entered the outer hall where Lord Ivywood stood with the white face of a statue. He was the only statue the New Moslems were allowed to worship.

On a sofa, like a purple island in the middle of the sea of floor, sat Enid Wimpole, talking eagerly to her cousin Dorian; being, in fact, fighting her best to prevent the family quarrel which threatened to follow hard on the incident at Westminster. In the deeper perspective of the rooms Lady Joan Brett was floating about. And if her attitudes before the Post-Futurist pictures could not be called humble, or even inquiring, it is but just to that school to say that she seemed to be quite as bored with the floor that she walked on and the parasol she held. Bit by bit other figures or groups of that world drifted through the Exhibition of the Post-Futurists. It is a very small world: but it is just big enough and just small enough to govern a country—that is, a country with no religion. And it has all the vanity of a mob; and all the reticence of a secret society.

Leveson instantly went up to Lord Ivywood, pulled papers from his pocket, and was plainly telling him of the escape from Peaceways. Ivywood's face hardly changed; he was, or felt, above some things; and one of them was blaming a servant before the servant's social superiors. But no one could say he looked less like cold marble than before.

"I made all possible inquiries about their subsequent route," the Secretary was heard saying, "and the most serious feature is that they seem to have taken the road for London."

"Quite so," replied the statue. "They will be easier to capture here."

Lady Enid, by a series of assurances (most of which were, I regret to say, lies) had succeeded in preventing the scandal of her cousin Dorian actually cutting her cousin Philip. But she knew very little of the masculine temper if she really thought she had prevented the profound intellectual revolt of the poet against the politician. Ever since he heard Mr. Hibbs say "Yars! Yars!" and order his arrest by a common policeman, the feelings of Dorian Wimpole had flowed for some four days and nights in a direction highly contrary to the ideals of Mr. Hibbs; and the sudden appearance of that blameless diplomatist quickened the mental current to a cataract. But as he could not insult Hibbs, whom socially he did not even know; and could not insult Ivywood, with whom he had just had a formal reconciliation, it was absolutely necessary that he should insult something else instead. All watchers for the Dawn will be deeply distressed to know that the Post-Futurist School of Painting received the full effects of this perverted wrath. In vain did Mr. Leveson affirm from time to time "People always prejudiced against new ideas." Vainly did Mr. Hibbs say, at the proper intervals, "After all, they said the same of Whistler." Not by such decent formalities was the frenzy of Dorian to be appeased

"That little Turk has more sense than you have," he said; "he passes it as a good wall-paper. I should say it was a bad wall-paper; the sort of wall-paper that gives a sick man fever when he hasn't got it. But to call it pictures—you might as well call it seats for the Lord Mayor's Show. A seat isn't a seat if you can't see the Lord Mayor's Show. A picture isn't a picture if you can't see any picture. You can sit down at home more comfortably than you can at a procession. And you can walk about at home more comfortably than you can at a picture gallery. There's only one thing to be said for a street show or a picture show—and that is whether there is anything to be shown. Now then! Show me something!"

"Well," said Lord Ivywood good-humouredly motioning towards the wall in front of him, "let me show you the 'Portrait of an Old Lady.'"

"Well," said Dorian stolidly, "which is it?"

Mr. Hibbs made a hasty gesture of identification, but was so unfortunate as to point to the picture of "Rain in the Apennines" instead of the "Portrait of an Old Lady," and his intervention increased the irritation of Dorian Wimpole. Most probably, as Mr. Hibbs afterwards explained, it was because a vivacious movement of the elbow of Mr. Wimpole interfered with the exact pointing of the forefinger of Mr. Hibbs. In any case, Mr. Hibbs was sharply and horridly fixed by embarrassment: so that he had to go away to the refreshment bar, and eat three lobster-patties and even a glass of that champagne that had once been his ruin. But he stopped at one glass; and returned with a full diplomatic responsibility.

He returned to find that Dorian Wimpole had forgotten all the facts of time, place, and personal pride, in an argument with Lord Ivywood, exactly as he had forgotten such facts in an argument with Patrick Dalroy, in a dark wood with a donkey-cart. And Philip Ivywood was interested also; his cold eyes even shone; for though his pleasure was almost purely intellectual, it was utterly sincere.

"And I do trust the untried; I do follow the inexperienced," he was saying quietly, with his fine inflections of voice. "You say this is changing the very nature of Art. I want to change the very nature of Art. Everything lives by turning into something else. Exaggeration is growth."

"But exaggeration of what?" demanded Dorian. "I cannot see a trace of exaggeration in these pictures; because I cannot find a hint of what it is they want to exaggerate. You can't exaggerate the feathers of a cow or the legs of a whale. You can draw a cow with feathers or a whale with legs for a joke—though I hardly think such jokes are in your line. But don't you see, my good Philip, that even then the joke depends upon its looking like a cow and not only like a thing with feathers. Even then the joke depends upon the whale as well as the legs. You can combine up to a certain point; you can distort up to a certain point: after that you lose the identity: and with that you lose everything. A Centaur is so much of a man with so much of a horse. The Centaur must not be hastily identified with the Horsy Man. And the Mermaid must be maidenly; even if there is something fishy about her social conduct."

"No," said Lord Ivywood, in the same quiet way, "I understand what you mean; and I don't agree. I should like the Centaur to turn into something else, that is neither man nor horse."

"But not something that has nothing of either?" asked the poet.

"Yes," answered Ivywood, with the same queer quiet gleam in his colourless eyes, "something that has nothing of either."

"But what's the good?" argued Dorian. "A thing that has changed entirely has not changed at all. It has no bridge of crisis. It can remember no change. If you wake up to-morrow and you simply *are* Mrs. Dope, an old woman who lets lodgings at Broadstairs—well, I don't doubt Mrs. Dope is a saner and happier person than you are. But in what way have *you* progressed? What part of *you* is better? Don't you see this prime fact of identity is the limit set on all living things."

"No!" said Philip, with suppressed but sudden violence. "I deny that any limit is set upon living things!"

"Why, then I understand," said Dorian, "why, though you make such good speeches, you have never written any poetry."

Lady Joan, who was looking with tedium at a rich pattern of purple and green in which Misysra attempted to interest her (imploring her to disregard the mere title, which idolatrously stated it as "First Communion in the Snow"), abruptly turned her full face to Dorian. It was a face to which few men could feel indifferent, especially when thus suddenly shown them.

"Why can't he write poetry?" she asked "Do you mean he would resent the limits of metre and rhyme and so on?"

The poet reflected for a moment and then said, "Well, partly; but I mean more than that too. As one can be candid in the family, I may say that what every one says about him is that he has no humour. But that's not my complaint at all. I think my complaint is that he has no pathos. That is, he does not feel human limitations. That is, he will not write poetry."

Lord Ivywood was looking with his cold, unconscious profile into a little black and yellow picture called "Enthusiasm"; but Joan Brett leaned across to him with swarthy eagerness and cried quite provocatively:

"Dorian says you've no pathos. Have you any pathos? He says it's a sense of human limitations."

Ivywood did not remove his gaze from the picture of "Enthusiasm," but simply said "No; I have no sense of human limitations." Then he put up his elderly eye-glass to examine the picture better. Then he dropped it again and confronted Joan with a face paler than usual.

"Joan," he said, "I would walk where no man has walked; and find something beyond tears and laughter. My road shall be my road indeed; for I will make it, like the Romans. And my adventures shall not be in the hedges and the gutters; but in the borders of the ever-advancing brain. I will think what was unthinkable until I thought it; I will love what never lived until I loved it—I will be as lonely as the first man."

"They say," she said, after a silence, "that the first man fell."

"You mean the priests?" he answered. "Yes; but even they admit that he discovered good and evil. So are these artists trying to discover some distinction that is still dark to us."

"Oh," said Joan, looking at him with a real and unusual interest, "then you don't *see* anything in the pictures yourself?"

"I see the breaking of the barriers," he answered; "beyond that I see nothing."

She looked at the floor for a little time and traced patterns with her parasol, like one who has really received food for thought. Then she said suddenly:

"But perhaps the breaking of barriers might be the breaking of everything."

The clear and colourless eyes looked at her quite steadily.

"Perhaps," said Lord Ivywood.

Dorian Wimpole made a sudden movement a few yards off, where he was looking at a picture, and said, "Hullo! what's this?" Mr. Hibbs was literally gaping in the direction of the entrance.

Framed in that fine Byzantine archway stood a great big bony man in threadbare but careful clothes, with a harsh, high-featured, intelligent face, to which a dark beard under the chin gave something of the Puritanic cast. Somehow his whole personality seemed to be pulled together and explained when he spoke with a North Country accent.

"Weel, lards," he said genially, "t'hoose be main great on t'pictures. But I coom for suthin' in a moog. Haw! Haw!"

Leveson and Hibbs looked at each other. Then Leveson rushed from the room. Lord Ivywood did not move a finger; but Mr. Wimpole, with a sort of poetic curiosity, drew nearer to the stranger, and studied him.

"It's perfectly awful," cried Enid Wimpole, in a loud whisper. "The man must be drunk."

"Na, lass," said the man, with gallantry. "A've not been droonk, nobbut at Hurley Fair, these years and all; a'm a decent lad and workin' ma way back t'Wharfedale. No harm in a moog of ale, lass."

"Are you quite sure," asked Dorian Wimpole, with a singular sort of delicate curiosity,—"are you quite *sure* you're not drunk."

"A'm not droonk," said the man jovially.

"Even if these were licensed premises," began Dorian, in the same diplomatic manner.

"There's t'sign on t'hoose," said the stranger.

The black, bewildered look on the face of Joan Brett suddenly altered. She took four steps towards the doorway; and then went back and sat on the purple ottoman. But Dorian seemed fascinated with his inquiry into the alleged decency of the lad who was working his way to Wharfedale.

"Even if these were licensed premises," he repeated, "drink could be refused you if you were drunk. Now, are you *really* sure you're not drunk. Would you know if it was raining, say?"

"Aye," said the man, with great conviction.

"Would you know any common object of your country-side," inquired Dorian scientifically, "a woman—let us say an old woman."

"Aye," said the man, with good-humour.

"What on earth are you doing with the creature?" whispered Enid feverishly.

"I am trying," answered the poet, "to prevent a very sensible man from smashing a very silly shop. I beg your pardon, sir. As I was saying, would you know these things in a picture, now? Do you know what a landscape is and what a portrait is? Forgive my asking; you see, we are responsible while we keep the place going."

There soared up into the sky like a cloud of rooks the eager vanity of the North.

"We collier lads are none so badly educated, lad," he said. "In the town a' was born in there was a gallery of pictures as fine as Lunnon. Aye, and a' knew 'em too."

"Thank you," said Wimpole, pointing suddenly at the wall. "Would you be so kind, for instance, as to look at those two pictures. One represents an old woman and the other rain in the hills. It's a mere formality. You shall have your drink when you've said which is which."

The northerner bowed his huge body before the two frames and peered into them patiently. The long stillness that followed seemed to be something of a strain on Joan, who rose in a restless manner, first went to look out of a window and then went out of the front doors.

At length the art-critic lifted a large, puzzled, but still philosophical face.

"Soomehow or other," he said, "a' mun be droonk after all."

"You have testified," cried Dorian, with animation. "You have all but saved civilization. And, by God, you shall have your drink."

And he brought from the refreshment table a huge bumper of the Hibbsian champagne; and declined payment by the rapid method of running out of the gallery on to the steps outside.

Joan was already standing there. Out the little side window she had seen the incredible thing she expected to see: which explained the ludicrous scene inside. She saw the red and blue wooden flag of Mr. Pump standing up in the flower-beds in the sun, as serenely as if it were a tall and tropical flower. And yet, in the brief interval between the window and the door it had vanished, as if to remind her it was a flying dream. But two men were in a little motor outside, which was in the very act of starting. They were in motoring disguise; but she knew who they were. All that was deep in her, all that was sceptical, all that was stoical, all that was noble, made her stand as still as one of the pillars of the porch. But a dog, bearing the name of Quoodle, sprang up in the moving car, and barked with joy at the mere sight of her. And though she had borne all else, something in that bestial innocence of an animal, suddenly blinded her with tears.

It could not, however, blind her to the extraordinary fact that followed. Mr. Dorian Wimpole, attired in anything but motoring costume, dressed in that compromise between fashion and art which seems proper to the visiting of picture galleries, did not by any means stand as still as one of the pillars of the porch. He rushed down the steps, ran after the car and actually sprang into it, without disarranging his Whistlerian silk hat

"Good afternoon," he said to Dalroy pleasantly. "You owe me a motor-ride, you know."

XXI

THE ROAD TO ROUNDABOUT

Patrick Dalroy looked at the invader with a heavy and yet humorous expression, and merely said, "I didn't steal your car; really I didn't."

"Oh, no," answered Dorian, "I've heard all about it since; and as you're rather the persecuted party, so to speak, it wouldn't be fair not to tell you that I don't agree much with Ivywood about all this. I disagree with him. Or rather, to speak medically, he disagrees with me. He has; ever since I woke up after an oyster supper, and found myself in the House of Commons with policemen calling out, 'Who Goes Home?'"

"Indeed," inquired Dalroy, drawing his red bushy eyebrows together. "Do the officials in Parliament say 'Who Goes Home?'"

"Yes," answered Wimpole indifferently. "It's a part of some old custom in the days when members of Parliament might be attacked in the street."

"Well," inquired Patrick, in a rational tone, "why aren't they attacked in the street?"

There was a silence. "It is a holy mystery," said the Captain at last. "But 'Who Goes Home?'—that is uncommonly good."

The Captain had received the poet into the car with all possible expressions of affability and satisfaction, but the poet, who was keen-sighted enough about people of his own sort, could not help thinking that the Captain was a little absent-minded. As they flew thundering through the mazes of South London (for Pump had crossed West-minster Bridge and was making for the Surrey hills), the big blue eye of the big red-haired man rolled perpetually up and down the streets; and after longer and longer silences he found expression for his thoughts.

"Doesn't it strike you that there are a very large number of chem-ists in London nowadays?"

"Are there?" asked Wimpole carelessly. "Well, there certainly are two very close to each other just over there."

"Yes, and both the same name," replied Dalroy,—"Crooke. And I saw the same Mr. Crooke chemicalizing round the corner. He seems to be a highly omnipresent deity."

"A large business, I suppose," observed Dorian Wimpole.

"Too large for its profits, I should say," said Dalroy. "What can people want with two chemists of the same sort within a few yards of each other? Do they put one leg into one shop and one into the other, and have their corns done in both at once? Or do they take an acid in one shop and an alkali in the next, and wait for the fizz? Or do they take the poison in the first shop and the emetic in the second shop? It seems like carrying delicacy too far. It almost amounts to living a double life."

"But perhaps," said Dorian, "he is an uproariously popular chemist, this Mr. Crooke. Perhaps there's a rush on some speciality of his."

"It seems to me," said the Captain, "that there are certain limitations to such popularity in the case of a chemist. If a man sells very good tobacco, people may smoke more and more of it from sheer self-indulgence. But I never heard of anybody exceeding in cod-liver oil. Even castor oil, I should say, is regarded with respect rather than true affection."

After a few minutes of silence he said, "Is it safe to stop here for an instant, Pump?"

"I think so," replied Humphrey, "if you'll promise me not to have any adventures in the shop."

The motor-car stopped before yet a fourth arsenal of Mr. Crooke and his pharmacy; and Dalroy went in. Before Pump and his companion could exchange a word, the Captain came out again, with a curious expression on his countenance, especially round the mouth.

"Mr. Wimpole," said Dalroy, "will you give us the pleasure of dining with us this evening? Many would consider it an unceremonious invitation to an unconventional meal; and it may be necessary to eat it under a hedge or even up a tree. But you are a man of taste; and one does not apologize for Hump's rum or Hump's cheese to persons of taste. We will eat and drink of our best to-night. It is a banquet. I am not very certain whether you and I are friends or enemies; but at least there shall be peace to-night."

"Friends, I hope," said the poet, smiling. "But why peace especially to-night?"

"Because there will be war to-morrow," answered Patrick Dalroy, "whichever side of it you may be on. I have just made a singular discovery."

And he relapsed into his silence as they flew out of the fringe of London into the woods and hills beyond Croydon. Dalroy remained in the same mood of brooding. Dorian was brushed by the butterfly wing of that fleeting slumber that will come on a man hurried through the air after long lounging in hot drawing-rooms; even the dog Quoodle was asleep at the bottom of the car. As for Humphrey Pump, he very seldom talked when he had anything else to do. Thus it happened that long landscapes and perspectives were shot past them like suddenly shifted slides, and long stretches of time elapsed before any of them spoke again. The sky was changing from the pale golds and greens of evening to the burning blue of a strong summer night, a night of strong stars. The walls of woodland that flew past them like long assegais were mostly, at first, of the fenced and park-like sort; endless oblong blocks of blank pine-wood shut in by boxes of thin grey wood. But soon fences began to sink and pine-woods to straggle and roads to split and even to sprawl. Half an hour later Dalroy had begun to realize something romantic and even faintly reminiscent in the roll of the country; and Humphrey Pump had long known he was on the marches of his native land.

So far as the difference could be defined by a detail, it seemed to consist not so much in the road rising as in the road perpetually winding. It was more like a path; and even where it was abrupt or aimless, it seemed the more alive. They appeared to be ascending a big dim hill that was built of a crowd of little hills with rounded tops; it was like a cluster of domes. Among these domes the road climbed and curled in multitudinous curves and angles. It was almost impossible to believe that it could turn itself and round on itself so often without tying itself in a knot and choking.

"I say," said Dalroy, breaking the silence suddenly, "this car will get giddy and fall down."

"Perhaps," said Dorian, beaming at him; "my car, as you may have noticed, was much steadier."

Patrick laughed, but not without a shade of confusion. "I hope you got back your car all right," he said. "This is really nothing for speed; but it is an uncommonly good little climber. And it seems to have some climbing to do just now. And even more wandering."

"The roads certainly seem to be very irregular," said Dorian reflectively.

"Well," cried Patrick, with a queer kind of impatience, "you're English, and I'm not. You ought to know why the road winds about like this. Why, the Saints deliver us," he cried, "it's one of the wrongs of Ireland that she can't understand England. England won't understand herself. England won't tell us why these roads go wriggling about. Englishmen won't tell us! You won't tell us!"

"Don't be too sure," said Dorian, with a quiet irony.

Dalroy, with an irony far from quiet, emitted a loud yell of victory.

"Right," he shouted. "More Songs of the Car Club! We're all poets here, I hope. Each shall write something about why the road jerks about so much. So much as this, for example," he added, as the whole vehicle nearly rolled over in a ditch.

For indeed Pump appeared to be attacking such inclines as are more suitable for a goat than a small motor-car. This may have been exaggerated in the emotions of his companions, who had both, for different reasons, seen much of mere flat country lately. The sensation was like a combination of trying to get into the middle of the maze at Hampton Court, and climbing the spiral staircase to the Belfry at Bruges.

"This is the right way to roundabout," said Dalroy cheerfully. "Charming place. Salubrious spot. You can't miss it. First to the left and right and straight on round the corner and back again. That'll do for my poem. Get on, you slackers; why aren't you writing your poems?"

"I'll try one if you like," said Dorian, treating his flattered egotism lightly. "But it's too dark to write; and getting darker."

Indeed they had come under a shadow between them and the stars like the brim of a giant's hat; only through the holes and rents in which the summer stars could now look down on them. The hill like a cluster of domes, though smooth and even bare in its lower contours, was topped with a tangle of spreading trees that sat above them like a bird brooding over its nest. The wood was larger and vaguer than the clump that is the crown of the hill at Chanctonbury; but was rather like it and held much the same high and romantic position. The next moment they were in the wood itself, and winding in and out among the trees by a ribbon of paths. The emerald twilight between the stems, combined with the dragon-like contortions of the great grey roots of the beeches, had a suggestion of monsters and the deep sea; especially as a long litter of crimson and copper-coloured fungi, which might well have been the more gorgeous types of anemone or jelly-fish, reddened the ground like a sunset dropped from the sky. And yet, contradictorily enough, they had also a strong sense of being high up; and even near to heaven; and the brilliant summer stars that stared through the chinks of the leafy roof, might almost have been white starry blossoms on the trees of the wood.

But though they had entered the wood as if it were a house, their strongest sensation still was the rotatory; it seemed as if that high green house went round and round like a revolving lighthouse or the whizzygig temple in the old pantomimes. The stars seemed to circle over their heads; and Dorian felt almost certain he had seen the same beech-tree twice.

At length they came to a central place where the hill rose in a sort of cone in the thick of its trees, lifting its trees with it. Here Pump stopped the car; and clambering up the slope came to the crawling colossal roots of a very large but very low beech-tree. It spread out to the four quarters of heaven more in the manner of an octopus than a tree; and within its low crown branches there was a kind of hollow, like a cup, into which Mr. Humphrey Pump, of "The Old Ship," Pebbleswick, suddenly and entirely disappeared.

When he appeared it was with a kind of rope ladder, which he politely hung over the side for his companions to ascend by; but the Captain preferred to swing himself on to one of the octopine branches with a whirl of large wild legs worthy of a chimpanzee. When they were established there, each propped in a hollow against a branch, almost as comfortably as in an arm-chair, Humphrey himself descended once more and began to take out their simple stores. The dog was still asleep in the car.

"An old haunt of yours, Hump, I suppose," said the Captain. "You seem quite at home."

"I am at home," answered Pump, with gravity. "At the sign of 'The Old Ship.'" And he stuck the old blue and red sign-board erect among the toadstools, as if inviting the passer-by to climb the tree for a drink.

The tree just topped the mound or clump of trees, and from it they could see the whole champaign of the country they had passed; with the silver roads roaming about in it like rivers. They were so exalted they could almost fancy the stars would burn them.

"Those roads remind me of the songs you've all promised," said Dalroy at last. "Let's have some supper, Hump, and then recite."

Humphrey had hung one of the motor lanterns on to a branch above him, and proceeded, by the light of it, to tap the keg of rum and hand round the cheese.

"What an extraordinary thing!" exclaimed Dorian Wimpole suddenly. "Why, I'm quite comfortable! Such a thing has never happened before, I should imagine. And how holy this cheese tastes!"

"It has gone on a pilgrimage," answered Dalroy, "or rather a crusade. It's a heroic, a fighting cheese. 'Cheese of all Cheeses, Cheese of all the world,' as my compatriot, Mr. Yeats,[37] says to the Something-or-other of Battle. It's almost impossible that this cheese can have come out of such a coward as a cow. I suppose," he added, wistfully,—"I suppose it wouldn't do to explain that in this case Hump had milked the bull. That would be classed by scientists among Irish legends— those that have the Celtic glamour and all that. No, I think this cheese must have come from that Dun Cow of Dunsmore Heath,[38] who had horns bigger than elephant's tusks; and who was so ferocious that one of the greatest of the old heroes of chivalry was required to do battle

[37] William Butler Yeats (1865–1939) was an Irish poet. The line Chesterton is here parodying is the opening line of Yeats' poem "The Rose of Battle", which begins, "Rose of all Roses,/Rose of all the World!"

[38] The dun cow of Dunsmore heath was a savage beast slain by Sir Guy, Earl of Warwick, who was an Anglo-Danish hero of wonderful strength and legendary adventures, including the slaying of the dun cow. A huge tusk, probably that of an elephant, is still shown at Harwich Castle as one of the horns of the dun cow.

with it. The rum's good, too. I've earned this glass of rum—earned it by Christian humility. For nearly a month I've lowered myself to the beasts of the field, and gone about on all fours like a teetotaller. Hump, circulate the bottle—I mean the cask—and let us have some of this poetry you're so keen about. Each poem must have the same title, you know; it's a rattling good title. It's called 'An Inquiry into the causes geological, historical, agricultural, psychological, psychical, moral, spiritual, and theological of the alleged cases of double, treble, quadruple, and other curvature in the English Road, conducted by a specially appointed secret commission in a hole in a tree by admittedly judicious and academic authorities specially appointed by themselves to report to the Dog Quoodle, having power to add to their number and also to take away the number they first thought of; God save the King.' " Having delivered this formula with blinding rapidity, he added rather breathlessly, "That's the note to strike. The lyric note."

For all his rather formless hilarity, Dalroy still impressed the poet as being more *distrait* than the others, as if his mind were labouring with some bigger thing in the background. He was in a sort of creative trance; and Humphrey Pump, who knew him like his own soul, knew well that it was not mere literary creation. Rather it was a kind of creation which many modern moralists would call destruction. For Patrick Dalroy was, not a little to his misfortune, what is called a man of action; as Captain Dawson realized, when he found his entire person a bright pea-green. Fond as he was of jokes and rhymes, nothing he could write, or even sing, ever satisfied him like something he could do.

Thus it happened that his contribution to the metrical inquiry into the crooked roads was avowedly hasty and flippant: while Dorian, who was of the opposite temper, the temper that receives impressions instead of pushing out to make them, found his artist's love of beauty fulfilled as it had never been before in that noble nest; and was far more serious and human than usual. Patrick's verses ran:

> "Some say that Guy of Warwick,
> The man that killed the Cow
> And brake the mighty Boar alive
> Beyond the Bridge at Slough;

Went up against a Loathly Worm
That wasted all the Downs,
And so the roads they twist and squirm
(If I may be allowed the term)
From the writhing of the stricken Worm
That died in seven towns.
    I see no scientific proof
    That this idea is sound,
    And I should say they wound about
    To find the town of Roundabout,
    The merry town of Roundabout,
    That makes the world go round.

Some say that Robin Goodfellow,
Whose lantern lights the meads
(To steal a phrase Sir Walter Scott
In heaven no longer needs)
Such dance around the trysting-place
The moonstruck lover leads;
Which superstition I should scout
There is more faith in honest doubt
(As Tennyson has pointed out)
Than in those nasty creeds.
    But peace and righteousness (St. John)
    In Roundabout can kiss,
    And since that's all that's found about
    The pleasant town of Roundabout,
    The roads they simply bound about
    To find out where it is.

Some say that when Sir Lancelot
Went forth to find the Grail,
Grey Merlin wrinkled up the roads
For hope that he should fail;
All roads led back to Lyonesse
And Camelot in the Vale,
I cannot yield assent to this
Extravagant hypothesis,
The plain, shrewd Briton will dismiss
Such rumours *(Daily Mail).*

> But in the streets of Roundabout
> Are no such factions found,
> Or theories to expound about,
> Or roll upon the ground about,
> In the happy town of Roundabout,
> That makes the world go round."

Patrick Dalroy relieved his feelings by finishing with a shout, draining a stiff glass of his sailor's wine, turning restlessly on his elbow and looking across the landscape towards London.

Dorian Wimpole had been drinking golden rum and strong starlight and the fragrance of forests; and though his verses too were burlesque, he read them more emotionally than was his wont:

"Before the Roman came to Rye or out to Severn strode,
The rolling English drunkard made the rolling English road.
A reeling road, a rolling road, that rambles round the shire,
And after him the parson ran, the sexton and the squire;
A merry road, a mazy road, and such as we did tread
The night we went to Birmingham by way of Beachy Head.

I knew no harm of Bonaparte and plenty of the Squire,
And for to fight the Frenchman I did not much desire;
But I did bash their baggonets because they came arrayed
To straighten out the crooked road an English drunkard made,
Where you and I went down the lane with ale-mugs in our hands,
The night we went to Glastonbury by way of Goodwin Sands.

His sins they were forgiven him; or why do flowers run
Behind him; and the hedges all strengthing in the sun?
The wild thing went from left to right and knew not which was which,
But the wild rose was above him when they found him in the ditch.
God pardon us, nor harden us; we did not see so clear
The night we went to Bannockburn by way of Brighton Pier.

My friends, we will not go again or ape an ancient rage,
Or stretch the folly of our youth to be the shame of age,
But walk with clearer eyes and ears this path that wandereth,
And see undrugged in evening light the decent inn of death;
For there is good news yet to hear and fine things to be seen,
Before we go to Paradise by way of Kensal Green."

"Have you written one, Hump?" asked Dalroy. Humphrey, who had been scribbling hard under the lamp, looked up with a dismal face.

"Yes," he said. "But I write under a great disadvantage. You see, I know why the road curves about." And he read very rapidly all on one note:

> "The road turned first towards the left
> Where Pinker's quarry made the cleft;
> The path turned next towards the right,
> Because the mastiff used to bite,
> Then left, because of Slippery Height,
> And then again towards the right—
> We could not take the left because
> It would have been against the laws:
> Squire closed it in King William's day
> Because it was a Right of Way.
> Still right; to dodge the ridge of chalk
> Where Parson's Ghost it used to walk,
> Till someone Parson used to know
> Met him blind drunk in Callao.
> Then left, a long way round, to skirt
> The good land, where old Doggy Burt
> Was owner of the 'Crown and Cup,'
> And would not give his freehold up;
> Right, missing the old river-bed,
> They tried to make him take instead
> Right, since they say Sir Gregory
> Went mad and let the Gipsies be
> And so they have their camp secure:
> And though not honest, they are poor;
> And that is something; then along
> And first to right—no, I am wrong!
> Second to right of course; the first
> Is what the holy sisters cursed,
> And none defy their awful oaths
> Since the policeman lost his clothes
> Because of fairies; right again
> What used to be High Toby Lane

> Left by the double larch and right
> Until the milestone is in sight,
> Because the road is firm and good
> From past the milestone to the wood.
> And I was told by Dr. Lowe,
> Whom Mr. Wimpole's aunt would know,
> Who lives at Oxford writing books,
> And ain't so silly as he looks,
> The Romans did that little bit
> And we've done all the rest of it,
> By which we hardly seem to score.
> Left and then forward as before
> To where they nearly hanged Miss Browne,
> Who told them not to cut her down,
> But loose the rope or let her swing
> Because it was a waste of string;
> Left once again by Hunker's Cleft
> And right beyond the elm, and left
> By Pills's, right by Nineteen Nicks
> And left——"

"No! No! No! Hump! Hump! Hump!" cried Dalroy, in a sort of terror. "Don't be exhaustive! Don't be a scientist, Hump, and lay waste fairyland! How long does it go on? Is there a lot more of it?"

"Yes," said Pump, in a stony manner. "There is a lot more of it."

"And it's all true?" inquired Dorian Wimpole, with interest.

"Yes," replied Pump, with a smile, "it's all true."

"My complaint exactly," said the Captain. "What you want is legends. What you want is lies, especially at this time of night, and on rum like this, and on our first and our last holiday. What do you think about rum?" he asked Wimpole.

"About this particular rum, in this particular tree, at this particular moment," answered Wimpole, "I think it is the nectar of the younger gods. If you ask me in a general, synthetic sense what I think of rum—well, I think it's rather rum."

"You find it a trifle sweet, I suppose," said Dalroy, with some bitterness. "Sybarite! By the way," he said abruptly, "what a silly word that word 'Hedonist' is! The really self-indulgent people generally like sour things and not sweet, bitter things like caviare and curries or what-not. It's the saints who like the sweets. Anyhow, I've known at least five women who were practically saints; and they all preferred sweet champagne. Look here, Wimpole. Shall I tell you the ancient oral legend about the origin of rum? I told you what you wanted was legends. Be careful to preserve this one, and hand it on to your children; for unfortunately my parents carelessly neglected the duty of handing it on to me. After the words 'A Farmer had three sons ...' all that I owe to tradition ceases. But when the three boys last met in the village market-place, they were all sucking sugar-sticks. Nevertheless, they were all discontented; and on that day parted for ever. One remained on his father's farm, hungering for his inheritance. One went up to London to seek his fortune, as fortunes are found to-day in that town forgotten by God. The third ran away to sea. And the first two flung away their sugar-sticks in shame; and he on the farm was always drinking smaller and sourer beer for the love of money. And he that was in town was always drinking richer and richer wines, that men might see that he was rich. But he who ran away to sea actually ran on board with the sugar-stick in his mouth. And St. Peter or St. Andrew, or whoever is the patron of men in boats, touched it and turned it into a fountain for the comfort of men upon the sea. That is the sailor's theory of the origin of the rum. Inquiry addressed to any busy captain with a new crew in the act of shipping an unprecedented cargo, will elicit a sympathetic agreement."

"Your rum at least," said Dorian good-humouredly, "may well produce a fairy-tale. But, indeed, I think all this would have been a fairy-tale without it."

Patrick raised himself from his arboreal throne; and leaned against his branch with a curious and sincere sense of being rebuked.

"Yours was a good poem," he said, with seeming irrelevance, "and mine was a bad one. Mine was bad, partly because I'm not a poet as you are; but almost as much because I was trying to make up another song at the same time. And it went to another tune, you see."

He looked out over the rolling roads and said almost to himself:

"In the city set upon slime and loam
They cry in their parliament 'Who goes home?'
And there comes no answer in arch or dome,
For none in the city of graves goes home.
Yet these shall perish and understand,
For God has pity on this great land.
Men that are men again; who goes home?
Tocsin and trumpeter! Who goes home?
For there's blood on the field and blood on the foam
And blood on the body when Man goes home.
And a voice valedictory.... Who is for Victory?
Who is for Liberty? Who goes home?"

Softly and idly as he had said this second rhyme, there were circumstances about his attitude that must have troubled or interested any one who did not know him well.

"May I ask," asked Dorian, laughing, "why it is necessary to draw your sword at this stage of the affair?"

"Because we have left the place called Roundabout," answered Patrick, "and we have come to a place called Rightabout."

And he lifted his sword towards London; and the grey glint upon it came from a low grey light in the east.

XXII

THE CHEMISTRY OF MR. CROOKE

When the celebrated Hibbs next visited the shop of Crooke, that mystic and criminologist chemist, he found the premises were impressively and even amazingly enlarged with decorations in the Eastern style. Indeed, it would not have been too much to say that Mr. Crooke's shop occupied the whole of one side of a showy street in the West End; the other side being a blank facade of public buildings. It would be no exaggeration to say that Mr. Crooke was the only shopkeeper for some distance round. Mr. Crooke still served in his shop, however; and politely hastened to serve his customer with the medicine that was customary. Unfortunately, for some reason or other, history was, in connexion with this shop, only too prone to repeat itself. And after a vague but soothing conversation with the chemist (on the subject of vitriol and its effects on human happiness) Mr. Hibbs experienced the acute annoyance of once more beholding his most intimate friend, Mr. Joseph Leveson, enter the same fashionable emporium. But, indeed, Leveson's own annoyance was much too acute for him to notice any on the part of Hibbs.

"Well," he said, stopping dead in the middle of the shop. "Here is a fine confounded kettle of fish!"

It is one of the tragedies of the diplomatic that they are not allowed to admit either knowledge or ignorance. So Hibbs looked gloomily wise; and said, pursing his lips, "You mean the *general* situation."

"I mean the situation about this everlasting business of the inn signs," said Leveson impatiently. "Lord Ivywood went up specially, when his leg was really bad, to get it settled in the House in a small noncontentious bill, providing that the sign shouldn't be enough if the liquor hadn't been on the spot three days."

"Oh, but," said Hibbs, sinking his voice to soft solemnity, as being one of the initiate. "A thing like *that* can be managed, don't you know."

"Of course it can," said the other, still with the same slightly irritable air. "It was. But it doesn't seem to occur to you, any more than it did to his lordship, that there is rather a weak point after all in this business of passing Acts quietly before they're unpopular. Has it ever occurred to you that if a law is really kept too quiet to be opposed, it may also be kept too quiet to be obeyed? It's not so easy to hush it up from a big politician without running the risk of hushing it up even from a common policeman."

"But surely that can't happen, by the nature of things?"

"Can't it, by God!" said J. Leveson, appealing to a less pantheistic authority.

He unfolded a number of papers from his pocket, chiefly cheap local newspapers, but some of them letters and telegrams.

"Listen to this!" he said. " 'A curious incident occurred in the village of Poltwell in Surrey yesterday morning. The baker's shop of Mr. Whiteman was suddenly besieged by a knot of the looser types of the locality, who appear to have demanded beer instead of bread; basing their claim on some ornamental object erected outside the shop; which object they asserted to be a sign-board within the meaning of the Act.' There, you see, they haven't even heard of the new Act! What do you think of this, from the *Clapton Conservator*? 'The contempt of Socialists for the law was well illustrated yesterday; when a crowd, collected round some wooden ensign of Socialism, set up before Mr. Dugdale's Drapery Stores, refused to disperse, though told that their action was contrary to the law. Eventually the malcontents joined the procession following the wooden emblem.' And what do you say to this? '*Stop Press News*. A chemist in Pimlico has been invaded by a huge crowd, demanding beer; and asserting the provision of it to be among his duties. The chemist is, of course, well acquainted with his immunities in the matter, especially under the new Act; but the old notion of the importance of the sign seems still to possess the populace and even, to a certain extent paralyse the police.' What do you say to that? Isn't it as plain as Monday morning that this Flying Inn has flown a day in front of us, as all such lies do?" There was a diplomatic silence.

"Well," asked the still angry Leveson of the still dubious Hibbs, "what do you make of all that?"

One ill-acquainted with that relativity essential to all modern minds might possibly have fancied that Mr. Hibbs could not make much of it. However that may be, his explanations, or incapacity for explanations, were soon tested with a fairly positive test. For Lord Ivywood actually walked into the shop of Mr. Crooke.

"Good-day, gentlemen," he said, looking at them with an expression which they both thought baffling and even a little disconcerting. "Good morning, Mr. Crooke. I have a celebrated visitor for you." And he introduced the smiling Misysra. The Prophet had fallen back on a comparatively quiet costume this morning; a mere matter of purple and orange or what-not; but his aged face was now perennially festive.

"The Cause progresses," he said. "Everywhere the Cause progresses. You hear his lordship's beau-utiful speech?"

"I have heard many," said Hibbs gracefully, "that can be so described."

"The Prophet means what I was saying about the Ballot Paper Amendment Act," said Ivywood, casually. "It seems to me the alphabet of statesmanship to recognize now that the great Oriental British Empire has become one corporate whole with the Occidental one. Look at our universities, with their Mohammedan students; soon they may be a majority. Now are we," he went on, still more quietly,— "are we to rule this country under the forms of representative government? I do not pretend to believe in democracy, as you know; but I think it would be extremely unsettling and incalculable to destroy representative government. If we are to give Moslem Britain representative government, we must not make the mistake we made about the Hindoos and military organization—which led to the Mutiny. We must not ask them to make a cross on their ballot papers; for though it seems a small thing, it may offend them. So I brought in a little bill to make it optional between the old-fashioned cross and an upward curved mark that might stand for a crescent—and as it's rather easier to make, I believe it will be generally adopted."

"And so," said the radiant old Turk, "the little, light, easily made, curly mark is substituted for the hard, difficult, double-made, cutting-both-ways mark. It is the more good for hygi-e-ene. For you must know, and indeed our good and wise chemist will tell you, that the Saracenic and the Arabian and the Turkish physicians were the first of all physicians; and taught all medicals to the barbarians of the Frank-ish territotories. And many of the moost modern, the moost fash-ionable remedies are thus of the Oriental origin."

"Yes, that is quite true," said Crooke, in his rather cryptic and unsym-pathetic way. "The powder called Arenine, lately popularized by Mr. Boze, now Lord Helvellyn, who tried it first on birds, is made of plain desert sand. And what you see in prescriptions as *Cannabis Indi-ensis* is what our lively neighbours of Asia describe more energetically as bhang."

"And so-o—in the sa-ame way," said Misysra, making soothing passes with his brown hand like a mesmerist—"in the sa-ame way the making of the crescent is hy ... gienic; the making of the cross is non-hy ... gienic. The crescent was a little wave, as a leaf, as a little curling feather," and he waved his hand with real artistic enthusiasm towards the capering curves of the new Turkish decoration which Ivywood made fashionable in many of the fashionable shops. "But when you make the cross you must make the one line *so-o*," and he swept the horizon with the brown hand, "and then you go back and make the other line so-o"; and he made an upward gesture, sugges-tive of one constrained to lift a pine-tree. "And then you become very ill."

"As a matter of fact, Mr. Crooke," said Ivywood, in his polite man-ner, "I brought the Prophet here to consult you, as the best authority, on the very point you have just mentioned—the use of hashish, or the hemp-plant. I have it on my conscience to decide whether these Oriental stimulants or sedatives shall come under the general veto we are attempting to impose on the vulgar intoxicants. Of course, one has heard of the horrible and voluptuous visions, and a kind of insan-ity attributed to the Assassins and the Old Man of the Mountain. But, on the one hand, we must clearly discount much for the illimitable pro-Christian bias with which the history of these Eastern tribes is told in this country. Would you say the effect of hashish was extremely bad?" And he turned first to the Prophet.

"You will see mosques," said that seer, with candour, "many mosques—more mosques—taller and taller mosques till they reach the moon, and you hear a dreadful voice in the very high mosque calling the muezzin; and you will think it is Allah. Then you will see wives—many, many wives—more wives than you yet have. Then you will be rolled over and over in a great pink and purple sea—which is still wives. Then you will go to sleep. I have only done it once," he concluded mildly.

"And what do you think about hashish, Mr. Crooke?" asked Ivywood thoughtfully.

"I think it's hemp at both ends," said the chemist

"I fear," said Lord Ivywood, "I don't quite understand you."

"A hempen drink, a murder, and a hempen rope. That's my experience in India," said Mr. Crooke.

"It is true," said Ivywood, yet more reflectively, "that the thing is not Moslem in any sense in its origin. There is that against the Assassins always. And of course," he added, with a simplicity that had something noble about it, "their connexion with St. Louis discredits them rather."

After a space of silence, he said suddenly, looking at Crooke:

"So it isn't the sort of thing you chiefly sell?"

"No, my lord; it isn't what I chiefly sell," said the chemist. He also looked steadily; and the wrinkles of his young-old face were like hieroglyphics.

"The Cause progress! Everywhere it progress!" cried Misysra, spreading his arms and relieving a momentary tension of which he was totally unaware. "The hygienic curve of the crescent will soon super-impose himself for your plus sign. You already use him for the short syllables in your dactyl; which is doubtless of Oriental origin. You see the new game?"

He said this so suddenly that everyone turned round, to see him produce from his purple clothing a brightly coloured and highly polished apparatus from one of the grand toy-shops; which on examination seemed to consist of a kind of blue slate in a red and yellow frame; a number of divisions being already marked on the slate, about seventeen slate pencils with covers of different colours, and a vast number of printed instructions, stating that it was but recently introduced from the remote East, and was called Naughts and Crescents.

Strangely enough, Lord Ivywood, with all his enthusiasm, seemed almost annoyed at the emergence of this Asiatic discovery; more especially as he really wanted to look at Mr. Crooke as hard as Mr. Crooke was looking at him.

Hibbs coughed considerably and said, "Of course all our things came from the East, and——" and he paused, being suddenly unable to remember anything but curry; to which he was very rightly attached. He then remembered Christianity; and mentioned that too. "Everything from the East good, of course," he ended, with an air of light omniscience.

Those who in later ages and other fashions failed to understand how Misysra had ever got a mental hold on men like Lord Ivywood, left out two elements in the man which are very attractive, especially to other men. One was that there was *no* subject on which the little Turk could not instantly produce a theory. The other was that though the theories were crowded, they were consistent. He was never known to accept an illogical compliment

"You are in error," he said solemnly to Hibbs, "because you say all things from the East are good. There is the east wind. I do not like him. He is not good. And I think very much that all the warmth and all the wealthiness and the colours and the poems and the religiousness, that the East was meant to give you have been much poisoned by this accident, this east wind. When you see the green flag of the Prophet, you do not think of a green field in summer, you think of a green wave in your seas of winter; for you think it blown by the east wind. When you read of the moon-faced houris, you think not of our moons like oranges, but of your moons like snowballs——"

Here a new voice contributed to the conversation. Its contribution, though imperfectly understood, appeared to be:

"Nar! Why sh'd I wite for a little Jew in 'is dressin'-gown? Little Jews in their dressin'-gowns 'as their drinks, as we 'as our drinks. Bitter, miss."

The speaker, who appeared to be a powerful person of the plastering occupation, looked round for the unmarried female he had ceremonially addressed; and seemed honestly abashed that she was not present.

Ivywood looked at the man with that expression of one turned to stone which his physique made so effective in him. But J. Leveson, Secretary, could summon no such powers of self-petrification. Upon his soul the slaughter red of that unhallowed eve arose when first "The Ship" and he were foes; when he discovered that the poor are human beings, and therefore are polite and brutal within a comparatively short space of time. He saw that two other men were standing behind the plastering person, one of them apparently urging him to counsels of moderation: which was an ominous sign. And then he lifted his eyes and saw something worse than any omen.

All the glass frontage of the shop was a cloud of crowding faces. They could not be clearly seen, since night was closing in on the street; and the dazzling fires of ruby and amethyst which the lighted shop gave to its great globes of liquid, rather veiled than revealed them. But the foremost actually flattened and whitened their noses on the glass: and the most distant were nearer than Mr. Leveson wanted them. Also he saw a shape erect outside the shop; the shape of an upright staff and a square board. He could not see what was on the board. He did not need to see.

Those who saw Lord Ivywood at such moments understood why he stood out so strongly in the history of his time, in spite of his frozen face and his fanciful dogmas. He had all the negative nobility that is possible to man. Unlike Nelson and most of the great heroes, he knew not fear. Thus he was never conquered by a surprise; but was cold and collected when other men had lost their heads, even if they had not lost their nerve.

"I will not conceal from you, gentlemen," said Lord Ivywood, "that I have been expecting this. I will not even conceal from you that I have been occupying Mr. Crooke's time until it occurred. So far from excluding the crowd, I suggest it would be an excellent thing if Mr. Crooke could accommodate them all in this shop. I want to tell as soon as possible as large a crowd as possible that the law is altered and this folly about the Flying Inn has ceased. Come in, all of you! Come in and listen!"

"Thank yer," said a man connected in some way with motor-buses, who lurched in behind the plasterer.

"Thanky, sir," said a bright little clock-mender from Croydon, who immediately followed him.

"Thanks," said a rather bewildered clerk from Camberwell, who came next in the rather bewildered procession.

"Thank you," said Mr. Dorian Wimpole, who entered, carrying a large round cheese.

"Thank you," said Captain Dalroy, who entered carrying a large cask of rum.

"Thank you very much," said Mr. Humphrey Pump, who entered the shop carrying the sign of "The Old Ship."

I fear it must be recorded that the crowd which followed them dispensed with all expressions of gratitude. But though the crowd filled the shop so that there was no standing room to spare, Leveson still lifted his gloomy eyes and beheld his gloomy omen. For though there were very many more people standing in the shop, there seemed to be no less people looking in at the window.

"Gentlemen," said Ivywood, "all jokes come to an end. This one has gone so far as to be serious: and it might have become impossible to correct public opinion, and expound to law-abiding citizens the true state of the law, had I not been able to meet so representative an assembly in so central a place. It is not pertinent to my purpose to indicate what I think of the jest which Captain Dalroy and his friends have been playing upon you for the last few weeks. But I think Captain Dalroy will himself concede that I am not jesting."

"With all my heart," said Dalroy, in a manner that was unusually serious and even sad. Then he added, with a sigh, "And as you truly say, my jest has come to an end."

"That wooden sign," said Ivywood, pointing at the queer blue ship, "can be cut up for firewood. It shall lead decent citizens a devil's dance no more. Understand it once and for all, before you learn it from policemen or prison warders. You are under a new law. That sign is the sign of nothing. You can no more buy and sell alcohol by having that outside your house than if it were a lamp-post."

"D'you meanter say, guv'ner," said the plasterer, with a dawn of intelligence on his large face which was almost awful to watch, "that I ain't to 'ave a glass of bitter?"

"Try a glass of rum," said Patrick.

"Captain Dalroy," said Lord Ivywood, "if you give one drop from that cask to that man, you are breaking the law and you shall sleep in jail."

"Are you quite sure?" asked Dalroy, with a strange sort of anxiety. "I might escape."

"I am quite sure," said Ivywood. "I have posted the police with full powers for the purpose, as you will find. I mean that this business shall end here to-night."

"If I find that pleeceman what told me I could 'ave a drink just now, I'll knock 'is 'elmet into a fancy necktie, I will," said the plasterer. "Why ain't people allowed to know the law?"

"They ain't got no right to alter the law in the dark like that," said the clock-mender. "Damn the new law!"

"What is the new law?" asked the clerk.

"The words inserted by the recent Act," said Lord Ivywood, with the cold courtesy of the conqueror, "are to the effect that alcohol cannot be sold, even under a lawful sign, unless alcoholic liquors have been kept for three days on the premises. Captain Dalroy, that cask of yours has not, I think, been three days on these premises. I command you to seal it up and take it away."

"Surely," said Patrick, with an innocent air, "the best remedy would be to wait till it *has* been three days on the premises. We might all get to know each other better." And he looked round at the ever-increasing multitude with hazy benevolence.

"You shall do nothing of the kind," said his lordship, with sudden fierceness.

"Well," answered Patrick wearily, "now I come to think of it, perhaps I won't. I'll have one drink here and go home to bed like a good little boy."

"And the constables shall arrest you!" thundered Ivywood.

"Why, nothing seems to suit you," said the surprised Dalroy. "Thank you, however for explaining the new law so clearly—'unless alcoholic liquors have been three days on the premises'—I shall remember it now. You always explain such things so clearly. You only made one legal slip. The constables will not arrest me."

"And why not?" demanded the nobleman, white with passion.

"Because," cried Patrick Dalroy, and his voice lifted itself like a lonely trumpet before the charge,—"because I shall not have broken the law. Because alcoholic liquors *have* been three days on these premises. Three months, more likely. Because this is a common grog-shop, Philip Ivywood. Because that man behind the counter lives by selling spirits to all the cowards and hypocrites who are rich enough to bribe a bad doctor."

And he pointed suddenly at the small medicine-glass on the counter by Hibbs and Leveson.

"What is that man drinking?" he demanded.

Hibbs put out his hand hastily for his glass, but the indignant clock-mender had snatched it first and drained it at a gulp.

"Scortch," he said, and dashed the glass to atoms on the floor. "Right you are too," roared the plasterer, seizing a big medicine-bottle in each hand. "We're goin' to 'ave a little of the fun now, we are. What's in that big red bowl up there—I reckon it's port. Fetch it down, Bill."

Ivywood turned to Crooke and said, scarcely moving his lips of marble, "This is a lie."

"It is the truth," answered Crooke, looking back at him with equal steadiness. "Do you think you made the world, that you should make it over again so easily?"

"The world was made badly," said Philip, with a terrible note in his voice, "and I *will* make it over again."

Almost as he spoke the glass front of the shop fell inward, shattered; and there was wreckage among the moonlike coloured bowls; almost as if spheres of celestial crystal cracked at his blasphemy. Through the broken windows came the roar of that confused tongue that is more terrible than the elements; the cry that the deaf kings have heard at last; the terrible voice of mankind. All the way down the long, fashionable street, lined with the Crooke plate-glass, that glass was crashing amid the cries of a crowd. Rivers of gold and purple wines sprawled about the pavement.

"Out in the open!" shouted Dalroy, rushing out of the shop sign-board in hand, the dog Quoodle barking furiously at his heels; while

Dorian with the cheese and Humphrey with the keg followed as rapidly as they could. "Good-night, my lord.

> Perhaps our meeting next may fall
> At Tamworth, in your castle hall.

Come along, friends, and form up. Don't waste time destroying property. We're all to start now."

"Where are we all going to?" asked the plasterer.

"We're all going into Parliament," answered the Captain, as he went to the head of the crowd.

The marching crowd turned two or three corners, and at the end of the next long street Dorian Wimpole, who was towards the tail of the procession, saw again the grey cyclops tower of St. Stephen's, with its one great golden eye, as he had seen it against that pale green sunset that was at once quiet and volcanic, on the night he was betrayed by sleep and by a friend. Almost as far off, at the head of the procession, he could see the sign with the ship and the cross going before them like an ensign; and hear a great voice singing:

> "Men that are men again, Who goes home?
> Tocsin and trumpeter; Who goes home?
> The voice valedictory—who is for Victory?
> Who is for Liberty? Who goes home?"

XXIII

THE MARCH ON IVYWOOD

That storm-spirit or eagle of liberty which is the sudden soul in a crowd, had descended upon London after a foreign tour of some centuries in which it had commonly alighted upon other capitals. It is always impossible to define the instant and the turn of mood which makes the whole difference between danger being worse than endurance and endurance being worse than danger. The actual outbreak generally has a symbolic or artistic, or, what some would call whimsical cause. Somebody fires off a pistol, or appears in an unpopular uniform, or refers in a loud voice to a scandal that is never mentioned in the newspapers; somebody takes off his hat, or somebody doesn't take off his hat; and a city is sacked before midnight. When the ever-swelling army of revolt smashed a whole street full of the shops of Mr. Crooke the chemist, and then went on to Parliament, the Tower of London and the road to the sea, the sociologists hiding in their coal-cellars could think (in that clarifying darkness) of many material and spiritual explanations of such a storm in human souls; but of none that explained it quite enough. Doubtless there was a great deal of sheer drunkenness when the urns and goblets of Æsculapius[39] were reclaimed as belonging to Bacchus:[40] and many who went roaring down that road were merely stored with rich wines and liqueurs, which are more comfortably and quietly digested at a City banquet or a West End restaurant. But many of these had been blind drunk twenty times without a thought of rebellion; you could not stretch the material explanation to cover a corner of the case. Much more general was a savage sense of the meanness of Crooke's wealthy patrons, in keeping a door open for themselves which they had wantonly shut on less

[39] In Greek Mythology Æsculapius was the son of Coronis who became so skilled in surgery and the use of drugs that he became, in effect, the founder of medicine (hence, in this context, the containers from the chemist's shop).

[40] In Greek Mythology Bacchus (also known as Dionysius) was the son of Zeus who was chiefly celebrated for inventing wine.

happy people. But no explanation can explain it; and no man can say when it will come.

Dorian Wimpole was at the tail of the procession which grew more and more crowded every moment. For one space of the march he even had the misfortune to lose it altogether; owing to the startling activity which the rotund cheese, when it escaped from his hands showed, in descending a somewhat steep road towards the river. But in recent days he had gained a pleasure in practical events which was like a second youth. He managed to find a stray taxi-cab; and had little difficulty in picking up again the trail of the extraordinary cortège. Inquiries addressed to a policeman with a black eye outside the House of Commons informed him sufficiently of the rebels' line of retreat or advance, or whatever it was; and in a very short time he beheld the unmistakable legion once more. It was unmistakable, because in front of it there walked a red-headed giant, apparently carrying with him a wooden portion of some public building; and also because so big a crowd had never followed any man in England for a long time past. But except for such things the unmistakable crowd might well have been mistaken for another one. Its aspect had been altered almost as much as if it had grown horns or tusks; for many of the company walked with outlandish weapons like iron teeth or horns, bills and pole-axes, and spears with strangely shaped heads. What was stranger still, whole rows and rows of them had rifles, and even marched with a certain discipline; and yet again others seemed to have snatched up household or workshop tools, meataxes and pickaxes, hammers, and even carving knives. Such things need be none the less deadly because they are domestic. They have figured in millions of private murders before they appeared in any public war.

Dorian was so fortunate as to meet the flame-haired Captain almost face to face, and easily fell into step with him at the head of the march. Humphrey Pump walked on the other side, with the celebrated cask suspended round his neck by something resembling braces, as if it were a drum. Mr. Wimpole had himself taken the opportunity of his brief estrangement to carry the cheese somewhat more easily in a very large loose waterproof knapsack on his shoulders. The effect in both cases was to suggest dreadful deformities in two persons who happened to be exceptionally cleanly built. The Captain, who seemed to be in tearing and towering spirits, gained great pleasure from this. But Dorian had his sources of amusement too.

"What have you been doing with yourselves since you lost my judicious guidance?" he asked laughing, "and why are parts of you a dull review and parts of you a fancy dress ball? What have you been up to?"

"We've been shopping," said Mr. Patrick Dalroy, with some pride. "We are country cousins. I know all about shopping; let us see, what are the phrases about it? Look at those rifles now! We got them quite at a bargain. We went to all the best gunsmiths in London, and we didn't pay much. In fact, we didn't pay anything. That's what is called a bargain, isn't it? Surely I've seen in those things they send to ladies, something about 'giving them away.' Then we went to a remnant sale. At least, it was a remnant sale when we left. And we bought that piece of stuff we've tied round the sign. Surely it must be what ladies called chiffon?"

Dorian lifted his eyes and perceived that a very coarse strip of red rag, possibly collected from a dust-bin, had been tied round the wooden sign-post by way of a red flag of revolution.

"Not what ladies call chiffon?" inquired the Captain, with anxiety. "Well, anyhow it is what *chiffoniers* call it. But as I'm going to call on a lady shortly, I'll try to remember the distinction."

"Is your shopping over, may I ask?" asked Mr. Wimpole.

"All but one thing," answered the other. "I must find a music shop—you know what I mean. Place where they sell pianos and things of that sort."

"Look here," said Dorian, "this cheese is pretty heavy as it is. Have I got to carry a piano too?"

"You misunderstand me," said the Captain calmly; and as he had never thought of music shops until his eye had caught one an instant before, he darted into the doorway. Returning almost immediately with a long parcel under his arm, he resumed the conversation.

"Did you go anywhere else," asked Dorian, "except to shops?"

"Anywhere else!" cried Patrick indignantly. "Haven't you got any country cousins? Of course we went to all the right places. We went

to the Houses of Parliament. But Parliament isn't sitting: so there are
no eggs of the quality suitable for elections. We went to the Tower of
London—you can't tire country cousins like us. We took away some
curiosities of steel and iron. We even took away the halberds from the
Beef-eaters. We pointed out that for the purpose of eating beef (their
only avowed public object) knives and forks had always been found
more convenient. To tell the truth, they seemed rather relieved to be
relieved of them."

"And may I ask," said the other, with a smile, "where you are off
to now?"

"Another beauty spot!" cried the Captain boisterously; "no tiring
the country cousin! I am going to show my young friends from the
provinces what is perhaps the finest old country house in England.
We are going to Ivywood, not far from that big watering-place they
call Pebbleswick."

"I see," said Dorian; and for the first time looked back with intelligent trouble on his face on the marching ranks behind him.

"Captain Dalroy," said Dorian Wimpole in a slightly altered tone,
"there is one thing that puzzles me. Ivywood talked about having set
the police to catch us; and though this is a pretty big crowd, I simply
cannot believe that the police, as I knew them in my youth, could not
catch us. But where are the police? You seem to have marched through
half London with much (if you'll excuse me) of the appearance of
carrying murderous weapons. Lord Ivywood threatened that the police
would stop us. Well, why didn't they stop us?"

"Your subject," said Patrick cheerfully, "divides itself into three
heads."

"I hope not," said Dorian.

"There really are three reasons why the police should not be prominent in this business; as their worst enemy cannot say that they were."

He began ticking off the three on his own huge fingers; and seemed
to be quite serious about it.

"First," he said, "you have been a long time away from town. Probably you do not know a policeman when you see him. They do not
wear helmets, as our line regiments did after the Prussians had won.
They wear fezes, because the Turks have won. Shortly, I have little

doubt, they will wear pigtails, because the Chinese have won. It is a very interesting branch of moral science. It is called Efficiency."

"Second," explained the Captain, "you have perhaps omitted to notice that a very considerable number of those wearing such fezes are walking just behind us. Oh, yes, it's quite true. Don't you remember that the whole French Revolution really began because a sort of City Militia refused to fire on their own fathers and wives; and even showed some slight traces of a taste for firing on the other side? You'll see lots of them behind; and you can tell them by their revolver belts and their walking in step; but don't look back on them too much; it makes them nervous."

"And the third reason?" asked Dorian.

"For the real reason," answered Patrick. "I am not fighting a hopeless fight. People who have fought in real fights don't, as a rule. But I noticed something singular about the very point you mention. Why are there no more police? Why are there no more soldiers? I will tell you. There really are very few policemen or soldiers left in England to-day."

"Surely that," said Wimpole, "is an unusual complaint."

"But very clear," said the Captain gravely, "to any one who has ever seen sailors or soldiers. I will tell you the truth. Our rulers have come to count on the bare bodily cowardice of a mass of Englishmen as a sheep-dog counts on the cowardice of a flock of sheep. Now, look here, Mr. Wimpole. Wouldn't a shepherd be wise to limit the number of his dogs if he could make his sheep pay by it? At the end you might find millions of sheep managed by a solitary dog. But that is because they are sheep. Suppose the sheep were turned by a miracle into wolves. There are very few dogs they could not tear in peices. But, what is my practical point, there are really very few dogs to tear."

"You don't mean," said Dorian, "that the British Army is practically disbanded?"

"There are the sentinels outside Whitehall," replied Patrick, in a low voice. "But indeed your question puts me in a difficulty. No; the army is not entirely disbanded, of course. But the *British* army—Did you ever hear, Wimpole, of the great destiny of the Empire?"

"I seem to have heard the phrase," replied his companion.

"It is in four acts," said Dalroy. "Victory over barbarians. Employment of barbarians. Alliance with barbarians. Conquest by barbarians. That is the great destiny of Empire."

"I think I begin to see what you mean," returned Dorian Wimpole. "Of course Ivywood and the authorities do seem very prone to rely on the sepoy troops."[41]

"And other troops as well," said Patrick. "I think you will be surprised when you see them."

He tramped on for a little in silence and then said, with some air of abruptness, which yet did not seem to be entirely a changing of the subject:

"Do you know the man who lives now on the estate next to Ivywood?"

"No," replied Dorian, "I am told he keeps himself very much to himself."

"And his estate too," said Patrick rather gloomily. "If you would climb his garden-wall, Wimpole, I think you would find an answer to a good many of your questions. Oh yes, the right honourable gentlemen are making full provision for public order and national defence—in a way."

He fell into an almost sullen silence again; and several villages had been passed before he spoke again.

They tramped through the darkness: and dawn surprised them somewhere in the wilder and more wooded parts where the roads began to rise and roam. Dalroy gave an exclamation of pleasure and pointed ahead, drawing the attention to Dorian of the distance. Against the silver and scarlet bars of the daybreak could be seen afar a dark purple dome, with a crown of dark green leaves; the place they had called Roundabout.

Dalroy's spirits seemed to revive at the sight, with the customary accompaniment of the threat of vocalism.

"Been making any poems lately?" he asked of Wimpole.

"Nothing particular," replied the poet

---

[41] Sepoy troops were native Indian soldiers under European (usually British) discipline.

"Then," said the Captain, portentously clearing his throat, "you shall listen to one of mine, whether you like it or not—nay, the more you dislike it the longer and longer it will be. I begin to understand why soldiers want to sing when on the march; and also why they put up with such rotten songs.

"The Druids waved their golden knives
And danced around the Oak
When they had sacrificed a man;
But though the learned search and scan,
No single modern person can
Entirely see the joke.
But though they cut the throats of men
They cut not down the tree,
And from the blood the saplings sprang
Of oak-woods yet to be.
But Ivywood, Lord Ivywood,
He rots the tree as ivy would,
He clings and crawls as ivy would
About the sacred tree.

King Charles he fled from Worcester fight
And hid him in an Oak;
In convent schools no man of tact
Would trace and praise his every act,
Or argue that he was in fact
A strict and sainted bloke,
But not by him the sacred woods
Have lost their fancies free,
And though he was extremely big
He did not break the tree.
But Ivywood, Lord Ivywood,
He breaks the tree as ivy would,
And eats the woods as ivy would
Between us and the sea.

Great Collingwood walked down the glade
And flung the acorns free,
That oaks might still be in the grove
As oaken as the beams above,

When the great Lover sailors love
Was kissed by Death at sea.
But though for him the oak-trees fell
To build the oaken ships,
The woodman worshipped what he smote
And honoured even the chips.
    But Ivywood, Lord Ivywood,
    He hates the tree as ivy would,
    As the dragon of the ivy would
    That has us in his grips."

They were ascending a sloping road, walled in on both sides by solemn woods, which somehow seemed as watchful as owls awake. Though daybreak was going over them with banners, scrolls of scarlet and gold, and with a wind like trumpets of triumph, the dark woods screened their secret like dark cool cellars; nor was the strong sunlight seen in them, save in one or two brilliant scars, that looked like splintered emeralds.

"I should not wonder," said Dorian, "if the ivy does not find the tree knows a thing or two also."

"The tree does," assented the Captain. "The trouble was that until a little while ago the tree did not know that it knew."

There was a silence; and as they went up the incline grew steeper and steeper and the tall trees seemed more and more to be guarding something from sight as with the grey shields of giants.

"Do you remember this road, Hump?" asked Dalroy of the innkeeper.

"Yes," answered Humphrey Pump, and said no more; but few have ever heard such fullness in an affirmative.

They marched on in silence, and about two hours afterwards, towards eleven o'clock, Dalroy called a halt in the forest, and said that everybody had better have a few hours' sleep. The impenetrable quality in the woods and the comparative softness of the carpet of beech-mast, made the spot as appropriate as the time was inappropriate. And if someone thinks that common people, casually picked up in the street, could not follow a random leader on such a journey or sleep at his command in such a spot, given the state of the soul, then some one knows no history.

"I'm afraid," said Dalroy, "you'll have to have your supper for breakfast. I know an excellent place for having breakfast; but it's too exposed for sleep. And sleep you must have; so we won't unpack the stores just now. We'll lie down like Babes in the Wood, and any bird of an industrious disposition is free to start covering me with leaves. Really, there are things coming before which you will want sleep."

When they resumed the march it was nearly the middle of the afternoon; and the meal which Dalroy insisted buoyantly on describing as breakfast was taken about that mysterious hour when ladies die without tea. The steep road had consistently grown steeper and steeper; and at last Dalroy said to Dorian Wimpole:

"Don't drop that cheese again just here, or it will roll right away down into the woods. I know it will. No scientific calculations of grades and angles are necessary: because I have seen it do so myself. In fact, I have run after it."

Wimpole realized they were mounting to the sharp edge of a ridge; and in a few moments he knew by the oddness in the shape of the trees what it had been that the trees were hiding.

They had been walking along a swelling woodland path beside the sea. On a particular high plateau, projecting above the shore stood some dwarfed and crippled apple-trees, of whose apples no man alive would have eaten, so sour and salt they must be. All the rest of the plateau was bald and featureless, but Dalroy looked at every inch of it, as if at an inhabited place.

"This is where we'll have breakfast," he said, pointing to the naked grassy waste. "It's the best inn in England." Then as if introducing Humphrey: "The Parish Pump."

Some of his audience began to laugh; but somehow suddenly ceased doing so, as Dalroy strode forward and planted the sign of "The Old Ship" on the desolate sea-shore.

"And now," he said, "you have charge of the stores we brought, Hump, and we will picnic. As it said in a song I once sang:

> " 'The Saracen's Head out of Araby came,
> King Richard riding in arms like flame,
> And where he established his folk to be fed
> He set up his spear, and the Saracen's Head.' "

It was nearly dusk before the mob, much swelled by the many discontented on the Ivywood estates, reached the gates of Ivywood House. Strategically, and for the purposes of a night surprise, this might have done credit to the Captain's military capacity. But the use to which he put it actually was what some might call eccentric. When he had disposed his forces, with swift injunctions of silence for the first few minutes, he turned to Pump and said:

"And now, before we do anything else, I'm going to make a noise."

And he produced from under brown paper what appeared to be a musical instrument.

"A summons to parley?" inquired Dorian, with interest; "a trumpet of defiance, or something of that kind?"

"No," said Patrick, "a serenade."

XXIV

THE ENIGMAS OF LADY JOAN

On an evening when the sky was clear and only its fringes embroidered with the purple arabesques of the sunset, Joan Brett was walking on the upper lawn of the terraced garden at Ivywood, where the peacocks trail themselves about. She was not unlike one of the peacocks herself in beauty, and some might have said in inutility; she had the proud head and the sweeping train; nor was she, in these days, devoid of the occasional disposition to scream. For indeed, for some time past she had felt her existence closing round her with an incomprehensible quietude; and that is harder for the patience than an incomprehensible noise. Whenever she looked at the old yew hedges of the garden they seemed to be higher than when she saw them last; as if those living walls could still grow to shut her in. Whenever from the turret windows she had a sight of the sea, it seemed to be farther away. Indeed, the whole closing of the end of the turret wing with the new wall of Eastern woodwork seemed to symbolize all her shapeless sensations. In her childhood the wing had ended with a broken-down door and a disused staircase. They led to an uncultivated copse and an abandoned railway tunnel, to which neither she nor any one else ever wanted to go. Still she knew what they led to. Now it seemed that this scrap of land had been sold and added to the adjoining estate; and about the adjoining estate nobody seemed to know anything in particular. The sense of things closing in increased upon her. All sorts of silly little details magnified the sensation. She could discover nothing about this new landlord next door, so to speak, since he was, it seemed, an elderly man who preferred to live in the greatest privacy. Miss Browning, Lord Ivywood's secretary, could give her no further information than that he was a gentleman from the Mediterranean coast; which singular form of words seemed to have been put into her mouth. As a Mediterranean gentleman might mean anything from an American gentleman living in Venice to a black African on the edge of the Atlas, the description did not illuminate; and probably was not intended to do so. She occasionally saw his liveried servants going about; and their liveries were not like English liveries. She was also, in her somewhat morbid state, annoyed by the fact that the uniforms of the old Pebbleswick militia had been changed, under the influence of the Turkish prestige in the recent war. They wore fezes like the French Zouaves;[42] they were certainly much more practical than the heavy helmets they used to wear. It was a small matter; but it annoyed Lady Joan, who was like so many clever women, at once subtle and conservative. It made her feel as if the whole world was being altered outside; and she was not allowed to know about it.

But she had deeper spiritual troubles also, while, under the pathetic entreaties of old Lady Ivywood and her own sick mother, she stayed on week after week at Ivywood House. If the matter be stated cynically (as she herself was quite capable of stating it) she was engaged in the feminine occupation of trying to like a man. But the cynicism would have been false; as cynicism nearly always is; for during the most crucial days of that period, she had really liked the man.

She had liked him when he was brought in with Pump's bullet in his leg; and was still the strongest and calmest man in the room. She had liked him when the hurt took a dangerous turn; and when he bore pain to admiration. She had liked him when he showed no malice against the angry Dorian; she had liked him with something like enthusiasm on the night he rose rigid on his rude crutch, and crushing all remonstrance, made his rash and swift rush to London. But, despite the queer closing-in sensations of which we have spoken, she never liked him better than that evening, when he lifted himself laboriously on his crutch up the terraces of the old garden and came to speak to her as she stood among the peacocks. He even tried to pat a peacock in a hazy way, as if it were a dog. He told her that these beautiful birds were; of course, imported from the East—by the semi-Eastern empire of Macedonia. But, all the same, Joan had a dim suspicion that he had never noticed before that there were any peacocks

---

[42]The French Zouaves were the French light-infantry corps originally formed in Algeria. The style referred to is exotic, namely wide-topped trousers tapering to a narrow ankle.

at Ivywood. His greatest fault was a pride in the faultlessness of his mental and moral strength; but, if he had only known, something faintly comic in the unconscious side of him did him more good with the woman than all the rest.

"They were said to be the birds of Juno," he said; "but I have little doubt that Juno, like so much else of the Homeric mythology, has also an Asiatic origin."

"I always thought," said Joan, "that Juno was rather too stately for the seraglio."

"You ought to know," replied Ivywood, with a courteous gesture, "for I never saw any one who looked so like Juno as you do. But indeed there is a great deal of misunderstanding; about the Arabian or Indian view of women. It is, somehow, too simple and solid for our paradoxical Christendom to comprehend. Even the vulgar joke against the Turks, that they like their brides fat, has in it a sort of distorted shadow of what I mean. They do not look so much at the individual, as at Womanhood and the power of Nature."

"I sometimes think," said Joan, "that these fascinating theories are a little strained. Your friend Misysra told me the other day that women had the highest freedom in Turkey; as they were allowed to wear trousers."

Ivywood smiled his rare and dry smile. "The Prophet has something of a simplicity often found with genius," he answered. "I will not deny that some of the arguments he has employed have seemed to me crude and even fanciful. But he is right at the root. There is a kind of freedom that consists in never rebelling against Nature; and I think they understand it in the Orient better than we do in the West. You see, Joan, it is all very well to talk about love in our narrow, personal, romantic way; but there is something higher than the love of a lover or the love of love."

"What is that?" asked Joan, looking down.

"The love of Fate," said Lord Ivywood, with something like spiritual passion in his eyes. "Doesn't Nietzsche[43] say somewhere that the

---

[43] Nietzsche (1844–1900) was a German philosopher. The principal features of his writing is contempt for Christianity and its compassion for the weak and his praise for the "will to power" and the superman. His contempt for ordinary people, whom he referred to as the "herd", and belief that the "master-class" should rule over them was influential to, amongst others, Adolf Hitler, who presented a set of the collected works

delight in destiny is the mark of the hero? We are mistaken if we think that the heroes and saints of Islam say 'Kismet' [44] with bowed heads and in sorrow. They say 'Kismet' with a shout of joy. That which is fitting—that is what they really mean. In the Arabian tales, the most perfect prince is wedded to the most perfect princess—because it is fitting. The spiritual giants, the Genii, achieve it—that is, the purposes of Nature, In the selfish, sentimental European novels, the loveliest princess on earth might have run away with her middle-aged drawing-master. These things are not in the Path. The Turk rides out to wed the fairest queen of the earth; he conquers empires to do it; and he is not ashamed of his laurels."

The crumpled violet clouds around the edge of the silver evening looked to Lady Joan more and more like vivid violet embroideries hemming some silver curtain in the closed corridor at Ivywood. The peacocks looked more lustrous and beautiful than they ever had before; but for the first time she really felt they came out of the land of the Arabian Nights.

"Joan," said Philip Ivywood, very softly in the twilight, "I am not ashamed of my laurels. I see no meaning in what these Christians call humility. I will be the greatest man in the world if I can; and I think I can. Therefore something that is higher than love itself, Fate and what is fitting, make it right that I should wed the most beautiful woman in the world. And she stands among the peacocks; and is more beautiful and more proud than they."

Joan's troubled eyes were on the violet horizon and her troubled lips could utter nothing but something like "don't."

"Joan," said Philip again, "I have told you you are the woman one of the great heroes could have desired. Let me now tell you something I could have told no one to whom I had not thus spoken of love

---

of the philosopher to Mussolini, the Italian Fascist leader. Chesterton, on the other hand, once wrote that there is no such person as "the ordinary man". The philosophy of power and fate reappear again in the character of Morrice Wimpey in Chesterton's novel *The Ball and the Cross*.

[44] *Kismet* is the Turkish form of the Arabic *qismah*, which means "portion, lot, destiny or fate".

and betrothal. When I was twenty years old, in a town in Germany, pursuing my education, I did what the West calls falling in love. She was a fisher-girl from the coast; for this town was near the sea. My story might have ended there. I could not have entered diplomacy with such a wife; but I should not have minded then. But a little while after I wandered into the edges of Flanders, and found myself standing above some of the last great reaches of the Rhine. And things came over me, but for which I might be crying stinking fish to this day. I thought how many holy or lovely nooks that river had left behind, and gone on. It might anywhere in Switzerland have spent its weak youth in a spirt over a high crag; or anywhere in the Rhine-lands, lost itself in a marsh covered with flowers. But it went on to the perfect sea, which is the fulfilment of a river."

Again Joan could not speak; and again it was Philip who went on:

"Here is yet another thing that could not be said, till the hand of the prince had been offered to the princess. It may be that in the East they carry too far this matter of infant marriages. But look round on the mad young marriages that go to pieces everywhere, and ask yourself whether you don't wish they had been infant marriages! People talk in the newspapers of the heartlessness of royal weddings. But you and I do not believe the newspapers, I suppose. We know there is no King in England; nor has been since his head fell before Whitehall. You know that you and I and the families are the Kings of England: and our marriages are royal marriages. Let the suburbs call them heartless. Let us say they need the brave heart that is the only badge of aristocracy. Joan," he said very gently, "perhaps you have been near a crag in Switzerland, or a marsh covered with flowers. Perhaps you have known—a fisher-girl. But there is something greater and simpler than all that; something you find in the great epics of the East—the beautiful woman, and the great man, and Fate."

"My lord," said Joan, using the formal phrase by an unfathomable instinct, "will you allow me a little more time to think of this? And let there be no notion of disloyalty, if my decision is one way or the other?"

"Why, of course," said Ivywood, bowing over his crutch; and he limped off, picking his way among the peacocks.

For days afterwards Joan tried to build the foundations of her earthly destiny. She was still quite young; but she felt as if she had lived thousands of years, worrying over the same question. She told herself again and again, and truly, that many a better woman than she had taken a second-best which was not so first-class a second best. But there was something complicated in the very atmosphere. She liked listening to Philip Ivywood at his best, as any one likes listening to a man who can really play the violin. But the great trouble always is that at certain awful moments you cannot be certain whether it is the violin or the man.

Moreover there was a curious tone and spirit in the Ivywood household, especially after the wound and convalescence of Ivywood, about which she could say nothing except that it annoyed her somehow. There was something in it glorious—but also languorous. By an impulse by no means uncommon among intelligent fashionable people, she felt a desire to talk to a sensible woman of the middle or lower classes; and almost threw herself on the bosom of Miss Browning for sympathy.

But Miss Browning, with her curling reddish hair and white, very clever face, struck the same indescribable note. Lord Ivywood was assumed as a first principle; as if he were Father Time, or the Clerk of the Weather. He was called "He." The fifth time he was called "He," Joan could not understand why she seemed to smell the plants in the hot conservatory.

"You see," said Miss Browning, "we mustn't interfere with his career; that is the important thing. And, really, I think the quieter we keep about everything the better. I am sure he is maturing very big plans. You heard what the Prophet said the other night?"

"The last thing the Prophet said to me," said the darker lady in a dogged manner, "was that when we English see the English youth, we cry out, 'He is crescent!' But when we see the English aged man we cry out, 'He is cross!'"

A lady with so clever a face could not but laugh faintly; but she continued on a determined theme. "The Prophet said, you know, that all real love had in it an element of fate. And I am sure that is his view, too. People cluster round a centre as little stars do round a star; because a star is a magnet. You are never wrong when destiny blows behind you like a great big wind; and I think many things have been judged unfairly that way. It's all very well to talk about the infant marriages in India——"

"Miss Browning," said Joan, "are you interested in the infant marriages in India?"

"Well——" said Miss Browning.

"Is your sister interested in them? I'll run and ask her," cried Joan, plunging across the room to where Mrs. Mackintosh was sitting at a table scribbling secretarial notes.

"Well," said Mrs. Mackintosh, turning up a rich-haired, resolute head, more handsome than her sister's. "I believe the Indian way is the best. When people are left to themselves in early youth, any of them might marry anything. We might have married a nigger or a fish-wife or—a criminal."

"Now, Mrs. Mackintosh," said Joan, with black-browed severity, "you well know you would never have married a fish-wife. Where is Enid?" she ended suddenly.

"Lady Enid," said Miss Browning, "is looking out music in the music-room, I think."

Joan walked swiftly through several long salons, and found her fair-haired and pallid relative actually at the piano.

"Enid," cried Joan, "you know I've always been fond of you. For God's sake tell me what is the matter with this house? I admire Philip as everybody does. But what is the matter with the house? Why do all these rooms and gardens seem to be shutting me in and in and in? Why does everything look more and more the same? Why does everybody say the same thing? Oh, I don't often talk metaphysics; but there is a purpose in this. That's the only way of putting it; there is a purpose. And I don't know what it is."

Lady Enid Wimpole played a preliminary bar or two on the piano. Then she said:

"Nor do I, Joan. I don't indeed. I know exactly what you mean. But it's just because there is a purpose that I have faith in him and trust him." She began softly to play a ballad tune of the Rhineland; and perhaps the music suggested her next remark. "Suppose you were looking at some of the last reaches of the Rhine, where it flows——"

"Enid!" cried Joan, "if you say 'into the North Sea,' I shall scream. Scream, do you hear, louder than all the peacocks together."

"Well," expostulated Lady Enid, looking up rather wildly. "The Rhine *does* flow into the North Sea, doesn't it?"

"I dare say" said Joan recklessly; "but the Rhine might have flowed into the Round Pond, before you would have known or cared, until——"

"Until what?" asked Enid; and her music suddenly ceased.

"Until something happened that I cannot understand," said Joan, moving away.

"*You* are something I cannot understand," said Enid Wimpole. "But I will play something else if this annoys you." And she fingered the music again with an eye to choice.

Joan walked back again through the corridor of the music-room, and restlessly resumed her seat in the room with the two lady secretaries.

"Well," asked the red-haired and good-humoured Mrs. Mackintosh, without looking up from her work of scribbling, "have you discovered anything?"

For some moments Joan appeared to be in a blacker state of brooding than usual; then she said, in a candid and friendly tone, which somehow contrasted with her knit and swarthy brows:

"No, really. At least, I think I've only found out two things; and they are only things about myself. I've discovered that I do like heroism, but I don't like hero worship."

"Surely," said Miss Browning, in the Girton manner,[45] "the one always flows from the other."

"I hope not," said Joan.

"But what else can you do with the hero?" asked Mrs. Mackintosh, still without looking up from her writing, "except worship him?"

"You might crucify him," said Joan, with a sudden return of savage restlessness, as she rose from her chair. "Things seem to happen then."

"Aren't you tired?" said unmarried Browning, who had the clever face.

---

[45] "Girton manner" is a reference to Girton College Cambridge (1869), which was, until relatively recently, a college for women only.

"Yes," said Joan, "and the worst sort of tiredness; when you don't even know what you're tired of. To tell the honest truth, I think I'm tired of this house."

"It's very old, of course, and parts of it are still dismal," said Miss Browning, "but he has enormously improved it. The decoration, with the moon and stars, down in the wing with the turret is really——"

Away in the distant music-room, Lady Enid, having found the music she preferred, was fingering its prelude on the piano. At the first few notes, Joan Brett stood up like a tigress.

"Thanks," she said, with a hoarse softness, "that's it, of course! and that's just what we all are! She's found the right tune now."

"What tune is it?" asked the wondering secretary.

"The tune of harp, sacbut, psaltery, dulcimer, and all kinds of music," said Joan softly and fiercely, "when we shall bow down and worship the Golden Image that Nebuchadnezzar the King[46] has set up. Girls! Women! Do you know what this place is? Do you know why it is all doors within doors and lattice behind lattice; and everything is cur-tained and cushioned; and why the flowers that are so fragrant here are not the flowers of our hills?"

From the distant and slowly darkening music-room Enid Wim-pole's song came thin and clear:

> "Less than the dust beneath thy chariot wheel,
> Less than the rust that never stained thy sword——"

"Do you know what we are?" demanded Joan Brett again. "We are a harem."

"Why, what can you mean?" cried the younger girl in great agi-tation. "Why, Lord Ivywood has never——"

"I know he has never. I am not sure," said Joan, "even whether he would ever. I shall never understand that man, nor will anybody else. But I tell you that is the spirit. That is what we *are*, and this room stinks of polygamy as certainly as it smells of lilies."

---

[46] Nebuchadnezzar (c. 630–562 B.C.) was a king of Babylon (605–562 B.C.), the erection of a golden statue at his direction is detailed in Daniel 3:1–7.

"Why, Joan," cried Lady Enid, entering the room like a well-bred ghost, "what on earth is the matter with you? You all look as white as sheets."

Joan took no heed of her, but went on with her own obstinate argument.

"And besides," she said, "if there's one thing we do know about him, it is that he believes on principle in doing things slowly. He calls it evolution and relativity, and the expanding of an idea into larger ideas. How do we know he isn't doing that slowly; getting us accustomed to living like this, so that it may be the less shock when he goes farther—steeping us in the atmosphere before he actually introduces"—and she shuddered—"the institution? Is it any more calmly outrageous a scheme than any other of Ivywood's schemes; than a Sepoy Commander-in-Chief or Misysra preaching in Westminster Abbey, or the destruction of all the inns in England? I will not wait and expand. I will not be evolved. I will not develop into something that is not me. My feet shall be outside these walls, if I walk the roads for it afterwards; or I will scream as I would scream trapped in any den by the Docks."

She swept down the rooms towards the turret, with a sudden passion for solitude; but as she passed the astronomical wood-carving that had closed up the end of the old wing, Enid saw her strike it with her clenched hand.

It was in the turret that she had a strange experience. She was again, later on, using its isolation to worry out the best way of having it out with Philip, when he should return from his visit to London. For to tell old Lady Ivywood what was on her mind, would be about as kind and useful as describing Chinese tortures to a baby. The evening was very quiet, of the pale grey sort, and all that side of Ivywood was always the most undisturbed. She was the more surprised when her dreaming took note of a sort of stirring in the grey-purple dusk of the bushes; of whisperings; and of many footsteps. Then the silence settled down again; and then it was startlingly broken by a big voice singing in the dark distance. It was accompanied by faint sounds that might have been the fingering of some lute or viol:

"Lady, the light is dying in the skies,
Lady, and let us die when honour dies;
Your dear, dropped glove was like a gauntlet flung
   When you and I were young,
For something more than splendour stood; and ease was not
  the only good,
About the woods in Ivywood, when you and I were young.

Lady, the stars are falling pale and small,
Lady, we will not live if life be all,
Forgetting those-good stars in heaven hung,
   When all the world was young;
For more than gold was in a ring, and love was not a little thing,
Between the trees in Ivywood, when all the world was young."

The singing ceased; and the bustle in the bushes could hardly be called more than a whisper. But sounds of the same sort and somewhat louder seemed wafted round corners from other sides of the house; and the whole night seemed full of something that was alive, but was more than a single man.

She heard a cry behind her; and Enid rushed into the room as white as one of the lilies.

"What awful thing is happening?" she cried. "The courtyard is full of men shouting; and there are torches everywhere and——"

Joan heard a tramp of men marching, and heard afar off another song, sung on a more derisive note, something like:

"But Ivywood, Lord Ivywood,
He rots the tree as ivy would."

"I think," said Joan thoughtfully, "it is the end of the world."

"But where are the police?" wailed her cousin, "They don't seem to be anywhere about since they wore those fezes. We shall be murdered or——"

Three thundering and measured blows shook the decorative wood panelling at the end of the wing; as if admittance were demanded with the club of a giant. Enid remembered that she had thought Joan's little blow energetic, and shuddered. Both the girls stared at the stars and moons and suns blazoned on that sacred wall that leapt and shuddered under the strokes of doom.

Then the sun fell from heaven, and the moon and stars dropped down, and were scattered about the Persian carpet; and by the opening of the end of the world, Patrick Dalroy came in, carrying a mandolin.

XXV

THE FINDING OF THE SUPERMAN

"I've brought you a little dog," said Mr. Dalroy, introducing the rampant Quoodle. "I had him brought down here in a large hamper labelled 'Explosives,' a title which appears to have been well selected."

He had bowed to Lady Enid on entering and taken Joan's hand with the least suggestion that he wanted to do something else with it. But he resolutely resumed his conversation, which was on the subject of dogs.

"People who bring back dogs," he said, "are always under a cloud of suspicion. Sometimes it is hideously hinted that the citizen who brings the dog back with him is identical with the citizen who took the dog away with him. In my case, of course, such conduct is inconceivable. But the returners of dogs, that prosperous and increasing class, are also accused," he went on, looking straight at Joan with blank blue eyes, "of coming back for a Reward. There is more truth in this charge."

Then, with a change of manner more extraordinary than any revolution, even the revolution that was roaring round the house, he took her hand again and kissed it; saying with a confounding seriousness:

"I know at least that you will pray for my soul."

"You had better pray for mine, if I have one," answered Joan; "but why now?"

"Because," said Patrick, "you will hear from outside, you may even see from that turret window, something which in brute fact has never been seen in England since poor Monmouth's army[47] went down. In

<hr/>

[47] James Scott, First Duke of Monmouth (1649–1685), was an English nobleman and illegitimate son of Charles II and Lucy Walter. Having being exiled to Holland to prevent his intrigues to be made heir to the throne he arrived back in England (1685) and asserted his claim to the throne. He had an army of between three thousand and four thousand, who were eventually defeated by royal troops at Sedgemoor. Monmouth was executed after the defeat.

spirit and in truth it has not happened since Saladin[48] and Cœur de Lion[49] crashed together. I only add one thing, and that you know already. I have lived loving you and I shall die loving you. It is the only dimension of the universe in which I have not wandered and gone astray. I leave the dog to guard you;" and he disappeared down the old broken staircase.

Lady Enid was much mystified that no popular pursuit assailed this stair or invaded the house. But Lady Joan knew better. She had gone, on the suggestion she most cared about, into the turret room and looked out of its many windows on to the abandoned copse and tunnel, which were now fenced off with high walls, the boundary of the mysterious property next door. Across that high barrier she could not even see the tunnel, and barely the tops of the tallest trees which hid its entrance from sight. But in an instant she knew that Dalroy was not hurling his forces on Ivywood at all, but on the house and estate beyond it.

And then followed a sight that was not an experience but rather a revolving vision. She could never describe it afterwards, nor could any of those involved in so violent and mystical a wheel. She had seen a huge wall of a breaker wash all over the parade at Pebbleswick; and wondered that so huge a hammer could be made merely of water. She had never had a notion of what it is like when it is made of men.

The palisade put up by the new landlord in front of the old tangled ground by the tunnel she had long regarded as something as settled and ordinary as one of the walls of the drawing-room. It swung and split and sprang into a thousand pieces under the mere blow of human bodies bursting with rage; and the great wave crested the obstacle more clearly than she had ever seen any great wave crest the parade. Only, when the fence was broken, she saw behind it something that

[48] Saladin, properly Salah al-Din Yusuf ibn Ayyub (1137–1193), was a sultan of Egypt and Syria and leader of the Muslims against the Crusaders in Palestine. He defeated the Christians near Tiberias in 1187, recapturing almost all their fortified places in Syria. He was defeated in 1191, at Acre, by a force assembled by the kings of England and France and died soon after at Damascus.

[49] "Coeur de Lion" is a reference to Richard I, the Lionheart (1157–1199), king of England and third son of Henry II of England and Eleanor of Aquitane. He spent most of his time as king on the Crusades and fought at Acre, where the encounter Chesterton refers to would have happened in 1191.

robbed her of reason; so that she seemed to be living in all ages and all lands at once. She never could describe the vision afterwards; but she always denied it was a dream. She said it was worse; it was something more real than reality. It was a line of real soldiers, which is always a magnificent sight. But they might have been the soldiers of Hannibal or of Attila, they might have been dug up from the cemeteries of Sidon and Babylon, for all Joan had to do with them. There, encamped in English meadows, with a hawthorn-tree in front of them and three beeches behind, was something that had never been in camp nearer than some leagues south of Paris, since that Carolus called the Hammer broke it backwards at Tours.

There flew the green standard of that great faith and strong civilization which has so often almost entered the great cities of the West; which long encircled Vienna, which was barely barred from Paris; but which had never before been seen in arms on the soil of England. At one end of the line stood Philip Ivywood, in a uniform of his own special creation, a compromise between the Sepoy and Turkish uniform. The compromise worked more and more wildly in Joan's mind. If any impression remained, it was merely that England had conquered India: and Turkey had conquered England. Then she saw that Ivywood, for all his uniform, was not the commander of these forces. For an old man with a great scar on his face, which was not a European face, set himself in front of the battle, as if it had been a battle in the old epics, and crossed swords with Patrick Dalroy. He had come to return the scar upon his forehead; and he returned it with many wounds, though at last it was he who sank under the sword-thrust. He fell on his face; and Dalroy looked at him with something that is much more great than pity. Blood was flowing from Patrick's wrist and forehead, but he made a salute with his sword. As he was doing so, the corpse, as it appeared, laboriously lifted a face with feeble eyelids. And seeming to understand the quarters of the sky by instinct, Oman Pasha dragged himself a foot or so to the left; and fell with his face towards Mecca.

And after that the turret turned round and round about Joan, and she knew not whether the things she saw were history or prophesy. Something in that last fact of being crushed by the weapons of brown men and yellow, secretly entrenched in English meadows, had made the English what they had not been for centuries. The hawthorn-tree was twisted and broken, as it was at the Battle of Ashdown when Alfred led his first charge against the Danes. The beech-trees were splashed up to their lowest branches with the mingling of brave heathen and brave Christian blood. She knew no more than that when a column of the Christian rebels, led by Humphrey of the Sign of the Ship, burst through the choked and forgotten tunnel and took the Turkish regiment in the rear, it was the end.

That violent and revolving vision became something beyond the human voice or human ear. She could not intelligently hear even the shots and shouts round the last magnificent rally of the Turks. It was natural, therefore, that she should not hear the words Lord Ivywood addressed to his next-door neighbour, a Turkish officer; or rather to himself. But his words were:

"I have gone where God has never dared to go. I am above the silly Supermen as they are above mere men. Where I walk in the heavens, no man has walked before me; and I am alone in the garden. All this passing about me is like the lonely plucking of garden flowers. I will have this blossom; I will have that ..."

The sentence ended so suddenly that the officer looked at him, as if expecting him to speak. But he did not speak.

But Patrick and Joan wandering together in a world made warm and fresh again, as it can be for few in a world that calls courage frenzy and love superstition, feeling every branching tree as a friend with arms open for the man, or every sweeping slope as a great train trailing behind the woman, did one day climb up to the little white cottage that was now the home of the Superman.

He sat playing, with a pale reposeful face, with scraps of stick and weed put before him on a wooden table. He did not notice them, nor anything else around him; scarcely even Enid Wimpole, who attended to all his wants.

"He is perfectly happy," she said quietly.

Joan, with the glow on her dark face, could not prevent herself from replying, "And we are so happy."

"Yes," said Enid, "but his happiness will last." And she wept.

"I understand," said Joan, and kissed her cousin, not without tears of her own. But they were of pity; which is the opposite of fear.

The text of this book has been set in Bembo type by Beljan, Ltd., Dexter, Michigan. Printed on Glatfelter Spring Grove Offset, B-18 text stock by Thomson-Shore, Inc., Dexter, Michigan. Bound by Thomson-Shore, Inc. The cover and jacket design are by Darlene Lawless O'Rourke of Loyola Graphics, San Bruno, California.